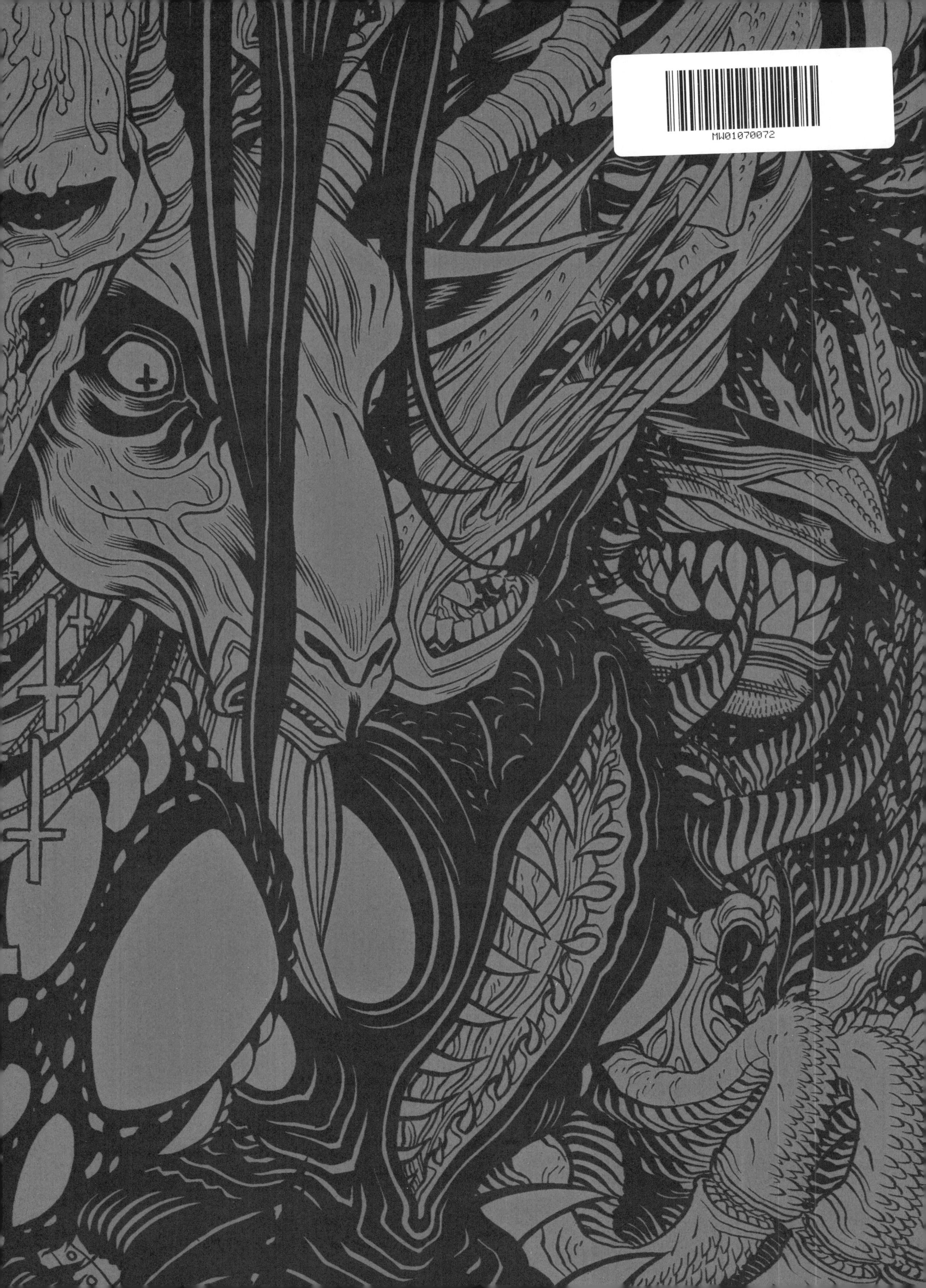

IN THE DARK

A HORROR ANTHOLOGY

Editor & Designer
RACHEL DEERING

Publishers
RACHEL DEERING
TED ADAMS

Cover Artwork
CHRISTIAN WILDGOOSE
JORDAN BOYD

Endpaper Artwork
TRADD MOORE

TINY BEHEMOTH PRESS

IDW PUBLISHING

PUBLISHED BY

TINY BEHEMOTH PRESS

RACHEL DEERING *Publisher*

IDW PUBLISHING

TED ADAMS *CEO & Publisher*
GREG GOLDSTEIN *President & COO*
ROBBIE ROBBINS *EVP & Sr. Graphic Artist*
CHRIS RYALL *CCO & EIC*
MATTHEW RUZICKA *CPA & CFO*
ALAN PAYNE *VP of Sales*

www.IDWPUBLISHING.com

SPECIAL THANKS TO
Ted Adams, Chris Ryall & Justin Eisinger

First Edition
April 2014
ISBN: 978-1-61377-934-7
17 16 15 14   1 2 3 4

PRINTED IN KOREA

INTRODUCTION

BY SCOTT SNYDER

When I was a kid growing up in New York City, there was a video store that was famous (or infamous) among the youth in my neighborhood. The Video Stop, on the corner of Twenty Sixth Street and Third Avenue, was a small place with only a few aisles to browse, nothing particularly special about it. The thing that made it remarkable to us, though, was that the staff there would rent horror movies – **R-RATED** horror movies – to kids under 17 years of age!

Not officially, of course. If you and your friends walked up to the counter with, say, *Critters 2* or *Friday the 13th Part Seven: The New Blood,* the clerk would give you a look and turn you around. No mature content for kids. That was the law, don't you know? But, the law was also such, or at least flexible enough in The Video Stop's interpretation of it to **be** such, that if you called the store from home and ordered an R-rated horror movie, they would deliver it to your house with no questions asked. You'd just leave the money in an envelope outside the door and wait, white-knuckled and drooling, for the sound of the doorbell. In this way, The Video Stop became our go-to place for horror. It truly was a neighborhood resource for all sorts of wonderfully nightmarish gems.

Truth be told, I have many vivid memories of grabbing a movie from outside the apartment and hurrying into the den to watch it with my friends. Why the den? Because it was always during the daylight hours that I would order the films, and the den was the only room in our house with no windows. It was a hideaway where we could watch these horrifying features entirely in the dark.

Looking back, some of the stories that really shaped my imagination came from that video store. The original *Night of the Living Dead. The Texas Chainsaw Massacre. The Shining. Psycho.* Nowadays, as a horror writer myself, I think back to those tender years and wonder why it always seemed to be horror films that grabbed me. What was it about monsters and ghouls and killers that, even at that early age, captured my imagination – and the imaginations of my friends? Was it just that we enjoyed seeing the popular kids being tormented? Was it the shock value of seeing things I wasn't supposed to?

Nah. I really don't believe so. Honestly, I think what attracted me to the genre then, and what still attracts me to it now, is that any good horror, at its core, pits a character against what they fear most in life. Sometimes this means taking the very totems of safety in our lives and turning them into murderous villains. Your neighbors turned against you, your mother, your father, your child, your car, the family dog, your new house, and sometimes, most terrifyingly, your own mind and body. You grow claws, you grow fangs, you develop a taste for brains, you can't help yourself, you lose control. All of this is unsettling because it takes what we think we know, takes something with which we identify and find comfort, and inverts it. Makes it into something menacing. Something unfamiliar and predatory. People up against things that terrify them about themselves, about their lives, about the world. Good horror is about facing the things that unnerve you most. Alone. **IN THE DARK!**

I can say, with all honesty, that this collection is filled with good horror. From creatures stalking the streets of Chicago to monsters hidden inside the human body. From urban ghosts to prairie ghouls, it's full of the kind of stories that, had I rented them in filmic form from The Video Stop as a child, I wouldn't have been able to sleep after consuming them, for both my terror, and that odd sense of inspiration that always accompanied a great scare. As a matter of fact, I wasn't even gonna have a story in this book originally. All I had planned to write was this introduction! But when I started reading some of the stories, I loved them so much I wanted to challenge myself to create a terror tale that could be printed right alongside them.

So, if you will, let's turn down the lights, turn the page, and begin.

Scott Snyder
December 12, 2013

CONTENTS

MURDER FARM

WRITER
CULLEN BUNN

ARTIST
DREW MOSS

COLORIST
TAMRA BONVILLAIN

LETTERER
RACHEL DEERING

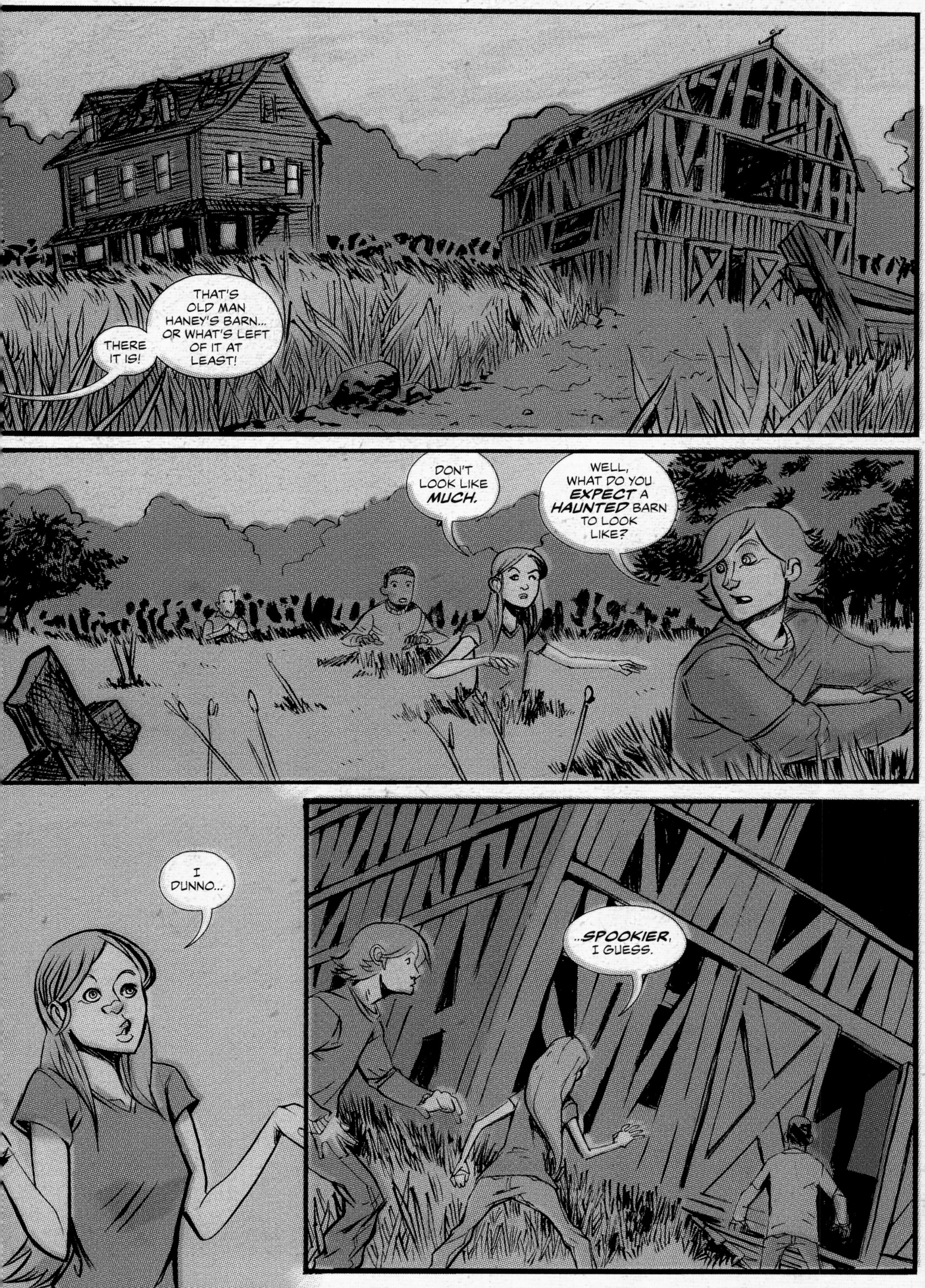
THERE IT IS!
THAT'S OLD MAN HANEY'S BARN... OR WHAT'S LEFT OF IT AT LEAST!
DON'T LOOK LIKE MUCH.
WELL, WHAT DO YOU EXPECT A HAUNTED BARN TO LOOK LIKE?
I DUNNO...
...SPOOKIER, I GUESS.

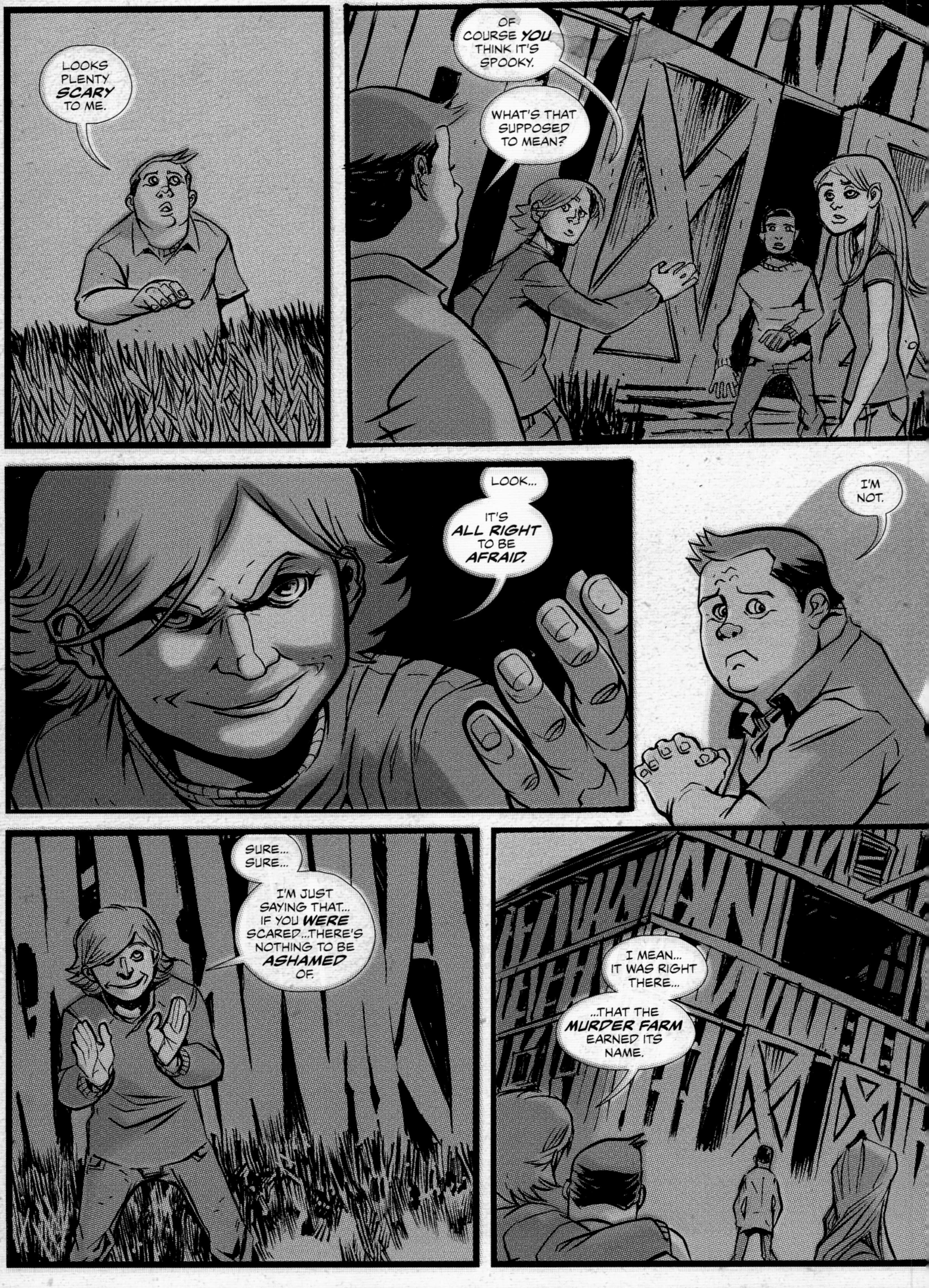
LOOKS PLENTY SCARY TO ME.
OF COURSE YOU THINK IT'S SPOOKY.
WHAT'S THAT SUPPOSED TO MEAN?
LOOK...
IT'S ALL RIGHT TO BE AFRAID.
I'M NOT.
SURE... SURE...
I'M JUST SAYING THAT... IF YOU WERE SCARED...THERE'S NOTHING TO BE ASHAMED OF.
I MEAN... IT WAS RIGHT THERE...
...THAT THE MURDER FARM EARNED ITS NAME.

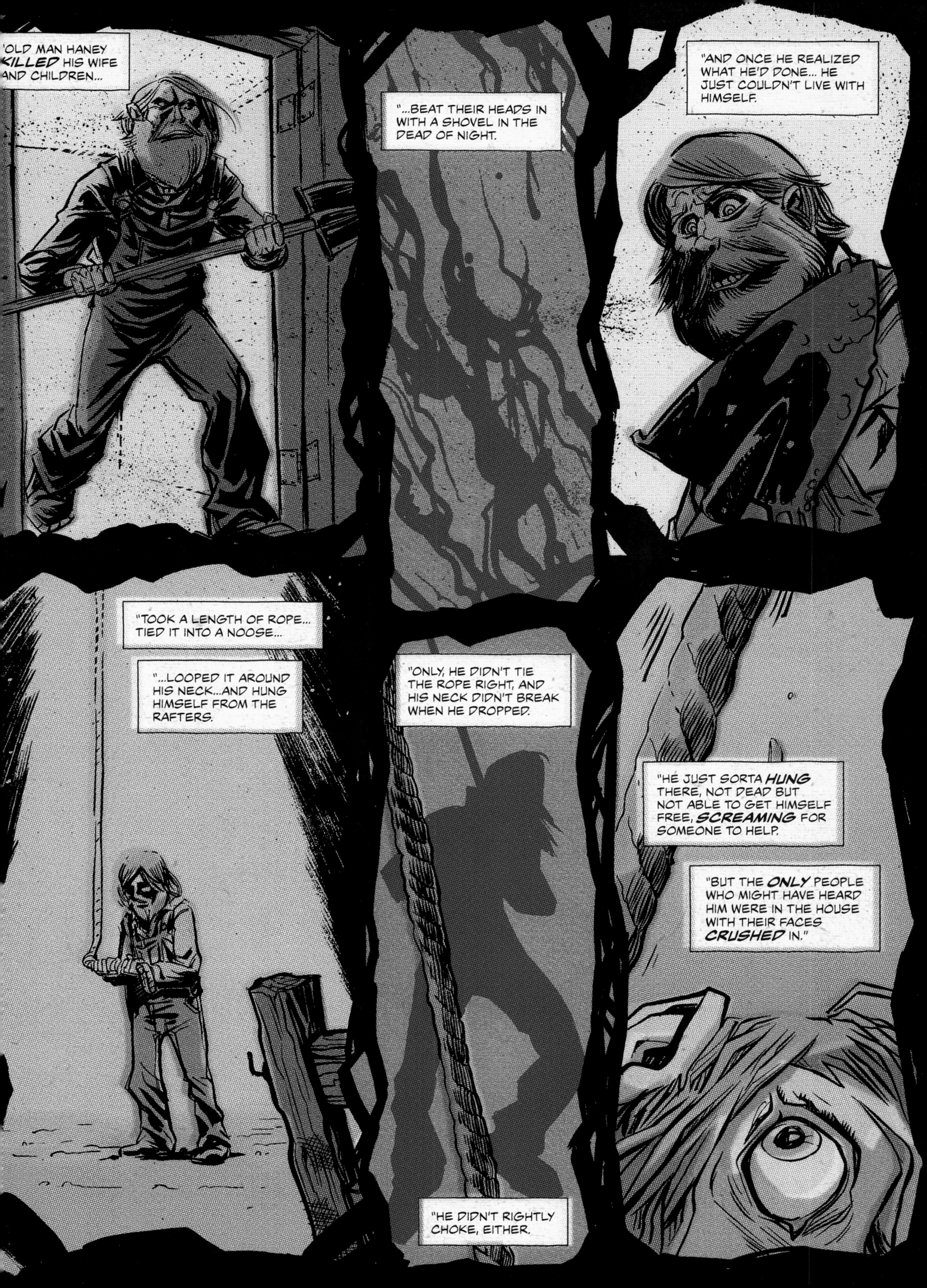
"OLD MAN HANEY KILLED HIS WIFE AND CHILDREN...
"...BEAT THEIR HEADS IN WITH A SHOVEL IN THE DEAD OF NIGHT.
"AND ONCE HE REALIZED WHAT HE'D DONE... HE JUST COULDN'T LIVE WITH HIMSELF.
"TOOK A LENGTH OF ROPE... TIED IT INTO A NOOSE...
"...LOOPED IT AROUND HIS NECK...AND HUNG HIMSELF FROM THE RAFTERS.
"ONLY, HE DIDN'T TIE THE ROPE RIGHT, AND HIS NECK DIDN'T BREAK WHEN HE DROPPED.
"HE DIDN'T RIGHTLY CHOKE, EITHER.
"HE JUST SORTA HUNG THERE, NOT DEAD BUT NOT ABLE TO GET HIMSELF FREE, SCREAMING FOR SOMEONE TO HELP.
"BUT THE ONLY PEOPLE WHO MIGHT HAVE HEARD HIM WERE IN THE HOUSE WITH THEIR FACES CRUSHED IN."

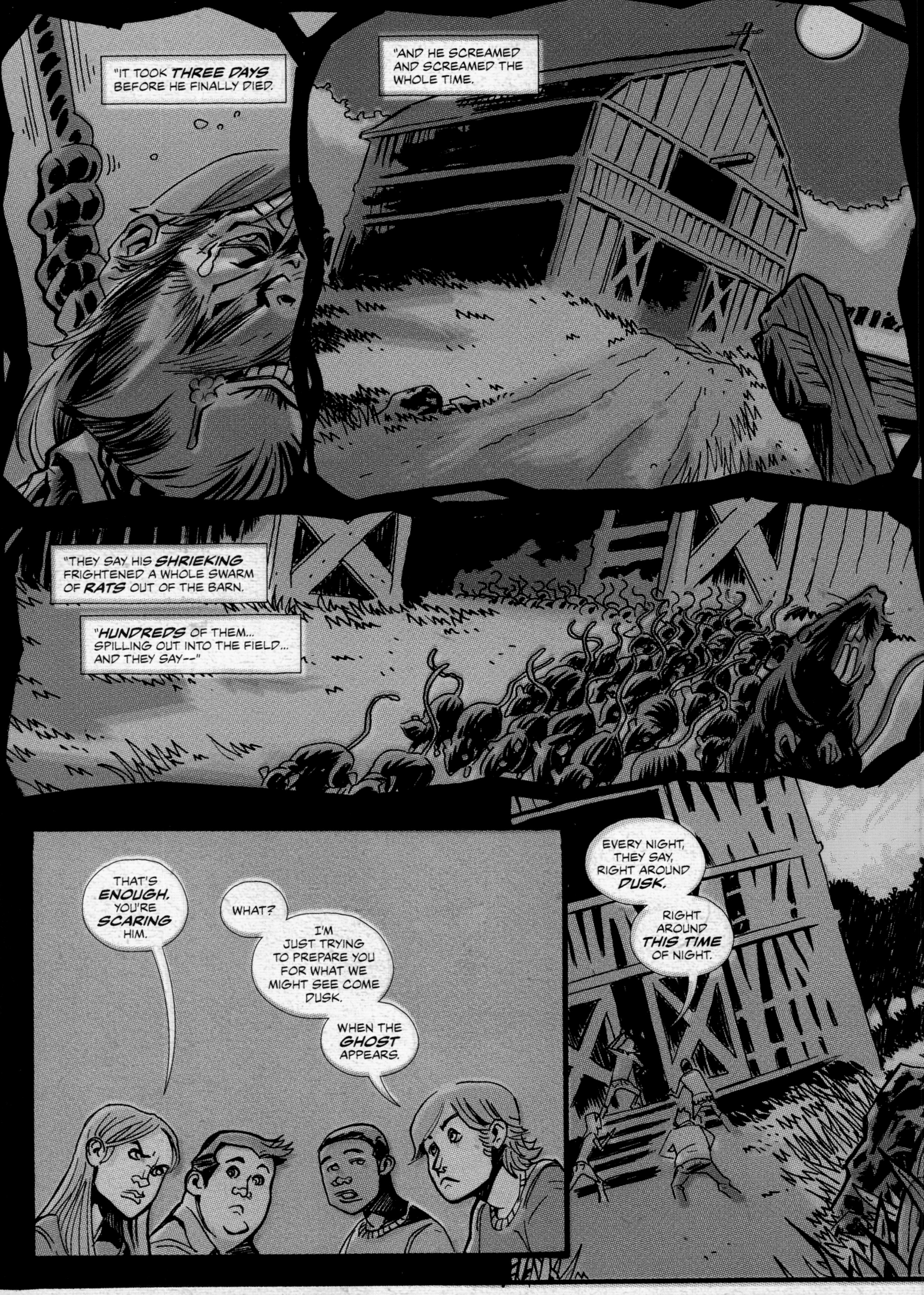
"IT TOOK THREE DAYS BEFORE HE FINALLY DIED.
"AND HE SCREAMED AND SCREAMED THE WHOLE TIME.
"THEY SAY HIS SHRIEKING FRIGHTENED A WHOLE SWARM OF RATS OUT OF THE BARN.
"HUNDREDS OF THEM... SPILLING OUT INTO THE FIELD... AND THEY SAY--"
THAT'S ENOUGH. YOU'RE SCARING HIM.
WHAT?
I'M JUST TRYING TO PREPARE YOU FOR WHAT WE MIGHT SEE COME DUSK.
WHEN THE GHOST APPEARS.
EVERY NIGHT, THEY SAY, RIGHT AROUND DUSK.
RIGHT AROUND THIS TIME OF NIGHT.

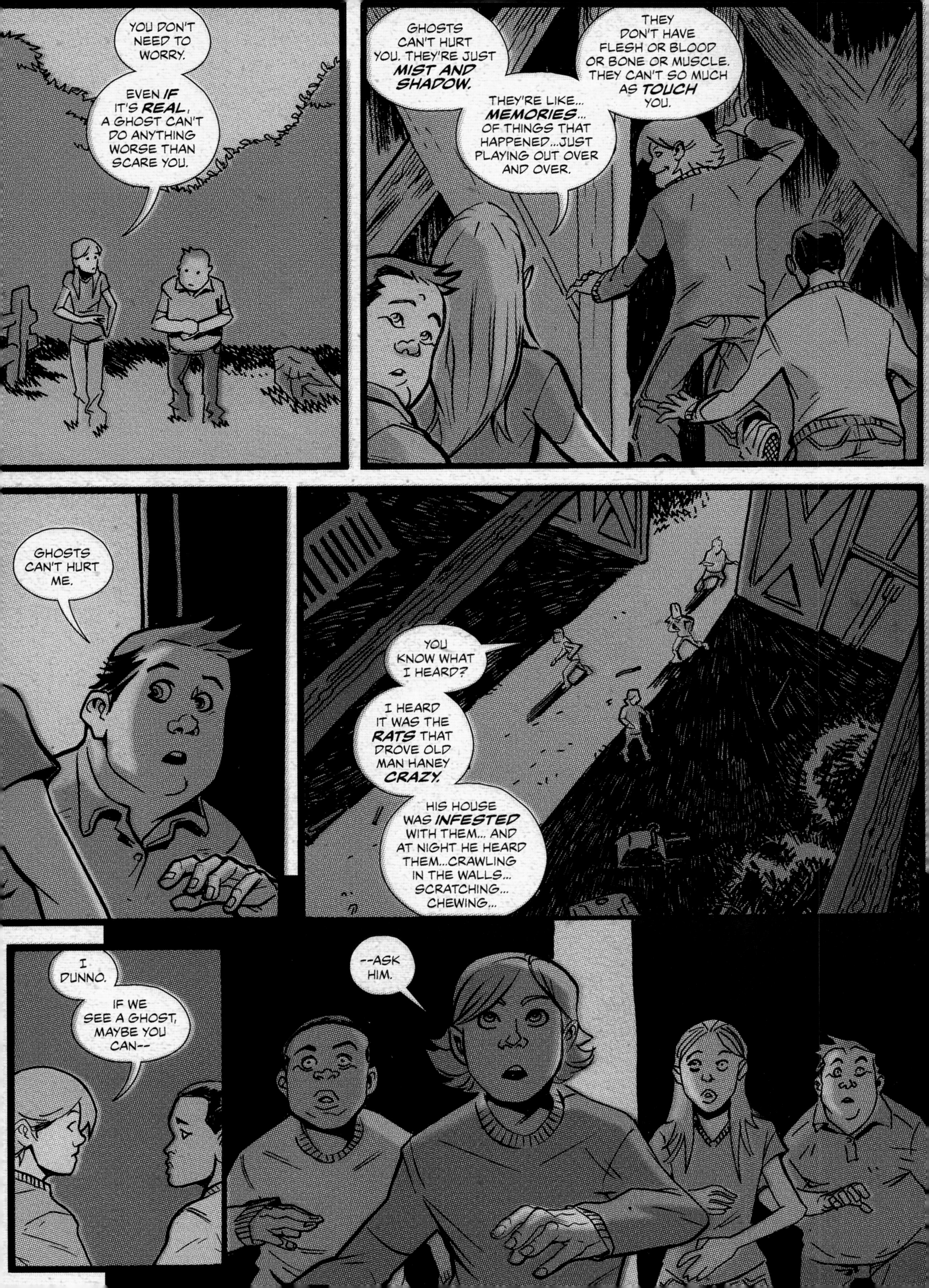
YOU DON'T NEED TO WORRY.
EVEN IF IT'S REAL, A GHOST CAN'T DO ANYTHING WORSE THAN SCARE YOU.
GHOSTS CAN'T HURT YOU. THEY'RE JUST MIST AND SHADOW.
THEY'RE LIKE... MEMORIES... OF THINGS THAT HAPPENED...JUST PLAYING OUT OVER AND OVER.
THEY DON'T HAVE FLESH OR BLOOD OR BONE OR MUSCLE. THEY CAN'T SO MUCH AS TOUCH YOU.
GHOSTS CAN'T HURT ME.
YOU KNOW WHAT I HEARD?
I HEARD IT WAS THE RATS THAT DROVE OLD MAN HANEY CRAZY.
HIS HOUSE WAS INFESTED WITH THEM... AND AT NIGHT HE HEARD THEM...CRAWLING IN THE WALLS... SCRATCHING... CHEWING...
I DUNNO.
IF WE SEE A GHOST, MAYBE YOU CAN--
--ASK HIM.

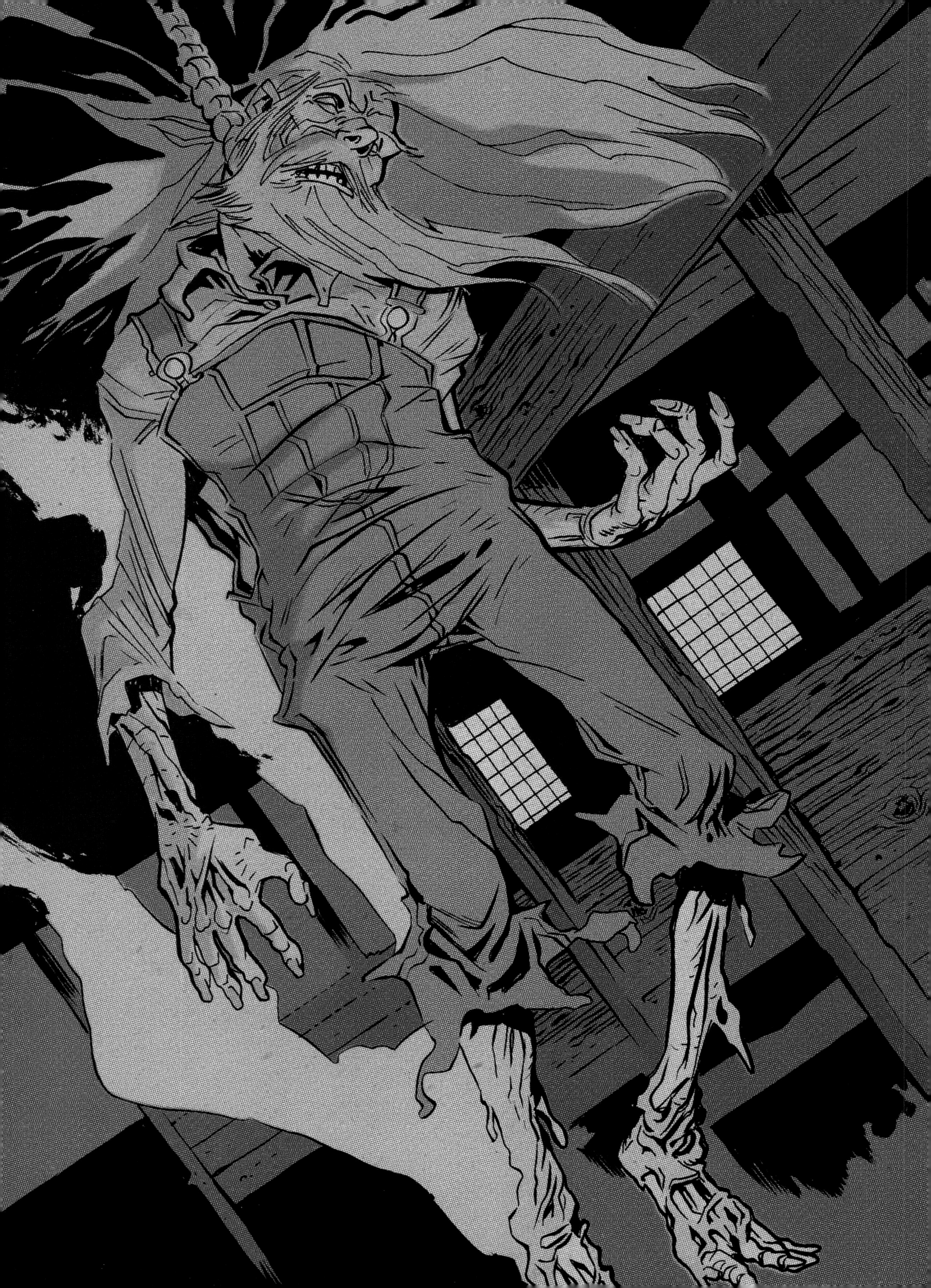

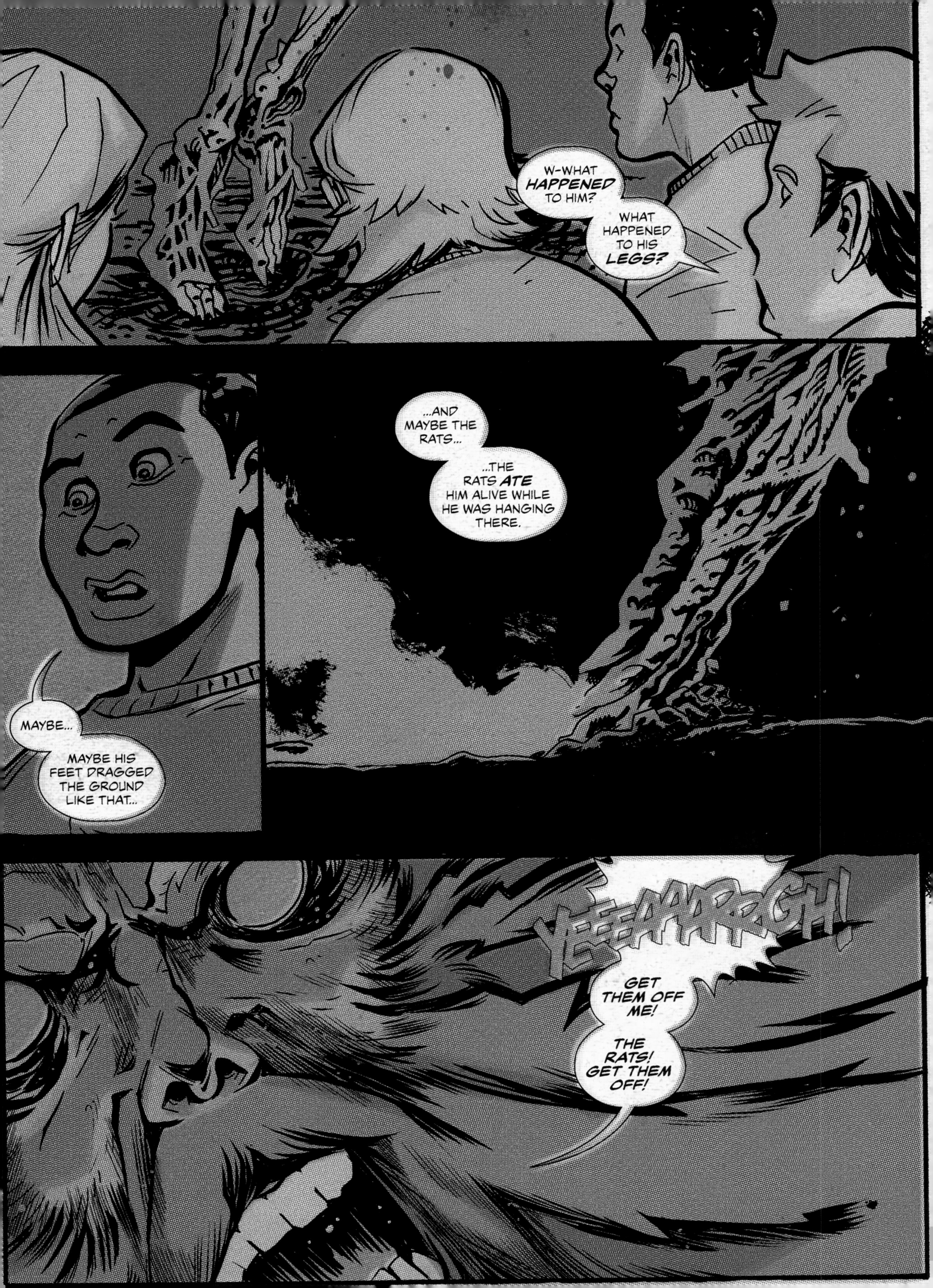
W-WHAT HAPPENED TO HIM?
WHAT HAPPENED TO HIS LEGS?
MAYBE...
MAYBE HIS FEET DRAGGED THE GROUND LIKE THAT...
...AND MAYBE THE RATS...
...THE RATS ATE HIM ALIVE WHILE HE WAS HANGING THERE.
YEEEAAARRGH!
GET THEM OFF ME!
THE RATS! GET THEM OFF!

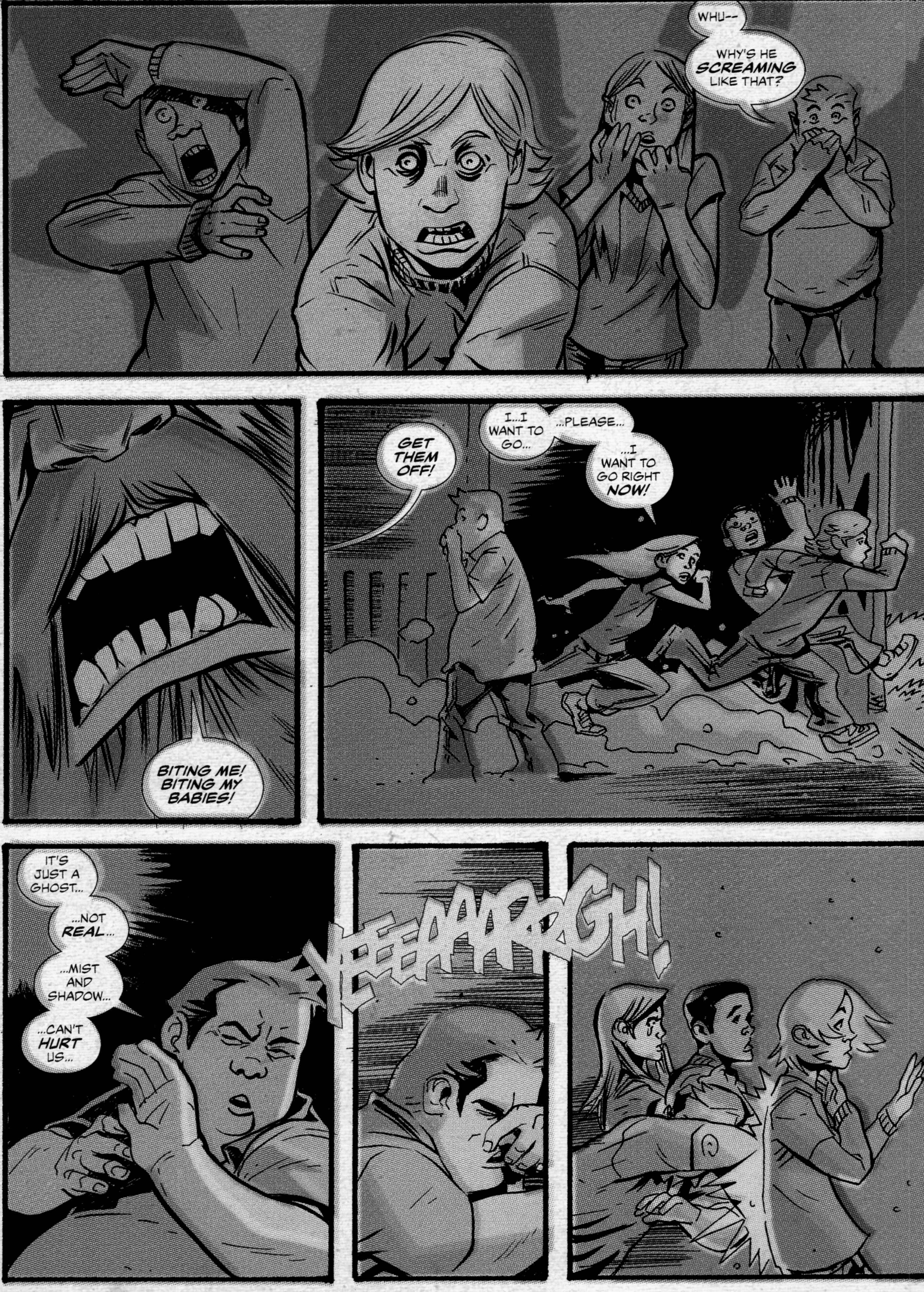
WHU--
WHY'S HE SCREAMING LIKE THAT?
BITING ME! BITING MY BABIES!
GET THEM OFF!
I...I WANT TO GO...
...PLEASE...
...I WANT TO GO RIGHT NOW!
IT'S JUST A GHOST...
...NOT REAL...
...MIST AND SHADOW...
...CAN'T HURT US...
YEEEAAARRGH!

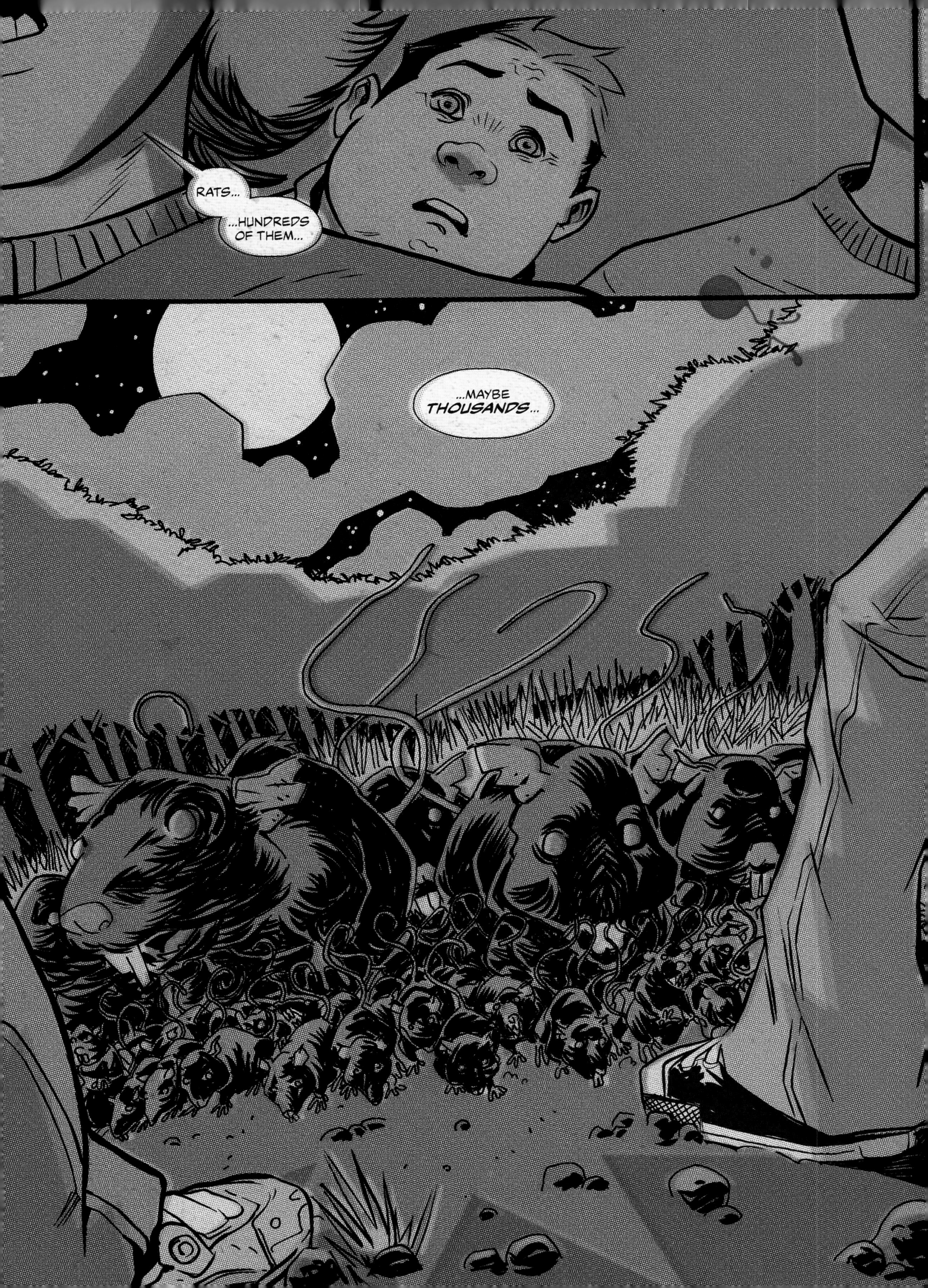
RATS...
...HUNDREDS OF THEM...
...MAYBE THOUSANDS...

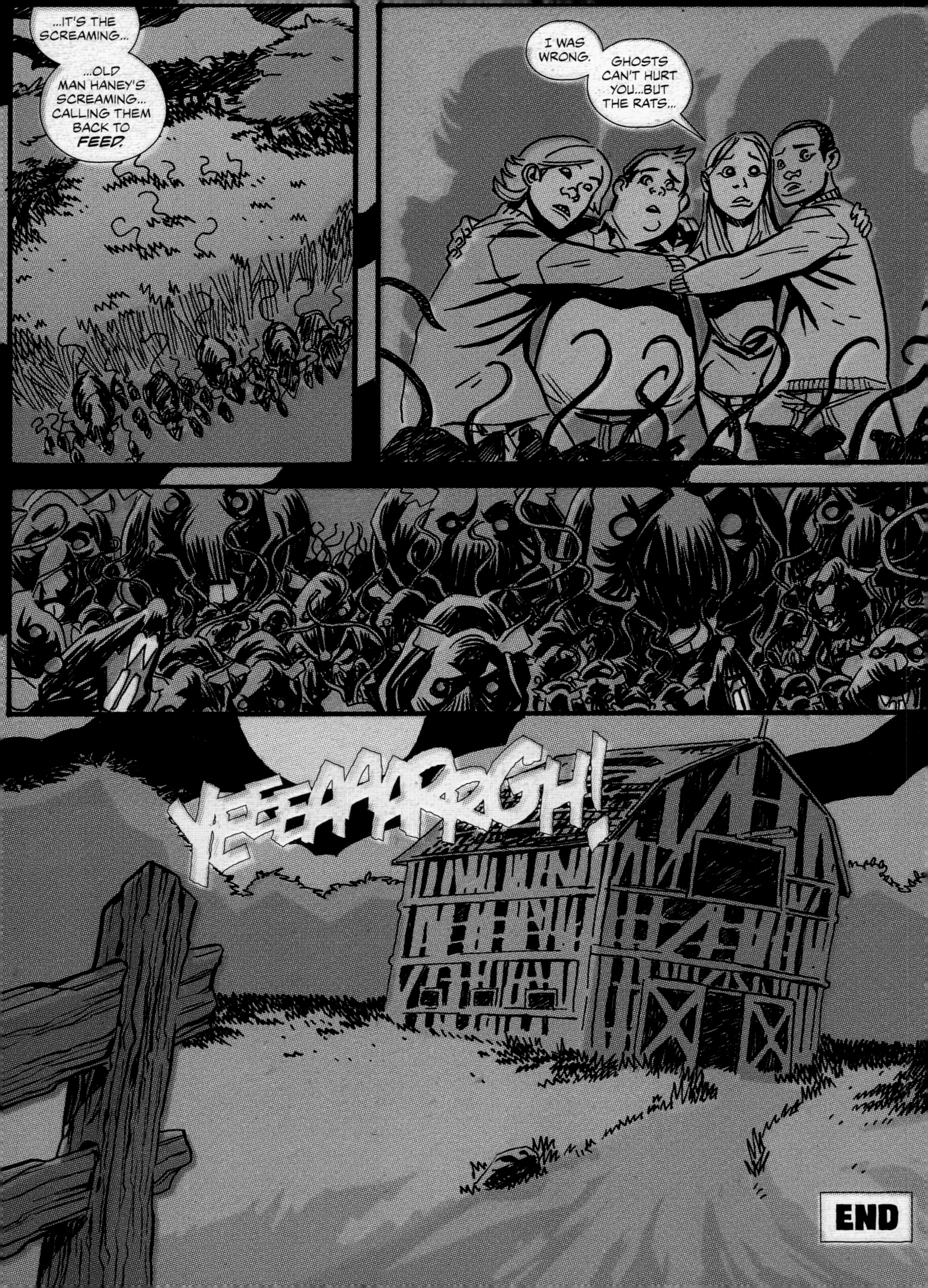
...IT'S THE SCREAMING...
...OLD MAN HANEY'S SCREAMING... CALLING THEM BACK TO FEED.
I WAS WRONG.
GHOSTS CAN'T HURT YOU...BUT THE RATS...
YEEEAAARRGH!
END

FOR THE THRILL of a LIFETIME
Don't Miss A Single, Chilling Issue!
VOODOO
HAUNTED THRILLS
STRANGE
DARK SHADOWS
SUSPOOKS
Bewitched
FANTASTIC fears
Dark Journey
ON SALE AT YOUR FAVORITE NEWSSTAND!

THE UNSEEN

WRITER
JUSTIN JORDAN

ARTIST
TYLER JENKINS

COLORIST
KELLY FITZPATRICK

LETTERER
RACHEL DEERING

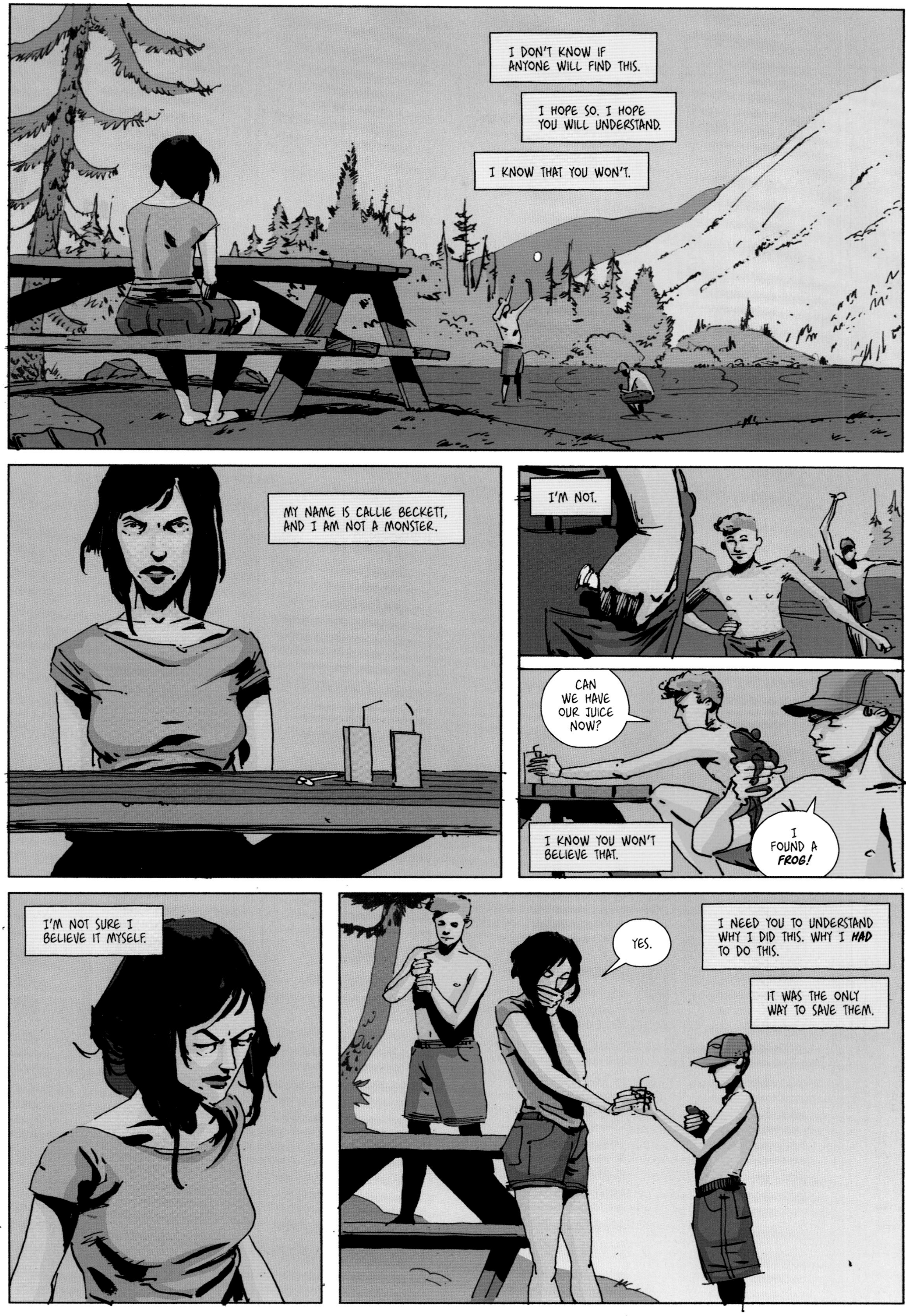
I DON'T KNOW IF ANYONE WILL FIND THIS.
I HOPE SO. I HOPE YOU WILL UNDERSTAND.
I KNOW THAT YOU WON'T.
MY NAME IS CALLIE BECKETT, AND I AM NOT A MONSTER.
I'M NOT.
CAN WE HAVE OUR JUICE NOW?
I FOUND A FROG!
I KNOW YOU WON'T BELIEVE THAT.
I'M NOT SURE I BELIEVE IT MYSELF.
YES.
I NEED YOU TO UNDERSTAND WHY I DID THIS. WHY I HAD TO DO THIS.
IT WAS THE ONLY WAY TO SAVE THEM.

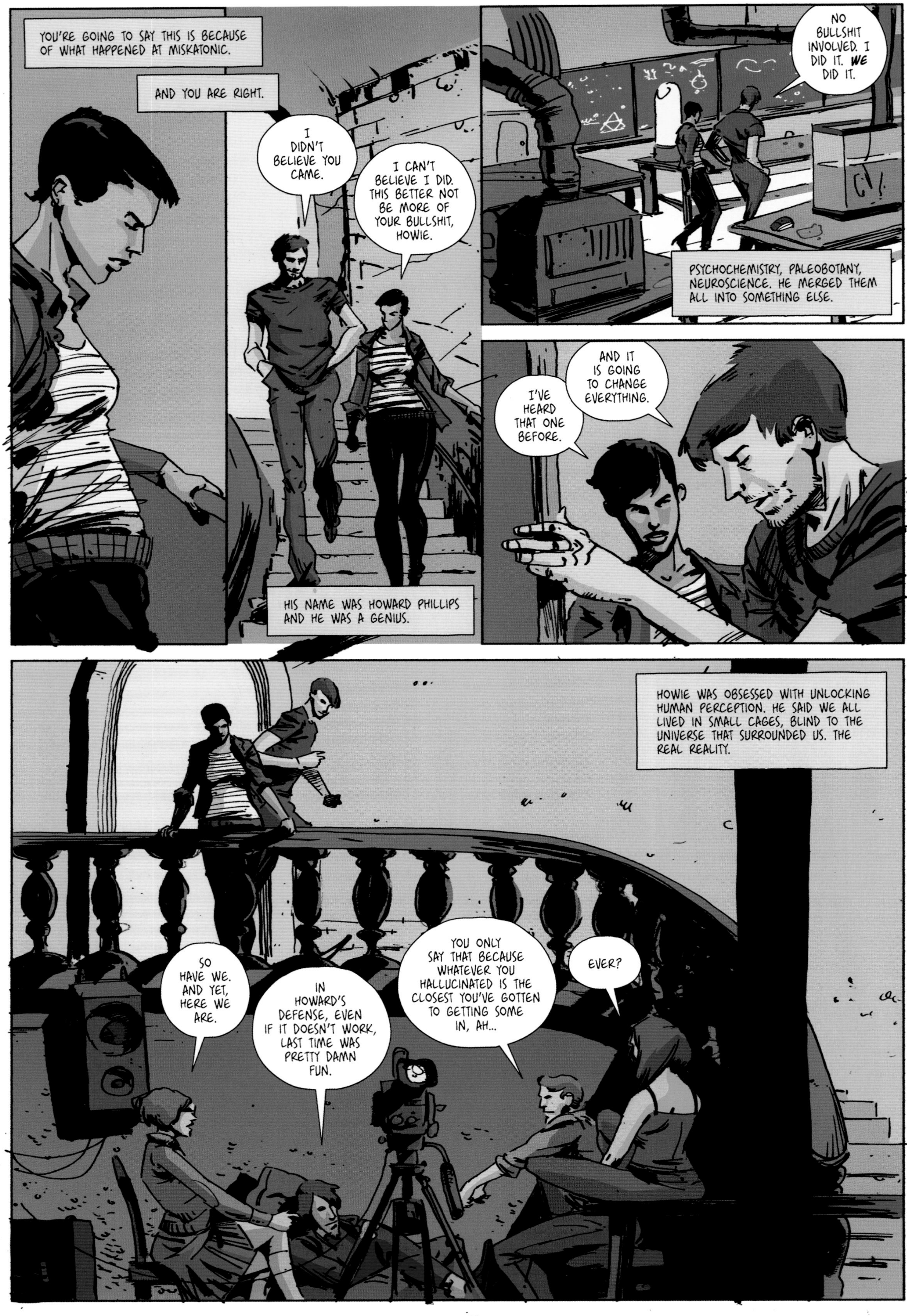
YOU'RE GOING TO SAY THIS IS BECAUSE OF WHAT HAPPENED AT MISKATONIC.
AND YOU ARE RIGHT.
I DIDN'T BELIEVE YOU CAME.
I CAN'T BELIEVE I DID. THIS BETTER NOT BE MORE OF YOUR BULLSHIT, HOWIE.
HIS NAME WAS HOWARD PHILLIPS AND HE WAS A GENIUS.
NO BULLSHIT INVOLVED. I DID IT. WE DID IT.
PSYCHOCHEMISTRY, PALEOBOTANY, NEUROSCIENCE. HE MERGED THEM ALL INTO SOMETHING ELSE.
AND IT IS GOING TO CHANGE EVERYTHING.
I'VE HEARD THAT ONE BEFORE.
HOWIE WAS OBSESSED WITH UNLOCKING HUMAN PERCEPTION. HE SAID WE ALL LIVED IN SMALL CAGES, BLIND TO THE UNIVERSE THAT SURROUNDED US. THE REAL REALITY.
SO HAVE WE. AND YET, HERE WE ARE.
IN HOWARD'S DEFENSE, EVEN IF IT DOESN'T WORK, LAST TIME WAS PRETTY DAMN FUN.
YOU ONLY SAY THAT BECAUSE WHATEVER YOU HALLUCINATED IS THE CLOSEST YOU'VE GOTTEN TO GETTING SOME IN, AH...
EVER?

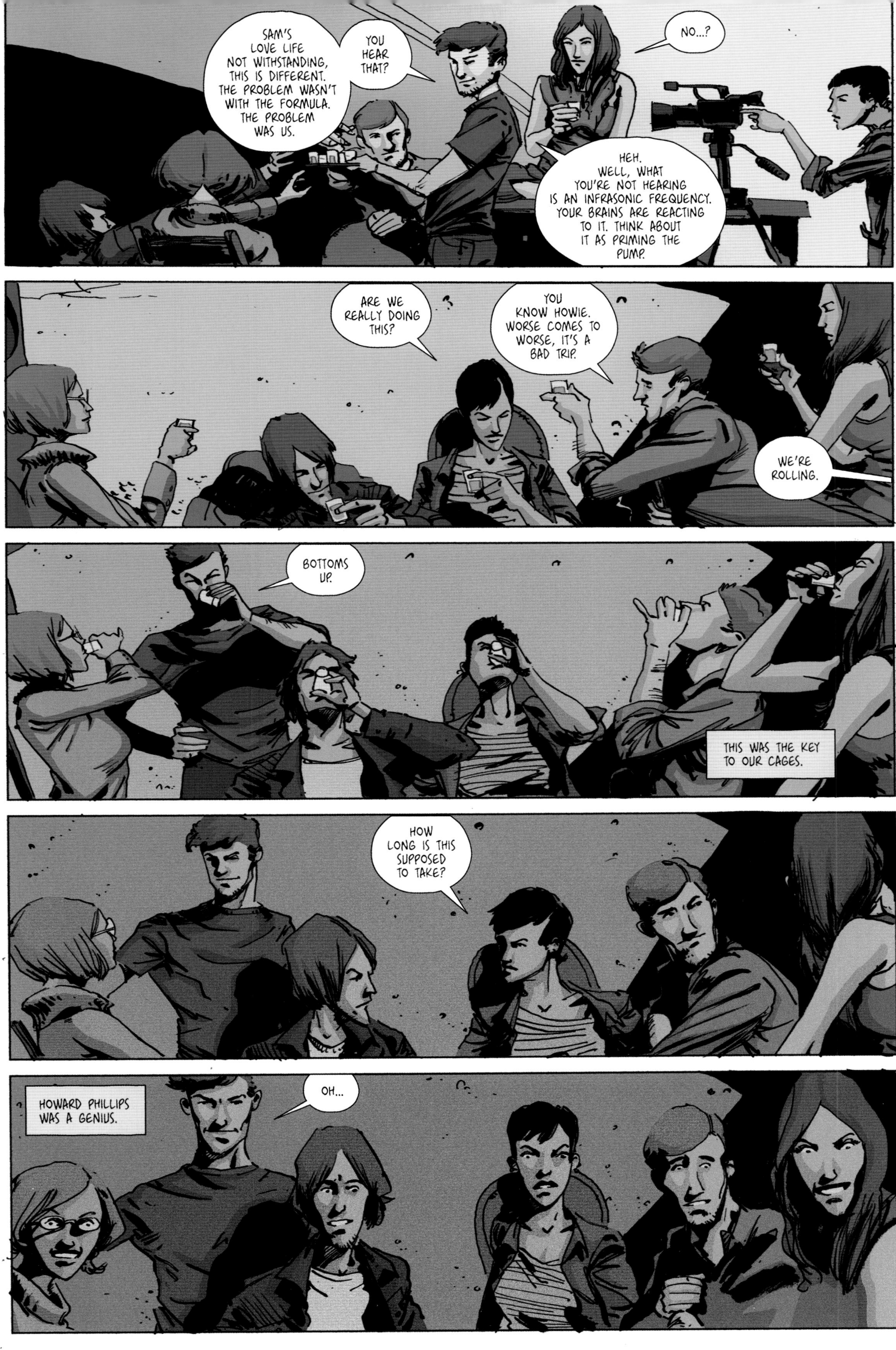
SAM'S LOVE LIFE NOT WITHSTANDING, THIS IS DIFFERENT. THE PROBLEM WASN'T WITH THE FORMULA. THE PROBLEM WAS US.
YOU HEAR THAT?
NO...?
HEH. WELL, WHAT YOU'RE NOT HEARING IS AN INFRASONIC FREQUENCY. YOUR BRAINS ARE REACTING TO IT. THINK ABOUT IT AS PRIMING THE PUMP.
ARE WE REALLY DOING THIS?
YOU KNOW HOWIE. WORSE COMES TO WORSE, IT'S A BAD TRIP.
WE'RE ROLLING.
BOTTOMS UP.
THIS WAS THE KEY TO OUR CAGES.
HOW LONG IS THIS SUPPOSED TO TAKE?
HOWARD PHILLIPS WAS A GENIUS.
OH...

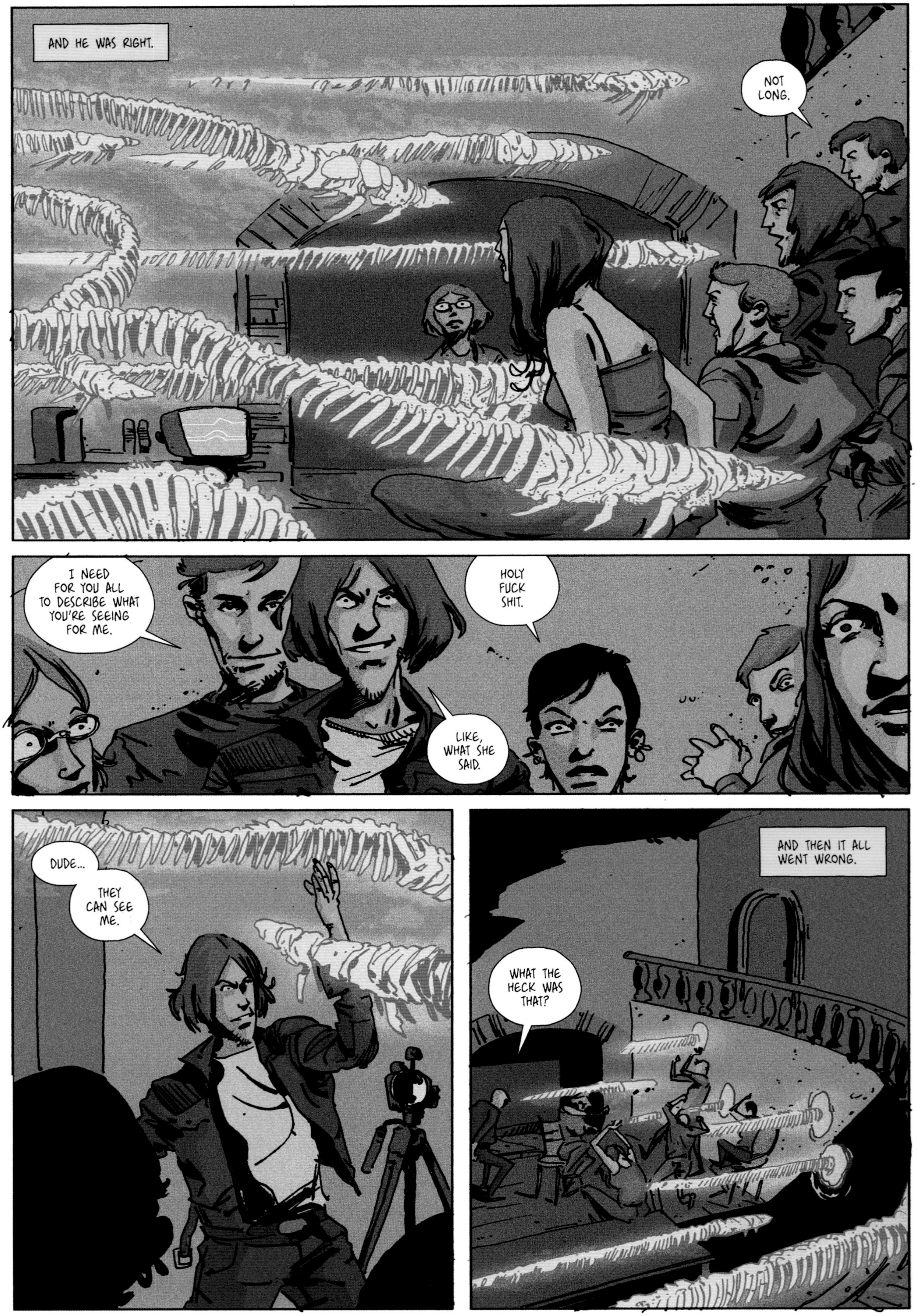
AND HE WAS RIGHT.
NOT LONG.
I NEED FOR YOU ALL TO DESCRIBE WHAT YOU'RE SEEING FOR ME.
LIKE, WHAT SHE SAID.
HOLY FUCK SHIT.
DUDE...
THEY CAN SEE ME.
AND THEN IT ALL WENT WRONG.
WHAT THE HECK WAS THAT?

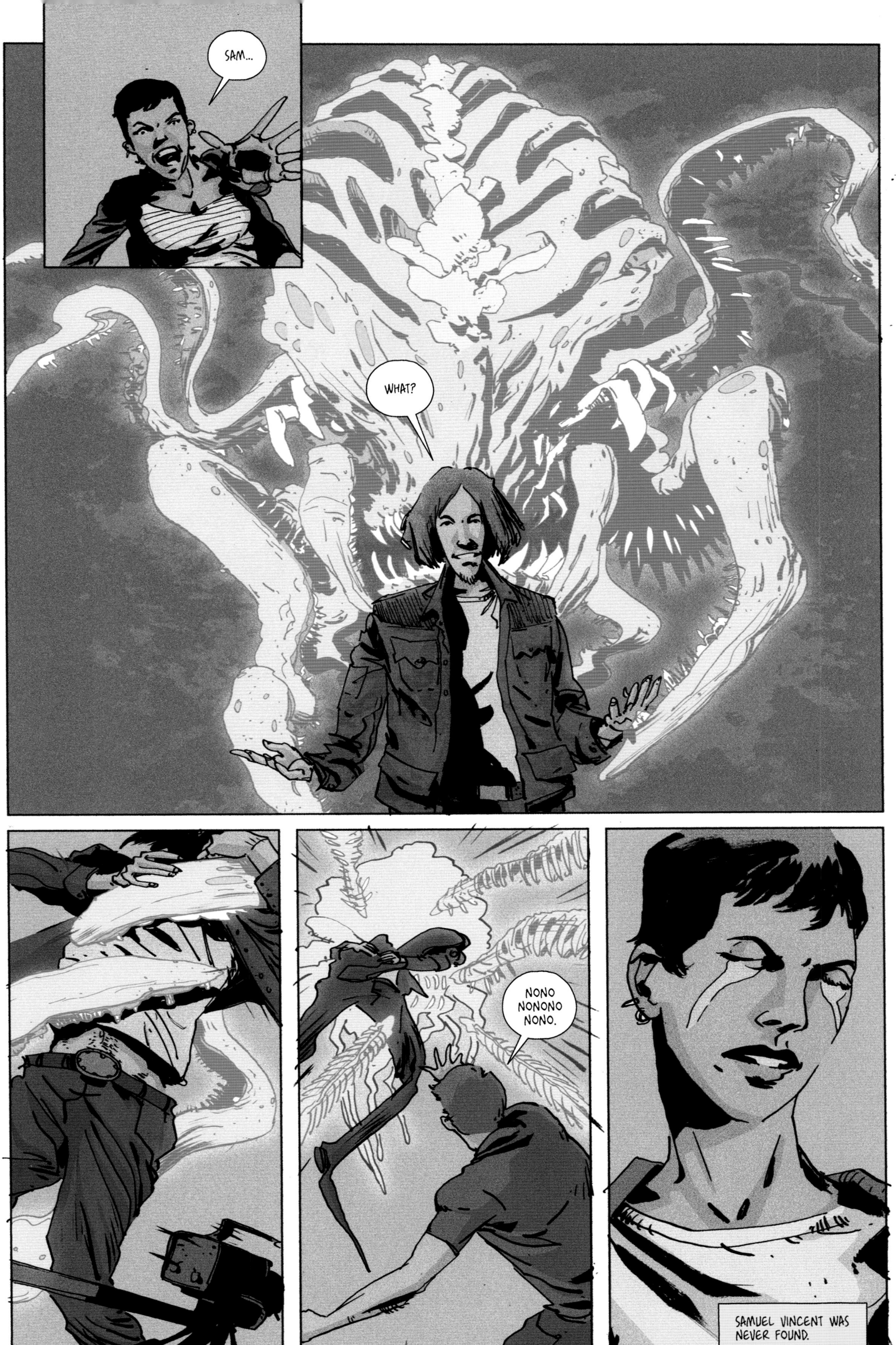
SAM...
WHAT?
NONO NONONO NONO.
SAMUEL VINCENT WAS NEVER FOUND.

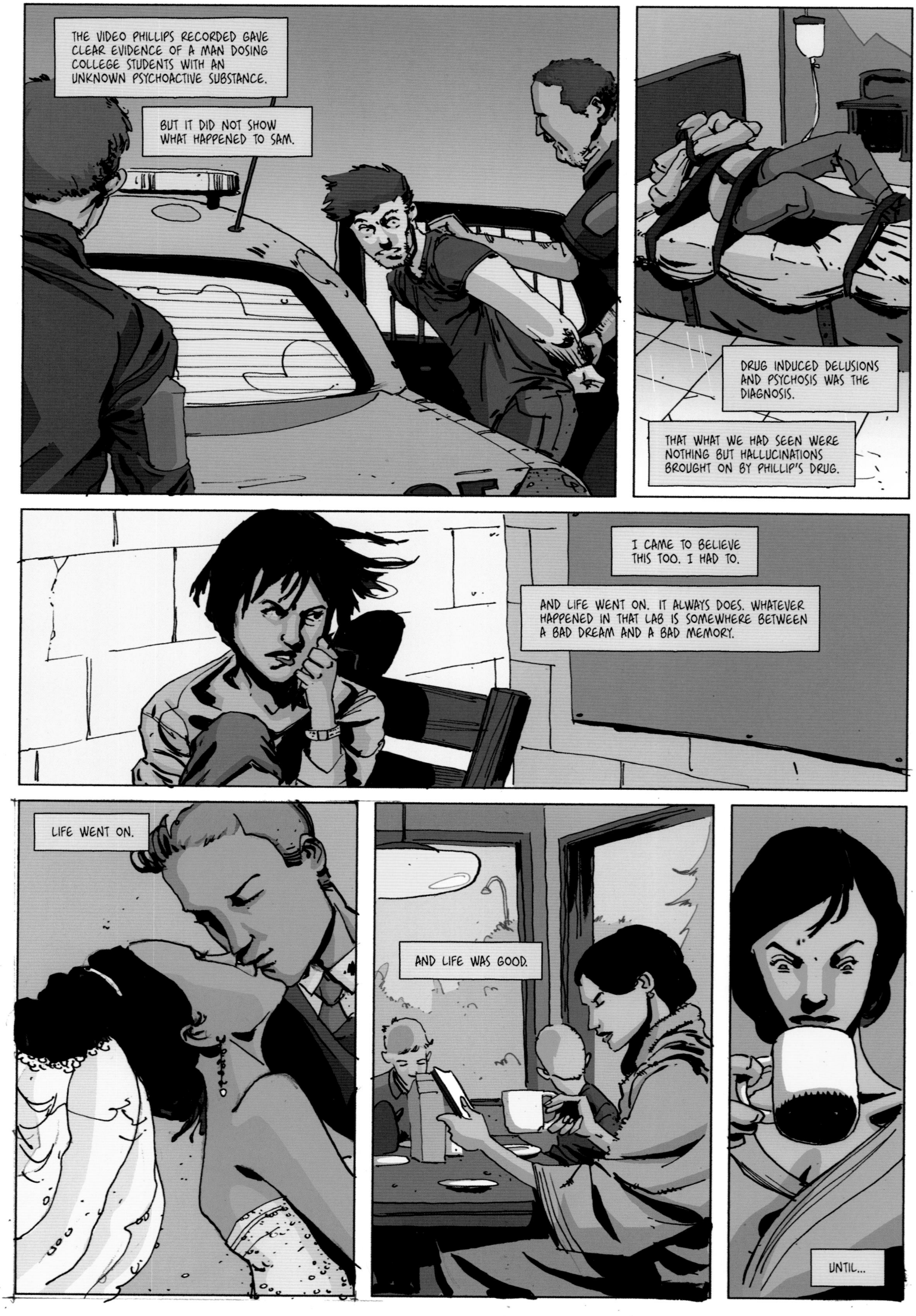
THE VIDEO PHILLIPS RECORDED GAVE CLEAR EVIDENCE OF A MAN DOSING COLLEGE STUDENTS WITH AN UNKNOWN PSYCHOACTIVE SUBSTANCE.
BUT IT DID NOT SHOW WHAT HAPPENED TO SAM.
DRUG INDUCED DELUSIONS AND PSYCHOSIS WAS THE DIAGNOSIS.
THAT WHAT WE HAD SEEN WERE NOTHING BUT HALLUCINATIONS BROUGHT ON BY PHILLIP'S DRUG.
I CAME TO BELIEVE THIS TOO. I HAD TO.
AND LIFE WENT ON. IT ALWAYS DOES. WHATEVER HAPPENED IN THAT LAB IS SOMEWHERE BETWEEN A BAD DREAM AND A BAD MEMORY.
LIFE WENT ON.
AND LIFE WAS GOOD.
UNTIL...

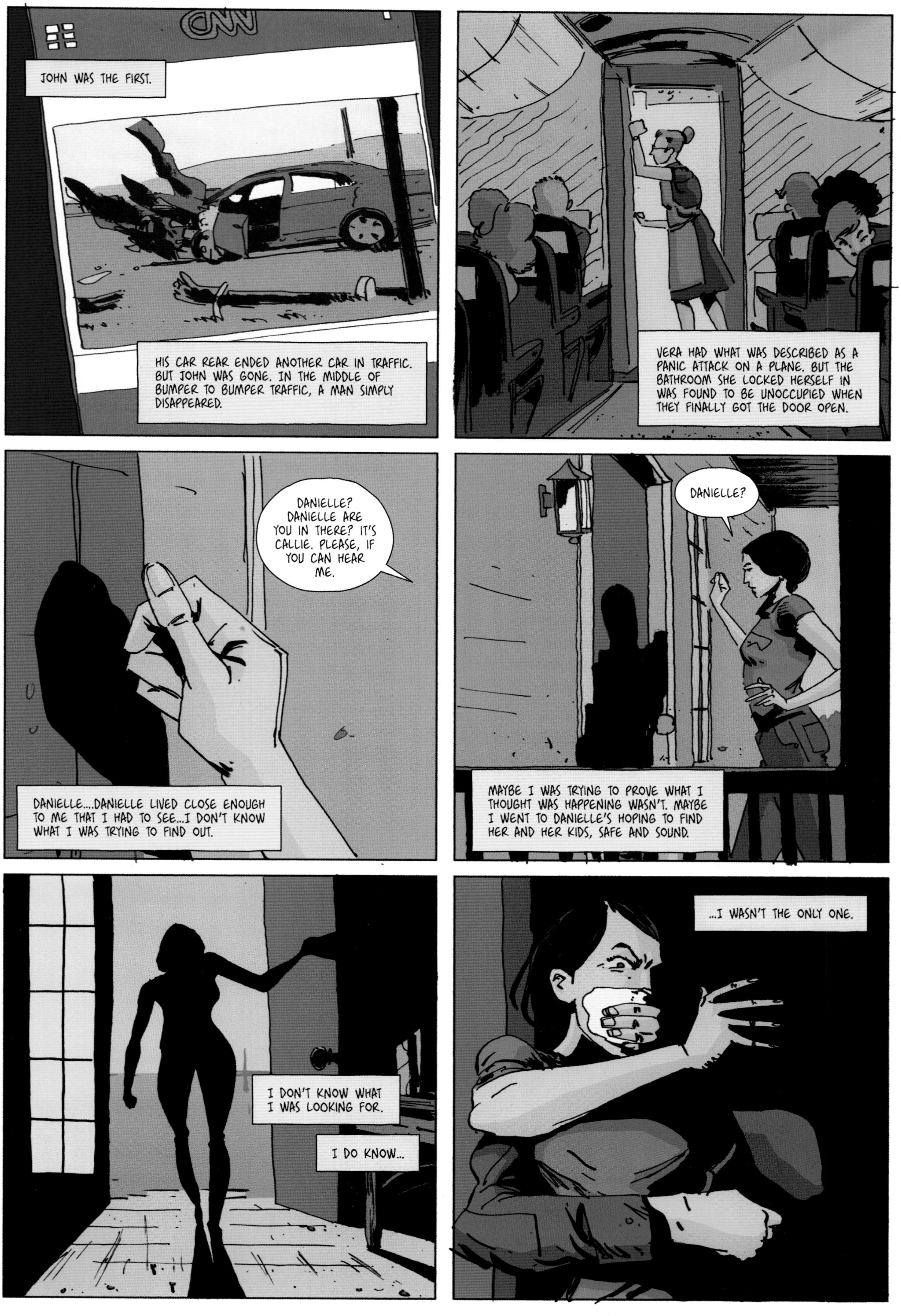
JOHN WAS THE FIRST.
HIS CAR REAR ENDED ANOTHER CAR IN TRAFFIC. BUT JOHN WAS GONE. IN THE MIDDLE OF BUMPER TO BUMPER TRAFFIC, A MAN SIMPLY DISAPPEARED.
VERA HAD WHAT WAS DESCRIBED AS A PANIC ATTACK ON A PLANE. BUT THE BATHROOM SHE LOCKED HERSELF IN WAS FOUND TO BE UNOCCUPIED WHEN THEY FINALLY GOT THE DOOR OPEN.
DANIELLE? DANIELLE ARE YOU IN THERE? IT'S CALLIE. PLEASE, IF YOU CAN HEAR ME.
DANIELLE....DANIELLE LIVED CLOSE ENOUGH TO ME THAT I HAD TO SEE...I DON'T KNOW WHAT I WAS TRYING TO FIND OUT.
DANIELLE?
MAYBE I WAS TRYING TO PROVE WHAT I THOUGHT WAS HAPPENING WASN'T. MAYBE I WENT TO DANIELLE'S HOPING TO FIND HER AND HER KIDS, SAFE AND SOUND.
I DON'T KNOW WHAT I WAS LOOKING FOR.
I DO KNOW...
...I WASN'T THE ONLY ONE.

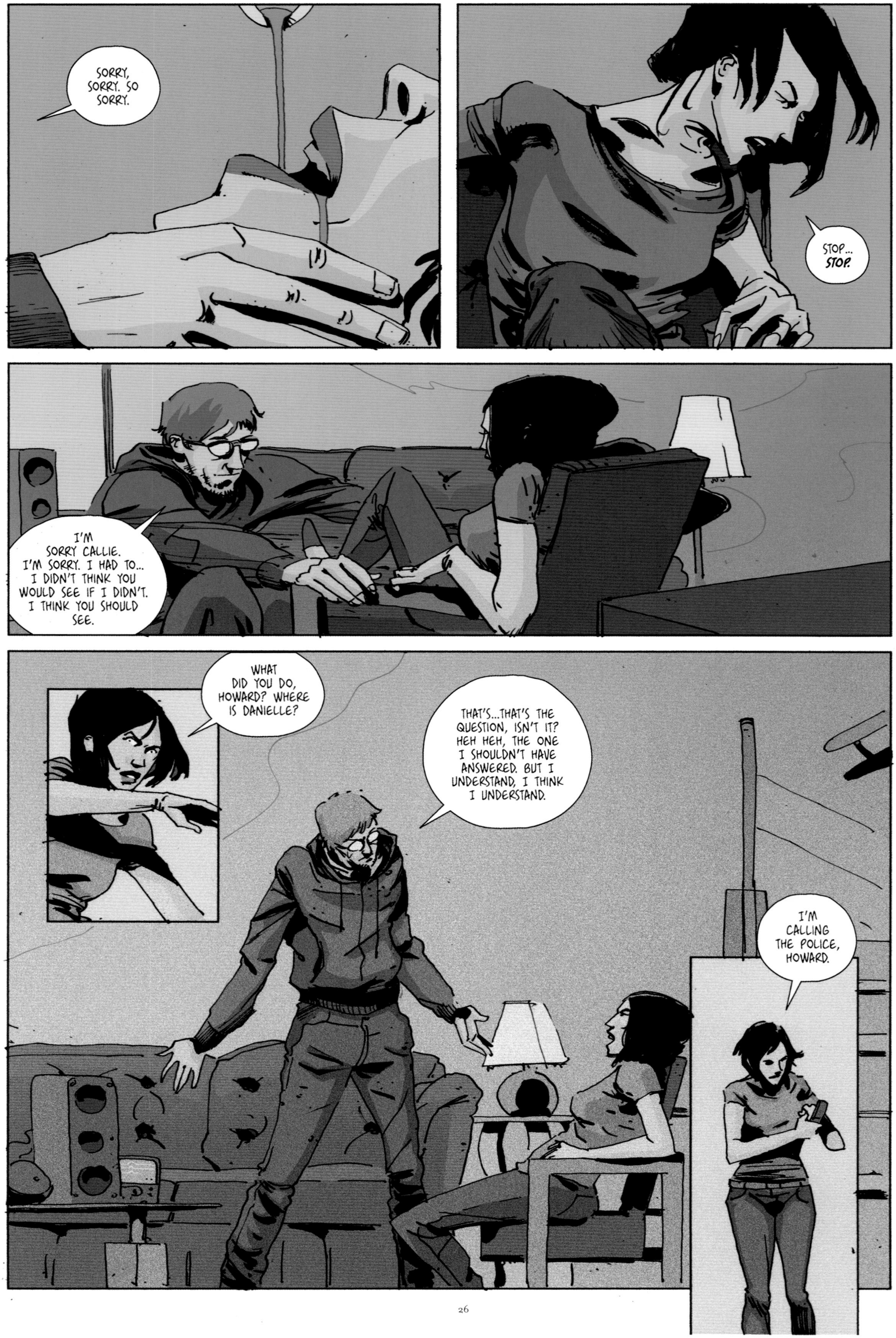
SORRY, SORRY. SO SORRY.
STOP... STOP.
I'M SORRY CALLIE. I'M SORRY. I HAD TO... I DIDN'T THINK YOU WOULD SEE IF I DIDN'T. I THINK YOU SHOULD SEE.
WHAT DID YOU DO, HOWARD? WHERE IS DANIELLE?
THAT'S...THAT'S THE QUESTION, ISN'T IT? HEH HEH, THE ONE I SHOULDN'T HAVE ANSWERED. BUT I UNDERSTAND, I THINK I UNDERSTAND.
I'M CALLING THE POLICE, HOWARD.

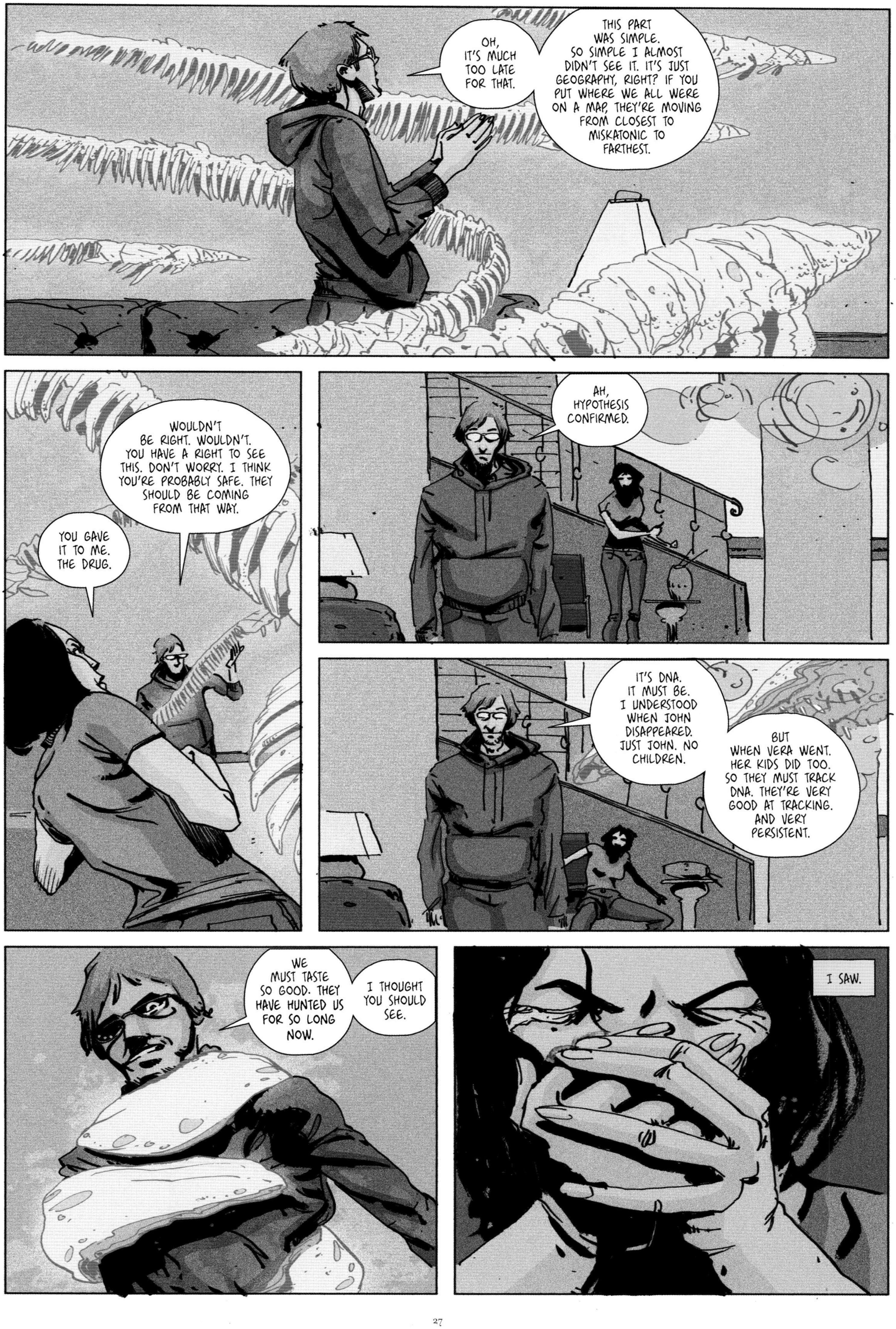
OH, IT'S MUCH TOO LATE FOR THAT.
THIS PART WAS SIMPLE. SO SIMPLE I ALMOST DIDN'T SEE IT. IT'S JUST GEOGRAPHY, RIGHT? IF YOU PUT WHERE WE ALL WERE ON A MAP, THEY'RE MOVING FROM CLOSEST TO MISKATONIC TO FARTHEST.
YOU GAVE IT TO ME. THE DRUG.
WOULDN'T BE RIGHT. WOULDN'T. YOU HAVE A RIGHT TO SEE THIS. DON'T WORRY. I THINK YOU'RE PROBABLY SAFE. THEY SHOULD BE COMING FROM THAT WAY.
AH, HYPOTHESIS CONFIRMED.
IT'S DNA. IT MUST BE. I UNDERSTOOD WHEN JOHN DISAPPEARED. JUST JOHN. NO CHILDREN.
BUT WHEN VERA WENT. HER KIDS DID TOO. SO THEY MUST TRACK DNA. THEY'RE VERY GOOD AT TRACKING. AND VERY PERSISTENT.
WE MUST TASTE SO GOOD. THEY HAVE HUNTED US FOR SO LONG NOW.
I THOUGHT YOU SHOULD SEE.
I SAW.

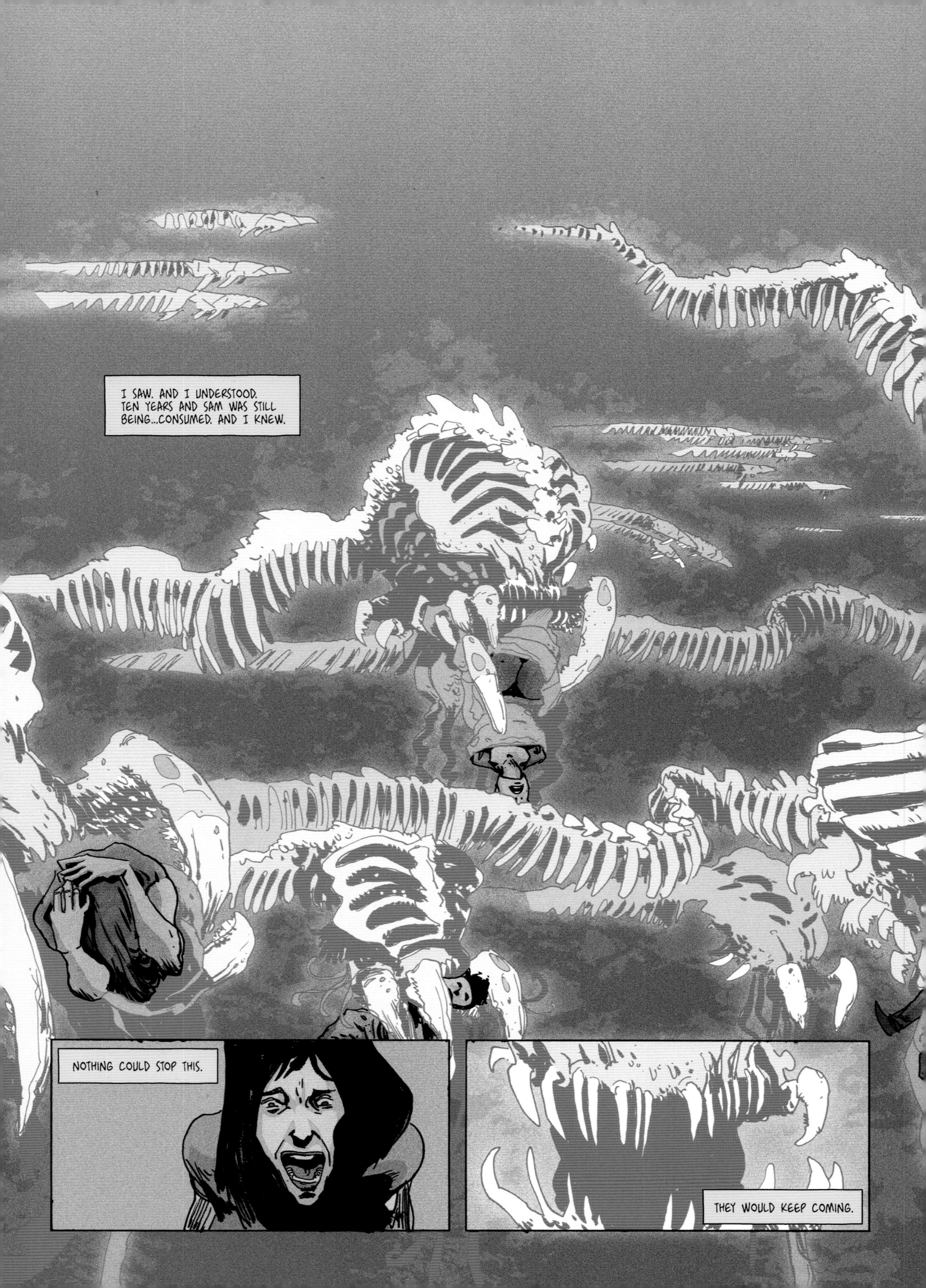
I SAW. AND I UNDERSTOOD. TEN YEARS AND SAM WAS STILL BEING...CONSUMED. AND I KNEW.
NOTHING COULD STOP THIS.
THEY WOULD KEEP COMING.

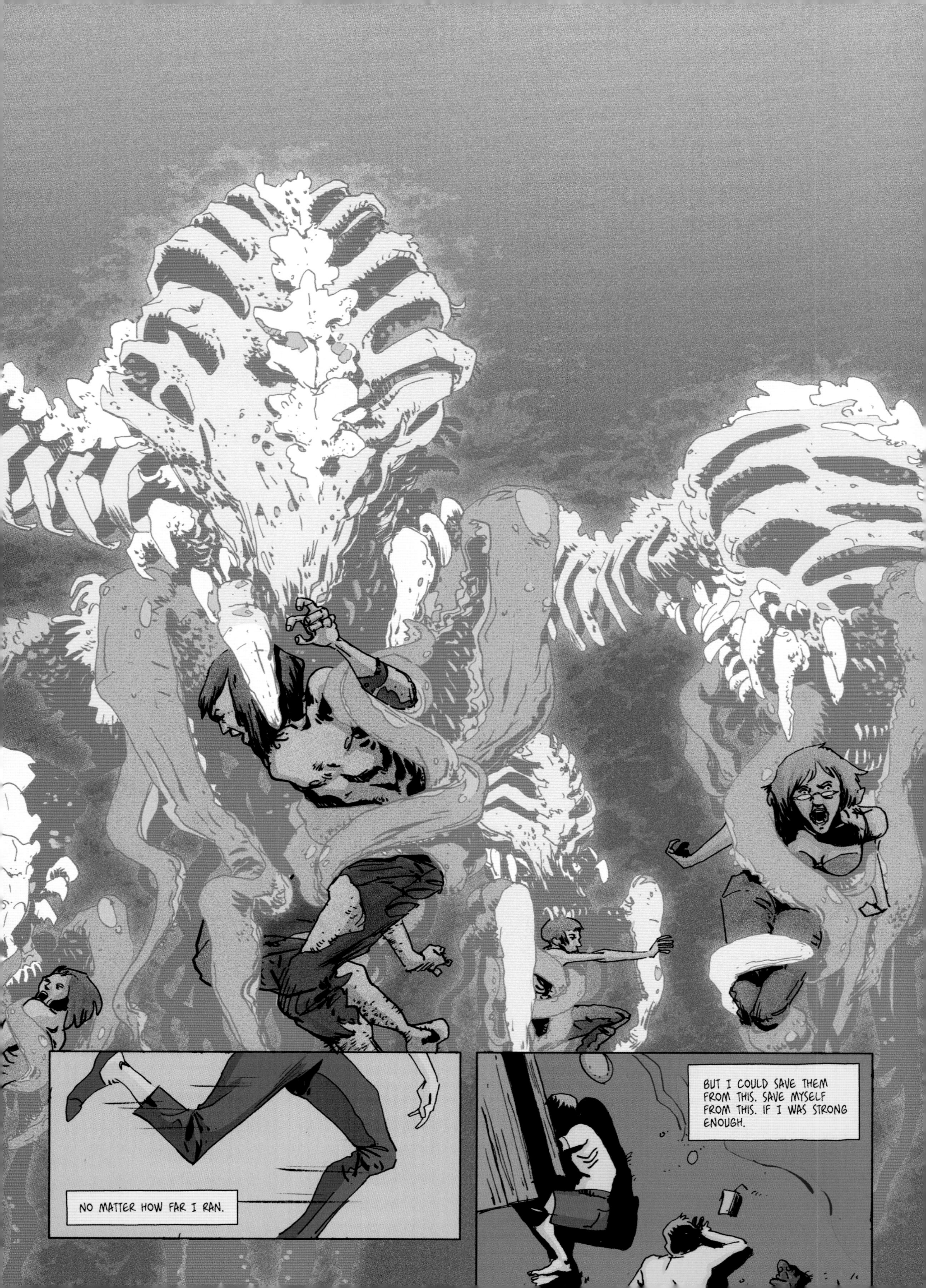
NO MATTER HOW FAR I RAN.
BUT I COULD SAVE THEM FROM THIS. SAVE MYSELF FROM THIS. IF I WAS STRONG ENOUGH.

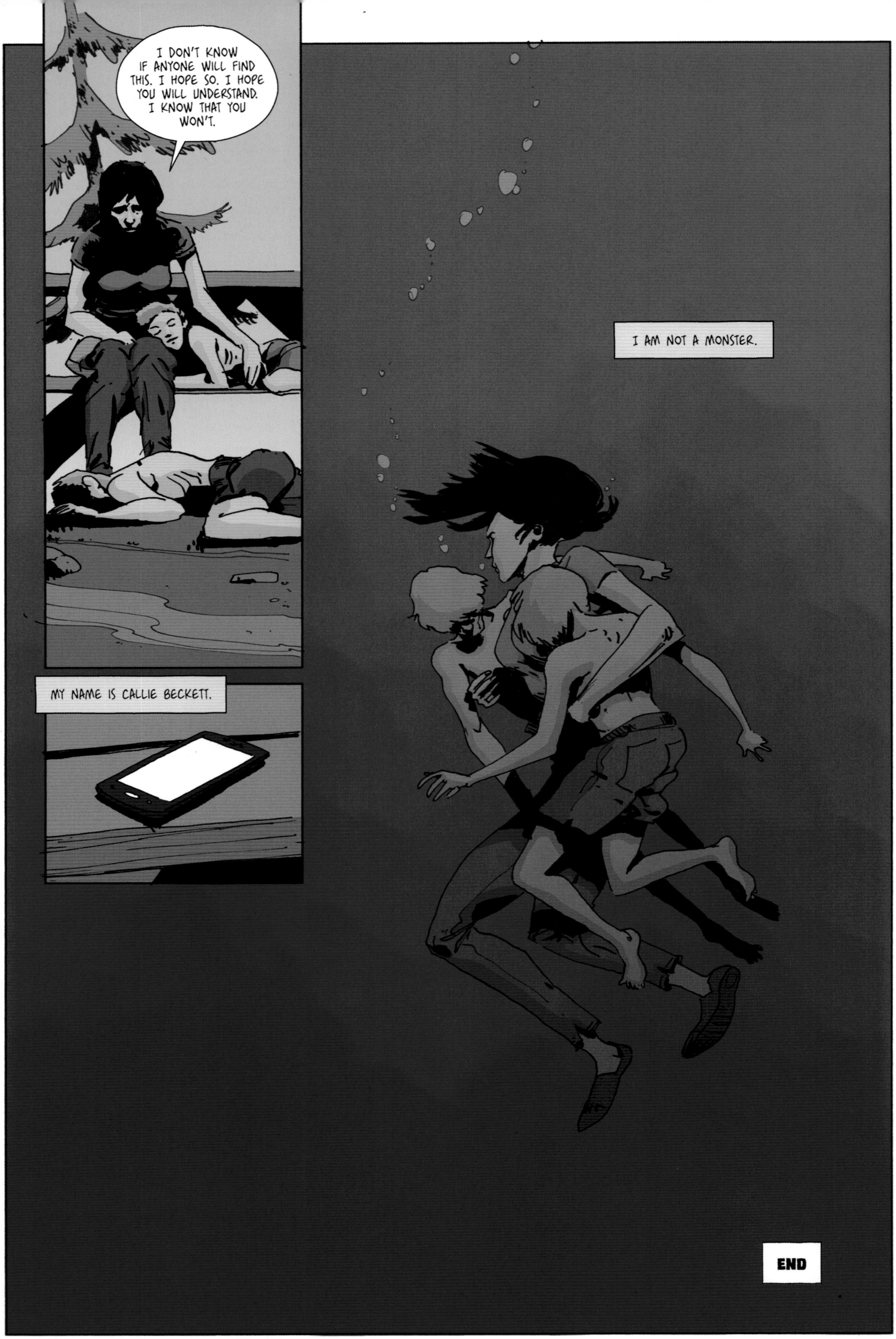
I DON'T KNOW IF ANYONE WILL FIND THIS. I HOPE SO. I HOPE YOU WILL UNDERSTAND. I KNOW THAT YOU WON'T.
MY NAME IS CALLIE BECKETT.
I AM NOT A MONSTER.
END

FEAR FOR YOUR EARS!

NEW L.P. RECORD ALBUM

Rush me the IN THE DARK audio drama!
I have enclosed $5.00.

Name:
Address:
City:
State:
Zip Code:

ORIGINAL SOUND TRACK NARRATIVES FROM YOUR FAVORITE IN THE DARK TERROR TALES!

12" VINYL RECORDS!

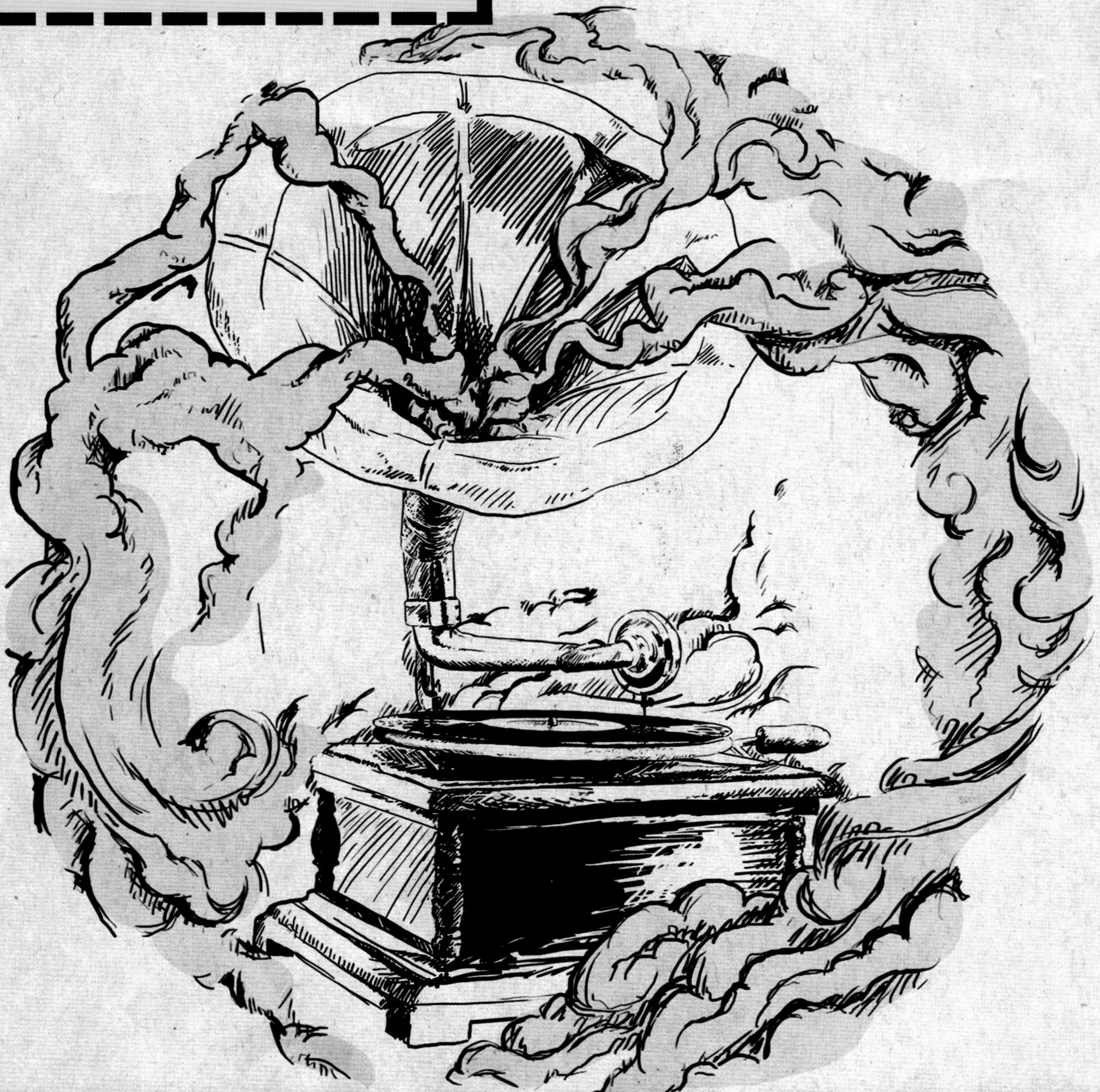

SEND TO: IN THE DARK 6669 Werewolf Way - Room 13 Columbus, OH 43230

FAMINE'S SHADOW

WRITER
RACHEL DEERING

ARTIST
CHRISTINE LARSEN

COLORIST
CHRISTINE LARSEN

LETTERER
RACHEL DEERING

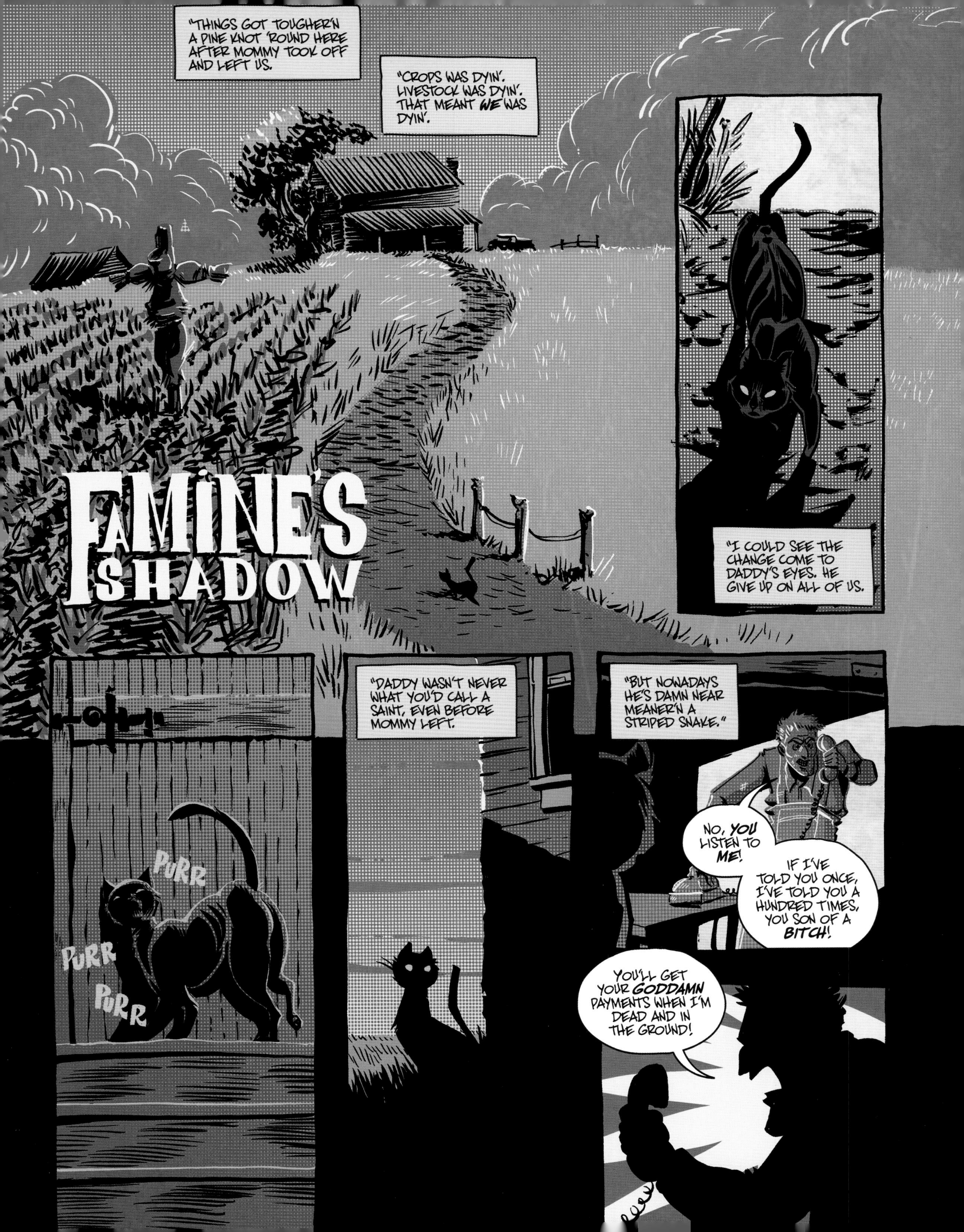
"THINGS GOT TOUGHER'N A PINE KNOT 'ROUND HERE AFTER MOMMY TOOK OFF AND LEFT US.
"CROPS WAS DYIN'. LIVESTOCK WAS DYIN'. THAT MEANT **WE** WAS DYIN'.
FAMINE'S SHADOW
"I COULD SEE THE CHANGE COME TO DADDY'S EYES. HE GIVE UP ON ALL OF US.
PURR
PURR
PURR
"DADDY WASN'T NEVER WHAT YOU'D CALL A SAINT, EVEN BEFORE MOMMY LEFT.
"BUT NOWADAYS HE'S DAMN NEAR MEANER'N A STRIPED SNAKE."
NO, **YOU** LISTEN TO **ME**!
IF I'VE TOLD YOU ONCE, I'VE TOLD YOU A HUNDRED TIMES, YOU SON OF A **BITCH**!
YOU'LL GET YOUR **GODDAMN** PAYMENTS WHEN I'M DEAD AND IN THE GROUND!

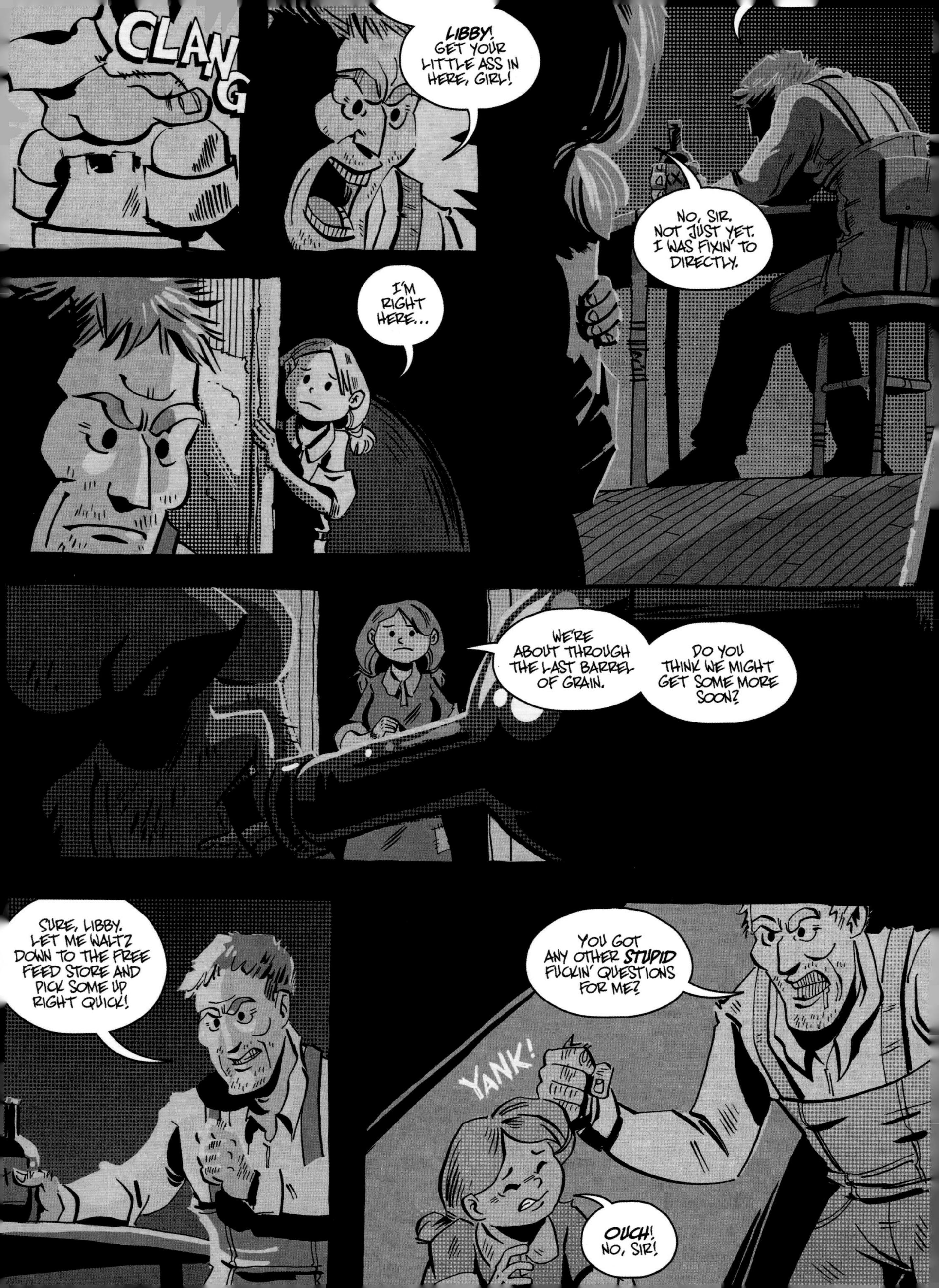
CLANG
LIBBY! GET YOUR LITTLE ASS IN HERE, GIRL!
NO, SIR. NOT JUST YET. I WAS FIXIN' TO DIRECTLY.
I'M RIGHT HERE...
WE'RE ABOUT THROUGH THE LAST BARREL OF GRAIN.
DO YOU THINK WE MIGHT GET SOME MORE SOON?
SURE, LIBBY. LET ME WALTZ DOWN TO THE FREE FEED STORE AND PICK SOME UP RIGHT QUICK!
YOU GOT ANY OTHER STUPID FUCKIN' QUESTIONS FOR ME?
YANK!
OUCH! NO, SIR!

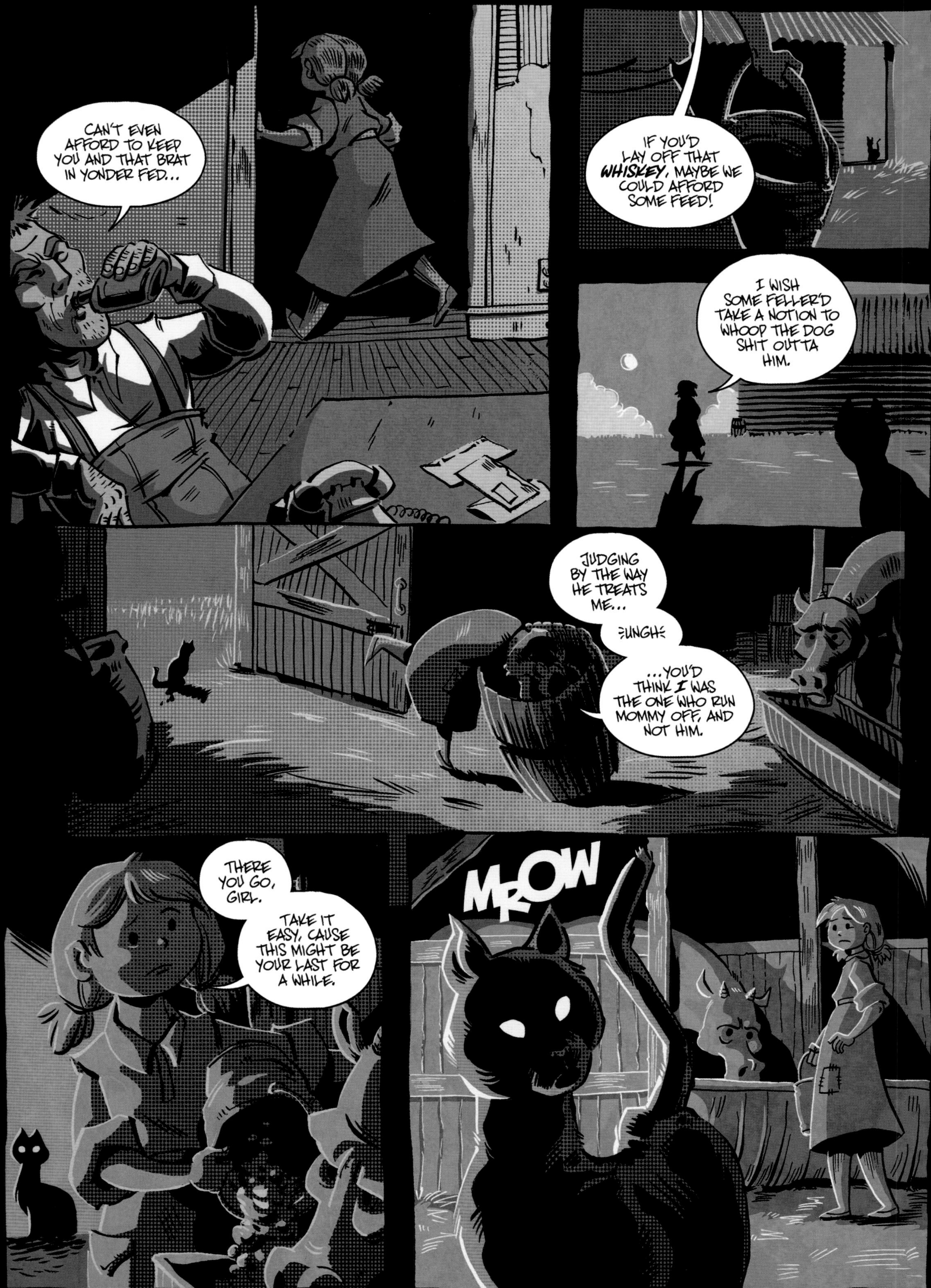
CAN'T EVEN AFFORD TO KEEP YOU AND THAT BRAT IN YONDER FED...
IF YOU'D LAY OFF THAT WHISKEY, MAYBE WE COULD AFFORD SOME FEED!
I WISH SOME FELLER'D TAKE A NOTION TO WHOOP THE DOG SHIT OUTTA HIM.
JUDGING BY THE WAY HE TREATS ME...
UNGH
...YOU'D THINK I WAS THE ONE WHO RUN MOMMY OFF, AND NOT HIM.
THERE YOU GO, GIRL.
TAKE IT EASY, CAUSE THIS MIGHT BE YOUR LAST FOR A WHILE.
MROW

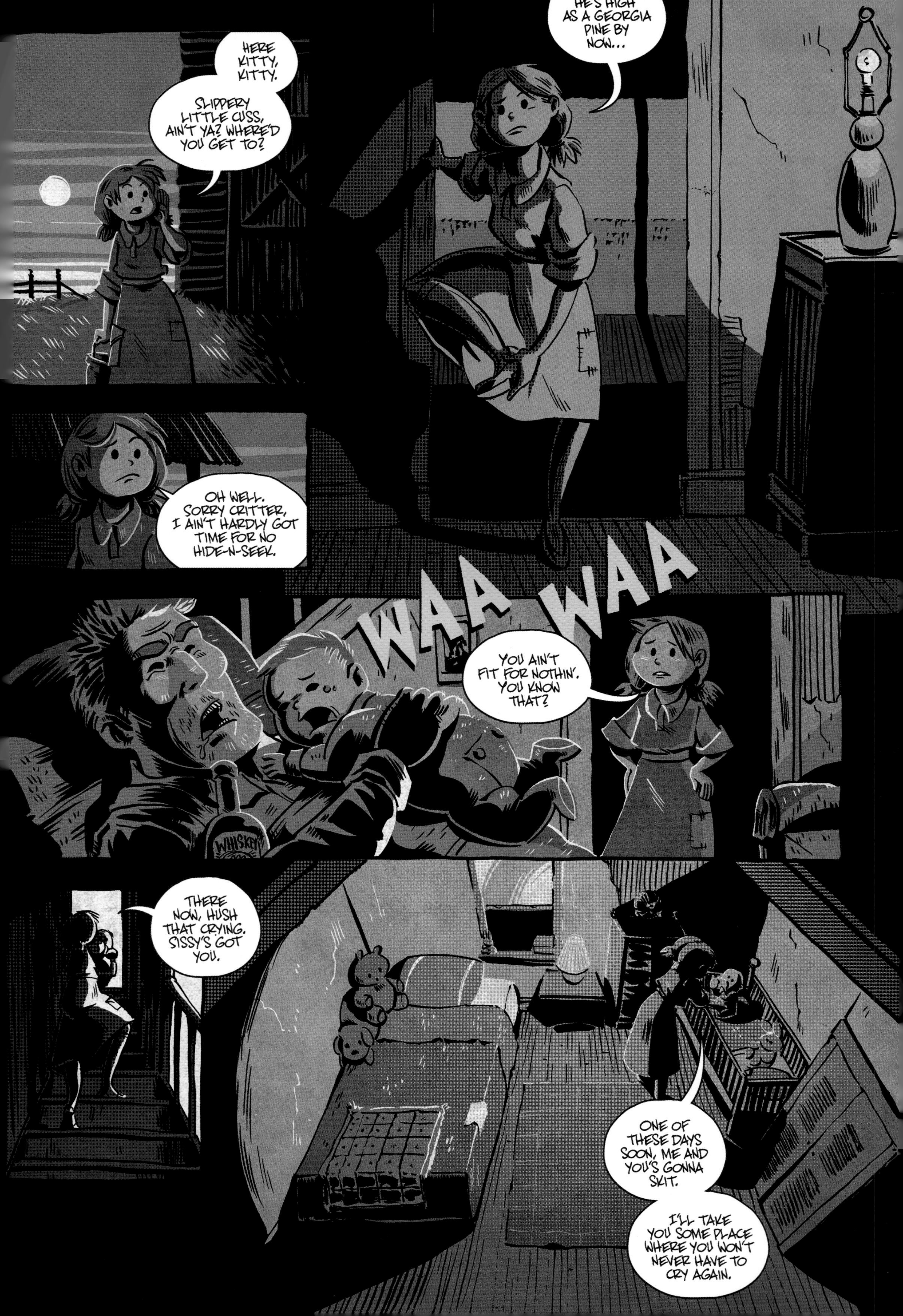
HERE KITTY, KITTY.
SLIPPERY LITTLE CUSS, AIN'T YA? WHERE'D YOU GET TO?
RECKON HE'S HIGH AS A GEORGIA PINE BY NOW...
OH WELL. SORRY CRITTER, I AIN'T HARDLY GOT TIME FOR NO HIDE-N-SEEK.
WAA WAA
YOU AIN'T FIT FOR NOTHIN'. YOU KNOW THAT?
WHISKEY
THERE NOW, HUSH THAT CRYING. SISSY'S GOT YOU.
ONE OF THESE DAYS SOON, ME AND YOU'S GONNA SKIT.
I'LL TAKE YOU SOME PLACE WHERE YOU WON'T NEVER HAVE TO CRY AGAIN.

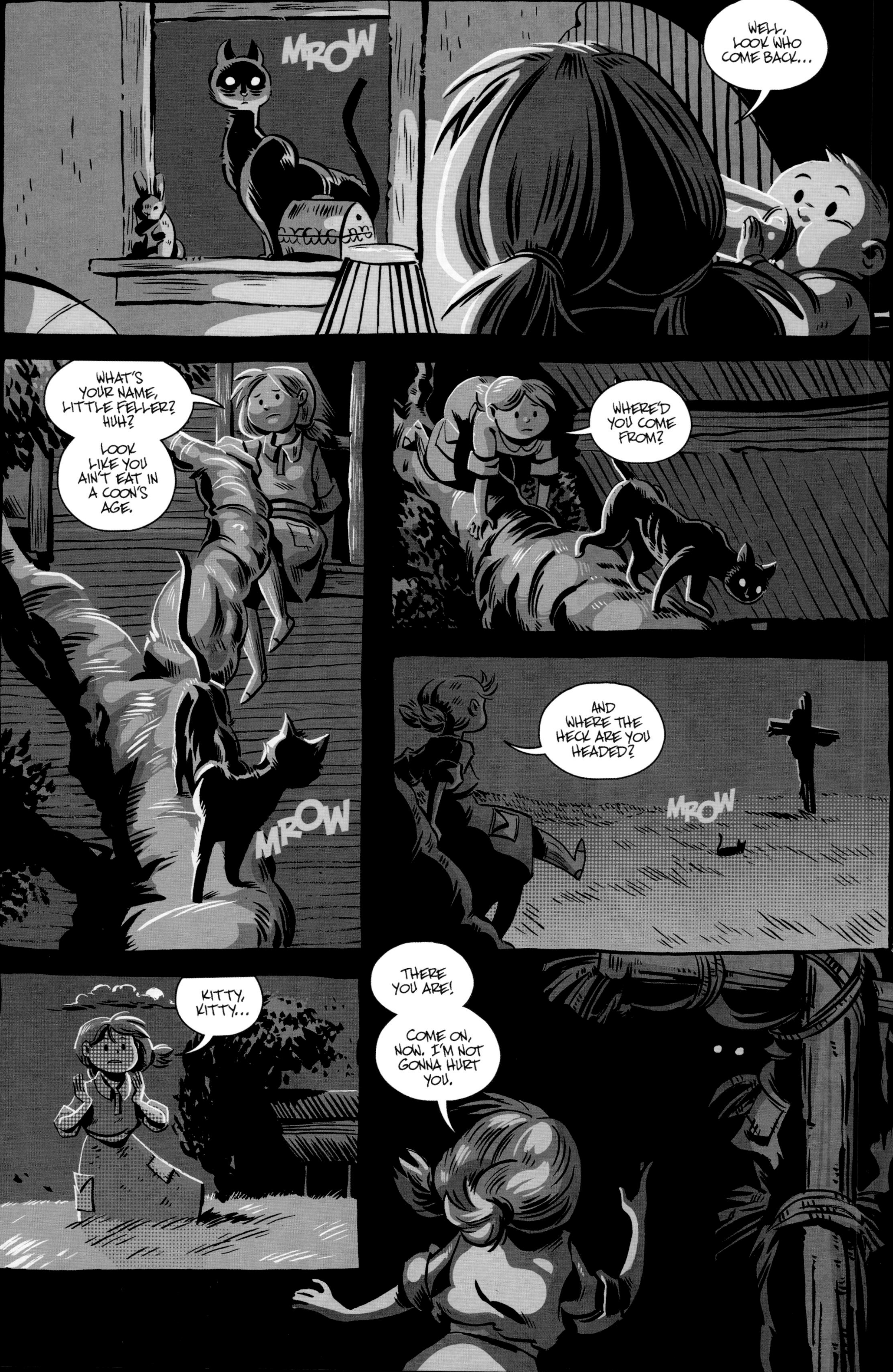
MROW
WELL, LOOK WHO COME BACK...
WHAT'S YOUR NAME, LITTLE FELLER? HUH?
LOOK LIKE YOU AIN'T EAT IN A COON'S AGE.
MROW
WHERE'D YOU COME FROM?
AND WHERE THE HECK ARE YOU HEADED?
MROW
KITTY, KITTY...
THERE YOU ARE!
COME ON, NOW. I'M NOT GONNA HURT YOU.

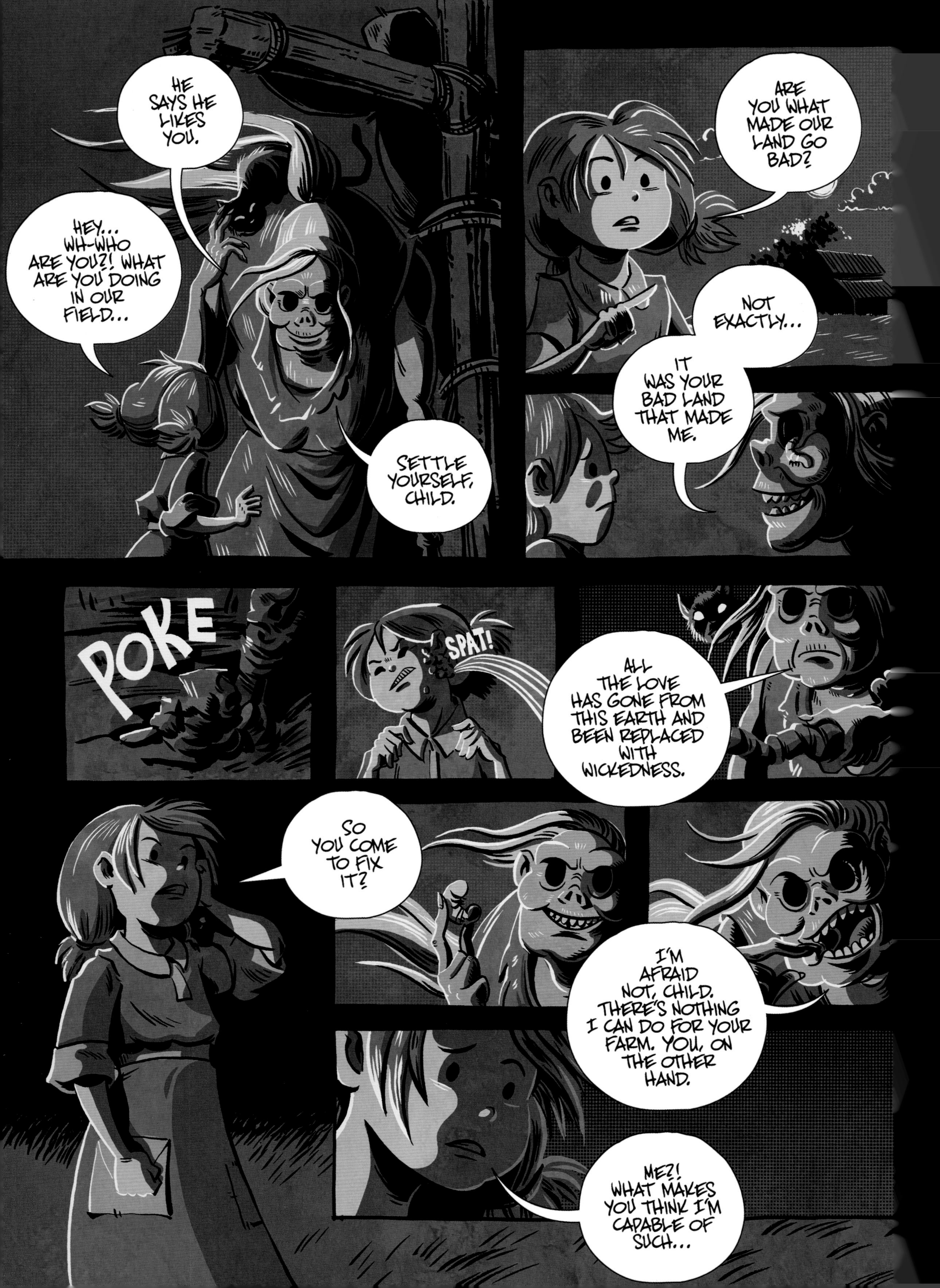
HEY... WH-WHO ARE YOU?! WHAT ARE YOU DOING IN OUR FIELD...
HE SAYS HE LIKES YOU.
SETTLE YOURSELF, CHILD.
ARE YOU WHAT MADE OUR LAND GO BAD?
NOT EXACTLY...
IT WAS YOUR BAD LAND THAT MADE ME.
POKE
SPAT!
ALL THE LOVE HAS GONE FROM THIS EARTH AND BEEN REPLACED WITH WICKEDNESS.
SO YOU COME TO FIX IT?
I'M AFRAID NOT, CHILD. THERE'S NOTHING I CAN DO FOR YOUR FARM. YOU, ON THE OTHER HAND.
ME?! WHAT MAKES YOU THINK I'M CAPABLE OF SUCH...

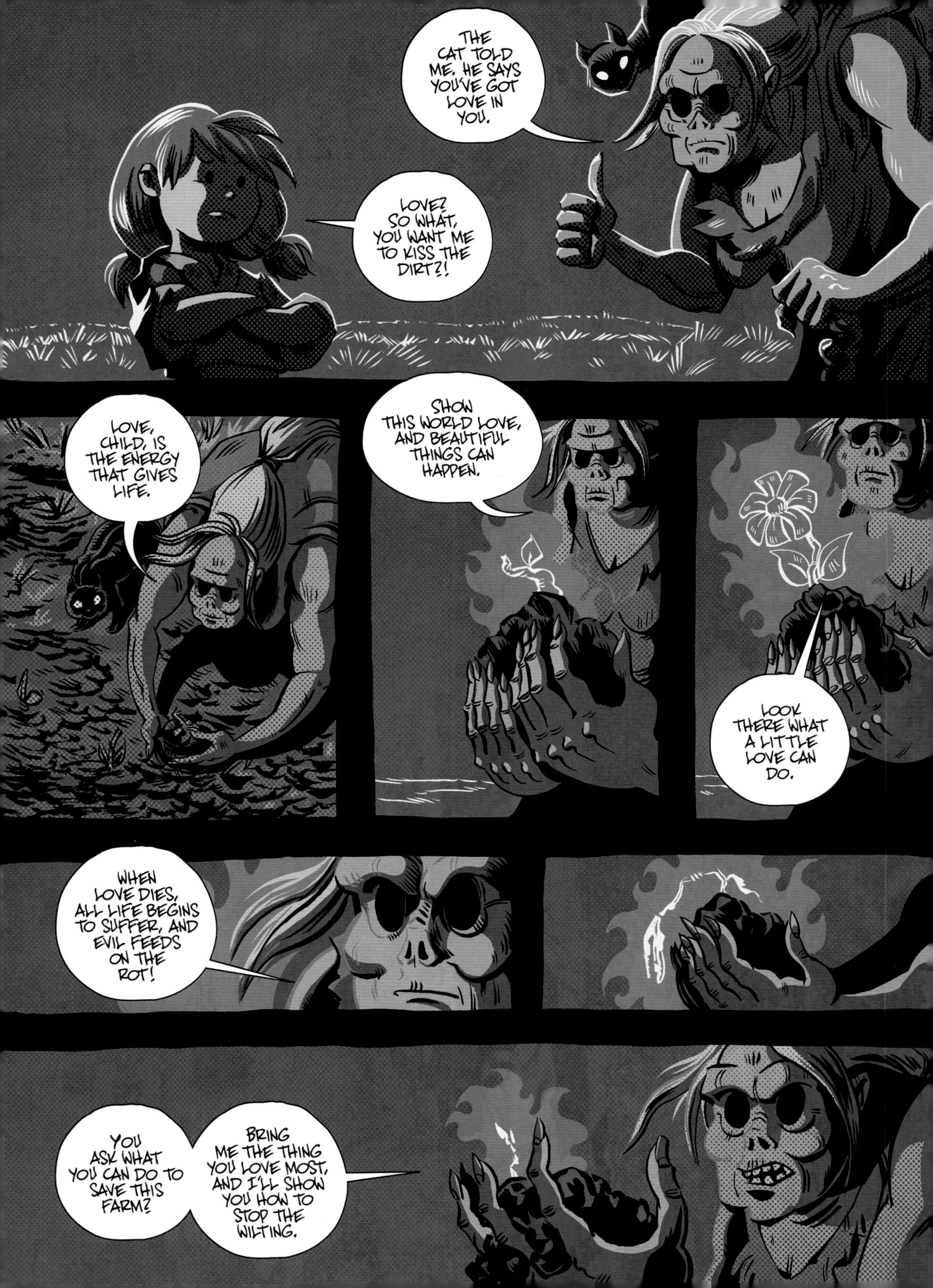
THE CAT TOLD ME. HE SAYS YOU'VE GOT LOVE IN YOU.
LOVE? SO WHAT, YOU WANT ME TO KISS THE DIRT?!
LOVE, CHILD, IS THE ENERGY THAT GIVES LIFE.
SHOW THIS WORLD LOVE, AND BEAUTIFUL THINGS CAN HAPPEN.
LOOK THERE WHAT A LITTLE LOVE CAN DO.
WHEN LOVE DIES, ALL LIFE BEGINS TO SUFFER, AND EVIL FEEDS ON THE ROT!
YOU ASK WHAT YOU CAN DO TO SAVE THIS FARM?
BRING ME THE THING YOU LOVE MOST, AND I'LL SHOW YOU HOW TO STOP THE WILTING.

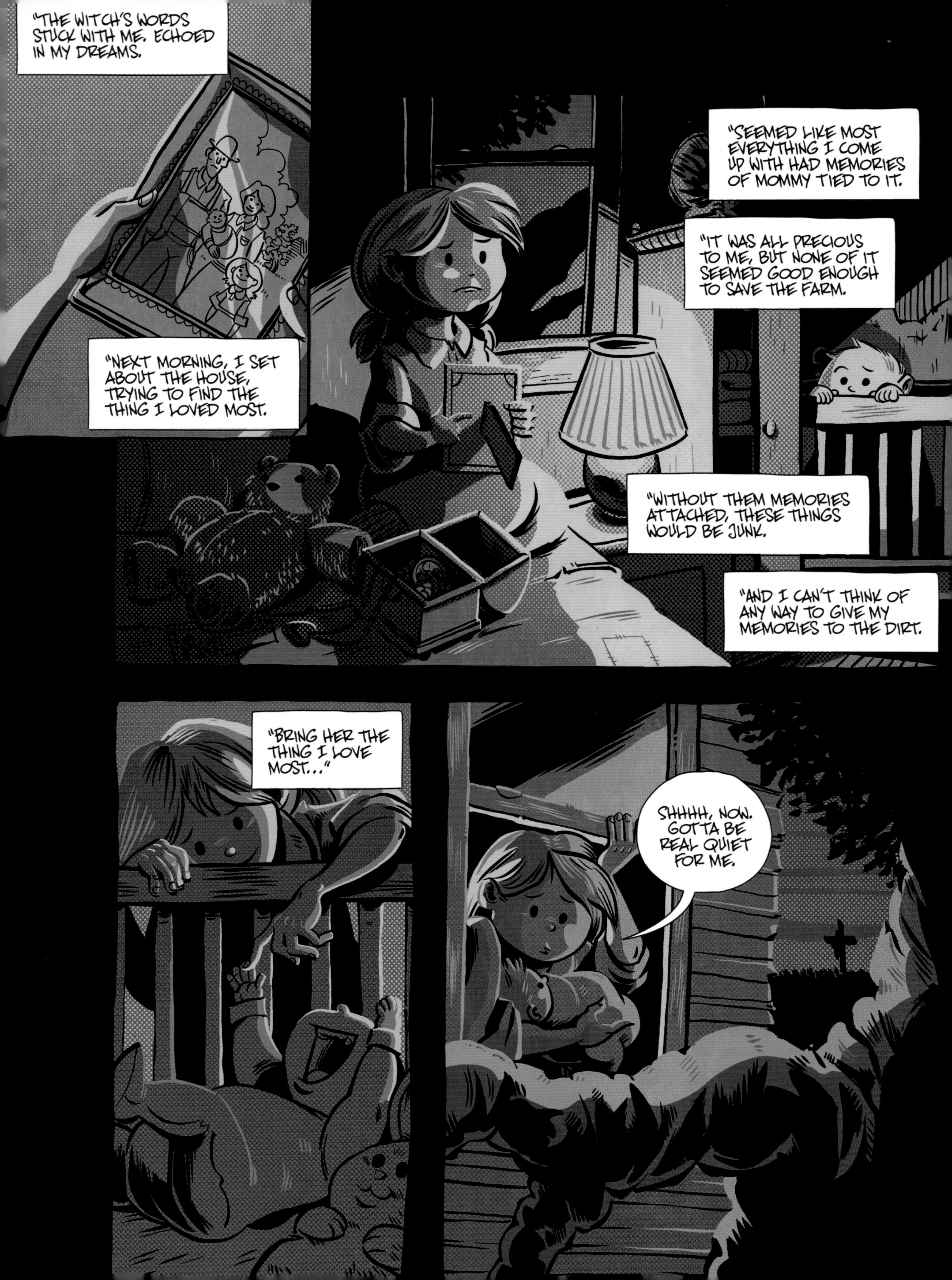
"THE WITCH'S WORDS STUCK WITH ME. ECHOED IN MY DREAMS.
"NEXT MORNING, I SET ABOUT THE HOUSE, TRYING TO FIND THE THING I LOVED MOST.
"SEEMED LIKE MOST EVERYTHING I COME UP WITH HAD MEMORIES OF MOMMY TIED TO IT.
"IT WAS ALL PRECIOUS TO ME, BUT NONE OF IT SEEMED GOOD ENOUGH TO SAVE THE FARM.
"WITHOUT THEM MEMORIES ATTACHED, THESE THINGS WOULD BE JUNK.
"AND I CAN'T THINK OF ANY WAY TO GIVE MY MEMORIES TO THE DIRT.
"BRING HER THE THING I LOVE MOST..."
SHHHH, NOW. GOTTA BE REAL QUIET FOR ME.

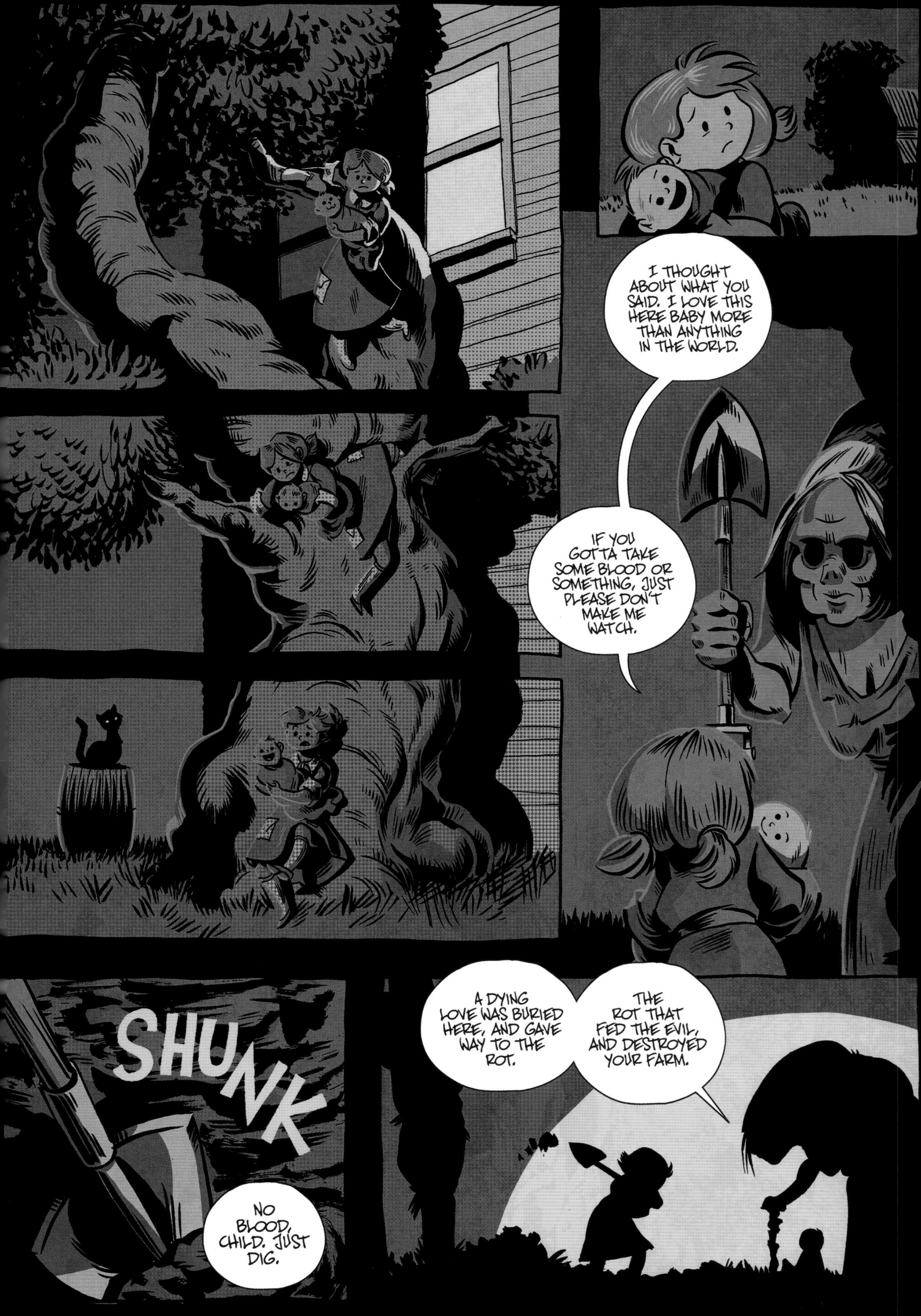
I THOUGHT ABOUT WHAT YOU SAID. I LOVE THIS HERE BABY MORE THAN ANYTHING IN THE WORLD.
IF YOU GOTTA TAKE SOME BLOOD OR SOMETHING, JUST PLEASE DON'T MAKE ME WATCH.
SHUNK
NO BLOOD, CHILD. JUST DIG.
A DYING LOVE WAS BURIED HERE, AND GAVE WAY TO THE ROT.
THE ROT THAT FED THE EVIL, AND DESTROYED YOUR FARM.

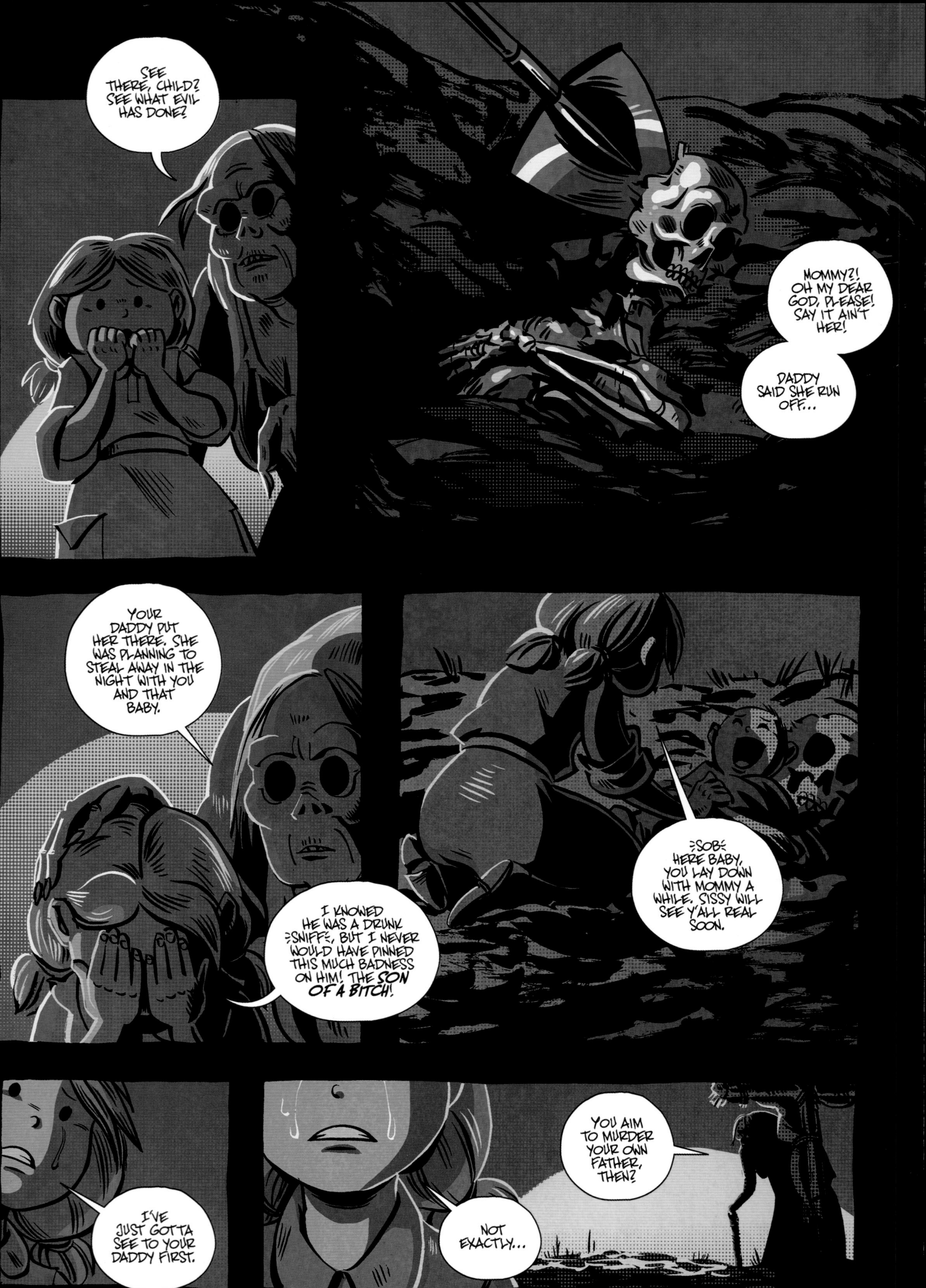
SEE THERE, CHILD? SEE WHAT EVIL HAS DONE?
MOMMY?! OH MY DEAR GOD, PLEASE! SAY IT AIN'T HER!
DADDY SAID SHE RUN OFF...
YOUR DADDY PUT HER THERE. SHE WAS PLANNING TO STEAL AWAY IN THE NIGHT WITH YOU AND THAT BABY.
I KNOWED HE WAS A DRUNK *SNIFF*, BUT I NEVER WOULD HAVE PINNED THIS MUCH BADNESS ON HIM! THE SON OF A BITCH!
SOB HERE BABY, YOU LAY DOWN WITH MOMMY A WHILE. SISSY WILL SEE Y'ALL REAL SOON.
I'VE JUST GOTTA SEE TO YOUR DADDY FIRST.
YOU AIM TO MURDER YOUR OWN FATHER, THEN?
NOT EXACTLY...

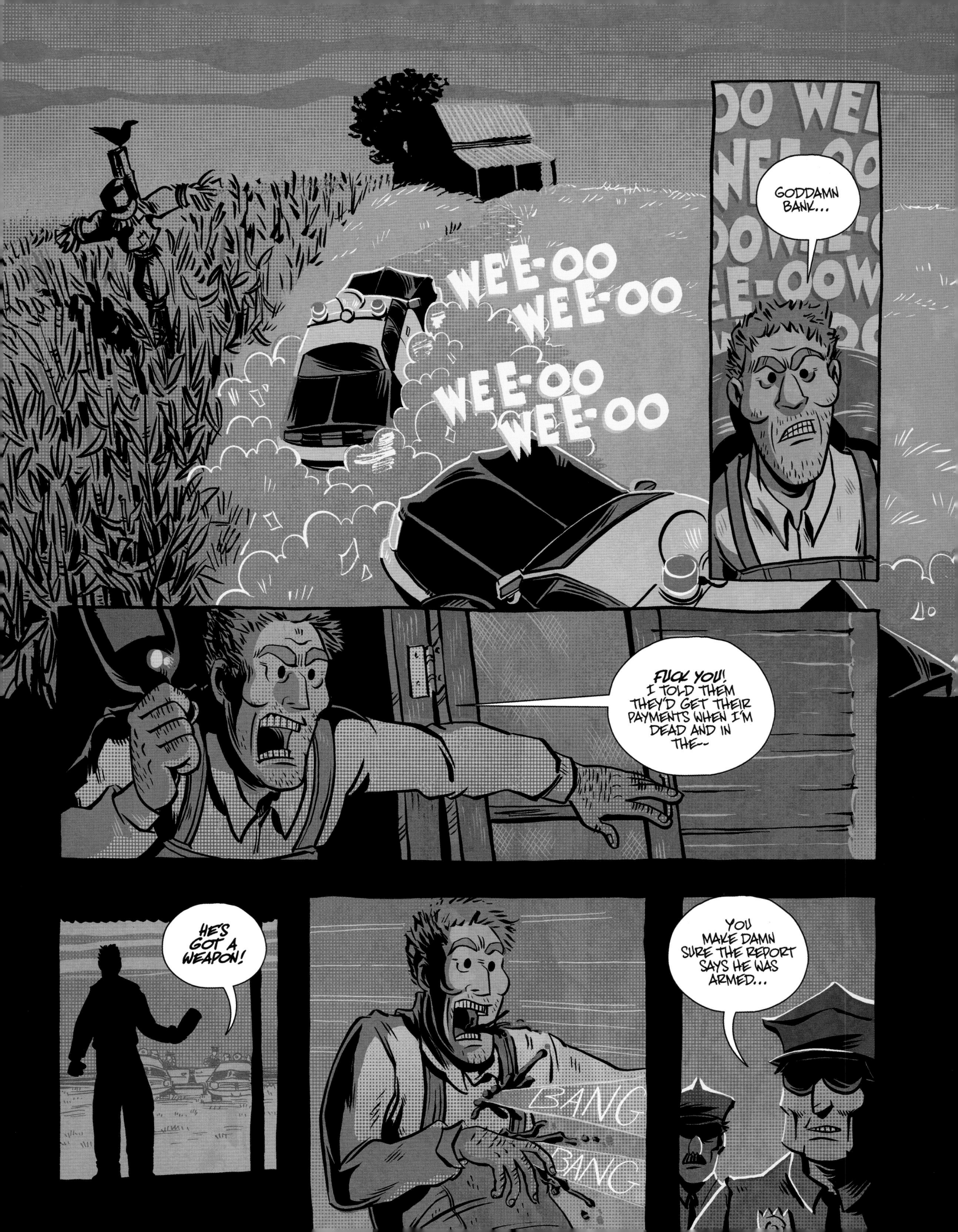
WEE-OO
WEE-OO
WEE-OO
WEE-OO
GODDAMN BANK...
FUCK YOU! I TOLD THEM THEY'D GET THEIR PAYMENTS WHEN I'M DEAD AND IN THE--
HE'S GOT A WEAPON!
BANG
BANG
YOU MAKE DAMN SURE THE REPORT SAYS HE WAS ARMED...

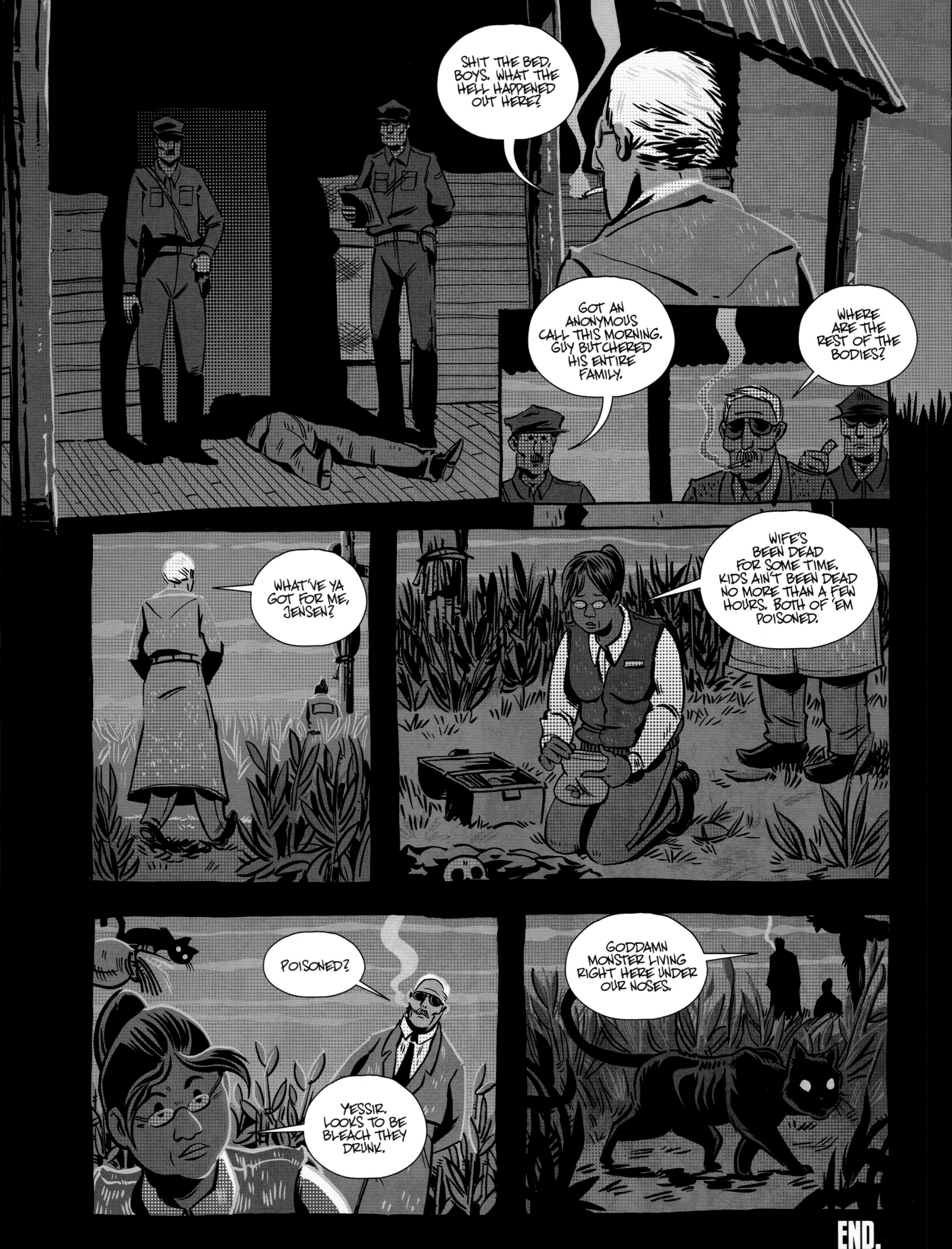
SHIT THE BED, BOYS. WHAT THE HELL HAPPENED OUT HERE?
GOT AN ANONYMOUS CALL THIS MORNING. GUY BUTCHERED HIS ENTIRE FAMILY.
WHERE ARE THE REST OF THE BODIES?
WHAT'VE YA GOT FOR ME, JENSEN?
WIFE'S BEEN DEAD FOR SOME TIME. KIDS AIN'T BEEN DEAD NO MORE THAN A FEW HOURS. BOTH OF 'EM POISONED.
POISONED?
YESSIR. LOOKS TO BE BLEACH THEY DRUNK.
GODDAMN MONSTER LIVING RIGHT HERE UNDER OUR NOSES.
END.

IF THE DEAD COULD BE
FRIGHTENED BACK TO LIFE . . .

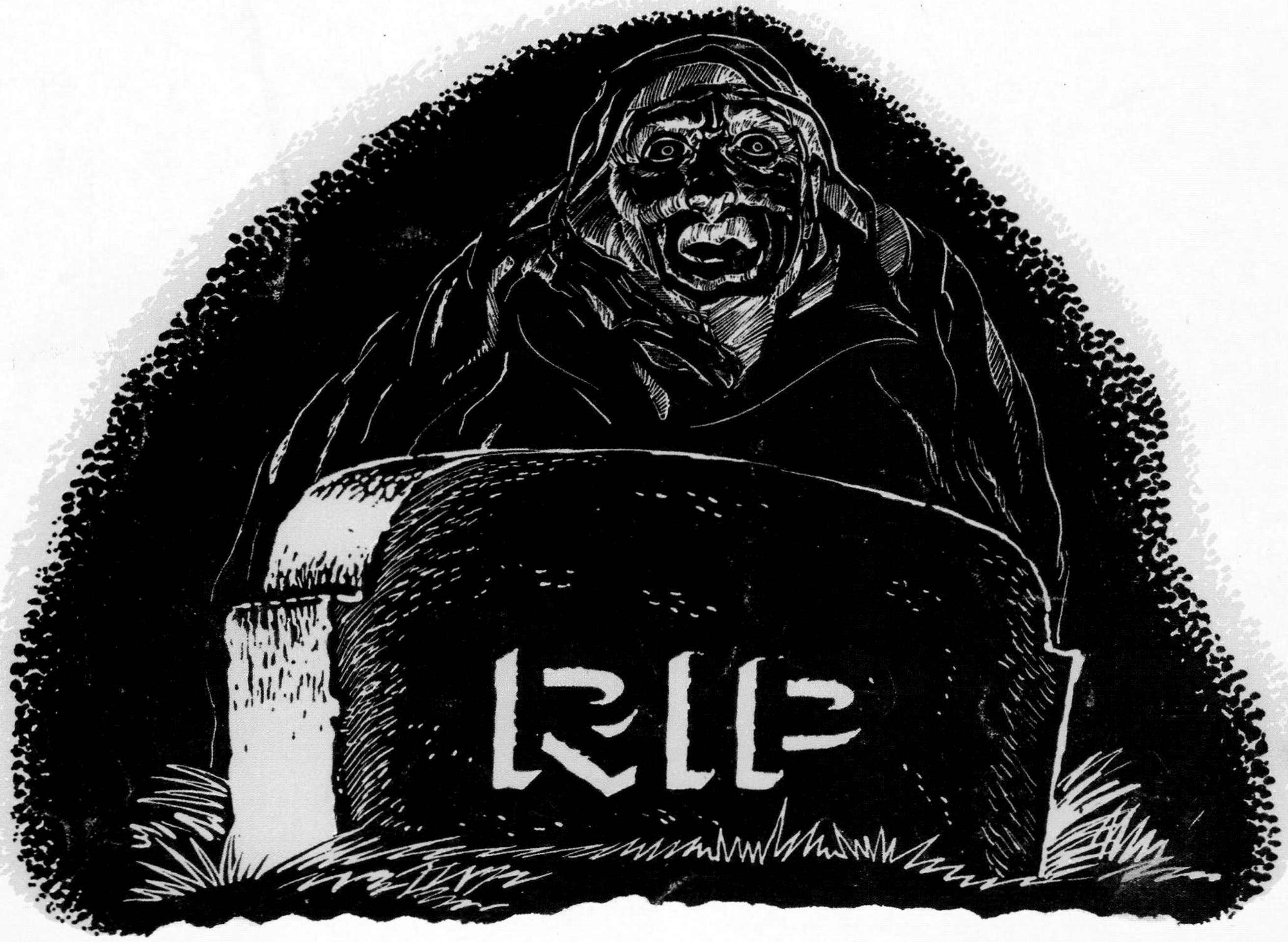
RIP

THIS MAGAZINE IS HAUNTED©

THE WEIRDEST OF ALL THE
SUPERNATURAL COMIC MAGAZINES
WOULD DO IT!

10¢ ON SALE AT YOUR FAVORITE NEWSSTAND 10¢

GUILLOTEENS

WRITER
MICHAEL MORECI
STEVE SEELEY

ARTIST
CHRISTIAN WILDGOOSE

COLORIST
FELIPE SOBREIRO

LETTERER
RACHEL DEERING

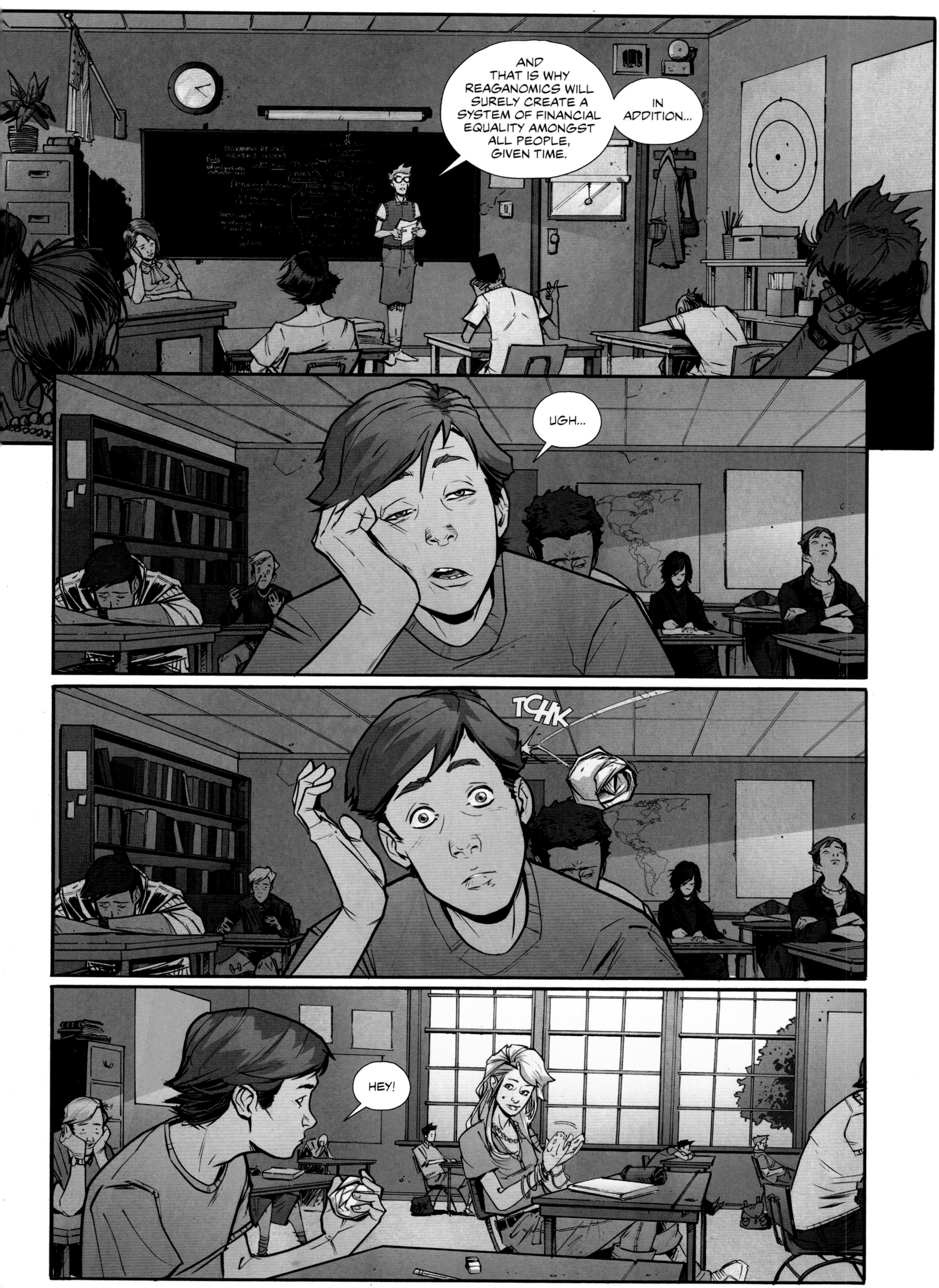
AND THAT IS WHY REAGANOMICS WILL SURELY CREATE A SYSTEM OF FINANCIAL EQUALITY AMONGST ALL PEOPLE, GIVEN TIME.
IN ADDITION...
UGH...
TCHK
HEY!

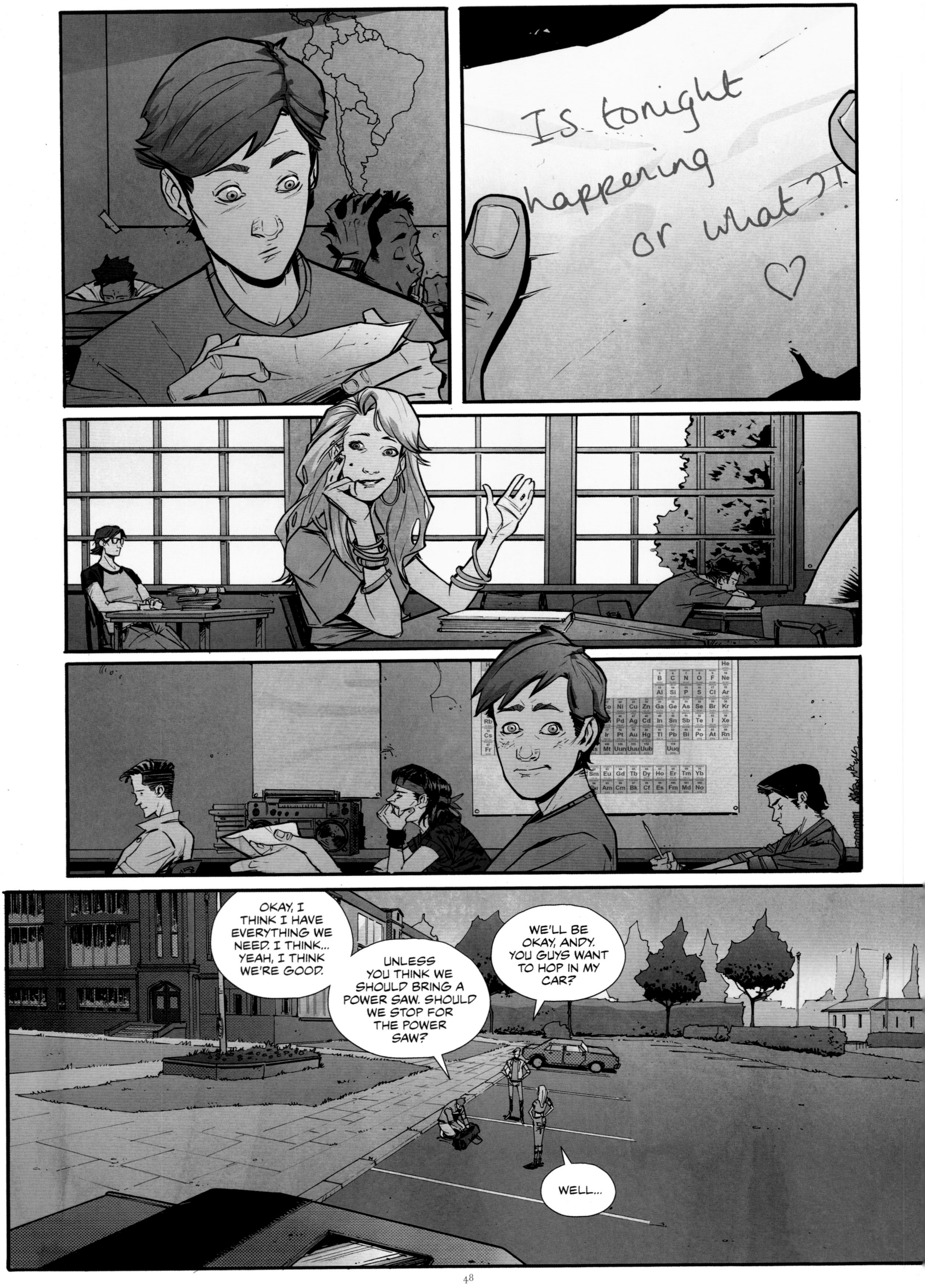
Is tonight happening or what?!
OKAY, I THINK I HAVE EVERYTHING WE NEED. I THINK... YEAH, I THINK WE'RE GOOD.
UNLESS YOU THINK WE SHOULD BRING A POWER SAW. SHOULD WE STOP FOR THE POWER SAW?
WE'LL BE OKAY, ANDY. YOU GUYS WANT TO HOP IN MY CAR?
WELL...

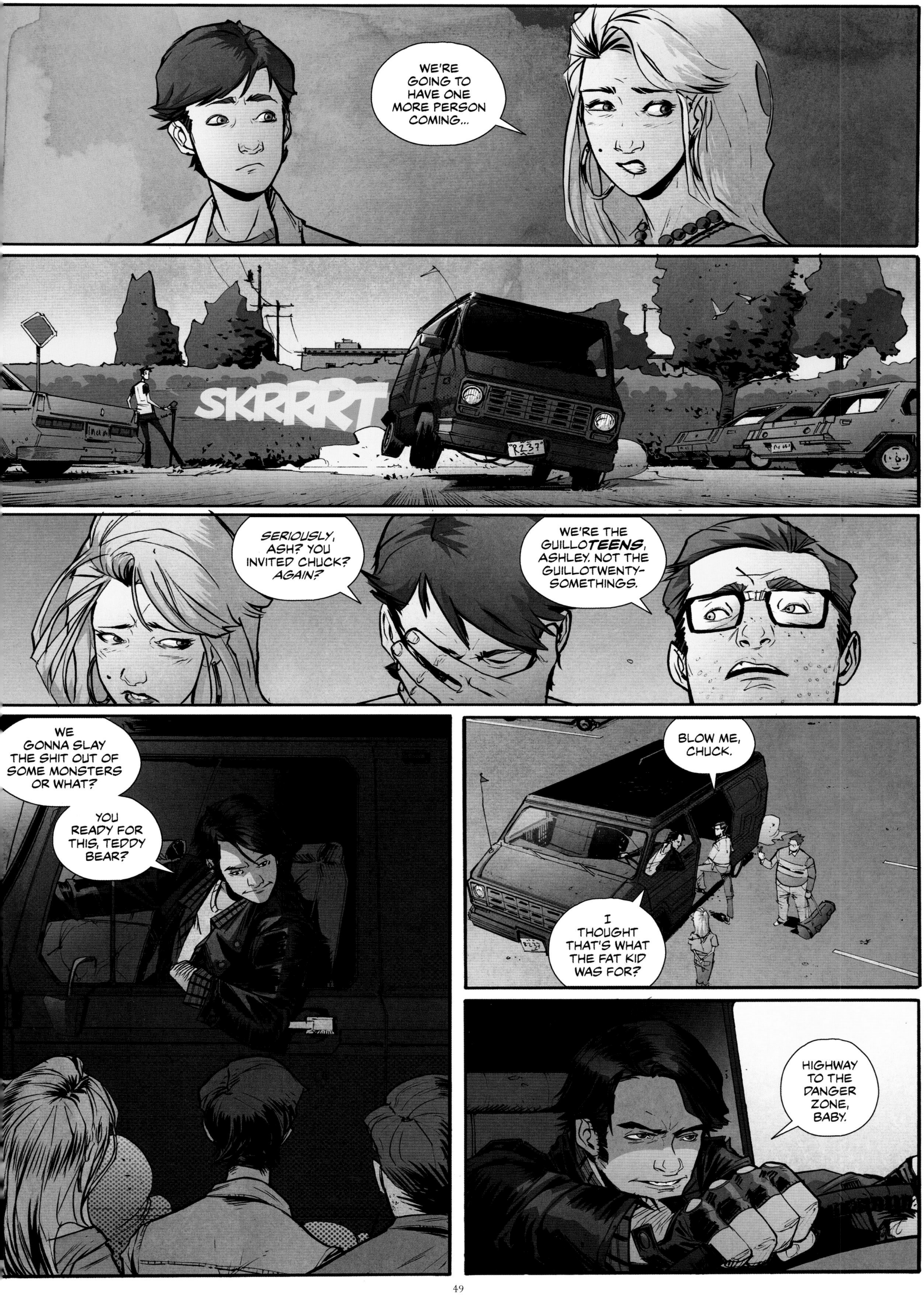
WE'RE GOING TO HAVE ONE MORE PERSON COMING...
SKRRRT
SERIOUSLY, ASH? YOU INVITED CHUCK? AGAIN?
WE'RE THE GUILLOTEENS, ASHLEY. NOT THE GUILLOTWENTY-SOMETHINGS.
WE GONNA SLAY THE SHIT OUT OF SOME MONSTERS OR WHAT?
YOU READY FOR THIS, TEDDY BEAR?
BLOW ME, CHUCK.
I THOUGHT THAT'S WHAT THE FAT KID WAS FOR?
HIGHWAY TO THE DANGER ZONE, BABY.

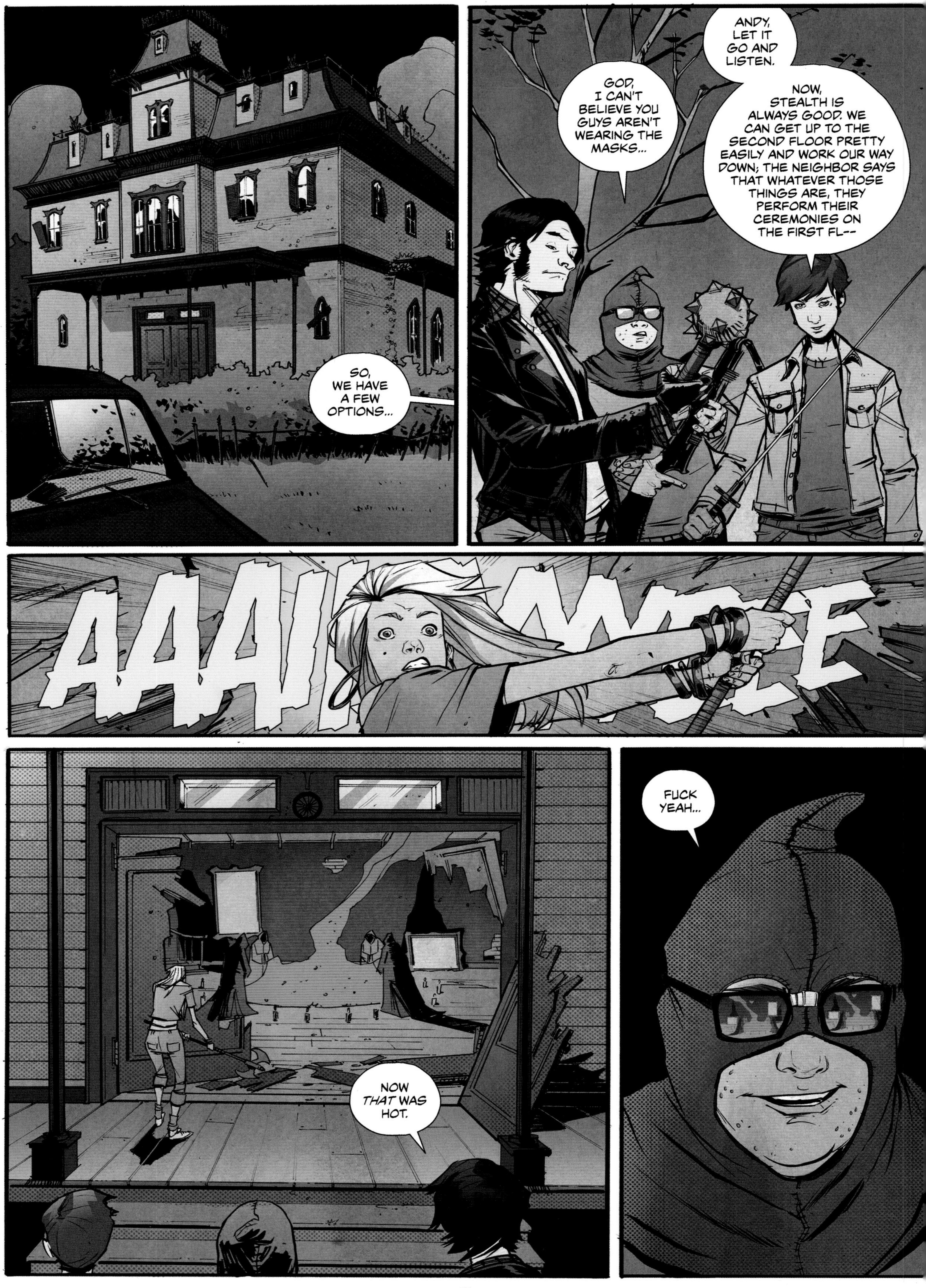
SO, WE HAVE A FEW OPTIONS...
GOD, I CAN'T BELIEVE YOU GUYS AREN'T WEARING THE MASKS...
ANDY, LET IT GO AND LISTEN.
NOW, STEALTH IS ALWAYS GOOD. WE CAN GET UP TO THE SECOND FLOOR PRETTY EASILY AND WORK OUR WAY DOWN; THE NEIGHBOR SAYS THAT WHATEVER THOSE THINGS ARE, THEY PERFORM THEIR CEREMONIES ON THE FIRST FL--
NOW *THAT* WAS HOT.
FUCK YEAH...

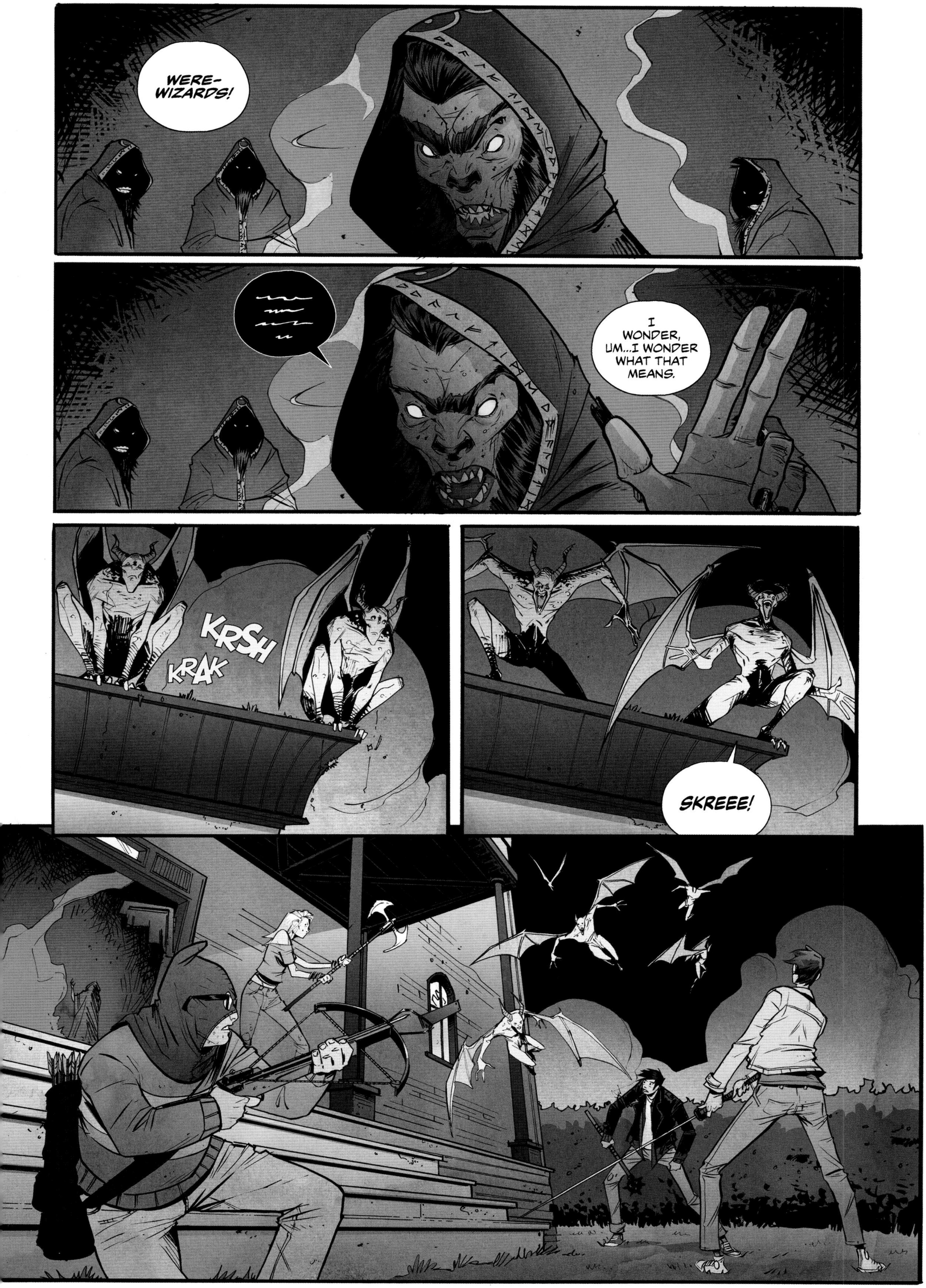
WERE-WIZARDS!
I WONDER, UM...I WONDER WHAT THAT MEANS.
KRSH
KRAK
SKREEE!

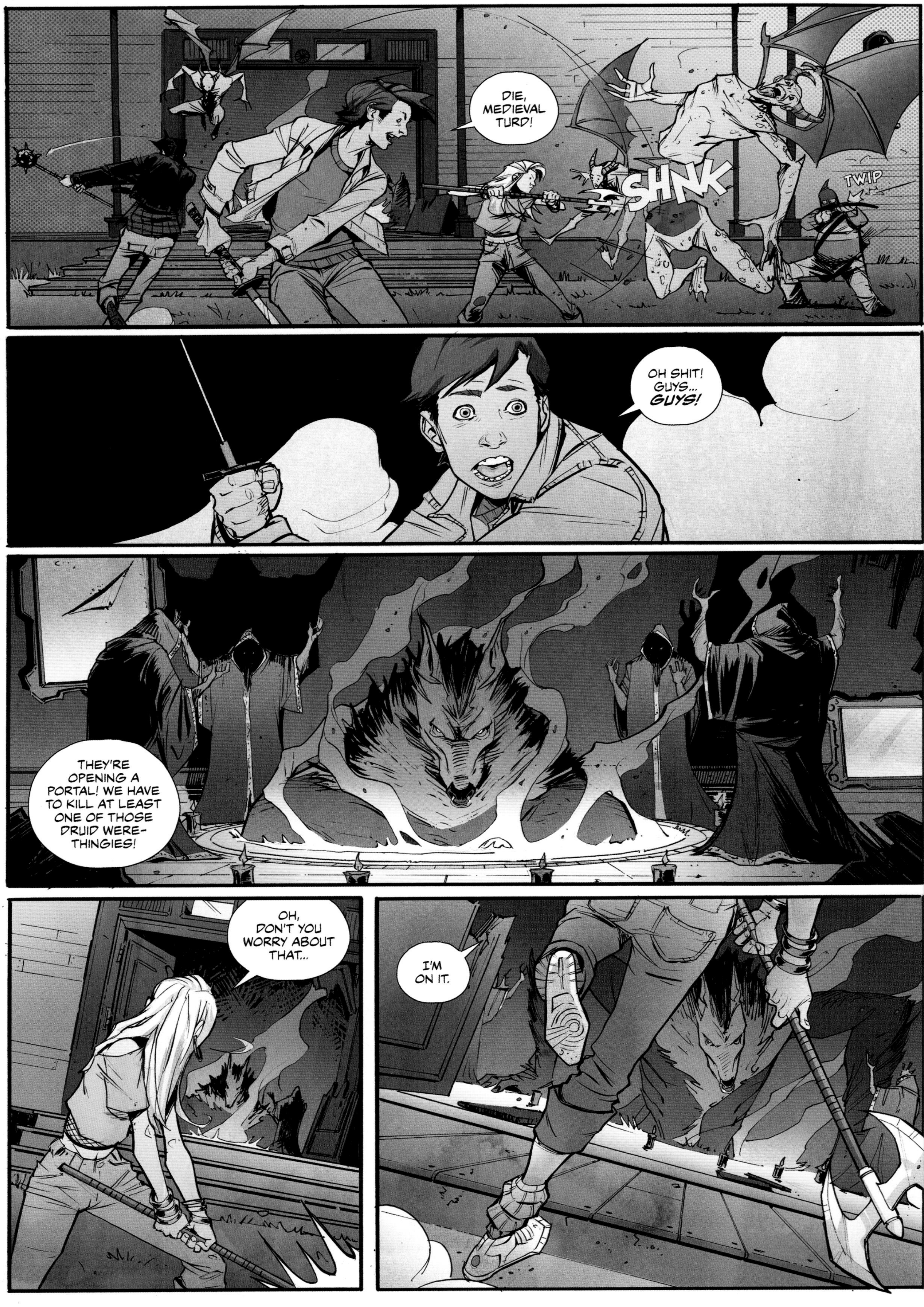
DIE, MEDIEVAL TURD!
SHNK
TWIP
OH SHIT! GUYS... GUYS!
THEY'RE OPENING A PORTAL! WE HAVE TO KILL AT LEAST ONE OF THOSE DRUID WERE-THINGIES!
OH, DON'T YOU WORRY ABOUT THAT...
I'M ON IT.

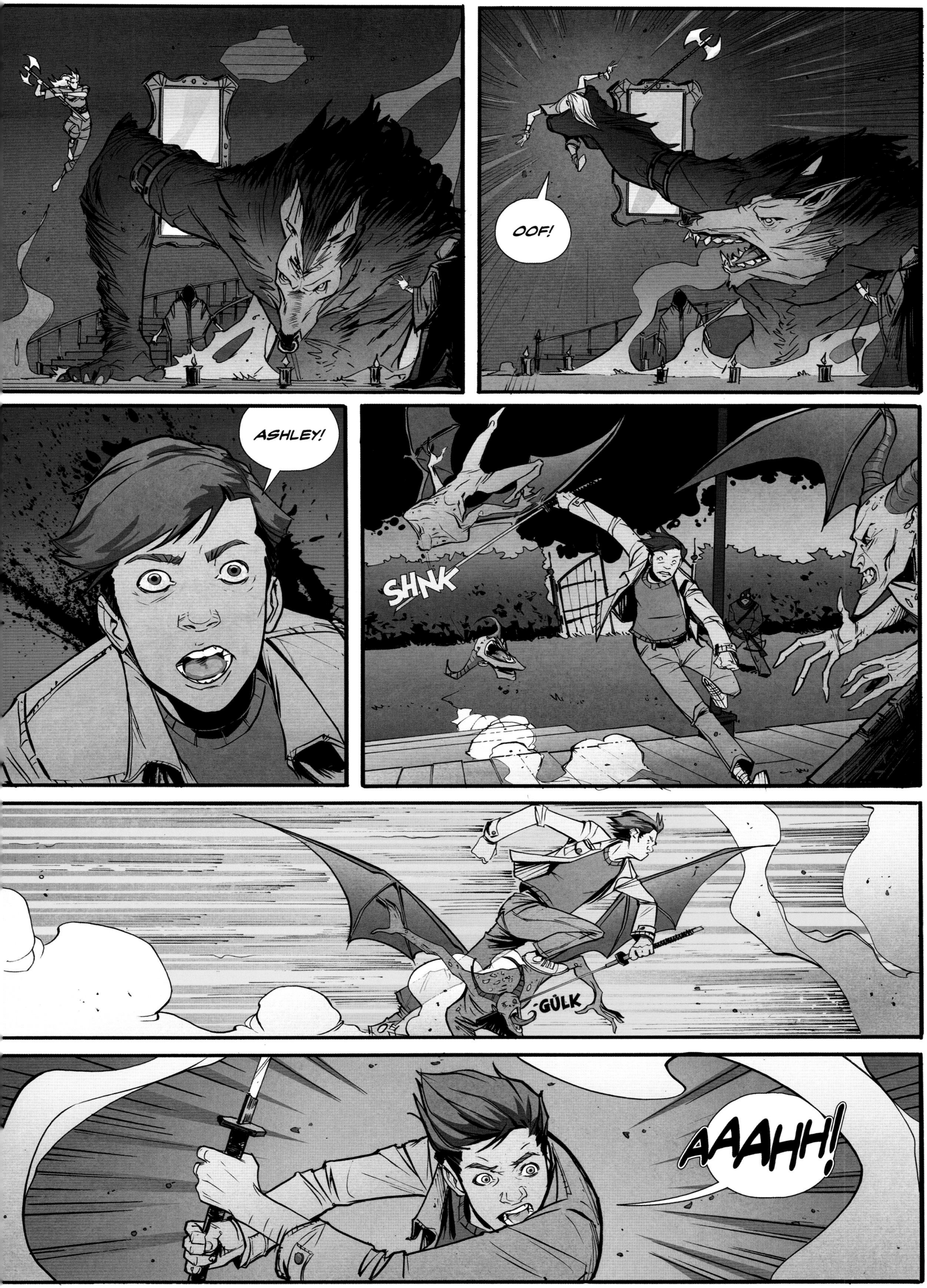
OOF!
ASHLEY!
SHNK
GULK
AAAHH!

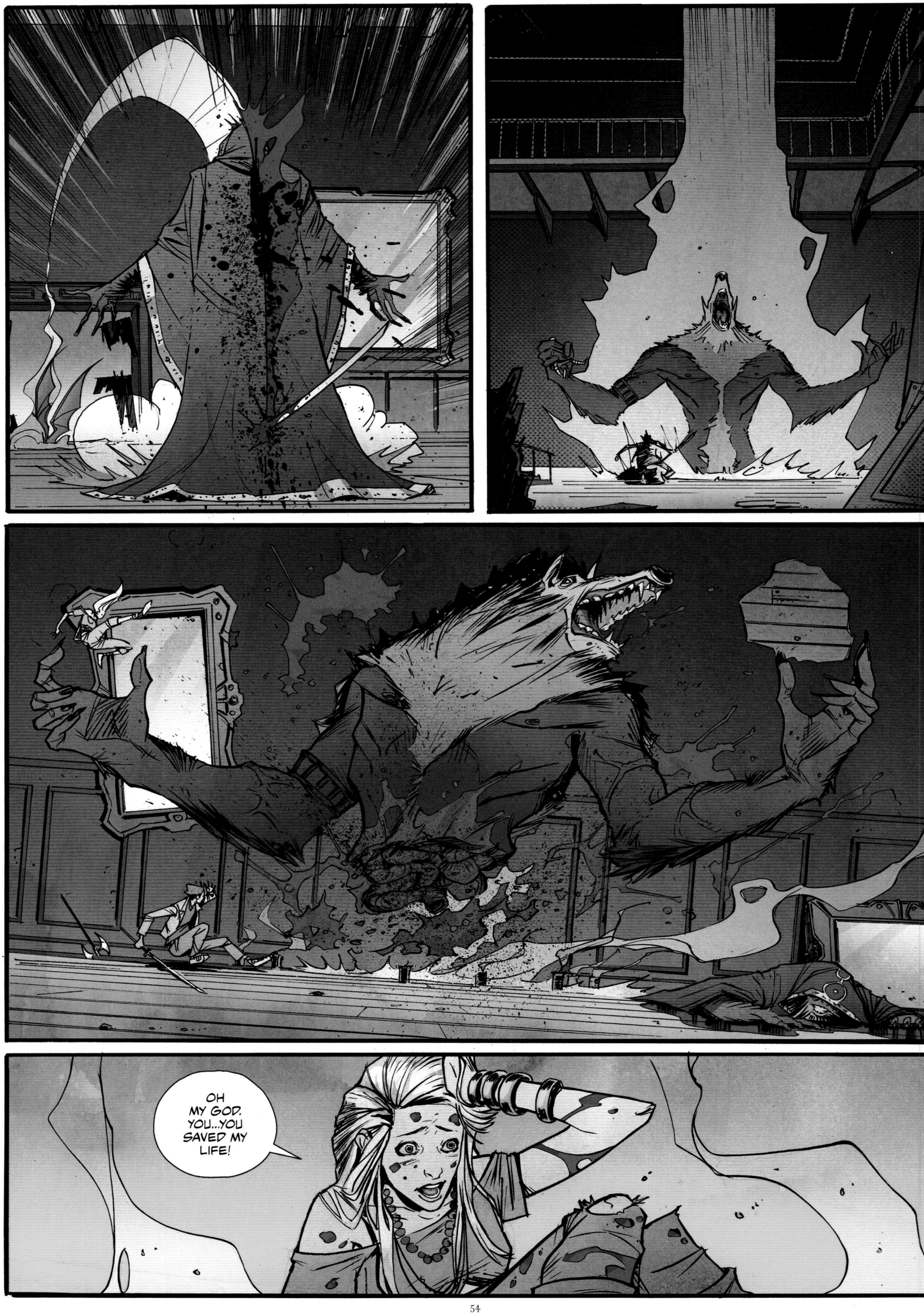
OH MY GOD. YOU...YOU SAVED MY LIFE!

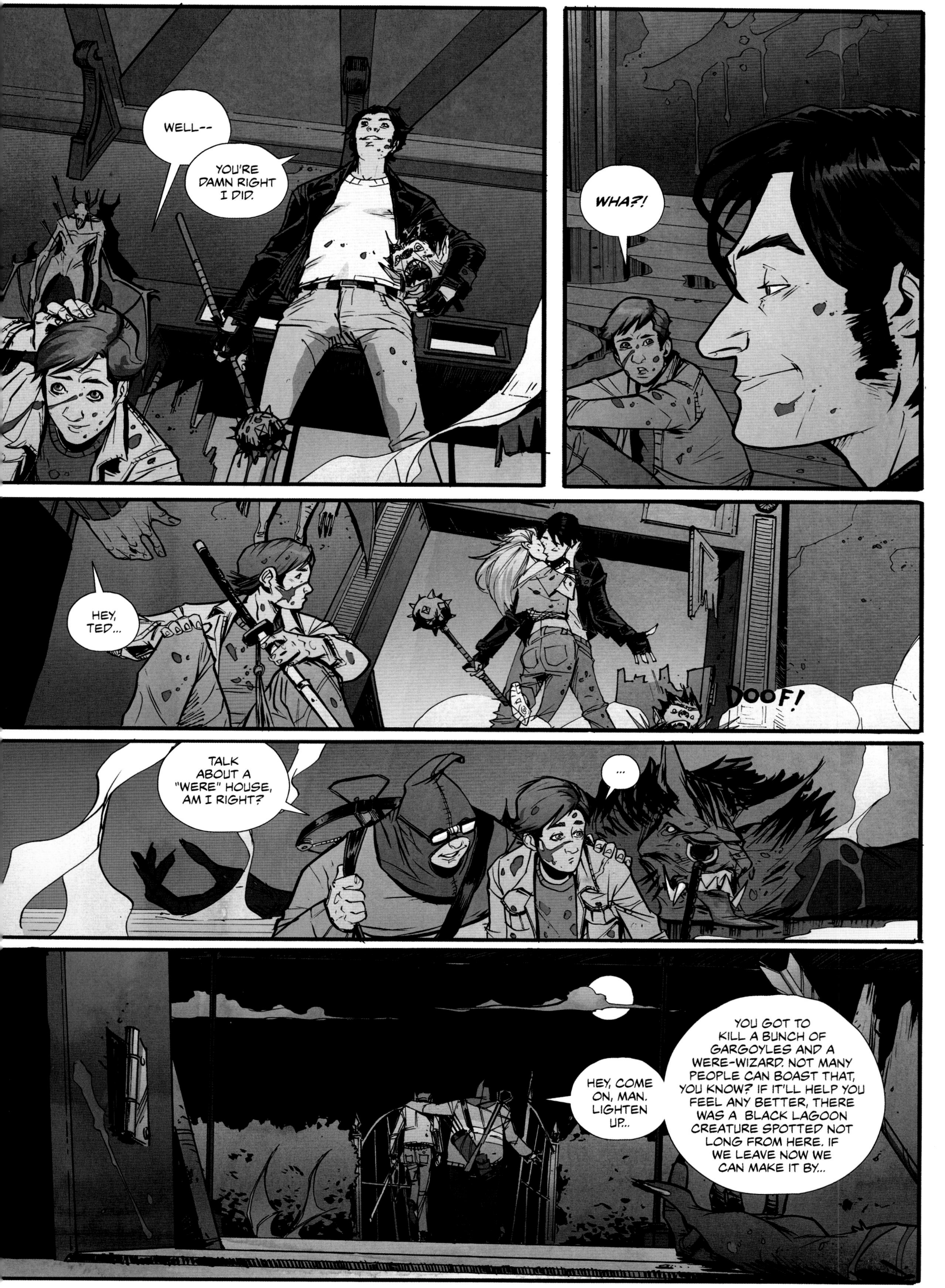
WELL--
YOU'RE DAMN RIGHT I DID.
WHA?!
HEY, TED...
DOOF!
TALK ABOUT A "WERE" HOUSE, AM I RIGHT?
...
HEY, COME ON, MAN. LIGHTEN UP...
YOU GOT TO KILL A BUNCH OF GARGOYLES AND A WERE-WIZARD. NOT MANY PEOPLE CAN BOAST THAT, YOU KNOW? IF IT'LL HELP YOU FEEL ANY BETTER, THERE WAS A BLACK LAGOON CREATURE SPOTTED NOT LONG FROM HERE. IF WE LEAVE NOW WE CAN MAKE IT BY...

ALL THINGS THROUGH ME

WRITER
MIKE OLIVERI

ARTIST
MIKE HENDERSON

COLORIST
JORDAN BOYD

LETTERER
RACHEL DEERING

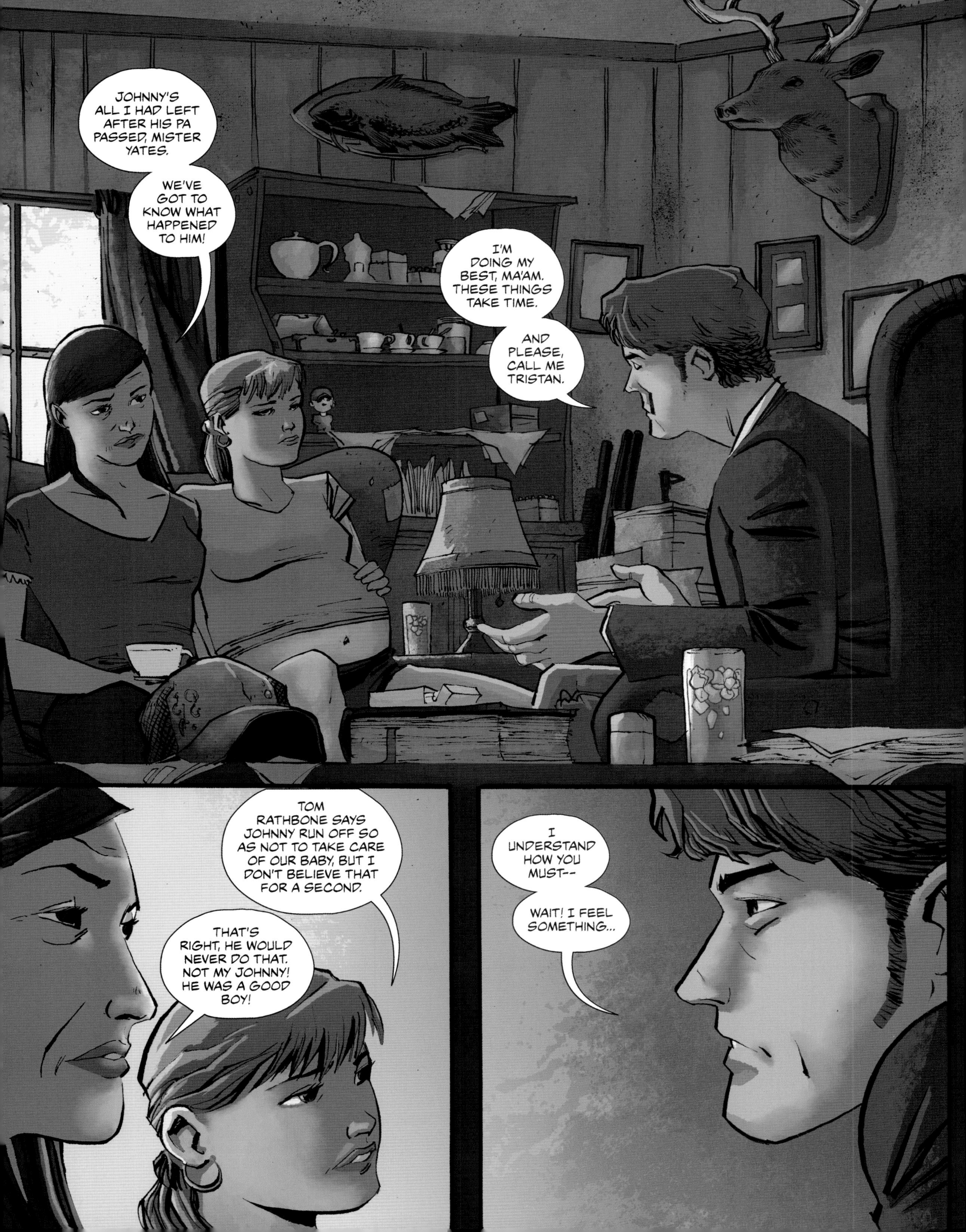
JOHNNY'S ALL I HAD LEFT AFTER HIS PA PASSED, MISTER YATES.
WE'VE GOT TO KNOW WHAT HAPPENED TO HIM!
I'M DOING MY BEST, MA'AM. THESE THINGS TAKE TIME.
AND PLEASE, CALL ME TRISTAN.
TOM RATHBONE SAYS JOHNNY RUN OFF SO AS NOT TO TAKE CARE OF OUR BABY, BUT I DON'T BELIEVE THAT FOR A SECOND.
THAT'S RIGHT, HE WOULD NEVER DO THAT. NOT MY JOHNNY! HE WAS A GOOD BOY!
I UNDERSTAND HOW YOU MUST--
WAIT! I FEEL SOMETHING...

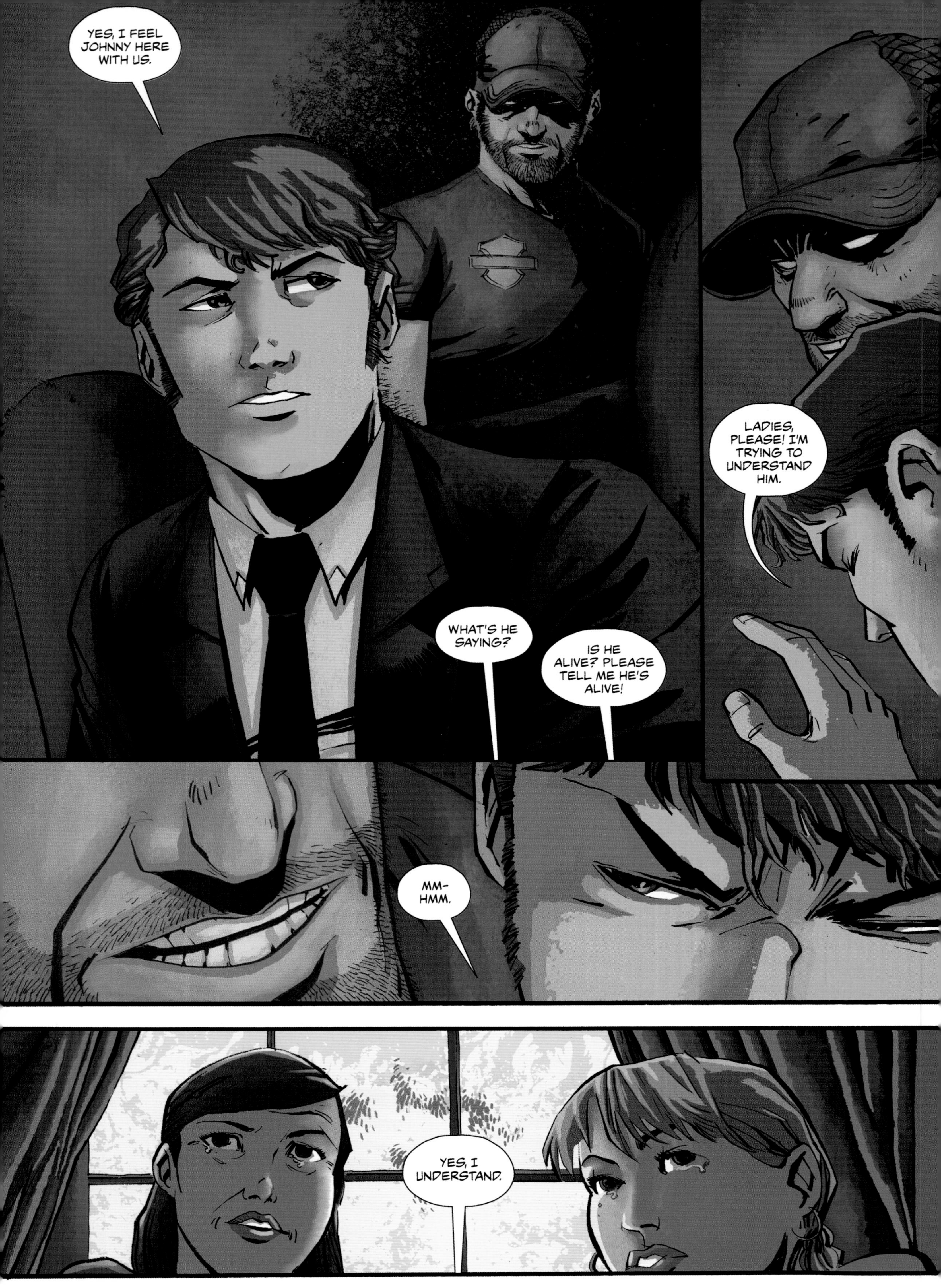
YES, I FEEL JOHNNY HERE WITH US.
LADIES, PLEASE! I'M TRYING TO UNDERSTAND HIM.
WHAT'S HE SAYING?
IS HE ALIVE? PLEASE TELL ME HE'S ALIVE!
MM-HMM.
YES, I UNDERSTAND.

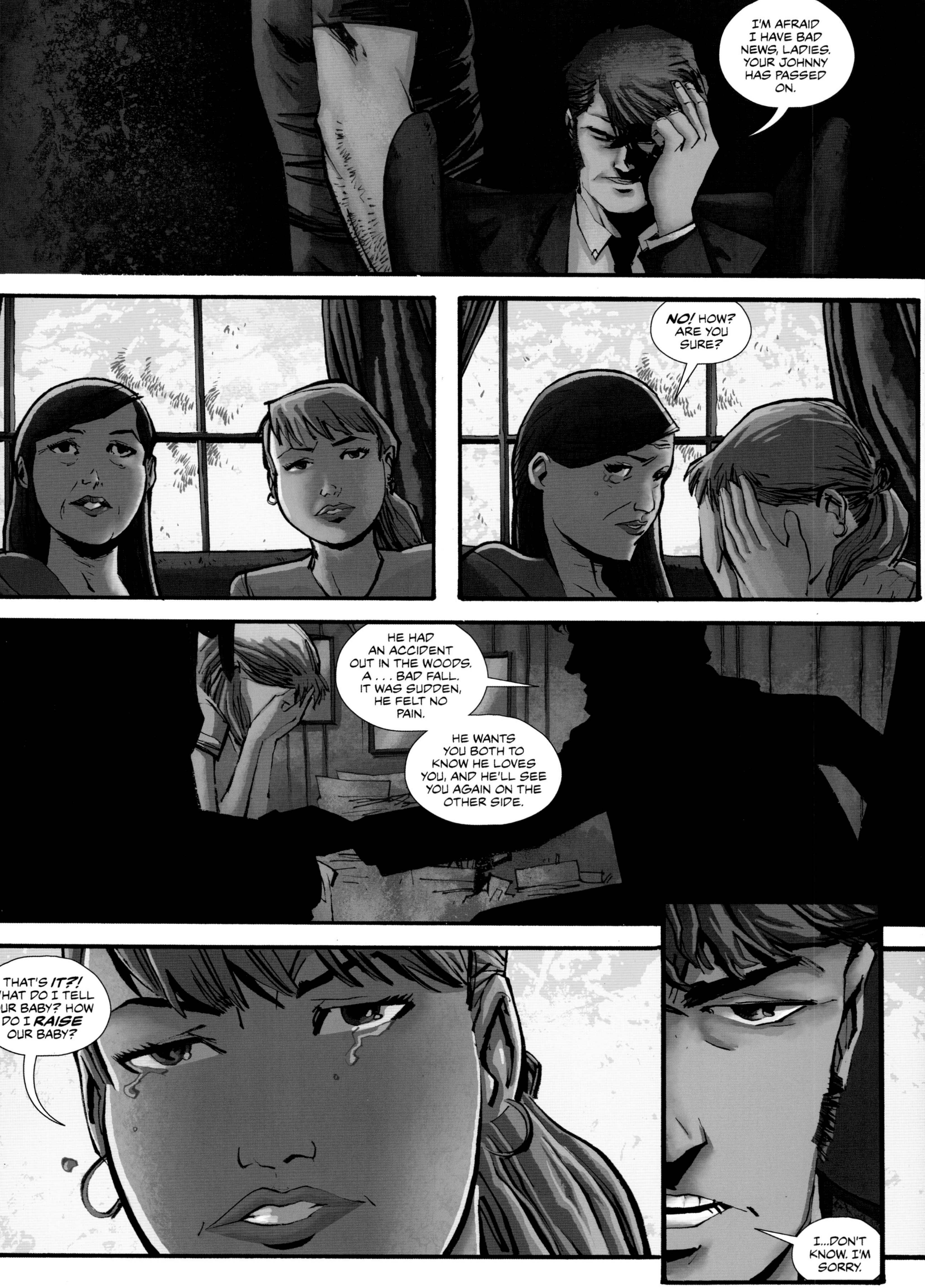
I'M AFRAID I HAVE BAD NEWS, LADIES. YOUR JOHNNY HAS PASSED ON.
NO! HOW? ARE YOU SURE?
HE HAD AN ACCIDENT OUT IN THE WOODS. A . . . BAD FALL. IT WAS SUDDEN, HE FELT NO PAIN.
HE WANTS YOU BOTH TO KNOW HE LOVES YOU, AND HE'LL SEE YOU AGAIN ON THE OTHER SIDE.
THAT'S IT?! WHAT DO I TELL OUR BABY? HOW DO I RAISE OUR BABY?
I...DON'T KNOW. I'M SORRY.

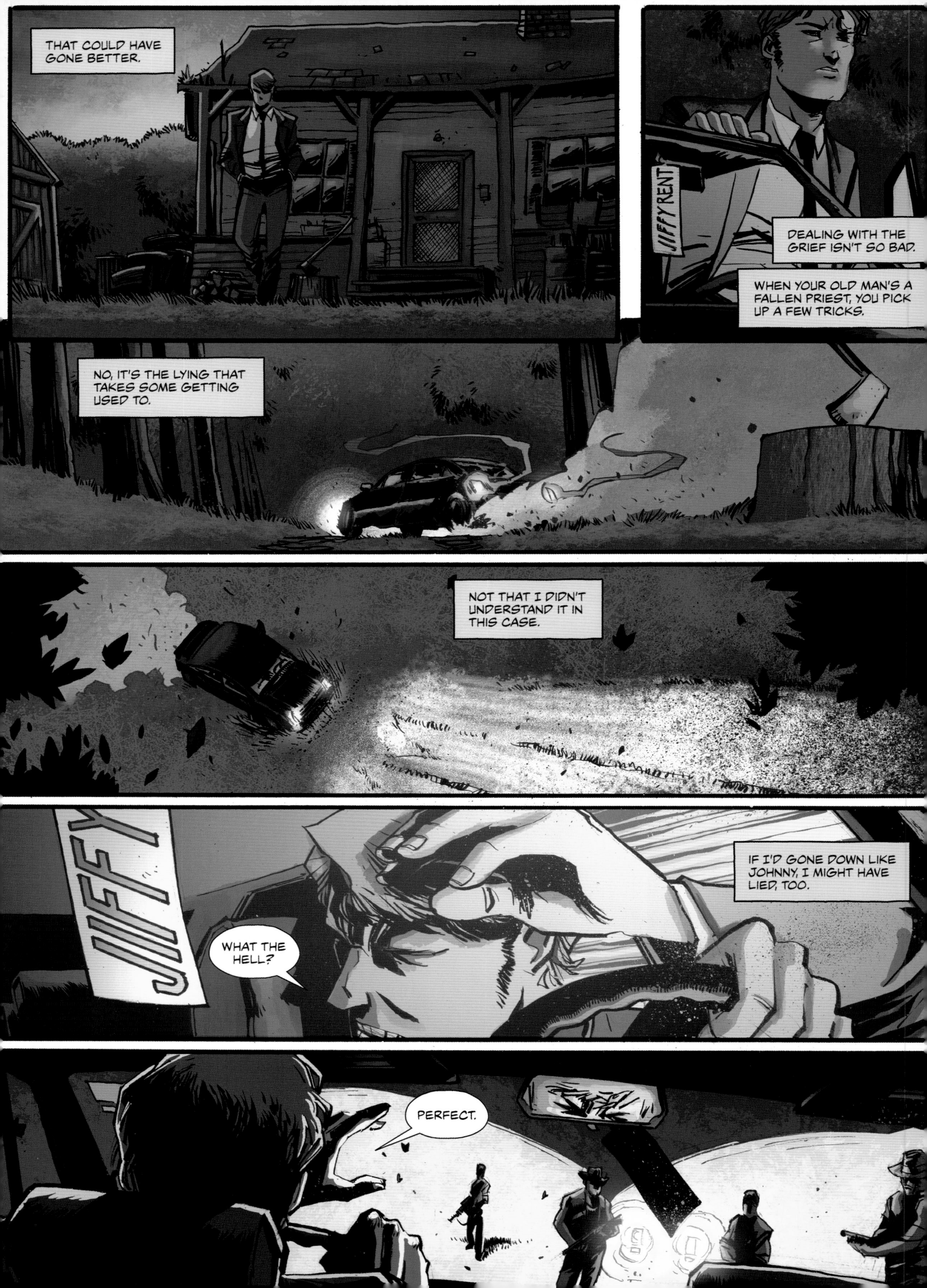
THAT COULD HAVE GONE BETTER.
JIFFY RENT
DEALING WITH THE GRIEF ISN'T SO BAD.
WHEN YOUR OLD MAN'S A FALLEN PRIEST, YOU PICK UP A FEW TRICKS.
NO, IT'S THE LYING THAT TAKES SOME GETTING USED TO.
NOT THAT I DIDN'T UNDERSTAND IT IN THIS CASE.
JIFFY
IF I'D GONE DOWN LIKE JOHNNY, I MIGHT HAVE LIED, TOO.
WHAT THE HELL?
PERFECT.

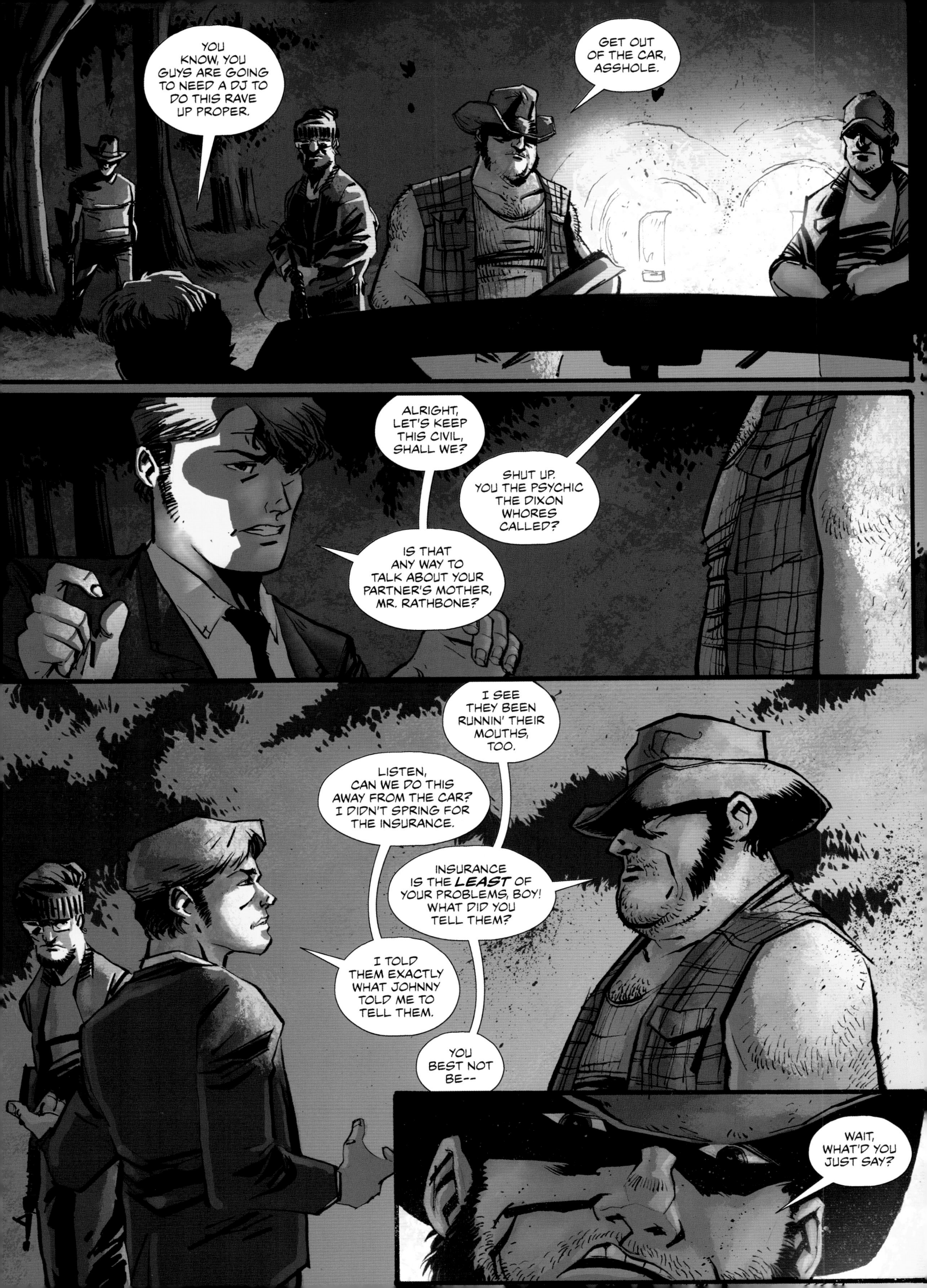
YOU KNOW, YOU GUYS ARE GOING TO NEED A DJ TO DO THIS RAVE UP PROPER.
GET OUT OF THE CAR, ASSHOLE.
ALRIGHT, LET'S KEEP THIS CIVIL, SHALL WE?
SHUT UP. YOU THE PSYCHIC THE DIXON WHORES CALLED?
IS THAT ANY WAY TO TALK ABOUT YOUR PARTNER'S MOTHER, MR. RATHBONE?
I SEE THEY BEEN RUNNIN' THEIR MOUTHS, TOO.
LISTEN, CAN WE DO THIS AWAY FROM THE CAR? I DIDN'T SPRING FOR THE INSURANCE.
INSURANCE IS THE *LEAST* OF YOUR PROBLEMS, BOY! WHAT DID YOU TELL THEM?
I TOLD THEM EXACTLY WHAT JOHNNY TOLD ME TO TELL THEM.
YOU BEST NOT BE--
WAIT, WHAT'D YOU JUST SAY?

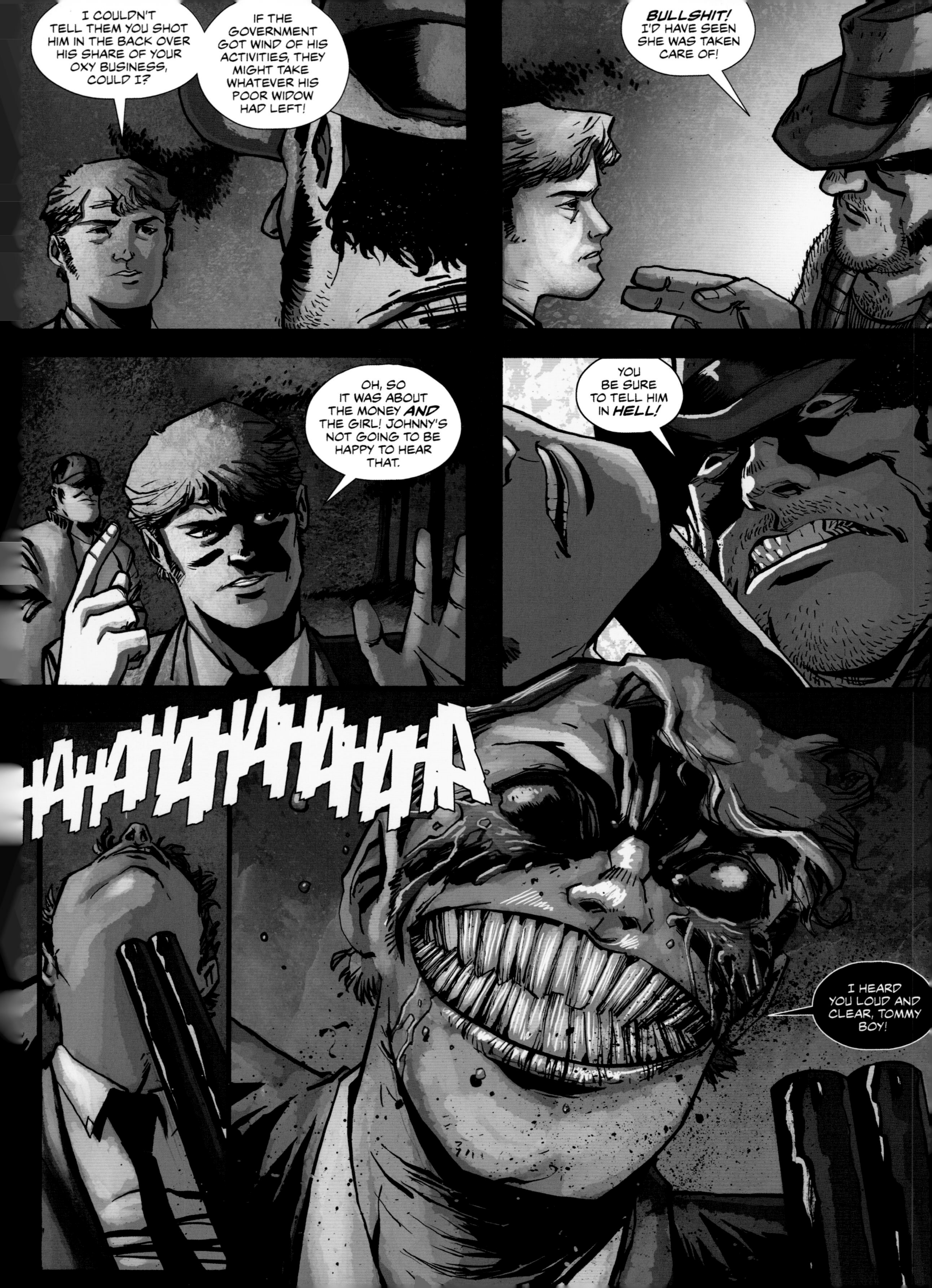

I COULDN'T TELL THEM YOU SHOT HIM IN THE BACK OVER HIS SHARE OF YOUR OXY BUSINESS, COULD I?
IF THE GOVERNMENT GOT WIND OF HIS ACTIVITIES, THEY MIGHT TAKE WHATEVER HIS POOR WIDOW HAD LEFT!
BULLSHIT! I'D HAVE SEEN SHE WAS TAKEN CARE OF!
OH, SO IT WAS ABOUT THE MONEY AND THE GIRL! JOHNNY'S NOT GOING TO BE HAPPY TO HEAR THAT.
YOU BE SURE TO TELL HIM IN HELL!
HAHAHAHAHAHAHA
I HEARD YOU LOUD AND CLEAR, TOMMY BOY!

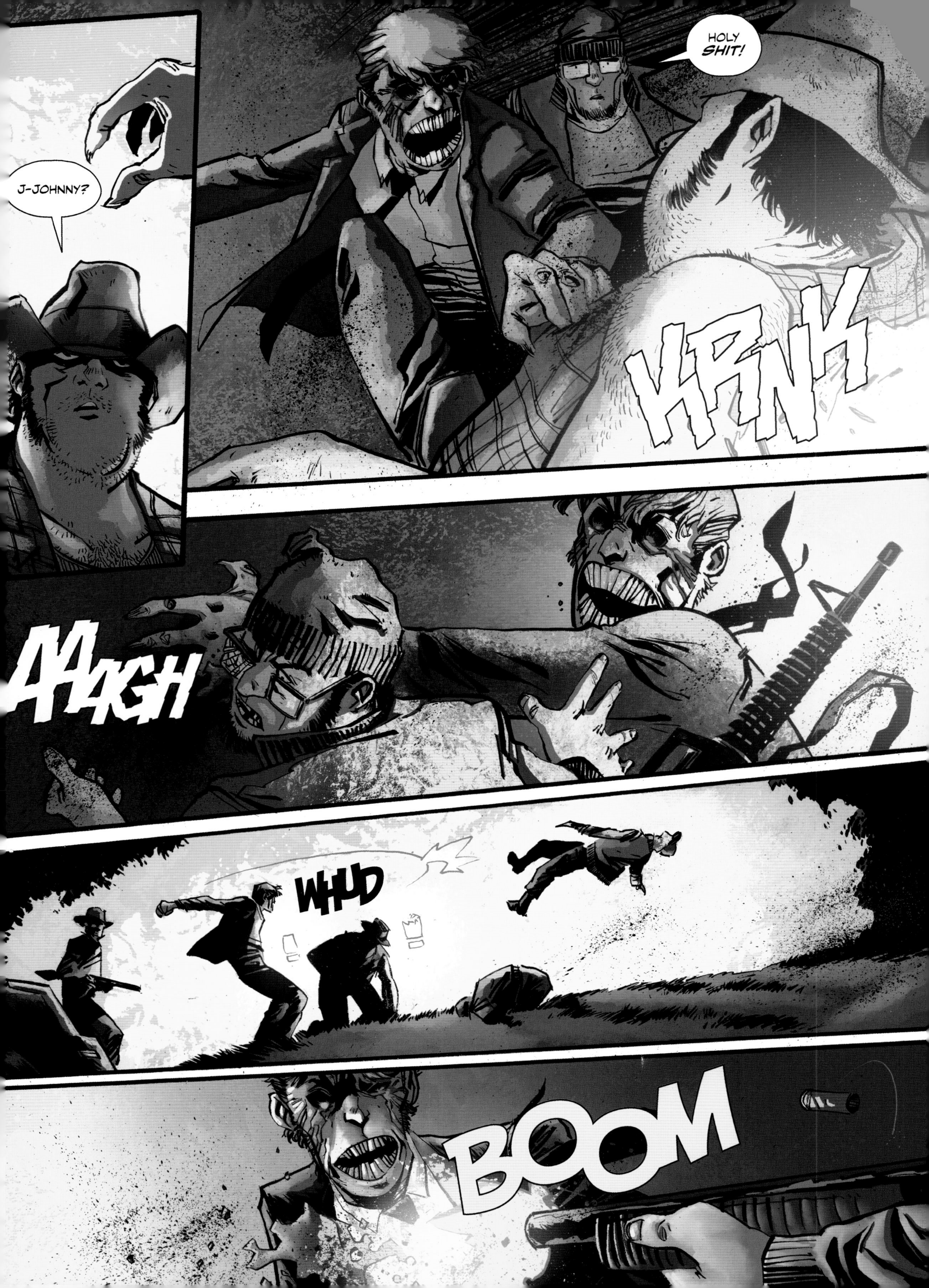
J-JOHNNY?
HOLY SHIT!
KRNK
AAAGH
WHUD
BOOM

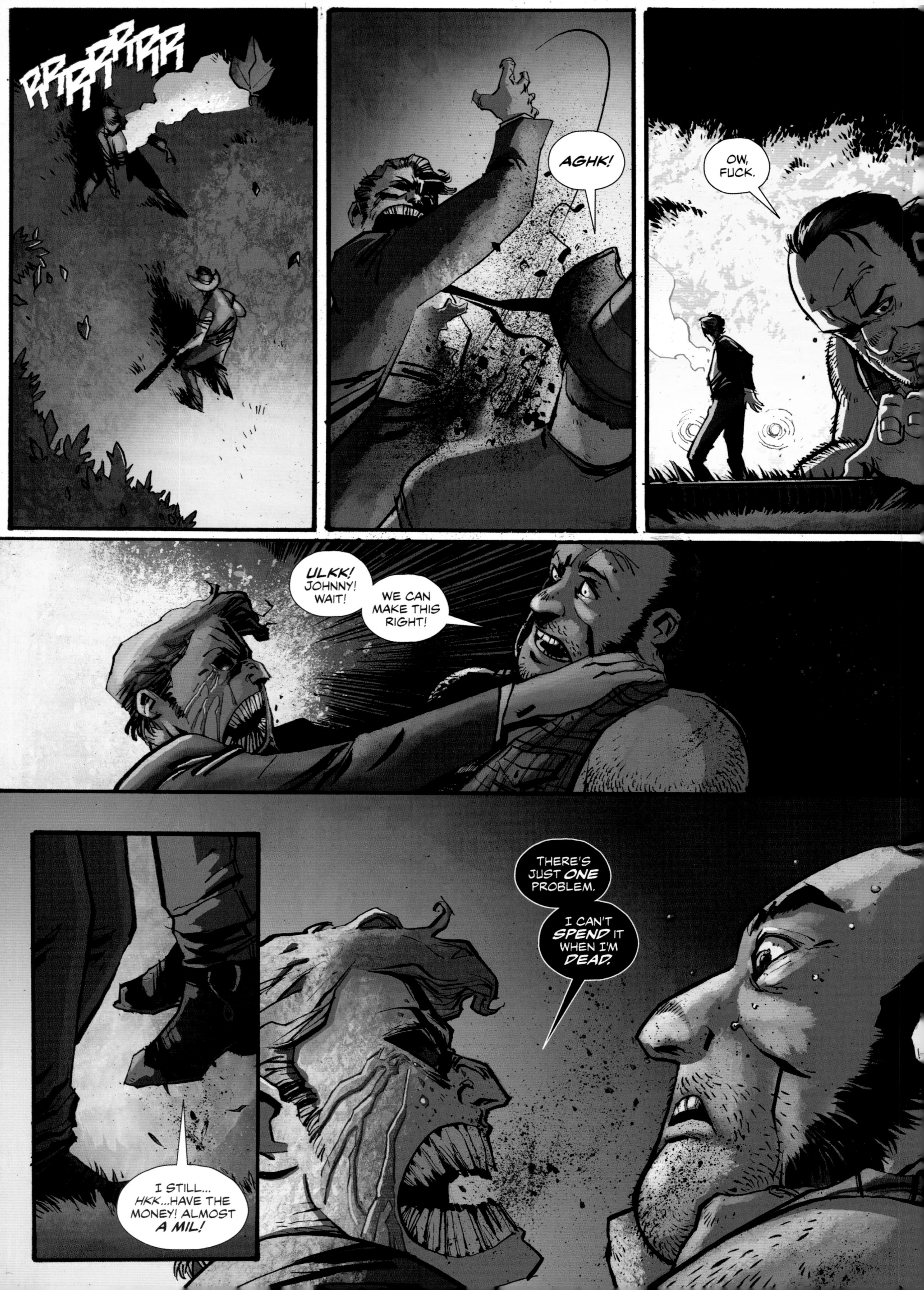
RRRRRRRR
AGHK!
OW, FUCK.
ULKK! JOHNNY! WAIT!
WE CAN MAKE THIS RIGHT!
THERE'S JUST ONE PROBLEM.
I CAN'T SPEND IT WHEN I'M DEAD.
I STILL... HKK...HAVE THE MONEY! ALMOST A MIL!

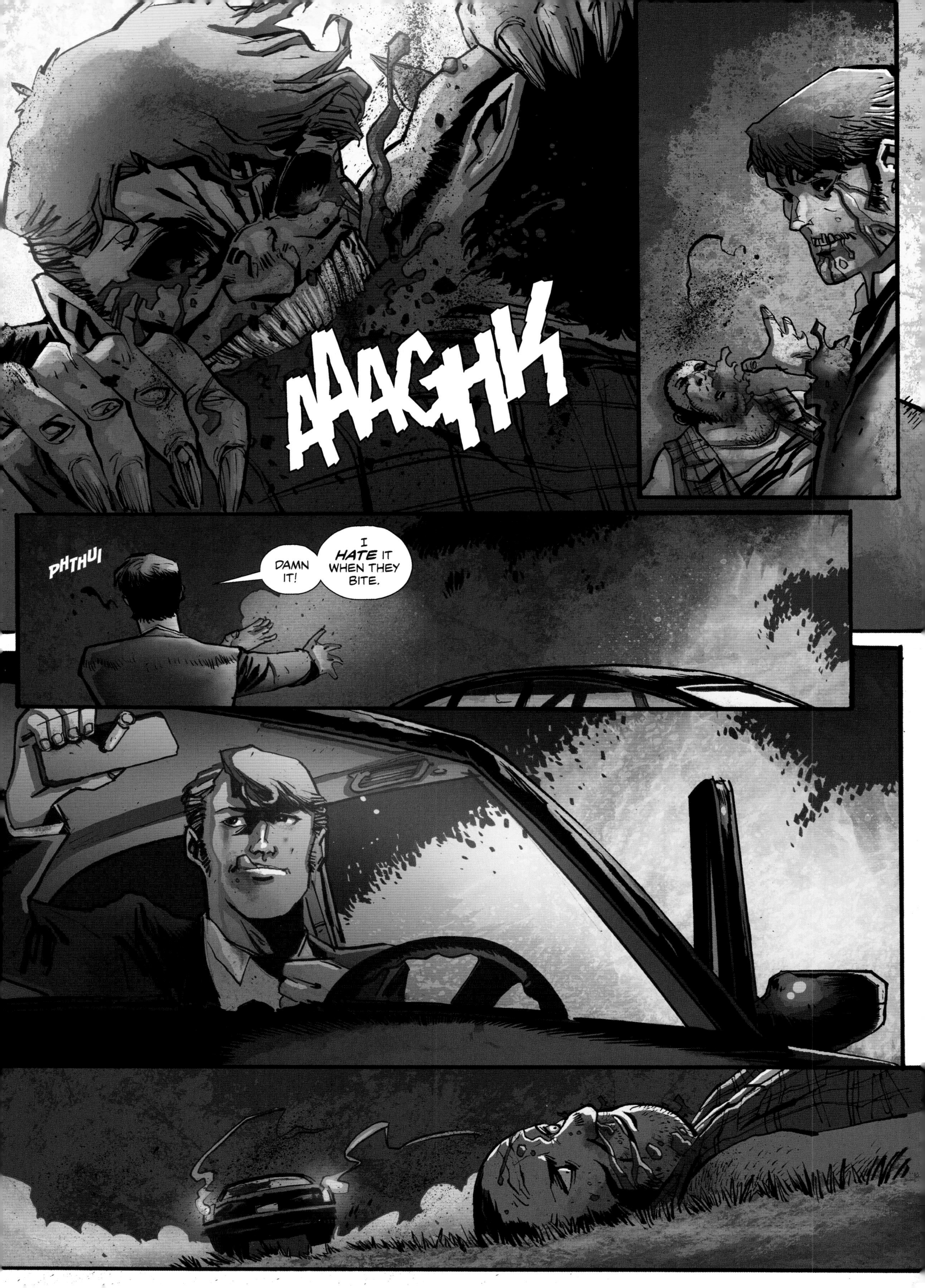
AAAGHK
PHTHUI
DAMN IT!
I HATE IT WHEN THEY BITE.

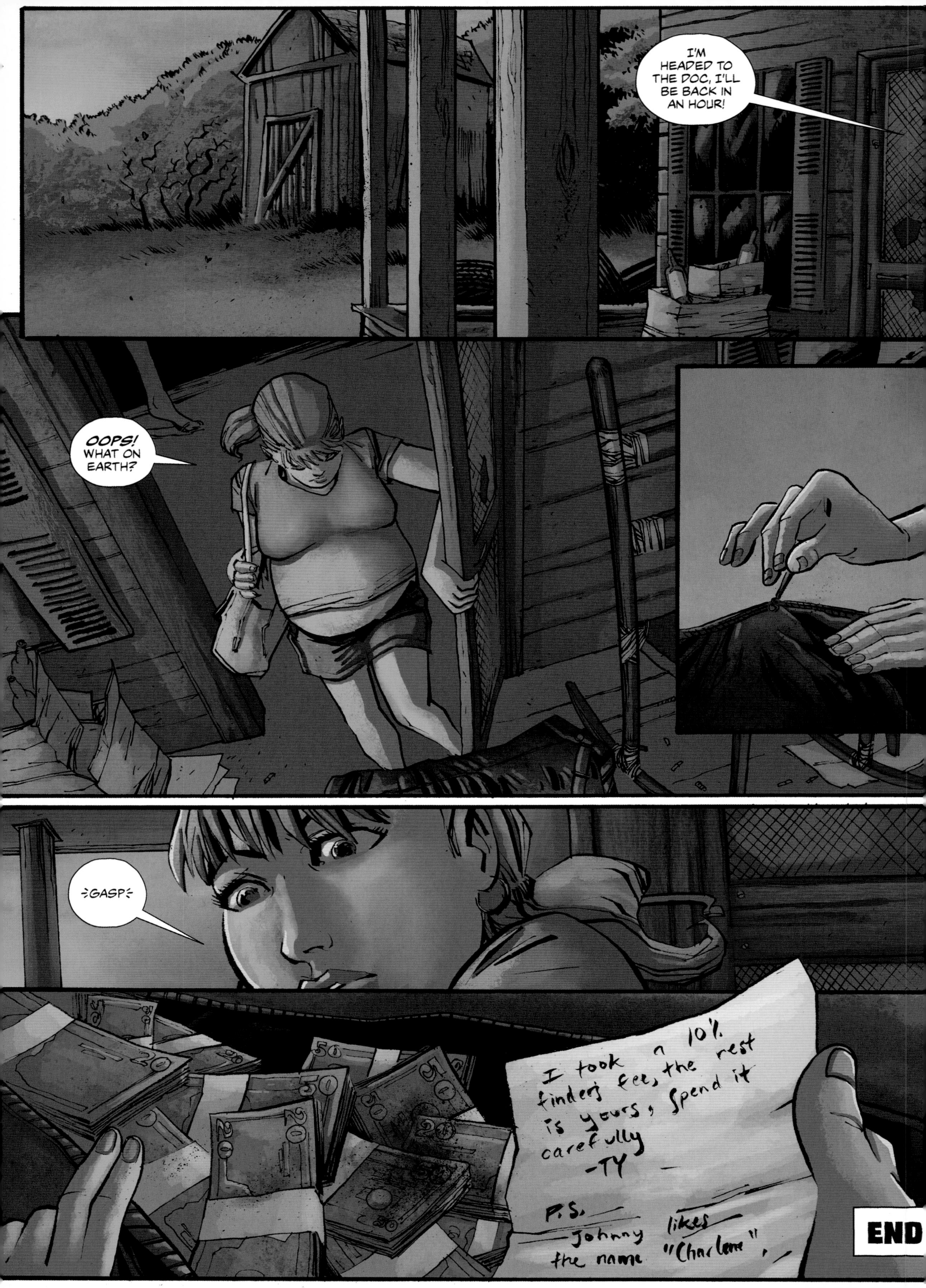
I'M HEADED TO THE DOC, I'LL BE BACK IN AN HOUR!
OOPS! WHAT ON EARTH?
GASP
I took a 10% finder's fee, the rest is yours, spend it carefully
-TY
P.S.
Johnny likes the name "Charlene".
END

MONSTERVISION SPECS!
LETS YOU SEE REAL LIVE MONSTERS

Catch the creatures that hide under your bed or in your closet! These MYSTERIOUS monstervision glasses will give you OTHERWORLDLY vision!

only $1.00

IN THE DARK
6669 WEREWOLF WAY - ROOM 13
COLUMBUS, OH 43230

Gentlemen:
Please send me my "Monstervision Specs" at once. I understand that if I am not 100% terrified after my 10 day FREE TRIAL I may return them and resume my boring life. I have enclosed $1.00 plus $.25 shipping charges in cash, check or money order.

Name:..
Address:..
City:...
State:...
Zip:..

HOW TO HYPNOTIZE

how to
HYPNOTIZE

IT'S EASY TO HYPNOTIZE...
when you know how!

Want the thrill of imposing your will over someone? Of making someone do exactly what you order? Try hypnotism! This amazing technique gives full personal satisfaction. You'll find it entertaining and gratifying. **HOW TO HYPNOTIZE** shows all you need to know. It is put so simply, anyone can follow it. And there are 24 revealing photographs for your guidance.

SEND NO MONEY

FREE ten days' examination of this system is offered to you if you send the coupon today. We will ship you our copy by return mail, in plain wrapper. If not delighted with results, return it in 10 days and your money will be refunded. Stravon Publishers, **DEPT. H-547** 113 West 57th St., New York 19, N. Y.

Mail Coupon Today

STRAVON PUBLISHERS, Dept. H-547
113 West 57th St., N. Y. 19, N. Y.

Send **HOW TO HYPNOTIZE** in plain wrapper.
☐ Send C.O.D. I will pay postman $1.98 plus postage.
☐ I enclose $1.98. Send postpaid.
If not delighted, I may return it in 10 days and get my money back.

Name ....
Address ....
City .... *Zone* .... *State* ....
Canada & Foreign—$2.50 with order

WHEN THE RAIN COMES

WRITER
STEVE NILES

ARTIST
DAMIEN WORM

COLORIST
DAMIEN WORM

LETTERER
DAMIEN WORM

THE RAINS CAME AT NIGHT.
HARD POUNDING WET,
DRENCHING THE DARKNESS.

MY BOY LOVED THE RAIN.
HE LOVED THE SOUNDS AND
THE FLASHING LIGHT THAT
LIT THE FARM FOR ONLY
SECONDS AT A TIME.

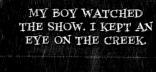

MY BOY WATCHED
THE SHOW. I KEPT AN
EYE ON THE CREEK.

WELL PAST MIDNIGHT
THE BOY AND ME SAT ON
THE PORCH WATCHING.

IT WAS KNOWN TO FLOOD, NOT
IN THE 25 YEARS I OWNED THE
FARM, BUT WE ALL HEARD STO-
RIES ABOUT THE LAST TIME
THE VALLEY FLOODED.

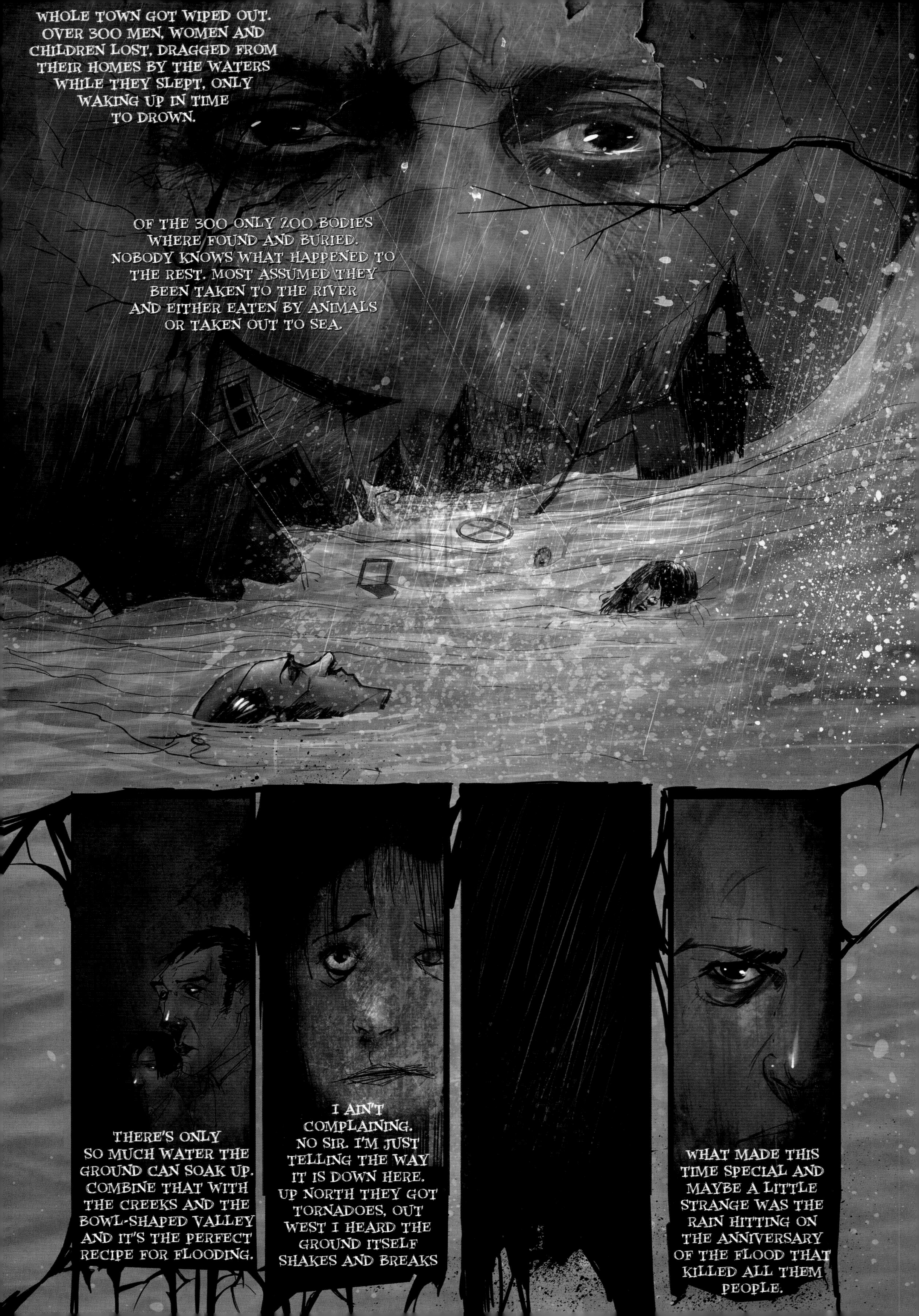
WHOLE TOWN GOT WIPED OUT. OVER 300 MEN, WOMEN AND CHILDREN LOST, DRAGGED FROM THEIR HOMES BY THE WATERS WHILE THEY SLEPT, ONLY WAKING UP IN TIME TO DROWN.
OF THE 300 ONLY 200 BODIES WHERE FOUND AND BURIED. NOBODY KNOWS WHAT HAPPENED TO THE REST. MOST ASSUMED THEY BEEN TAKEN TO THE RIVER AND EITHER EATEN BY ANIMALS OR TAKEN OUT TO SEA.
THERE'S ONLY SO MUCH WATER THE GROUND CAN SOAK UP. COMBINE THAT WITH THE CREEKS AND THE BOWL-SHAPED VALLEY AND IT'S THE PERFECT RECIPE FOR FLOODING.
I AIN'T COMPLAINING. NO SIR. I'M JUST TELLING THE WAY IT IS DOWN HERE. UP NORTH THEY GOT TORNADOES, OUT WEST I HEARD THE GROUND ITSELF SHAKES AND BREAKS
WHAT MADE THIS TIME SPECIAL AND MAYBE A LITTLE STRANGE WAS THE RAIN HITTING ON THE ANNIVERSARY OF THE FLOOD THAT KILLED ALL THEM PEOPLE.

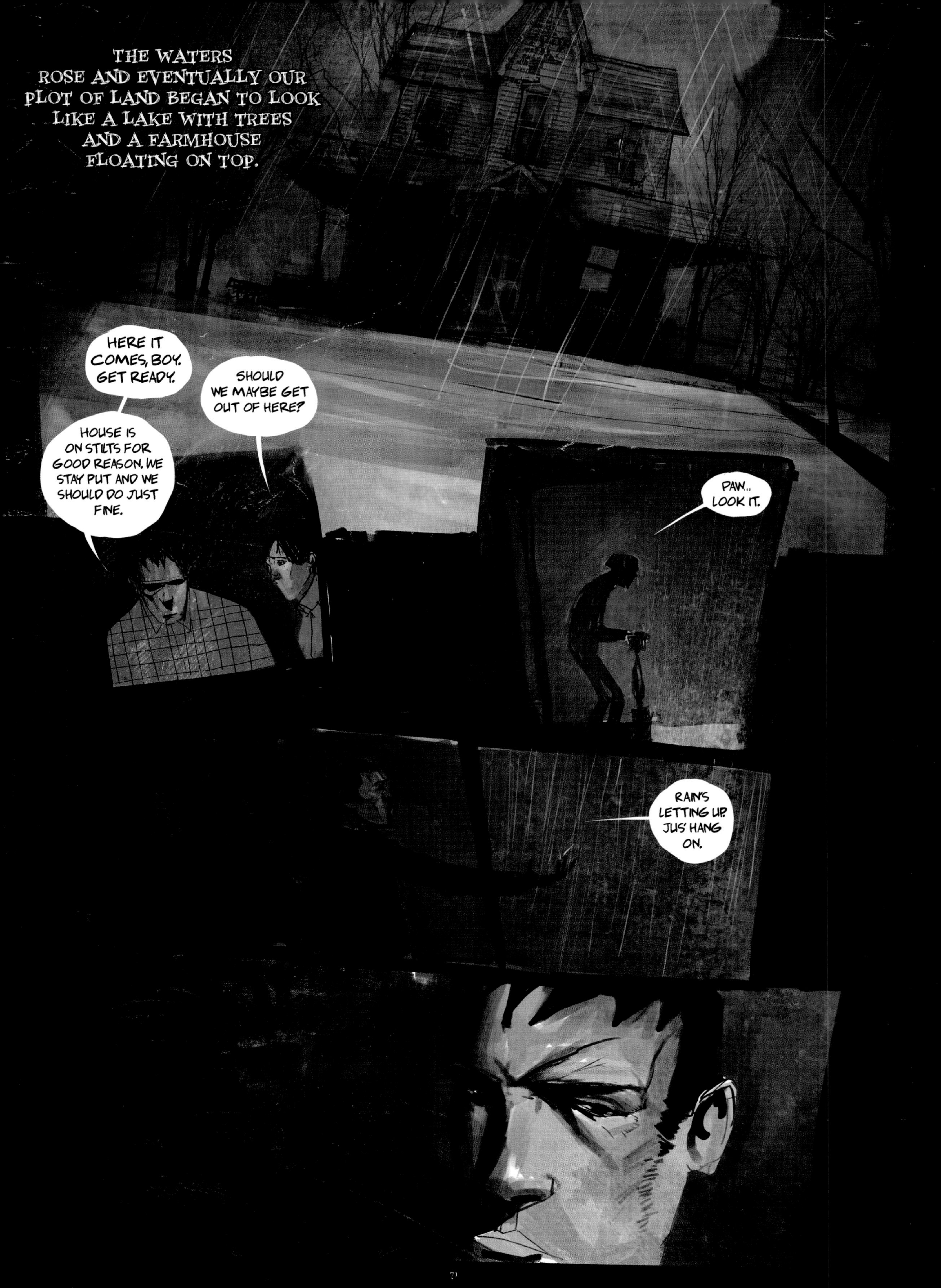
THE WATERS ROSE AND EVENTUALLY OUR PLOT OF LAND BEGAN TO LOOK LIKE A LAKE WITH TREES AND A FARMHOUSE FLOATING ON TOP.
HERE IT COMES, BOY. GET READY.
SHOULD WE MAYBE GET OUT OF HERE?
HOUSE IS ON STILTS FOR GOOD REASON. WE STAY PUT AND WE SHOULD DO JUST FINE.
PAW... LOOK IT.
RAIN'S LETTING UP. JUS' HANG ON.

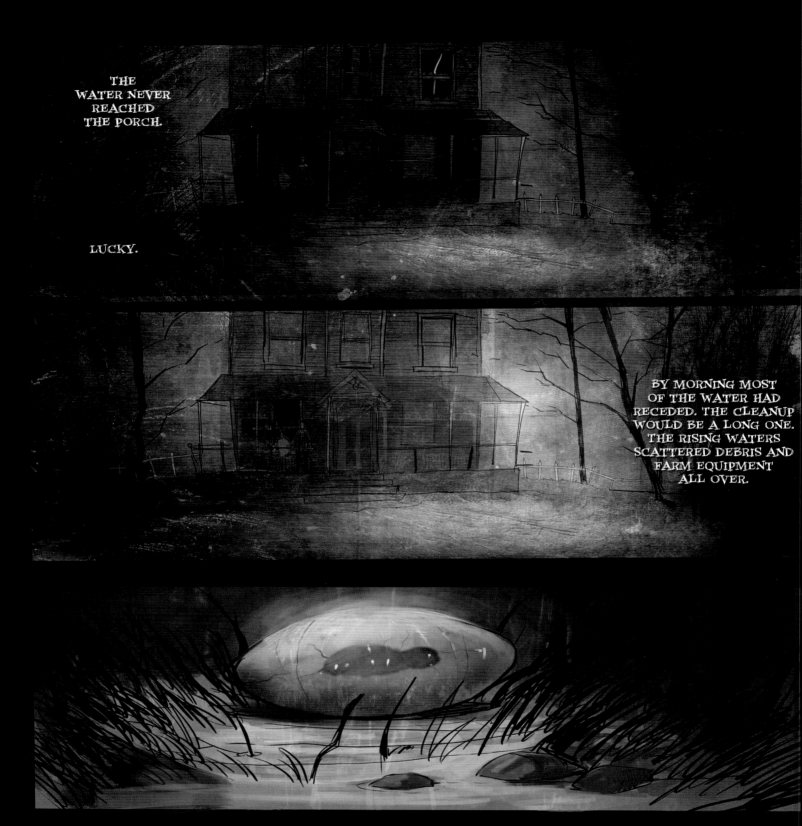

THE WATER NEVER REACHED THE PORCH.

LUCKY.

BY MORNING MOST OF THE WATER HAD RECEDED. THE CLEANUP WOULD BE A LONG ONE. THE RISING WATERS SCATTERED DEBRIS AND FARM EQUIPMENT ALL OVER.

AND THIS TIME...THE WATERS LEFT SOMETHING BEHIND.

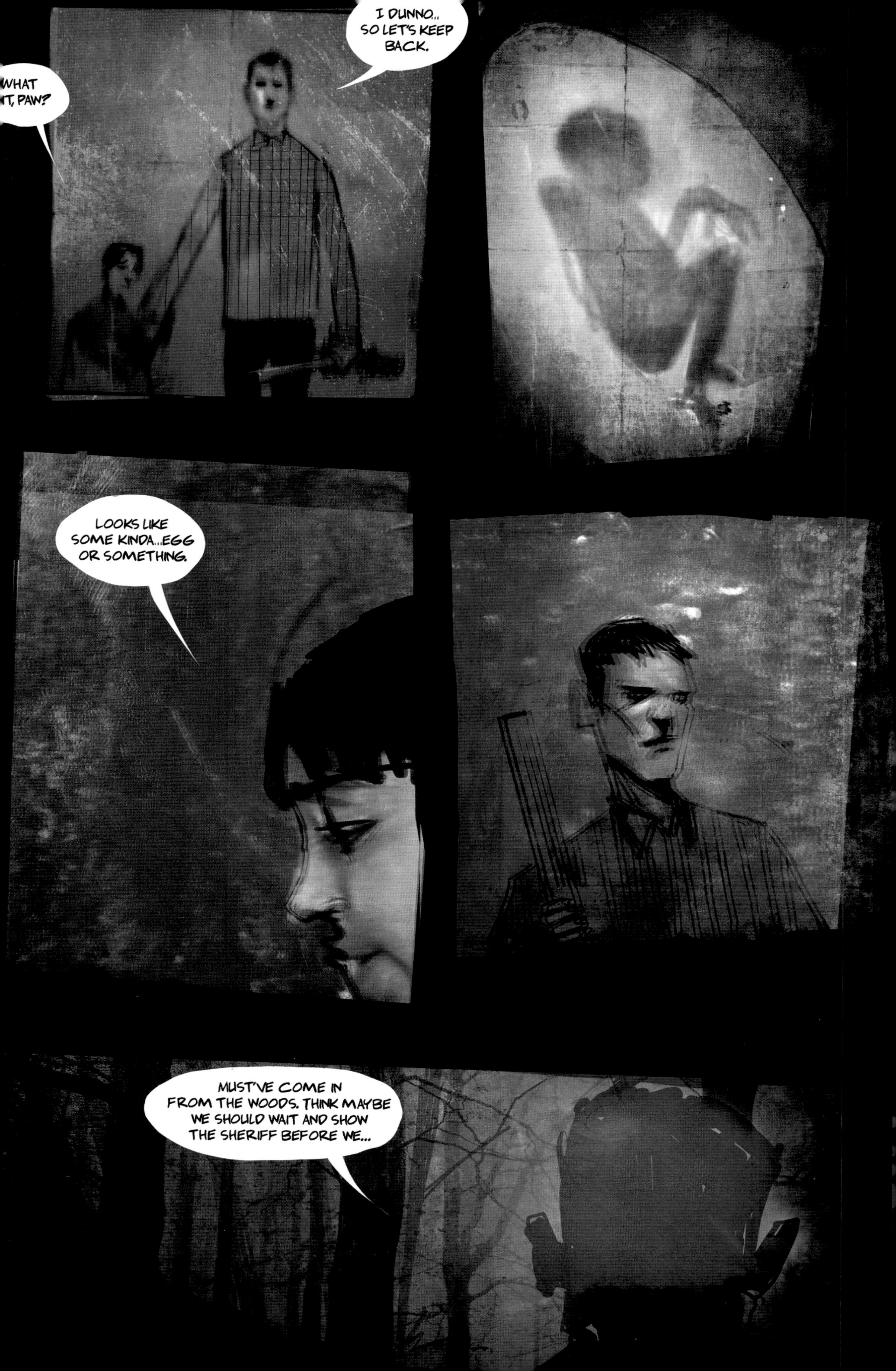
WHAT
T, PAW?
I DUNNO... SO LET'S KEEP BACK.
LOOKS LIKE SOME KINDA...EGG OR SOMETHING.
MUST'VE COME IN FROM THE WOODS. THINK MAYBE WE SHOULD WAIT AND SHOW THE SHERIFF BEFORE WE...

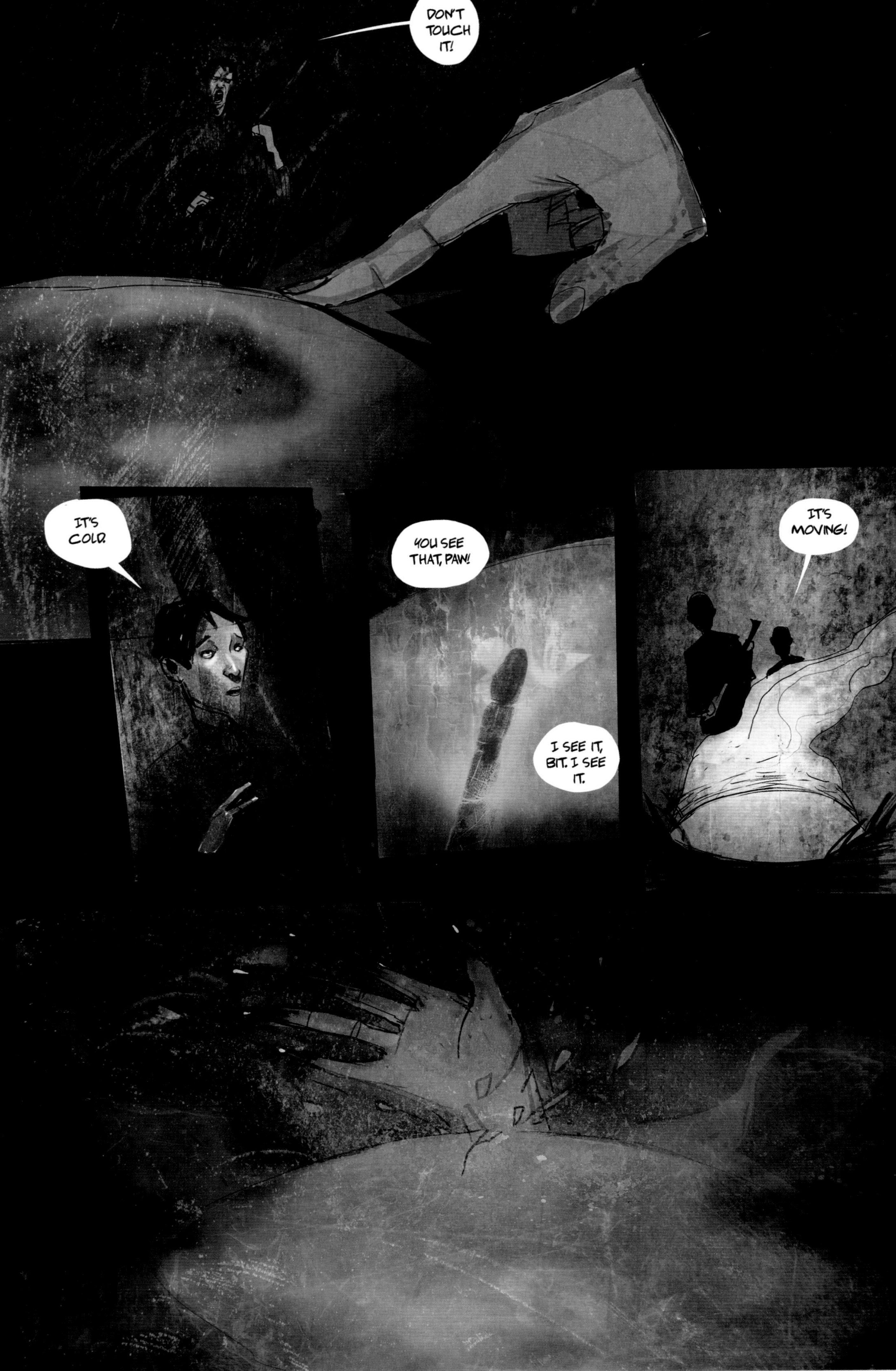
DON'T TOUCH IT!
IT'S COLD.
YOU SEE THAT, PAW!
I SEE IT, BIT. I SEE IT.
IT'S MOVING!

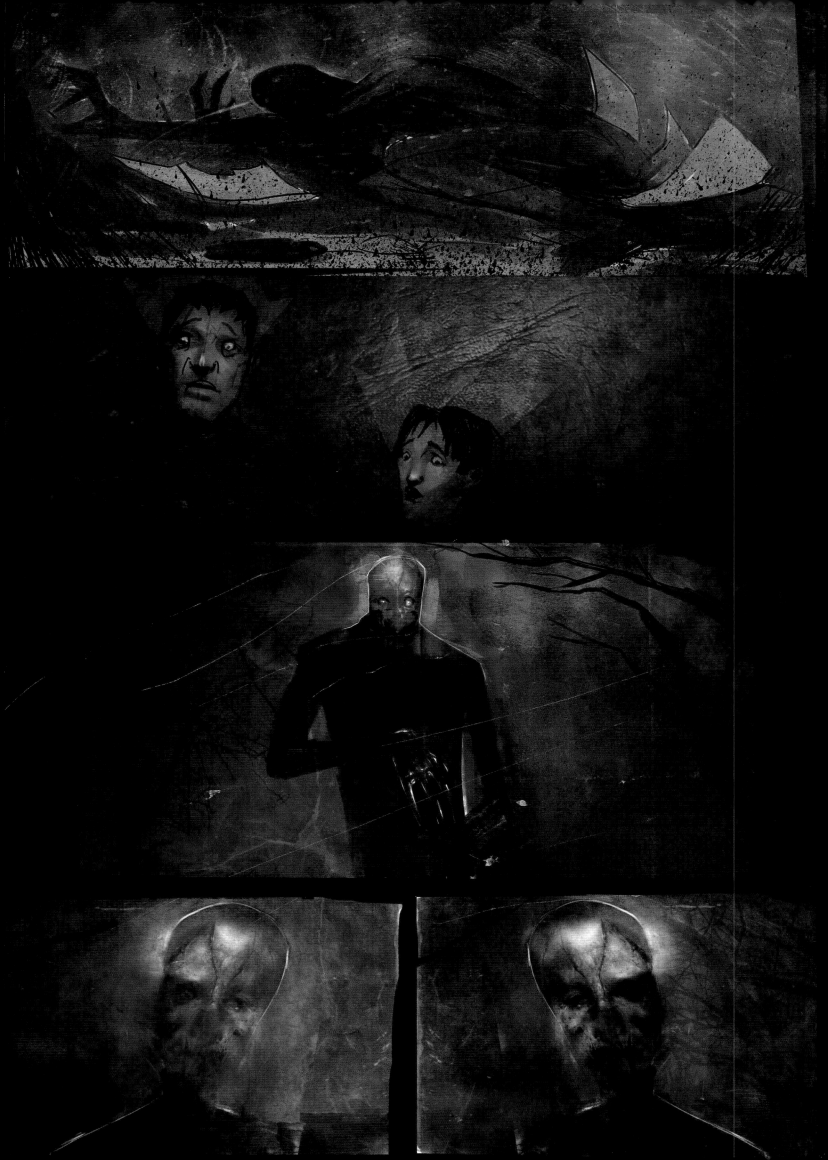

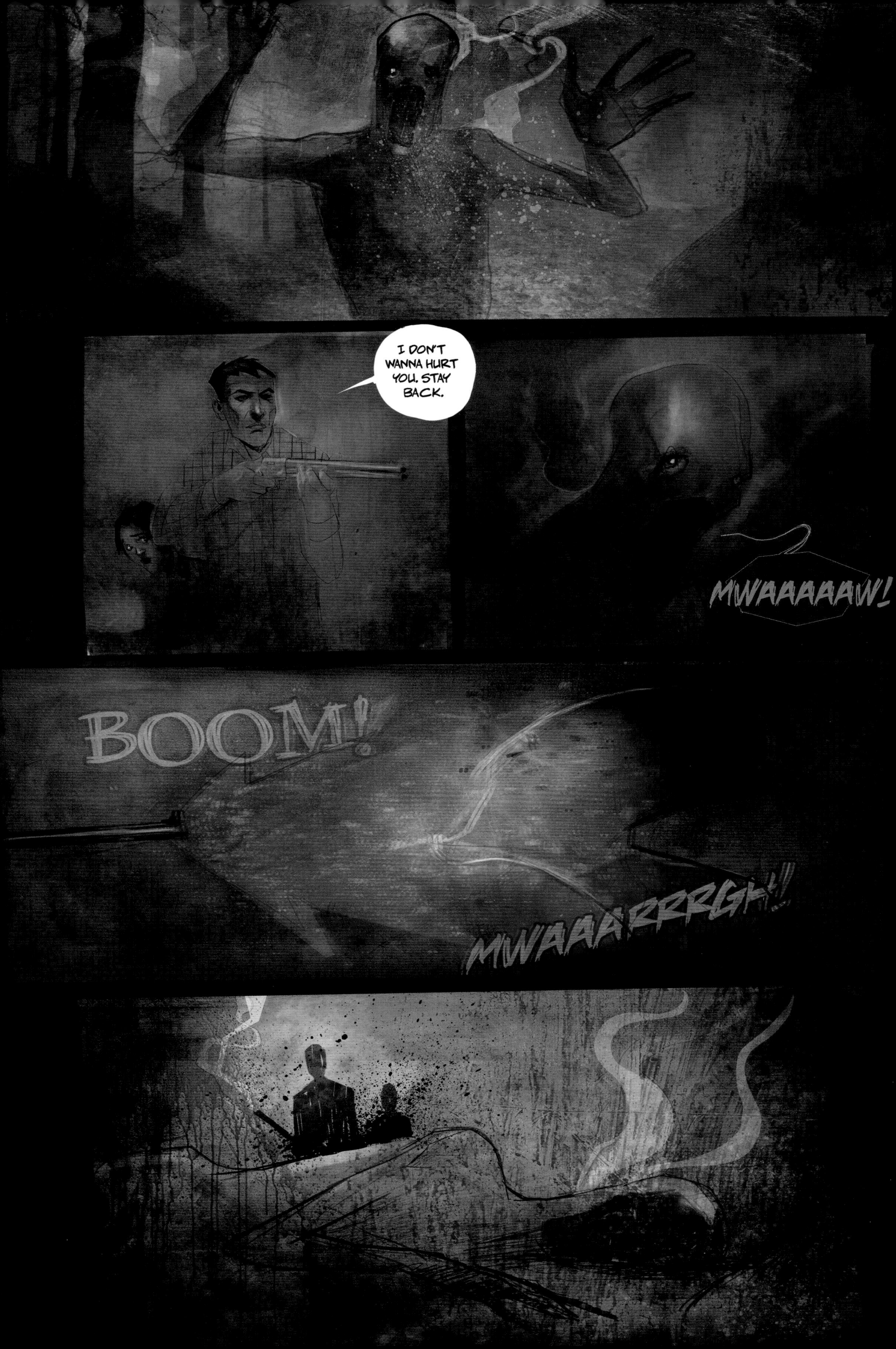
I DON'T WANNA HURT YOU. STAY BACK.
MWAAAAAAW!
BOOM!
MWAAAARRRGH!!

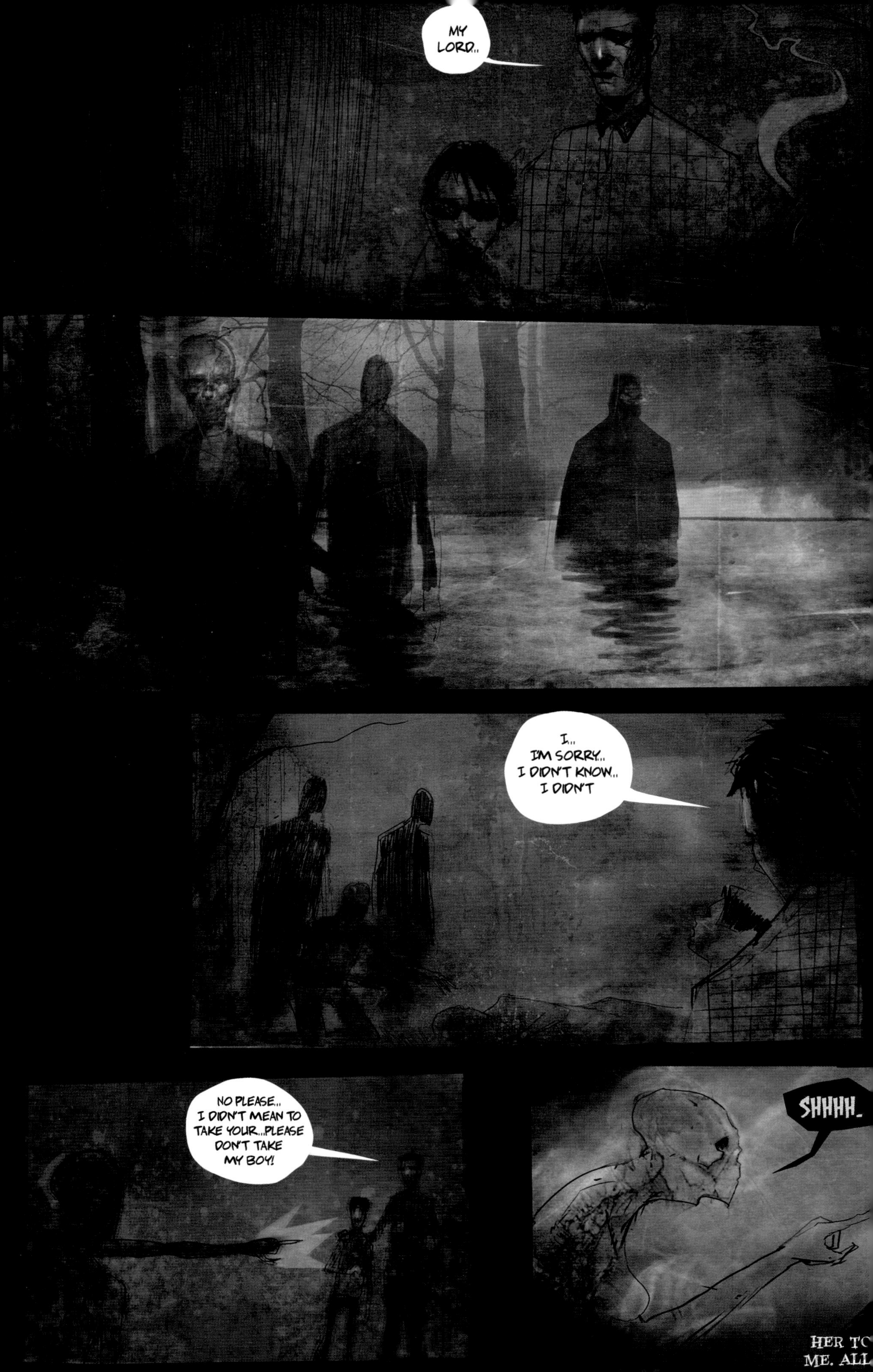
MY LORD...
I... I'M SORRY... I DIDN'T KNOW... I DIDN'T
NO PLEASE... I DIDN'T MEAN TO TAKE YOUR...PLEASE DON'T TAKE MY BOY!
SHHHH_
HER TO
ME. ALL
WAS

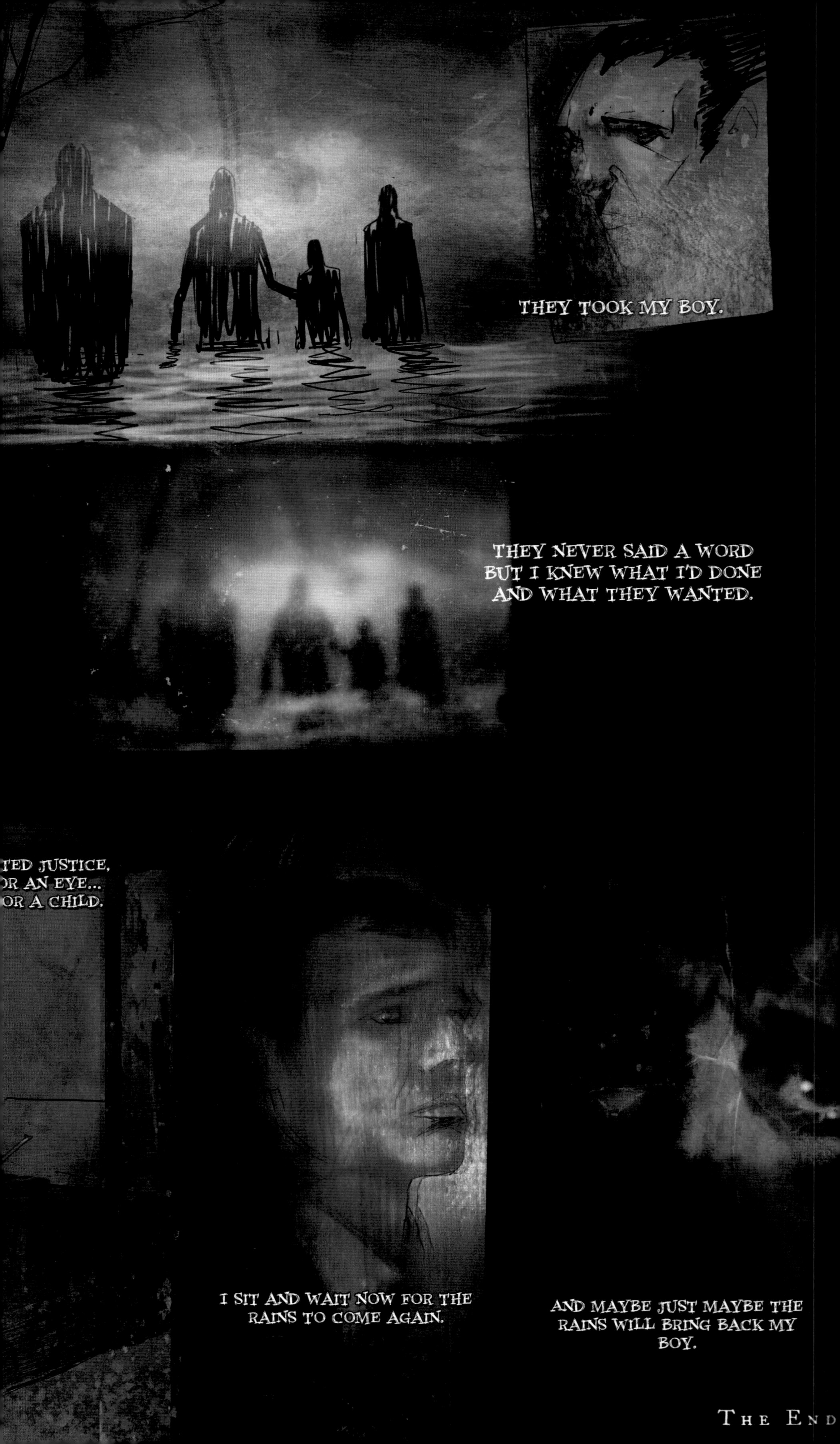

THEY TOOK MY BOY.
THEY NEVER SAID A WORD BUT I KNEW WHAT I'D DONE AND WHAT THEY WANTED.
JUSTICE, AN EYE... A CHILD.
I SIT AND WAIT NOW FOR THE RAINS TO COME AGAIN.
AND MAYBE JUST MAYBE THE RAINS WILL BRING BACK MY BOY.
THE END

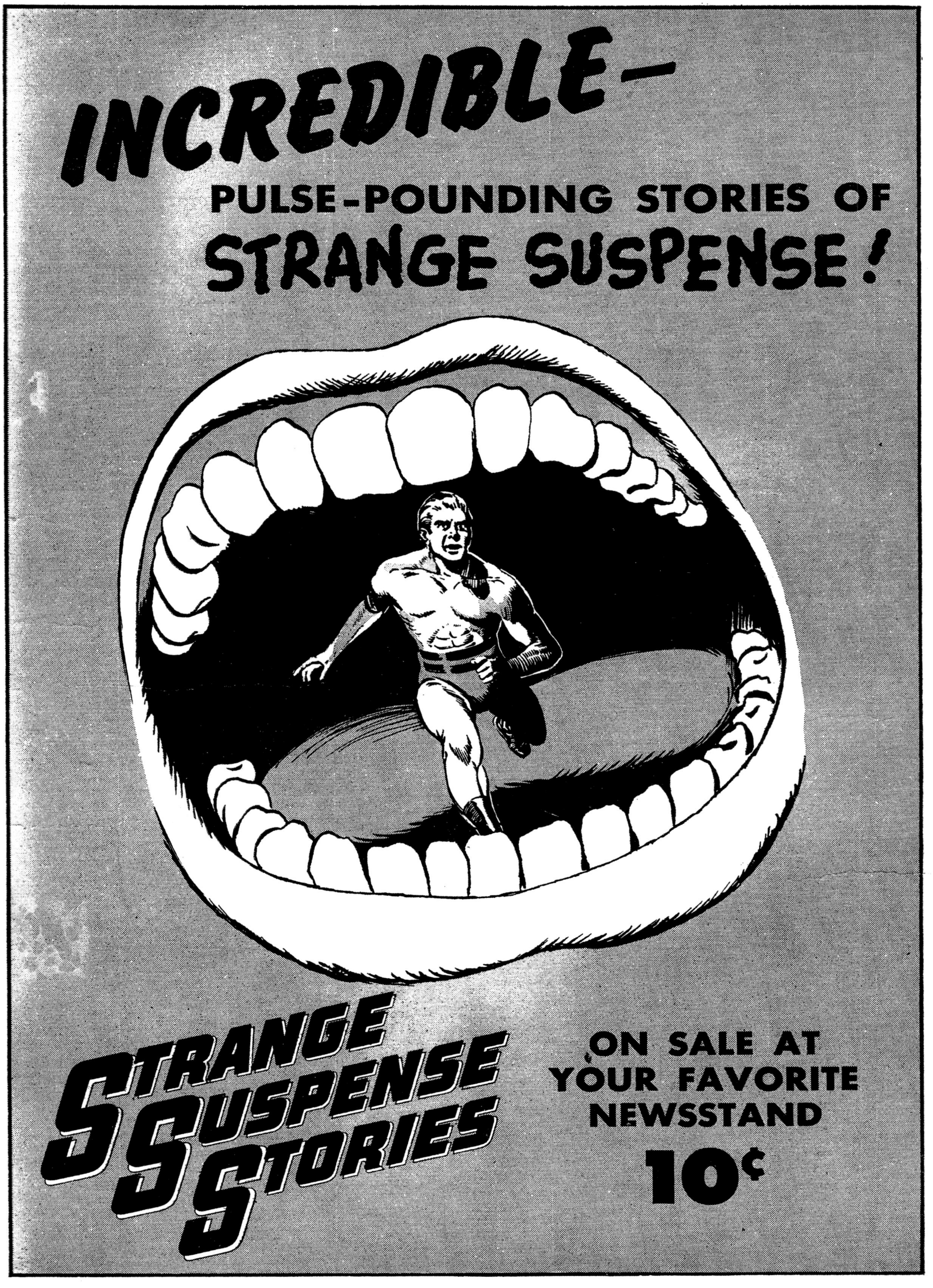
INCREDIBLE—
PULSE-POUNDING STORIES OF
STRANGE SUSPENSE!
STRANGE SUSPENSE STORIES
ON SALE AT
YOUR FAVORITE
NEWSSTAND
10¢

THE BODY

WRITER
TIM SEELEY

ARTIST
STEPHEN GREEN

COLORIST
K. MICHAEL RUSSELL

LETTERER
RACHEL DEERING

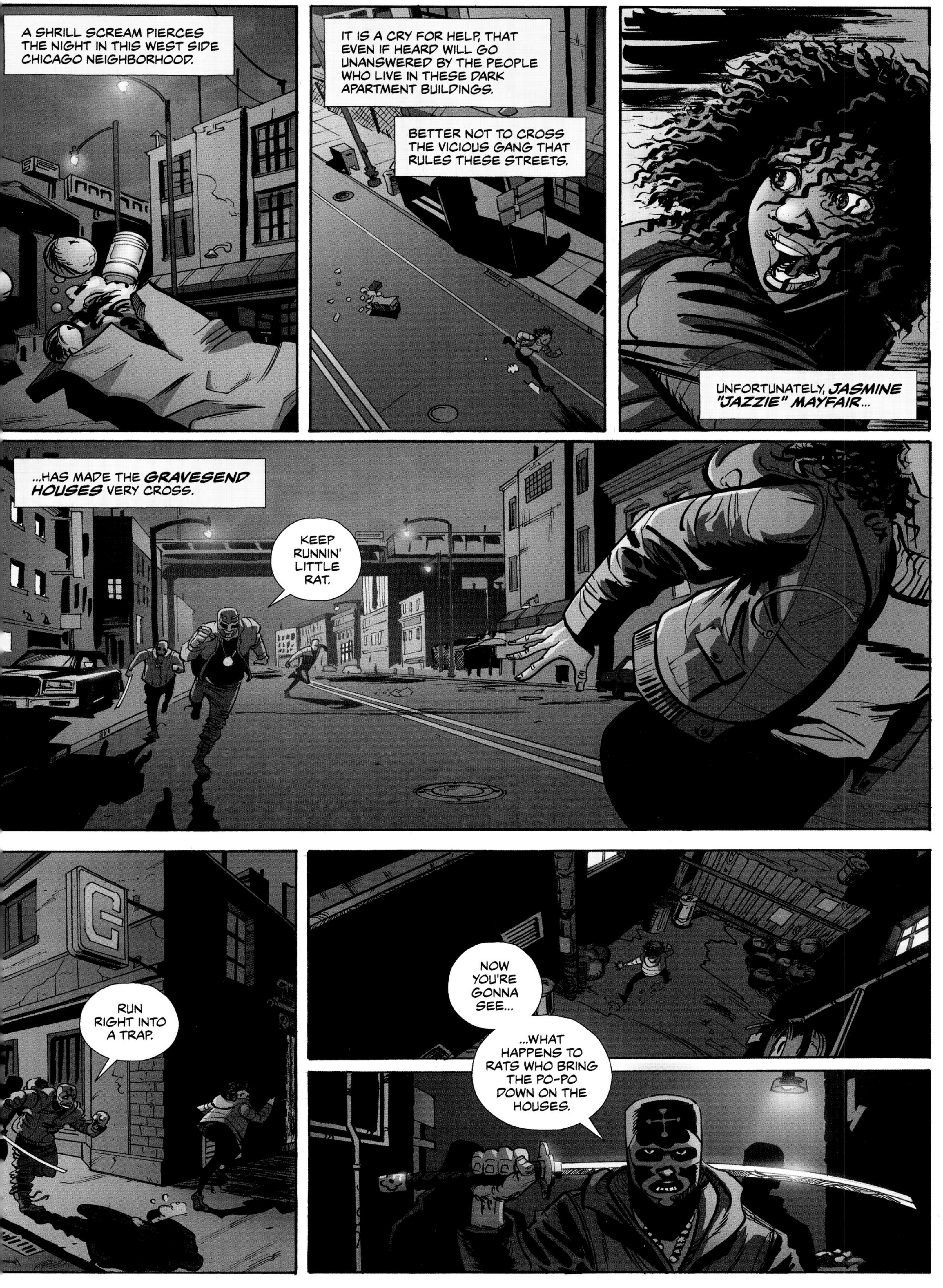
A SHRILL SCREAM PIERCES THE NIGHT IN THIS WEST SIDE CHICAGO NEIGHBORHOOD.
IT IS A CRY FOR HELP, THAT EVEN IF HEARD WILL GO UNANSWERED BY THE PEOPLE WHO LIVE IN THESE DARK APARTMENT BUILDINGS.
BETTER NOT TO CROSS THE VICIOUS GANG THAT RULES THESE STREETS.
UNFORTUNATELY, JASMINE "JAZZIE" MAYFAIR...
...HAS MADE THE GRAVESEND HOUSES VERY CROSS.
KEEP RUNNIN' LITTLE RAT.
RUN RIGHT INTO A TRAP.
NOW YOU'RE GONNA SEE...
...WHAT HAPPENS TO RATS WHO BRING THE PO-PO DOWN ON THE HOUSES.

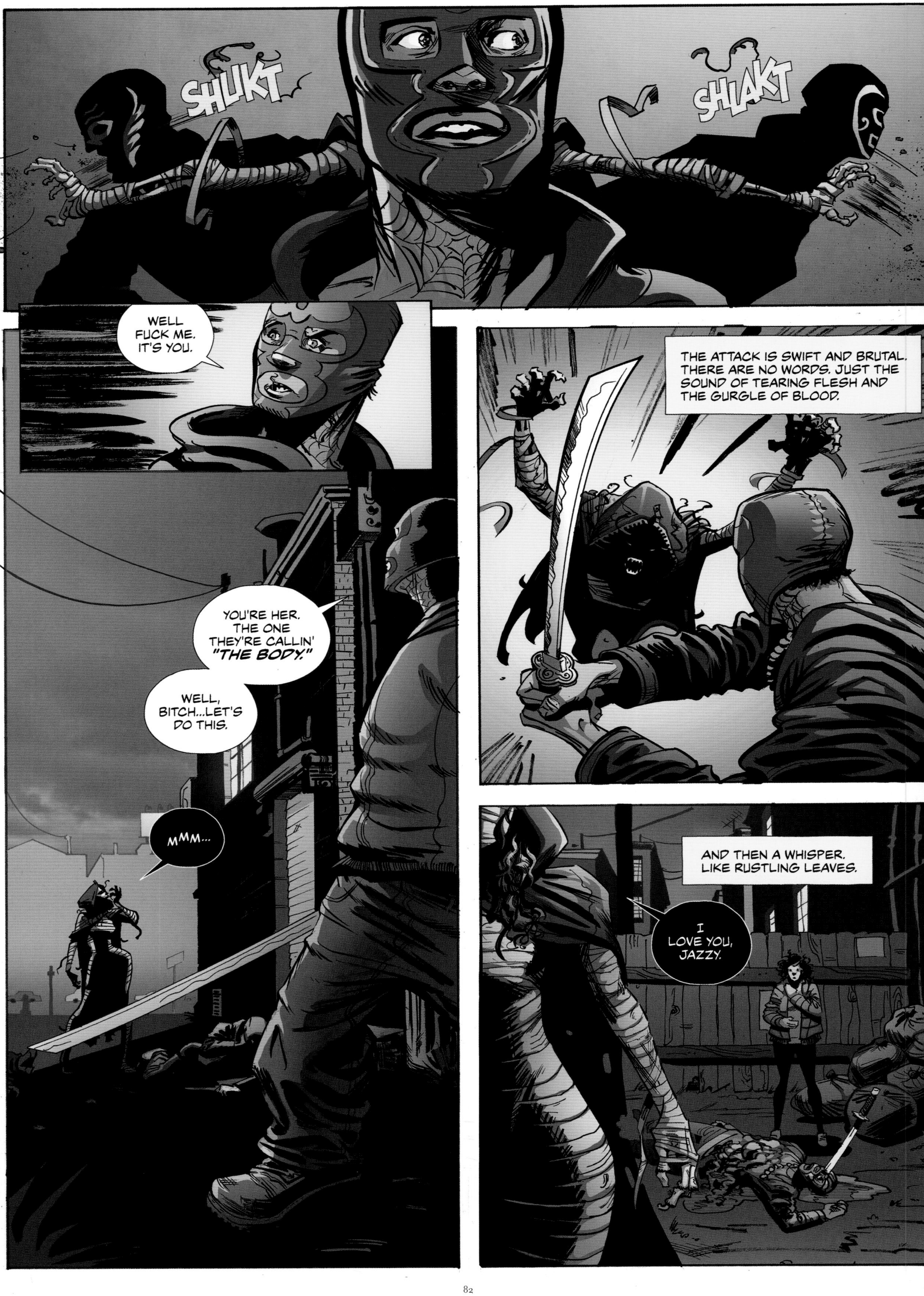
SHLIKT
SHLAKT
WELL FUCK ME. IT'S YOU.
THE ATTACK IS SWIFT AND BRUTAL. THERE ARE NO WORDS. JUST THE SOUND OF TEARING FLESH AND THE GURGLE OF BLOOD.
YOU'RE HER. THE ONE THEY'RE CALLIN' "THE BODY."
WELL, BITCH...LET'S DO THIS.
MMM...
AND THEN A WHISPER. LIKE RUSTLING LEAVES.
I LOVE YOU, JAZZY.

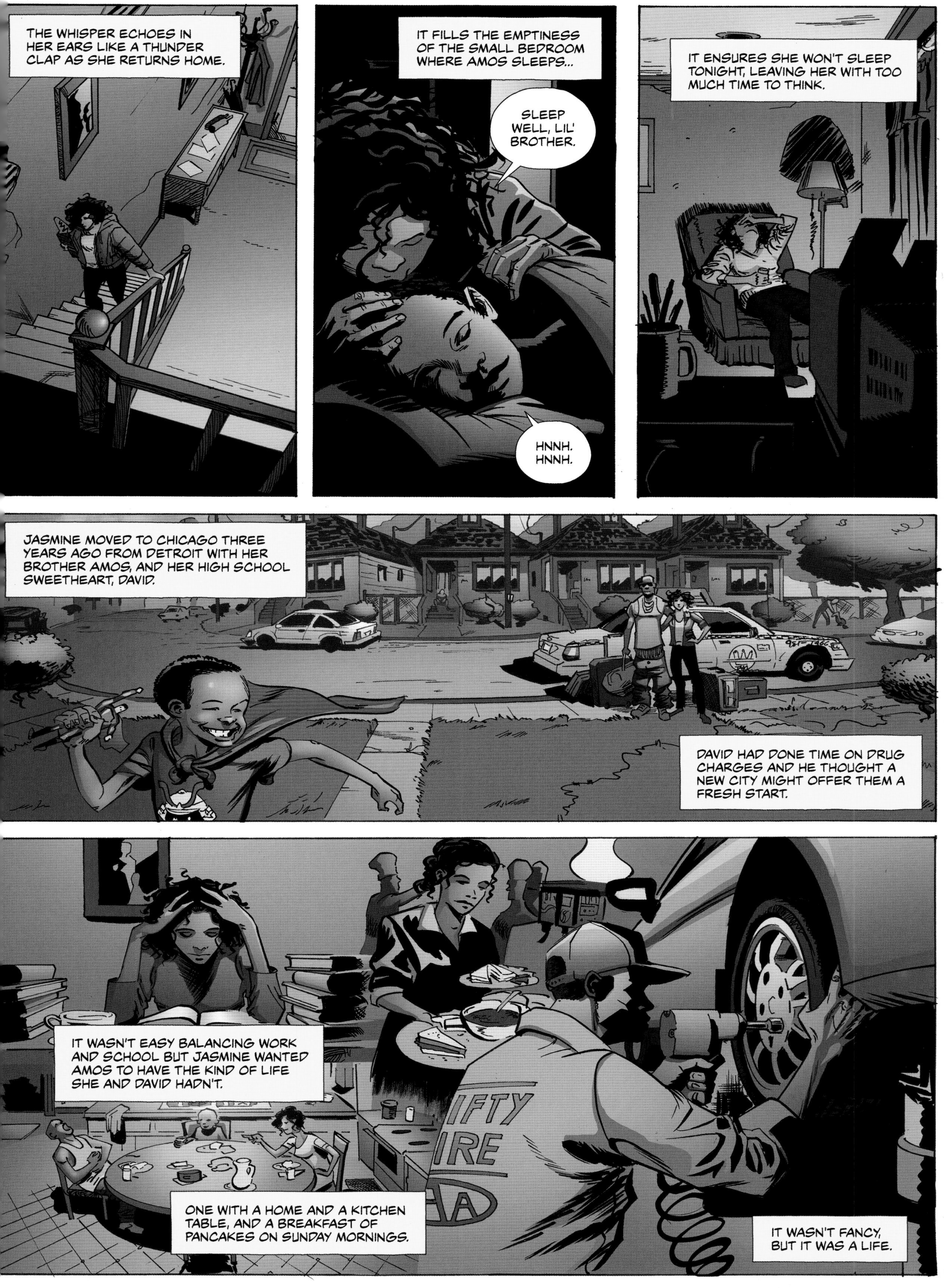
THE WHISPER ECHOES IN HER EARS LIKE A THUNDER CLAP AS SHE RETURNS HOME.
IT FILLS THE EMPTINESS OF THE SMALL BEDROOM WHERE AMOS SLEEPS...
SLEEP WELL, LIL' BROTHER.
HNNH. HNNH.
IT ENSURES SHE WON'T SLEEP TONIGHT, LEAVING HER WITH TOO MUCH TIME TO THINK.
JASMINE MOVED TO CHICAGO THREE YEARS AGO FROM DETROIT WITH HER BROTHER AMOS, AND HER HIGH SCHOOL SWEETHEART, DAVID.
DAVID HAD DONE TIME ON DRUG CHARGES AND HE THOUGHT A NEW CITY MIGHT OFFER THEM A FRESH START.
IT WASN'T EASY BALANCING WORK AND SCHOOL BUT JASMINE WANTED AMOS TO HAVE THE KIND OF LIFE SHE AND DAVID HADN'T.
ONE WITH A HOME AND A KITCHEN TABLE, AND A BREAKFAST OF PANCAKES ON SUNDAY MORNINGS.
IT WASN'T FANCY, BUT IT WAS A LIFE.

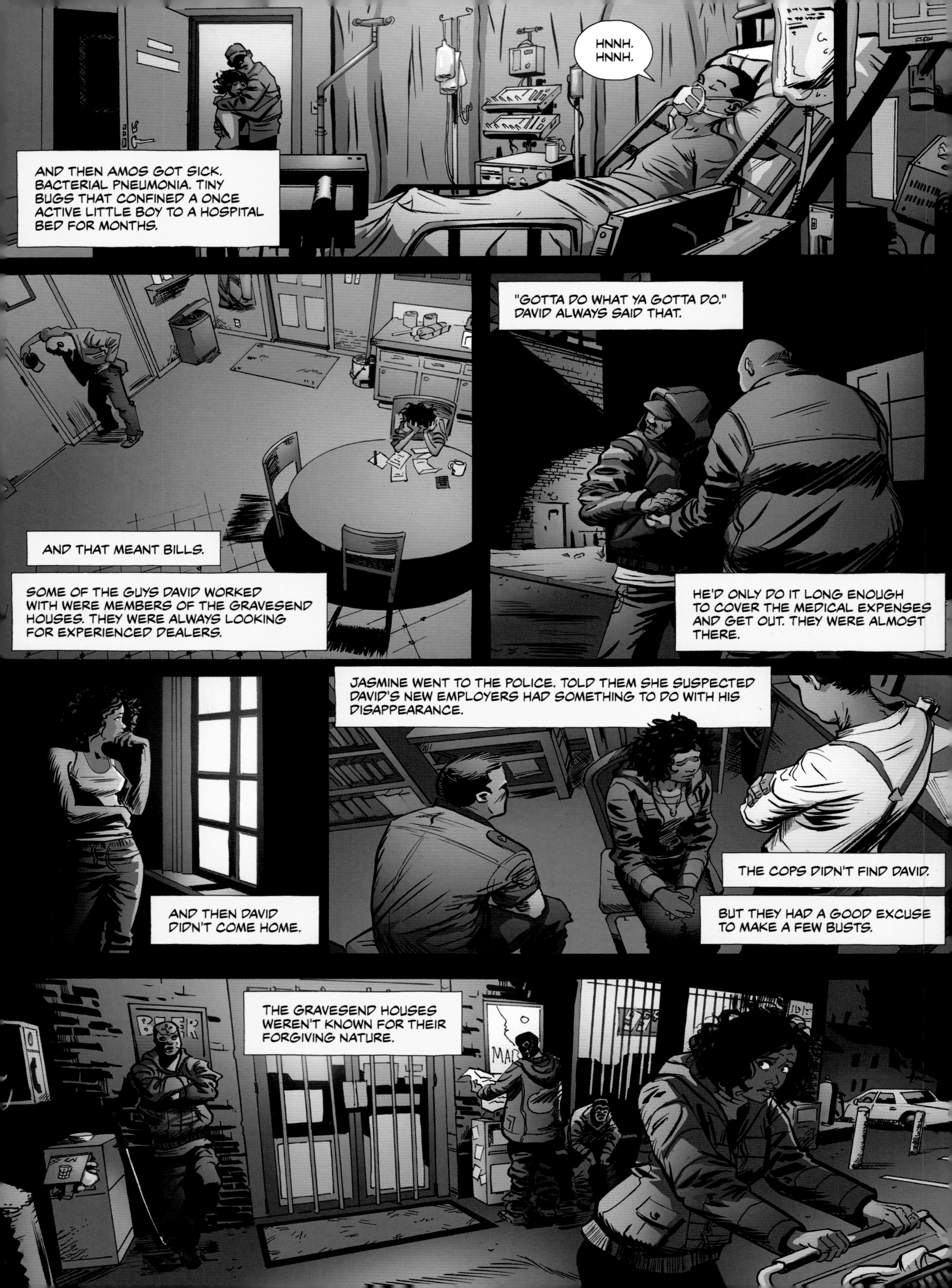
HNNH. HNNH.
AND THEN AMOS GOT SICK. BACTERIAL PNEUMONIA. TINY BUGS THAT CONFINED A ONCE ACTIVE LITTLE BOY TO A HOSPITAL BED FOR MONTHS.
AND THAT MEANT BILLS.
SOME OF THE GUYS DAVID WORKED WITH WERE MEMBERS OF THE GRAVESEND HOUSES. THEY WERE ALWAYS LOOKING FOR EXPERIENCED DEALERS.
"GOTTA DO WHAT YA GOTTA DO." DAVID ALWAYS SAID THAT.
HE'D ONLY DO IT LONG ENOUGH TO COVER THE MEDICAL EXPENSES AND GET OUT. THEY WERE ALMOST THERE.
AND THEN DAVID DIDN'T COME HOME.
JASMINE WENT TO THE POLICE. TOLD THEM SHE SUSPECTED DAVID'S NEW EMPLOYERS HAD SOMETHING TO DO WITH HIS DISAPPEARANCE.
THE COPS DIDN'T FIND DAVID.
BUT THEY HAD A GOOD EXCUSE TO MAKE A FEW BUSTS.
THE GRAVESEND HOUSES WEREN'T KNOWN FOR THEIR FORGIVING NATURE.

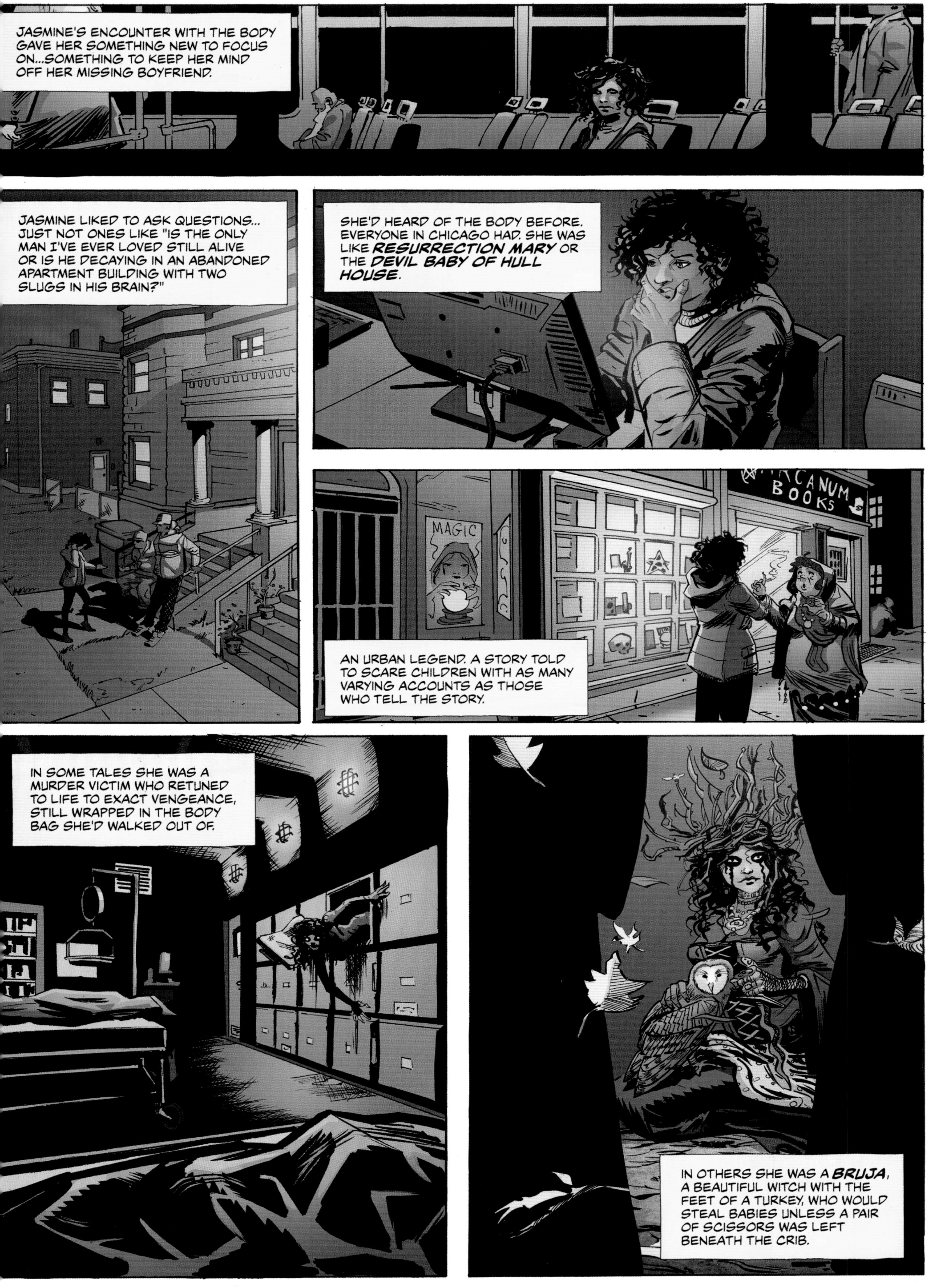
JASMINE'S ENCOUNTER WITH THE BODY GAVE HER SOMETHING NEW TO FOCUS ON...SOMETHING TO KEEP HER MIND OFF HER MISSING BOYFRIEND.
JASMINE LIKED TO ASK QUESTIONS... JUST NOT ONES LIKE "IS THE ONLY MAN I'VE EVER LOVED STILL ALIVE OR IS HE DECAYING IN AN ABANDONED APARTMENT BUILDING WITH TWO SLUGS IN HIS BRAIN?"
SHE'D HEARD OF THE BODY BEFORE. EVERYONE IN CHICAGO HAD. SHE WAS LIKE ***RESURRECTION MARY*** OR THE ***DEVIL BABY OF HULL HOUSE***.
MAGIC
BOOKS
AN URBAN LEGEND. A STORY TOLD TO SCARE CHILDREN WITH AS MANY VARYING ACCOUNTS AS THOSE WHO TELL THE STORY.
IN SOME TALES SHE WAS A MURDER VICTIM WHO RETUNED TO LIFE TO EXACT VENGEANCE, STILL WRAPPED IN THE BODY BAG SHE'D WALKED OUT OF.
IN OTHERS SHE WAS A ***BRUJA***, A BEAUTIFUL WITCH WITH THE FEET OF A TURKEY, WHO WOULD STEAL BABIES UNLESS A PAIR OF SCISSORS WAS LEFT BENEATH THE CRIB.

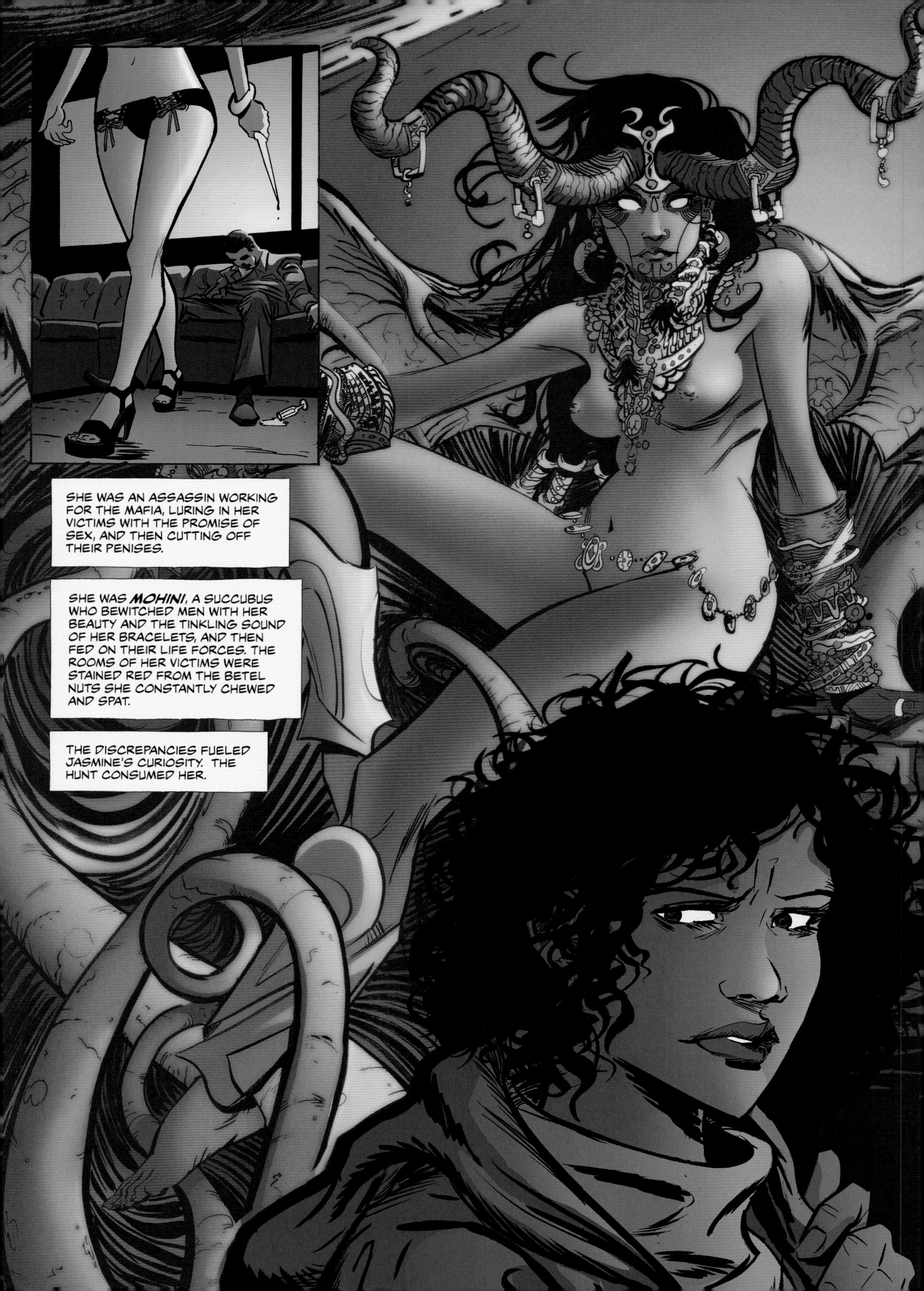
SHE WAS AN ASSASSIN WORKING FOR THE MAFIA, LURING IN HER VICTIMS WITH THE PROMISE OF SEX, AND THEN CUTTING OFF THEIR PENISES.
SHE WAS MOHINI, A SUCCUBUS WHO BEWITCHED MEN WITH HER BEAUTY AND THE TINKLING SOUND OF HER BRACELETS, AND THEN FED ON THEIR LIFE FORCES. THE ROOMS OF HER VICTIMS WERE STAINED RED FROM THE BETEL NUTS SHE CONSTANTLY CHEWED AND SPAT.
THE DISCREPANCIES FUELED JASMINE'S CURIOSITY. THE HUNT CONSUMED HER.

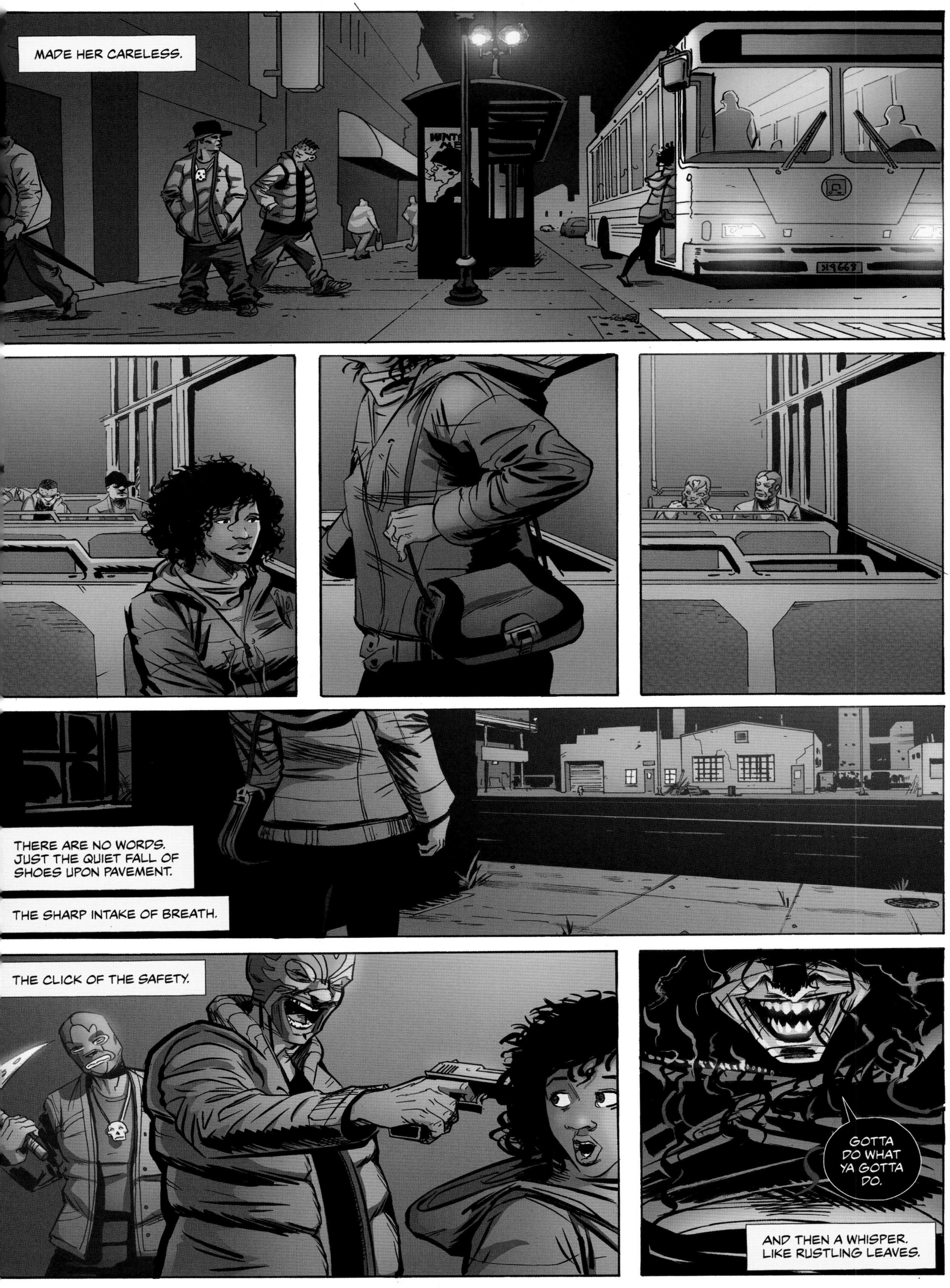
MADE HER CARELESS.
THERE ARE NO WORDS. JUST THE QUIET FALL OF SHOES UPON PAVEMENT.
THE SHARP INTAKE OF BREATH.
THE CLICK OF THE SAFETY.
GOTTA DO WHAT YA GOTTA DO.
AND THEN A WHISPER. LIKE RUSTLING LEAVES.

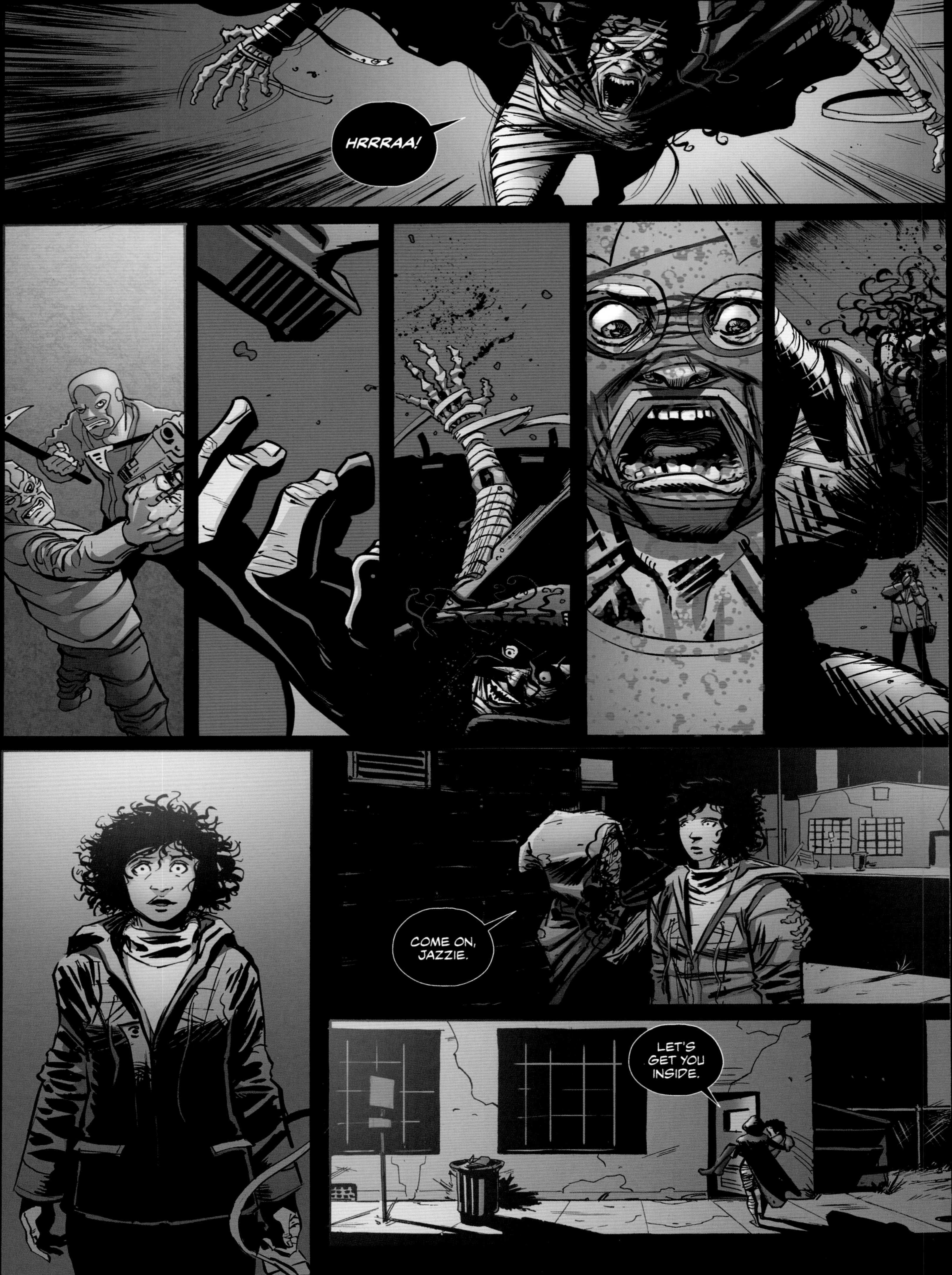
HRRRAA!
COME ON, JAZZIE.
LET'S GET YOU INSIDE.

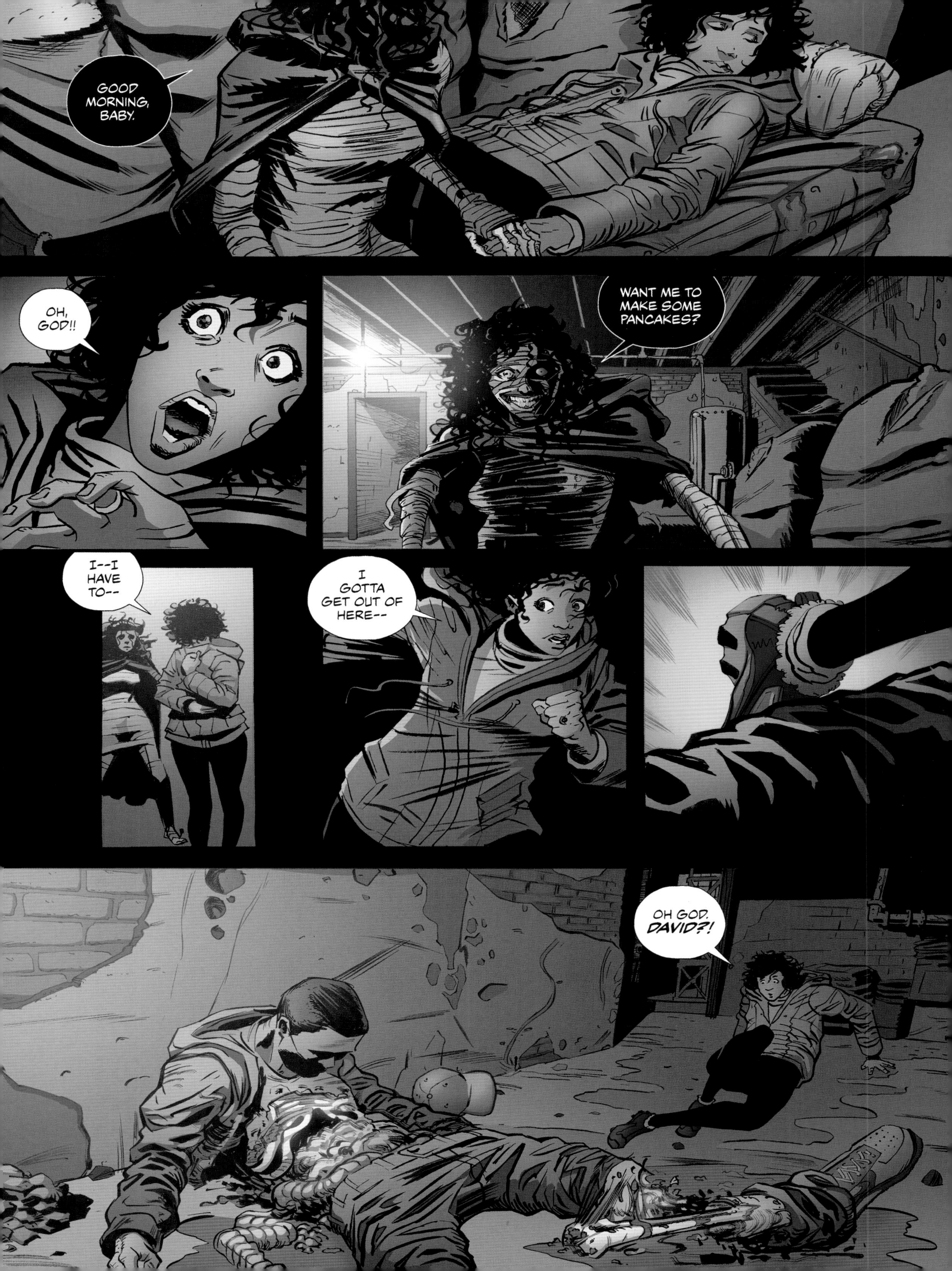
GOOD MORNING, BABY.
OH, GOD!!
WANT ME TO MAKE SOME PANCAKES?
I--I HAVE TO--
I GOTTA GET OUT OF HERE--
OH GOD. DAVID?!

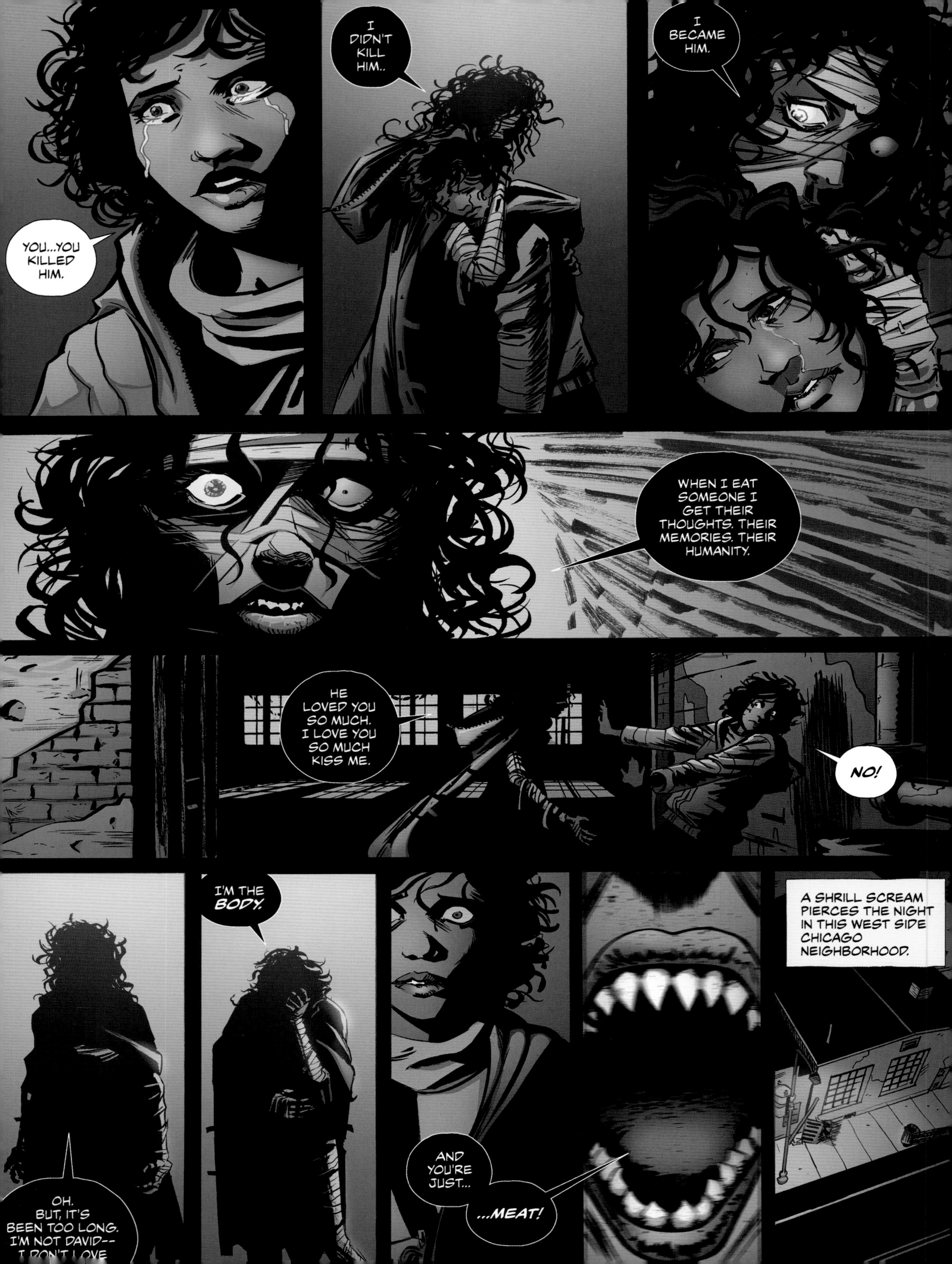
YOU...YOU KILLED HIM.
I DIDN'T KILL HIM..
I BECAME HIM.
WHEN I EAT SOMEONE I GET THEIR THOUGHTS. THEIR MEMORIES. THEIR HUMANITY.
HE LOVED YOU SO MUCH. I LOVE YOU SO MUCH KISS ME.
NO!
OH. BUT, IT'S BEEN TOO LONG. I'M NOT DAVID--
I'M THE BODY.
AND YOU'RE JUST...
...MEAT!
A SHRILL SCREAM PIERCES THE NIGHT IN THIS WEST SIDE CHICAGO NEIGHBORHOOD.

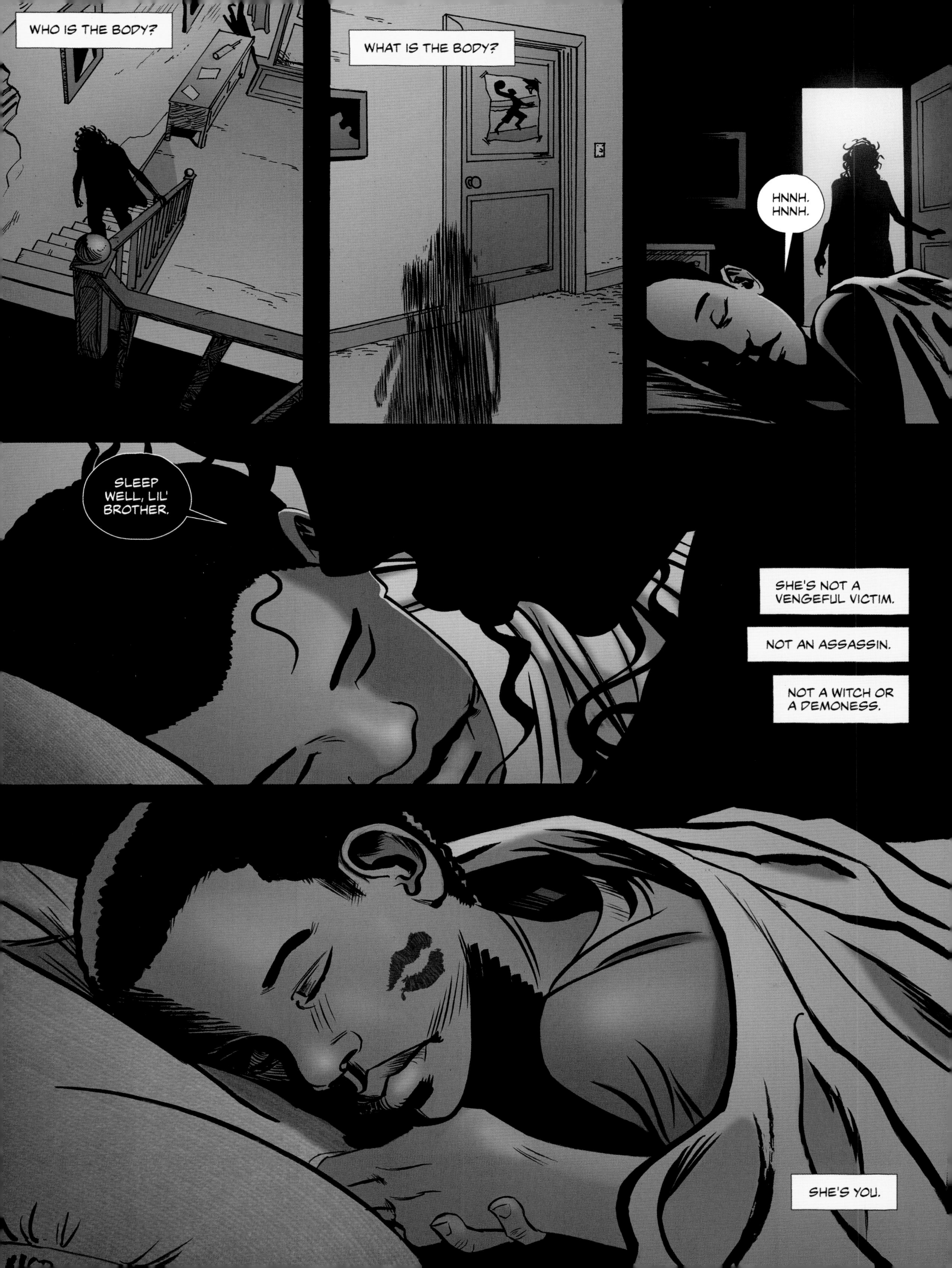
WHO IS THE BODY?
WHAT IS THE BODY?
HNNH. HNNH.
SLEEP WELL, LIL' BROTHER.
SHE'S NOT A VENGEFUL VICTIM.
NOT AN ASSASSIN.
NOT A WITCH OR A DEMONESS.
SHE'S YOU.

FINAL MEAL

WRITER
CHRISTOPHER SEBELA

ARTIST
ZACK SOTO

COLORIST
ZACK SOTO

LETTERER
RACHEL DEERING

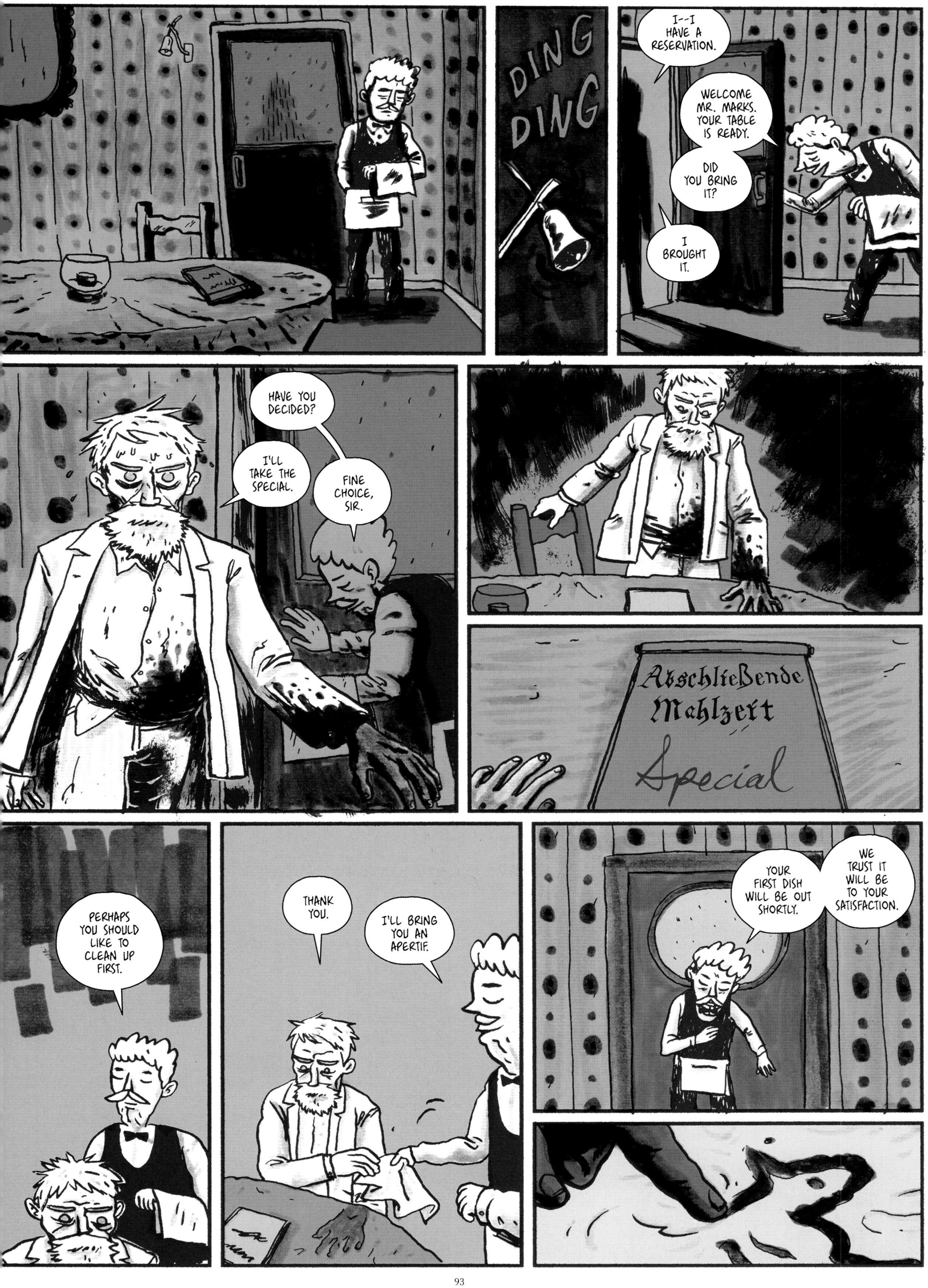
DING
DING
I--I HAVE A RESERVATION.
WELCOME MR. MARKS. YOUR TABLE IS READY.
DID YOU BRING IT?
I BROUGHT IT.
HAVE YOU DECIDED?
I'LL TAKE THE SPECIAL.
FINE CHOICE, SIR.
Abschließende Mahlzeit
Special
PERHAPS YOU SHOULD LIKE TO CLEAN UP FIRST.
THANK YOU.
I'LL BRING YOU AN APERTIF.
YOUR FIRST DISH WILL BE OUT SHORTLY.
WE TRUST IT WILL BE TO YOUR SATISFACTION.

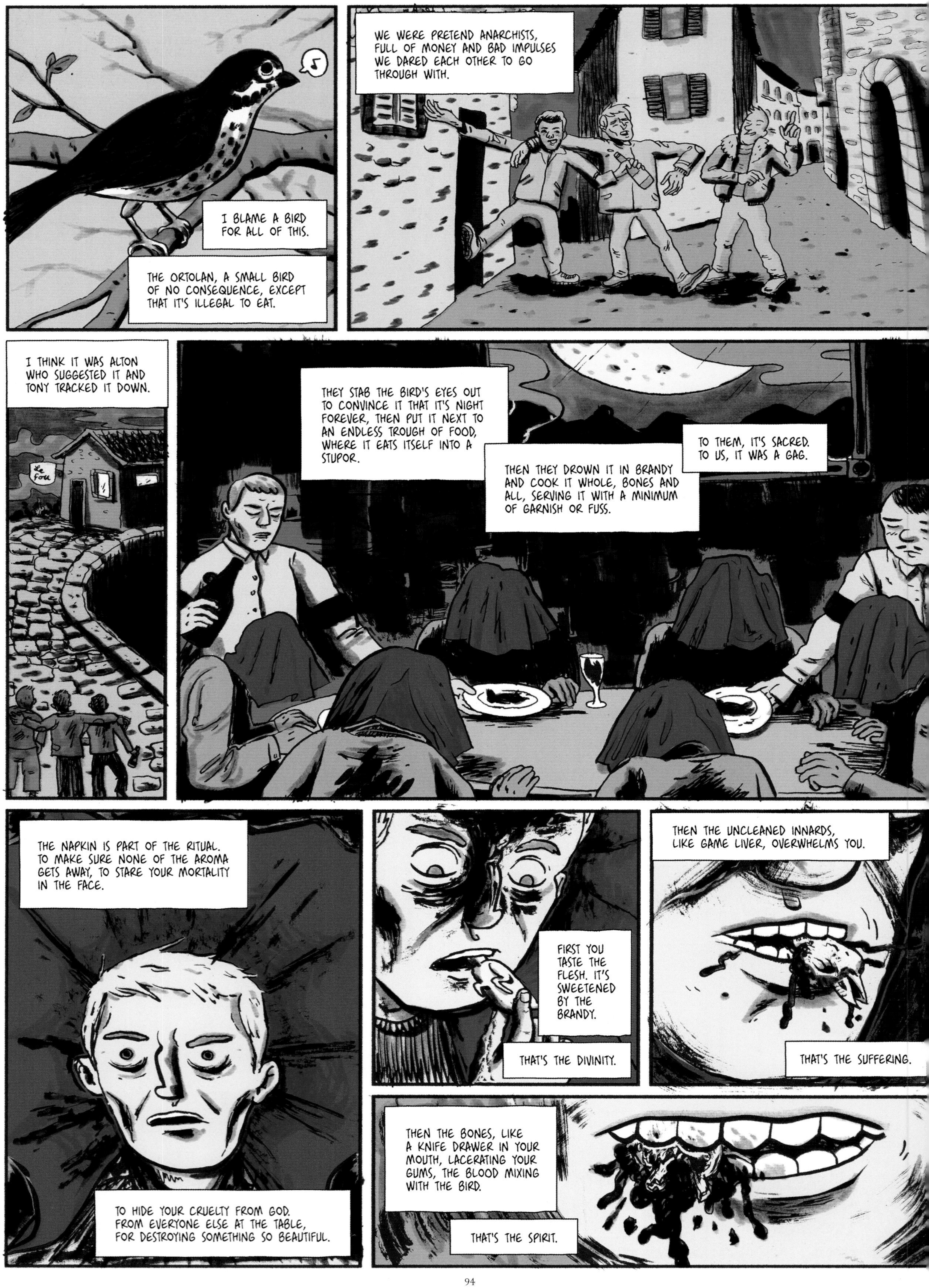
I BLAME A BIRD FOR ALL OF THIS.
THE ORTOLAN, A SMALL BIRD OF NO CONSEQUENCE, EXCEPT THAT IT'S ILLEGAL TO EAT.
WE WERE PRETEND ANARCHISTS, FULL OF MONEY AND BAD IMPULSES WE DARED EACH OTHER TO GO THROUGH WITH.
I THINK IT WAS ALTON WHO SUGGESTED IT AND TONY TRACKED IT DOWN.
THEY STAB THE BIRD'S EYES OUT TO CONVINCE IT THAT IT'S NIGHT FOREVER, THEN PUT IT NEXT TO AN ENDLESS TROUGH OF FOOD, WHERE IT EATS ITSELF INTO A STUPOR.
THEN THEY DROWN IT IN BRANDY AND COOK IT WHOLE, BONES AND ALL, SERVING IT WITH A MINIMUM OF GARNISH OR FUSS.
TO THEM, IT'S SACRED. TO US, IT WAS A GAG.
THE NAPKIN IS PART OF THE RITUAL. TO MAKE SURE NONE OF THE AROMA GETS AWAY, TO STARE YOUR MORTALITY IN THE FACE.
TO HIDE YOUR CRUELTY FROM GOD. FROM EVERYONE ELSE AT THE TABLE, FOR DESTROYING SOMETHING SO BEAUTIFUL.
FIRST YOU TASTE THE FLESH. IT'S SWEETENED BY THE BRANDY.
THAT'S THE DIVINITY.
THEN THE UNCLEANED INNARDS, LIKE GAME LIVER, OVERWHELMS YOU.
THAT'S THE SUFFERING.
THEN THE BONES, LIKE A KNIFE DRAWER IN YOUR MOUTH, LACERATING YOUR GUMS, THE BLOOD MIXING WITH THE BIRD.
THAT'S THE SPIRIT.

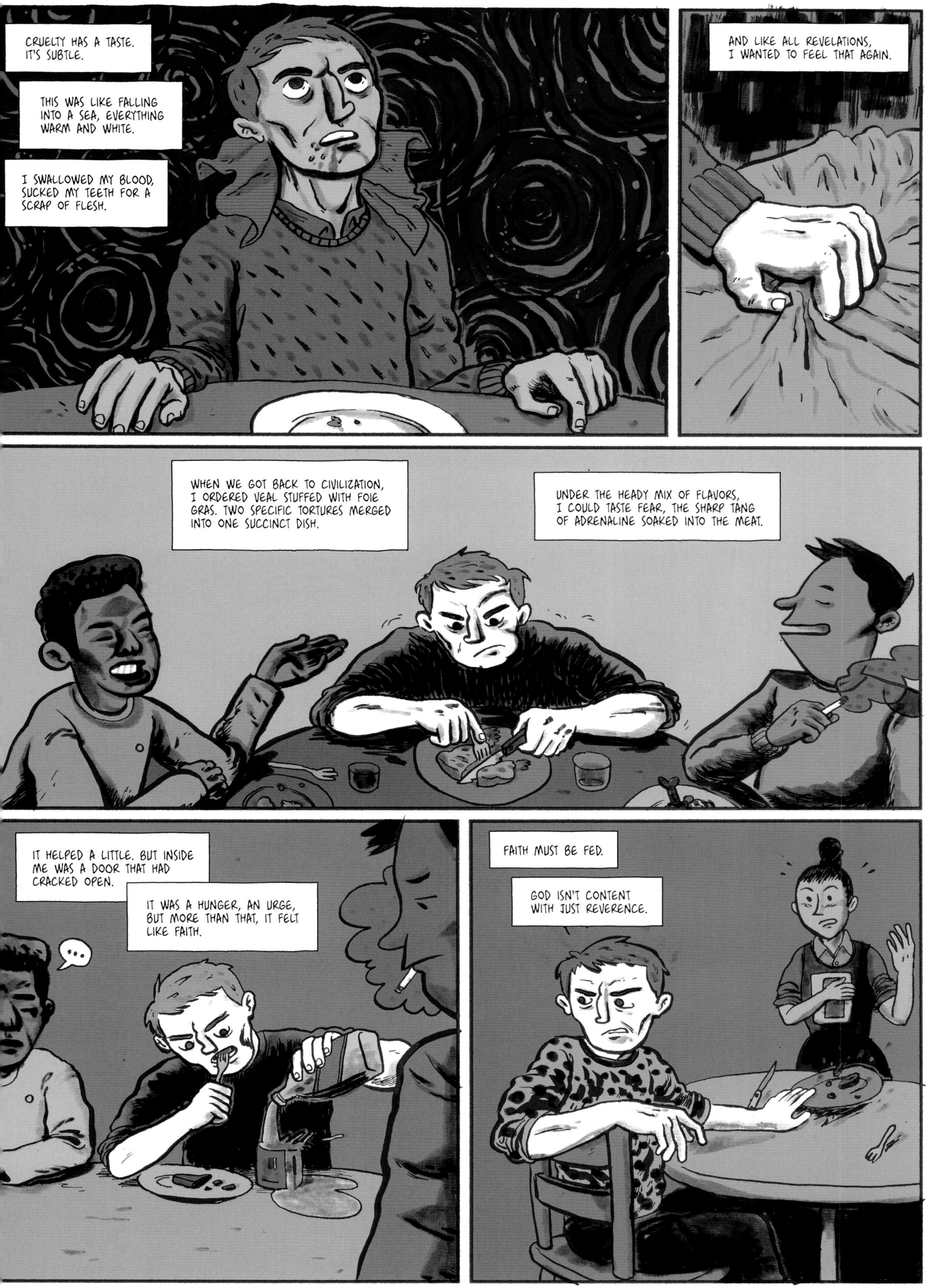
CRUELTY HAS A TASTE. IT'S SUBTLE.
THIS WAS LIKE FALLING INTO A SEA, EVERYTHING WARM AND WHITE.
I SWALLOWED MY BLOOD, SUCKED MY TEETH FOR A SCRAP OF FLESH.
AND LIKE ALL REVELATIONS, I WANTED TO FEEL THAT AGAIN.
WHEN WE GOT BACK TO CIVILIZATION, I ORDERED VEAL STUFFED WITH FOIE GRAS. TWO SPECIFIC TORTURES MERGED INTO ONE SUCCINCT DISH.
UNDER THE HEADY MIX OF FLAVORS, I COULD TASTE FEAR, THE SHARP TANG OF ADRENALINE SOAKED INTO THE MEAT.
IT HELPED A LITTLE. BUT INSIDE ME WAS A DOOR THAT HAD CRACKED OPEN.
IT WAS A HUNGER, AN URGE, BUT MORE THAN THAT, IT FELT LIKE FAITH.
...
FAITH MUST BE FED.
GOD ISN'T CONTENT WITH JUST REVERENCE.

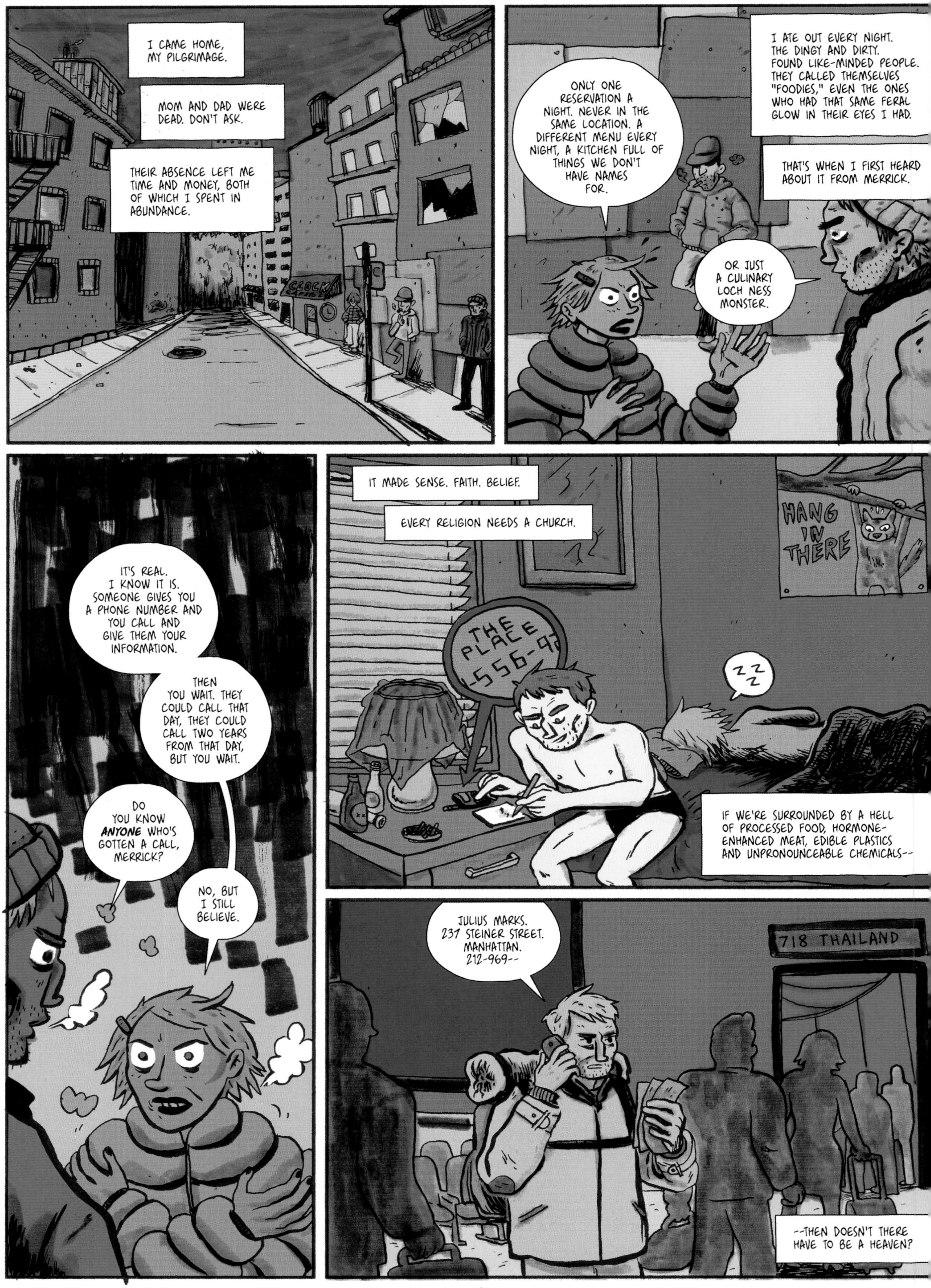

I CAME HOME, MY PILGRIMAGE.
MOM AND DAD WERE DEAD. DON'T ASK.
THEIR ABSENCE LEFT ME TIME AND MONEY, BOTH OF WHICH I SPENT IN ABUNDANCE.
CLOCK
I ATE OUT EVERY NIGHT. THE DINGY AND DIRTY. FOUND LIKE-MINDED PEOPLE. THEY CALLED THEMSELVES "FOODIES," EVEN THE ONES WHO HAD THAT SAME FERAL GLOW IN THEIR EYES I HAD.
ONLY ONE RESERVATION A NIGHT. NEVER IN THE SAME LOCATION. A DIFFERENT MENU EVERY NIGHT, A KITCHEN FULL OF THINGS WE DON'T HAVE NAMES FOR.
THAT'S WHEN I FIRST HEARD ABOUT IT FROM MERRICK.
OR JUST A CULINARY LOCH NESS MONSTER.
IT'S REAL. I KNOW IT IS. SOMEONE GIVES YOU A PHONE NUMBER AND YOU CALL AND GIVE THEM YOUR INFORMATION.
THEN YOU WAIT. THEY COULD CALL THAT DAY, THEY COULD CALL TWO YEARS FROM THAT DAY, BUT YOU WAIT.
DO YOU KNOW **ANYONE** WHO'S GOTTEN A CALL, MERRICK?
NO, BUT I STILL BELIEVE.
IT MADE SENSE. FAITH. BELIEF.
EVERY RELIGION NEEDS A CHURCH.
HANG IN THERE
THE PLACE -556-9
Z Z Z
IF WE'RE SURROUNDED BY A HELL OF PROCESSED FOOD, HORMONE-ENHANCED MEAT, EDIBLE PLASTICS AND UNPRONOUNCEABLE CHEMICALS--
JULIUS MARKS. 237 STEINER STREET. MANHATTAN. 212-969--
718 THAILAND
--THEN DOESN'T THERE HAVE TO BE A HEAVEN?

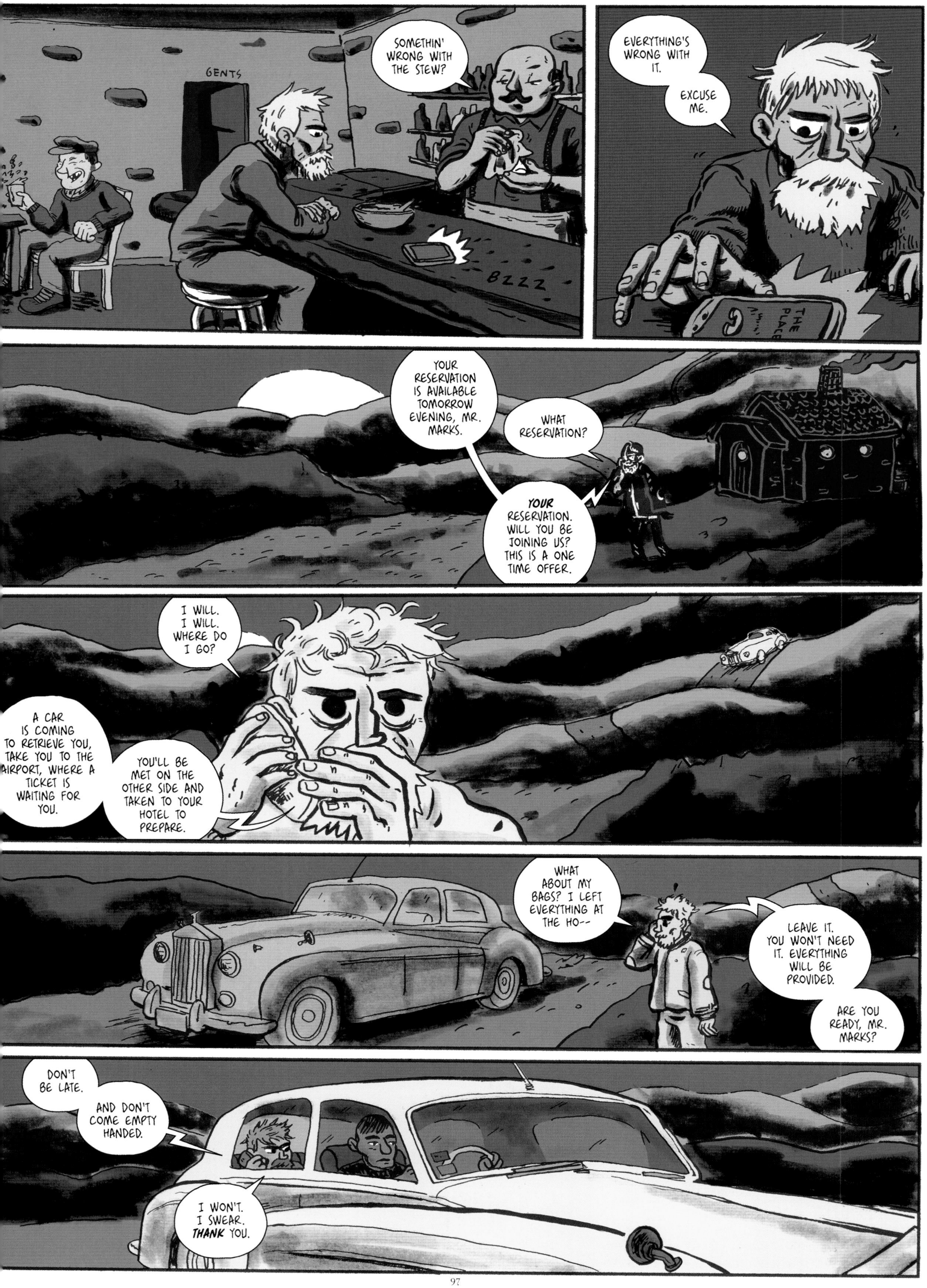
GENTS
SOMETHIN' WRONG WITH THE STEW?
BZZZ
EVERYTHING'S WRONG WITH IT.
EXCUSE ME.
THE PLACE
YOUR RESERVATION IS AVAILABLE TOMORROW EVENING, MR. MARKS.
WHAT RESERVATION?
YOUR RESERVATION. WILL YOU BE JOINING US? THIS IS A ONE TIME OFFER.
I WILL. I WILL. WHERE DO I GO?
A CAR IS COMING TO RETRIEVE YOU, TAKE YOU TO THE AIRPORT, WHERE A TICKET IS WAITING FOR YOU.
YOU'LL BE MET ON THE OTHER SIDE AND TAKEN TO YOUR HOTEL TO PREPARE.
WHAT ABOUT MY BAGS? I LEFT EVERYTHING AT THE HO--
LEAVE IT. YOU WON'T NEED IT. EVERYTHING WILL BE PROVIDED.
ARE YOU READY, MR. MARKS?
DON'T BE LATE.
AND DON'T COME EMPTY HANDED.
I WON'T. I SWEAR. *THANK* YOU.

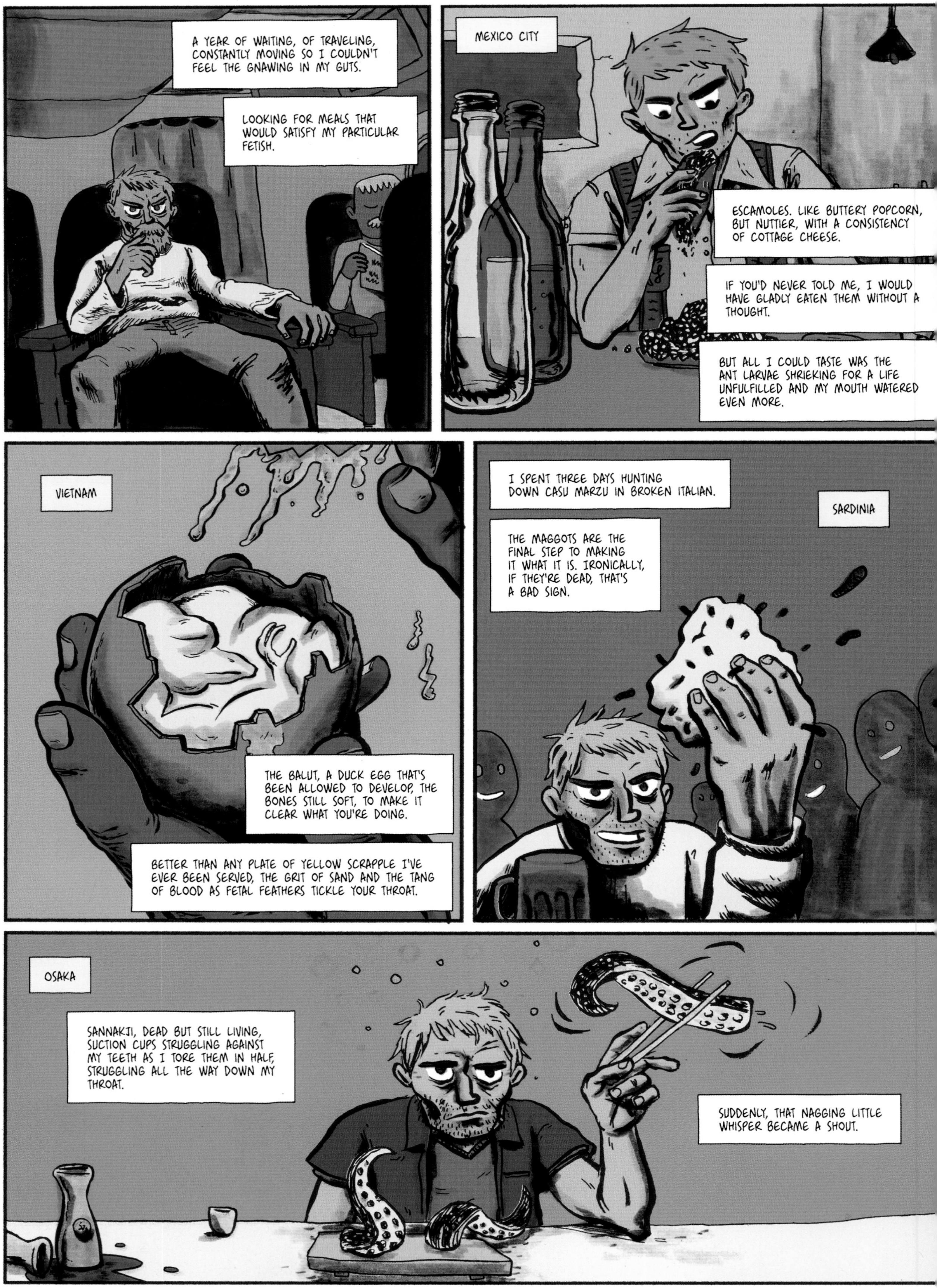
A YEAR OF WAITING, OF TRAVELING, CONSTANTLY MOVING SO I COULDN'T FEEL THE GNAWING IN MY GUTS.
LOOKING FOR MEALS THAT WOULD SATISFY MY PARTICULAR FETISH.
MEXICO CITY
ESCAMOLES. LIKE BUTTERY POPCORN, BUT NUTTIER, WITH A CONSISTENCY OF COTTAGE CHEESE.
IF YOU'D NEVER TOLD ME, I WOULD HAVE GLADLY EATEN THEM WITHOUT A THOUGHT.
BUT ALL I COULD TASTE WAS THE ANT LARVAE SHRIEKING FOR A LIFE UNFULFILLED AND MY MOUTH WATERED EVEN MORE.
VIETNAM
THE BALUT, A DUCK EGG THAT'S BEEN ALLOWED TO DEVELOP, THE BONES STILL SOFT, TO MAKE IT CLEAR WHAT YOU'RE DOING.
BETTER THAN ANY PLATE OF YELLOW SCRAPPLE I'VE EVER BEEN SERVED, THE GRIT OF SAND AND THE TANG OF BLOOD AS FETAL FEATHERS TICKLE YOUR THROAT.
I SPENT THREE DAYS HUNTING DOWN CASU MARZU IN BROKEN ITALIAN.
SARDINIA
THE MAGGOTS ARE THE FINAL STEP TO MAKING IT WHAT IT IS. IRONICALLY, IF THEY'RE DEAD, THAT'S A BAD SIGN.
OSAKA
SANNAKJI, DEAD BUT STILL LIVING, SUCTION CUPS STRUGGLING AGAINST MY TEETH AS I TORE THEM IN HALF, STRUGGLING ALL THE WAY DOWN MY THROAT.
SUDDENLY, THAT NAGGING LITTLE WHISPER BECAME A SHOUT.

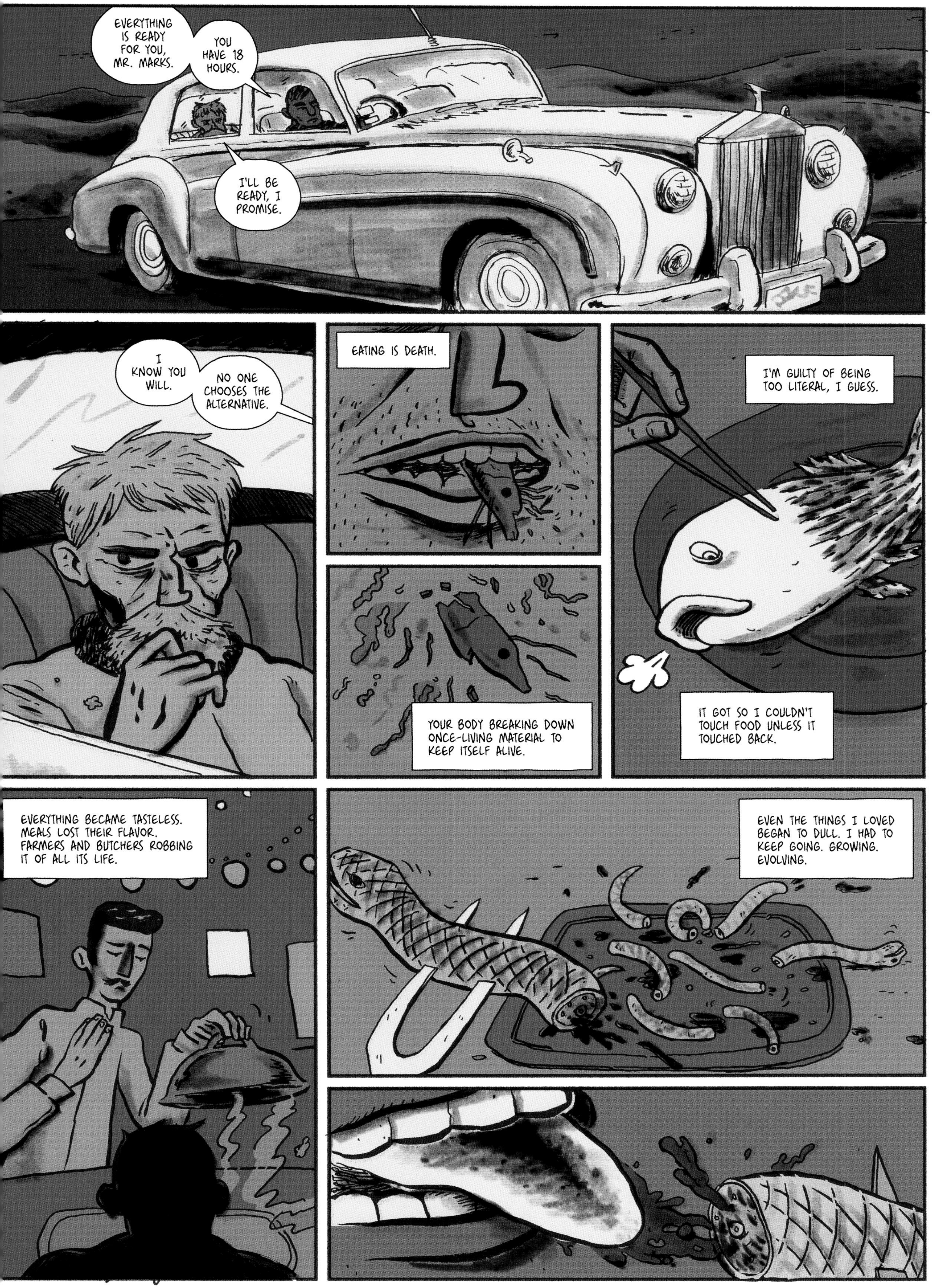
EVERYTHING IS READY FOR YOU, MR. MARKS.
YOU HAVE 18 HOURS.
I'LL BE READY, I PROMISE.
I KNOW YOU WILL.
NO ONE CHOOSES THE ALTERNATIVE.
EATING IS DEATH.
YOUR BODY BREAKING DOWN ONCE-LIVING MATERIAL TO KEEP ITSELF ALIVE.
I'M GUILTY OF BEING TOO LITERAL, I GUESS.
IT GOT SO I COULDN'T TOUCH FOOD UNLESS IT TOUCHED BACK.
EVERYTHING BECAME TASTELESS. MEALS LOST THEIR FLAVOR. FARMERS AND BUTCHERS ROBBING IT OF ALL ITS LIFE.
EVEN THE THINGS I LOVED BEGAN TO DULL. I HAD TO KEEP GOING. GROWING. EVOLVING.

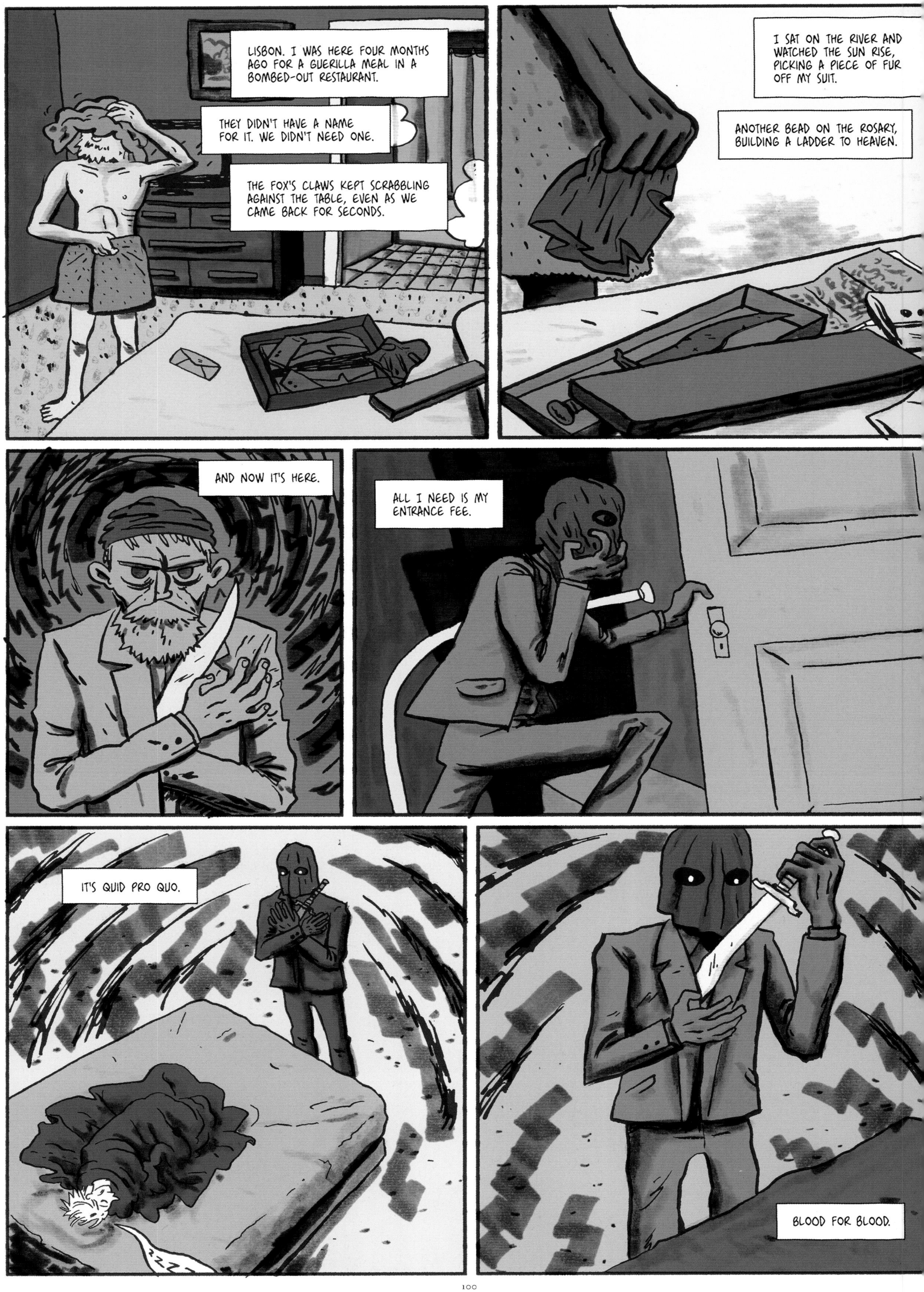
LISBON. I WAS HERE FOUR MONTHS AGO FOR A GUERILLA MEAL IN A BOMBED-OUT RESTAURANT.
THEY DIDN'T HAVE A NAME FOR IT. WE DIDN'T NEED ONE.
THE FOX'S CLAWS KEPT SCRABBLING AGAINST THE TABLE, EVEN AS WE CAME BACK FOR SECONDS.
I SAT ON THE RIVER AND WATCHED THE SUN RISE, PICKING A PIECE OF FUR OFF MY SUIT.
ANOTHER BEAD ON THE ROSARY, BUILDING A LADDER TO HEAVEN.
AND NOW IT'S HERE.
ALL I NEED IS MY ENTRANCE FEE.
IT'S QUID PRO QUO.
ZZZ
BLOOD FOR BLOOD.

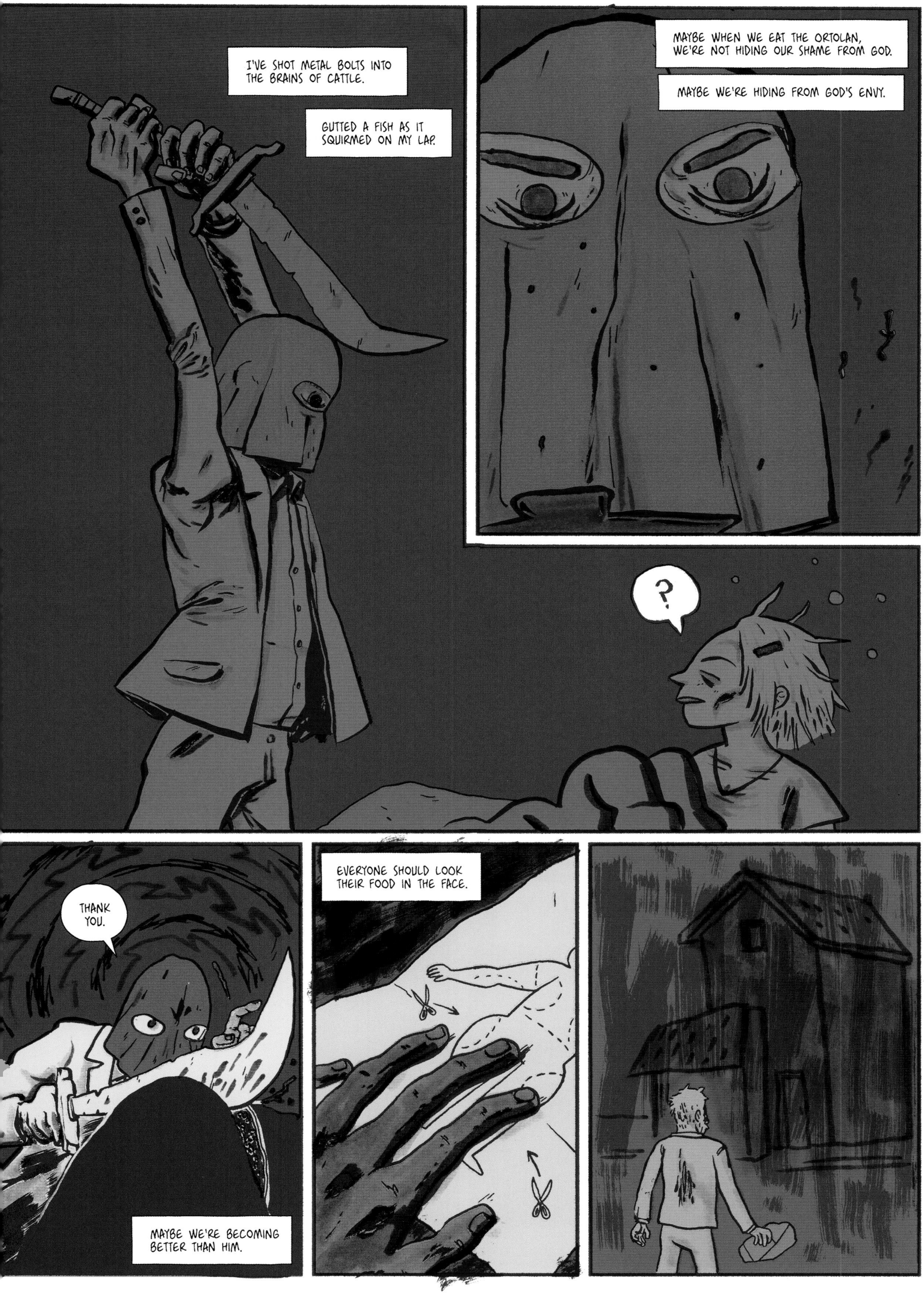
I'VE SHOT METAL BOLTS INTO THE BRAINS OF CATTLE.
GUTTED A FISH AS IT SQUIRMED ON MY LAP.
MAYBE WHEN WE EAT THE ORTOLAN, WE'RE NOT HIDING OUR SHAME FROM GOD.
MAYBE WE'RE HIDING FROM GOD'S ENVY.
?
THANK YOU.
MAYBE WE'RE BECOMING BETTER THAN HIM.
EVERYONE SHOULD LOOK THEIR FOOD IN THE FACE.

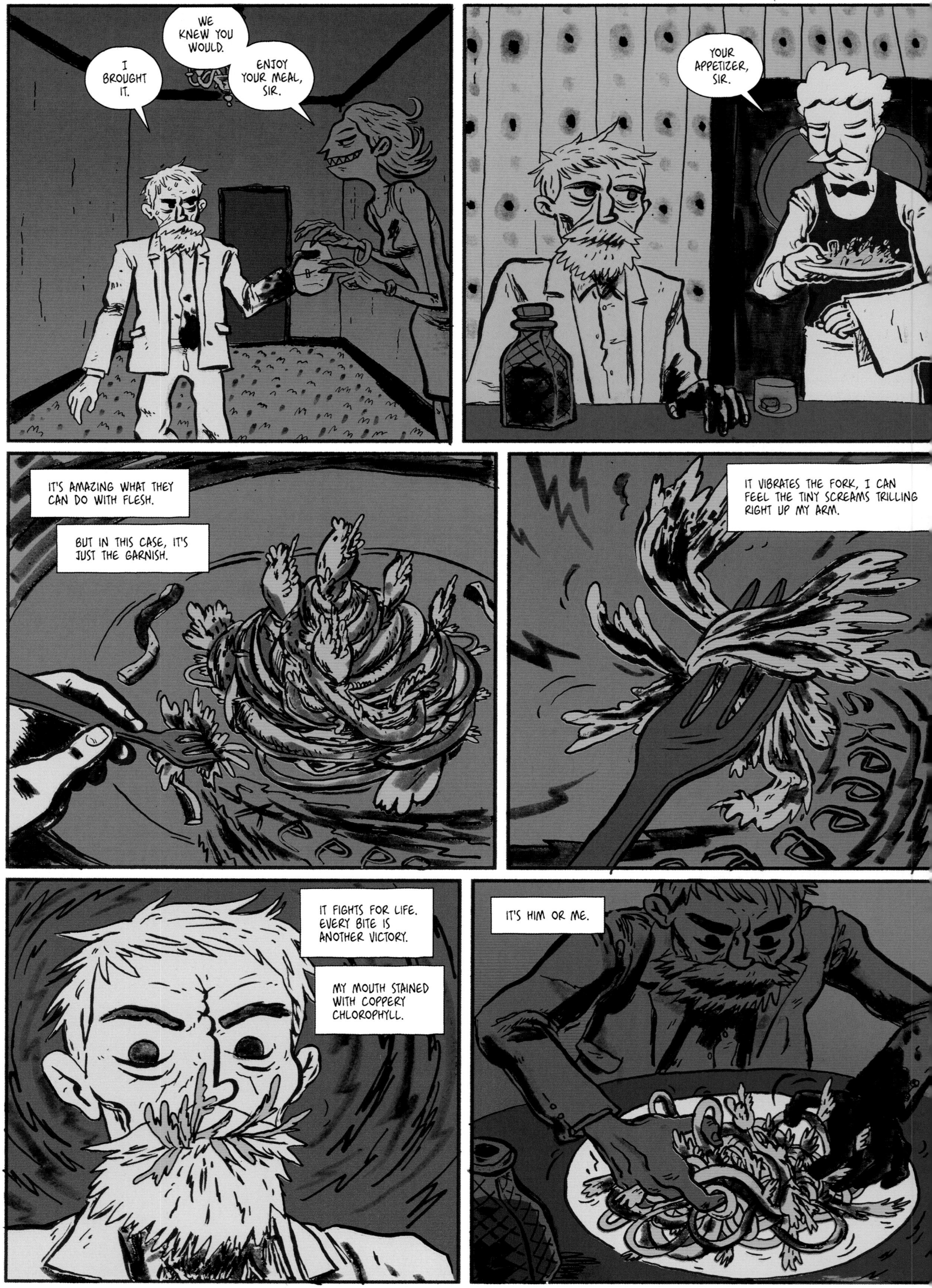
I BROUGHT IT.
WE KNEW YOU WOULD.
ENJOY YOUR MEAL, SIR.
YOUR APPETIZER, SIR.
IT'S AMAZING WHAT THEY CAN DO WITH FLESH.
BUT IN THIS CASE, IT'S JUST THE GARNISH.
IT VIBRATES THE FORK, I CAN FEEL THE TINY SCREAMS TRILLING RIGHT UP MY ARM.
IT FIGHTS FOR LIFE. EVERY BITE IS ANOTHER VICTORY.
MY MOUTH STAINED WITH COPPERY CHLOROPHYLL.
IT'S HIM OR ME.

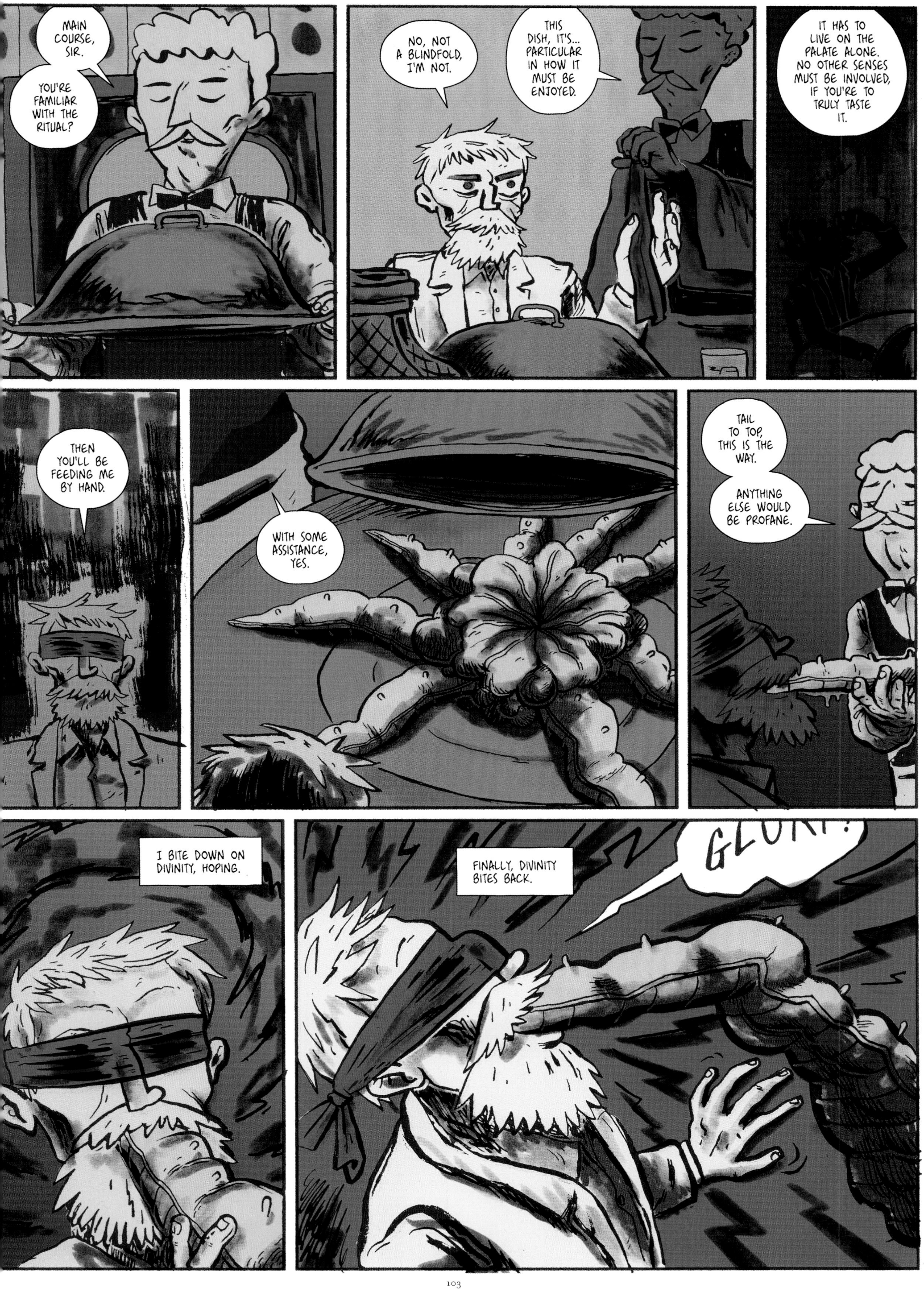
MAIN COURSE, SIR.
YOU'RE FAMILIAR WITH THE RITUAL?
NO, NOT A BLINDFOLD, I'M NOT.
THIS DISH, IT'S... PARTICULAR IN HOW IT MUST BE ENJOYED.
IT HAS TO LIVE ON THE PALATE ALONE. NO OTHER SENSES MUST BE INVOLVED, IF YOU'RE TO TRULY TASTE IT.
THEN YOU'LL BE FEEDING ME BY HAND.
WITH SOME ASSISTANCE, YES.
TAIL TO TOP, THIS IS THE WAY.
ANYTHING ELSE WOULD BE PROFANE.
I BITE DOWN ON DIVINITY, HOPING.
FINALLY, DIVINITY BITES BACK.

SIR, I MUST INSIST.

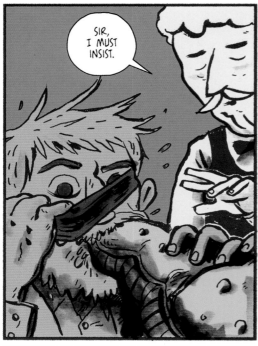

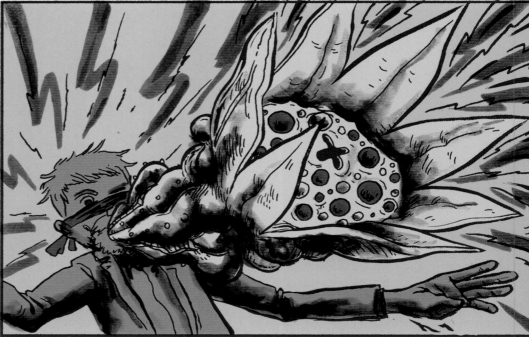

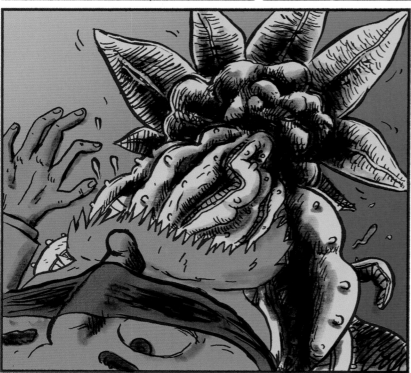

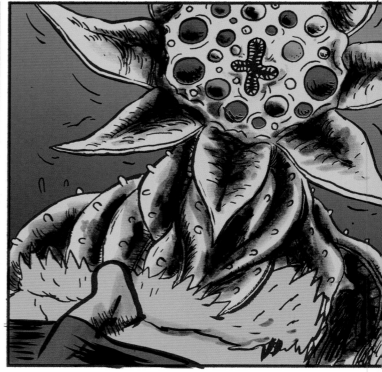

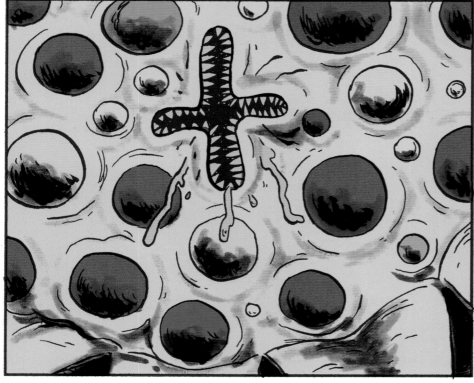

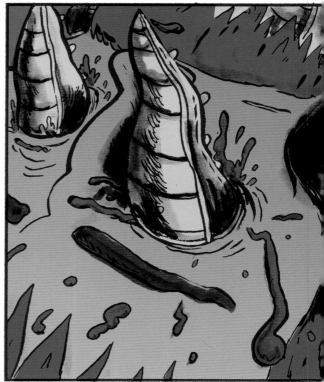

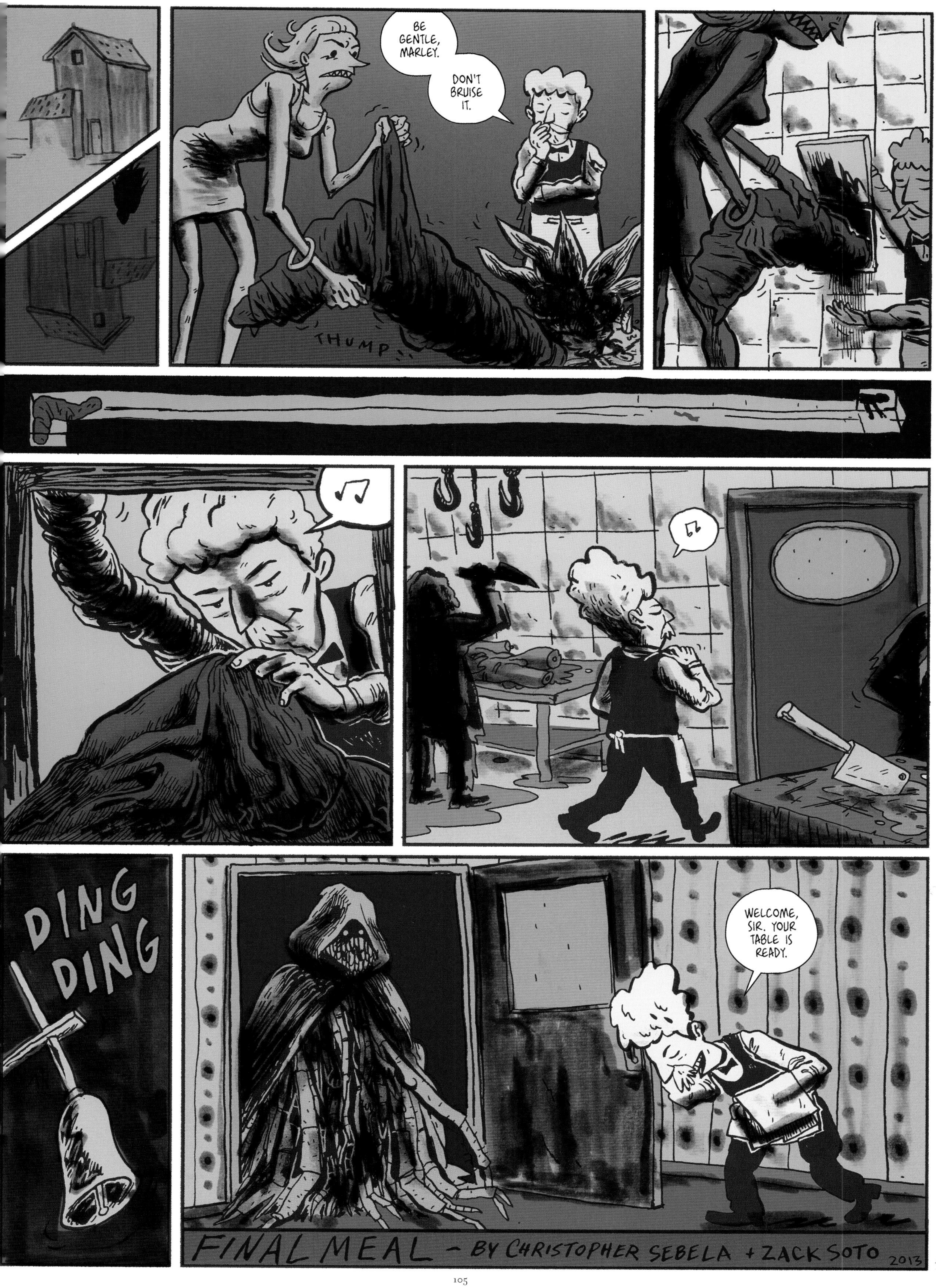
BE GENTLE, MARLEY.
DON'T BRUISE IT.
THUMP
DING DING
WELCOME, SIR. YOUR TABLE IS READY.
FINAL MEAL - BY CHRISTOPHER SEBELA + ZACK SOTO 2013

IN PLAIN SIGHT

WRITER
TOM TAYLOR

ARTIST
MACK CHATER

COLORIST
TAMRA BONVILLAIN

LETTERER
RACHEL DEERING

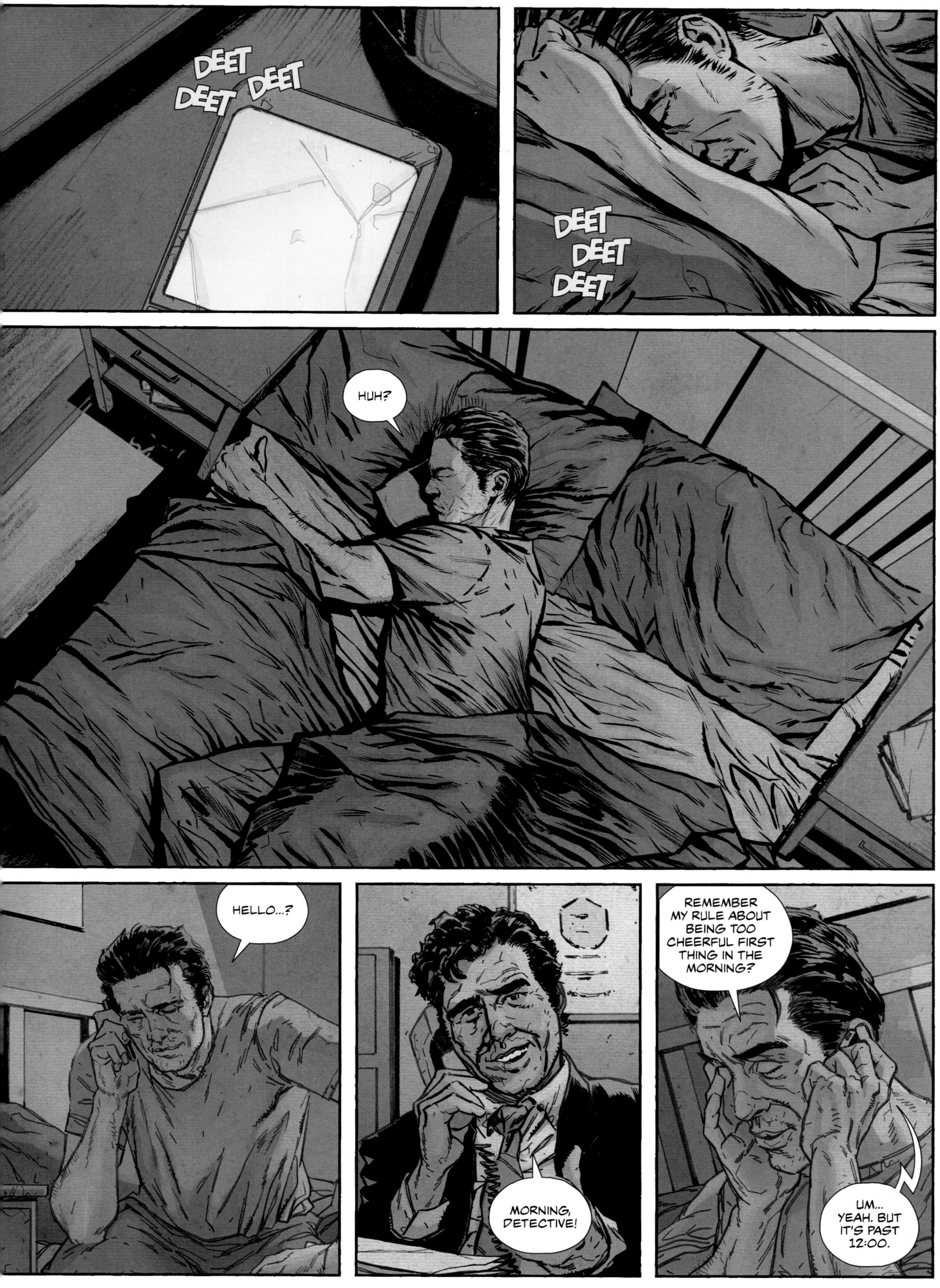
DEET DEET DEET
DEET DEET DEET
HUH?
HELLO...?
MORNING, DETECTIVE!
REMEMBER MY RULE ABOUT BEING TOO CHEERFUL FIRST THING IN THE MORNING?
UM... YEAH. BUT IT'S PAST 12:00.

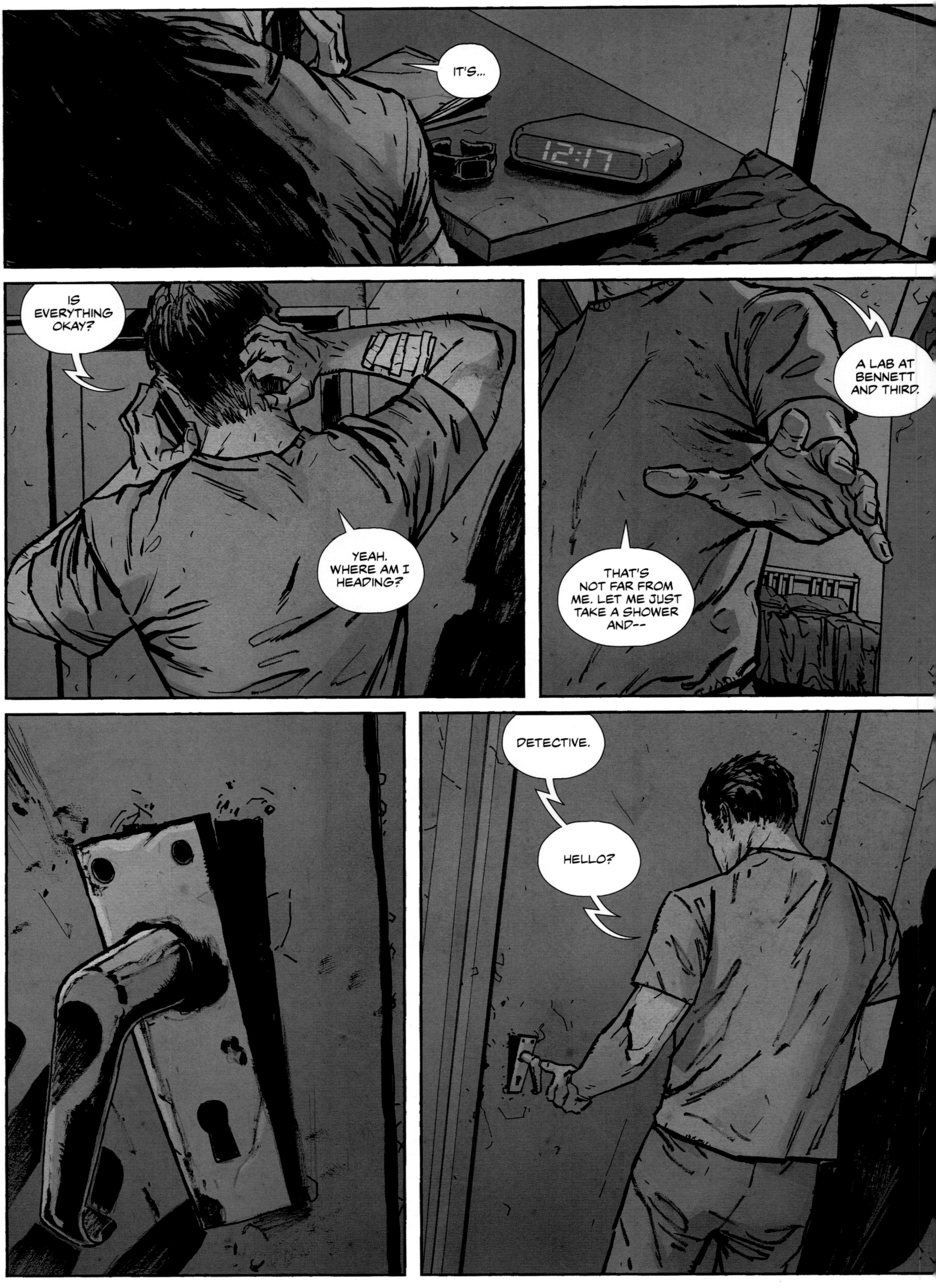
IT'S...
IS EVERYTHING OKAY?
YEAH. WHERE AM I HEADING?
A LAB AT BENNETT AND THIRD.
THAT'S NOT FAR FROM ME. LET ME JUST TAKE A SHOWER AND--
DETECTIVE.
HELLO?

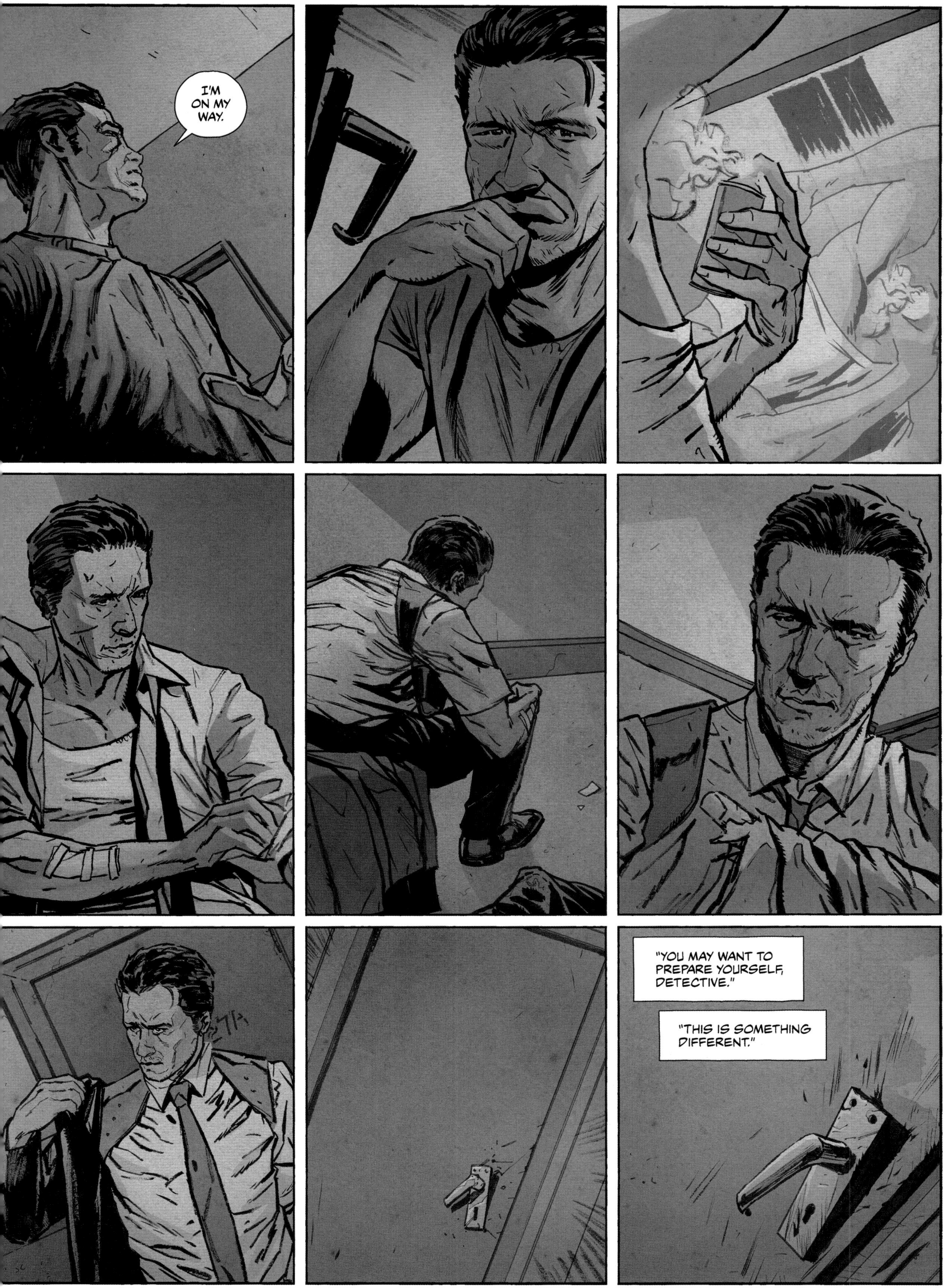
I'M ON MY WAY.
"YOU MAY WANT TO PREPARE YOURSELF, DETECTIVE."
"THIS IS SOMETHING DIFFERENT."

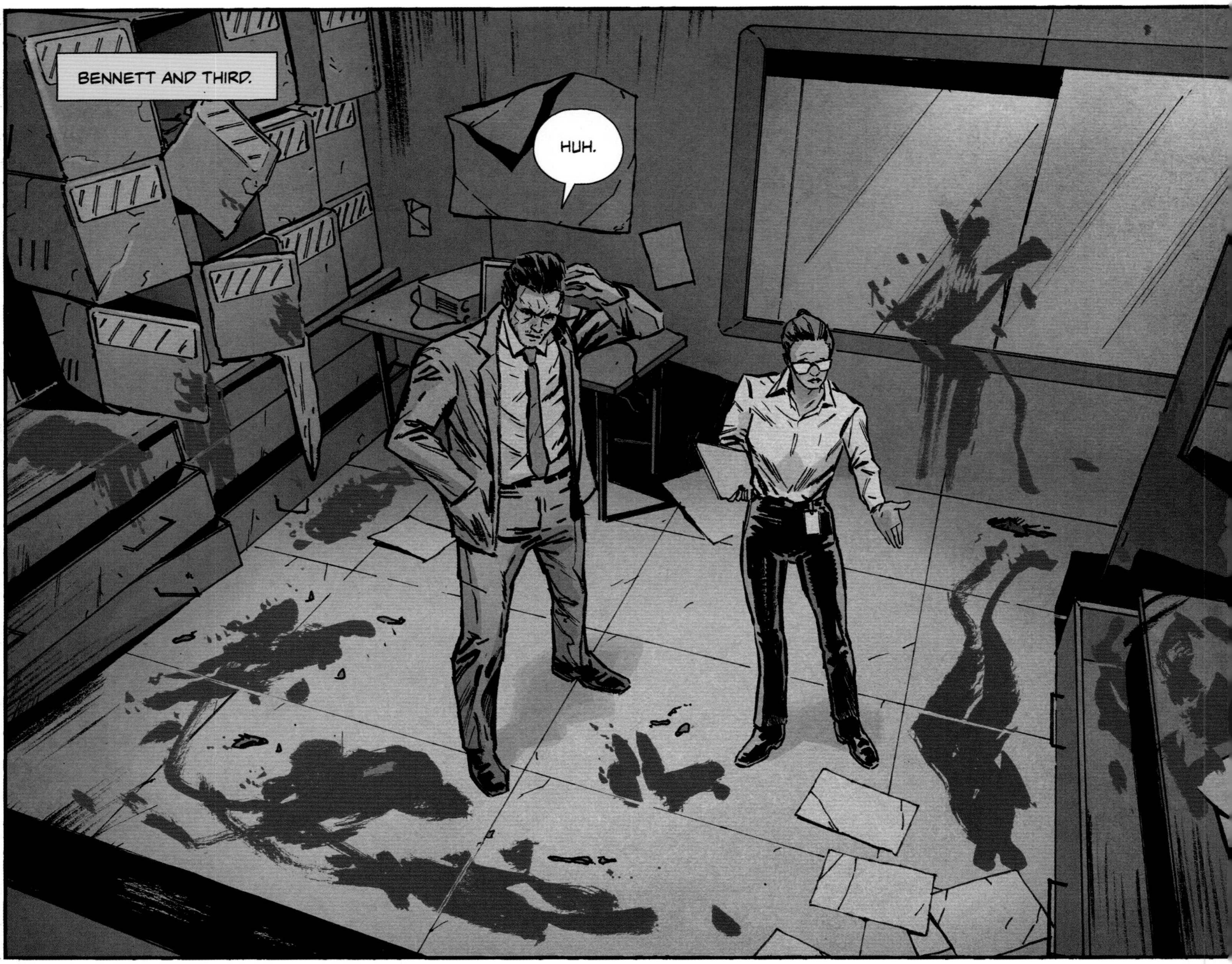
BENNETT AND THIRD.
HUH.

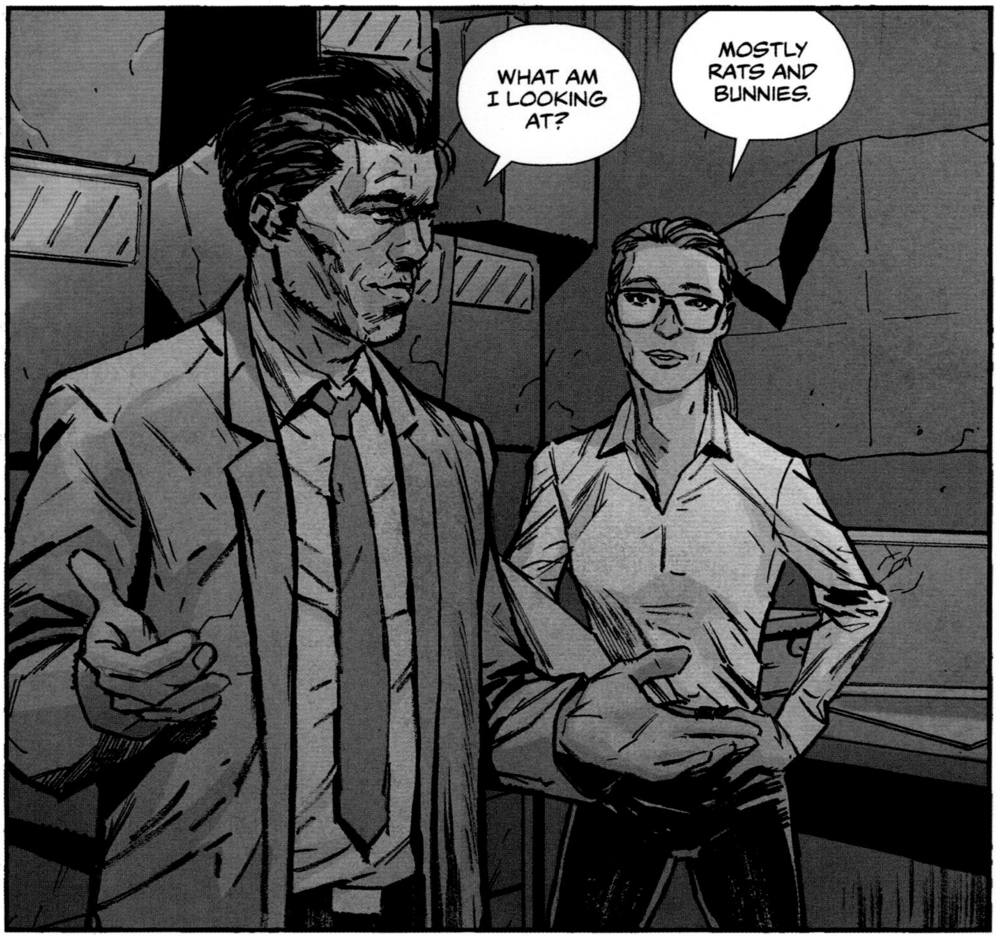
WHAT AM I LOOKING AT?
MOSTLY RATS AND BUNNIES.

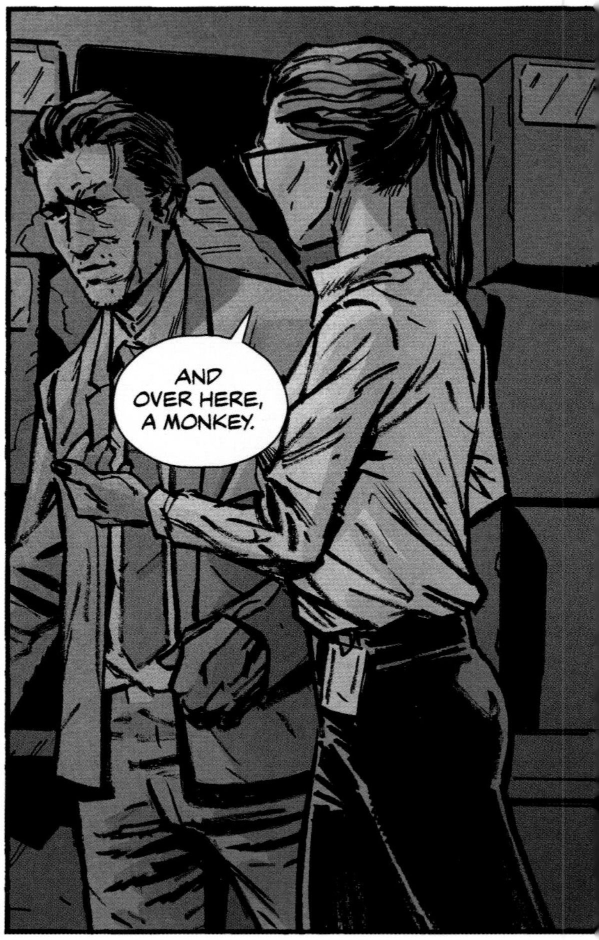
AND OVER HERE, A MONKEY.

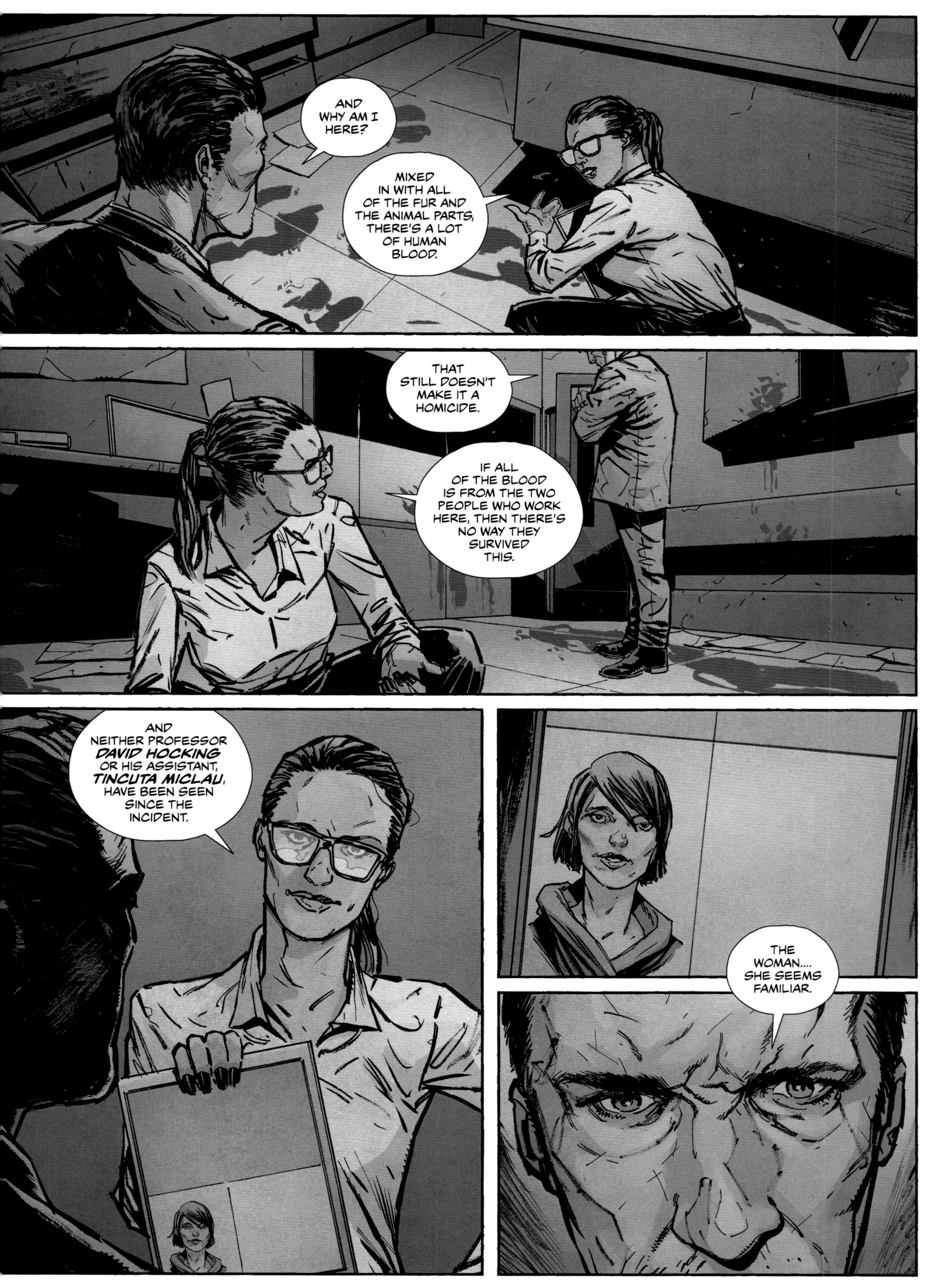
AND WHY AM I HERE?
MIXED IN WITH ALL OF THE FUR AND THE ANIMAL PARTS, THERE'S A LOT OF HUMAN BLOOD.
THAT STILL DOESN'T MAKE IT A HOMICIDE.
IF ALL OF THE BLOOD IS FROM THE TWO PEOPLE WHO WORK HERE, THEN THERE'S NO WAY THEY SURVIVED THIS.
AND NEITHER PROFESSOR DAVID HOCKING OR HIS ASSISTANT, TINCUTA MICLAU, HAVE BEEN SEEN SINCE THE INCIDENT.
THE WOMAN.... SHE SEEMS FAMILIAR.

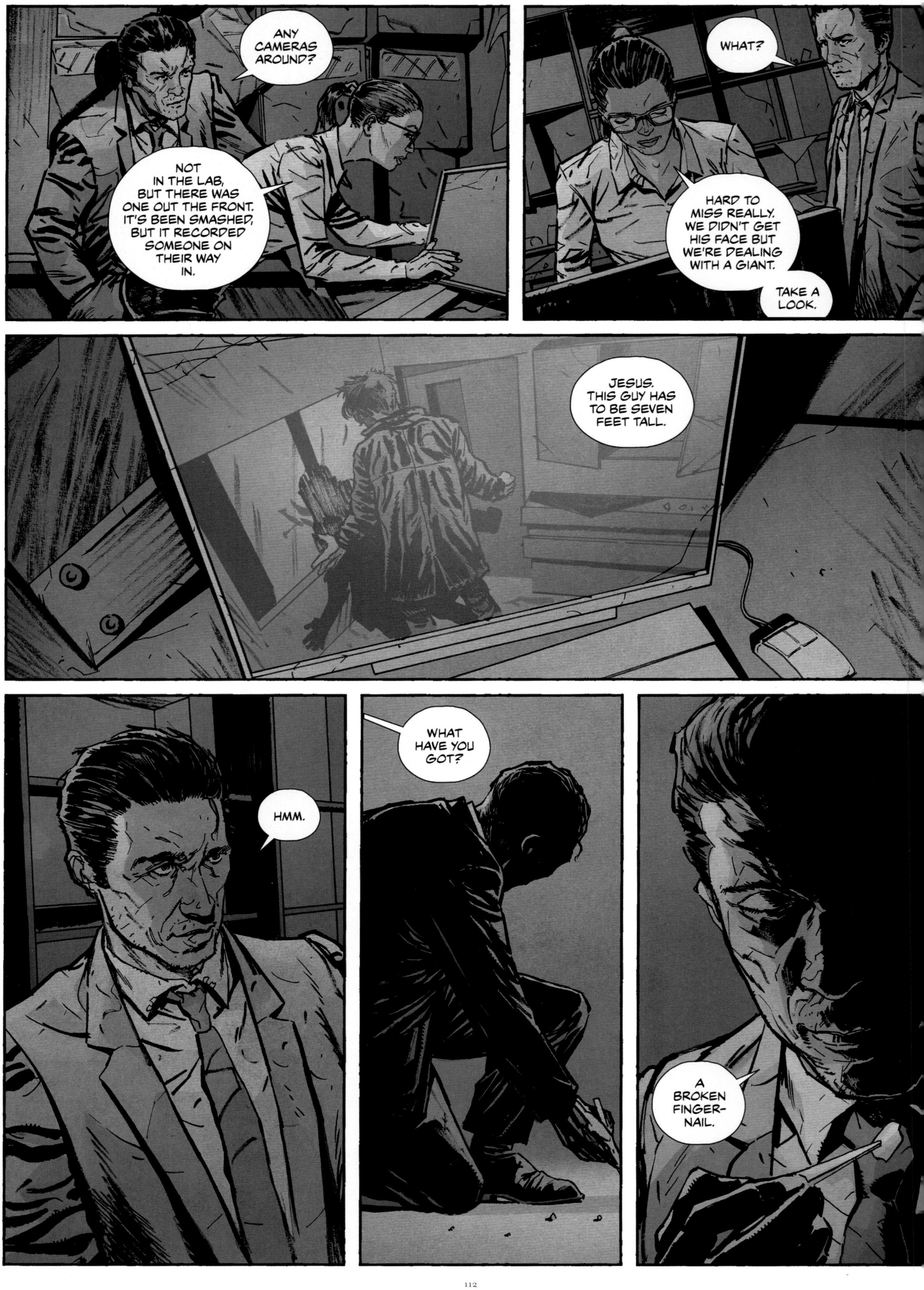
ANY CAMERAS AROUND?
NOT IN THE LAB, BUT THERE WAS ONE OUT THE FRONT. IT'S BEEN SMASHED, BUT IT RECORDED SOMEONE ON THEIR WAY IN.
WHAT?
HARD TO MISS REALLY. WE DIDN'T GET HIS FACE BUT WE'RE DEALING WITH A GIANT.
TAKE A LOOK.
JESUS. THIS GUY HAS TO BE SEVEN FEET TALL.
HMM.
WHAT HAVE YOU GOT?
A BROKEN FINGER-NAIL.

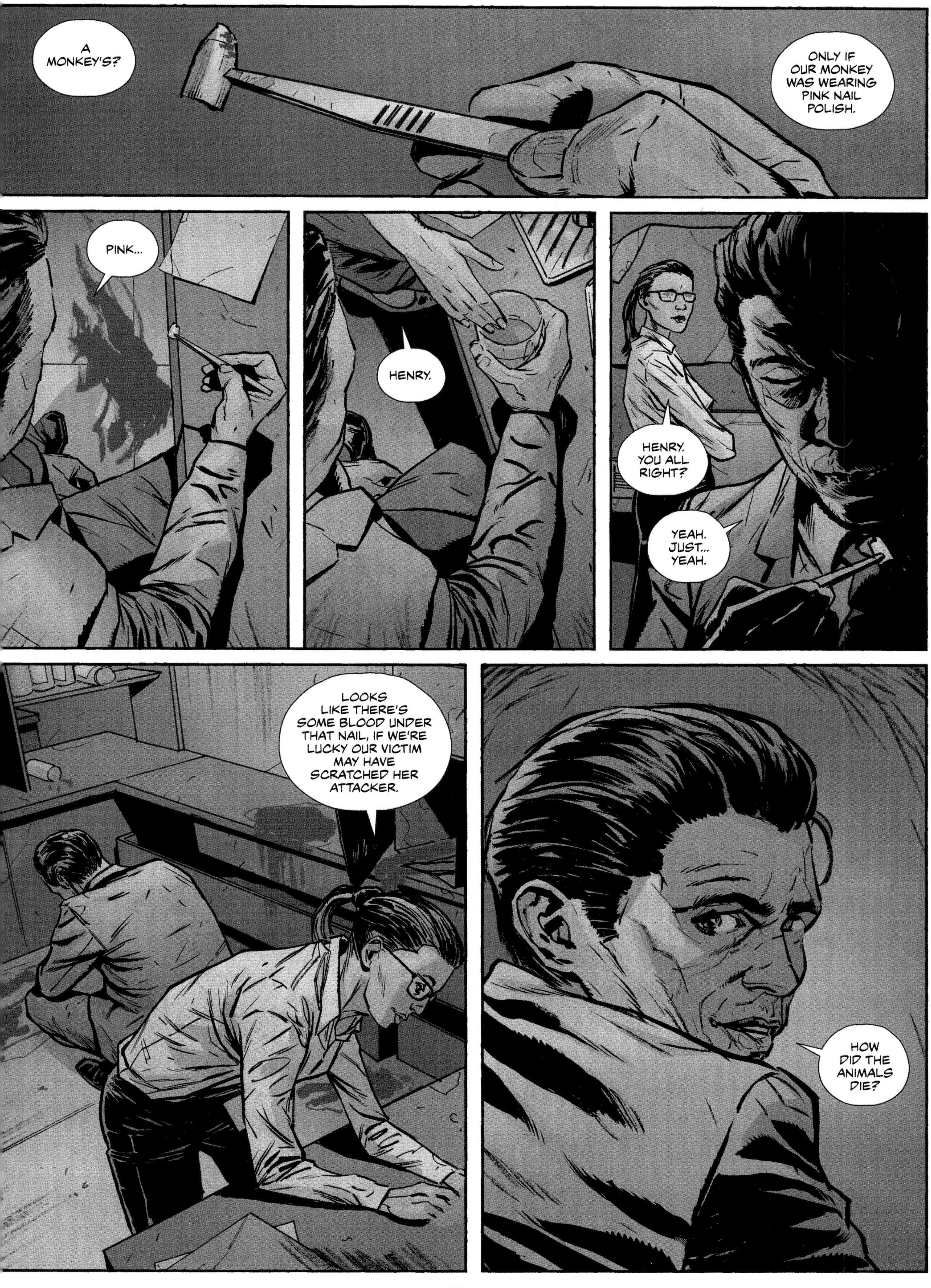
A MONKEY'S?
ONLY IF OUR MONKEY WAS WEARING PINK NAIL POLISH.
PINK...
HENRY.
HENRY. YOU ALL RIGHT?
YEAH. JUST... YEAH.
LOOKS LIKE THERE'S SOME BLOOD UNDER THAT NAIL, IF WE'RE LUCKY OUR VICTIM MAY HAVE SCRATCHED HER ATTACKER.
HOW DID THE ANIMALS DIE?

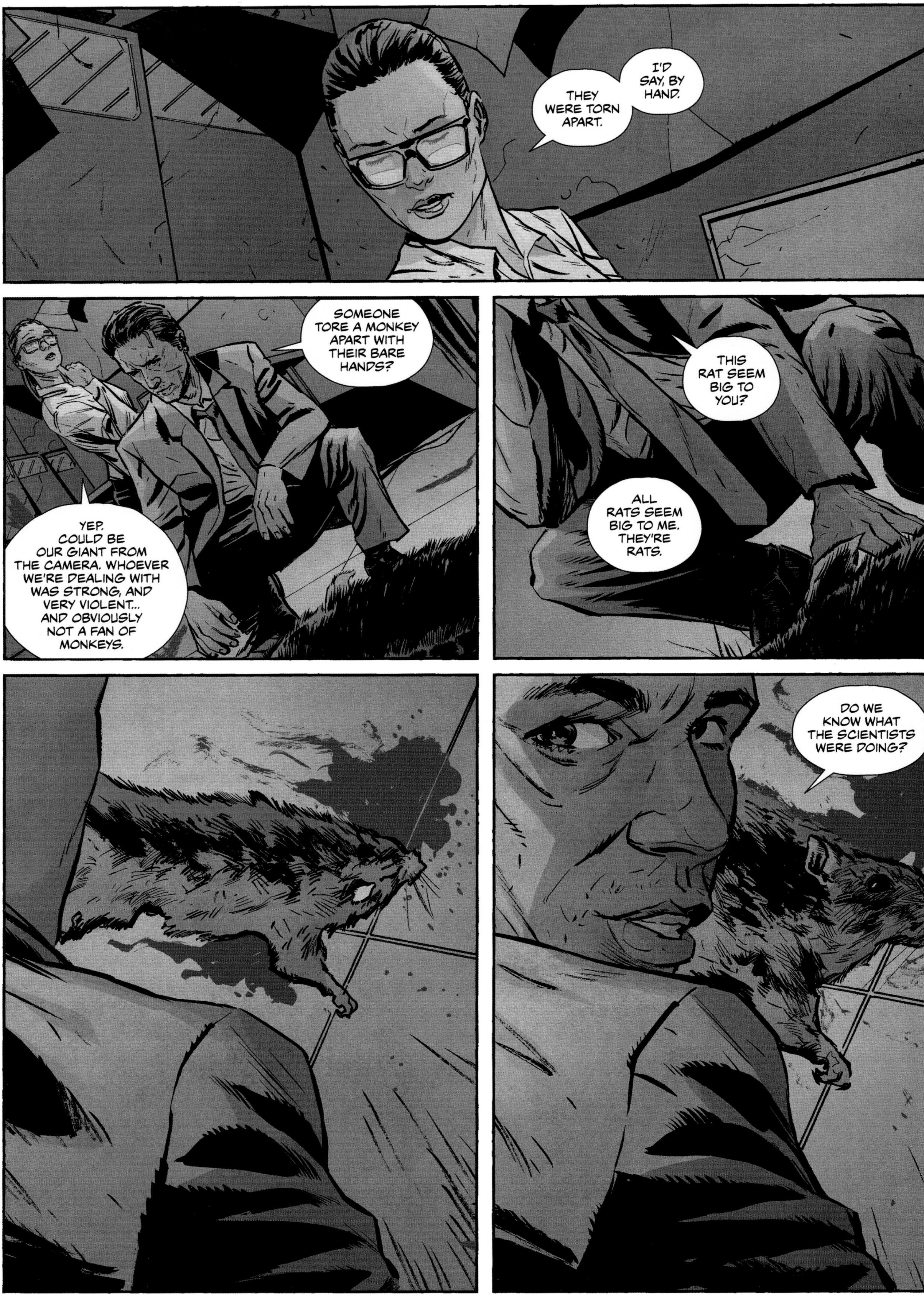

THEY WERE TORN APART.
I'D SAY, BY HAND.
SOMEONE TORE A MONKEY APART WITH THEIR BARE HANDS?
YEP. COULD BE OUR GIANT FROM THE CAMERA. WHOEVER WE'RE DEALING WITH WAS STRONG, AND VERY VIOLENT... AND OBVIOUSLY NOT A FAN OF MONKEYS.
THIS RAT SEEM BIG TO YOU?
ALL RATS SEEM BIG TO ME. THEY'RE RATS.
DO WE KNOW WHAT THE SCIENTISTS WERE DOING?

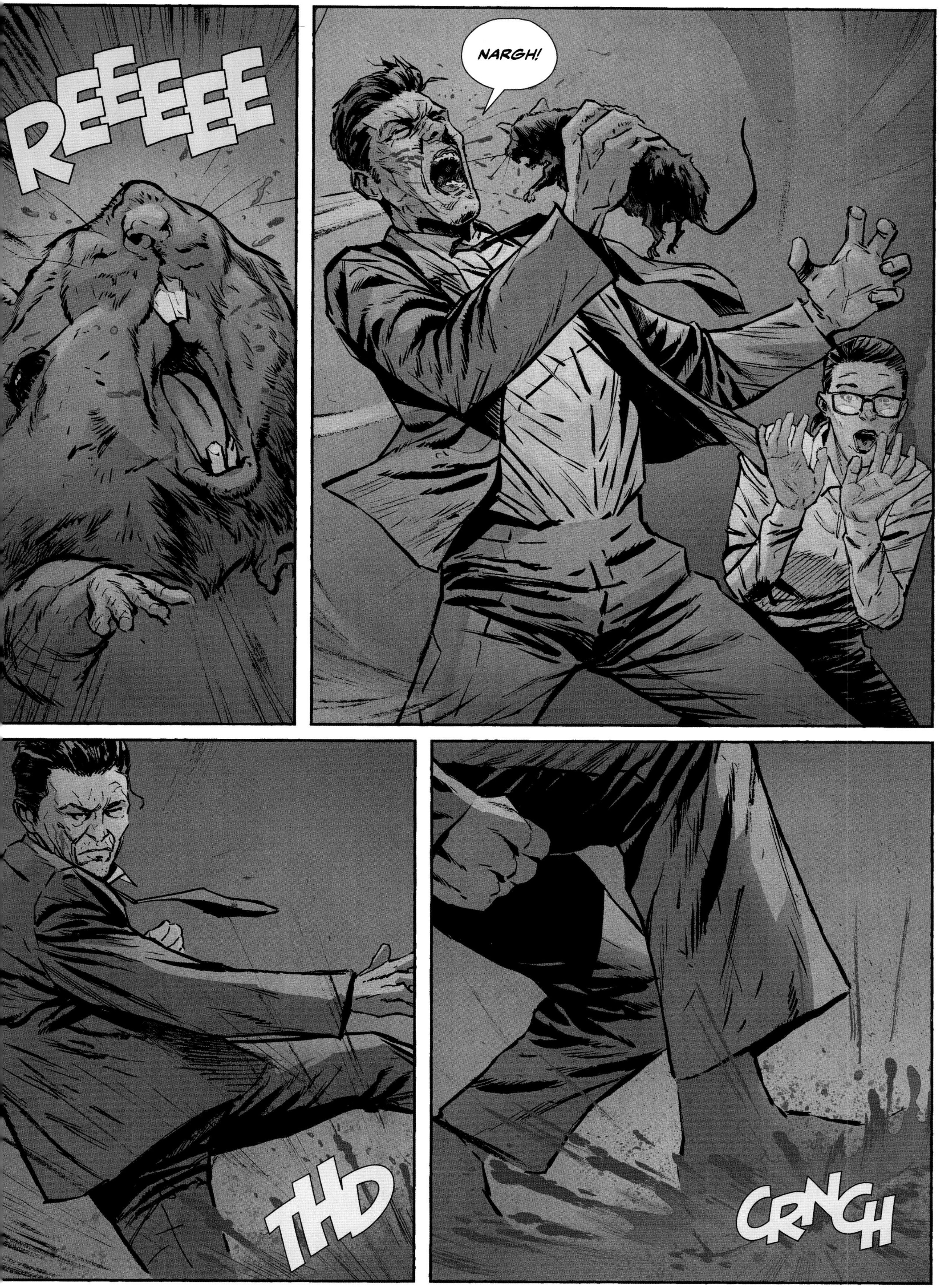
REEEEEE
NARGH!
THD
CRNCH

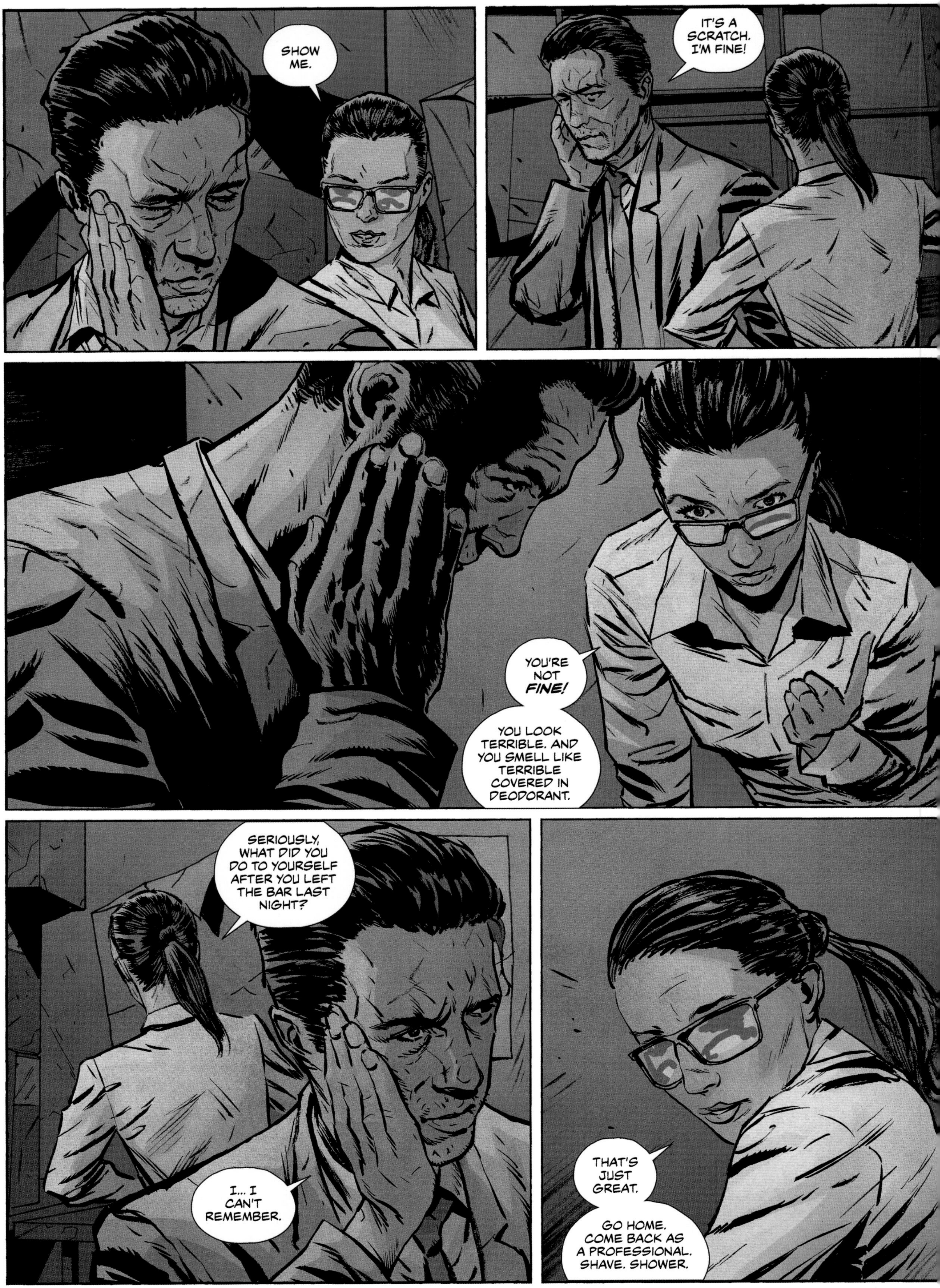
SHOW ME.
IT'S A SCRATCH. I'M FINE!
YOU'RE NOT *FINE!*
YOU LOOK TERRIBLE. AND YOU SMELL LIKE TERRIBLE COVERED IN DEODORANT.
SERIOUSLY, WHAT DID YOU DO TO YOURSELF AFTER YOU LEFT THE BAR LAST NIGHT?
I... I CAN'T REMEMBER.
THAT'S JUST GREAT.
GO HOME. COME BACK AS A PROFESSIONAL. SHAVE. SHOWER.

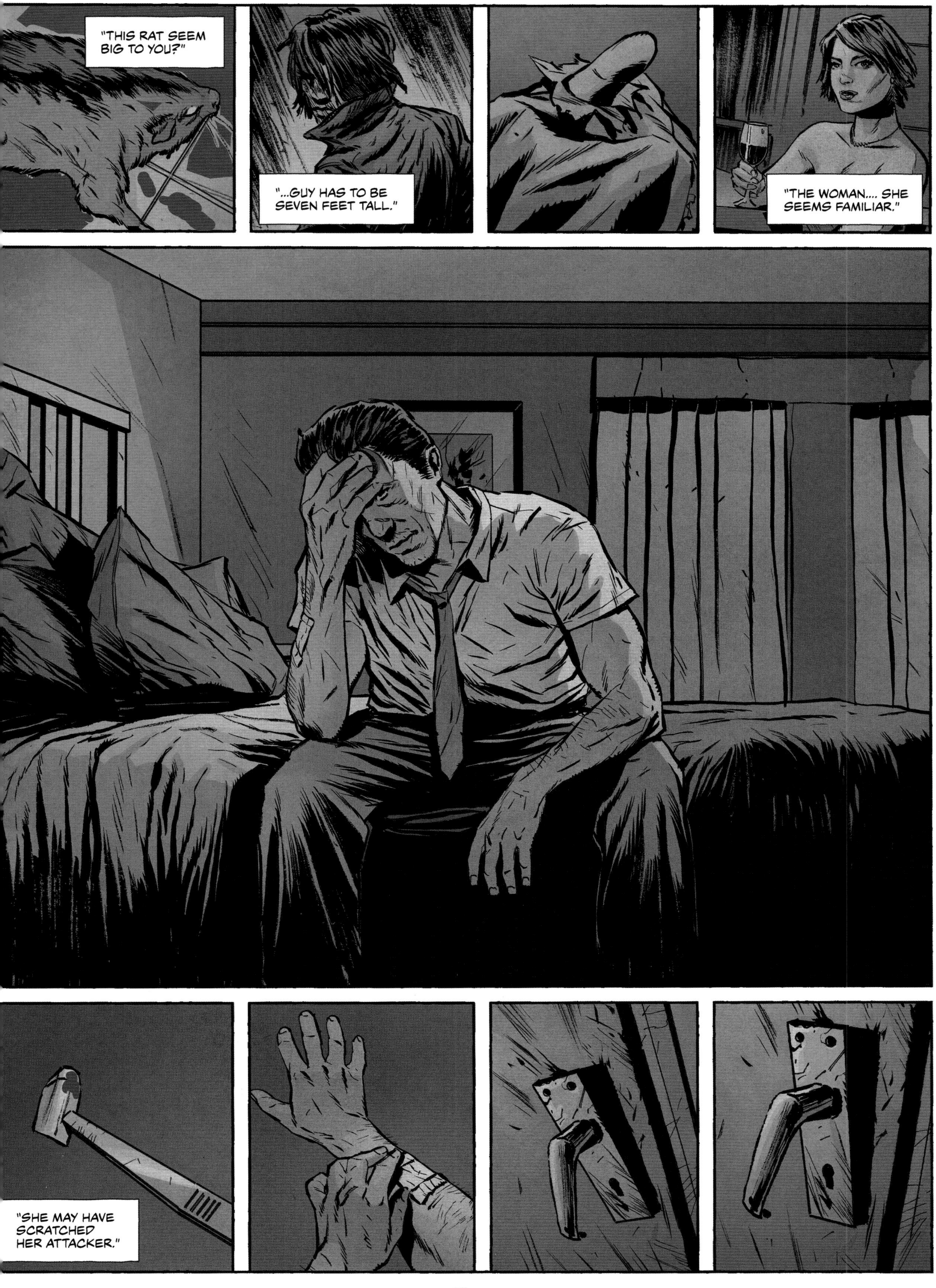
"THIS RAT SEEM BIG TO YOU?"
"...GUY HAS TO BE SEVEN FEET TALL."
"THE WOMAN.... SHE SEEMS FAMILIAR."
"SHE MAY HAVE SCRATCHED HER ATTACKER."

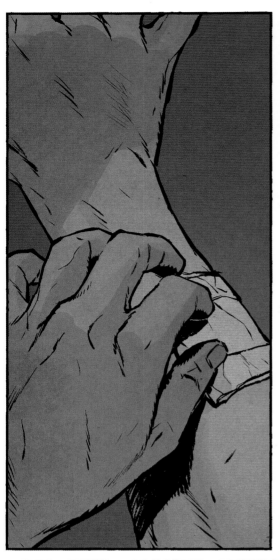

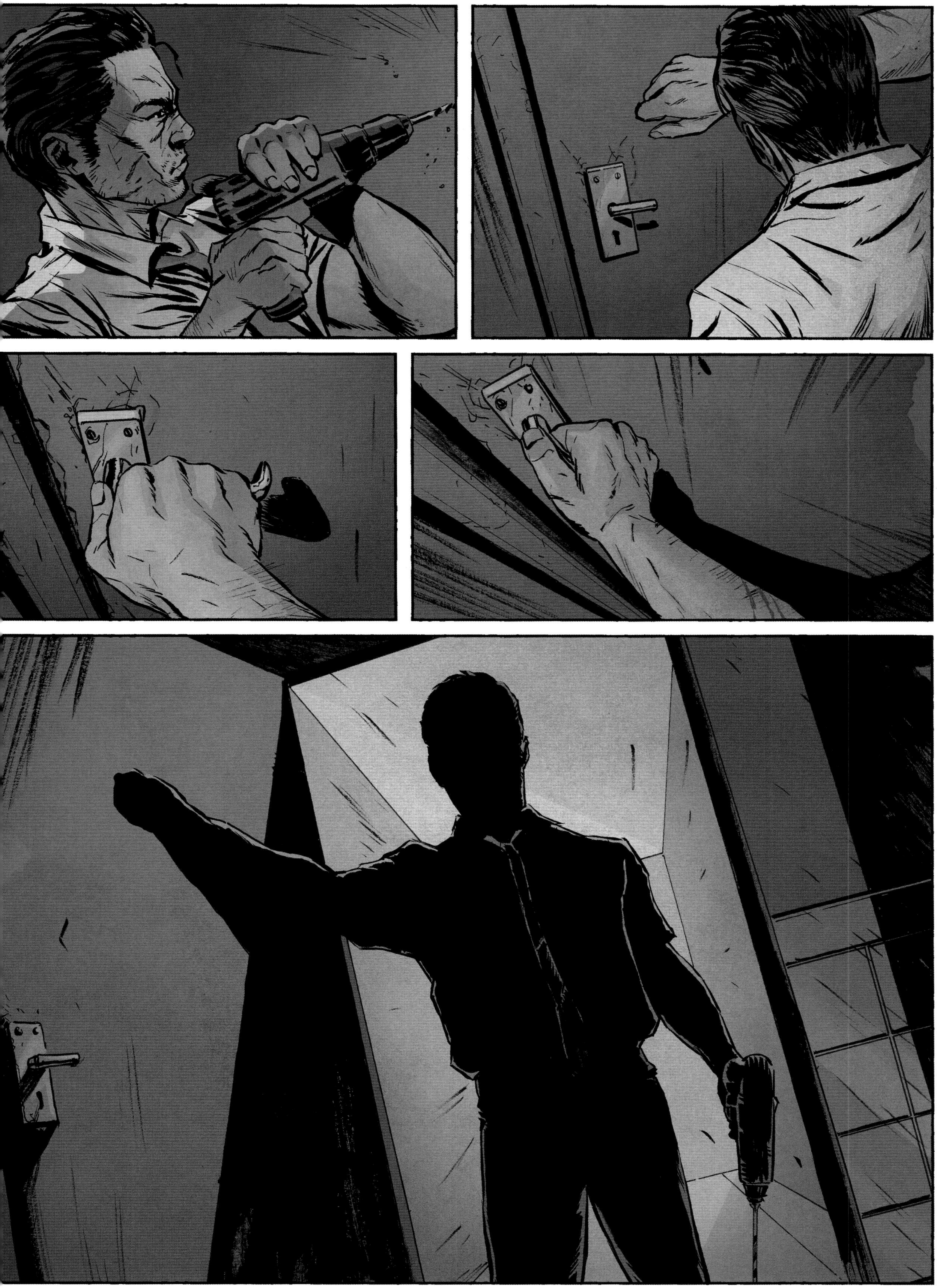

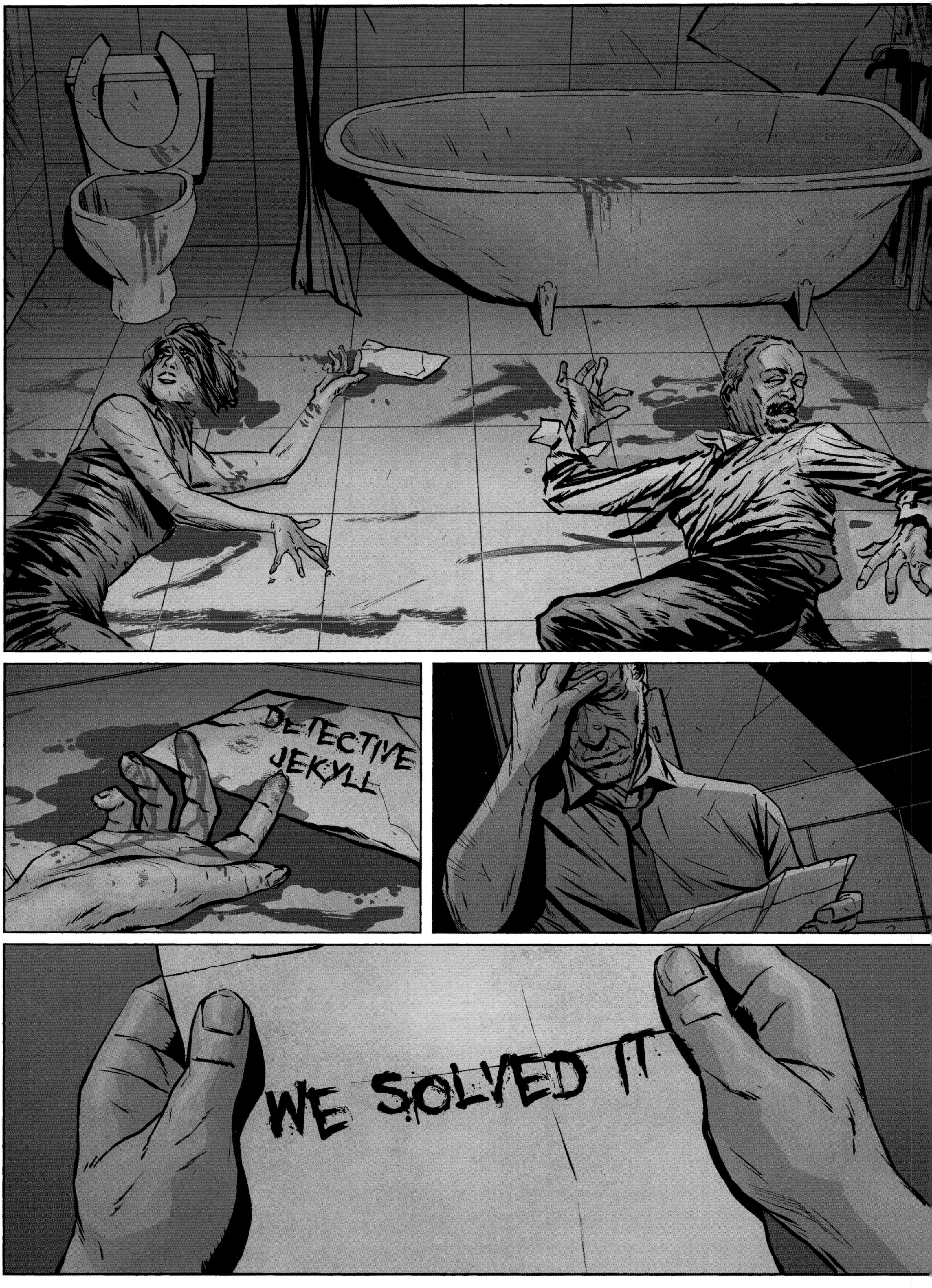
DETECTIVE
JEKYLL
WE SOLVED IT

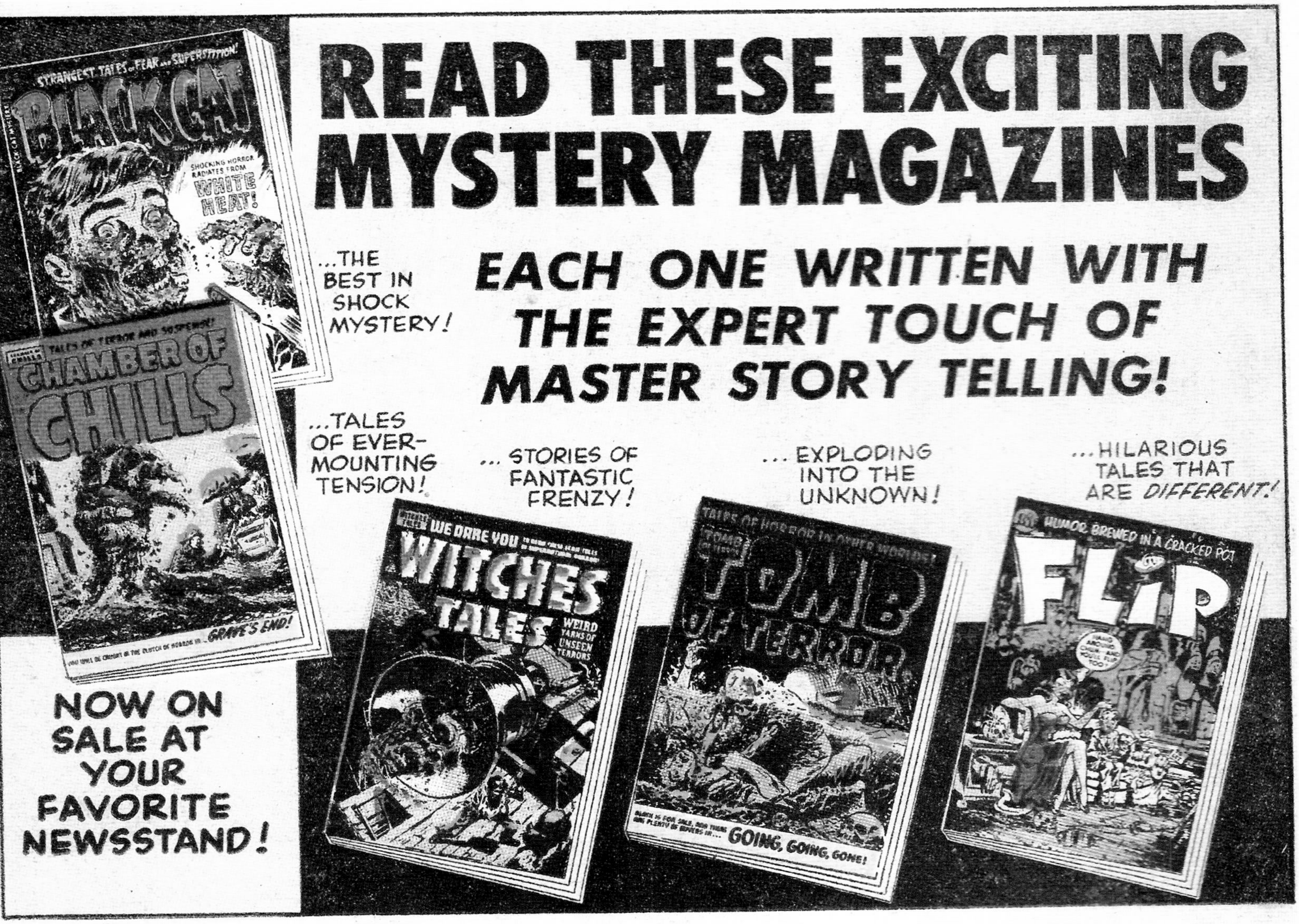
READ THESE EXCITING MYSTERY MAGAZINES
EACH ONE WRITTEN WITH THE EXPERT TOUCH OF MASTER STORY TELLING!
...THE BEST IN SHOCK MYSTERY!
...TALES OF EVER-MOUNTING TENSION!
... STORIES OF FANTASTIC FRENZY!
... EXPLODING INTO THE UNKNOWN!
...HILARIOUS TALES THAT ARE DIFFERENT!
STRANGEST TALES of FEAR and SUPERSTITION!
BLACK CAT
SHOCKING HORROR RADIATES FROM WHITE HEAT!
TALES OF TERROR AND SUSPENSE!
CHAMBER OF CHILLS
GRAVE'S END!
WE DARE YOU
WITCHES TALES
WEIRD YARNS OF UNSEEN TERRORS
TOMB OF TERROR
GOING, GOING, GONE!
HUMOR BREWED IN A CRACKED POT
FLIP
NOW ON SALE AT YOUR FAVORITE NEWSSTAND!

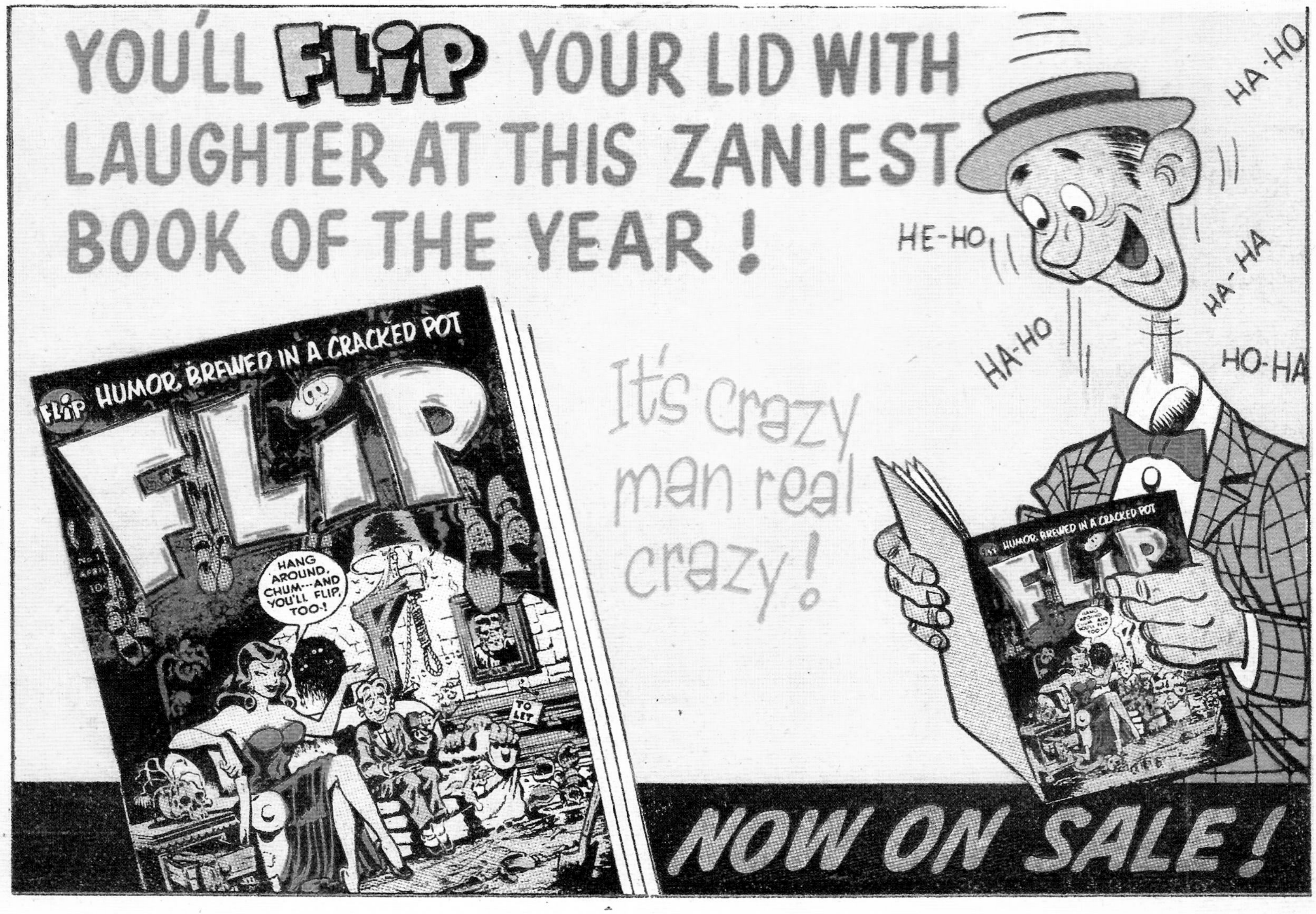
YOU'LL FLIP YOUR LID WITH LAUGHTER AT THIS ZANIEST BOOK OF THE YEAR!
HA-HO
HE-HO
HA-HA
HA-HO
HO-HA
FLIP HUMOR BREWED IN A CRACKED POT
FLIP
HANG AROUND, CHUM---AND YOU'LL FLIP, TOO!
TO LET
It's crazy man real crazy!
HUMOR BREWED IN A CRACKED POT
FLIP
NOW ON SALE!

WHY SO SAD?

WRITER
JAMES TYNION IV

ARTIST
ERYK DONOVAN

COLORIST
IAN HERRING

LETTERER
NATE PIEKOS

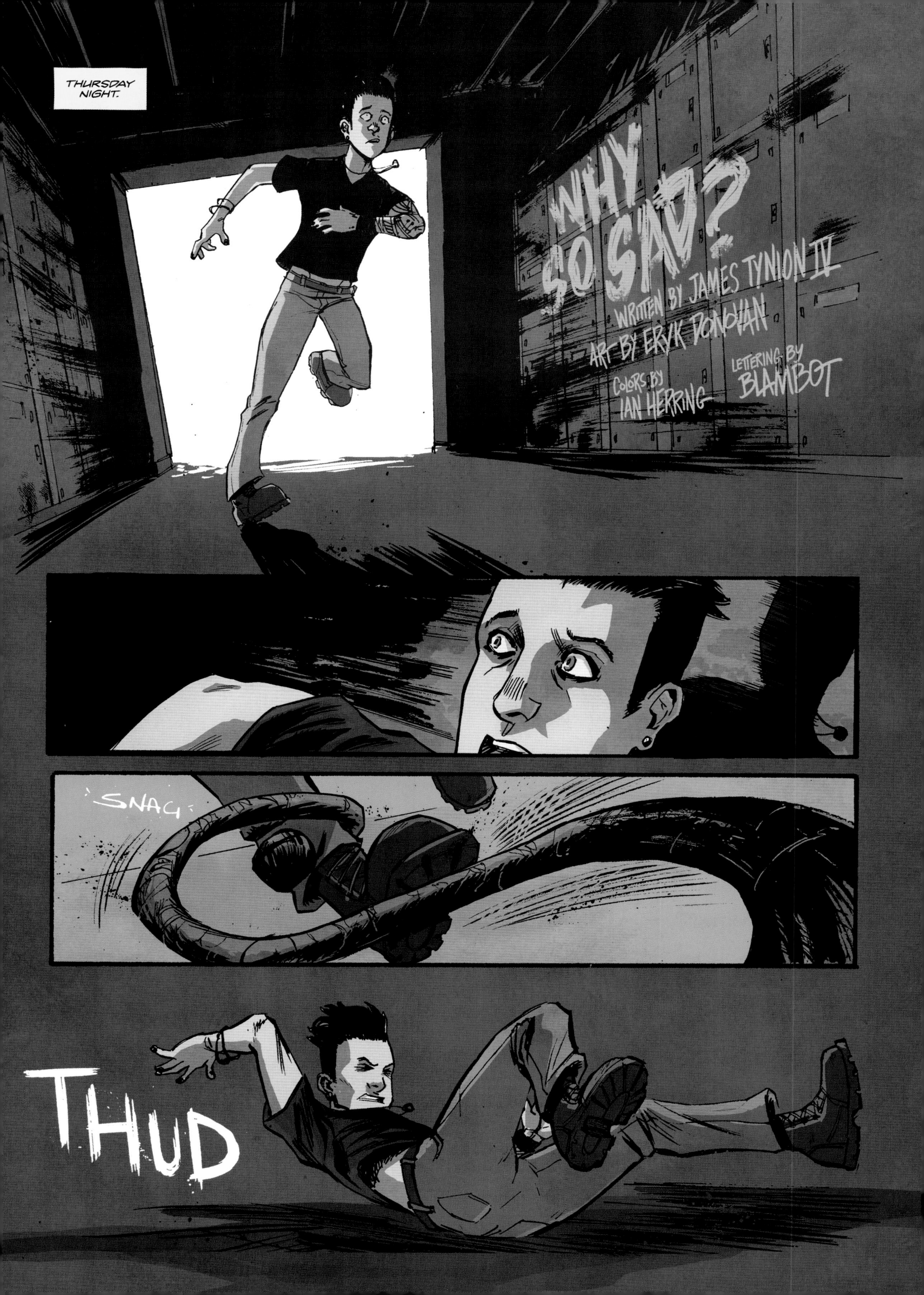
THURSDAY NIGHT.
WHY SO SAD?
WRITTEN BY JAMES TYNION IV
ART BY ERYK DONOVAN
COLORS BY IAN HERRING
LETTERING BY BLAMBOT
SNAG
THUD

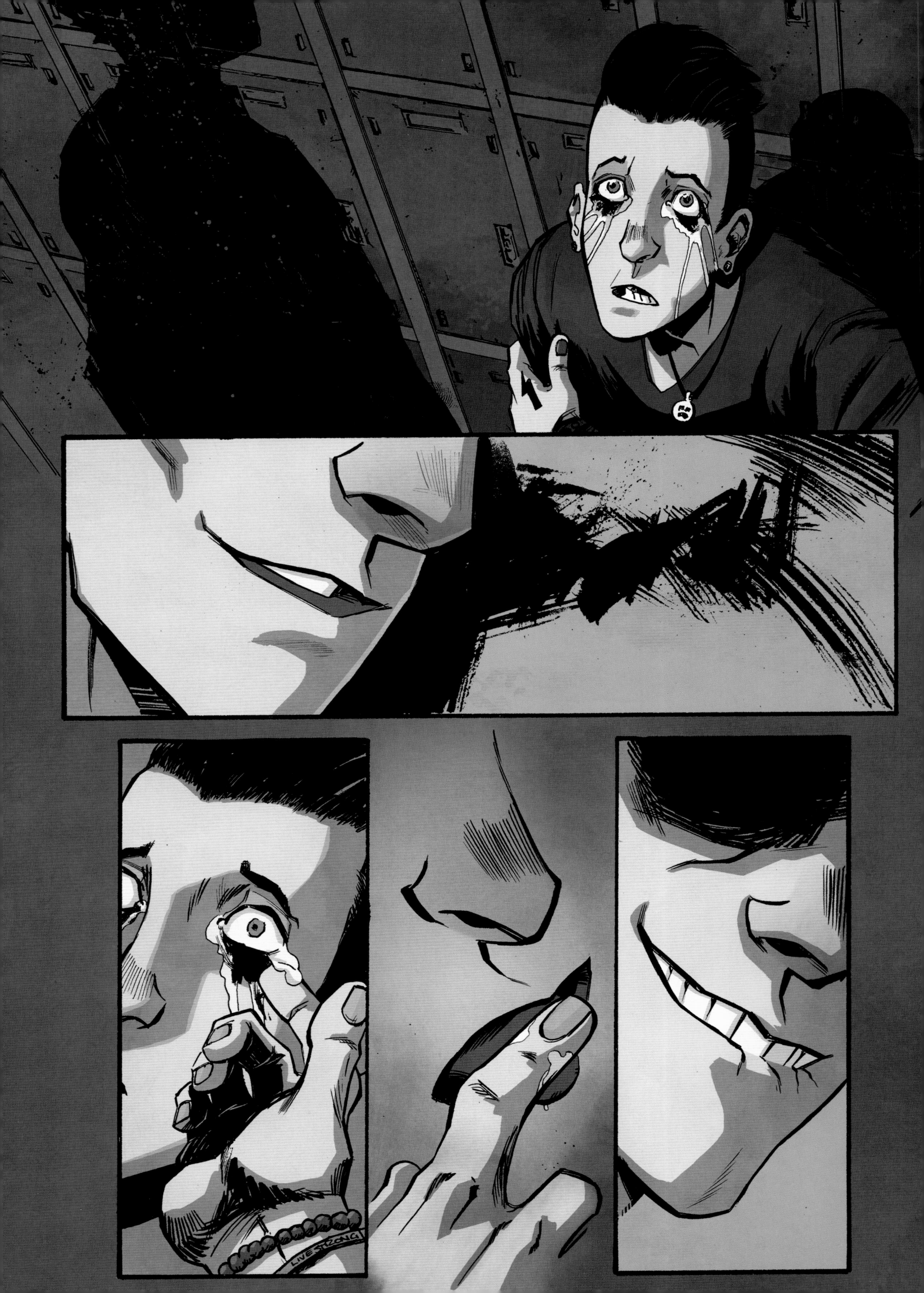
LIVESTRONG

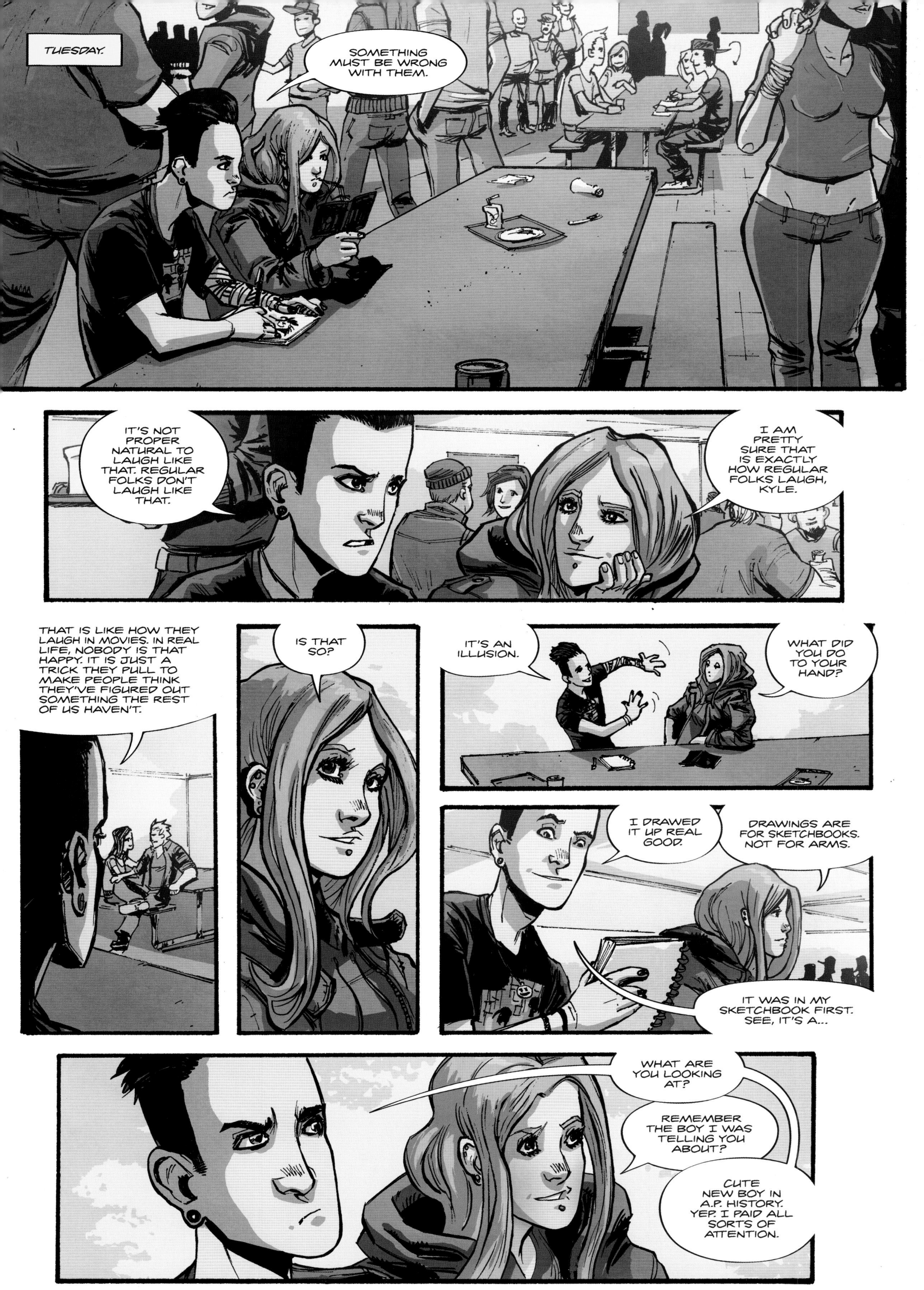
TUESDAY.
SOMETHING MUST BE WRONG WITH THEM.
IT'S NOT PROPER NATURAL TO LAUGH LIKE THAT. REGULAR FOLKS DON'T LAUGH LIKE THAT.
I AM PRETTY SURE THAT IS EXACTLY HOW REGULAR FOLKS LAUGH, KYLE.
THAT IS LIKE HOW THEY LAUGH IN MOVIES. IN REAL LIFE, NOBODY IS THAT HAPPY. IT IS JUST A TRICK THEY PULL TO MAKE PEOPLE THINK THEY'VE FIGURED OUT SOMETHING THE REST OF US HAVEN'T.
IS THAT SO?
IT'S AN ILLUSION.
WHAT DID YOU DO TO YOUR HAND?
I DRAWED IT UP REAL GOOD.
DRAWINGS ARE FOR SKETCHBOOKS. NOT FOR ARMS.
IT WAS IN MY SKETCHBOOK FIRST. SEE, IT'S A...
WHAT ARE YOU LOOKING AT?
REMEMBER THE BOY I WAS TELLING YOU ABOUT?
CUTE NEW BOY IN A.P. HISTORY. YEP. I PAID ALL SORTS OF ATTENTION.

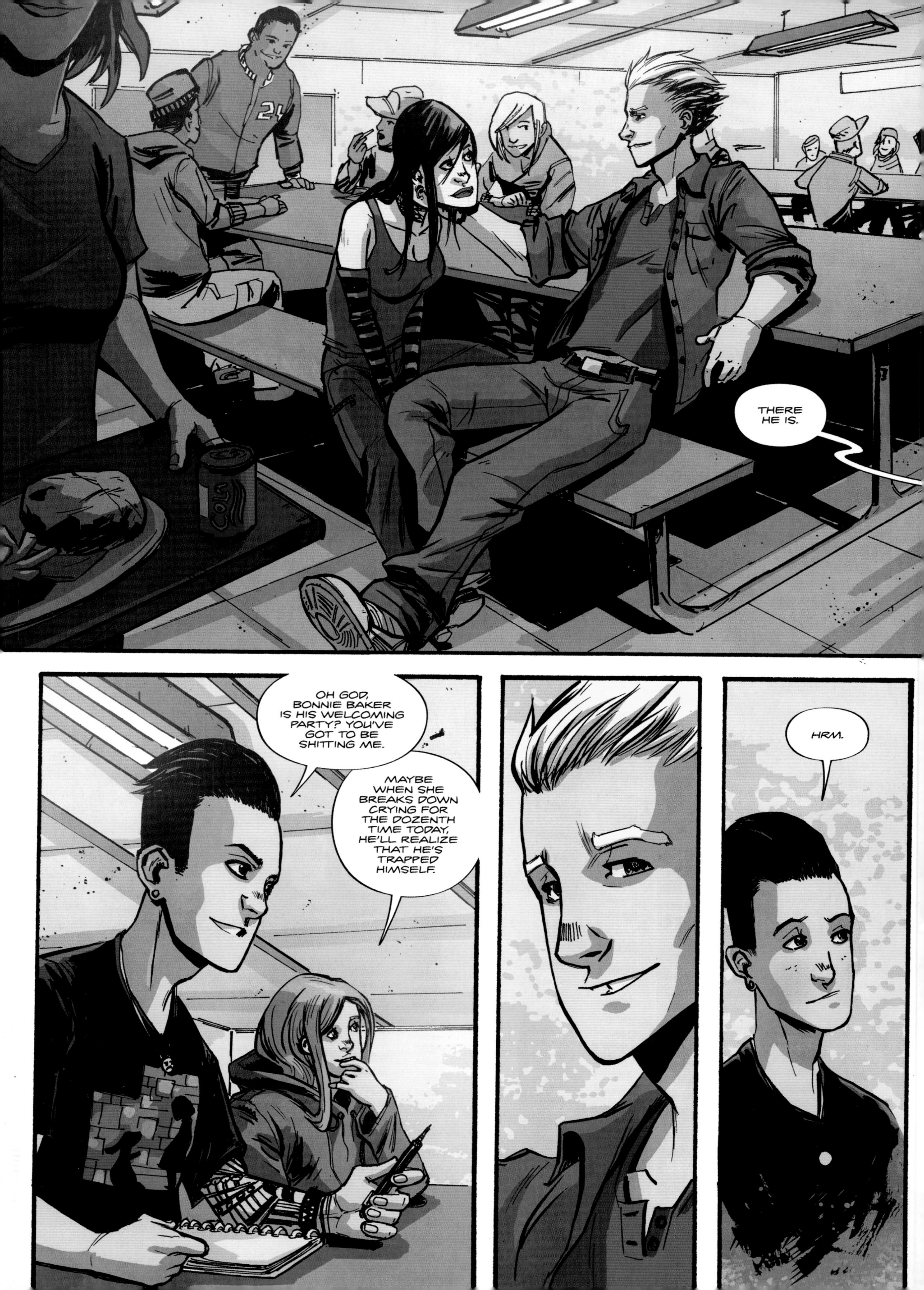
THERE HE IS.
OH GOD, BONNIE BAKER IS HIS WELCOMING PARTY? YOU'VE GOT TO BE SHITTING ME.
MAYBE WHEN SHE BREAKS DOWN CRYING FOR THE DOZENTH TIME TODAY, HE'LL REALIZE THAT HE'S TRAPPED HIMSELF.
HRM.

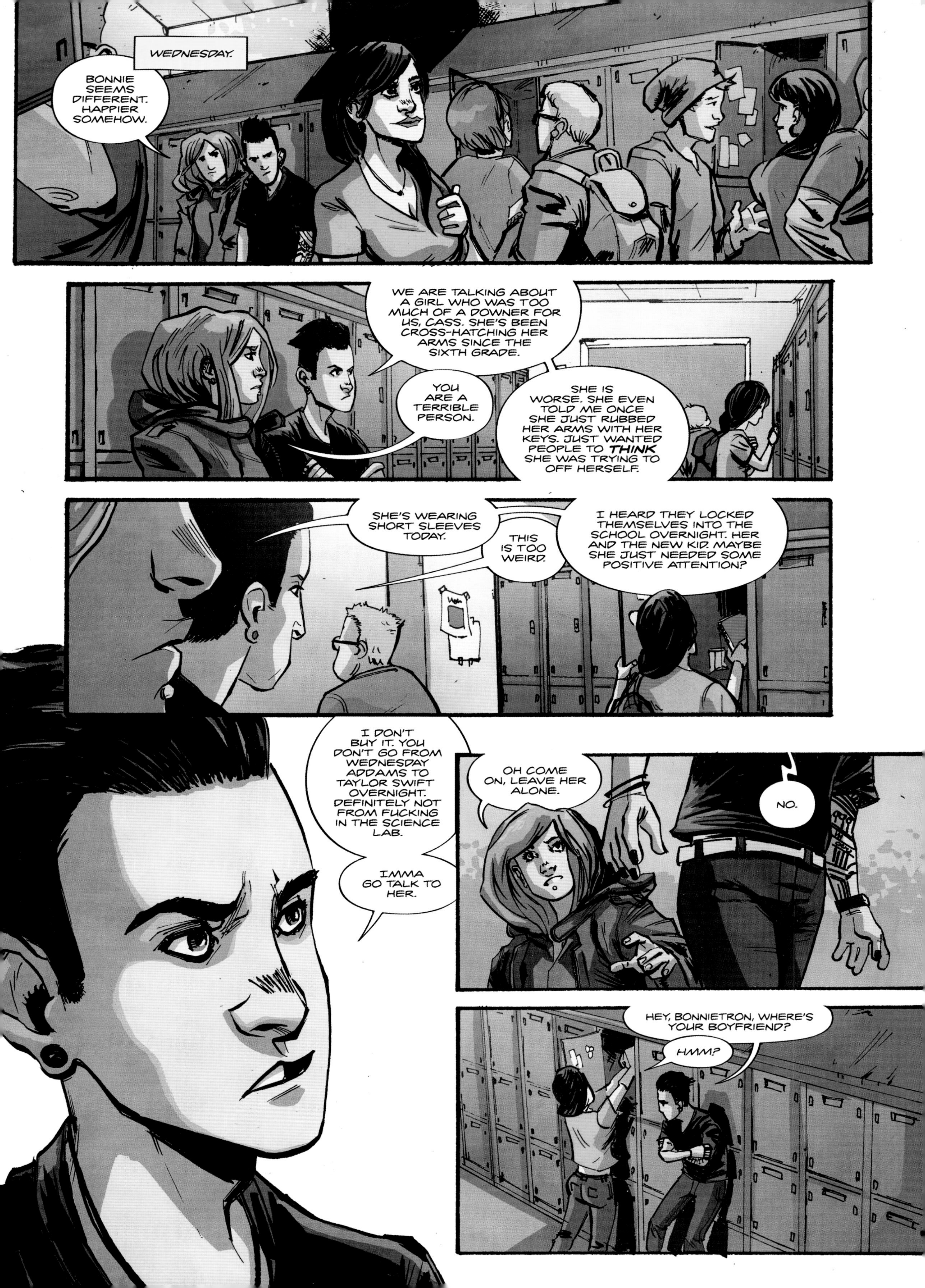
WEDNESDAY.
BONNIE SEEMS DIFFERENT. HAPPIER SOMEHOW.
WE ARE TALKING ABOUT A GIRL WHO WAS TOO MUCH OF A DOWNER FOR US, CASS. SHE'S BEEN CROSS-HATCHING HER ARMS SINCE THE SIXTH GRADE.
YOU ARE A TERRIBLE PERSON.
SHE IS WORSE. SHE EVEN TOLD ME ONCE SHE JUST RUBBED HER ARMS WITH HER KEYS. JUST WANTED PEOPLE TO THINK SHE WAS TRYING TO OFF HERSELF.
SHE'S WEARING SHORT SLEEVES TODAY.
THIS IS TOO WEIRD.
I HEARD THEY LOCKED THEMSELVES INTO THE SCHOOL OVERNIGHT. HER AND THE NEW KID. MAYBE SHE JUST NEEDED SOME POSITIVE ATTENTION?
I DON'T BUY IT. YOU DON'T GO FROM WEDNESDAY ADDAMS TO TAYLOR SWIFT OVERNIGHT. DEFINITELY NOT FROM FUCKING IN THE SCIENCE LAB.
IMMA GO TALK TO HER.
OH COME ON, LEAVE HER ALONE.
NO.
HEY, BONNIETRON, WHERE'S YOUR BOYFRIEND?
HMM?

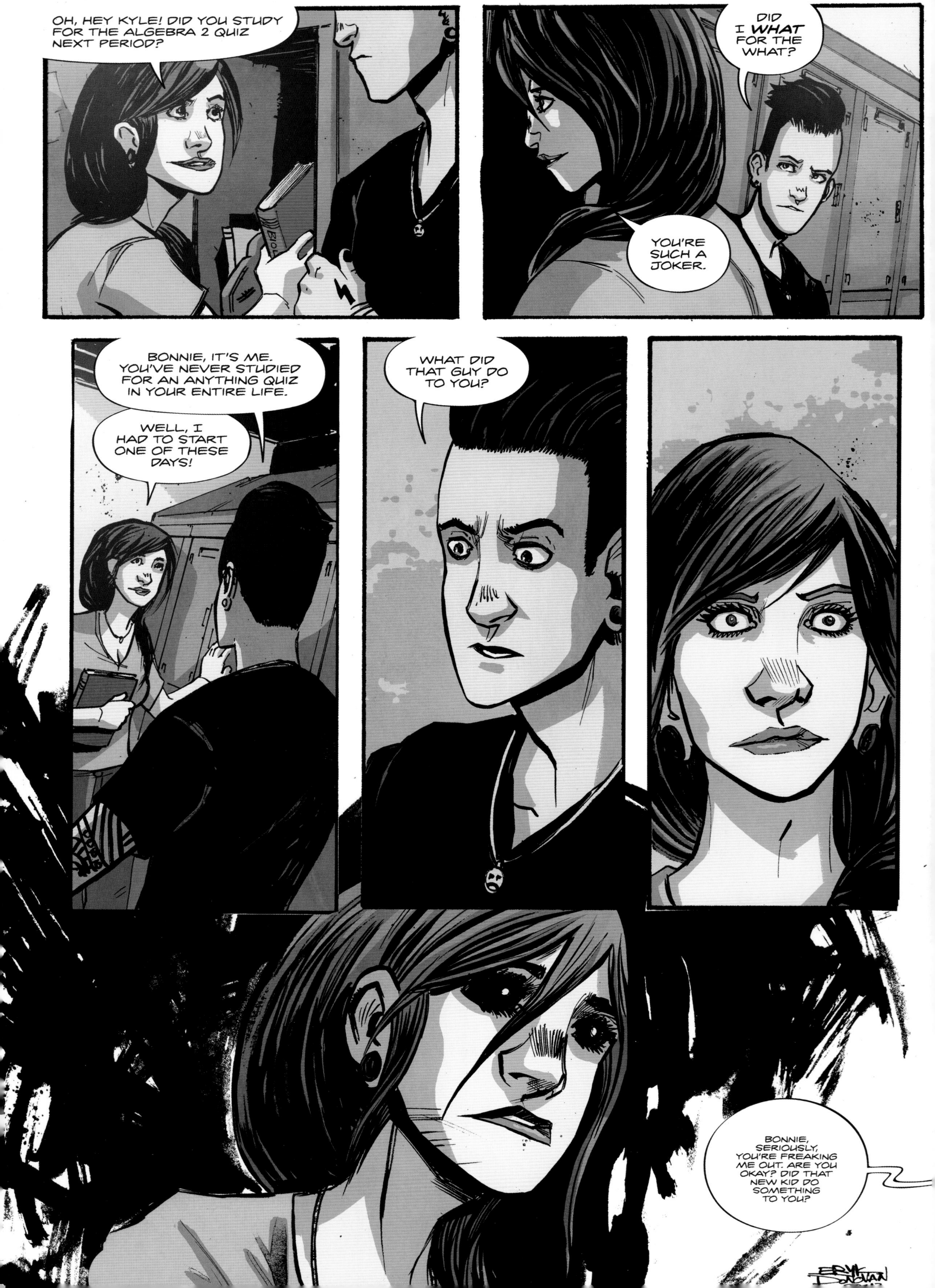

OH, HEY KYLE! DID YOU STUDY FOR THE ALGEBRA 2 QUIZ NEXT PERIOD?
DID I WHAT FOR THE WHAT?
YOU'RE SUCH A JOKER.
BONNIE, IT'S ME. YOU'VE NEVER STUDIED FOR AN ANYTHING QUIZ IN YOUR ENTIRE LIFE.
WELL, I HAD TO START ONE OF THESE DAYS!
WHAT DID THAT GUY DO TO YOU?
BONNIE, SERIOUSLY, YOU'RE FREAKING ME OUT. ARE YOU OKAY? DID THAT NEW KID DO SOMETHING TO YOU?

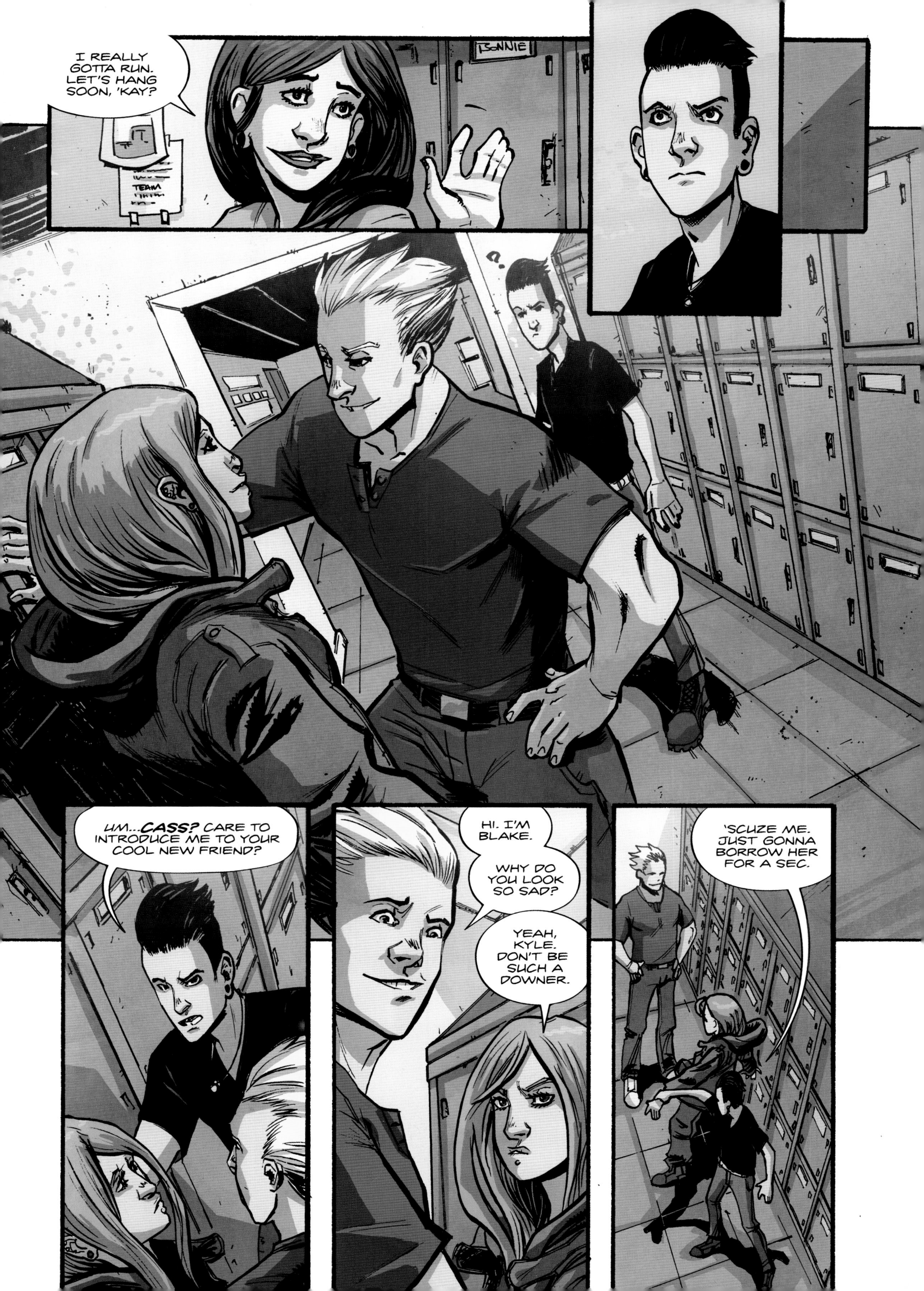
I REALLY GOTTA RUN. LET'S HANG SOON, 'KAY?
BONNIE
TEAM
?
UM...**CASS?** CARE TO INTRODUCE ME TO YOUR COOL NEW FRIEND?
HI. I'M BLAKE.
WHY DO YOU LOOK SO SAD?
YEAH, KYLE. DON'T BE SUCH A DOWNER.
'SCUZE ME. JUST GONNA BORROW HER FOR A SEC.

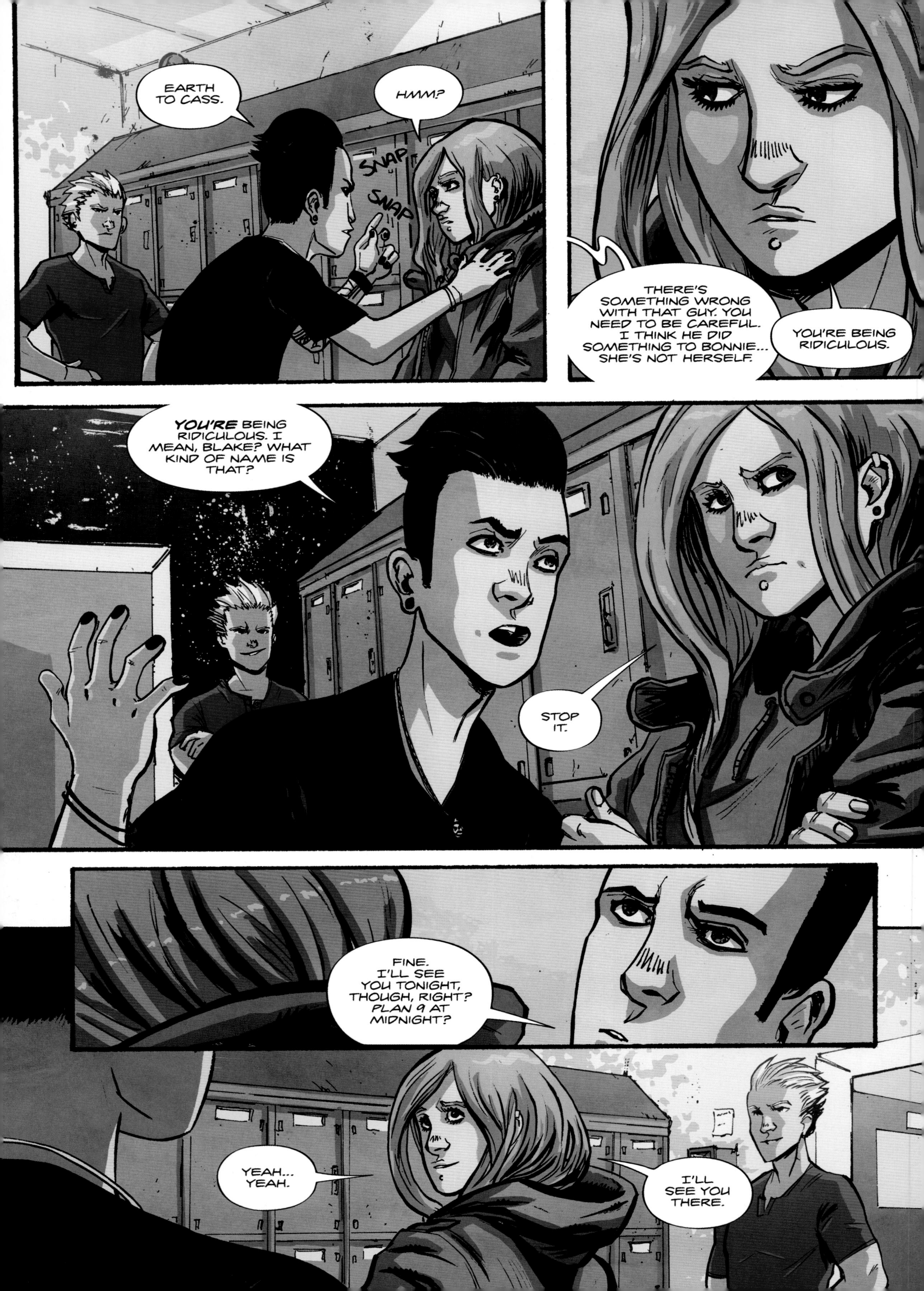
EARTH TO CASS.
HMM?
SNAP
SNAP
THERE'S SOMETHING WRONG WITH THAT GUY. YOU NEED TO BE CAREFUL. I THINK HE DID SOMETHING TO BONNIE... SHE'S NOT HERSELF.
YOU'RE BEING RIDICULOUS.
YOU'RE BEING RIDICULOUS. I MEAN, BLAKE? WHAT KIND OF NAME IS THAT?
STOP IT.
FINE. I'LL SEE YOU TONIGHT, THOUGH, RIGHT? PLAN 9 AT MIDNIGHT?
YEAH... YEAH.
I'LL SEE YOU THERE.

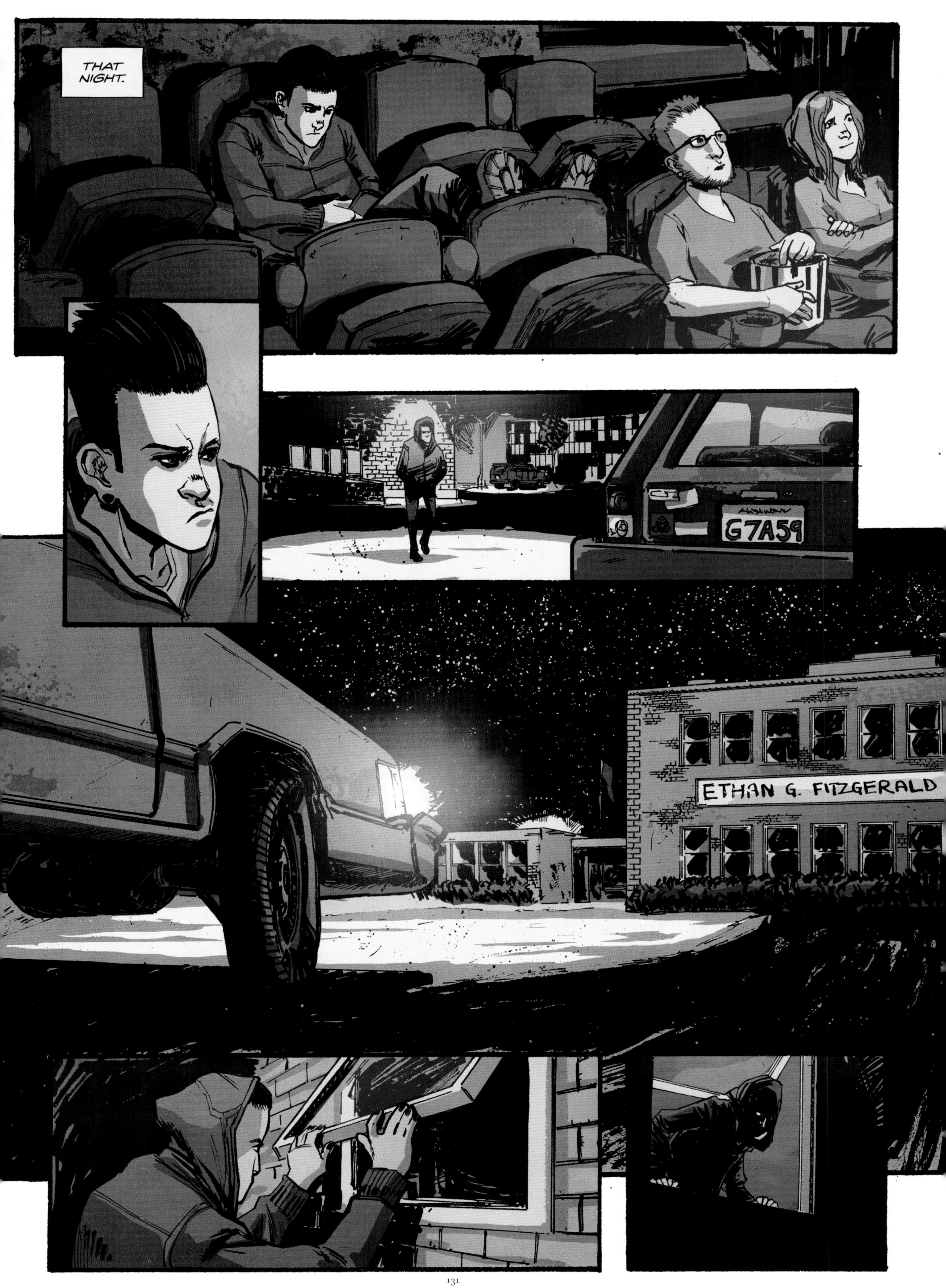
THAT NIGHT.
G7A59
ETHAN G. FITZGERALD

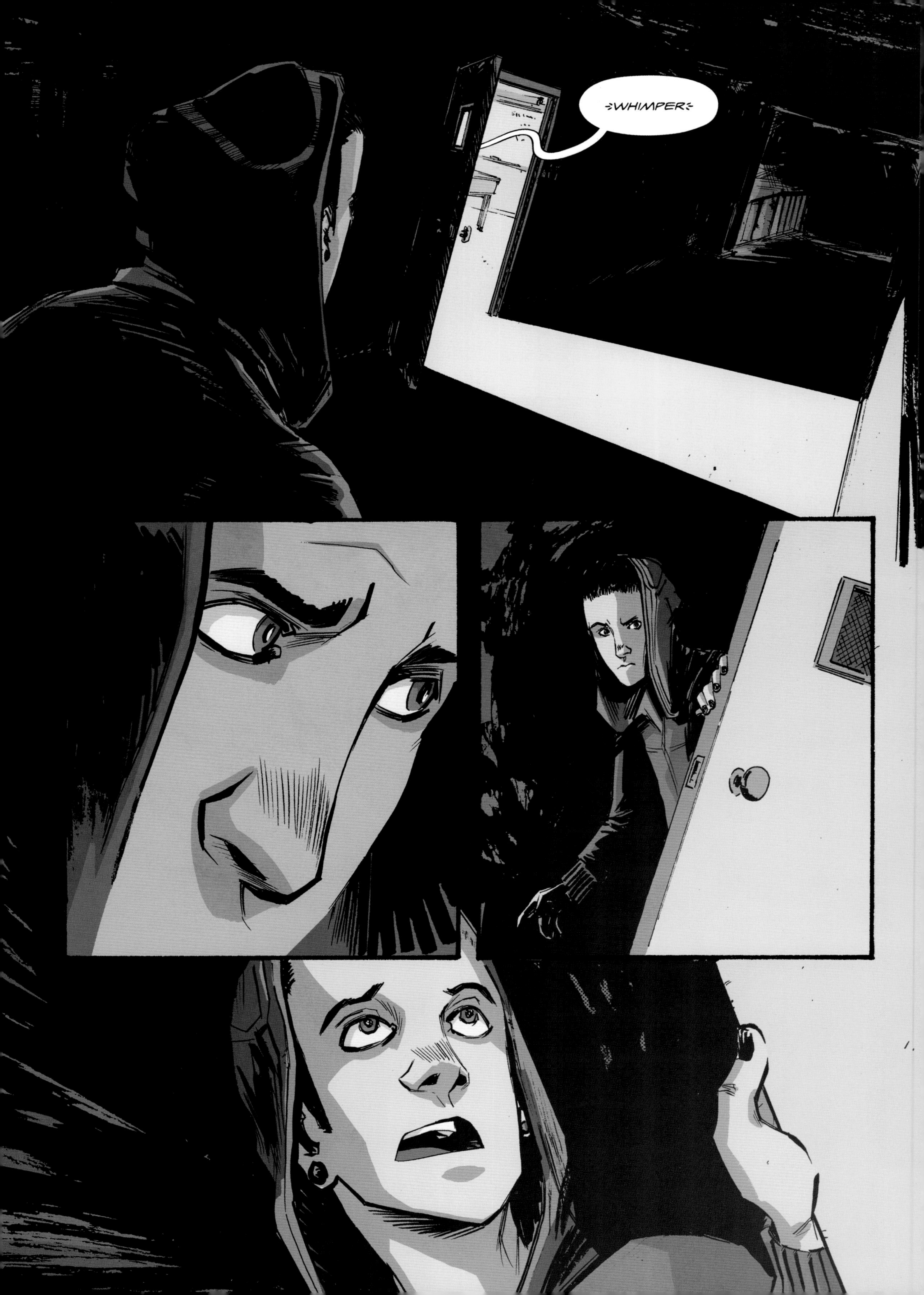
WHIMPER

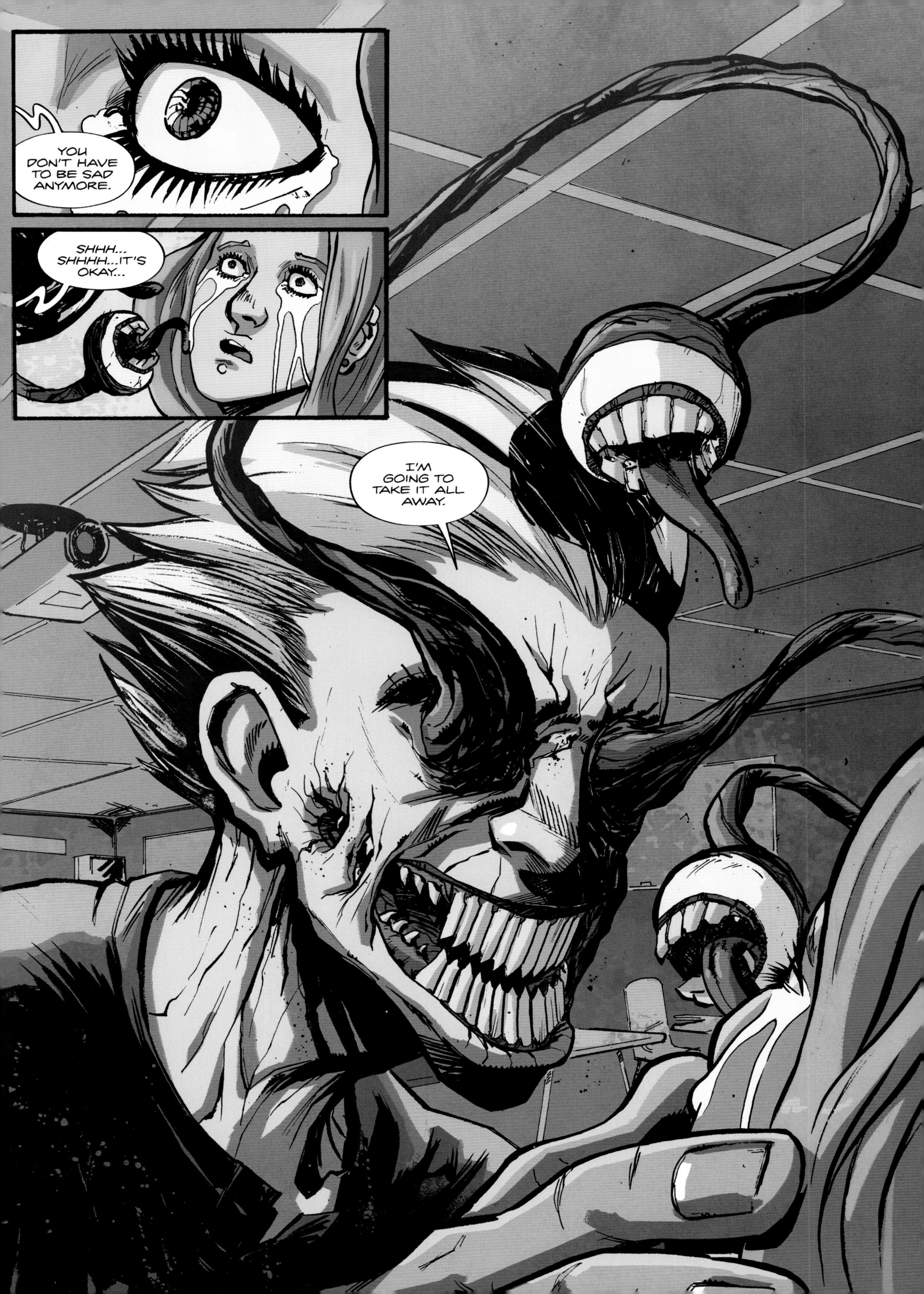
YOU DON'T HAVE TO BE SAD ANYMORE.
SHHH... SHHHH...IT'S OKAY...
I'M GOING TO TAKE IT ALL AWAY.

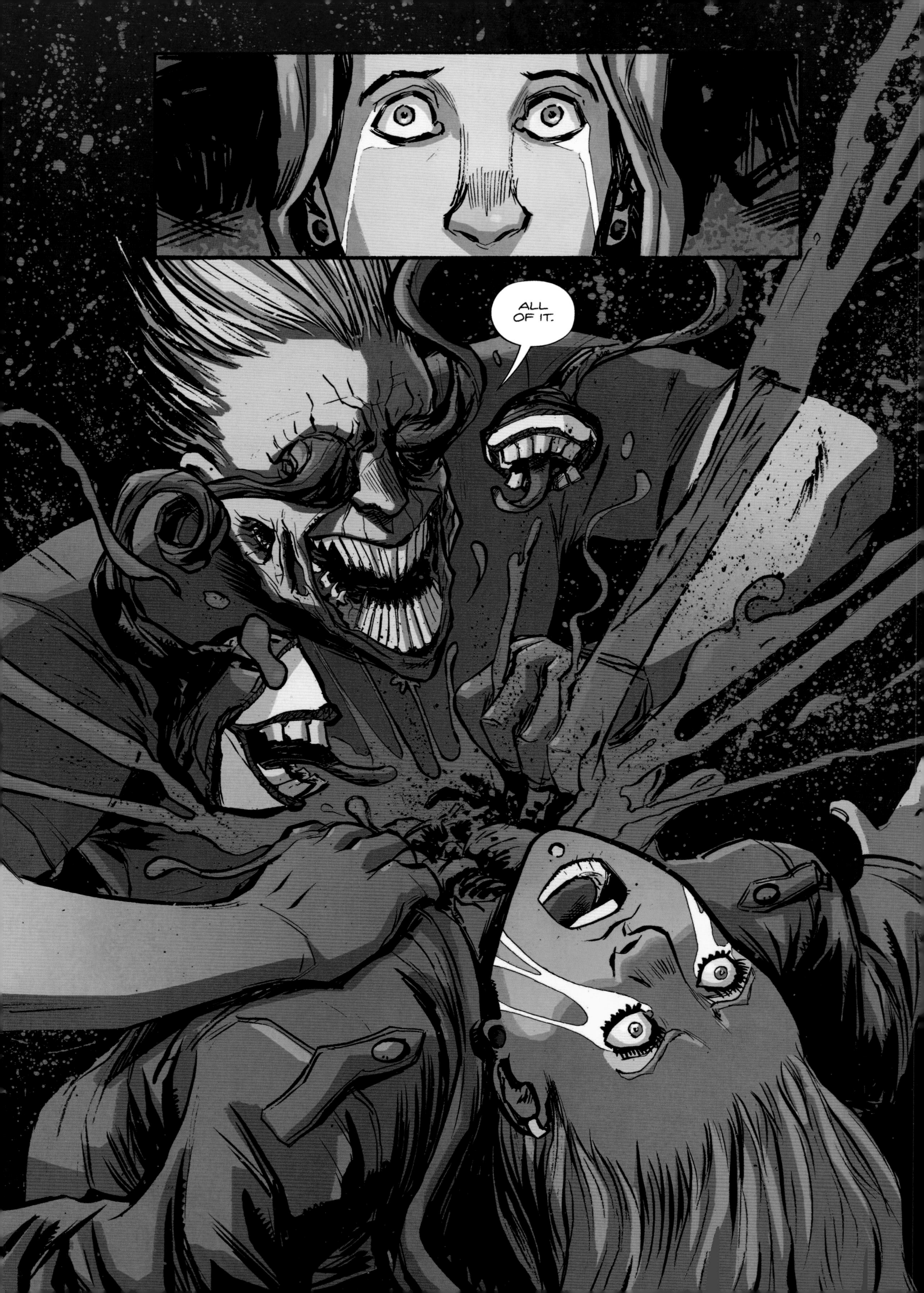
ALL OF IT.

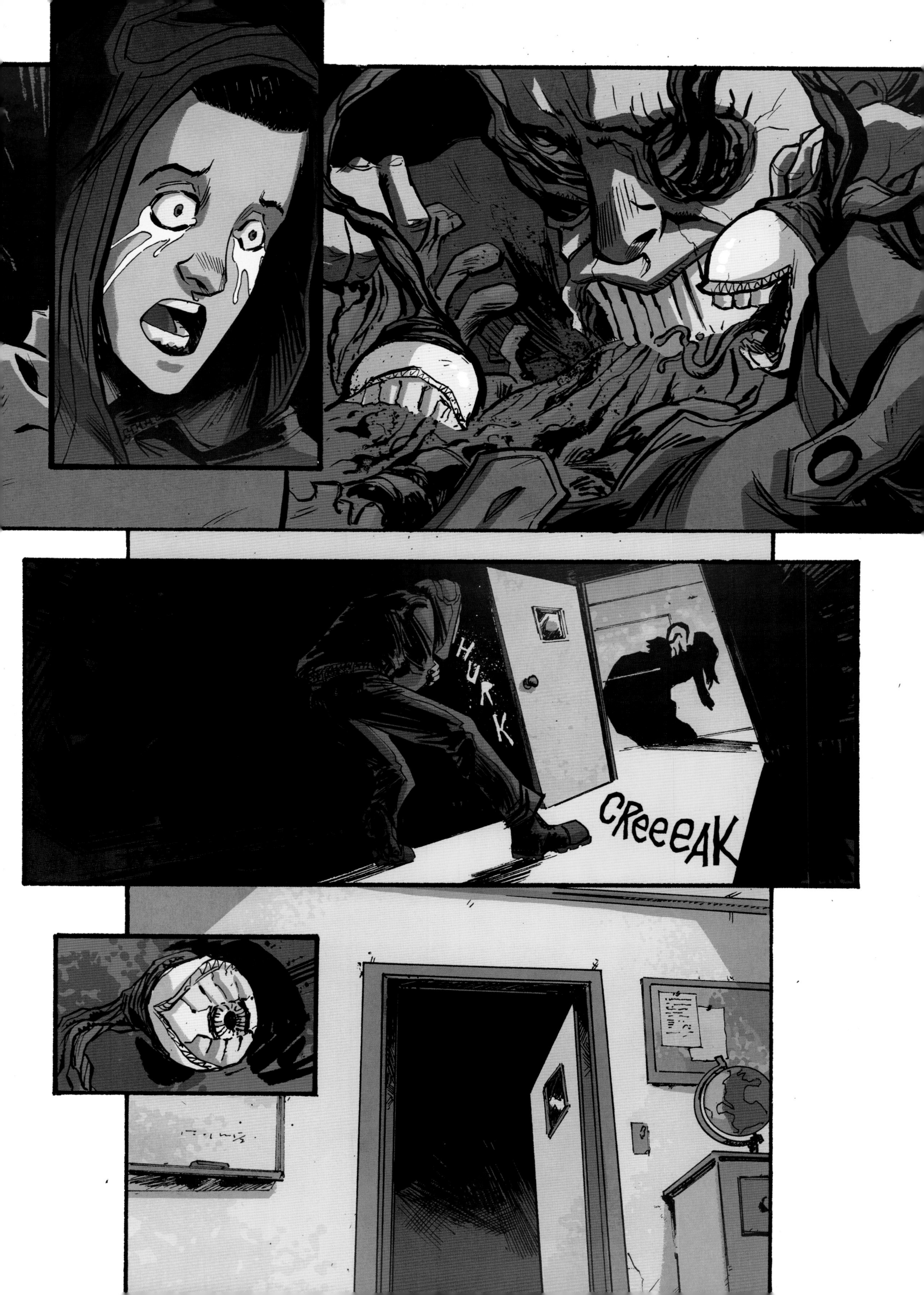
HURK
CREEEAK

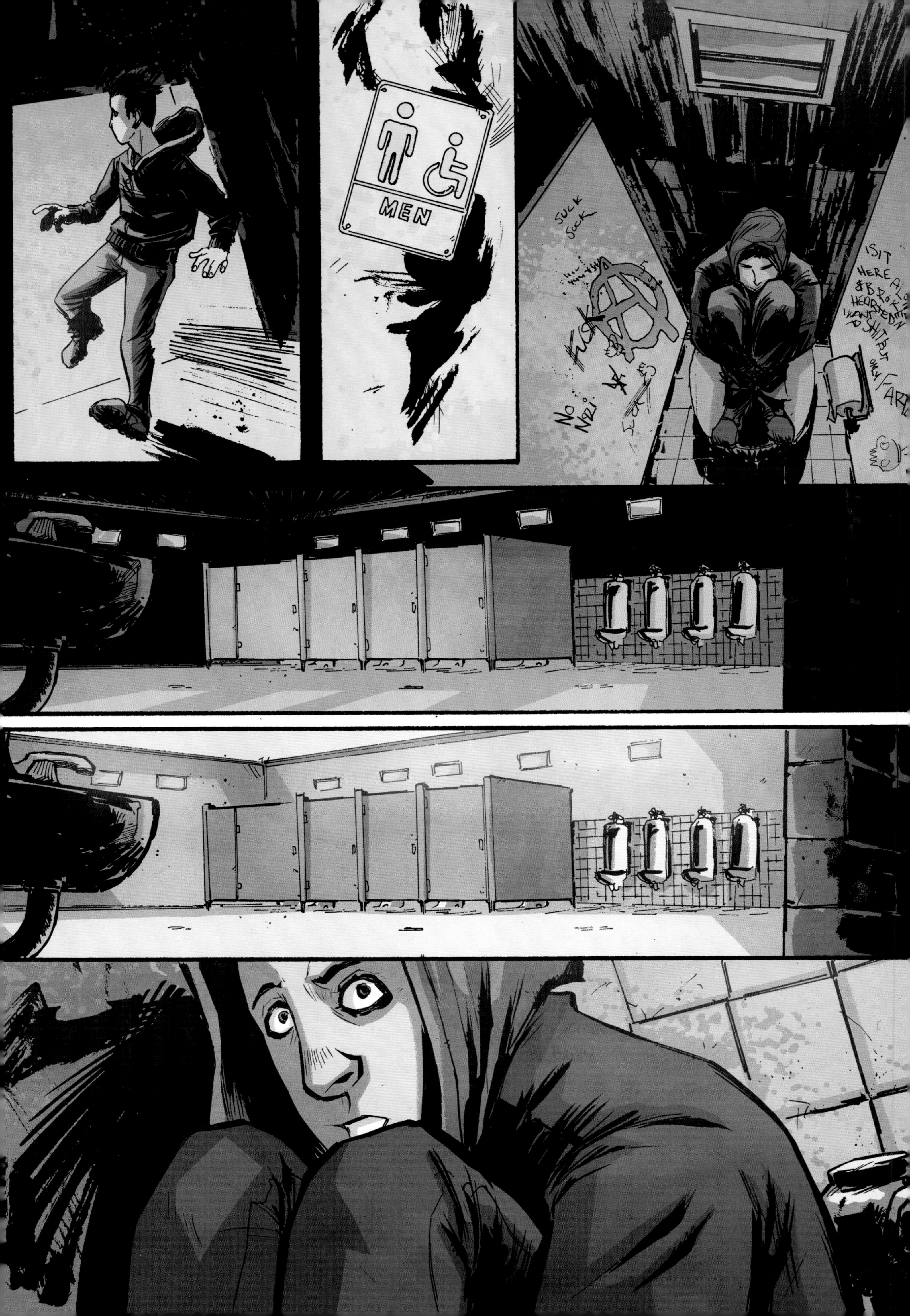
MEN
SUCK SUCK
FUCK
SUCK
No Nazi
ISIT HERE
ONLY

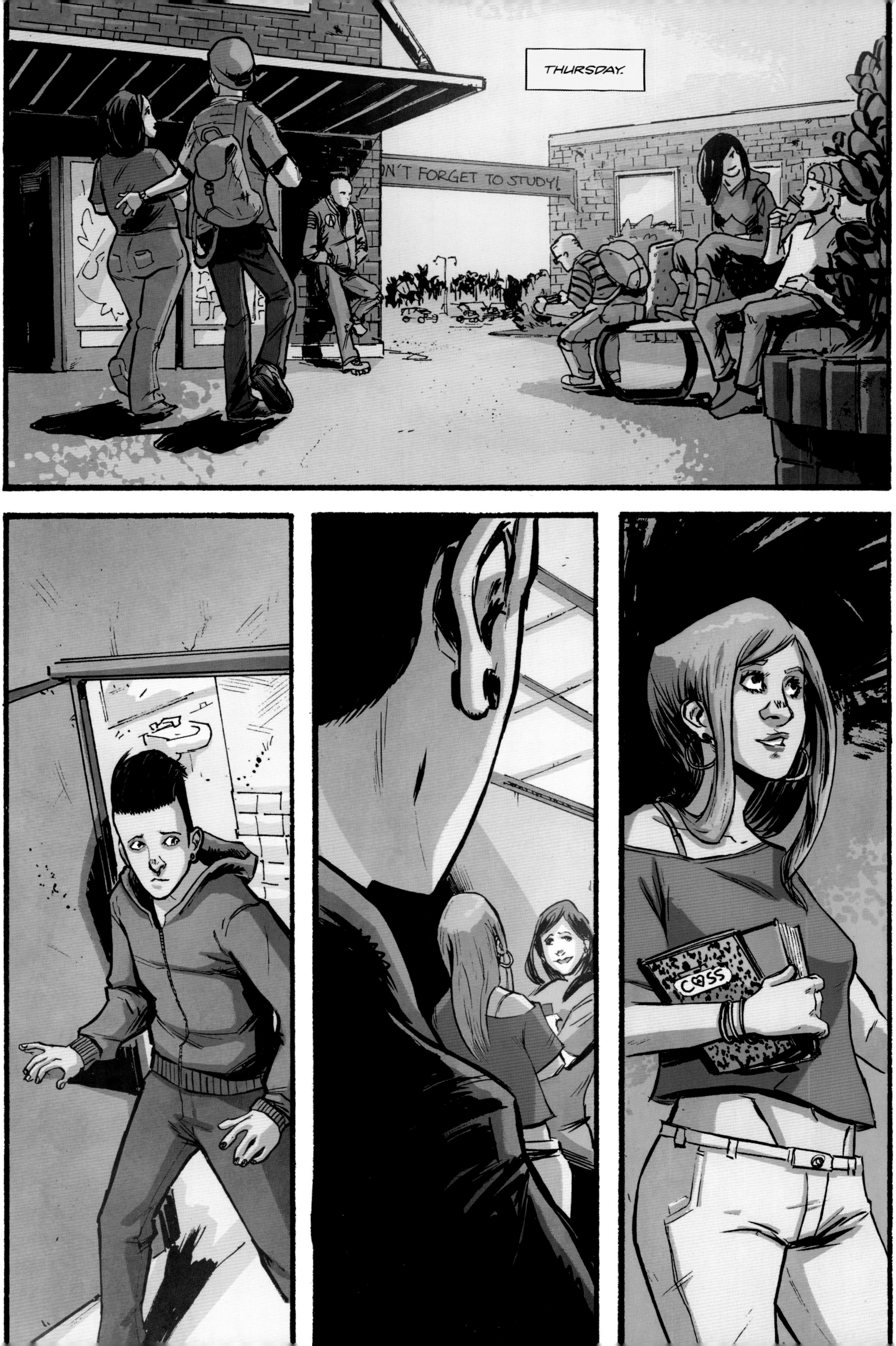
THURSDAY.
N'T FORGET TO STUDY!

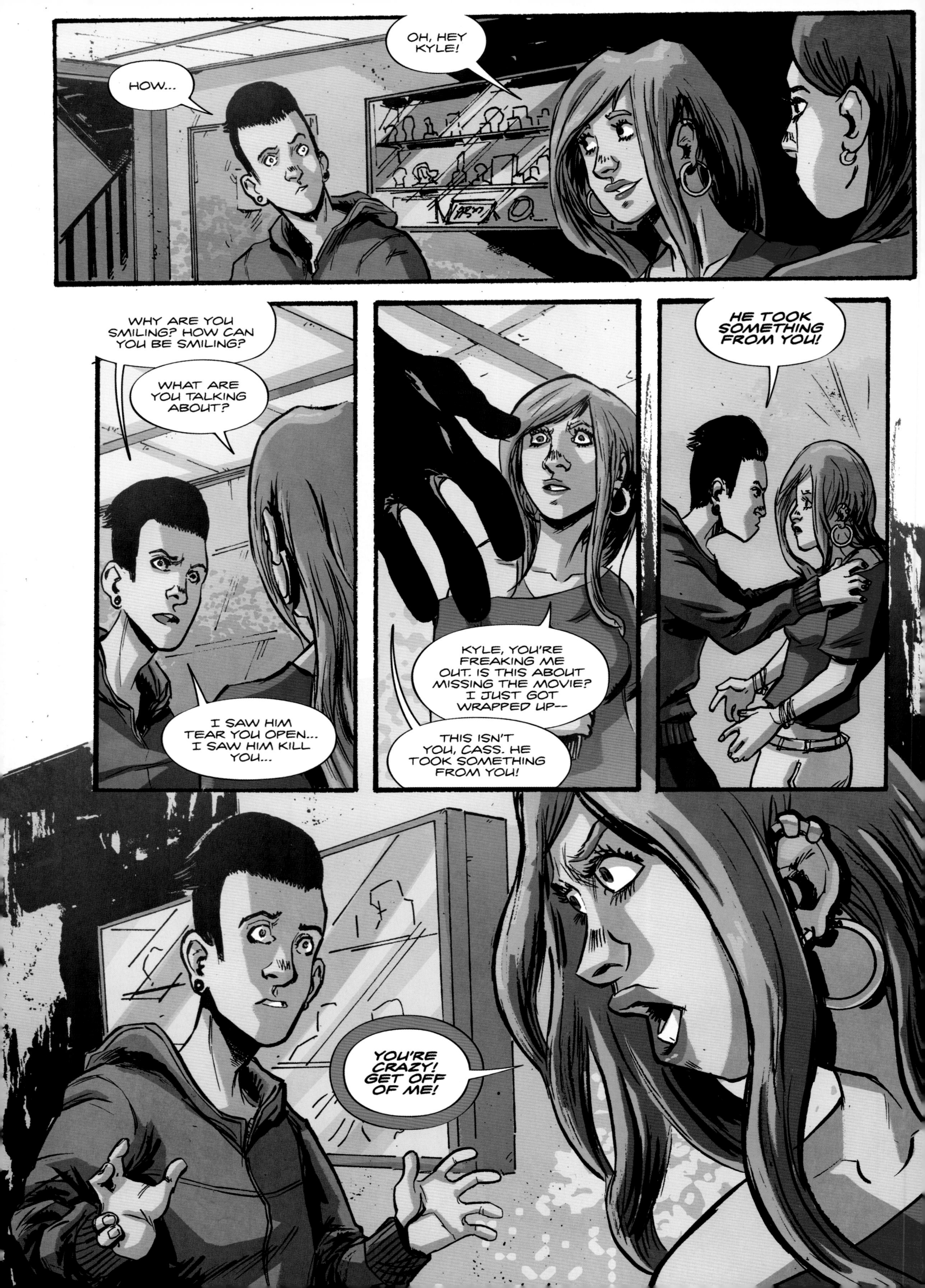
HOW...
OH, HEY KYLE!
WHY ARE YOU SMILING? HOW CAN YOU BE SMILING?
WHAT ARE YOU TALKING ABOUT?
I SAW HIM TEAR YOU OPEN... I SAW HIM KILL YOU...
KYLE, YOU'RE FREAKING ME OUT. IS THIS ABOUT MISSING THE MOVIE? I JUST GOT WRAPPED UP--
THIS ISN'T YOU, CASS. HE TOOK SOMETHING FROM YOU!
HE TOOK SOMETHING FROM YOU!
YOU'RE CRAZY! GET OFF OF ME!

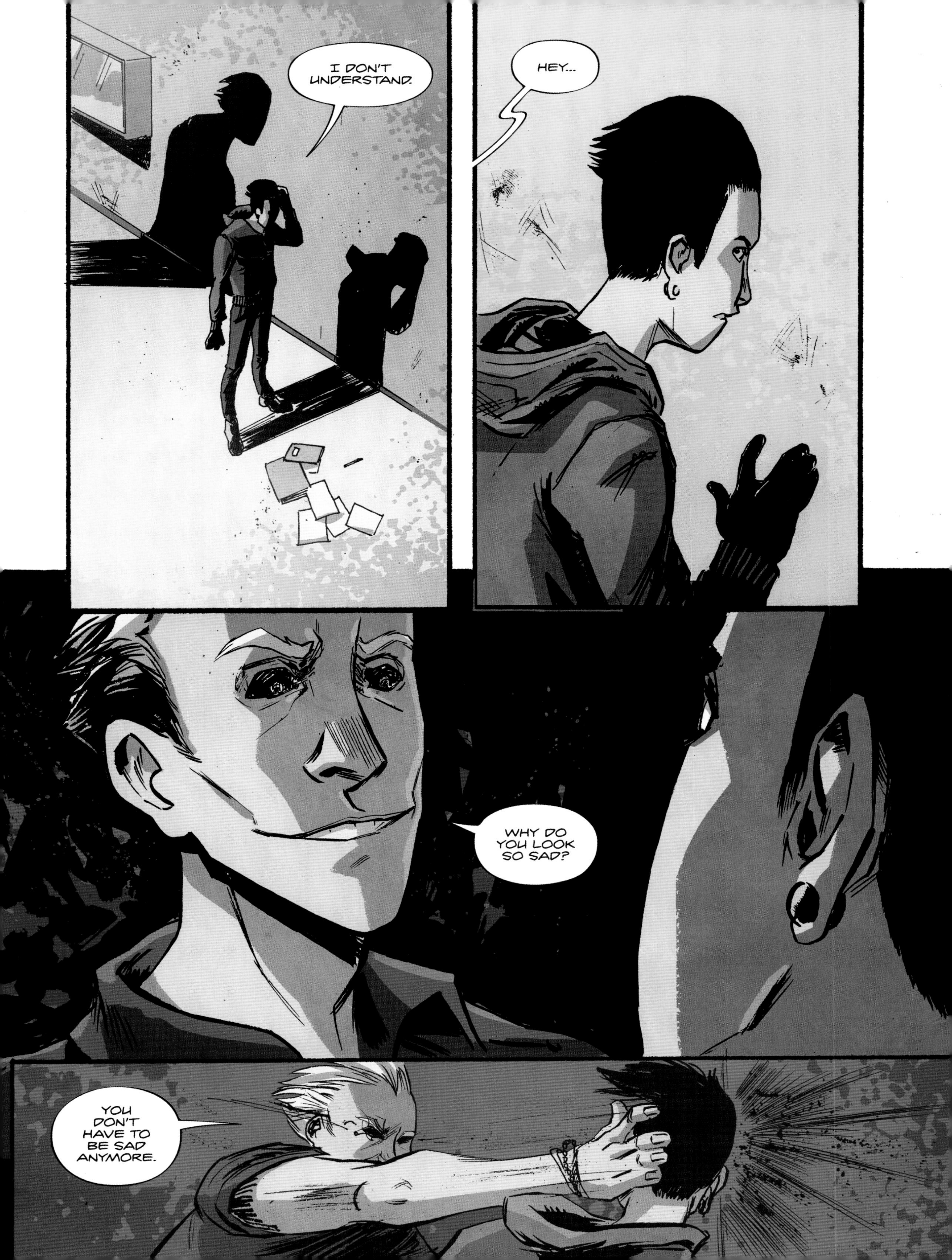
I DON'T UNDERSTAND.
HEY...
WHY DO YOU LOOK SO SAD?
YOU DON'T HAVE TO BE SAD ANYMORE.

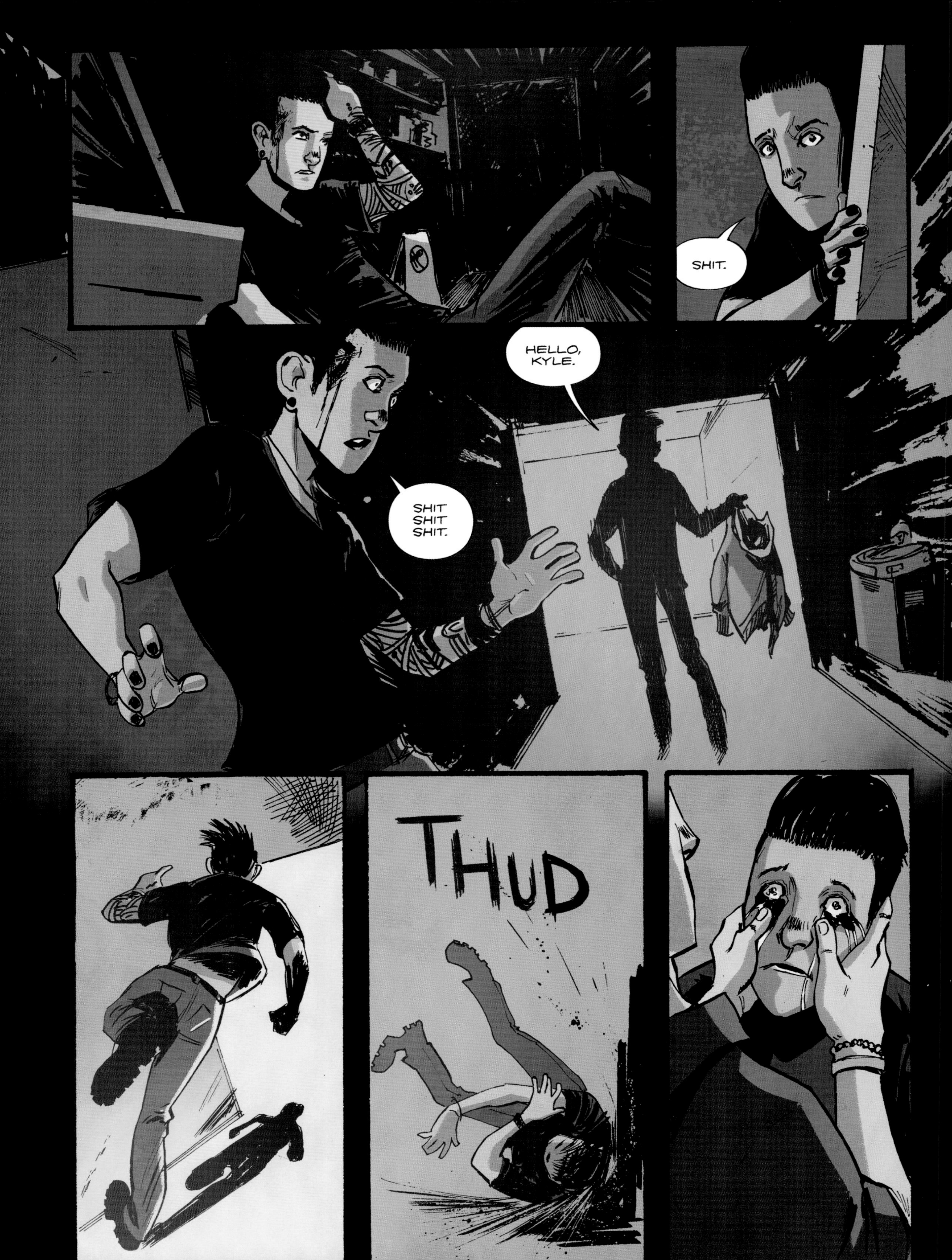
SHIT.
HELLO, KYLE.
SHIT SHIT SHIT.
THUD

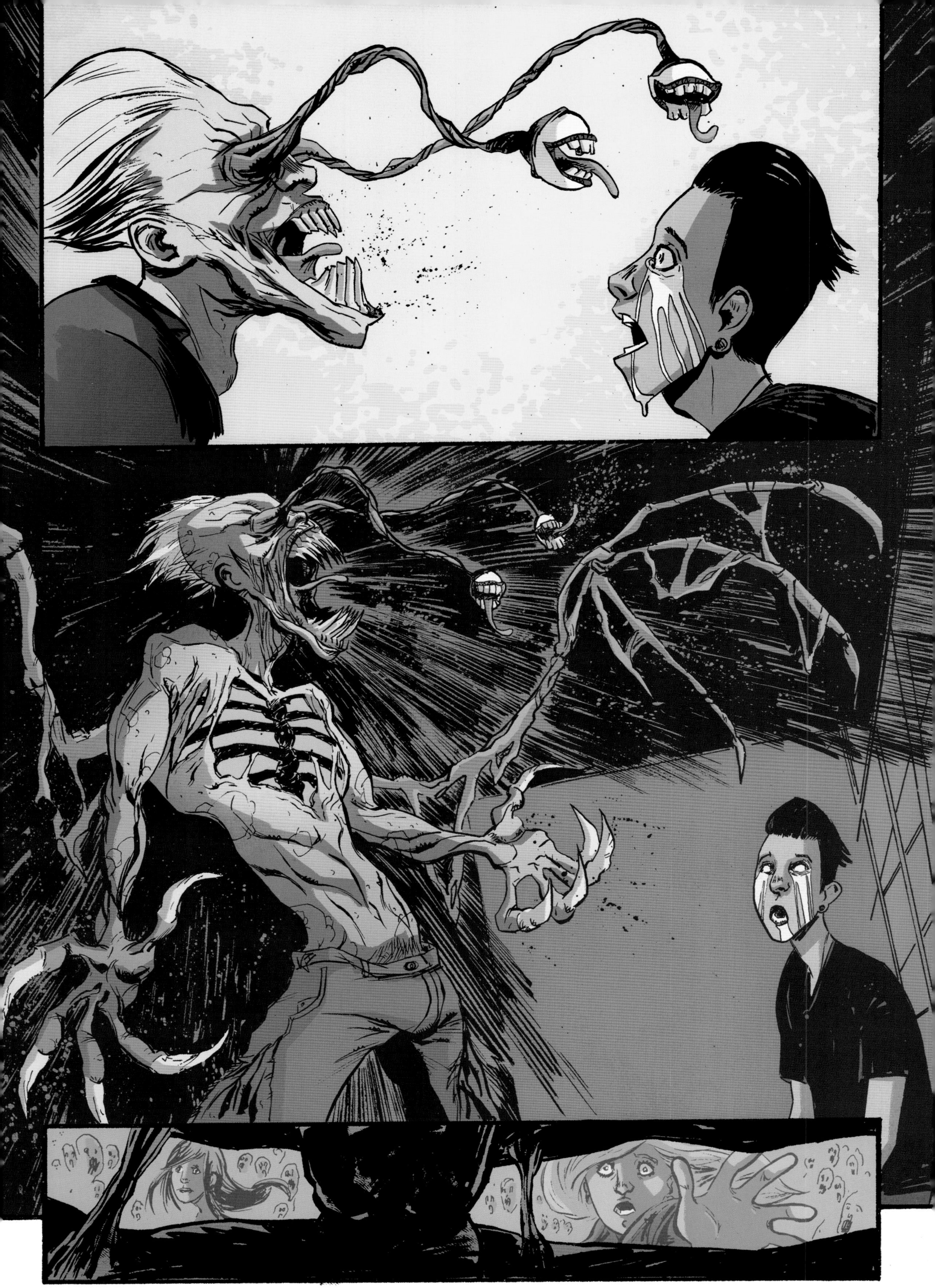

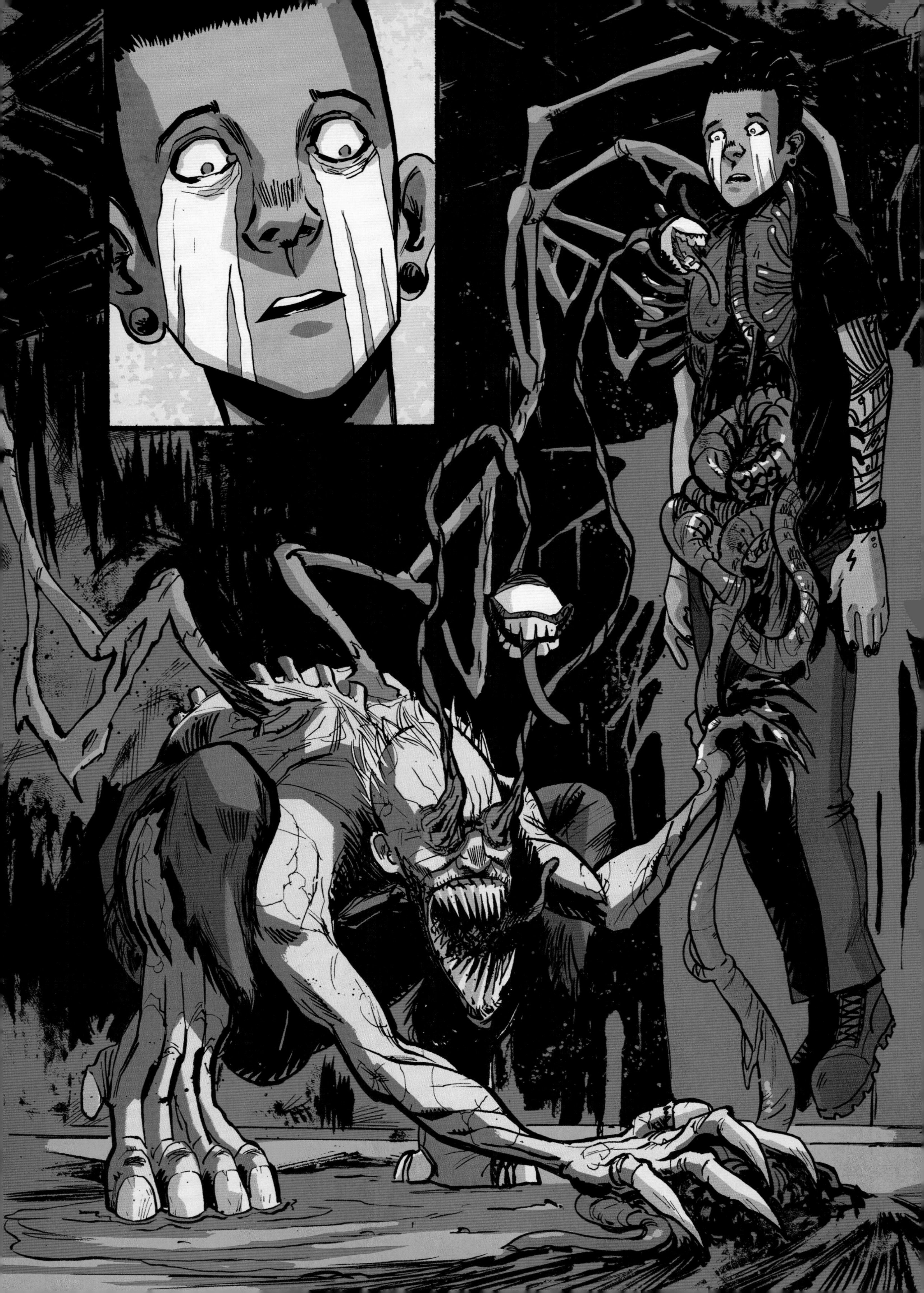

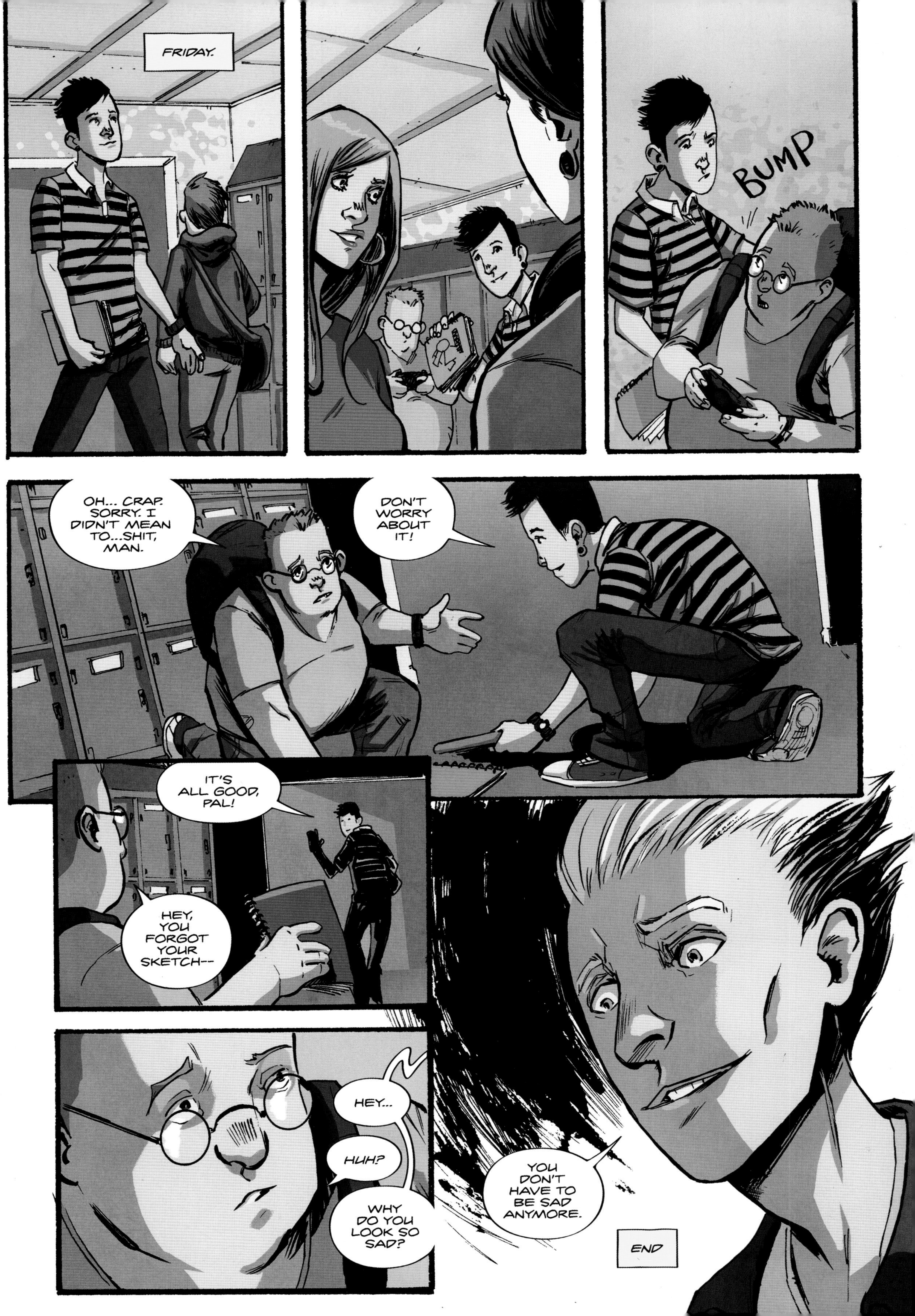
FRIDAY.
BUMP
OH... CRAP. SORRY. I DIDN'T MEAN TO...SHIT, MAN.
DON'T WORRY ABOUT IT!
IT'S ALL GOOD, PAL!
HEY, YOU FORGOT YOUR SKETCH--
HEY...
HUH?
WHY DO YOU LOOK SO SAD?
YOU DON'T HAVE TO BE SAD ANYMORE.
END

NOT ALL THERE

WRITER
DUANE SWIERCZYNSKI

ARTIST
RICHARD P. CLARK

COLORIST
TAMRA BONVILLAIN

LETTERER
RACHEL DEERING

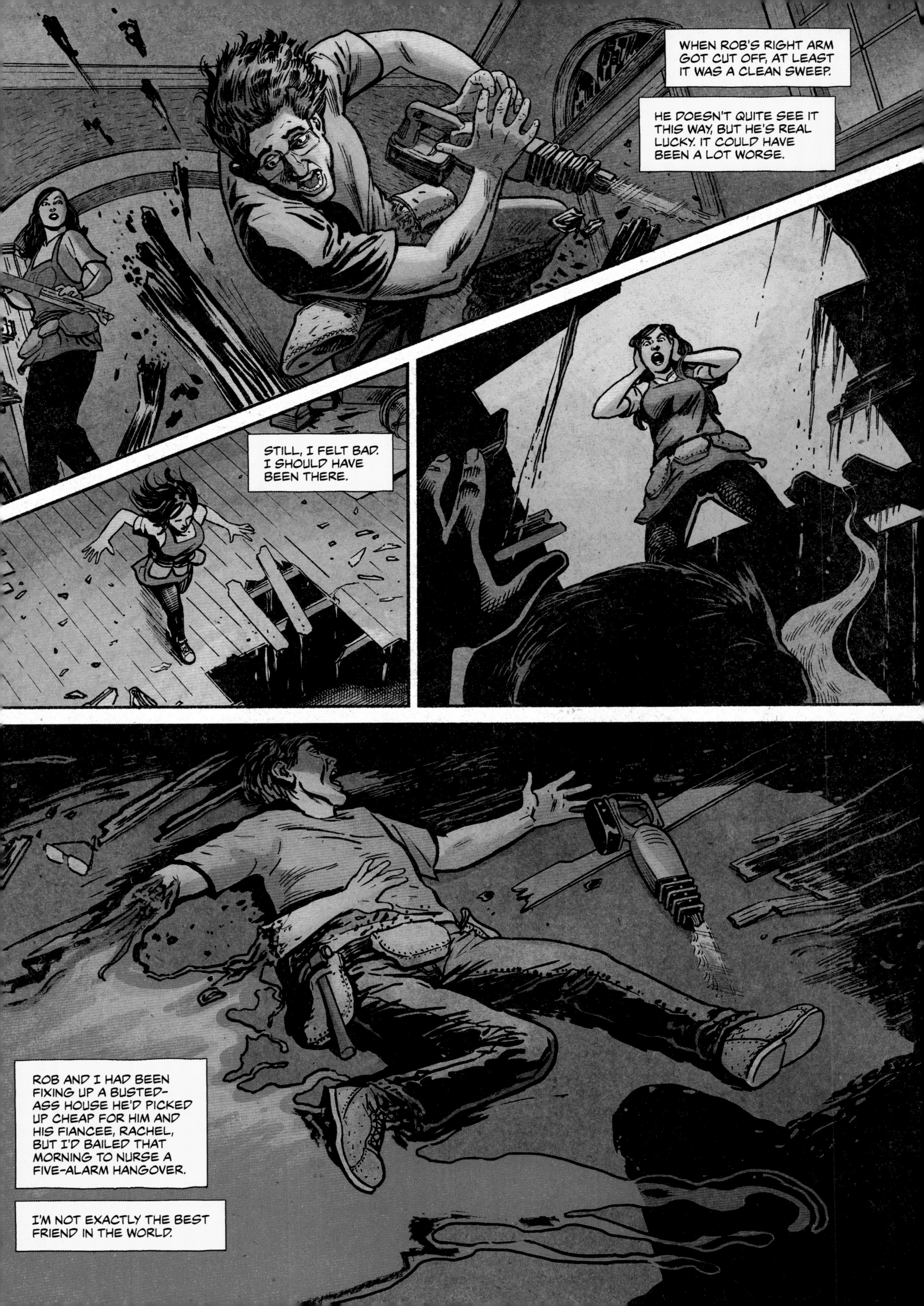
WHEN ROB'S RIGHT ARM GOT CUT OFF, AT LEAST IT WAS A CLEAN SWEEP.
HE DOESN'T QUITE SEE IT THIS WAY, BUT HE'S REAL LUCKY. IT COULD HAVE BEEN A LOT WORSE.
STILL, I FELT BAD. I SHOULD HAVE BEEN THERE.
ROB AND I HAD BEEN FIXING UP A BUSTED-ASS HOUSE HE'D PICKED UP CHEAP FOR HIM AND HIS FIANCEE, RACHEL, BUT I'D BAILED THAT MORNING TO NURSE A FIVE-ALARM HANGOVER.
I'M NOT EXACTLY THE BEST FRIEND IN THE WORLD.

I WENT TO VISIT ROB A FEW DAYS AFTER THE ACCIDENT TO CHEER HIM UP.

HEY.

HEY!

UHHH...

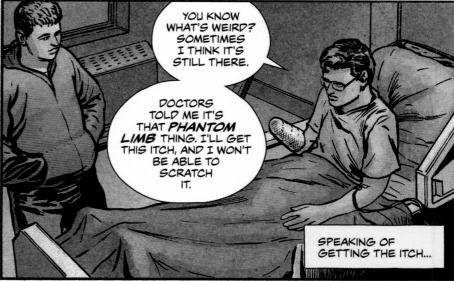

YOU KNOW WHAT'S WEIRD? SOMETIMES I THINK IT'S STILL THERE.

DOCTORS TOLD ME IT'S THAT *PHANTOM LIMB* THING. I'LL GET THIS ITCH, AND I WON'T BE ABLE TO SCRATCH IT.

SPEAKING OF GETTING THE ITCH...

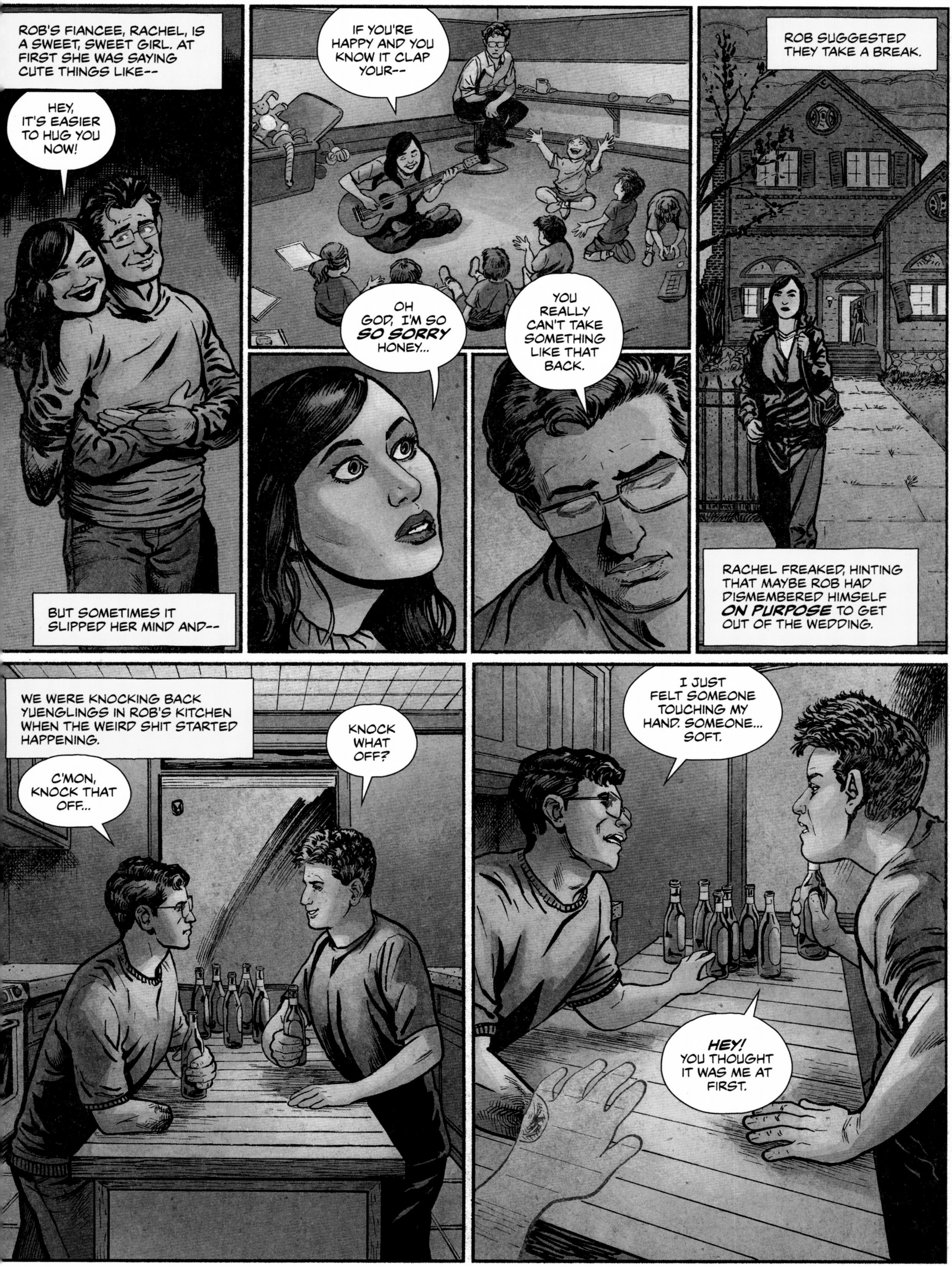

ROB'S FIANCEE, RACHEL, IS A SWEET, SWEET GIRL. AT FIRST SHE WAS SAYING CUTE THINGS LIKE--
HEY, IT'S EASIER TO HUG YOU NOW!
BUT SOMETIMES IT SLIPPED HER MIND AND--
IF YOU'RE HAPPY AND YOU KNOW IT CLAP YOUR--
OH GOD, I'M SO SO SORRY HONEY...
YOU REALLY CAN'T TAKE SOMETHING LIKE THAT BACK.
ROB SUGGESTED THEY TAKE A BREAK.
RACHEL FREAKED, HINTING THAT MAYBE ROB HAD DISMEMBERED HIMSELF ON PURPOSE TO GET OUT OF THE WEDDING.
WE WERE KNOCKING BACK YUENGLINGS IN ROB'S KITCHEN WHEN THE WEIRD SHIT STARTED HAPPENING.
C'MON, KNOCK THAT OFF...
KNOCK WHAT OFF?
I JUST FELT SOMEONE TOUCHING MY HAND. SOMEONE... SOFT.
HEY! YOU THOUGHT IT WAS ME AT FIRST.

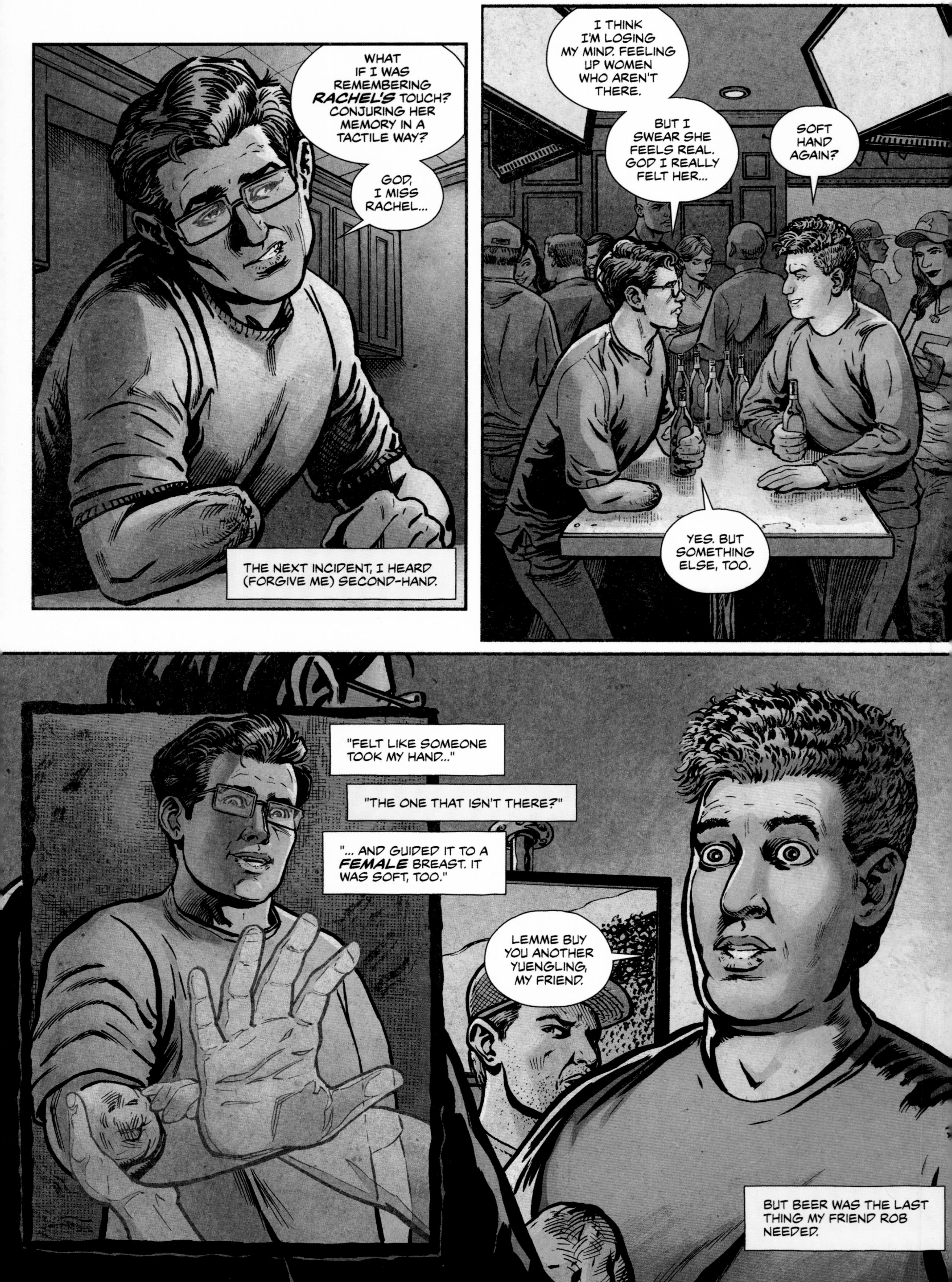
WHAT IF I WAS REMEMBERING RACHEL'S TOUCH? CONJURING HER MEMORY IN A TACTILE WAY?
GOD, I MISS RACHEL...
THE NEXT INCIDENT, I HEARD (FORGIVE ME) SECOND-HAND.
I THINK I'M LOSING MY MIND. FEELING UP WOMEN WHO AREN'T THERE.
BUT I SWEAR SHE FEELS REAL. GOD I REALLY FELT HER...
SOFT HAND AGAIN?
YES. BUT SOMETHING ELSE, TOO.
"FELT LIKE SOMEONE TOOK MY HAND..."
"THE ONE THAT ISN'T THERE?"
"... AND GUIDED IT TO A FEMALE BREAST. IT WAS SOFT, TOO."
LEMME BUY YOU ANOTHER YUENGLING, MY FRIEND.
BUT BEER WAS THE LAST THING MY FRIEND ROB NEEDED.

SOON ROB WENT INTO LOST WEEKEND MODE -- ONLY FOR HIM, IT WAS MORE LIKE A MONTH.

HE'D LINE UP HIS DEAD SOLDIERS...

... AND PLAY WILLIAM TELL WITH 'EM.

I WAS THINKING WE NEEDED TO HAVE THAT TALK YOU DREAD HAVING BECAUSE YOU KNOW SOMEDAY YOU'RE GONNA HEAR IT YOURSELF.

BUT THAT'S WHEN THE *SECOND* ACCIDENT HAPPENED.

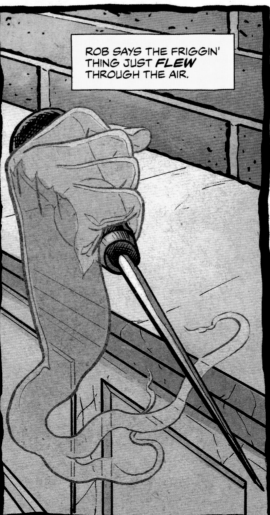

ROB SAYS THE FRIGGIN' THING JUST *FLEW* THROUGH THE AIR.

WHATEVER HAPPENED, RACHEL FOUND HIM PASSED OUT ON THE FLOOR LIKE A HALF-CORKED WINE BOTTLE.

THAT DAY, GOD BLESS HER, SHE MOVED BACK IN.

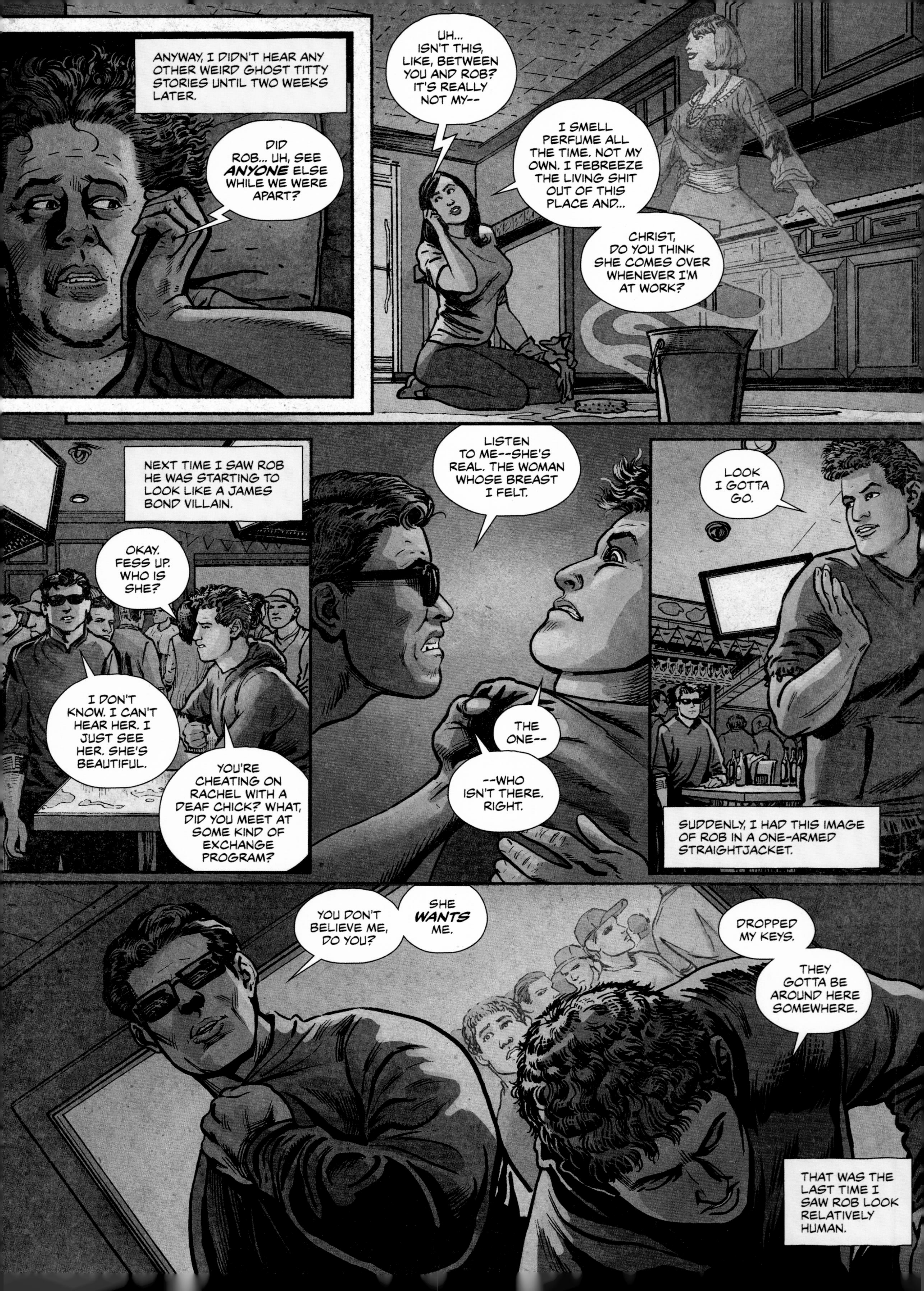

ANYWAY, I DIDN'T HEAR ANY OTHER WEIRD GHOST TITTY STORIES UNTIL TWO WEEKS LATER.
DID ROB... UH, SEE *ANYONE* ELSE WHILE WE WERE APART?
UH... ISN'T THIS, LIKE, BETWEEN YOU AND ROB? IT'S REALLY NOT MY--
I SMELL PERFUME ALL THE TIME. NOT MY OWN. I FEBREEZE THE LIVING SHIT OUT OF THIS PLACE AND...
CHRIST, DO YOU THINK SHE COMES OVER WHENEVER I'M AT WORK?
NEXT TIME I SAW ROB HE WAS STARTING TO LOOK LIKE A JAMES BOND VILLAIN.
OKAY. FESS UP. WHO IS SHE?
I DON'T KNOW. I CAN'T HEAR HER. I JUST SEE HER. SHE'S BEAUTIFUL.
YOU'RE CHEATING ON RACHEL WITH A DEAF CHICK? WHAT, DID YOU MEET AT SOME KIND OF EXCHANGE PROGRAM?
LISTEN TO ME--SHE'S REAL. THE WOMAN WHOSE BREAST I FELT.
THE ONE--
--WHO ISN'T THERE. RIGHT.
LOOK I GOTTA GO.
SUDDENLY, I HAD THIS IMAGE OF ROB IN A ONE-ARMED STRAIGHTJACKET.
YOU DON'T BELIEVE ME, DO YOU?
SHE *WANTS* ME.
DROPPED MY KEYS.
THEY GOTTA BE AROUND HERE SOMEWHERE.
THAT WAS THE LAST TIME I SAW ROB LOOK RELATIVELY HUMAN.

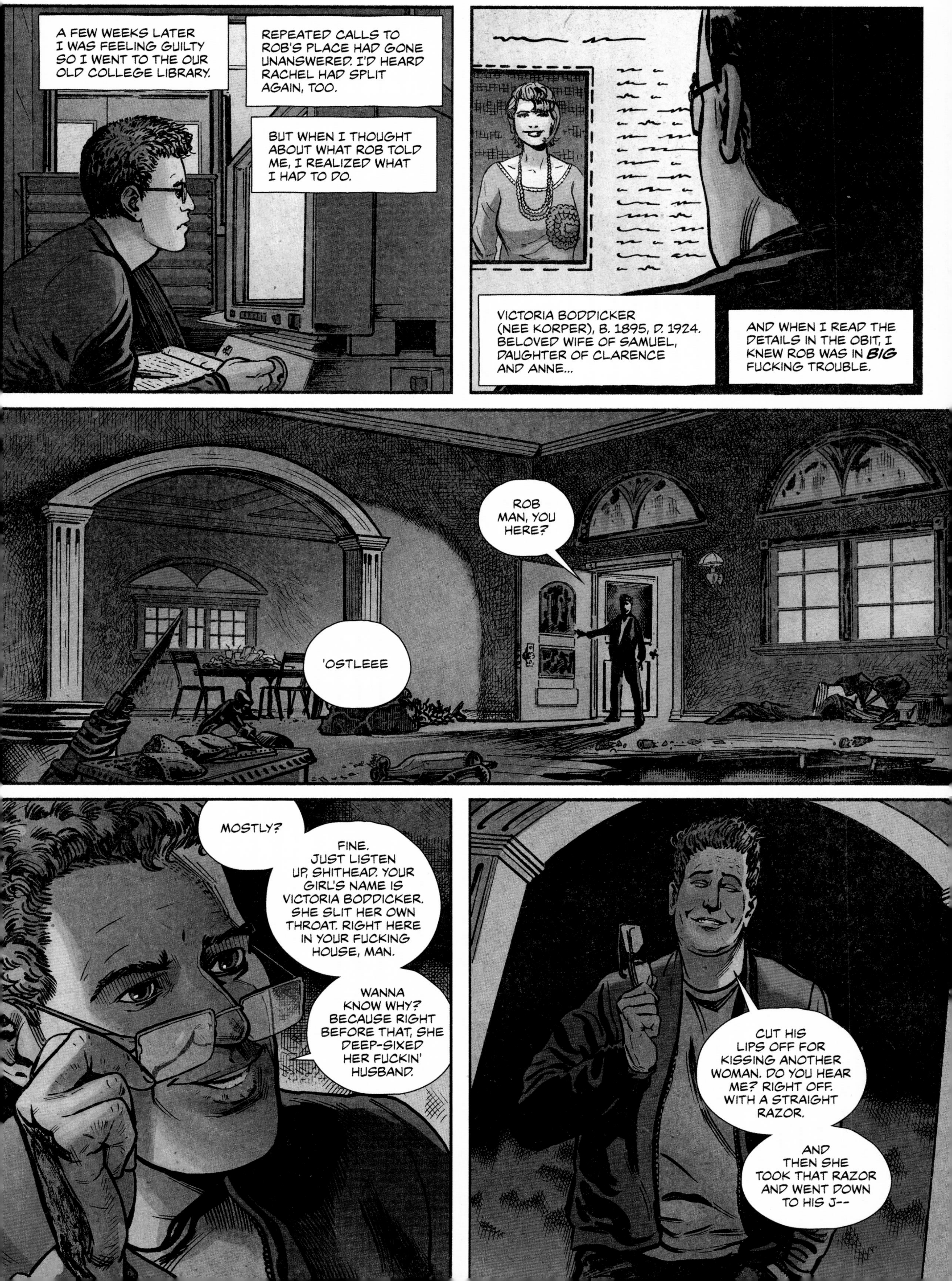

A FEW WEEKS LATER I WAS FEELING GUILTY SO I WENT TO THE OUR OLD COLLEGE LIBRARY.
REPEATED CALLS TO ROB'S PLACE HAD GONE UNANSWERED. I'D HEARD RACHEL HAD SPLIT AGAIN, TOO.
BUT WHEN I THOUGHT ABOUT WHAT ROB TOLD ME, I REALIZED WHAT I HAD TO DO.
VICTORIA BODDICKER (NEE KORPER), B. 1895, D. 1924. BELOVED WIFE OF SAMUEL, DAUGHTER OF CLARENCE AND ANNE...
AND WHEN I READ THE DETAILS IN THE OBIT, I KNEW ROB WAS IN BIG FUCKING TROUBLE.
ROB MAN, YOU HERE?
'OSTLEEE
MOSTLY?
FINE. JUST LISTEN UP, SHITHEAD. YOUR GIRL'S NAME IS VICTORIA BODDICKER. SHE SLIT HER OWN THROAT. RIGHT HERE IN YOUR FUCKING HOUSE, MAN.
WANNA KNOW WHY? BECAUSE RIGHT BEFORE THAT, SHE DEEP-SIXED HER FUCKIN' HUSBAND.
CUT HIS LIPS OFF FOR KISSING ANOTHER WOMAN. DO YOU HEAR ME? RIGHT OFF. WITH A STRAIGHT RAZOR.
AND THEN SHE TOOK THAT RAZOR AND WENT DOWN TO HIS J--

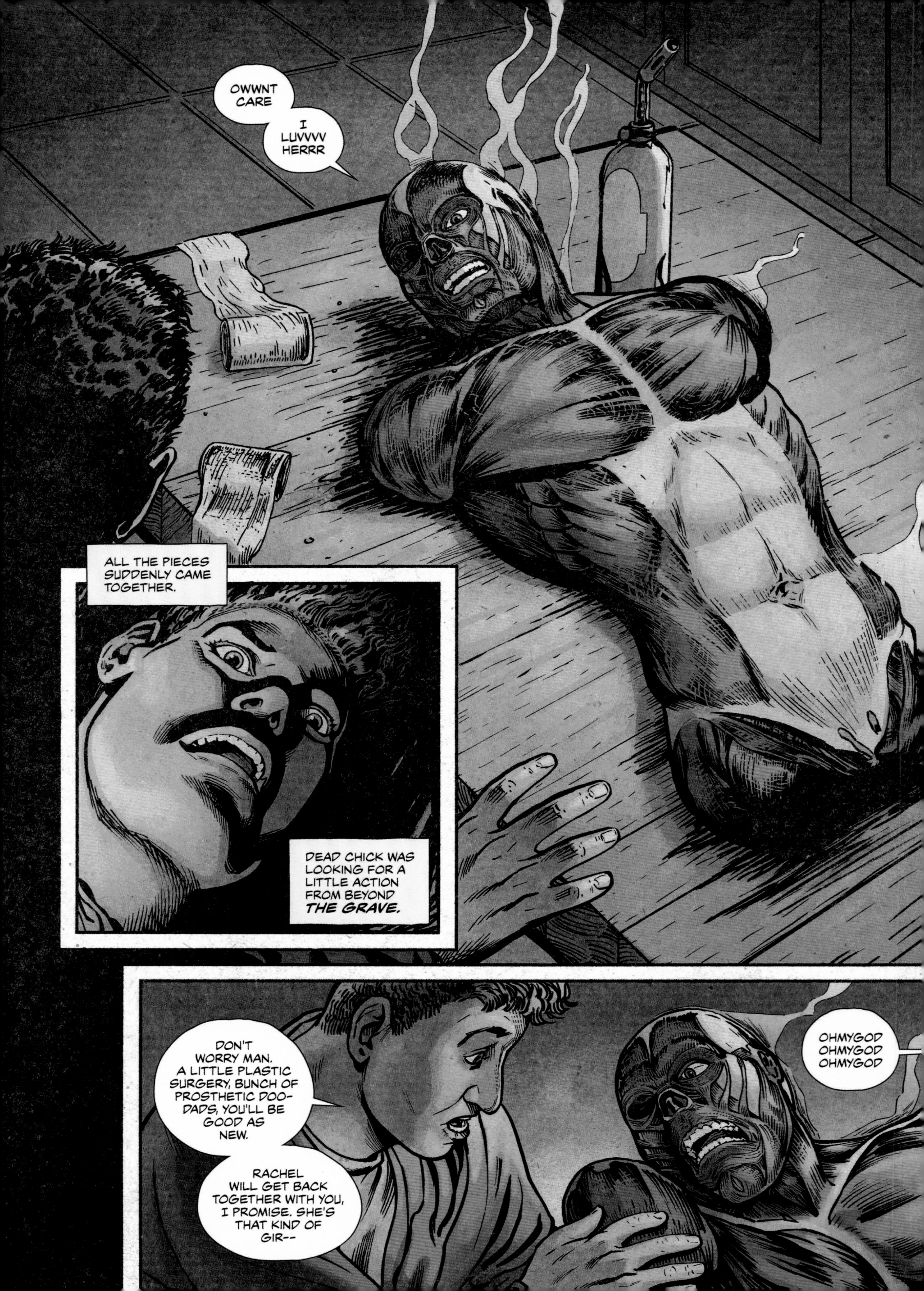
OWWNT CARE
I LUVVVV HERRR
ALL THE PIECES SUDDENLY CAME TOGETHER.
DEAD CHICK WAS LOOKING FOR A LITTLE ACTION FROM BEYOND THE GRAVE.
DON'T WORRY MAN. A LITTLE PLASTIC SURGERY, BUNCH OF PROSTHETIC DOO-DADS, YOU'LL BE GOOD AS NEW.
RACHEL WILL GET BACK TOGETHER WITH YOU, I PROMISE. SHE'S THAT KIND OF GIR--
OHMYGOD OHMYGOD OHMYGOD

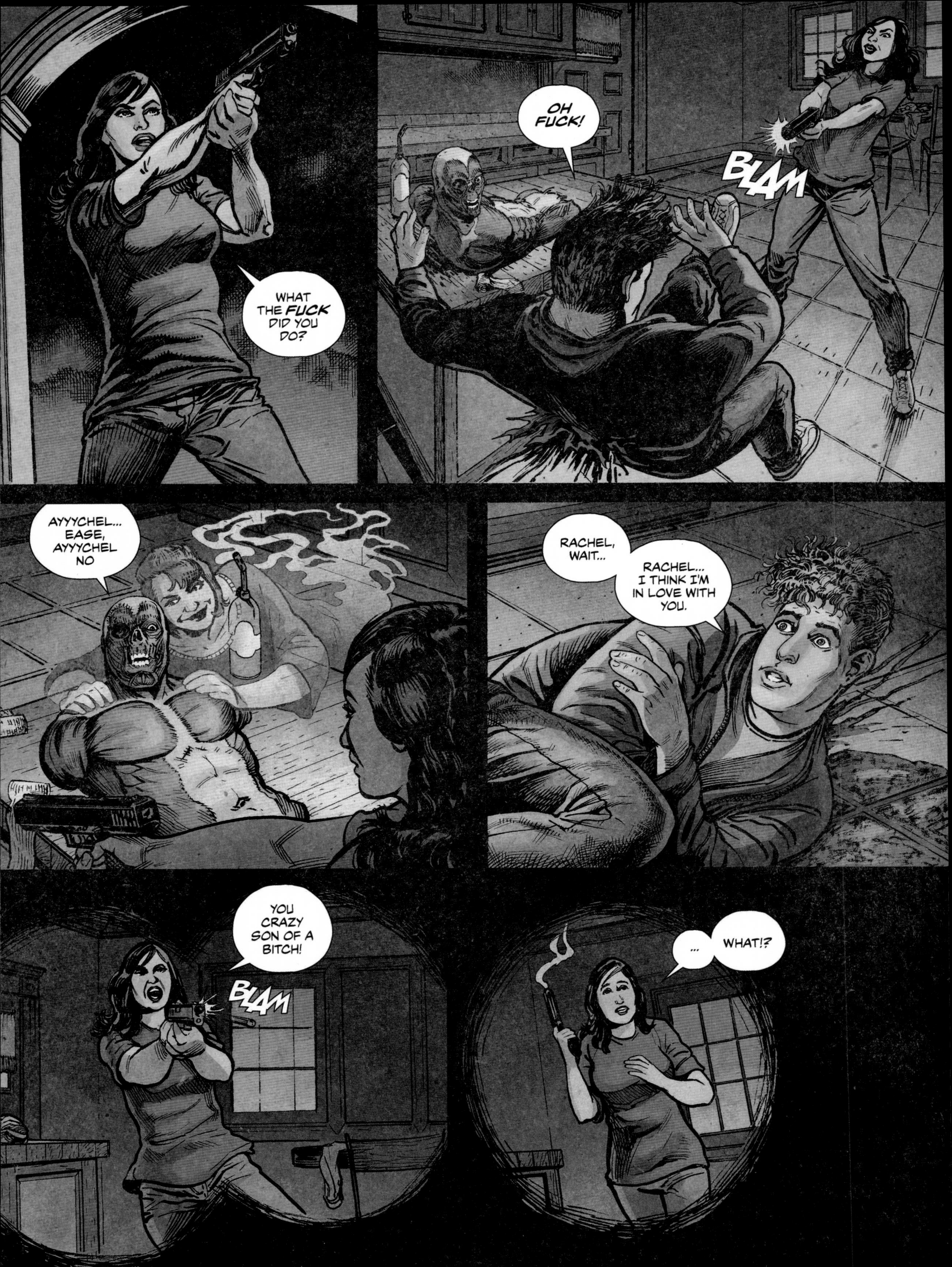
WHAT THE FUCK DID YOU DO?
OH FUCK!
BLAM
AYYYCHEL... EASE, AYYYCHEL NO
RACHEL, WAIT...
RACHEL... I THINK I'M IN LOVE WITH YOU.
YOU CRAZY SON OF A BITCH!
BLAM
...
WHAT!?

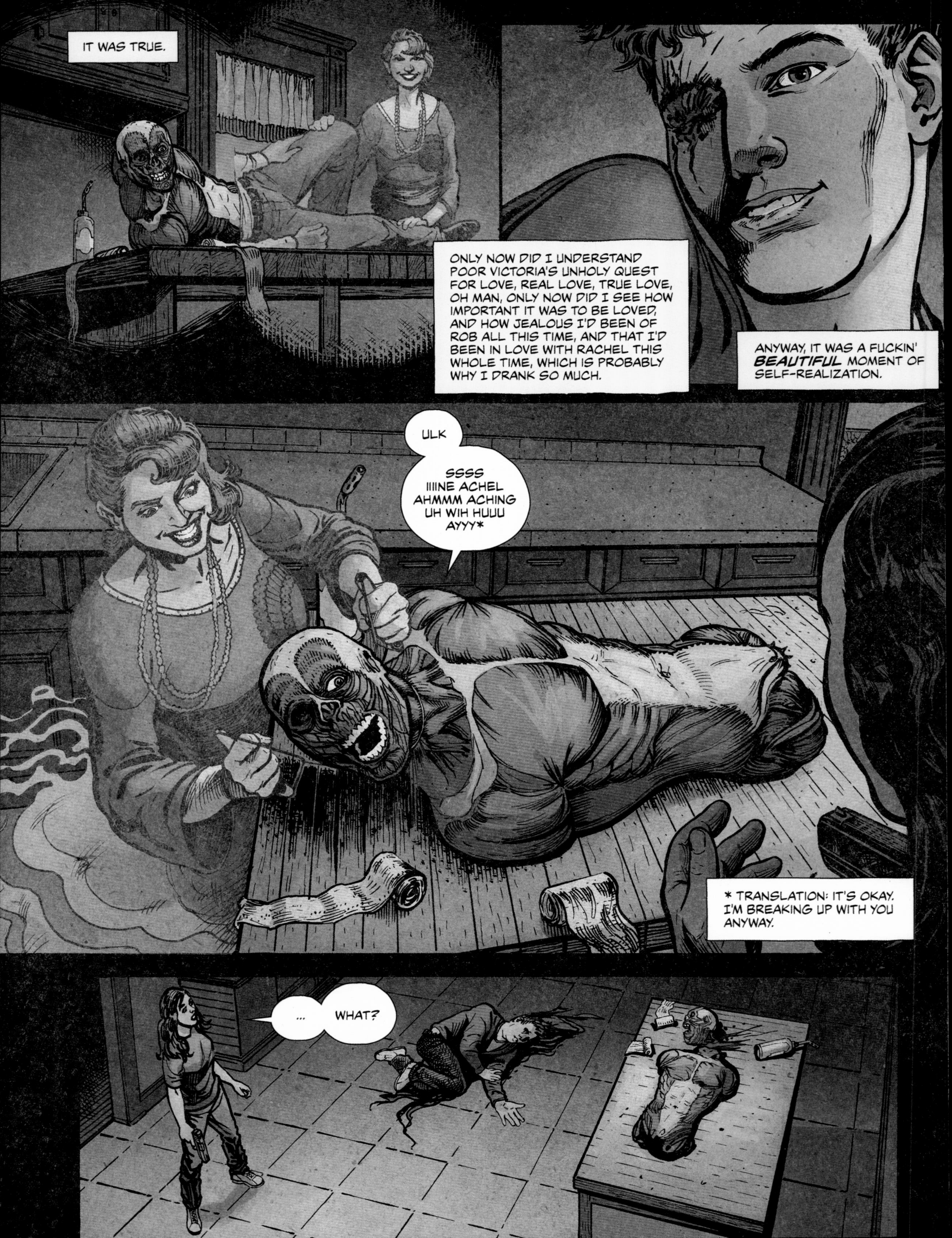
IT WAS TRUE.
ONLY NOW DID I UNDERSTAND POOR VICTORIA'S UNHOLY QUEST FOR LOVE, REAL LOVE, TRUE LOVE, OH MAN, ONLY NOW DID I SEE HOW IMPORTANT IT WAS TO BE LOVED, AND HOW JEALOUS I'D BEEN OF ROB ALL THIS TIME, AND THAT I'D BEEN IN LOVE WITH RACHEL THIS WHOLE TIME, WHICH IS PROBABLY WHY I DRANK SO MUCH.
ANYWAY, IT WAS A FUCKIN' **BEAUTIFUL** MOMENT OF SELF-REALIZATION.
ULK
SSSS IIIINE ACHEL AHMMM ACHING UH WIH HUUU AYYY*
* TRANSLATION: IT'S OKAY. I'M BREAKING UP WITH YOU ANYWAY.
...
WHAT?

HEY.

HEY.

ANYWAY, THAT'S HOW RACHEL AND I GOT TOGETHER, CRAZY AS IT SOUNDS.

I'M SUPPOSED TO LEAVE THE PATCH ALONE UNTIL I CAN BE FITTED FOR A GLASS PEEPER.

BUT SOME NIGHTS I CAN'T RESIST...

I TOLD YOU BEFORE, I'M NOT EXACTLY THE BEST FRIEND IN THE WORLD.

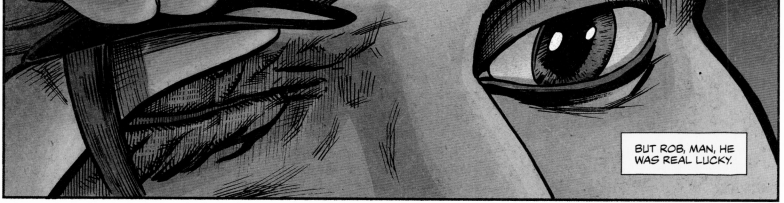

BUT ROB, MAN, HE WAS REAL LUCKY.

SHADOWS

WRITER
MATTHEW DOW SMITH

ARTIST
ALISON SAMPSON

COLORIST
IAN HERRING

LETTERER
RACHEL DEERING

I CAN FEEL HER.

IN THE DARK.

WATCHING.

WAITING.

ALWAYS WAITING.

SOMETIMES I WONDER IF SHE'S REALLY THERE.

OR IF SHE'S JUST A FIGMENT OF MY OVERBURDENED MIND.

A SHADOW CAST BY THE DARKNESS ALL AROUND ME.

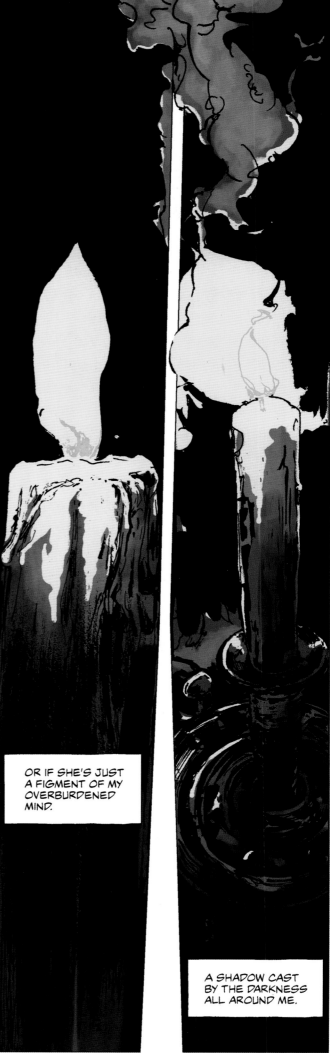

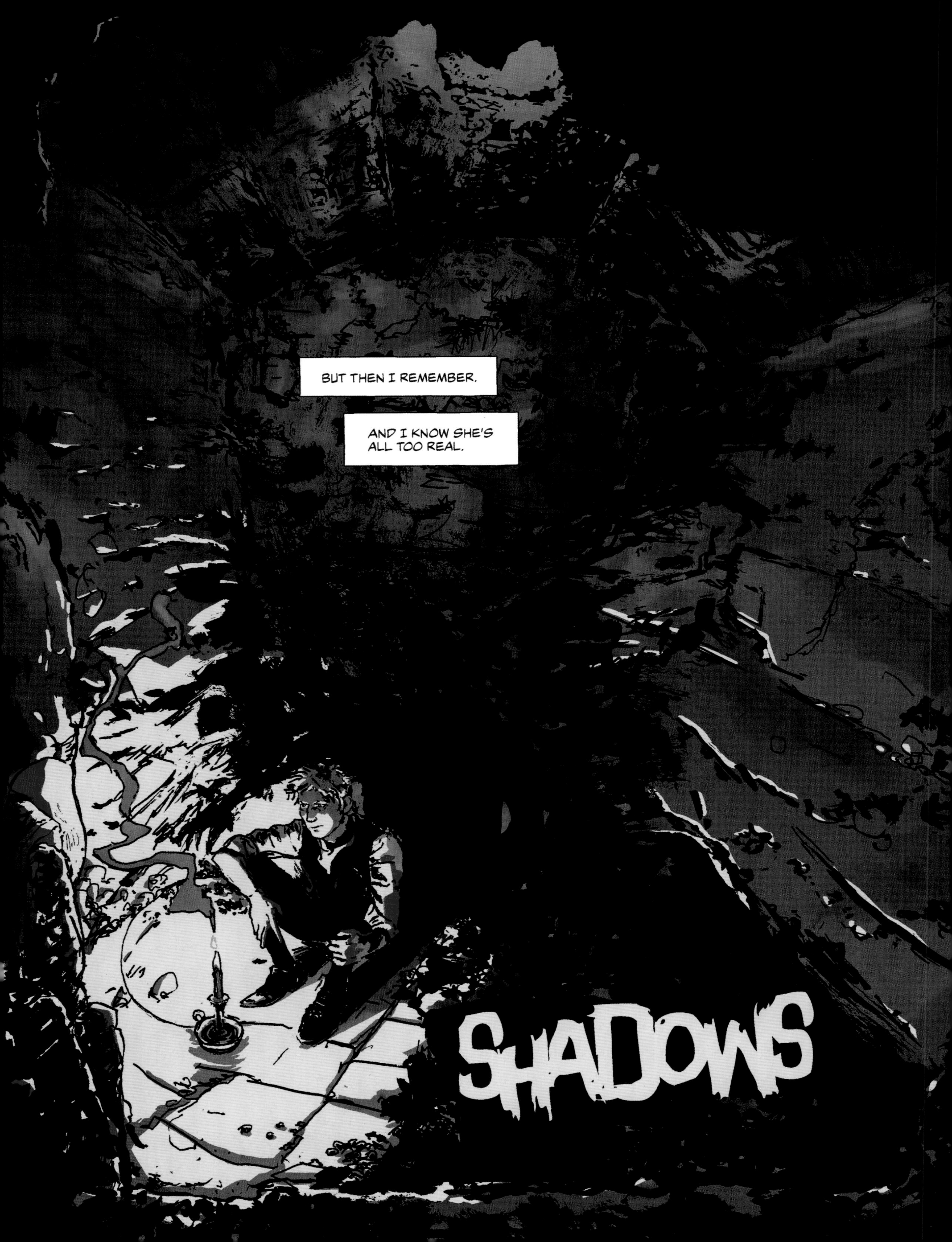
BUT THEN I REMEMBER.
AND I KNOW SHE'S ALL TOO REAL.
SHADOWS

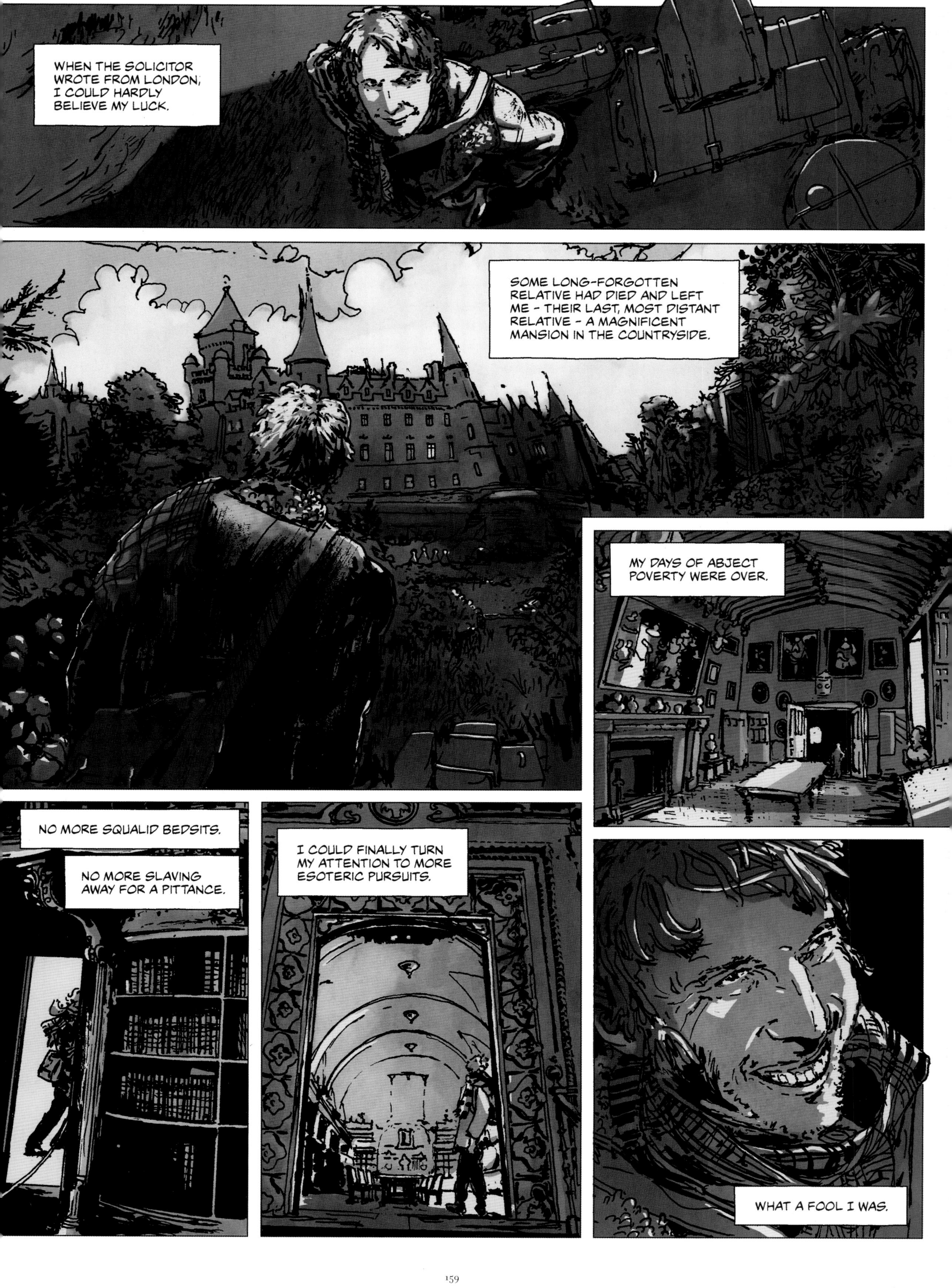
WHEN THE SOLICITOR WROTE FROM LONDON, I COULD HARDLY BELIEVE MY LUCK.
SOME LONG-FORGOTTEN RELATIVE HAD DIED AND LEFT ME - THEIR LAST, MOST DISTANT RELATIVE - A MAGNIFICENT MANSION IN THE COUNTRYSIDE.
MY DAYS OF ABJECT POVERTY WERE OVER.
NO MORE SQUALID BEDSITS.
NO MORE SLAVING AWAY FOR A PITTANCE.
I COULD FINALLY TURN MY ATTENTION TO MORE ESOTERIC PURSUITS.
WHAT A FOOL I WAS.

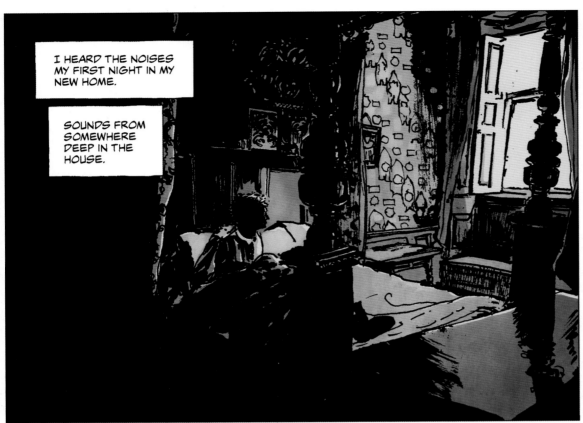

I HEARD THE NOISES MY FIRST NIGHT IN MY NEW HOME.

SOUNDS FROM SOMEWHERE DEEP IN THE HOUSE.

I WAS USED TO VERMIN.

RATS.

MICE.

THOUGH I SUSPECTED THE QUALITY OF VERMIN HERE WOULD BE SOMEWHAT HIGHER.

FOXES, PERHAPS.

OR SOMETHING EVEN MORE EXOTIC.

A SILLY THOUGHT, OF COURSE.

AND A SILENT HOPE.

I DESPERATELY WANTED IT TO BE SOMETHING MUNDANE.

ANYONE THERE?

BUT WHAT I FOUND WAS FAR FROM MUNDANE.

HELLO.

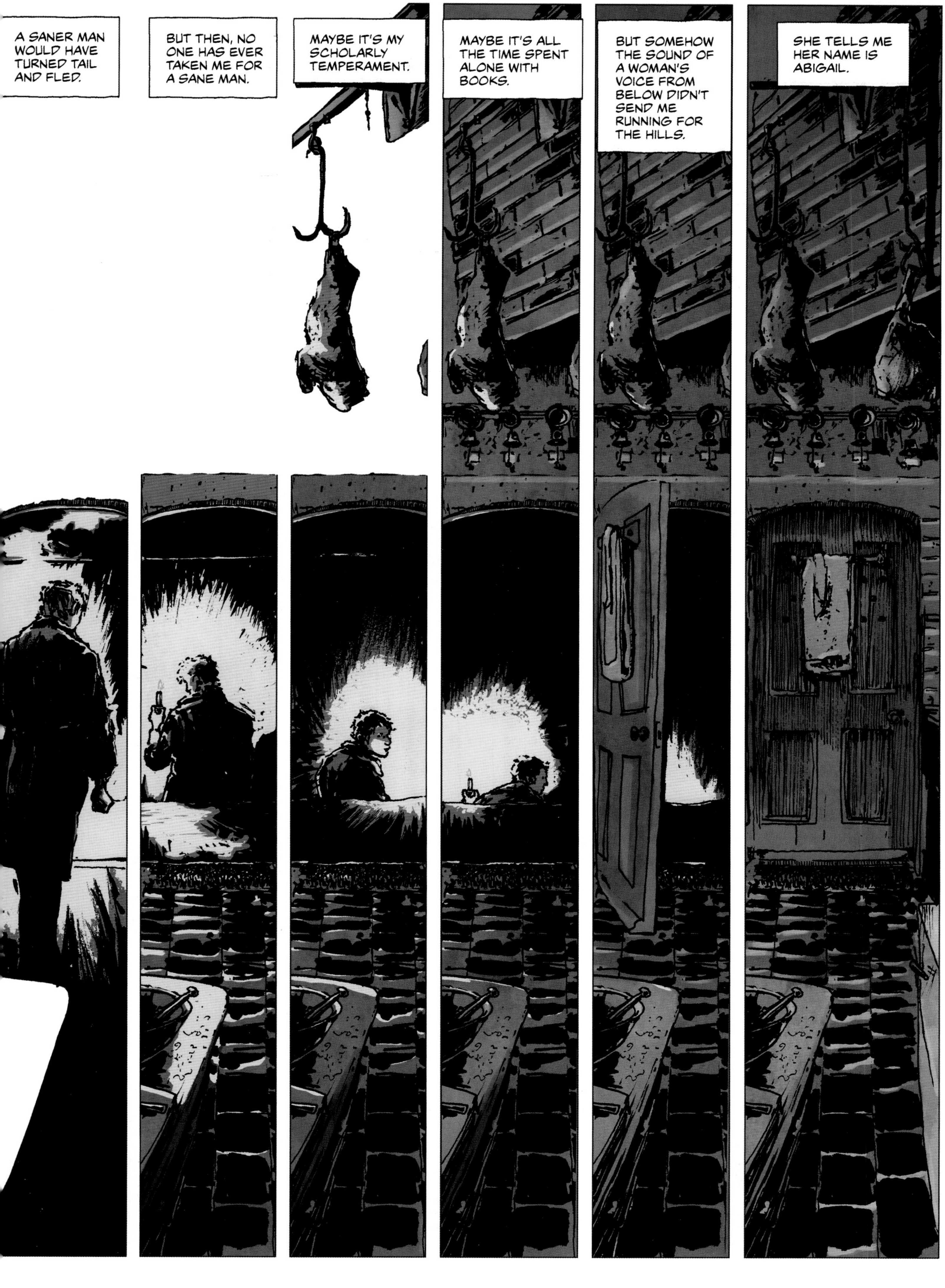
A SANER MAN WOULD HAVE TURNED TAIL AND FLED.
BUT THEN, NO ONE HAS EVER TAKEN ME FOR A SANE MAN.
MAYBE IT'S MY SCHOLARLY TEMPERAMENT.
MAYBE IT'S ALL THE TIME SPENT ALONE WITH BOOKS.
BUT SOMEHOW THE SOUND OF A WOMAN'S VOICE FROM BELOW DIDN'T SEND ME RUNNING FOR THE HILLS.
SHE TELLS ME HER NAME IS ABIGAIL.

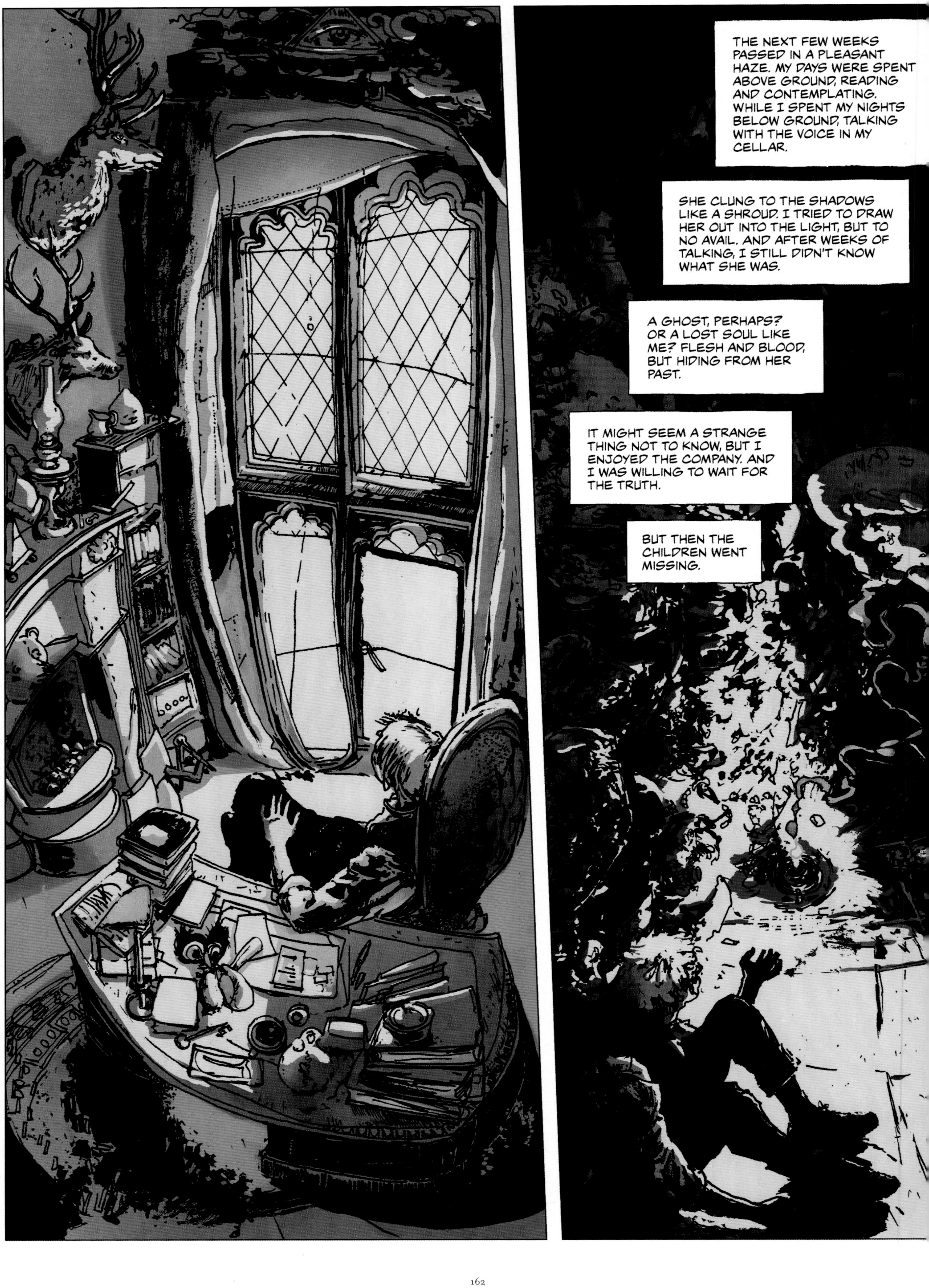
THE NEXT FEW WEEKS PASSED IN A PLEASANT HAZE. MY DAYS WERE SPENT ABOVE GROUND, READING AND CONTEMPLATING. WHILE I SPENT MY NIGHTS BELOW GROUND, TALKING WITH THE VOICE IN MY CELLAR.
SHE CLUNG TO THE SHADOWS LIKE A SHROUD. I TRIED TO DRAW HER OUT INTO THE LIGHT, BUT TO NO AVAIL. AND AFTER WEEKS OF TALKING, I STILL DIDN'T KNOW WHAT SHE WAS.
A GHOST, PERHAPS? OR A LOST SOUL LIKE ME? FLESH AND BLOOD, BUT HIDING FROM HER PAST.
IT MIGHT SEEM A STRANGE THING NOT TO KNOW, BUT I ENJOYED THE COMPANY. AND I WAS WILLING TO WAIT FOR THE TRUTH.
BUT THEN THE CHILDREN WENT MISSING.

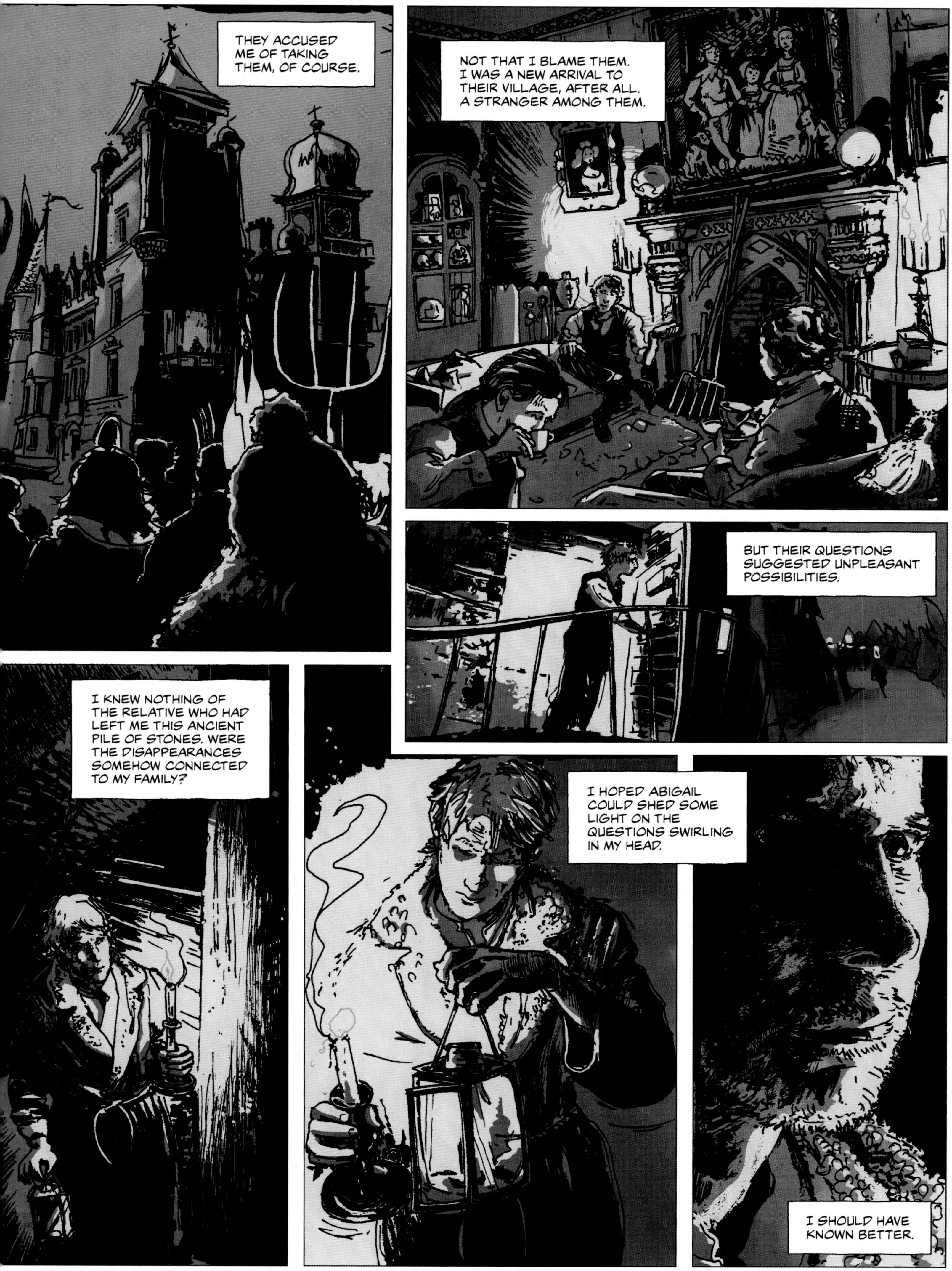
THEY ACCUSED ME OF TAKING THEM, OF COURSE.
NOT THAT I BLAME THEM. I WAS A NEW ARRIVAL TO THEIR VILLAGE, AFTER ALL. A STRANGER AMONG THEM.
BUT THEIR QUESTIONS SUGGESTED UNPLEASANT POSSIBILITIES.
I KNEW NOTHING OF THE RELATIVE WHO HAD LEFT ME THIS ANCIENT PILE OF STONES. WERE THE DISAPPEARANCES SOMEHOW CONNECTED TO MY FAMILY?
I HOPED ABIGAIL COULD SHED SOME LIGHT ON THE QUESTIONS SWIRLING IN MY HEAD.
I SHOULD HAVE KNOWN BETTER.

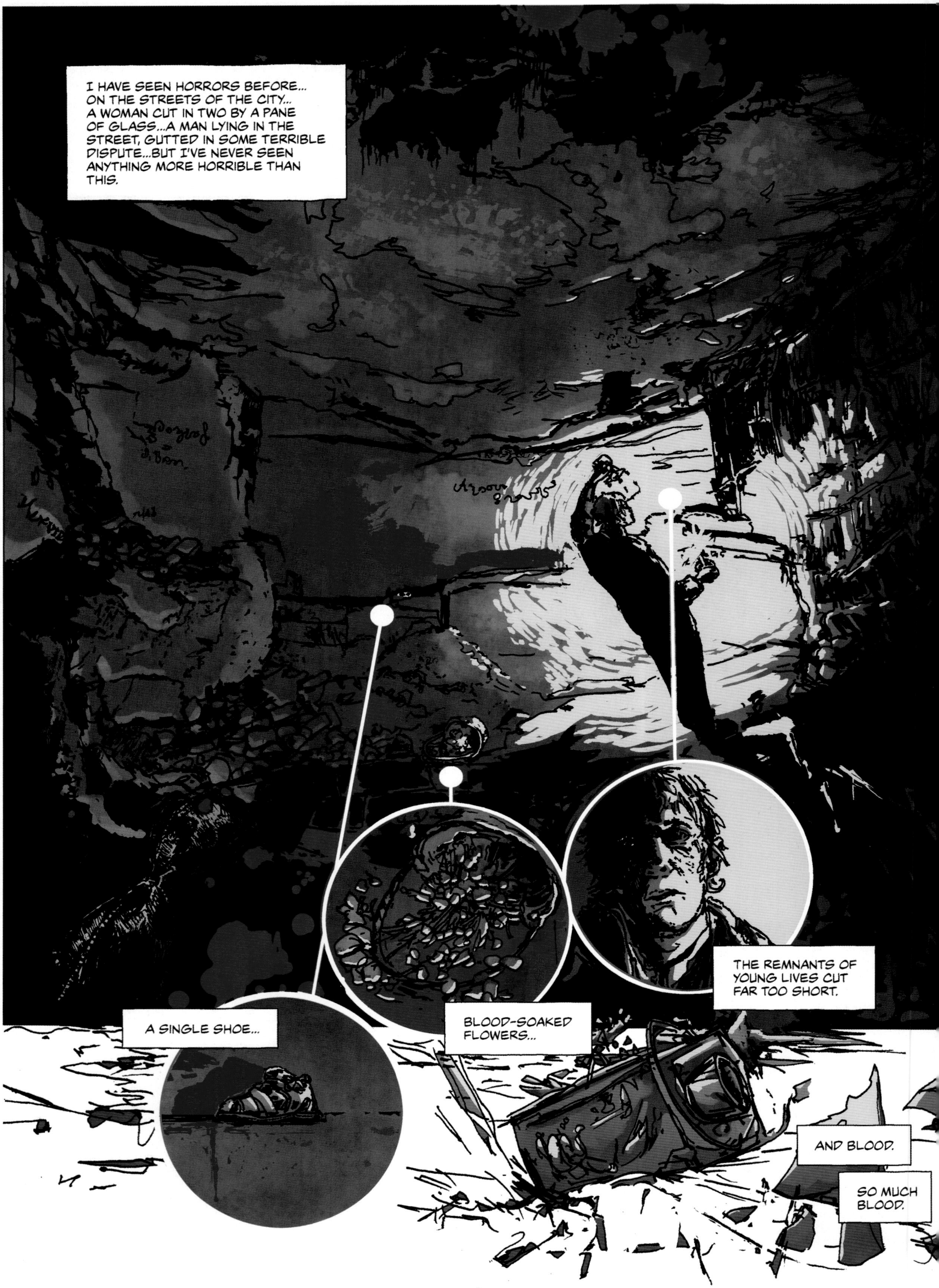
I HAVE SEEN HORRORS BEFORE... ON THE STREETS OF THE CITY... A WOMAN CUT IN TWO BY A PANE OF GLASS...A MAN LYING IN THE STREET, GUTTED IN SOME TERRIBLE DISPUTE...BUT I'VE NEVER SEEN ANYTHING MORE HORRIBLE THAN THIS.
A SINGLE SHOE...
BLOOD-SOAKED FLOWERS...
THE REMNANTS OF YOUNG LIVES CUT FAR TOO SHORT.
AND BLOOD.
SO MUCH BLOOD.

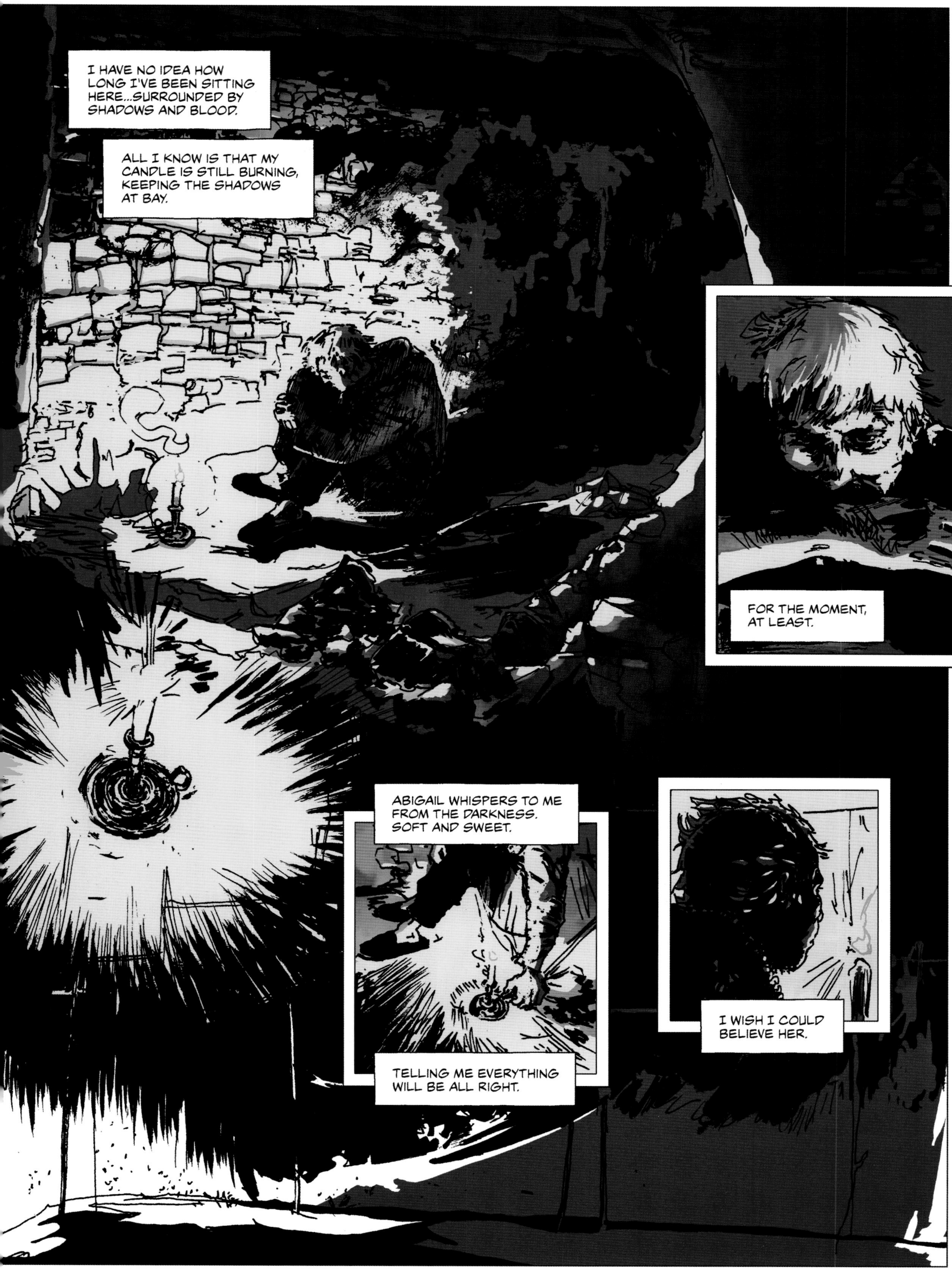
I HAVE NO IDEA HOW LONG I'VE BEEN SITTING HERE...SURROUNDED BY SHADOWS AND BLOOD.
ALL I KNOW IS THAT MY CANDLE IS STILL BURNING, KEEPING THE SHADOWS AT BAY.
FOR THE MOMENT, AT LEAST.
ABIGAIL WHISPERS TO ME FROM THE DARKNESS. SOFT AND SWEET.
TELLING ME EVERYTHING WILL BE ALL RIGHT.
I WISH I COULD BELIEVE HER.

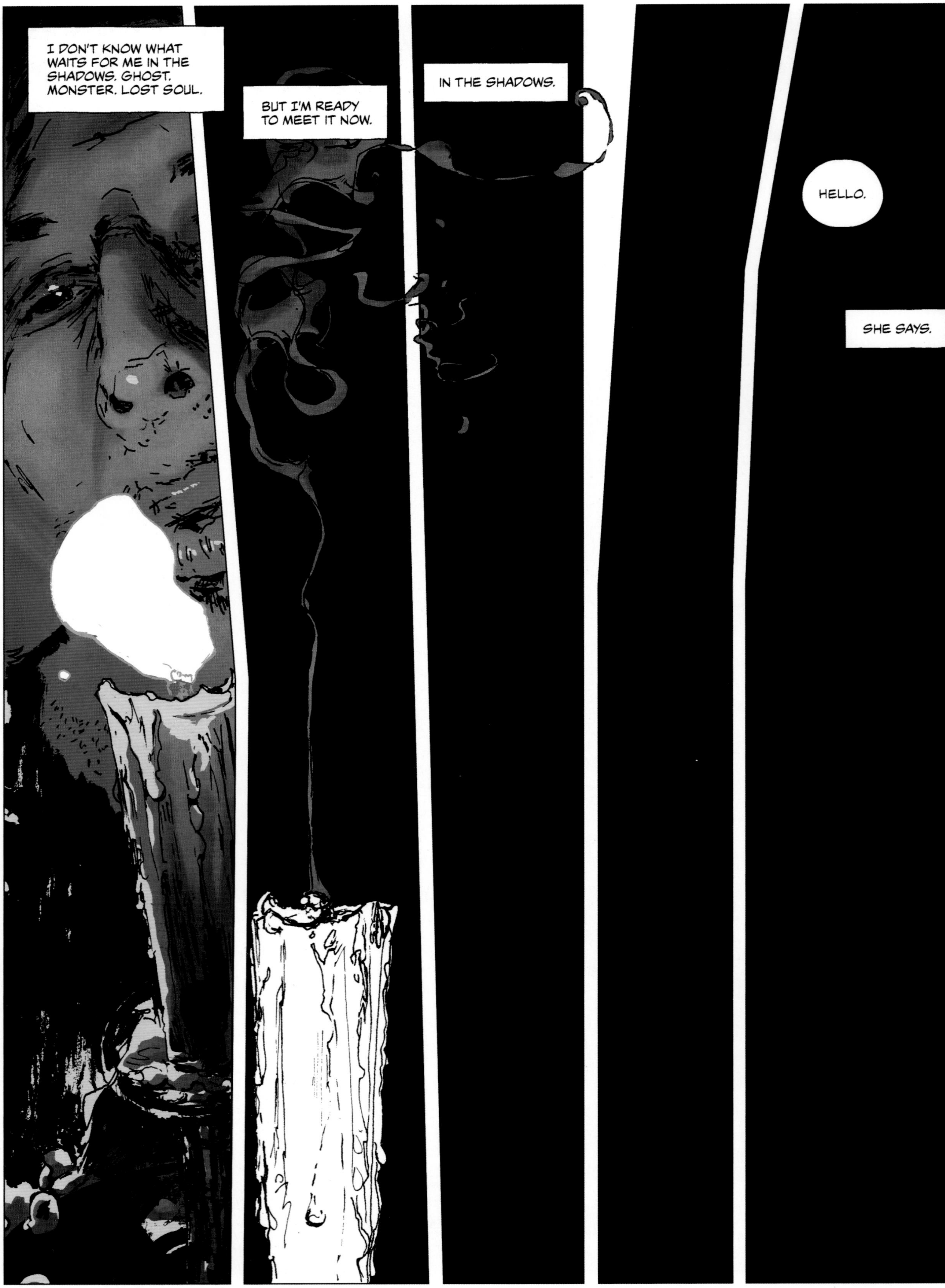
I DON'T KNOW WHAT WAITS FOR ME IN THE SHADOWS. GHOST. MONSTER. LOST SOUL.
BUT I'M READY TO MEET IT NOW.
IN THE SHADOWS.
HELLO.
SHE SAYS.

DOC JOHNSON

WRITER
F. PAUL WILSON

ARTIST
MATTHEW DOW SMITH

COLORIST
THOMAS BOATWRIGHT

LETTERER
RACHEL DEERING

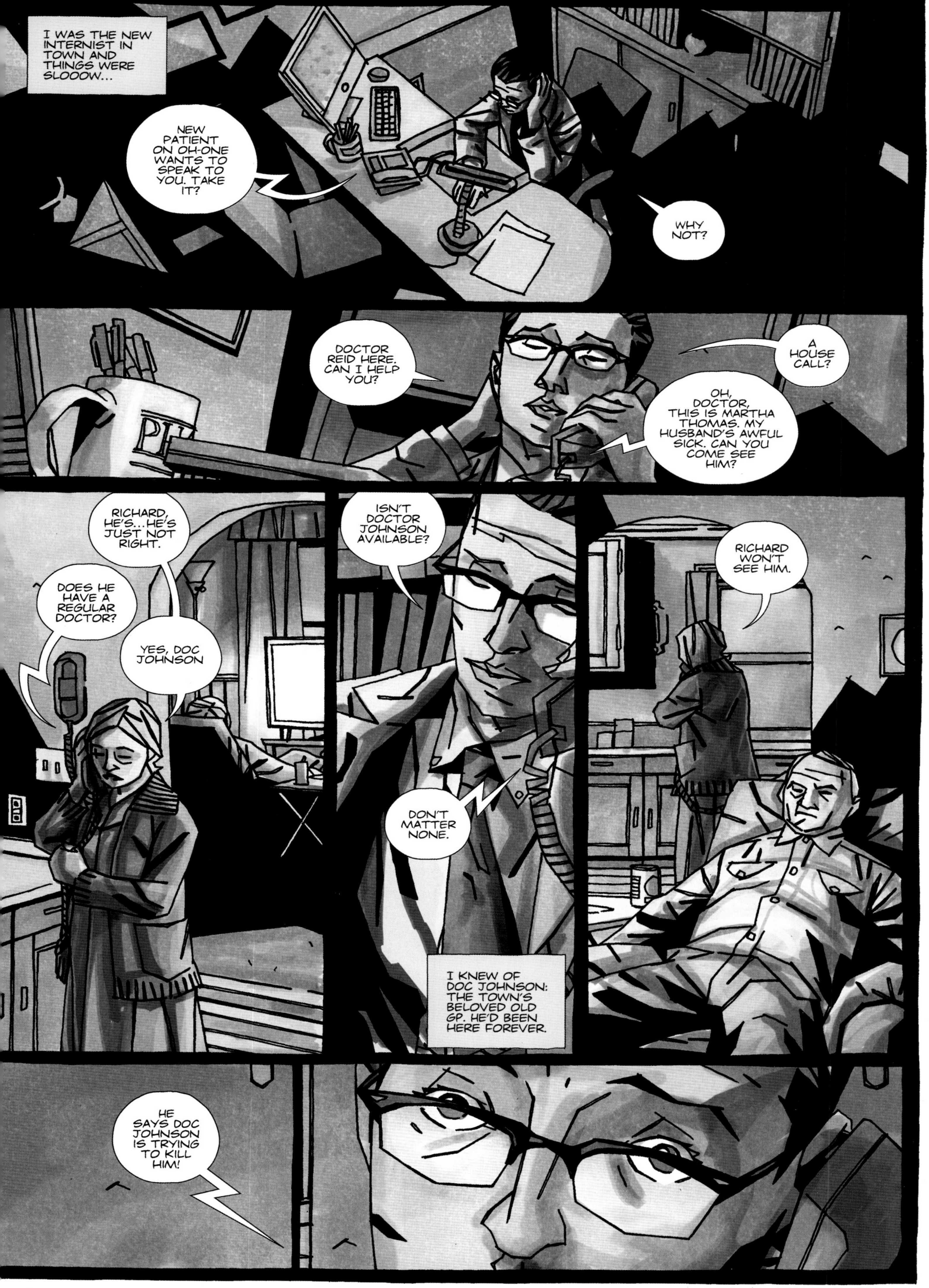
I WAS THE NEW INTERNIST IN TOWN AND THINGS WERE SLOOOW...
NEW PATIENT ON OH-ONE WANTS TO SPEAK TO YOU. TAKE IT?
WHY NOT?
DOCTOR REID HERE. CAN I HELP YOU?
OH, DOCTOR, THIS IS MARTHA THOMAS. MY HUSBAND'S AWFUL SICK. CAN YOU COME SEE HIM?
A HOUSE CALL?
RICHARD, HE'S...HE'S JUST NOT RIGHT.
DOES HE HAVE A REGULAR DOCTOR?
YES, DOC JOHNSON
ISN'T DOCTOR JOHNSON AVAILABLE?
RICHARD WON'T SEE HIM.
DON'T MATTER NONE.
I KNEW OF DOC JOHNSON: THE TOWN'S BELOVED OLD GP. HE'D BEEN HERE FOREVER.
HE SAYS DOC JOHNSON IS TRYING TO KILL HIM!

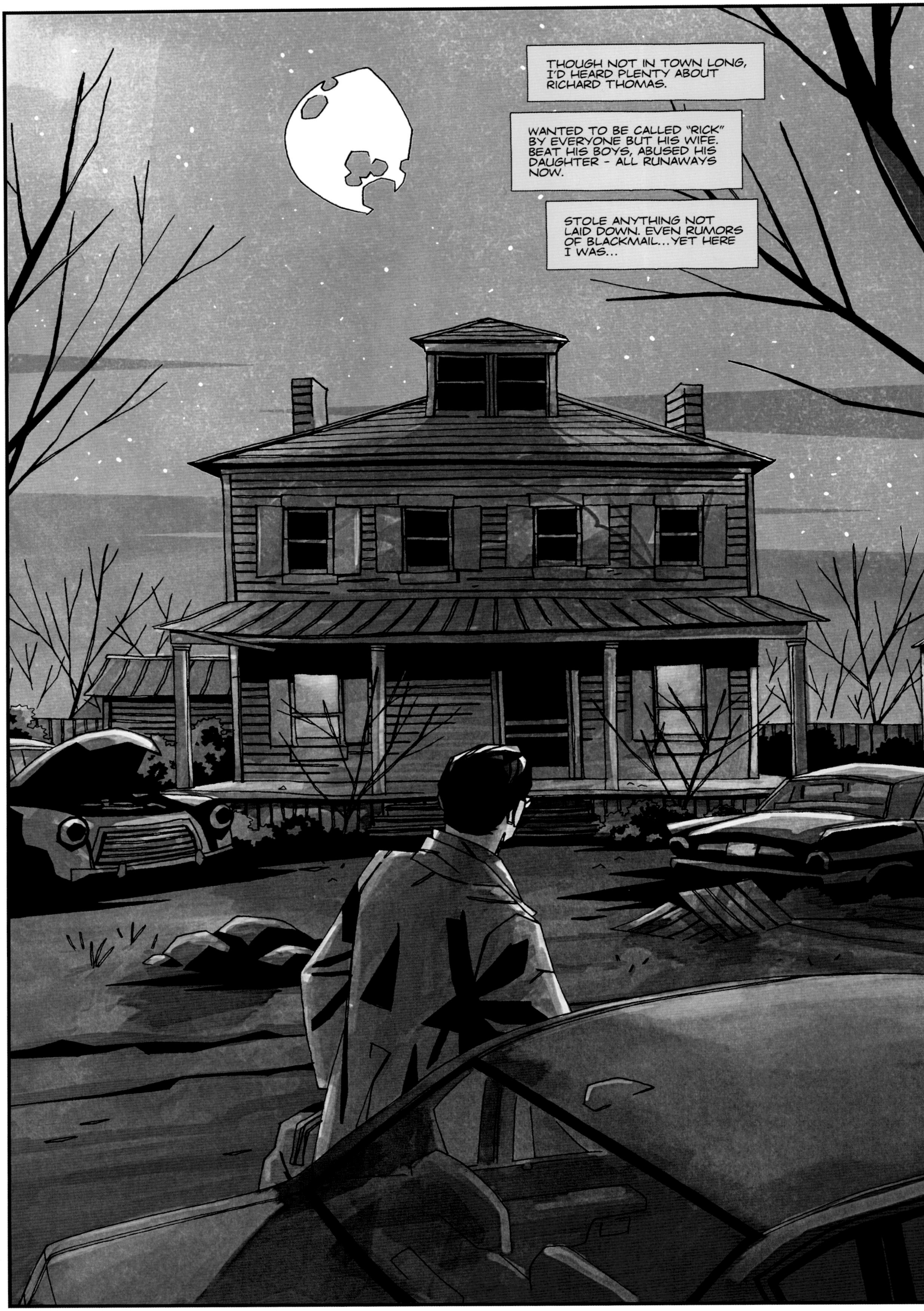
THOUGH NOT IN TOWN LONG, I'D HEARD PLENTY ABOUT RICHARD THOMAS.
WANTED TO BE CALLED "RICK" BY EVERYONE BUT HIS WIFE. BEAT HIS BOYS, ABUSED HIS DAUGHTER - ALL RUNAWAYS NOW.
STOLE ANYTHING NOT LAID DOWN. EVEN RUMORS OF BLACKMAIL...YET HERE I WAS...

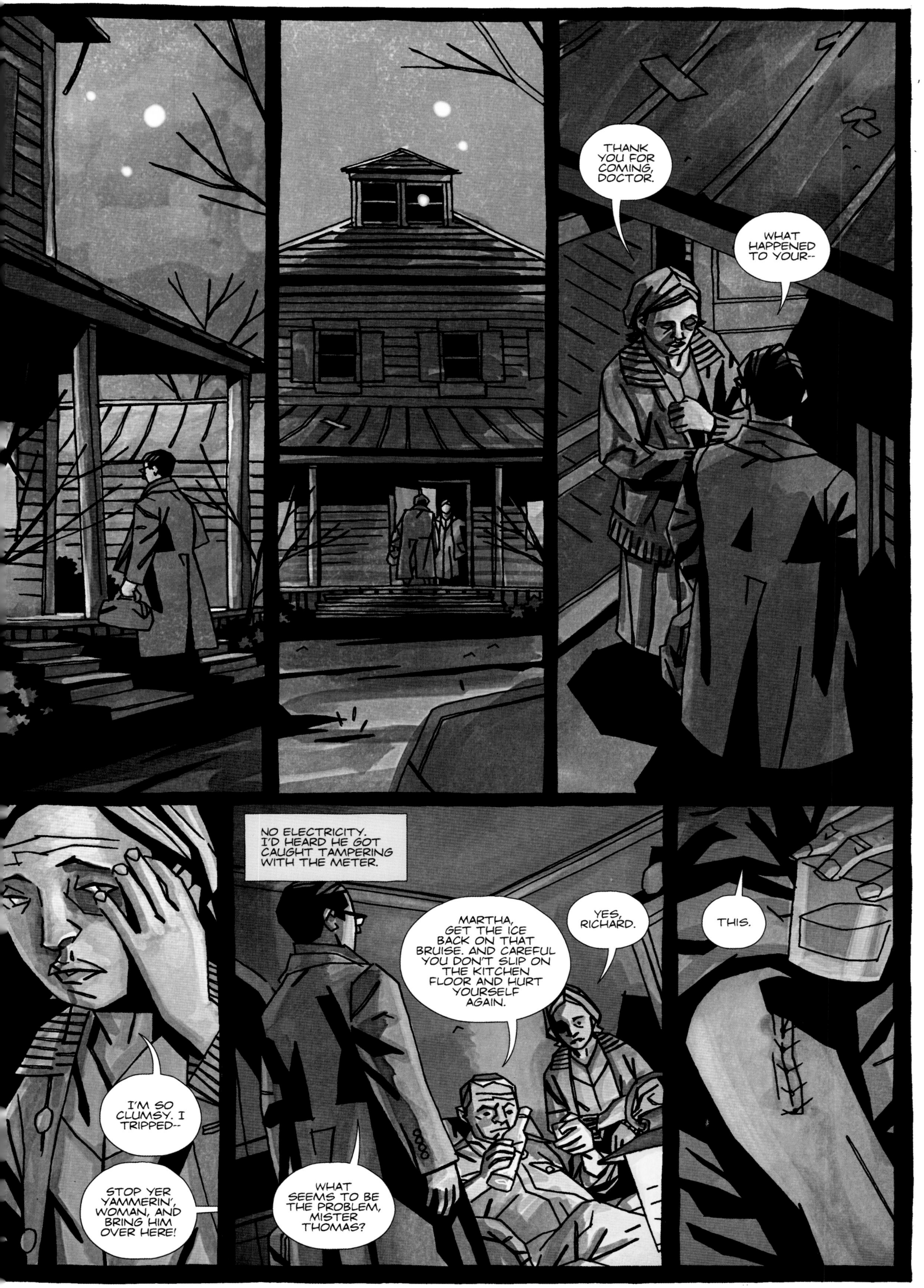
THANK YOU FOR COMING, DOCTOR.
WHAT HAPPENED TO YOUR--
I'M SO CLUMSY. I TRIPPED--
STOP YER YAMMERIN', WOMAN, AND BRING HIM OVER HERE!
NO ELECTRICITY. I'D HEARD HE GOT CAUGHT TAMPERING WITH THE METER.
WHAT SEEMS TO BE THE PROBLEM, MISTER THOMAS?
MARTHA, GET THE ICE BACK ON THAT BRUISE. AND CAREFUL YOU DON'T SLIP ON THE KITCHEN FLOOR AND HURT YOURSELF AGAIN.
YES, RICHARD.
THIS.

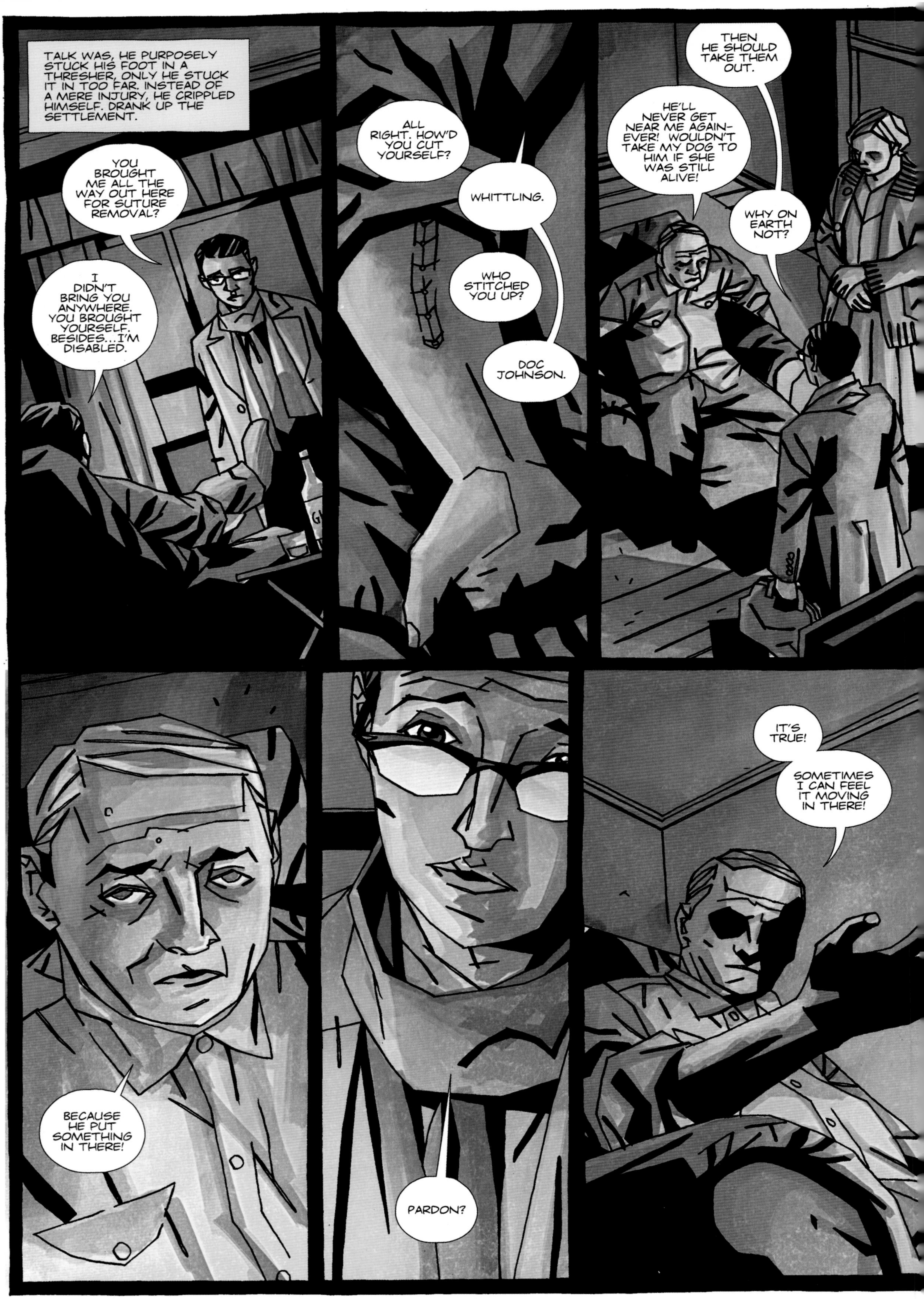
TALK WAS, HE PURPOSELY STUCK HIS FOOT IN A THRESHER, ONLY HE STUCK IT IN TOO FAR. INSTEAD OF A MERE INJURY, HE CRIPPLED HIMSELF. DRANK UP THE SETTLEMENT.
YOU BROUGHT ME ALL THE WAY OUT HERE FOR SUTURE REMOVAL?
I DIDN'T BRING YOU ANYWHERE. YOU BROUGHT YOURSELF. BESIDES... I'M DISABLED.
ALL RIGHT. HOW'D YOU CUT YOURSELF?
WHITTLING.
WHO STITCHED YOU UP?
DOC JOHNSON.
THEN HE SHOULD TAKE THEM OUT.
HE'LL NEVER GET NEAR ME AGAIN-EVER! WOULDN'T TAKE MY DOG TO HIM IF SHE WAS STILL ALIVE!
WHY ON EARTH NOT?
BECAUSE HE PUT SOMETHING IN THERE!
PARDON?
IT'S TRUE!
SOMETIMES I CAN FEEL IT MOVING IN THERE!

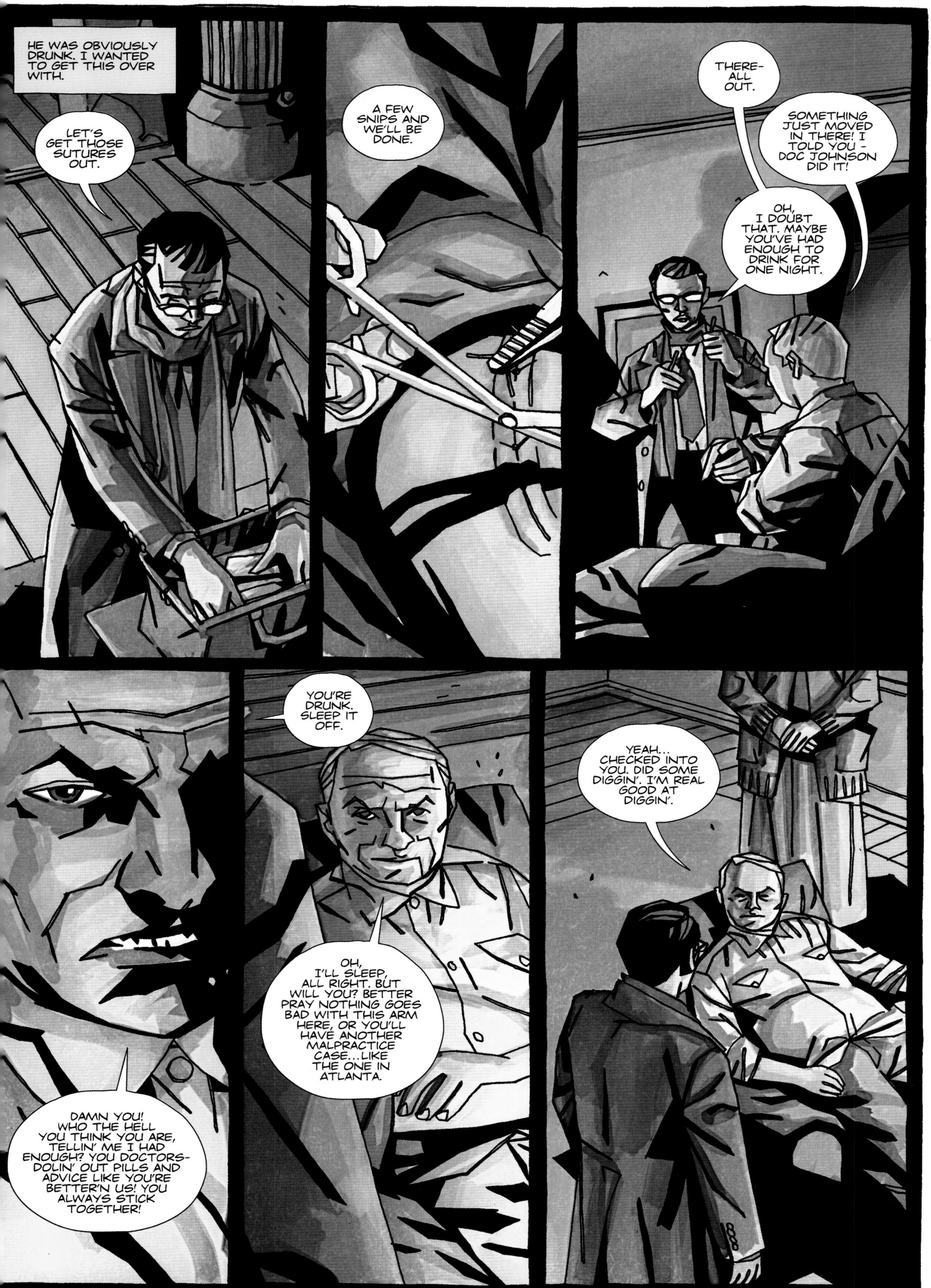
HE WAS OBVIOUSLY DRUNK. I WANTED TO GET THIS OVER WITH.
LET'S GET THOSE SUTURES OUT.
A FEW SNIPS AND WE'LL BE DONE.
THERE- ALL OUT.
SOMETHING JUST MOVED IN THERE! I TOLD YOU - DOC JOHNSON DID IT!
OH, I DOUBT THAT. MAYBE YOU'VE HAD ENOUGH TO DRINK FOR ONE NIGHT.
DAMN YOU! WHO THE HELL YOU THINK YOU ARE, TELLIN' ME I HAD ENOUGH? YOU DOCTORS- DOLIN' OUT PILLS AND ADVICE LIKE YOU'RE BETTER'N US! YOU ALWAYS STICK TOGETHER!
YOU'RE DRUNK. SLEEP IT OFF.
OH, I'LL SLEEP, ALL RIGHT. BUT WILL YOU? BETTER PRAY NOTHING GOES BAD WITH THIS ARM HERE, OR YOU'LL HAVE ANOTHER MALPRACTICE CASE...LIKE THE ONE IN ATLANTA.
YEAH... CHECKED INTO YOU. DID SOME DIGGIN'. I'M REAL GOOD AT DIGGIN'.

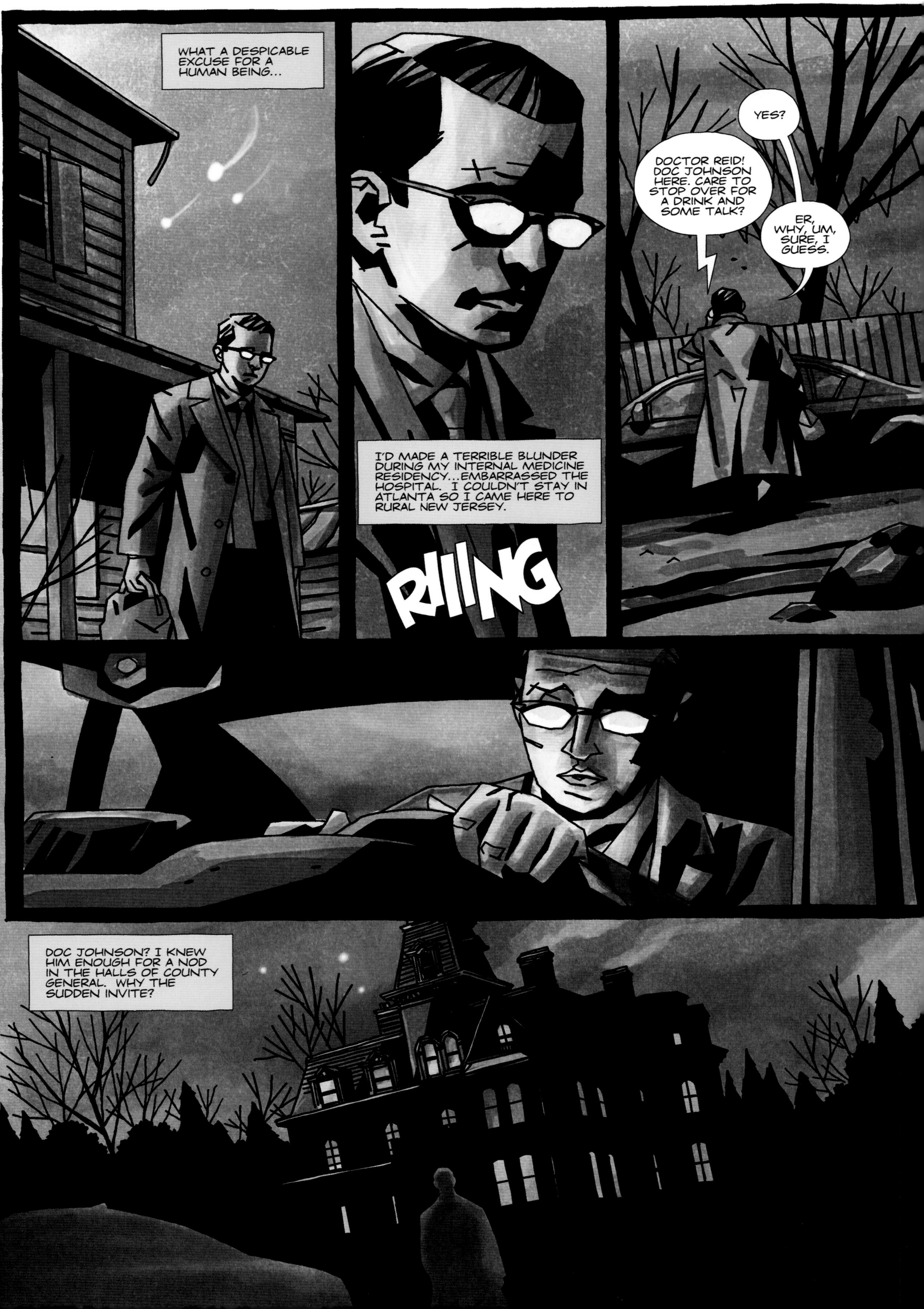
WHAT A DESPICABLE EXCUSE FOR A HUMAN BEING...
I'D MADE A TERRIBLE BLUNDER DURING MY INTERNAL MEDICINE RESIDENCY...EMBARRASSED THE HOSPITAL. I COULDN'T STAY IN ATLANTA SO I CAME HERE TO RURAL NEW JERSEY.
RIIING
YES?
DOCTOR REID! DOC JOHNSON HERE. CARE TO STOP OVER FOR A DRINK AND SOME TALK?
ER, WHY, UM, SURE, I GUESS.
DOC JOHNSON? I KNEW HIM ENOUGH FOR A NOD IN THE HALLS OF COUNTY GENERAL. WHY THE SUDDEN INVITE?

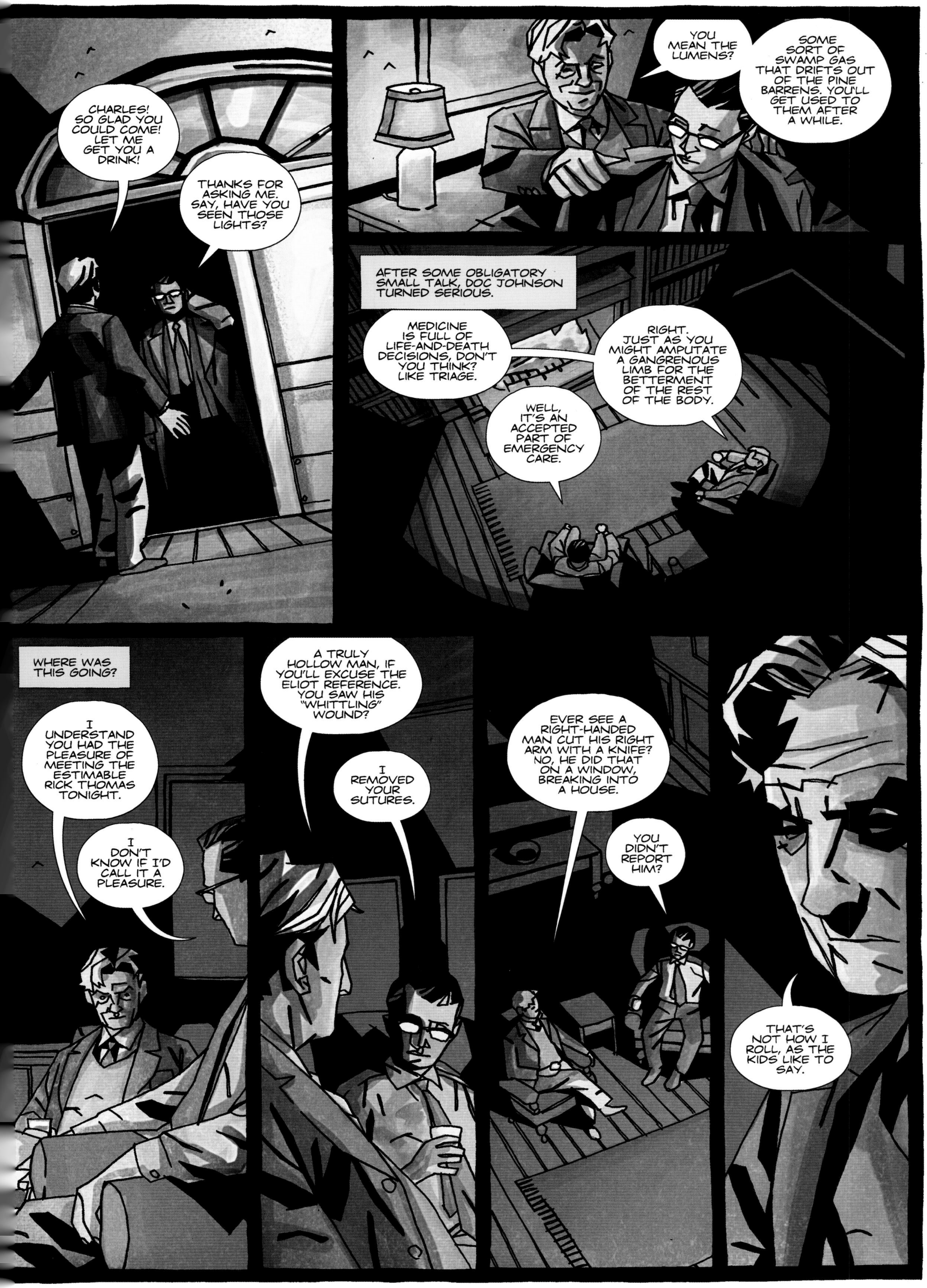
CHARLES! SO GLAD YOU COULD COME! LET ME GET YOU A DRINK!
THANKS FOR ASKING ME. SAY, HAVE YOU SEEN THOSE LIGHTS?
YOU MEAN THE LUMENS?
SOME SORT OF SWAMP GAS THAT DRIFTS OUT OF THE PINE BARRENS. YOU'LL GET USED TO THEM AFTER A WHILE.
AFTER SOME OBLIGATORY SMALL TALK, DOC JOHNSON TURNED SERIOUS.
MEDICINE IS FULL OF LIFE-AND-DEATH DECISIONS, DON'T YOU THINK? LIKE TRIAGE.
WELL, IT'S AN ACCEPTED PART OF EMERGENCY CARE.
RIGHT. JUST AS YOU MIGHT AMPUTATE A GANGRENOUS LIMB FOR THE BETTERMENT OF THE REST OF THE BODY.
WHERE WAS THIS GOING?
I UNDERSTAND YOU HAD THE PLEASURE OF MEETING THE ESTIMABLE RICK THOMAS TONIGHT.
I DON'T KNOW IF I'D CALL IT A PLEASURE.
A TRULY HOLLOW MAN, IF YOU'LL EXCUSE THE ELIOT REFERENCE. YOU SAW HIS "WHITTLING" WOUND?
I REMOVED YOUR SUTURES.
EVER SEE A RIGHT-HANDED MAN CUT HIS RIGHT ARM WITH A KNIFE? NO, HE DID THAT ON A WINDOW, BREAKING INTO A HOUSE.
YOU DIDN'T REPORT HIM?
THAT'S NOT HOW I ROLL, AS THE KIDS LIKE TO SAY.

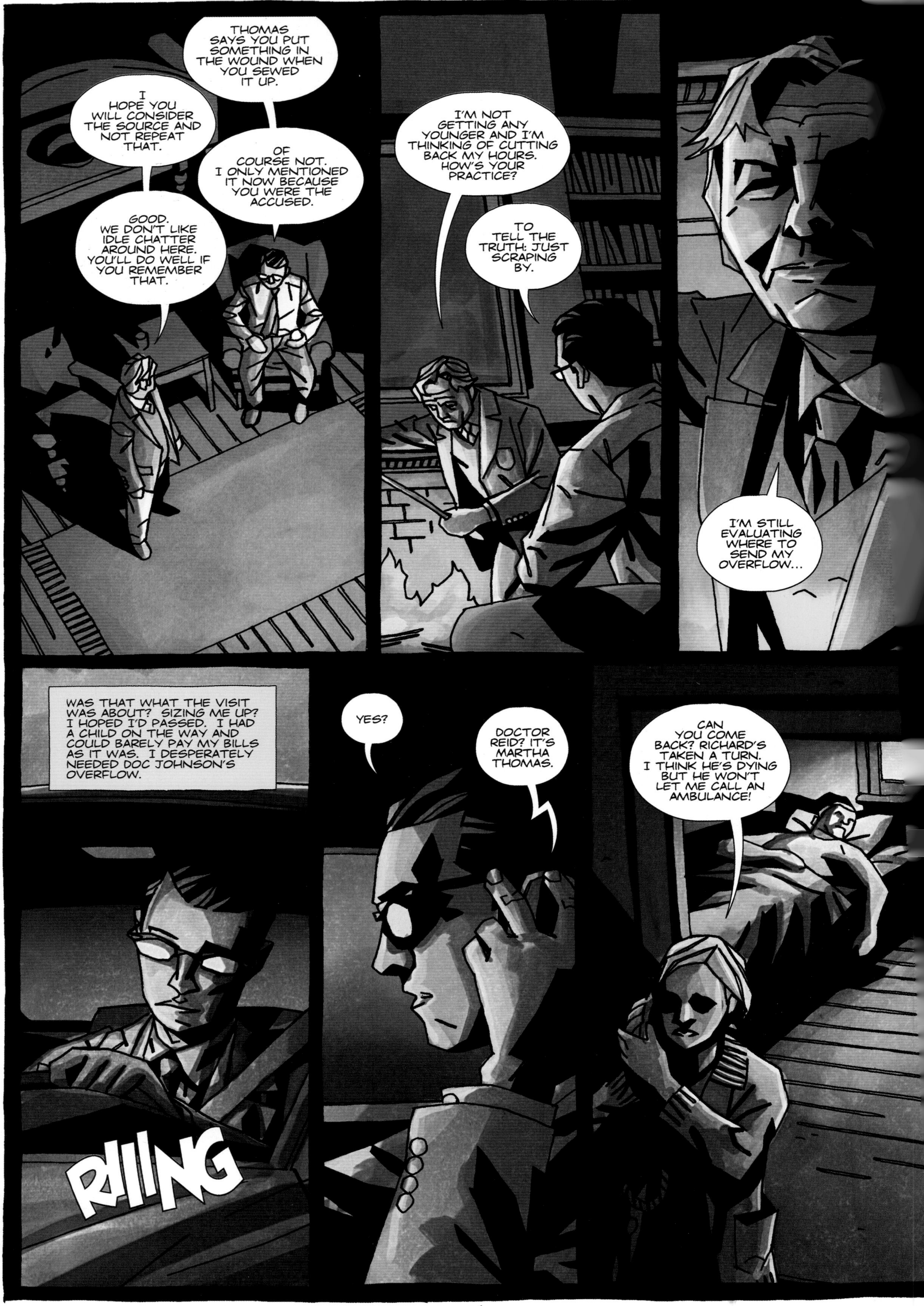
I HOPE YOU WILL CONSIDER THE SOURCE AND NOT REPEAT THAT.
THOMAS SAYS YOU PUT SOMETHING IN THE WOUND WHEN YOU SEWED IT UP.
OF COURSE NOT. I ONLY MENTIONED IT NOW BECAUSE YOU WERE THE ACCUSED.
GOOD. WE DON'T LIKE IDLE CHATTER AROUND HERE. YOU'LL DO WELL IF YOU REMEMBER THAT.
I'M NOT GETTING ANY YOUNGER AND I'M THINKING OF CUTTING BACK MY HOURS. HOW'S YOUR PRACTICE?
TO TELL THE TRUTH: JUST SCRAPING BY.
I'M STILL EVALUATING WHERE TO SEND MY OVERFLOW...
WAS THAT WHAT THE VISIT WAS ABOUT? SIZING ME UP? I HOPED I'D PASSED. I HAD A CHILD ON THE WAY AND COULD BARELY PAY MY BILLS AS IT WAS. I DESPERATELY NEEDED DOC JOHNSON'S OVERFLOW.
RIIING
YES?
DOCTOR REID? IT'S MARTHA THOMAS.
CAN YOU COME BACK? RICHARD'S TAKEN A TURN. I THINK HE'S DYING BUT HE WON'T LET ME CALL AN AMBULANCE!

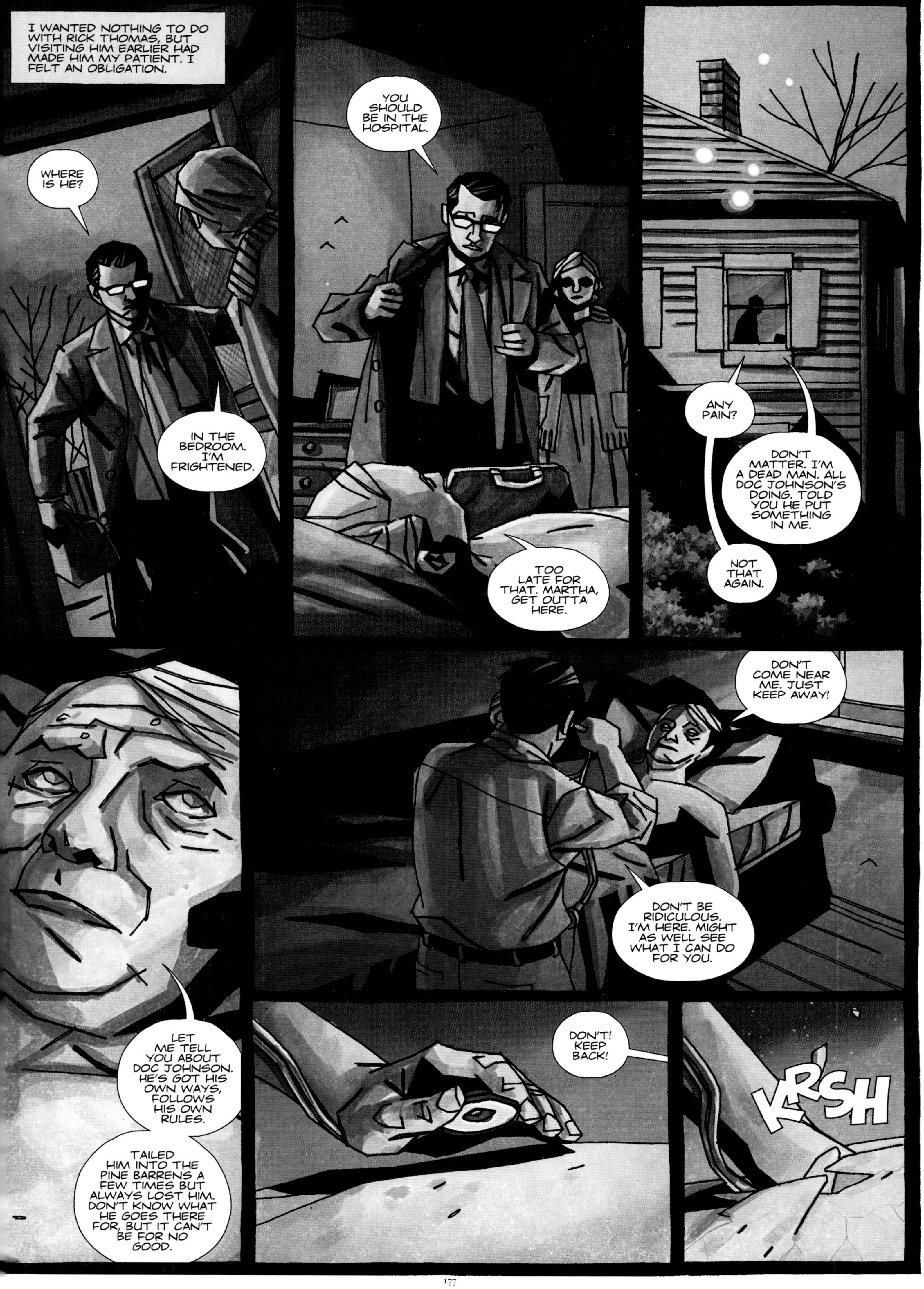
I WANTED NOTHING TO DO WITH RICK THOMAS, BUT VISITING HIM EARLIER HAD MADE HIM MY PATIENT. I FELT AN OBLIGATION.
WHERE IS HE?
IN THE BEDROOM. I'M FRIGHTENED.
YOU SHOULD BE IN THE HOSPITAL.
TOO LATE FOR THAT. MARTHA, GET OUTTA HERE.
ANY PAIN?
DON'T MATTER. I'M A DEAD MAN. ALL DOC JOHNSON'S DOING. TOLD YOU HE PUT SOMETHING IN ME.
NOT THAT AGAIN.
LET ME TELL YOU ABOUT DOC JOHNSON. HE'S GOT HIS OWN WAYS, FOLLOWS HIS OWN RULES.
TAILED HIM INTO THE PINE BARRENS A FEW TIMES BUT ALWAYS LOST HIM. DON'T KNOW WHAT HE GOES THERE FOR, BUT IT CAN'T BE FOR NO GOOD.
DON'T COME NEAR ME. JUST KEEP AWAY!
DON'T BE RIDICULOUS. I'M HERE. MIGHT AS WELL SEE WHAT I CAN DO FOR YOU.
DON'T! KEEP BACK!
KRSH

NOW YOU'VE DONE IT.

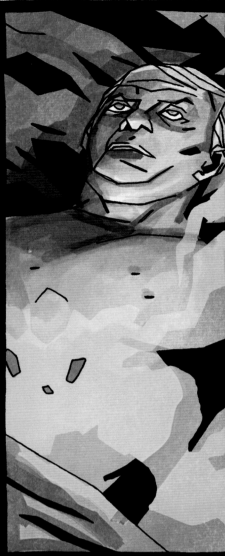

BANG

KRSH

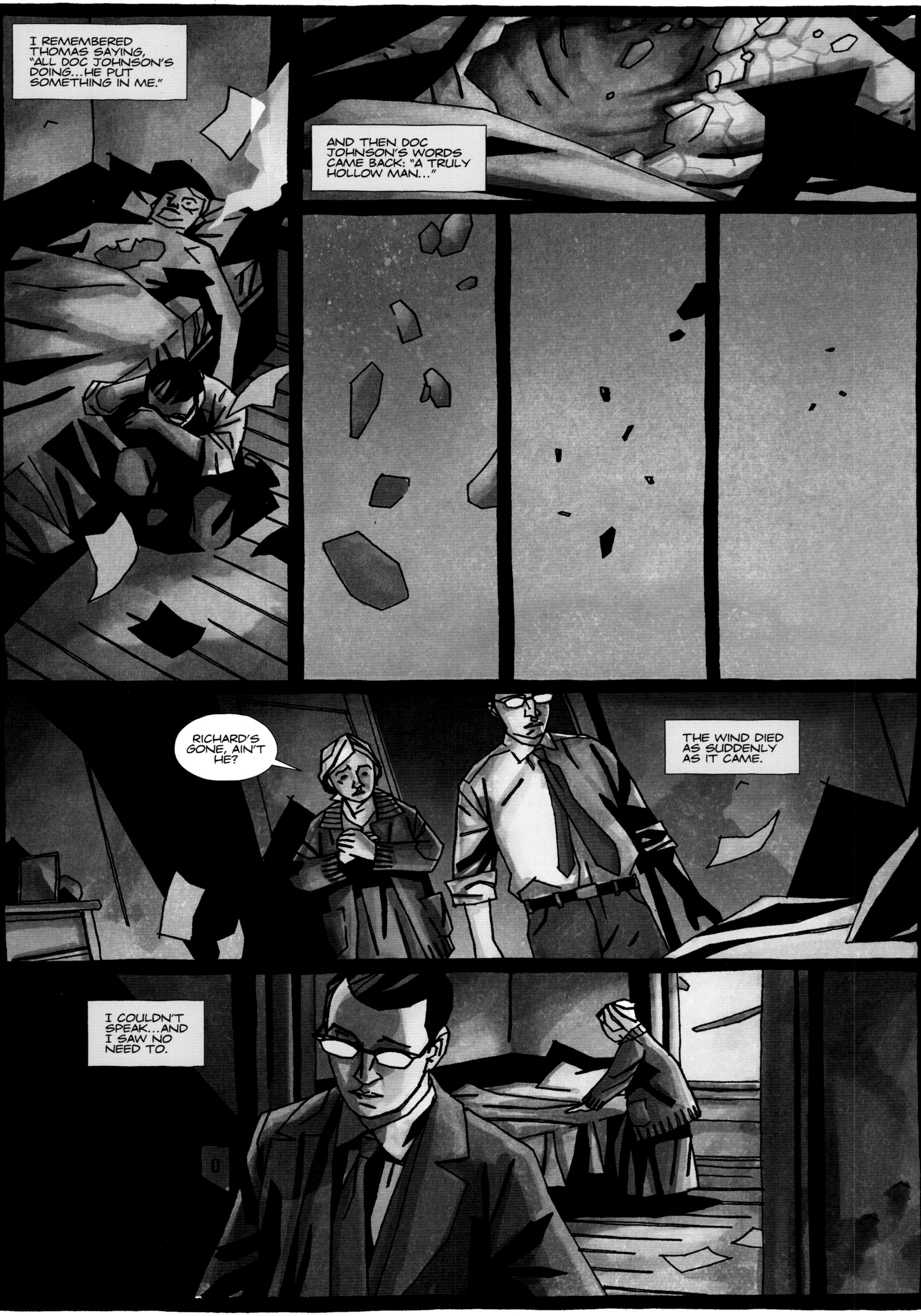
I REMEMBERED THOMAS SAYING, "ALL DOC JOHNSON'S DOING...HE PUT SOMETHING IN ME."
AND THEN DOC JOHNSON'S WORDS CAME BACK: "A TRULY HOLLOW MAN..."
RICHARD'S GONE, AIN'T HE?
THE WIND DIED AS SUDDENLY AS IT CAME.
I COULDN'T SPEAK...AND I SAW NO NEED TO.

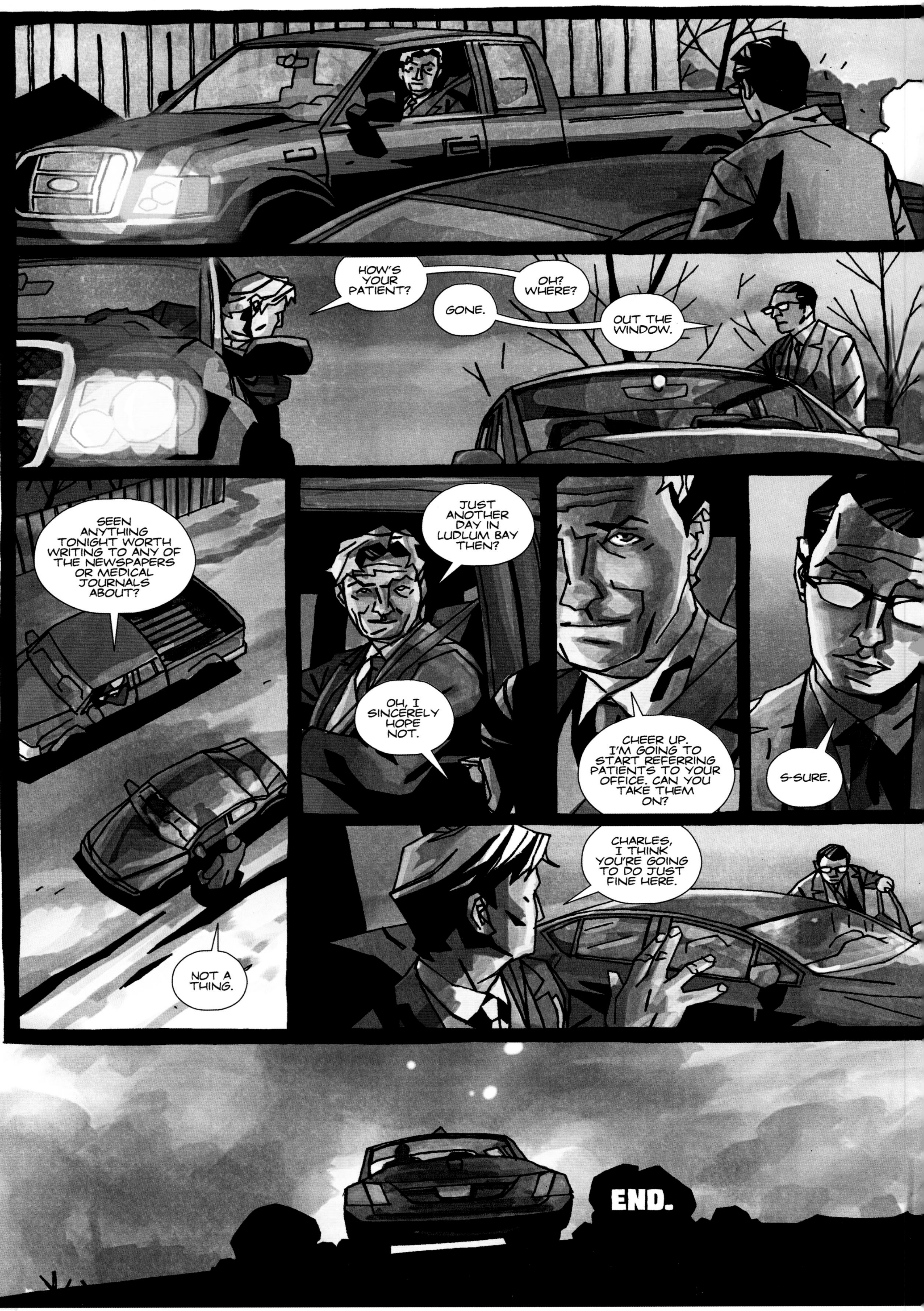
HOW'S YOUR PATIENT?
GONE.
OH? WHERE?
OUT THE WINDOW.
SEEN ANYTHING TONIGHT WORTH WRITING TO ANY OF THE NEWSPAPERS OR MEDICAL JOURNALS ABOUT?
NOT A THING.
JUST ANOTHER DAY IN LUDLUM BAY THEN?
OH, I SINCERELY HOPE NOT.
CHEER UP. I'M GOING TO START REFERRING PATIENTS TO YOUR OFFICE. CAN YOU TAKE THEM ON?
S-SURE.
CHARLES, I THINK YOU'RE GOING TO DO JUST FINE HERE.
END.

CREATURE CROSSWORD!

ACROSS:

3.) Leatherface clan surname.
7.) Jaws shark's name.
9.) _____ SuspenStories
13.) E.A. _____
16.) British film studio
17.) German Expressionist doctor.
18.) Skywald's darkly dreamy title.
19.) Carmilla's creator.
20.) She's written a letter to daddy.
22.) It's 12 O'Clock.
24.) Voodoo spirits.
25.) Howling horror.
29.) Poe's black cat.
30.) Publisher with the "Horror Mood."
31.) Warren vixen.
34.) Tibor Takacs demonic drama.
38.) Brandner's beastly book.
41.) Graham J. Ingels moniker.
42.) EC acronym.
45.) Hunchback and Phantom.
48.) Swamp Thing co-creator.
50.) Well-known denizens of Filmland.
53.) Shelley's creature creator.
54.) They mostly come at night...mostly.
55.) Mastermind behind Eerie pubs.
56.) Jason's surname.
57.) Peter Jackson's splatterfest.
58.) Classic horror author _____ Blackwood.
59.) Night of the Demons hostess.

DOWN:

1.) King's first novel.
2.) Laurence Olivier meets Hitchcock.
4.) Hammer: Hands of the _____.
5.) The Burning antagonist.
6.) The first of Le Tre Madri.
8.) Howard's hunter of horrors, Solomon _____.
10.) Charlton's ghostly title.
11.) Transylvanian terror.
12.) Peter Vincent's late night cable feature.
14.) Horror hound's holiday.
15.) _____ From the Mummy's Tomb.
20.) 1958 amorphous alien.
21.) Bald vampire.
23.) Do You Dare Enter The _____.
26.) Blatty's book.
27.) Dracula's daddy.
28.) Keep away from him unless you're tired of living.
32.) Gunnar Hansen role.
33.) Polanski's darling demon.
35.) Horror comic cover artist Nick _____.
36.) Philadelphia horror host.
37.) Fulci's feline film.
39.) Carpenter's sci-fi creeper.
40.) Warren horror host.
43.) Origin of EC's Tales.
44.) Tall Man's title.
46.) American Werewolf director.
47.) King's killer car.
49.) All work and no play makes Jack a dull boy.
51.) Mistress of the dark.
52.) Uncle Creepy's counterpart.

THE ONE THAT GOT AWAY

WRITER
SCOTT SNYDER

ARTIST
NATE POWELL

COLORIST
NATE POWELL

LETTERER
RACHEL DEERING

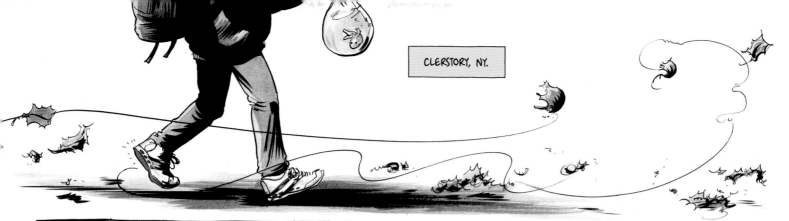

CLERSTORY, NY.

AW, DON'T BE SCARED, MAN.

YOU WON'T BE TRAPPED MUCH LONGER.

I PROMISE, BUD.

IN *JUST* A LITTLE WHILE...

...YOU'LL BE TOTALLY AND COMPLETELY FREE.

HEY THERE.

GET IN. I'LL GIVE YOU A RIDE.

THAT'S OKAY, I'M--

I SAID *GET IN.*

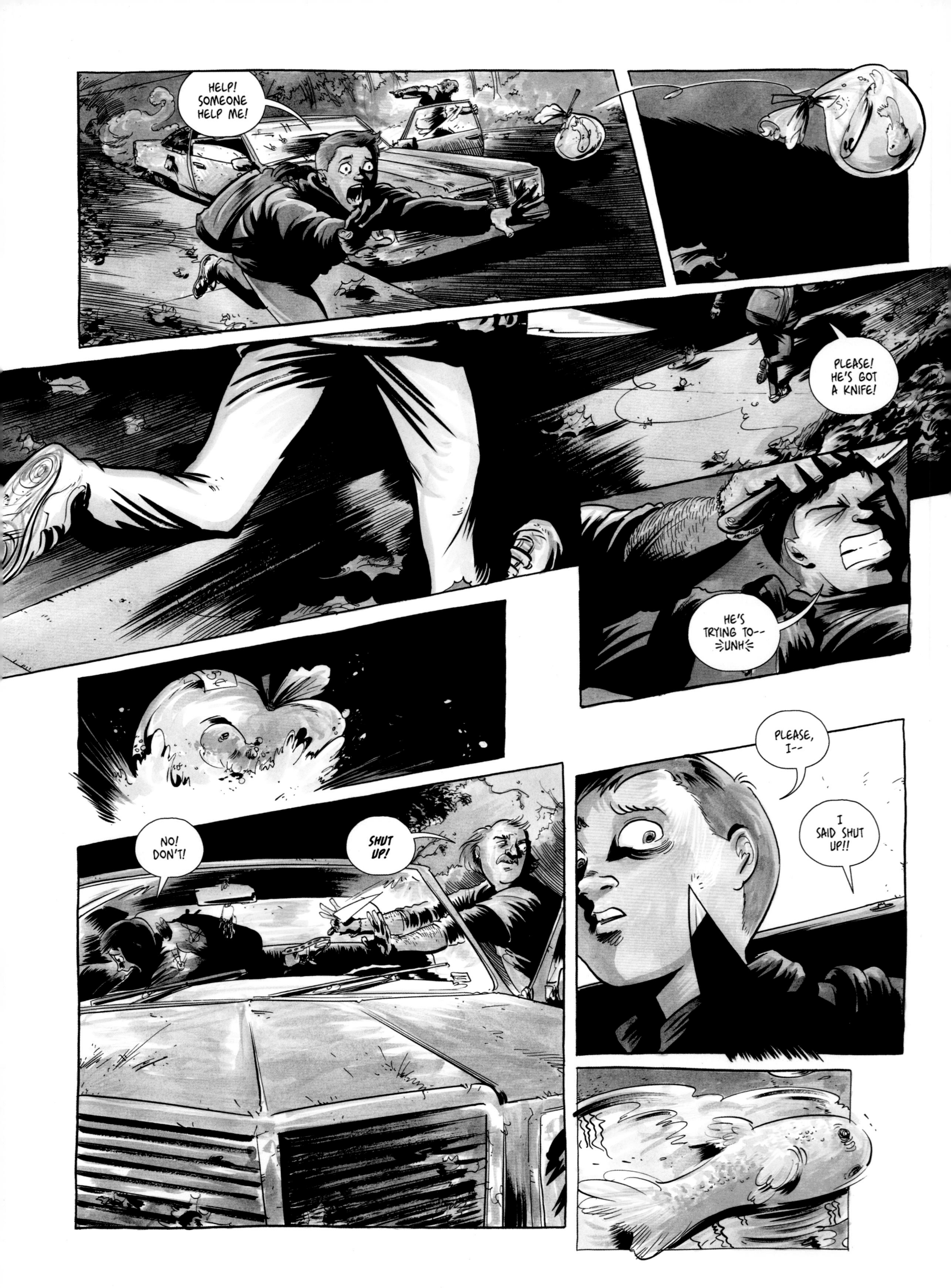
HELP! SOMEONE HELP ME!
PLEASE! HE'S GOT A KNIFE!
HE'S TRYING TO-- UNH
NO! DON'T!
SHUT UP!
PLEASE, I--
I SAID SHUT UP!!

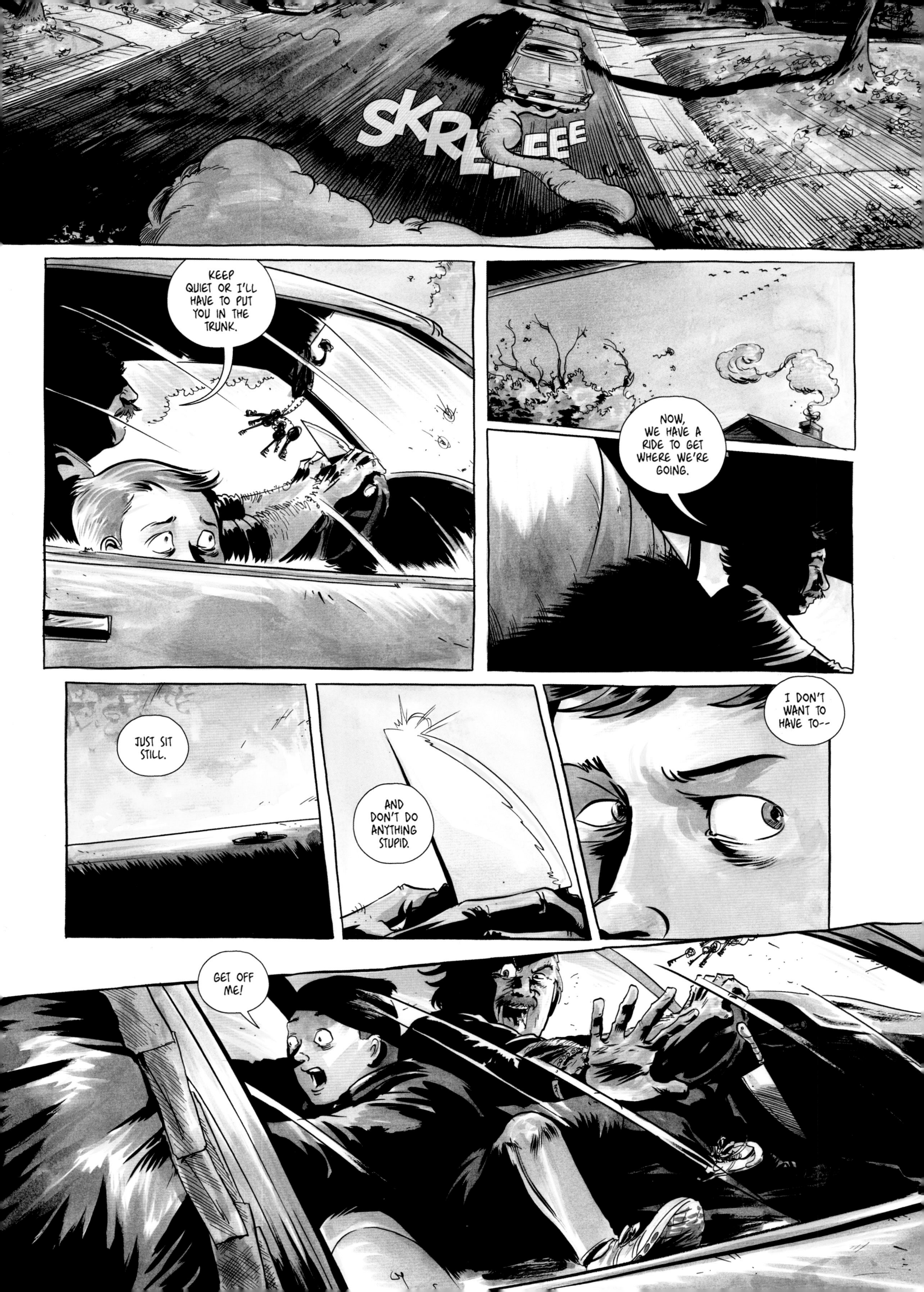
SKREEEEE
KEEP QUIET OR I'LL HAVE TO PUT YOU IN THE TRUNK.
NOW, WE HAVE A RIDE TO GET WHERE WE'RE GOING.
JUST SIT STILL.
AND DON'T DO ANYTHING STUPID.
I DON'T WANT TO HAVE TO--
GET OFF ME!

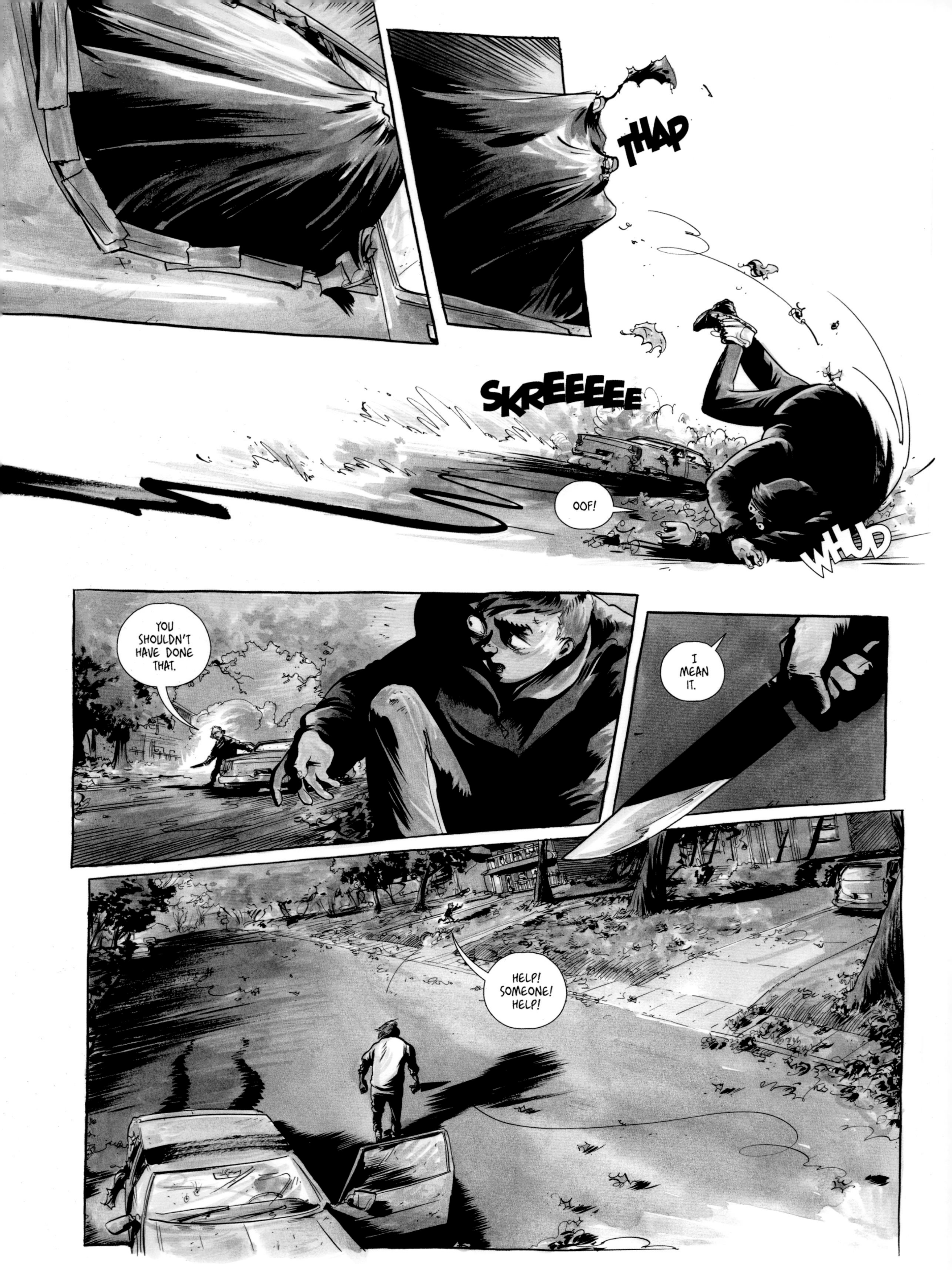
THAP
SKREEEEEE
OOF!
WHUD
YOU SHOULDN'T HAVE DONE THAT.
I MEAN IT.
HELP! SOMEONE! HELP!

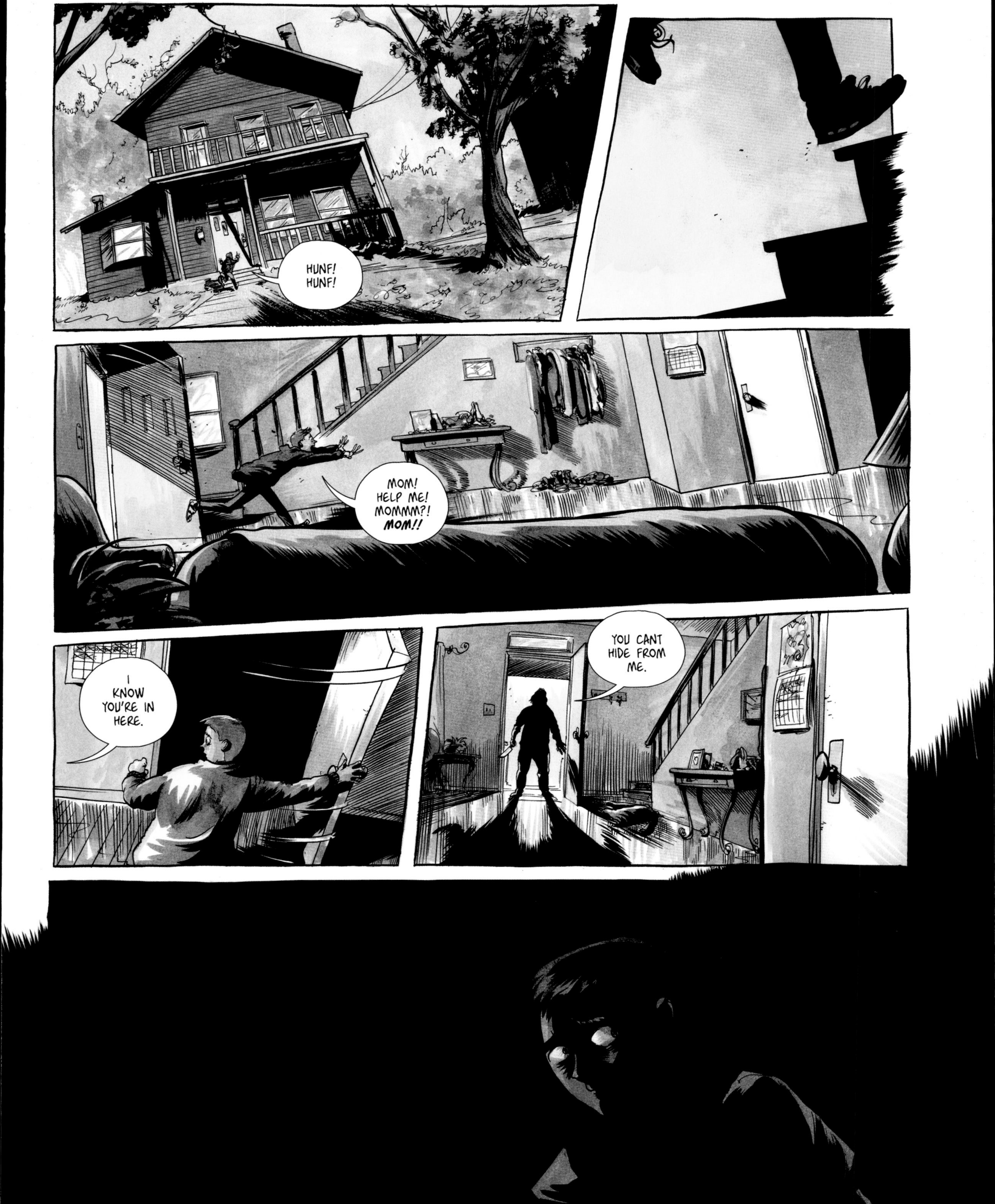
HUNF! HUNF!
MOM! HELP ME! MOMMM?! MOM!!
I KNOW YOU'RE IN HERE.
YOU CANT HIDE FROM ME.

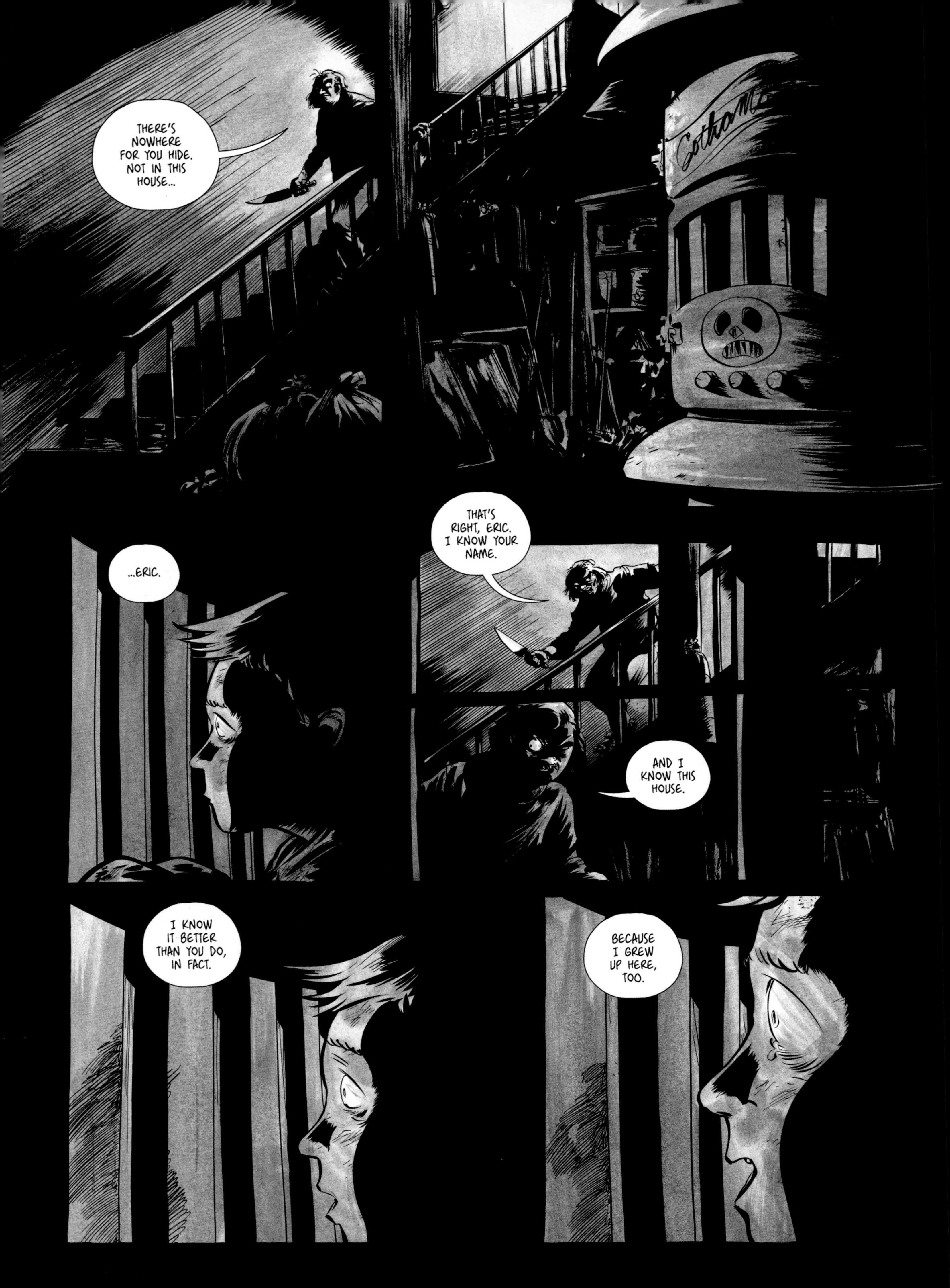
THERE'S NOWHERE FOR YOU HIDE. NOT IN THIS HOUSE...
...ERIC.
THAT'S RIGHT, ERIC. I KNOW YOUR NAME.
AND I KNOW THIS HOUSE.
I KNOW IT BETTER THAN YOU DO, IN FACT.
BECAUSE I GREW UP HERE, TOO.

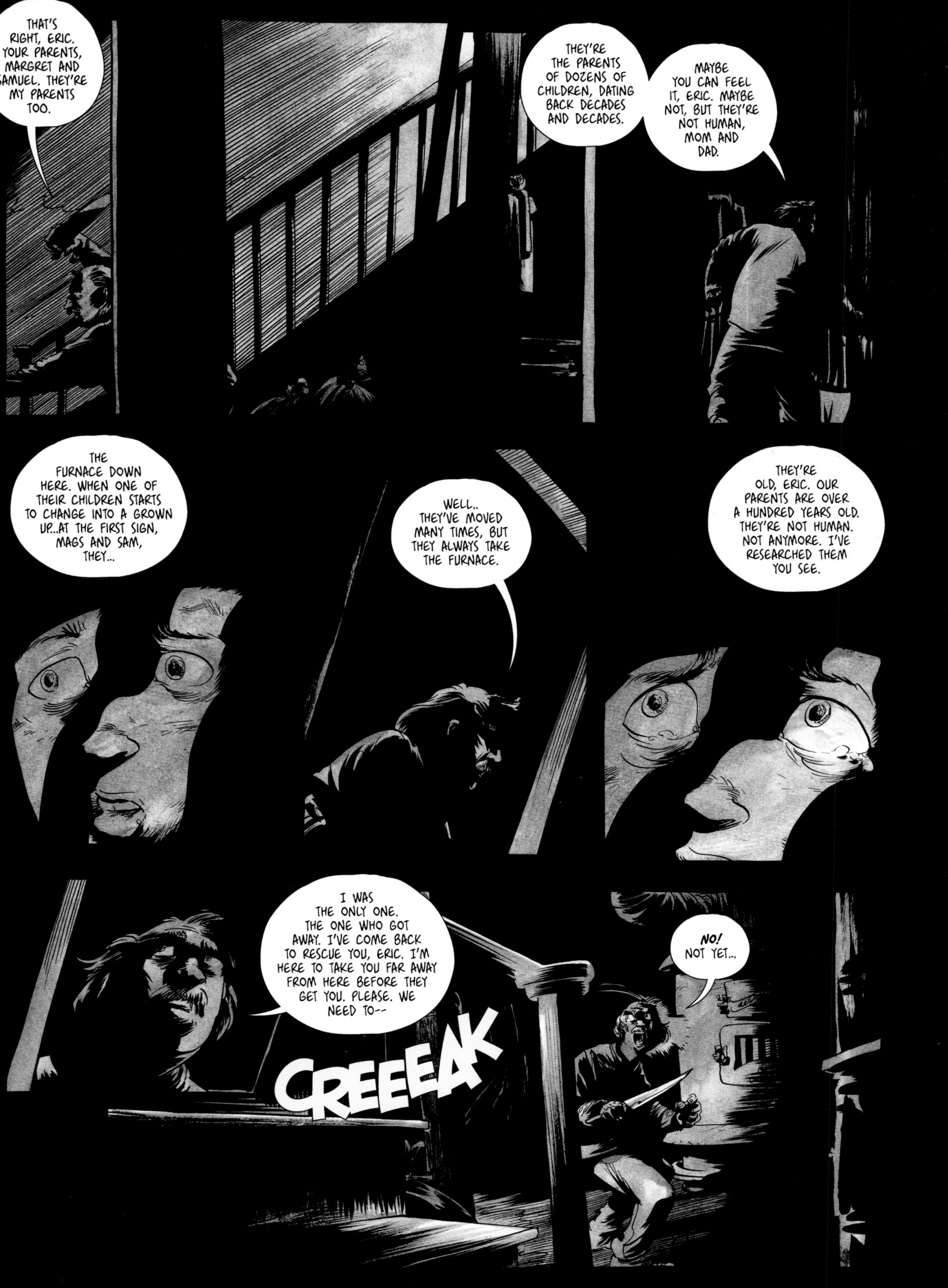

THAT'S RIGHT, ERIC. YOUR PARENTS, MARGRET AND SAMUEL. THEY'RE MY PARENTS TOO.
THEY'RE THE PARENTS OF DOZENS OF CHILDREN, DATING BACK DECADES AND DECADES.
MAYBE YOU CAN FEEL IT, ERIC. MAYBE NOT, BUT THEY'RE NOT HUMAN, MOM AND DAD.
THE FURNACE DOWN HERE. WHEN ONE OF THEIR CHILDREN STARTS TO CHANGE INTO A GROWN UP...AT THE FIRST SIGN, MAGS AND SAM, THEY...
WELL.. THEY'VE MOVED MANY TIMES, BUT THEY ALWAYS TAKE THE FURNACE.
THEY'RE OLD, ERIC. OUR PARENTS ARE OVER A HUNDRED YEARS OLD. THEY'RE NOT HUMAN. NOT ANYMORE. I'VE RESEARCHED THEM YOU SEE.
I WAS THE ONLY ONE. THE ONE WHO GOT AWAY. I'VE COME BACK TO RESCUE YOU, ERIC. I'M HERE TO TAKE YOU FAR AWAY FROM HERE BEFORE THEY GET YOU. PLEASE. WE NEED TO--
CREEEAK
NO! NOT YET...

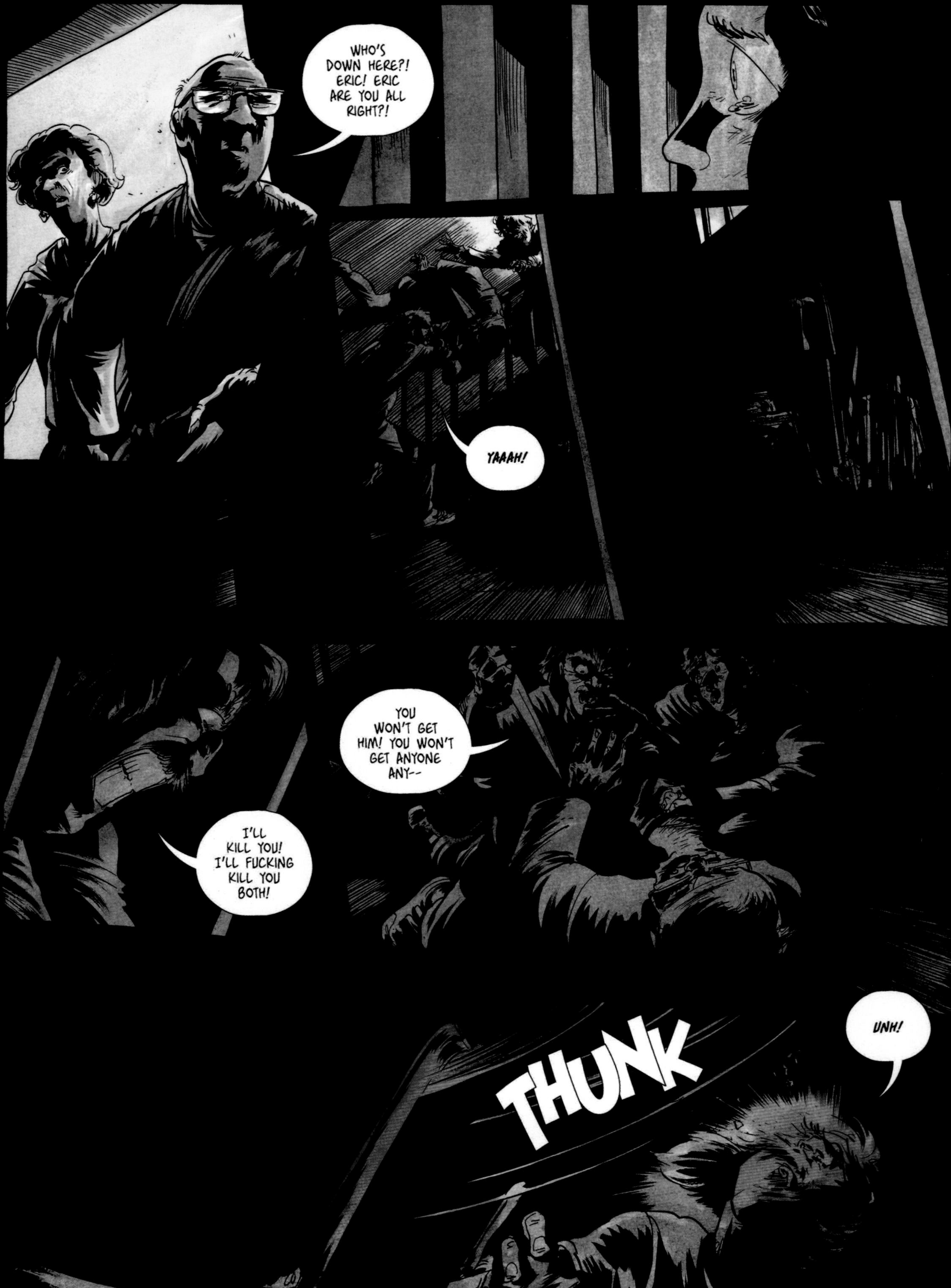
WHO'S DOWN HERE?! ERIC! ERIC ARE YOU ALL RIGHT?!
YAAAH!
YOU WON'T GET HIM! YOU WON'T GET ANYONE ANY--
I'LL KILL YOU! I'LL FUCKING KILL YOU BOTH!
THUNK
UNH!

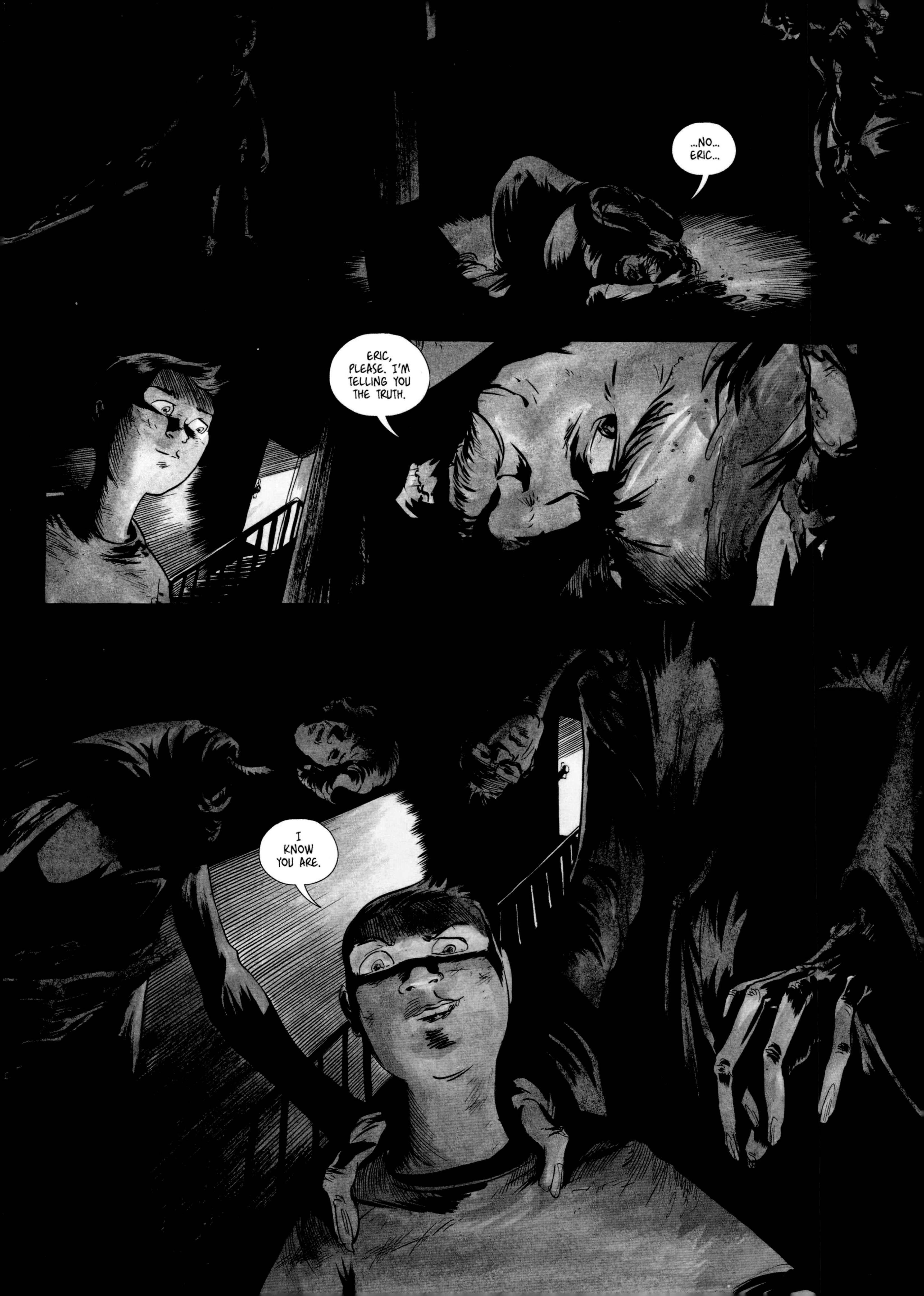
...NO...
ERIC...
ERIC, PLEASE. I'M TELLING YOU THE TRUTH.
I KNOW YOU ARE.

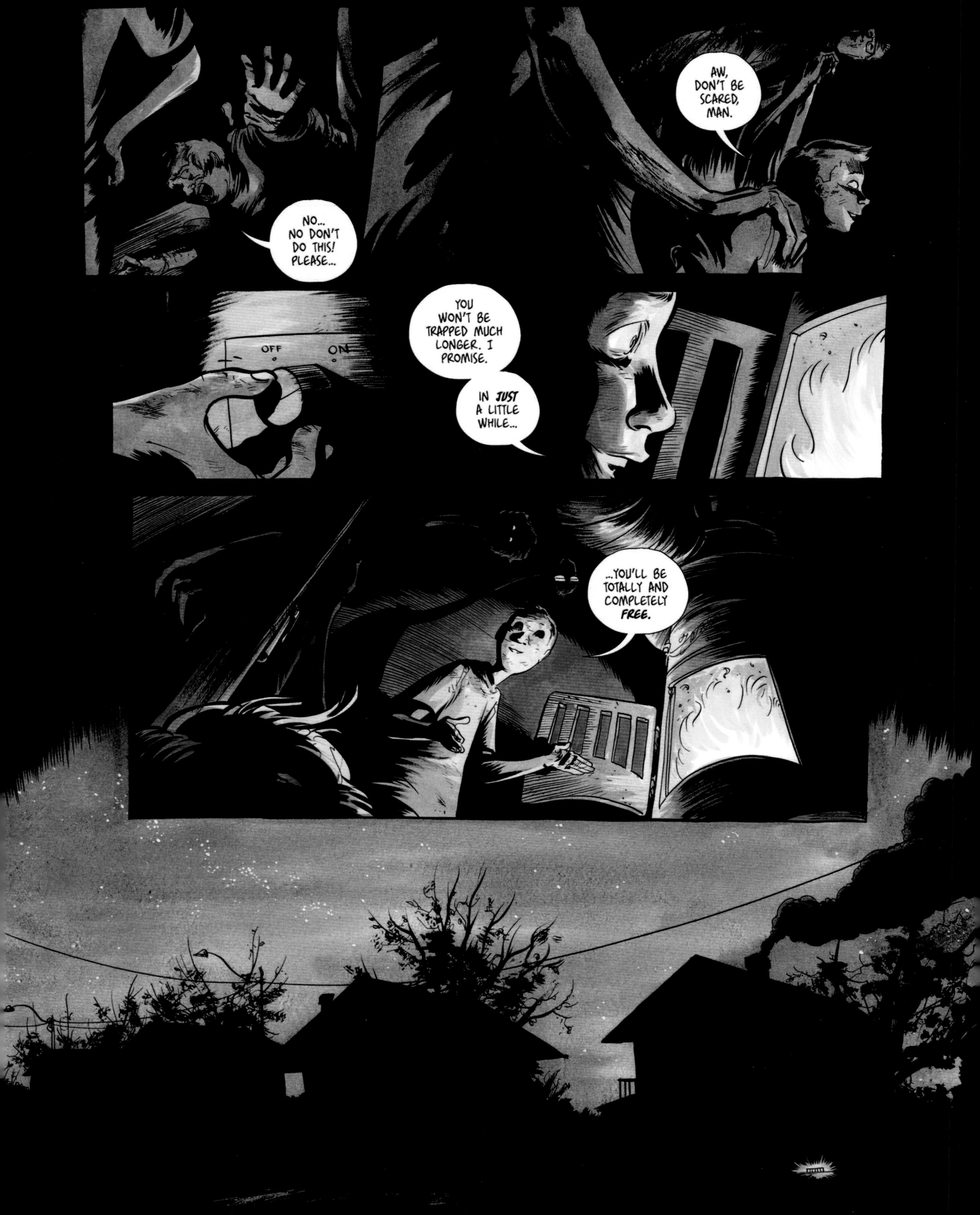
NO... NO DON'T DO THIS! PLEASE...
AW, DON'T BE SCARED, MAN.
OFF
ON
YOU WON'T BE TRAPPED MUCH LONGER. I PROMISE.
IN JUST A LITTLE WHILE...
...YOU'LL BE TOTALLY AND COMPLETELY FREE.

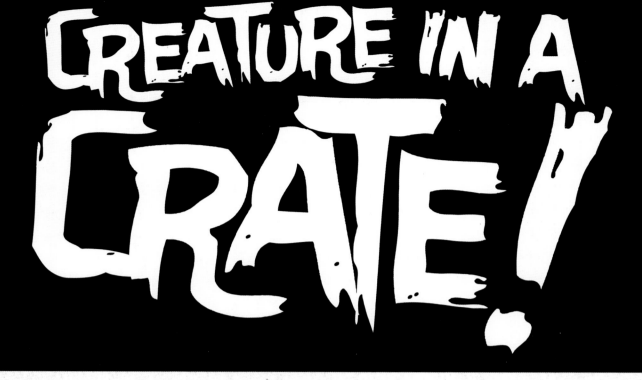

CREATURE IN A CRATE!

Watch your friends SHRIEK when they take a peek at your very own kooky CREATURE IN A CRATE!

Put him under your sister's bed for guaranteed night time TERROR!

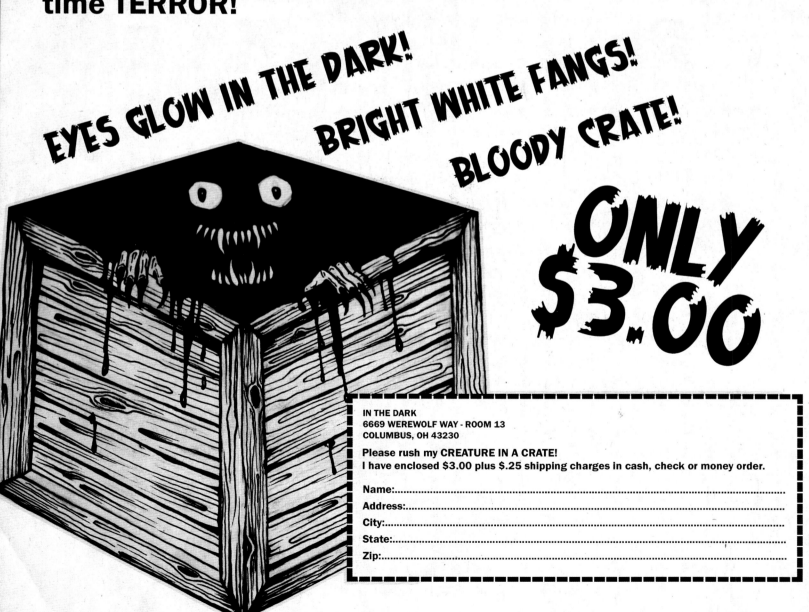

EYES GLOW IN THE DARK!

BRIGHT WHITE FANGS!

BLOODY CRATE!

ONLY $3.00

IN THE DARK
6669 WEREWOLF WAY - ROOM 13
COLUMBUS, OH 43230

Please rush my CREATURE IN A CRATE!
I have enclosed $3.00 plus $.25 shipping charges in cash, check or money order.

Name:..

Address:..

City:..

State:..

Zip:...

PROXIMITY

WRITER
SEAN E. WILLIAMS

ARTIST
ANDY BELANGER

COLORIST
THOMAS BOATWRIGHT

LETTERER
RACHEL DEERING

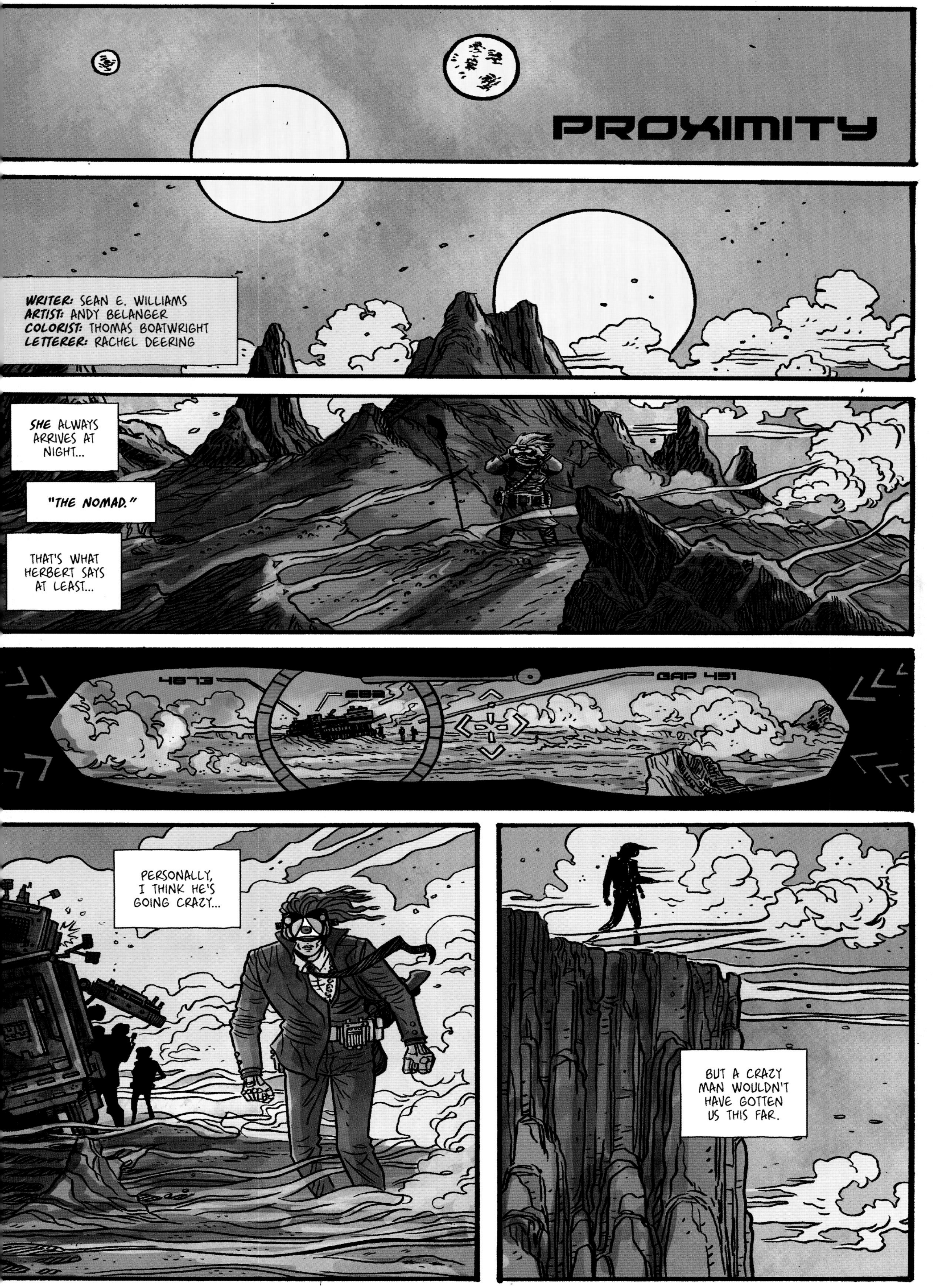
PROXIMITY
WRITER: SEAN E. WILLIAMS
ARTIST: ANDY BELANGER
COLORIST: THOMAS BOATWRIGHT
LETTERER: RACHEL DEERING
SHE ALWAYS ARRIVES AT NIGHT...
"THE NOMAD."
THAT'S WHAT HERBERT SAYS AT LEAST...
PERSONALLY, I THINK HE'S GOING CRAZY...
BUT A CRAZY MAN WOULDN'T HAVE GOTTEN US THIS FAR.

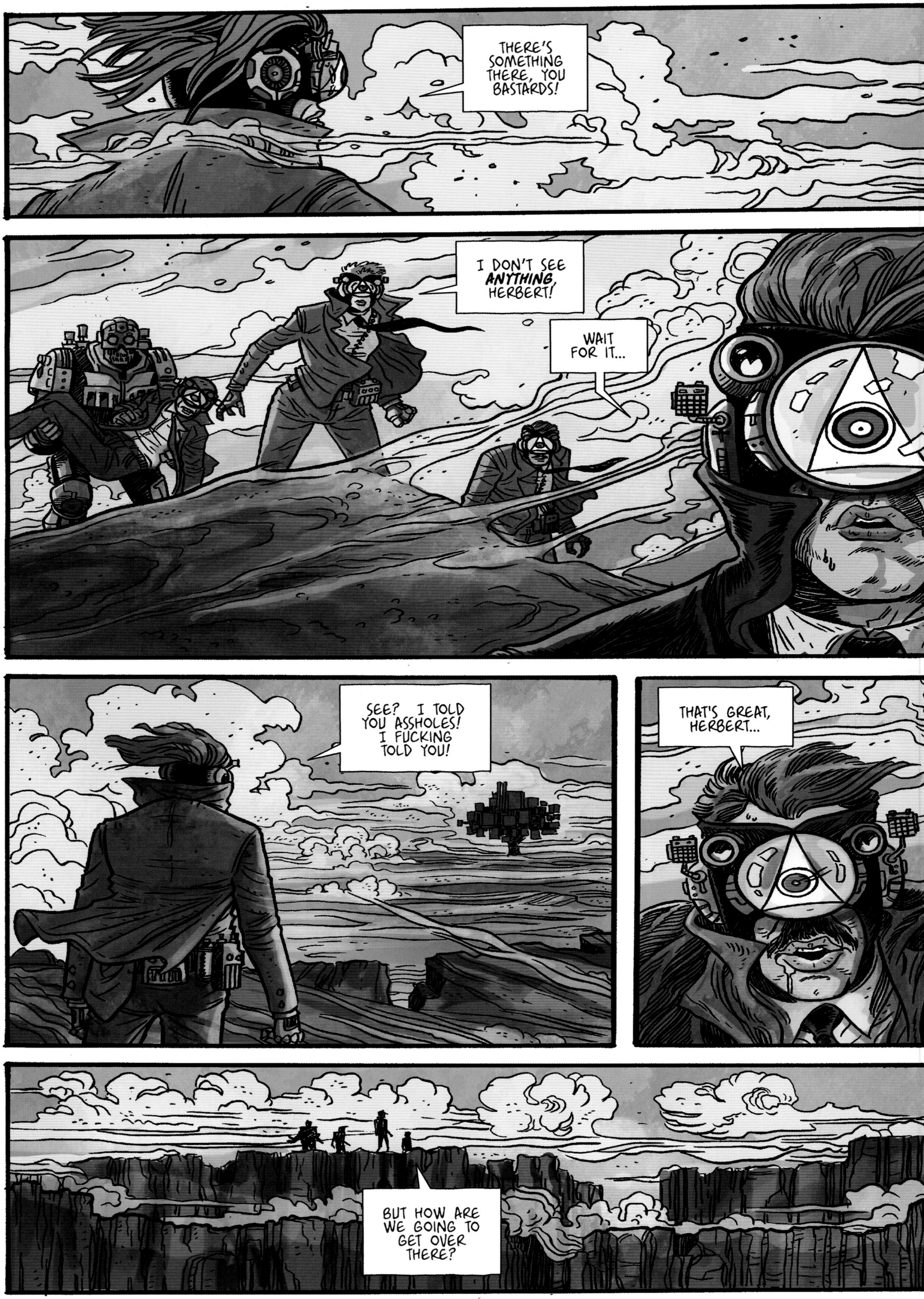
THERE'S SOMETHING THERE, YOU BASTARDS!
I DON'T SEE ANYTHING, HERBERT!
WAIT FOR IT...
SEE? I TOLD YOU ASSHOLES! I FUCKING TOLD YOU!
THAT'S GREAT, HERBERT...
BUT HOW ARE WE GOING TO GET OVER THERE?

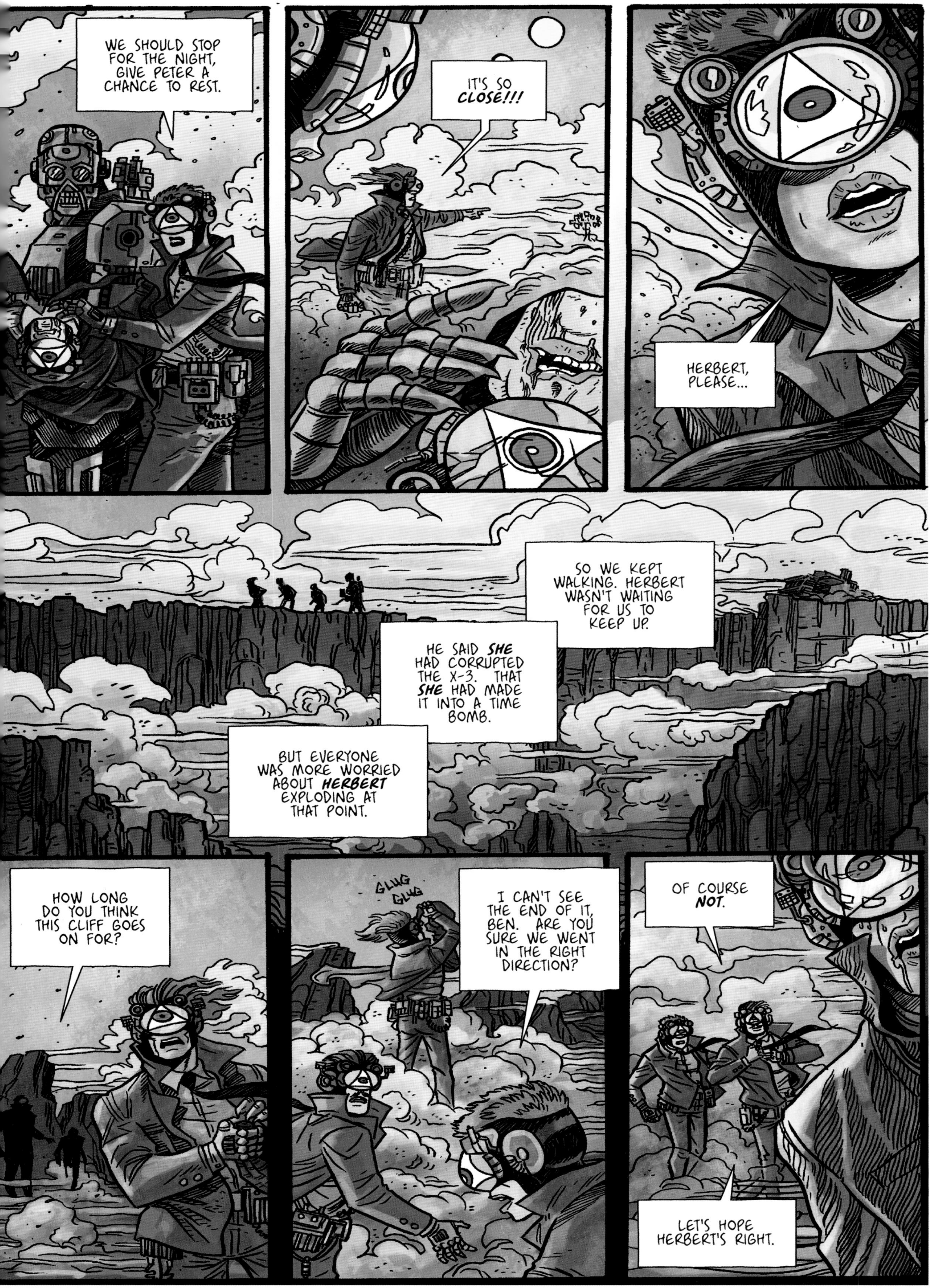
WE SHOULD STOP FOR THE NIGHT, GIVE PETER A CHANCE TO REST.
IT'S SO CLOSE!!!
HERBERT, PLEASE...
SO WE KEPT WALKING. HERBERT WASN'T WAITING FOR US TO KEEP UP.
HE SAID SHE HAD CORRUPTED THE X-3. THAT SHE HAD MADE IT INTO A TIME BOMB.
BUT EVERYONE WAS MORE WORRIED ABOUT HERBERT EXPLODING AT THAT POINT.
HOW LONG DO YOU THINK THIS CLIFF GOES ON FOR?
GLUG GLUG
I CAN'T SEE THE END OF IT, BEN. ARE YOU SURE WE WENT IN THE RIGHT DIRECTION?
OF COURSE NOT.
LET'S HOPE HERBERT'S RIGHT.

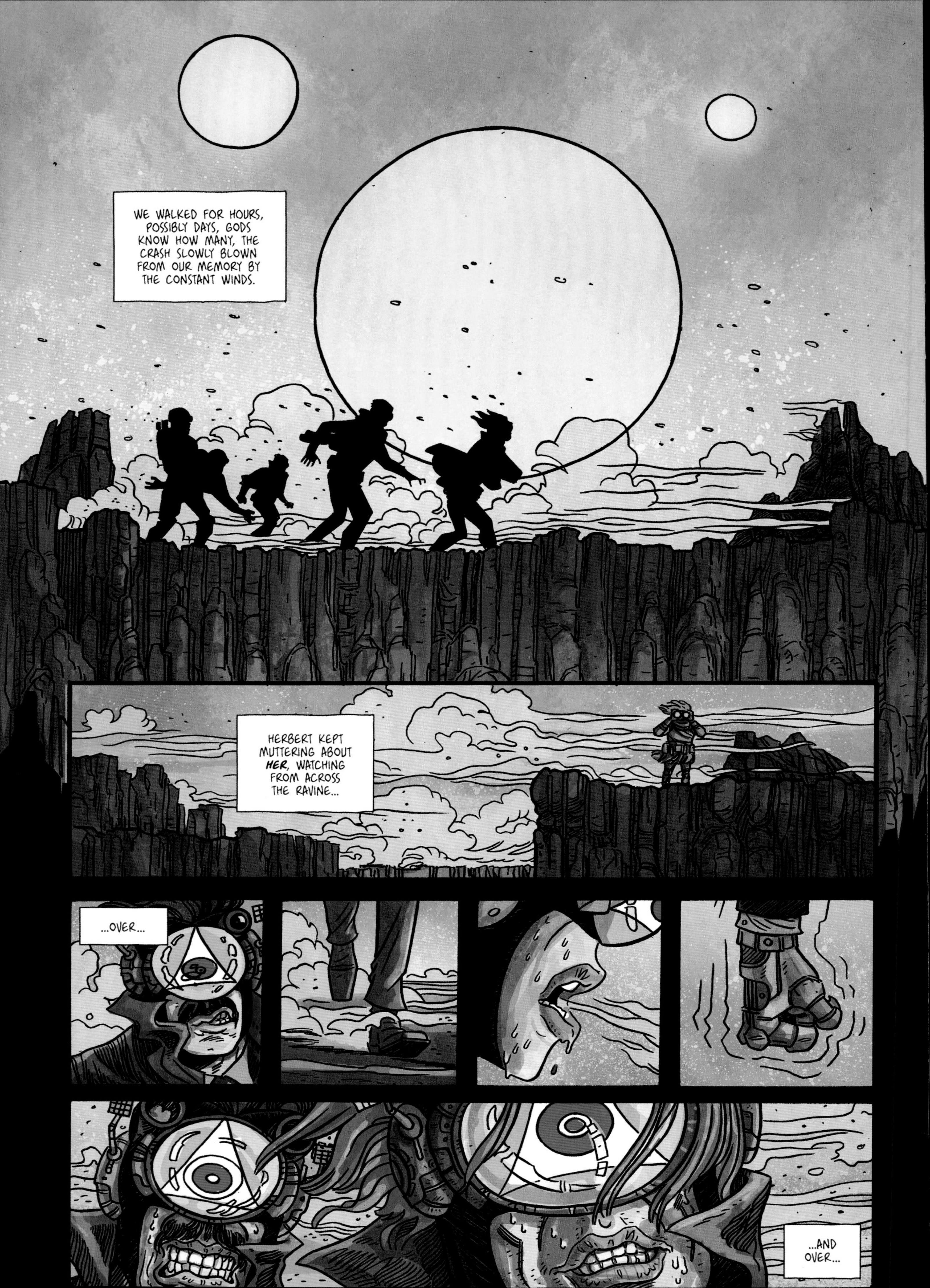
WE WALKED FOR HOURS, POSSIBLY DAYS, GODS KNOW HOW MANY, THE CRASH SLOWLY BLOWN FROM OUR MEMORY BY THE CONSTANT WINDS.
HERBERT KEPT MUTTERING ABOUT HER, WATCHING FROM ACROSS THE RAVINE...
...OVER...
...AND OVER...

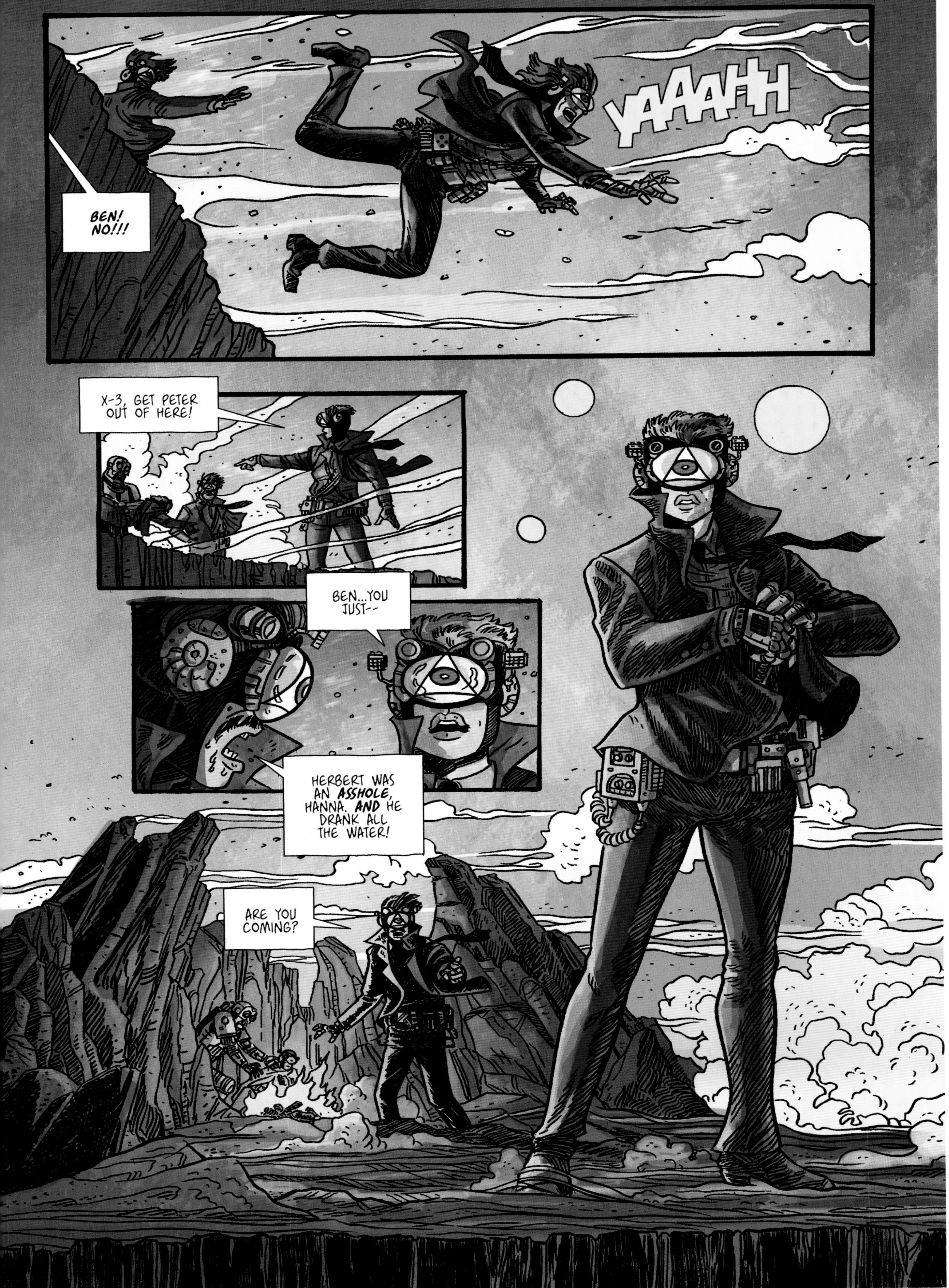
BEN! NO!!!
YAAAHH
X-3, GET PETER OUT OF HERE!
BEN...YOU JUST--
HERBERT WAS AN ASSHOLE, HANNA. AND HE DRANK ALL THE WATER!
ARE YOU COMING?

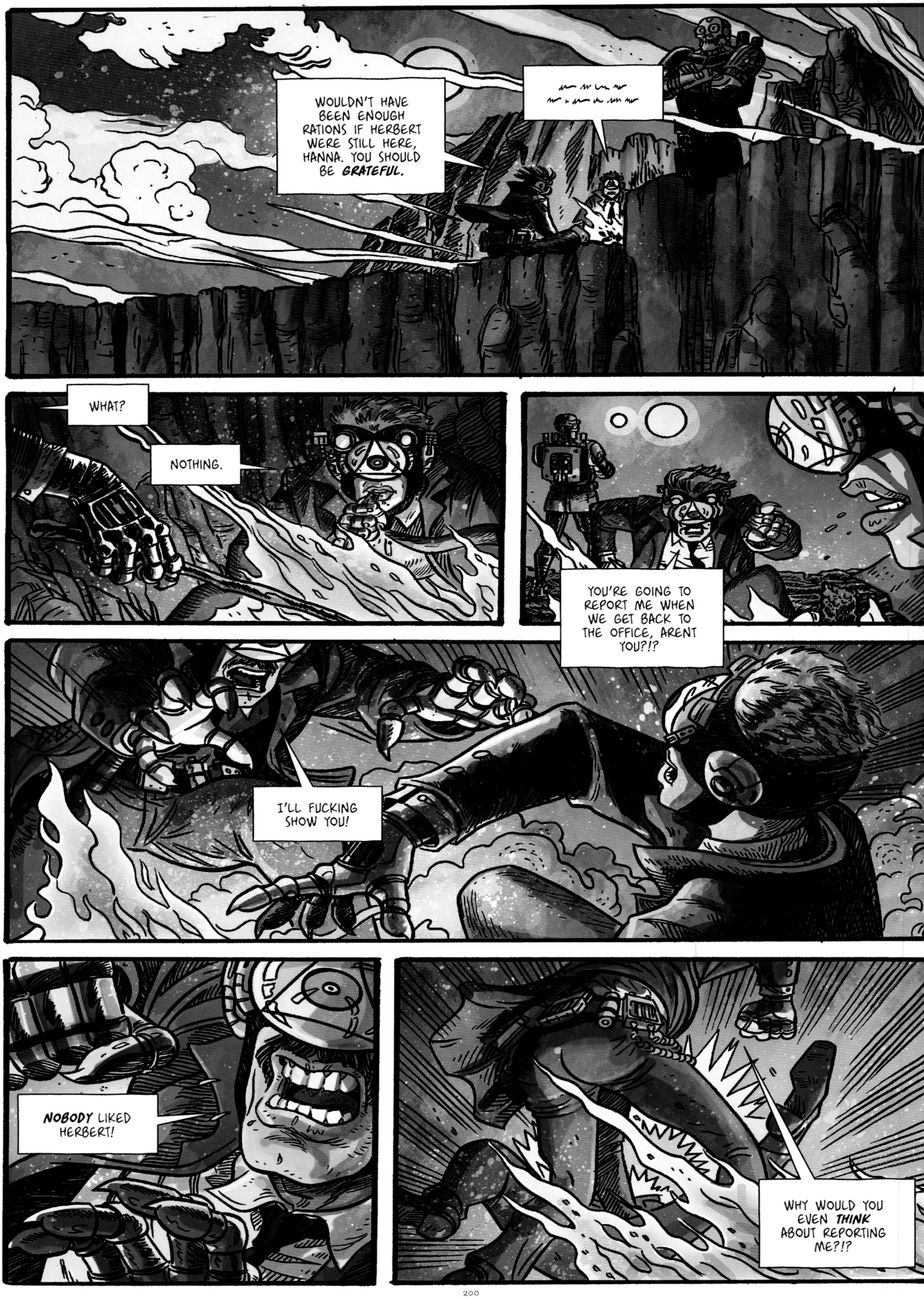
WOULDN'T HAVE BEEN ENOUGH RATIONS IF HERBERT WERE STILL HERE, HANNA. YOU SHOULD BE GRATEFUL.
WHAT?
NOTHING.
YOU'RE GOING TO REPORT ME WHEN WE GET BACK TO THE OFFICE, ARENT YOU?!?
I'LL FUCKING SHOW YOU!
NOBODY LIKED HERBERT!
WHY WOULD YOU EVEN THINK ABOUT REPORTING ME?!?

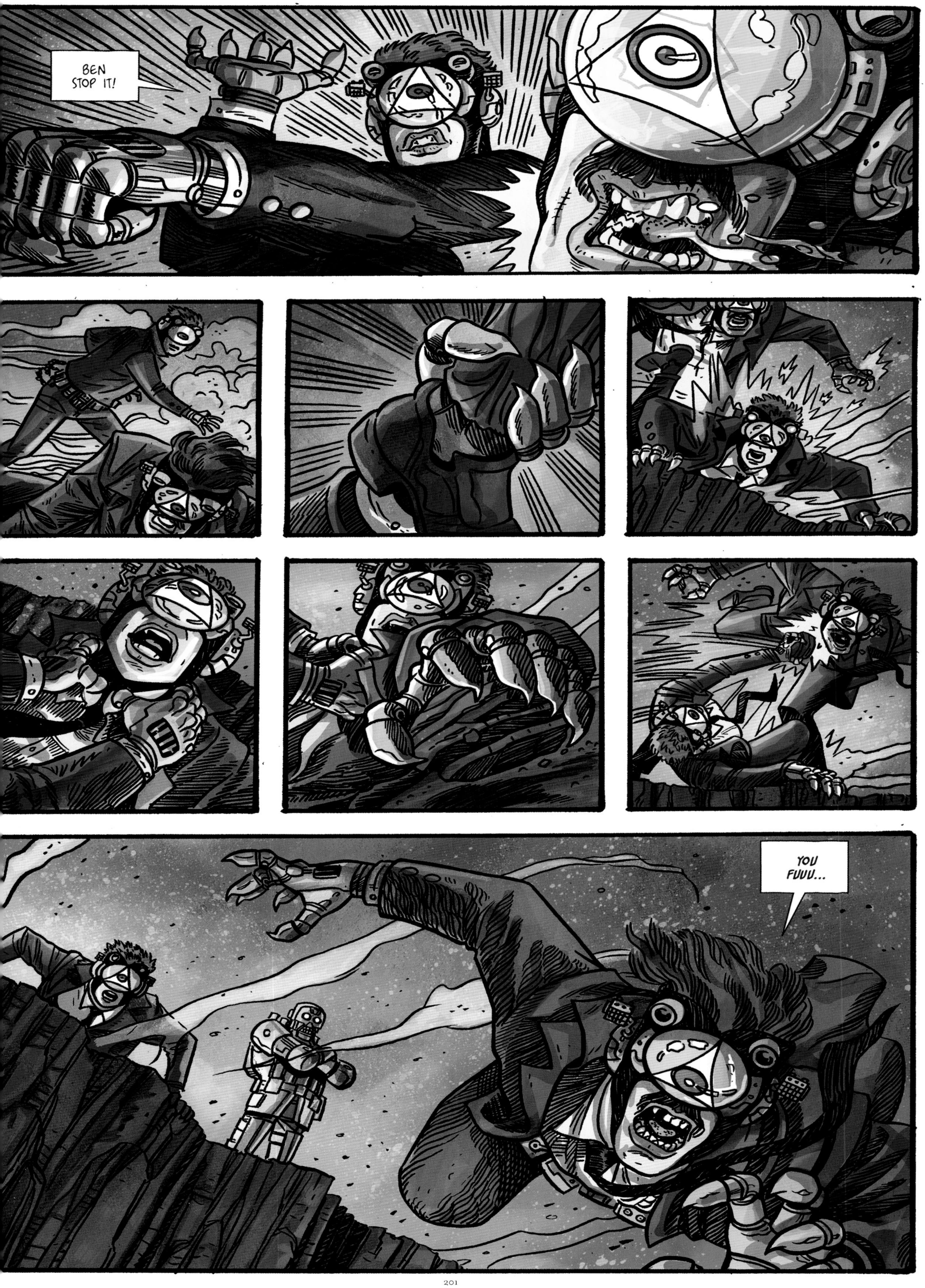
BEN
STOP IT!
YOU
FUUU...

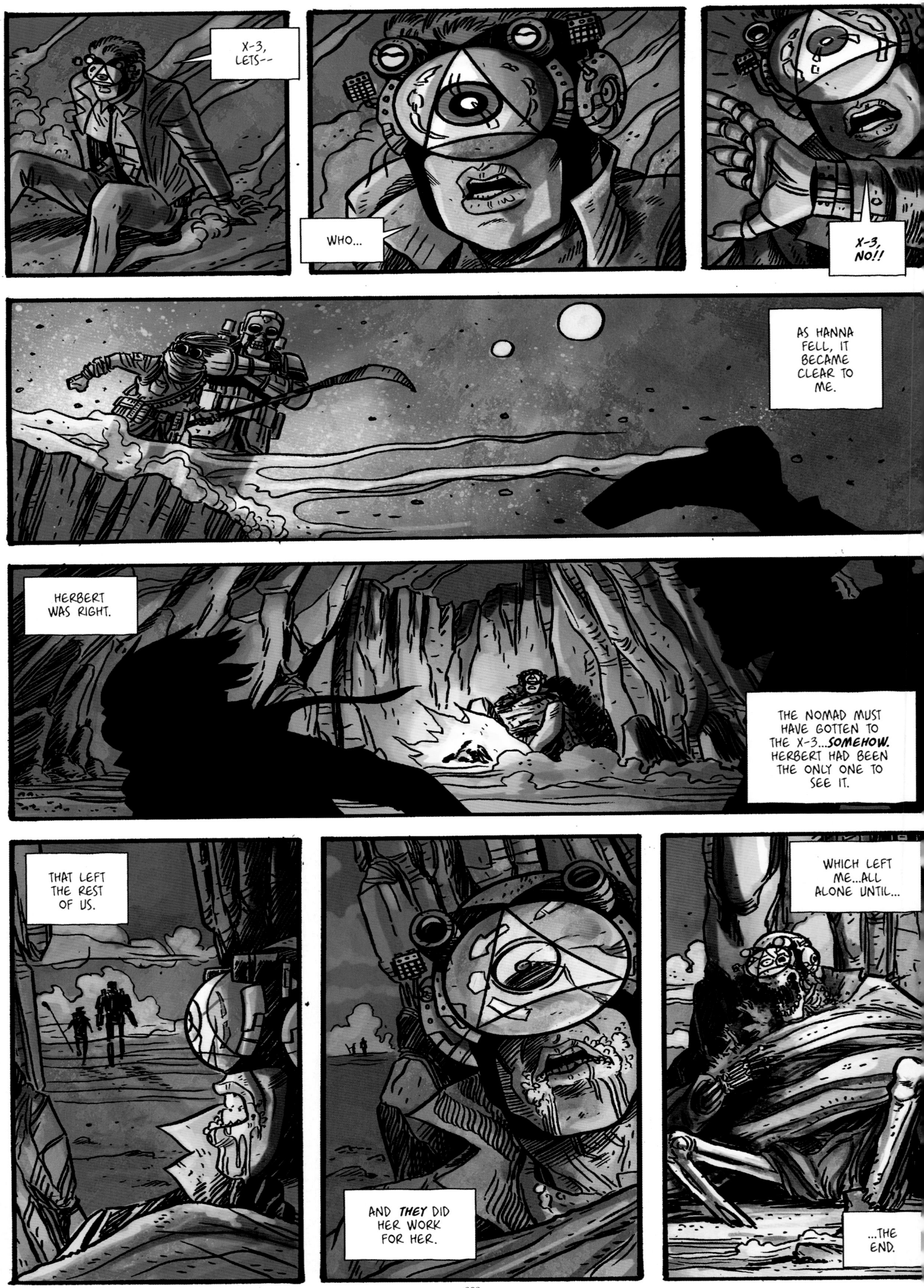
X-3, LETS--
WHO...
X-3, NO!!
AS HANNA FELL, IT BECAME CLEAR TO ME.
HERBERT WAS RIGHT.
THE NOMAD MUST HAVE GOTTEN TO THE X-3...SOMEHOW. HERBERT HAD BEEN THE ONLY ONE TO SEE IT.
THAT LEFT THE REST OF US.
AND THEY DID HER WORK FOR HER.
WHICH LEFT ME...ALL ALONE UNTIL...
...THE END.

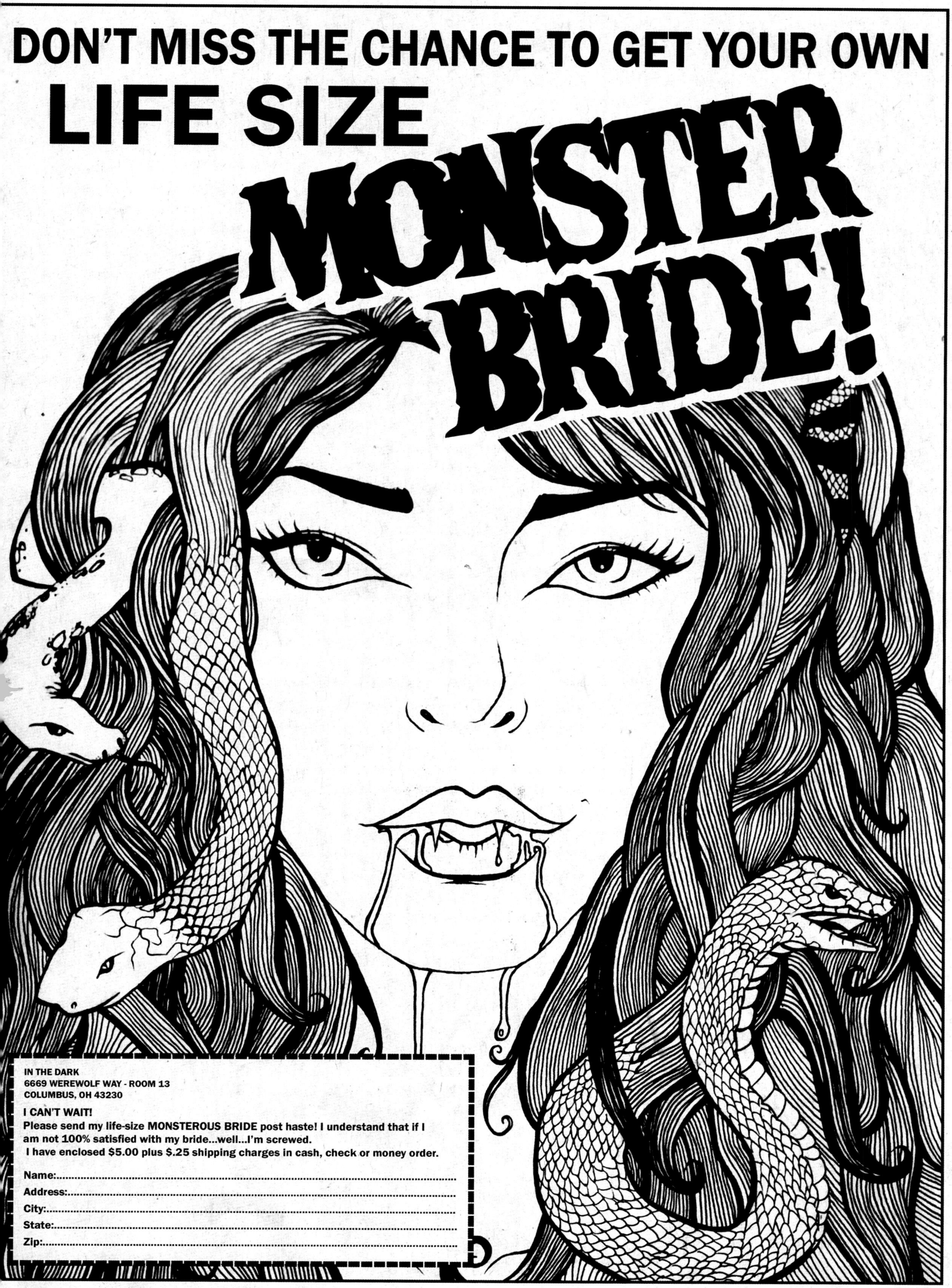
DON'T MISS THE CHANCE TO GET YOUR OWN
LIFE SIZE
MONSTER BRIDE!
IN THE DARK
6669 WEREWOLF WAY - ROOM 13
COLUMBUS, OH 43230
I CAN'T WAIT!
Please send my life-size MONSTEROUS BRIDE post haste! I understand that if I am not 100% satisfied with my bride...well...I'm screwed.
I have enclosed $5.00 plus $.25 shipping charges in cash, check or money order.
Name:
Address:
City:
State:
Zip:

THE LOST VALLEY OF THE DEAD

WRITER
BRIAN KEENE

ARTIST
TADD GALUSHA

COLORIST
THOMAS BOATWRIGHT

LETTERER
ADAM WOLLET

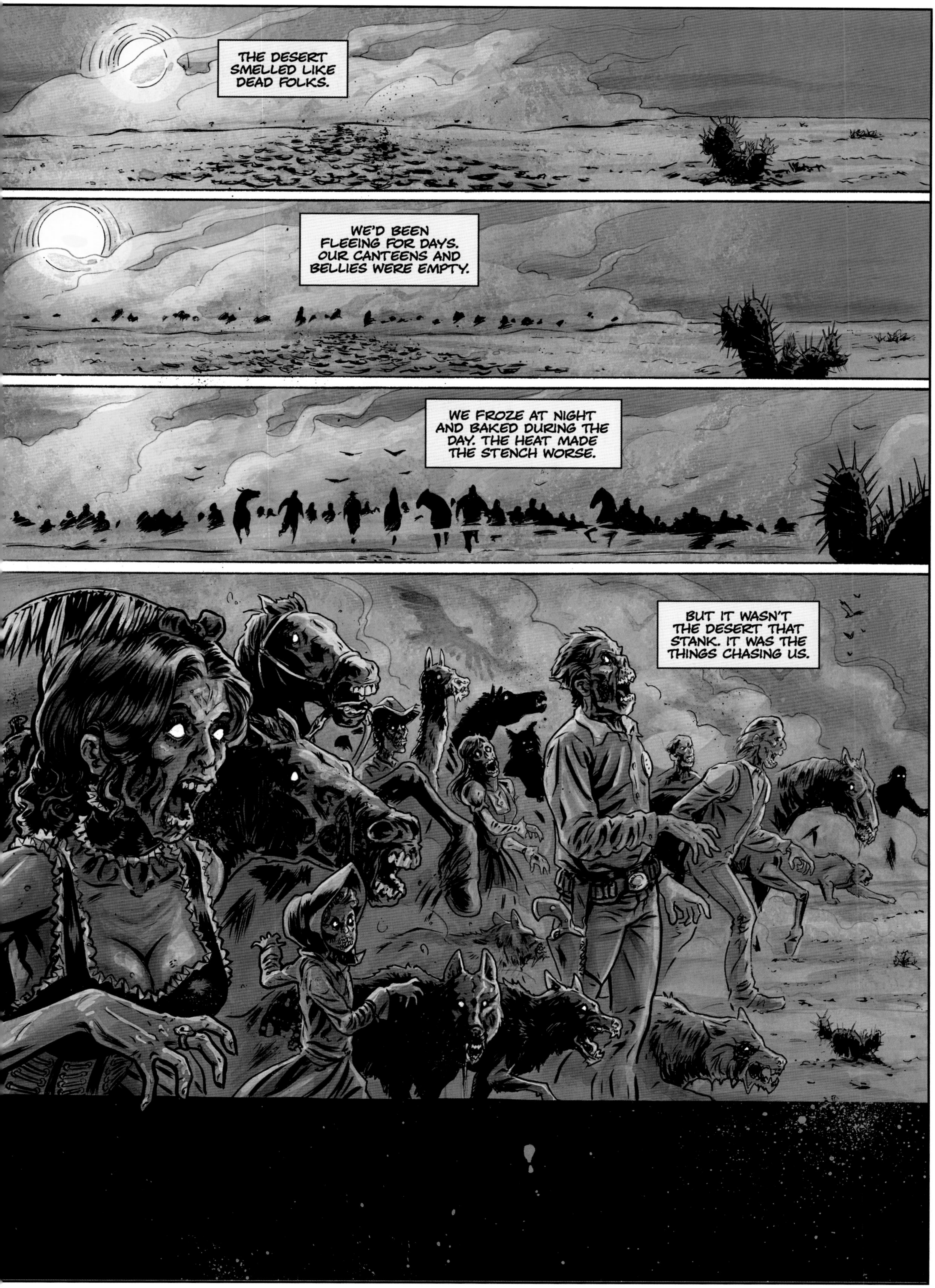
THE DESERT SMELLED LIKE DEAD FOLKS.
WE'D BEEN FLEEING FOR DAYS. OUR CANTEENS AND BELLIES WERE EMPTY.
WE FROZE AT NIGHT AND BAKED DURING THE DAY. THE HEAT MADE THE STENCH WORSE.
BUT IT WASN'T THE DESERT THAT STANK. IT WAS THE THINGS CHASING US.

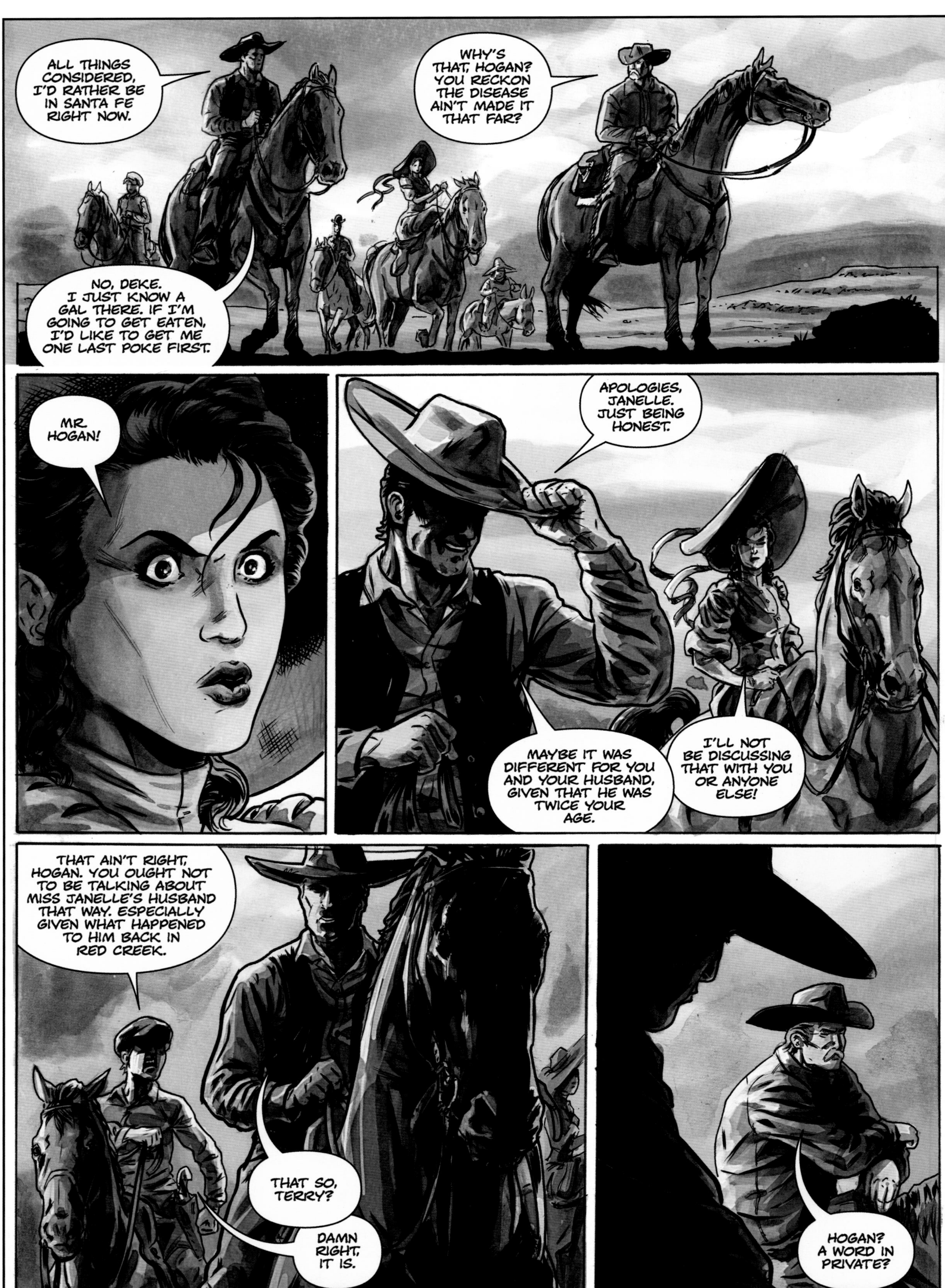
ALL THINGS CONSIDERED, I'D RATHER BE IN SANTA FE RIGHT NOW.
WHY'S THAT, HOGAN? YOU RECKON THE DISEASE AIN'T MADE IT THAT FAR?
NO, DEKE. I JUST KNOW A GAL THERE. IF I'M GOING TO GET EATEN, I'D LIKE TO GET ME ONE LAST POKE FIRST.
MR HOGAN!
APOLOGIES, JANELLE. JUST BEING HONEST.
MAYBE IT WAS DIFFERENT FOR YOU AND YOUR HUSBAND, GIVEN THAT HE WAS TWICE YOUR AGE.
I'LL NOT BE DISCUSSING THAT WITH YOU OR ANYONE ELSE!
THAT AIN'T RIGHT, HOGAN. YOU OUGHT NOT TO BE TALKING ABOUT MISS JANELLE'S HUSBAND THAT WAY. ESPECIALLY GIVEN WHAT HAPPENED TO HIM BACK IN RED CREEK.
THAT SO, TERRY?
DAMN RIGHT, IT IS.
HOGAN? A WORD IN PRIVATE?

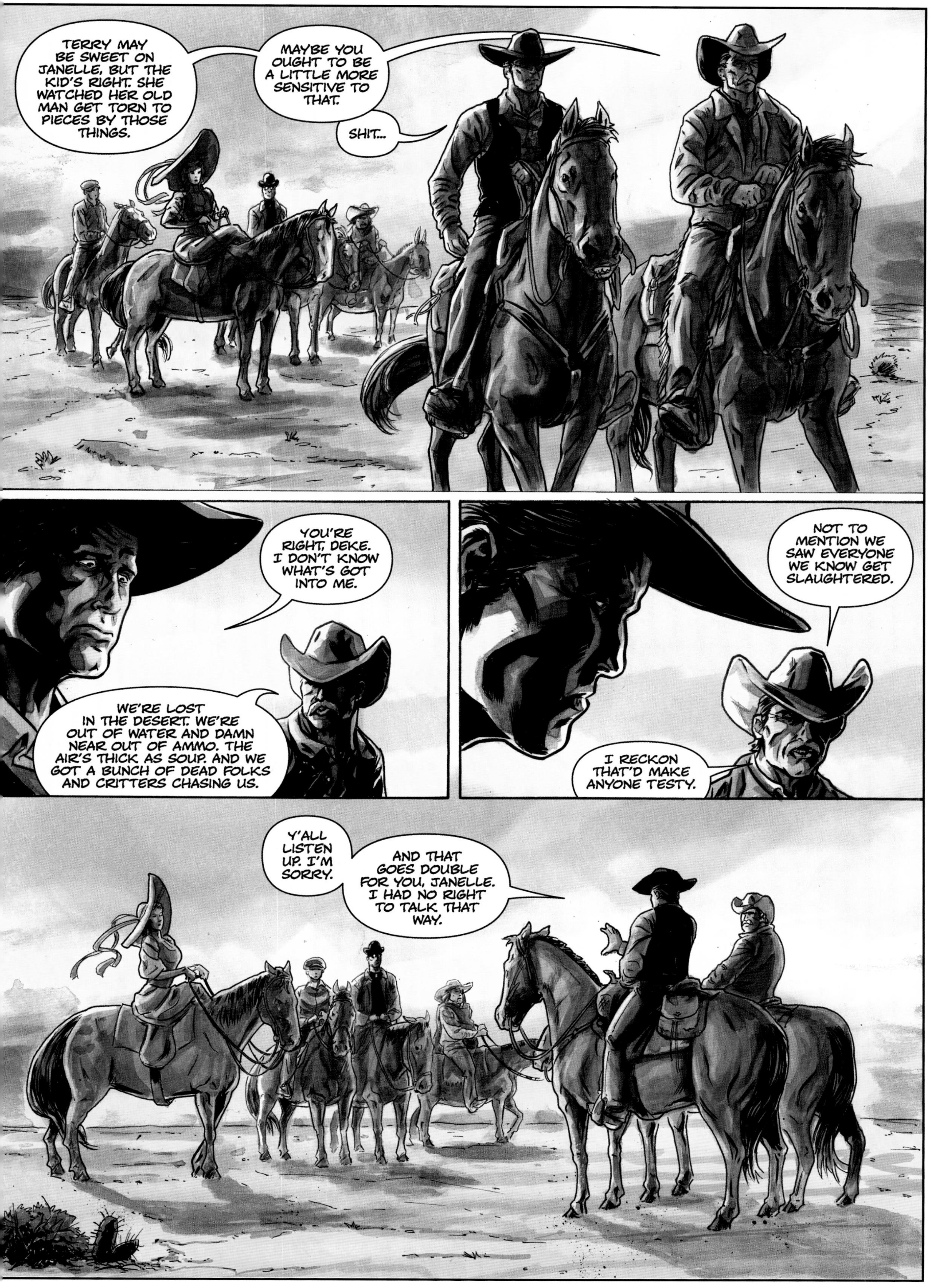
TERRY MAY BE SWEET ON JANELLE, BUT THE KID'S RIGHT. SHE WATCHED HER OLD MAN GET TORN TO PIECES BY THOSE THINGS.
MAYBE YOU OUGHT TO BE A LITTLE MORE SENSITIVE TO THAT.
SHIT...
YOU'RE RIGHT, DEKE. I DON'T KNOW WHAT'S GOT INTO ME.
WE'RE LOST IN THE DESERT. WE'RE OUT OF WATER AND DAMN NEAR OUT OF AMMO. THE AIR'S THICK AS SOUP. AND WE GOT A BUNCH OF DEAD FOLKS AND CRITTERS CHASING US.
NOT TO MENTION WE SAW EVERYONE WE KNOW GET SLAUGHTERED.
I RECKON THAT'D MAKE ANYONE TESTY.
Y'ALL LISTEN UP. I'M SORRY.
AND THAT GOES DOUBLE FOR YOU, JANELLE. I HAD NO RIGHT TO TALK THAT WAY.

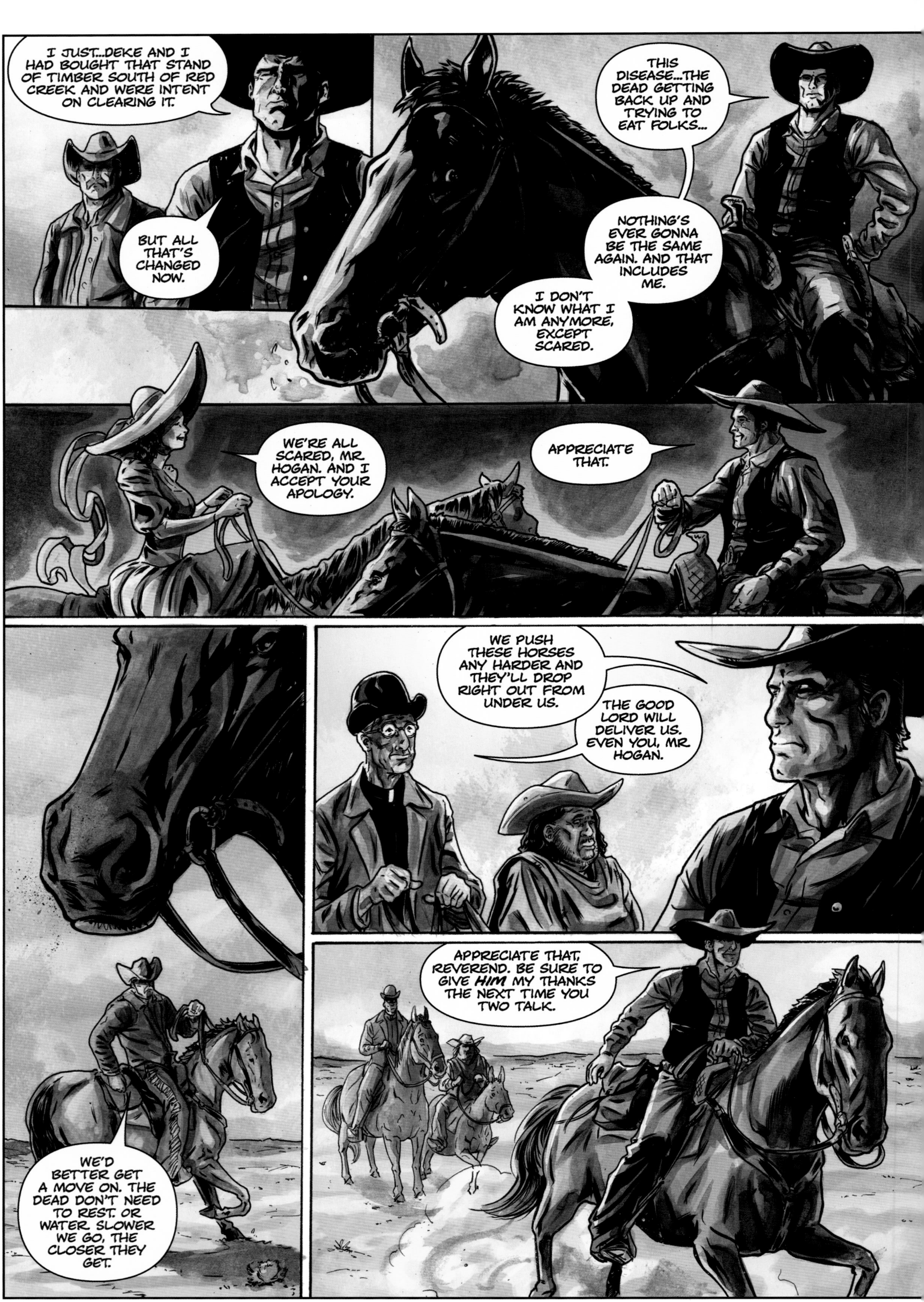

I JUST...DEKE AND I HAD BOUGHT THAT STAND OF TIMBER SOUTH OF RED CREEK AND WERE INTENT ON CLEARING IT.
BUT ALL THAT'S CHANGED NOW.
THIS DISEASE...THE DEAD GETTING BACK UP AND TRYING TO EAT FOLKS...
NOTHING'S EVER GONNA BE THE SAME AGAIN. AND THAT INCLUDES ME.
I DON'T KNOW WHAT I AM ANYMORE, EXCEPT SCARED.
WE'RE ALL SCARED, MR HOGAN. AND I ACCEPT YOUR APOLOGY.
APPRECIATE THAT.
WE PUSH THESE HORSES ANY HARDER AND THEY'LL DROP RIGHT OUT FROM UNDER US.
THE GOOD LORD WILL DELIVER US. EVEN YOU, MR HOGAN.
WE'D BETTER GET A MOVE ON. THE DEAD DON'T NEED TO REST. OR WATER. SLOWER WE GO, THE CLOSER THEY GET.
APPRECIATE THAT, REVEREND. BE SURE TO GIVE *HIM* MY THANKS THE NEXT TIME YOU TWO TALK.

HOW DO YOU KILL SOMETHING THAT'S ALREADY DEAD? SHOOTING THEM IN THE HEAD SEEMS TO WORK. SO DOES SMACKING THEM IN THE HEAD WITH A HAMMER OR A PICK-AXE OR A LENGTH OF KINDLING.

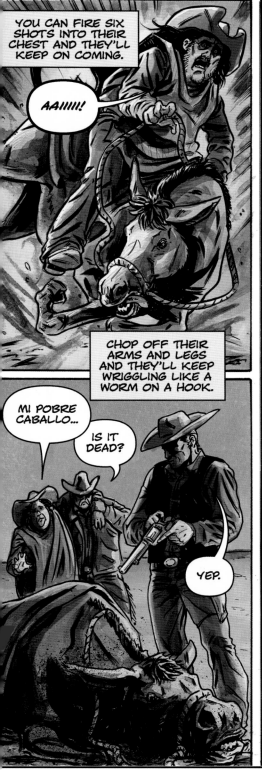

YOU CAN FIRE SIX SHOTS INTO THEIR CHEST AND THEY'LL KEEP ON COMING.

AAIIIII!

CHOP OFF THEIR ARMS AND LEGS AND THEY'LL KEEP WRIGGLING LIKE A WORM ON A HOOK.

MI POBRE CABALLO...

IS IT DEAD?

YEP.

BUT HIT THEM IN THE HEAD, AND THEY DROP LIKE A SACK OF GRAIN.

YEP...

THEN YOU KNOW WHAT WE GOTTA DO.

BOOM

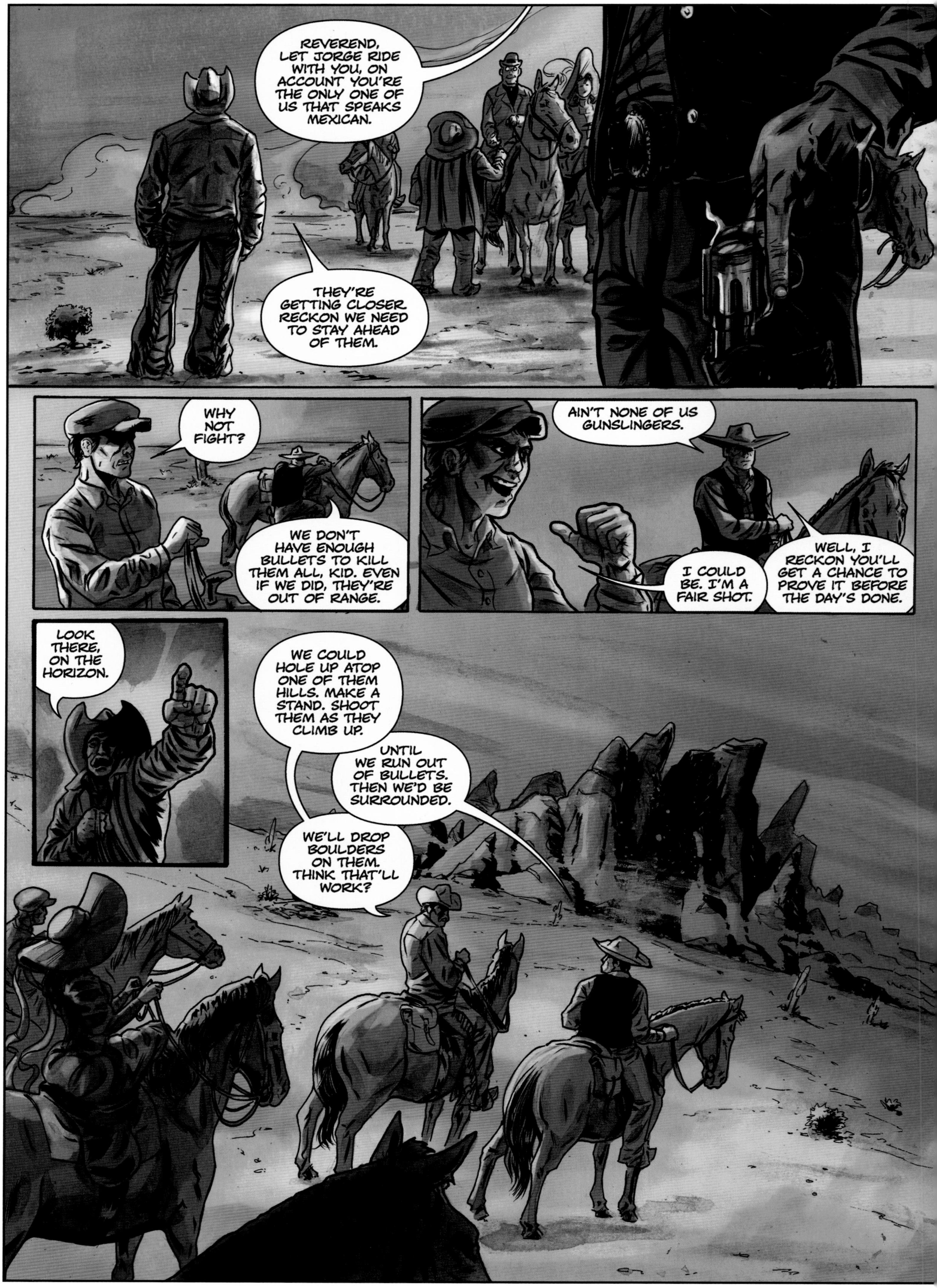
REVEREND, LET JORGE RIDE WITH YOU, ON ACCOUNT YOU'RE THE ONLY ONE OF US THAT SPEAKS MEXICAN.
THEY'RE GETTING CLOSER RECKON WE NEED TO STAY AHEAD OF THEM.
WHY NOT FIGHT?
WE DON'T HAVE ENOUGH BULLETS TO KILL THEM ALL, KID. EVEN IF WE DID, THEY'RE OUT OF RANGE.
AIN'T NONE OF US GUNSLINGERS.
I COULD BE. I'M A FAIR SHOT.
WELL, I RECKON YOU'LL GET A CHANCE TO PROVE IT BEFORE THE DAY'S DONE.
LOOK THERE, ON THE HORIZON.
WE COULD HOLE UP ATOP ONE OF THEM HILLS. MAKE A STAND. SHOOT THEM AS THEY CLIMB UP.
UNTIL WE RUN OUT OF BULLETS. THEN WE'D BE SURROUNDED.
WE'LL DROP BOULDERS ON THEM. THINK THAT'LL WORK?

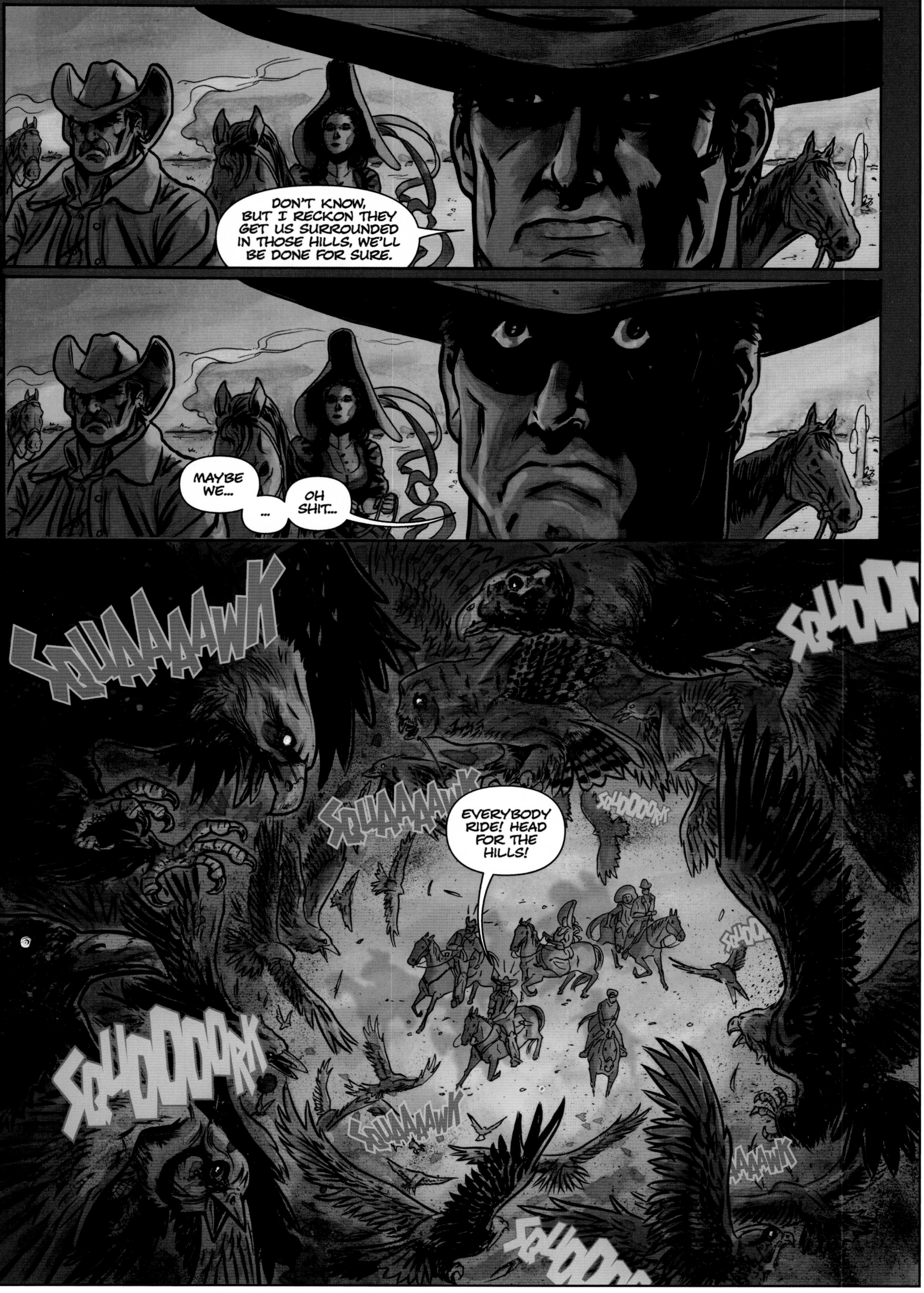
DON'T KNOW, BUT I RECKON THEY GET US SURROUNDED IN THOSE HILLS, WE'LL BE DONE FOR SURE.
MAYBE WE...
...
OH SHIT...
SQUAAAAAWK
SQUOOOORK
SQUAAAAWK
SQUOOOORK
EVERYBODY RIDE! HEAD FOR THE HILLS!
SQUOOOORK
SQUAAAAAWK
AAAWK

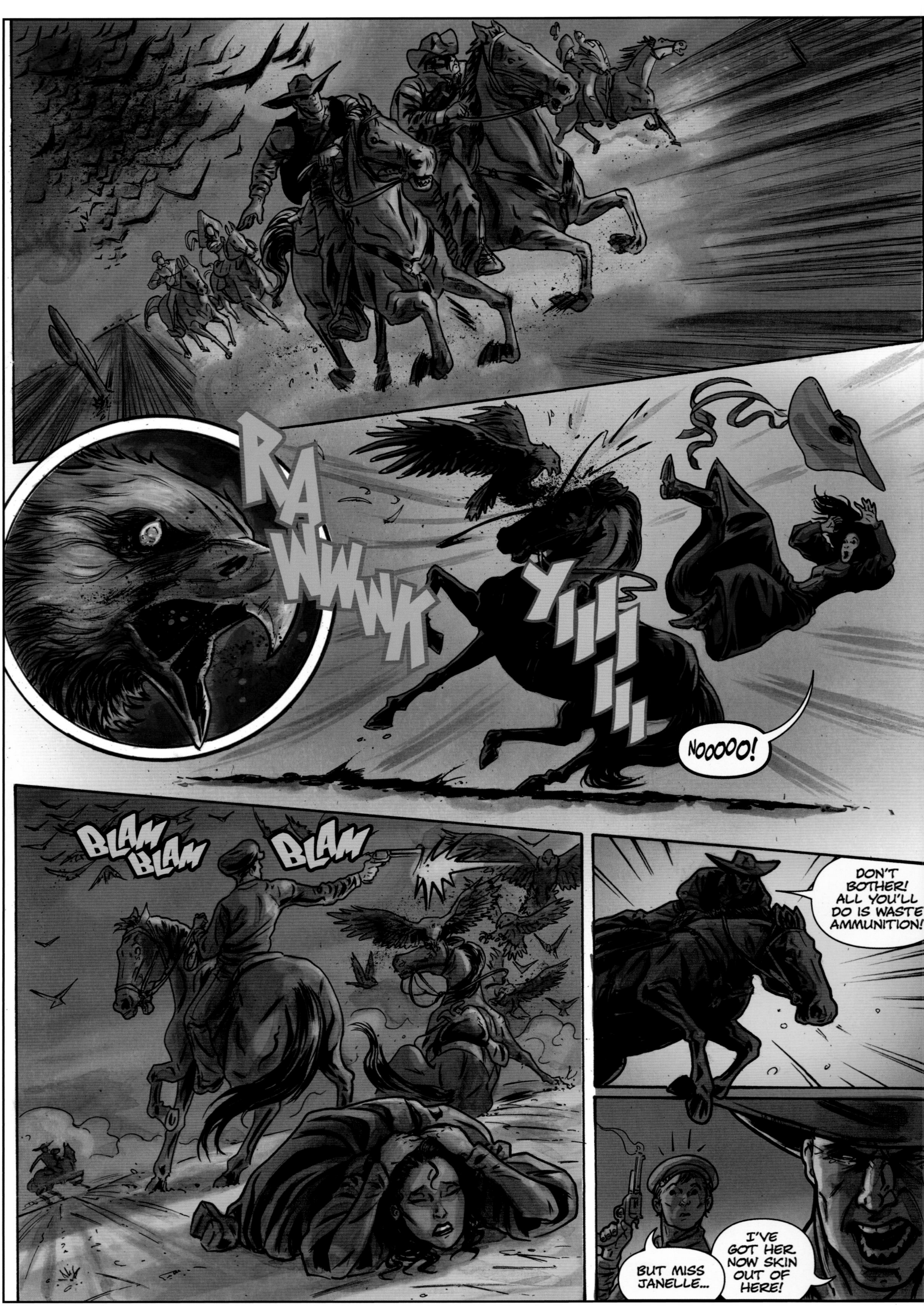
RAWWWWK
YIIIIIIII
NOOOOO!
BLAM BLAM
BLAM
DON'T BOTHER! ALL YOU'LL DO IS WASTE AMMUNITION!
BUT MISS JANELLE...
I'VE GOT HER NOW SKIN OUT OF HERE!

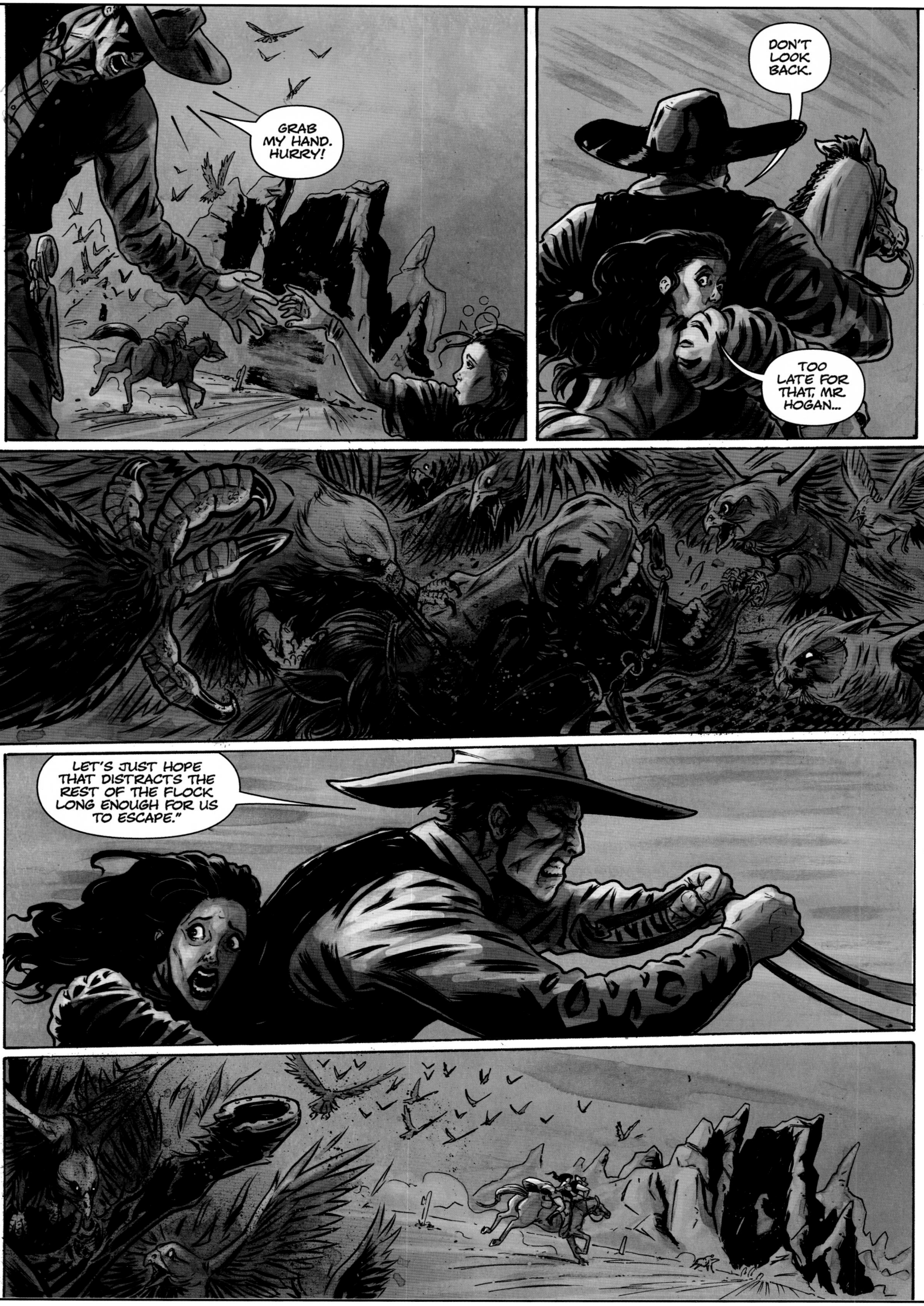
GRAB MY HAND. HURRY!
DON'T LOOK BACK.
TOO LATE FOR THAT, MR HOGAN...
LET'S JUST HOPE THAT DISTRACTS THE REST OF THE FLOCK LONG ENOUGH FOR US TO ESCAPE."

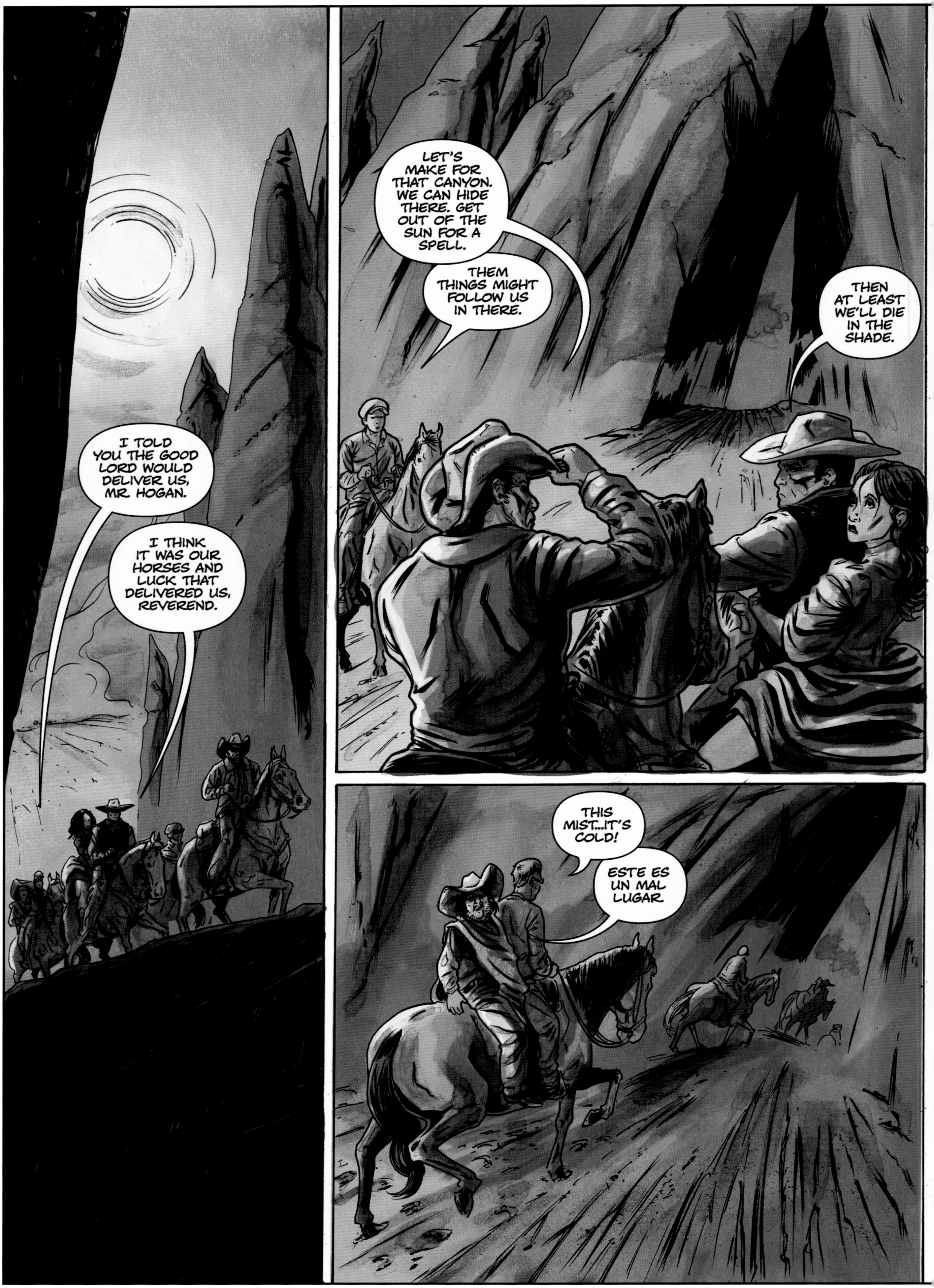
I TOLD YOU THE GOOD LORD WOULD DELIVER US, MR HOGAN.
I THINK IT WAS OUR HORSES AND LUCK THAT DELIVERED US, REVEREND.
LET'S MAKE FOR THAT CANYON. WE CAN HIDE THERE. GET OUT OF THE SUN FOR A SPELL.
THEM THINGS MIGHT FOLLOW US IN THERE.
THEN AT LEAST WE'LL DIE IN THE SHADE.
THIS MIST...IT'S COLD!
ESTE ES UN MAL LUGAR

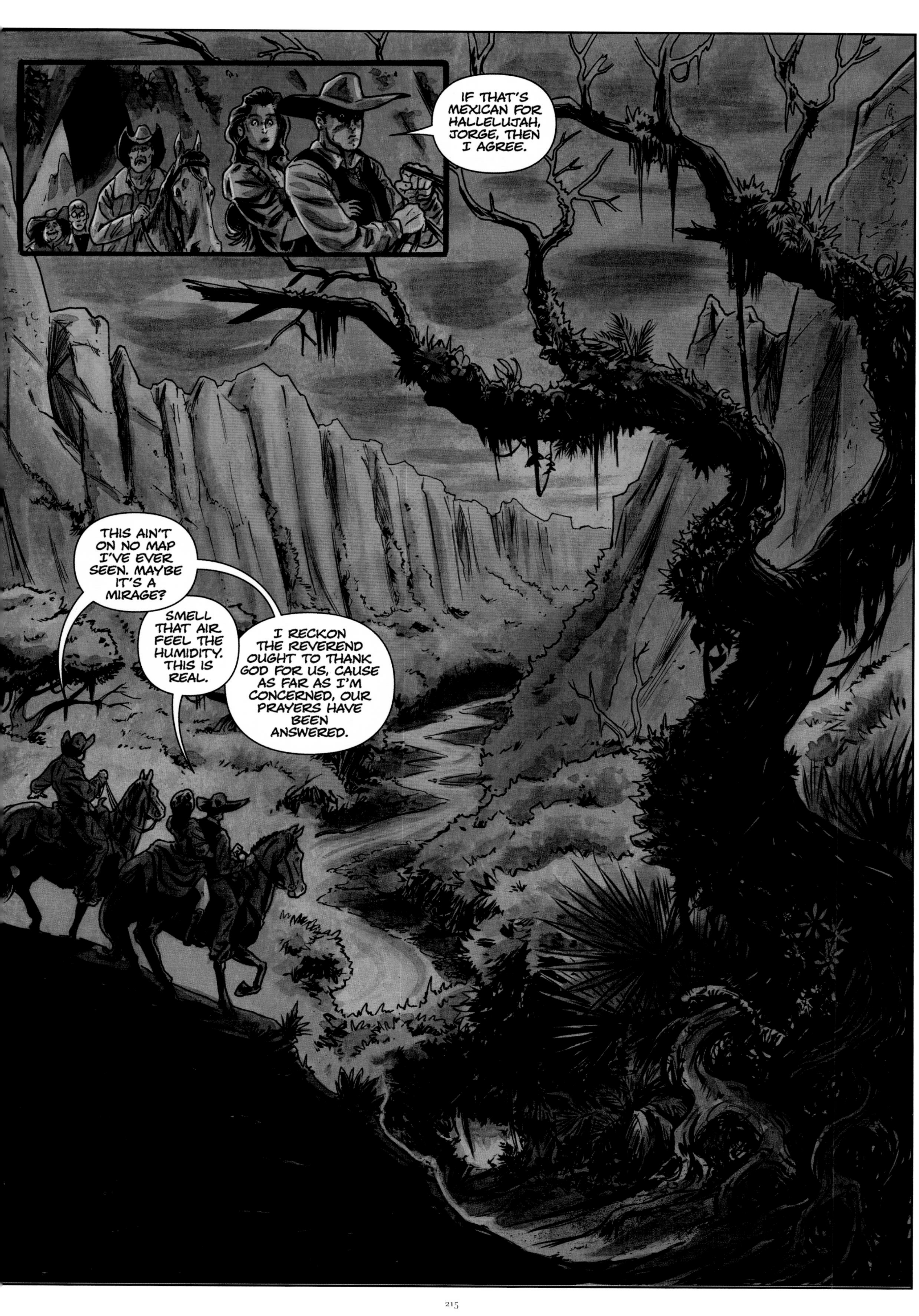
IF THAT'S MEXICAN FOR HALLELUJAH, JORGE, THEN I AGREE.
THIS AIN'T ON NO MAP I'VE EVER SEEN. MAYBE IT'S A MIRAGE?
SMELL THAT AIR FEEL THE HUMIDITY. THIS IS REAL.
I RECKON THE REVEREND OUGHT TO THANK GOD FOR US, CAUSE AS FAR AS I'M CONCERNED, OUR PRAYERS HAVE BEEN ANSWERED.

LET ME GIVE YOU A HAND.

THANK YOU, MR HOGAN.

MAYBE IT'S AN OASIS?

TOO BIG FOR THAT. IT'S A WHOLE VALLEY.

I DON'T CARE WHAT IT IS. WE'VE GOT SHELTER, SHADE, FOOD, AND WATER

TREES TO HIDE US FROM THOSE DEAD BIRDS.

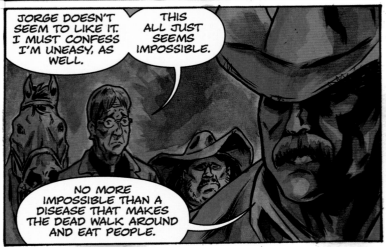

JORGE DOESN'T SEEM TO LIKE IT. I MUST CONFESS I'M UNEASY, AS WELL.

THIS ALL JUST SEEMS IMPOSSIBLE.

NO MORE IMPOSSIBLE THAN A DISEASE THAT MAKES THE DEAD WALK AROUND AND EAT PEOPLE.

BUT LOOK BEHIND US. WHERE HAS THE DESERT GONE? IT'S DISAPPEARED, ALONG WITH THE CANYON ENTRANCE.

DON'T GET YOUR BRITCHES IN AN UPROAR, REVEREND...

"...I'M SURE THE ENTRANCE IS STILL THERE."

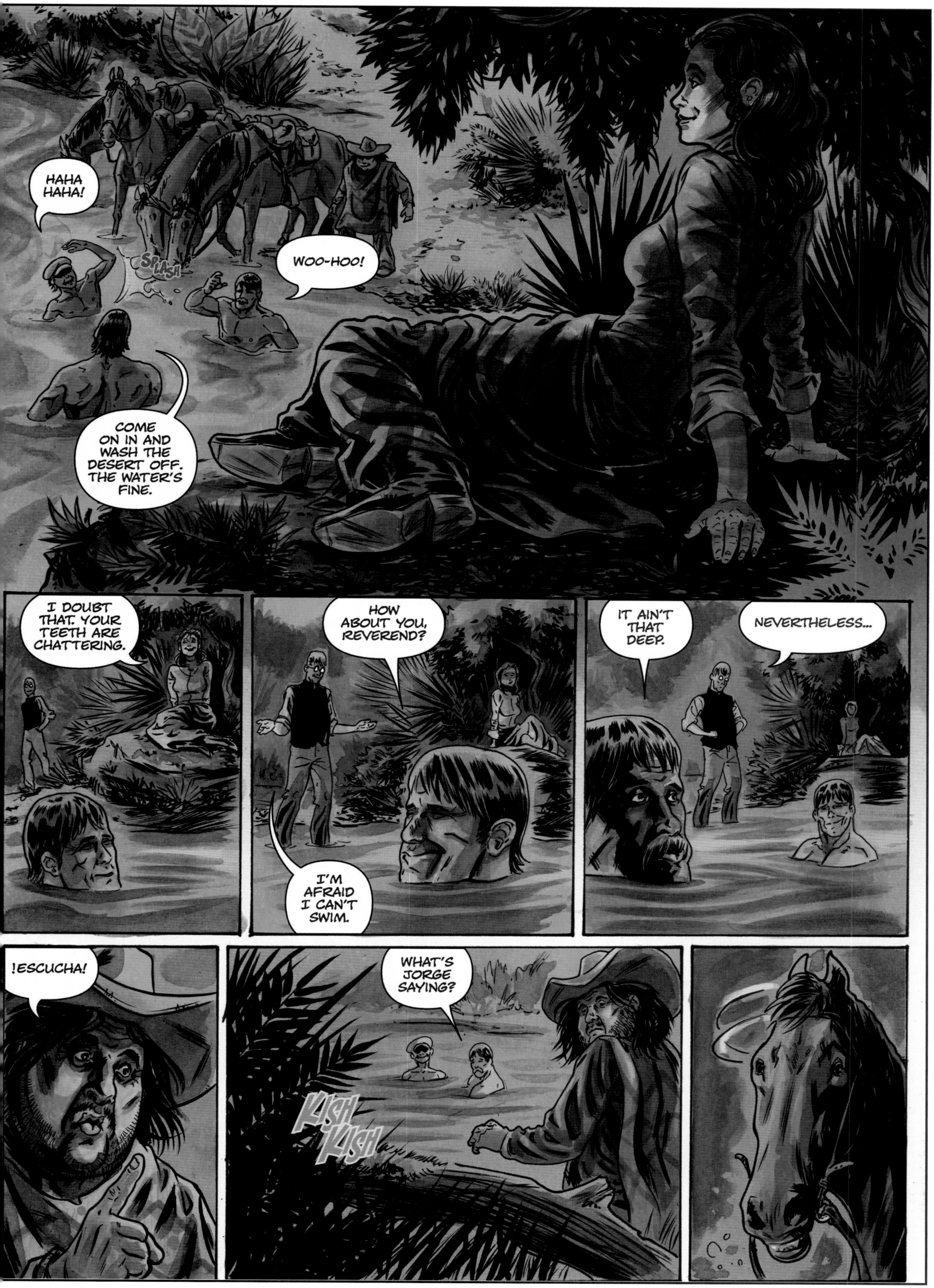

HAHA HAHA!
SPLASH
WOO-HOO!
COME ON IN AND WASH THE DESERT OFF. THE WATER'S FINE.
I DOUBT THAT. YOUR TEETH ARE CHATTERING.
HOW ABOUT YOU, REVEREND?
I'M AFRAID I CAN'T SWIM.
IT AIN'T THAT DEEP.
NEVERTHELESS...
!ESCUCHA!
WHAT'S JORGE SAYING?
KISH KISH

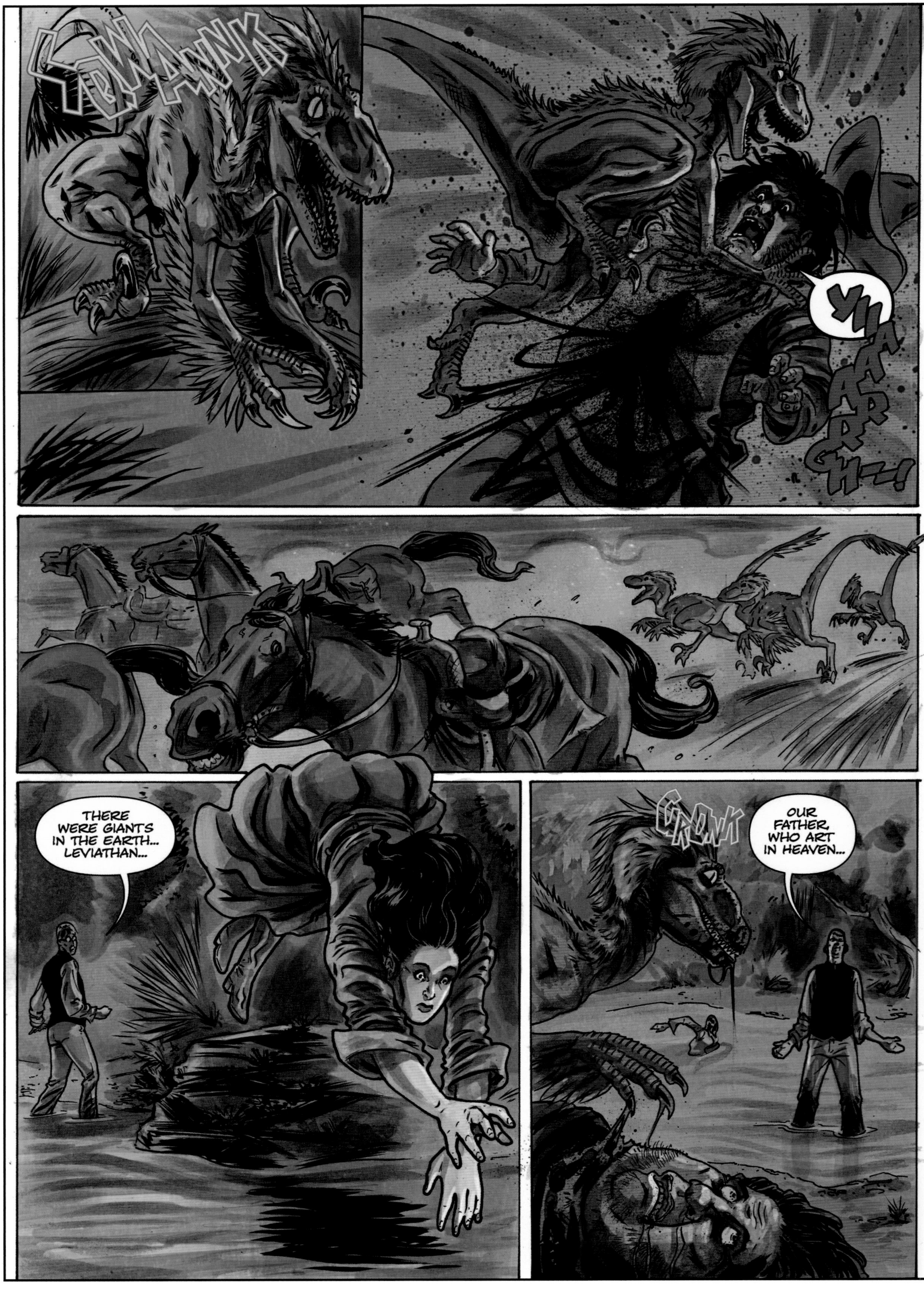
SKRWAANK
YAAARGH--!
THERE WERE GIANTS IN THE EARTH... LEVIATHAN...
GRONK
OUR FATHER WHO ART IN HEAVEN...

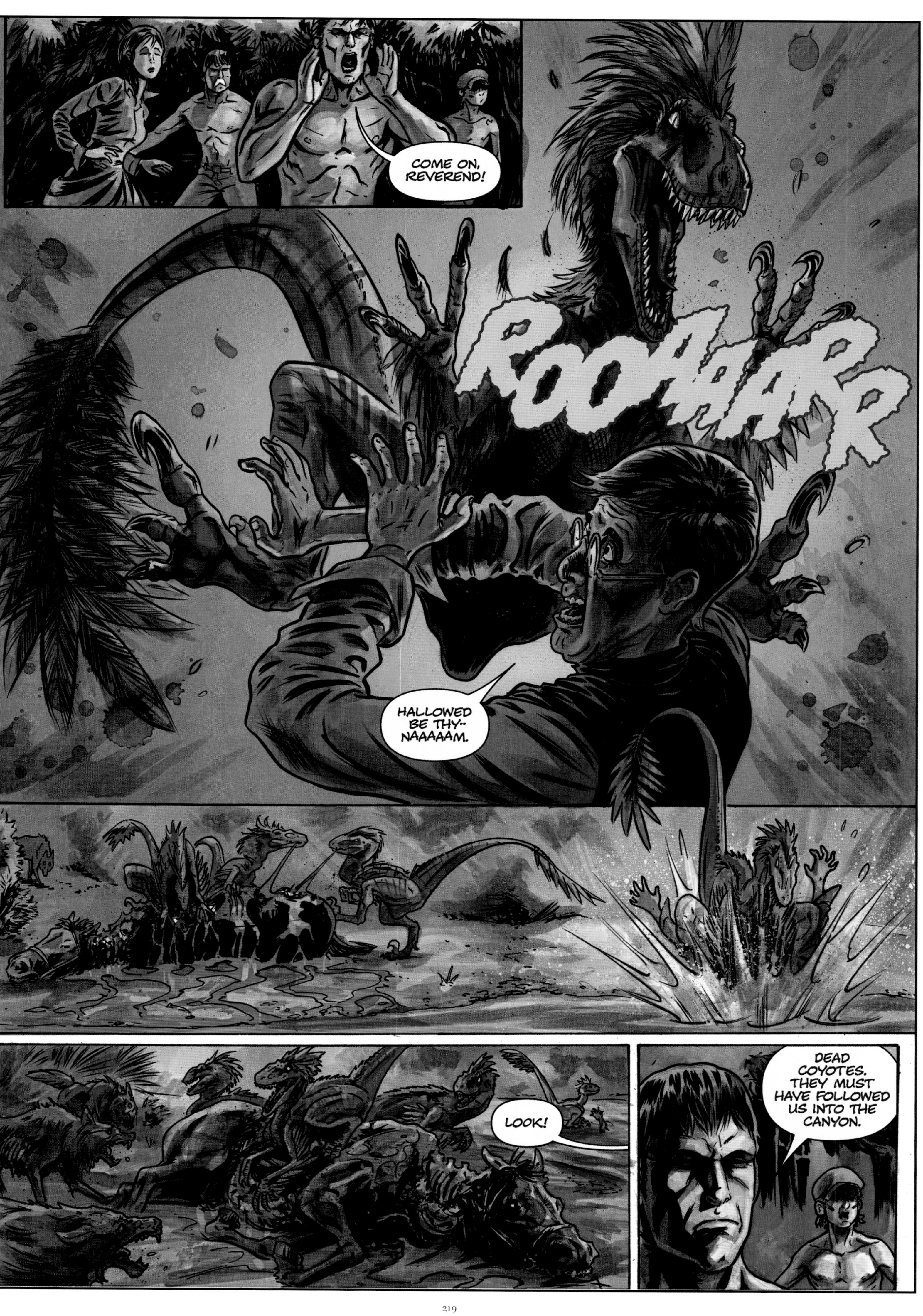
COME ON, REVEREND!
ROOAARR
HALLOWED BE THY.. NAAAAAM.
LOOK!
DEAD COYOTES. THEY MUST HAVE FOLLOWED US INTO THE CANYON.

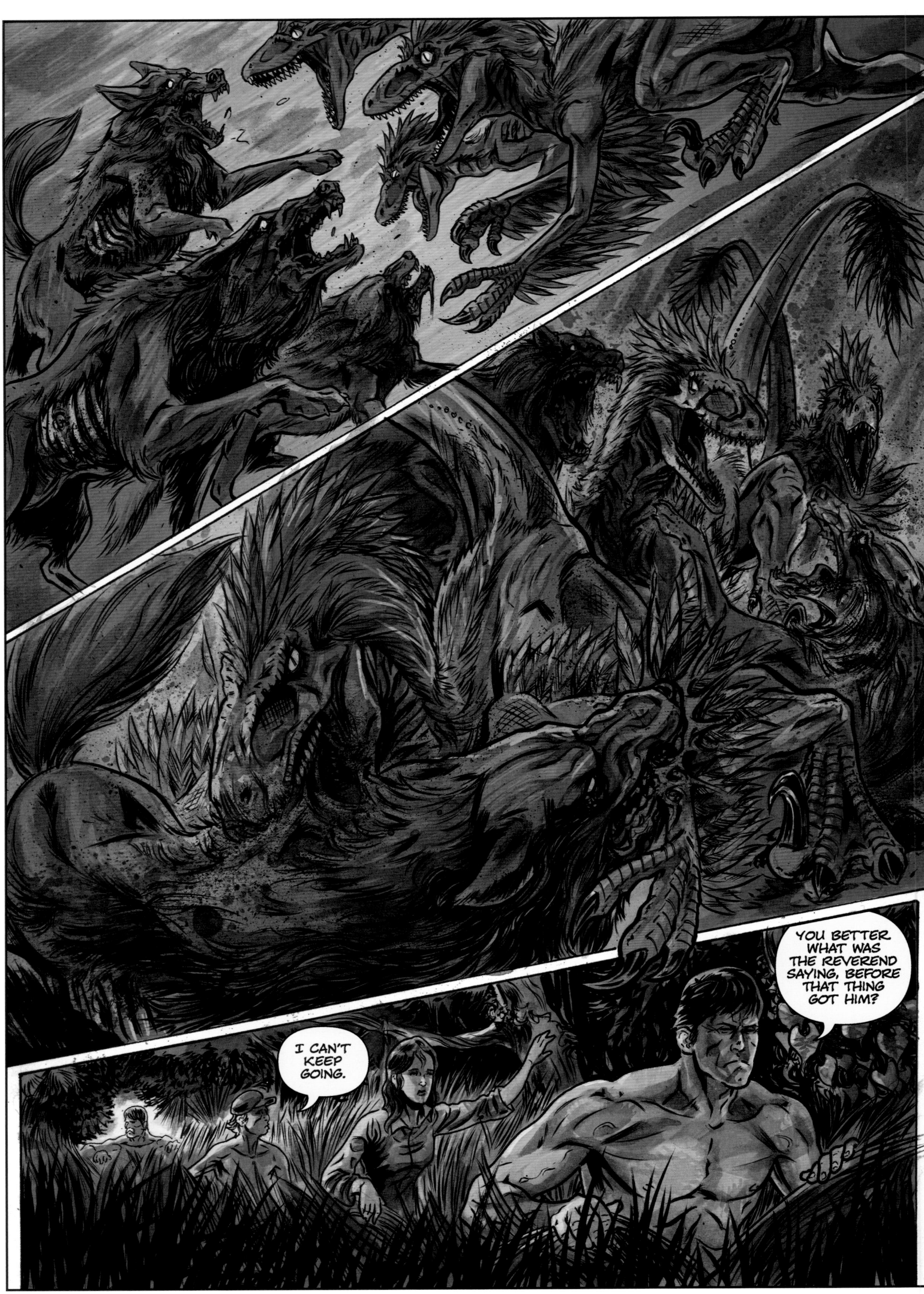
I CAN'T KEEP GOING.
YOU BETTER WHAT WAS THE REVEREND SAYING, BEFORE THAT THING GOT HIM?

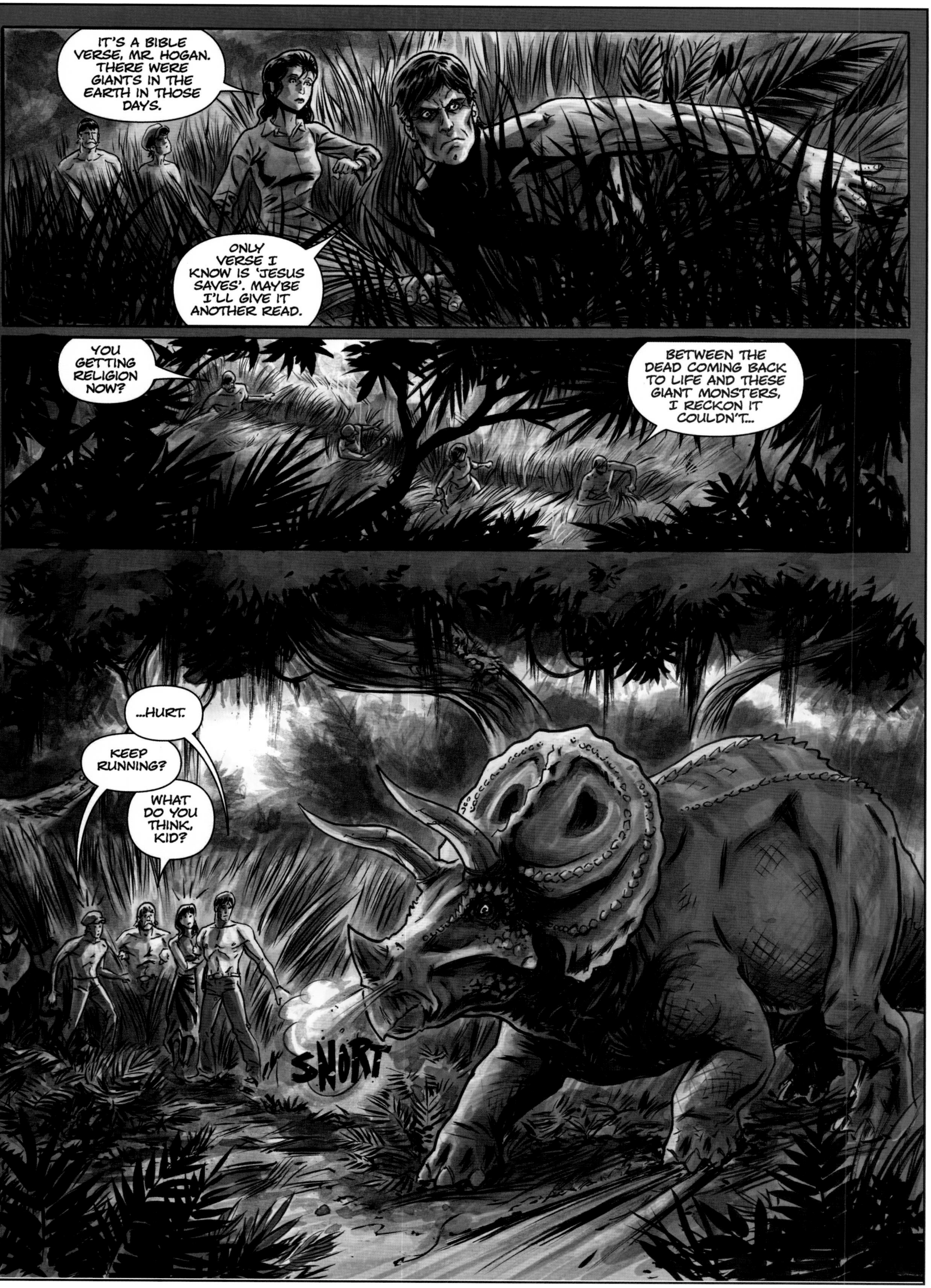
IT'S A BIBLE VERSE, MR. HOGAN. THERE WERE GIANTS IN THE EARTH IN THOSE DAYS.
ONLY VERSE I KNOW IS 'JESUS SAVES'. MAYBE I'LL GIVE IT ANOTHER READ.
YOU GETTING RELIGION NOW?
BETWEEN THE DEAD COMING BACK TO LIFE AND THESE GIANT MONSTERS, I RECKON IT COULDN'T...
...HURT.
KEEP RUNNING?
WHAT DO YOU THINK, KID?
SNORT

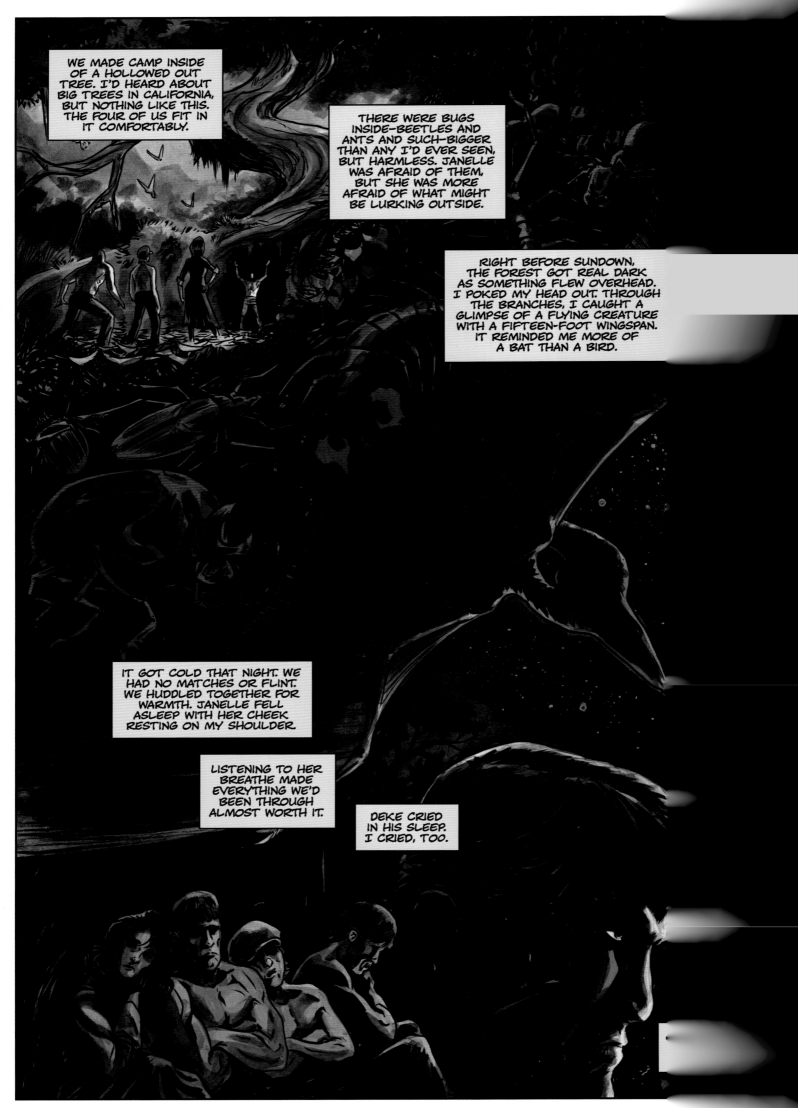

WE MADE CAMP INSIDE OF A HOLLOWED OUT TREE. I'D HEARD ABOUT BIG TREES IN CALIFORNIA, BUT NOTHING LIKE THIS. THE FOUR OF US FIT IN IT COMFORTABLY.

THERE WERE BUGS INSIDE—BEETLES AND ANTS AND SUCH—BIGGER THAN ANY I'D EVER SEEN, BUT HARMLESS. JANELLE WAS AFRAID OF THEM, BUT SHE WAS MORE AFRAID OF WHAT MIGHT BE LURKING OUTSIDE.

RIGHT BEFORE SUNDOWN, THE FOREST GOT REAL DARK AS SOMETHING FLEW OVERHEAD. I POKED MY HEAD OUT. THROUGH THE BRANCHES, I CAUGHT A GLIMPSE OF A FLYING CREATURE WITH A FIFTEEN-FOOT WINGSPAN. IT REMINDED ME MORE OF A BAT THAN A BIRD.

IT GOT COLD THAT NIGHT. WE HAD NO MATCHES OR FLINT. WE HUDDLED TOGETHER FOR WARMTH. JANELLE FELL ASLEEP WITH HER CHEEK RESTING ON MY SHOULDER.

LISTENING TO HER BREATHE MADE EVERYTHING WE'D BEEN THROUGH ALMOST WORTH IT.

DEKE CRIED IN HIS SLEEP. I CRIED, TOO.

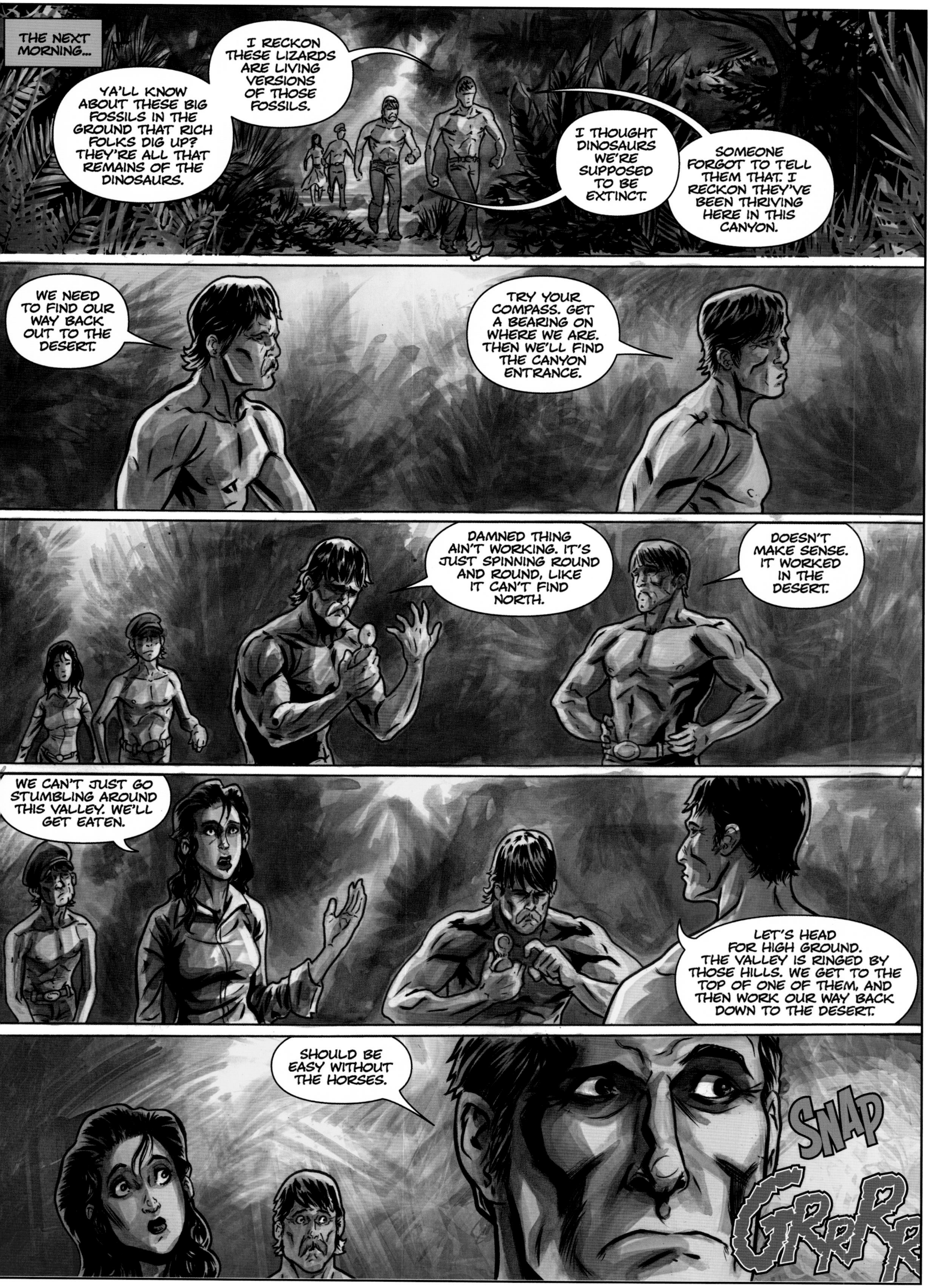
THE NEXT MORNING...
YA'LL KNOW ABOUT THESE BIG FOSSILS IN THE GROUND THAT RICH FOLKS DIG UP? THEY'RE ALL THAT REMAINS OF THE DINOSAURS.
I RECKON THESE LIZARDS ARE LIVING VERSIONS OF THOSE FOSSILS.
I THOUGHT DINOSAURS WE'RE SUPPOSED TO BE EXTINCT.
SOMEONE FORGOT TO TELL THEM THAT. I RECKON THEY'VE BEEN THRIVING HERE IN THIS CANYON.
WE NEED TO FIND OUR WAY BACK OUT TO THE DESERT.
TRY YOUR COMPASS. GET A BEARING ON WHERE WE ARE. THEN WE'LL FIND THE CANYON ENTRANCE.
DAMNED THING AIN'T WORKING. IT'S JUST SPINNING ROUND AND ROUND, LIKE IT CAN'T FIND NORTH.
DOESN'T MAKE SENSE. IT WORKED IN THE DESERT.
WE CAN'T JUST GO STUMBLING AROUND THIS VALLEY. WE'LL GET EATEN.
LET'S HEAD FOR HIGH GROUND. THE VALLEY IS RINGED BY THOSE HILLS. WE GET TO THE TOP OF ONE OF THEM, AND THEN WORK OUR WAY BACK DOWN TO THE DESERT.
SHOULD BE EASY WITHOUT THE HORSES.
SNAP
GRRRR

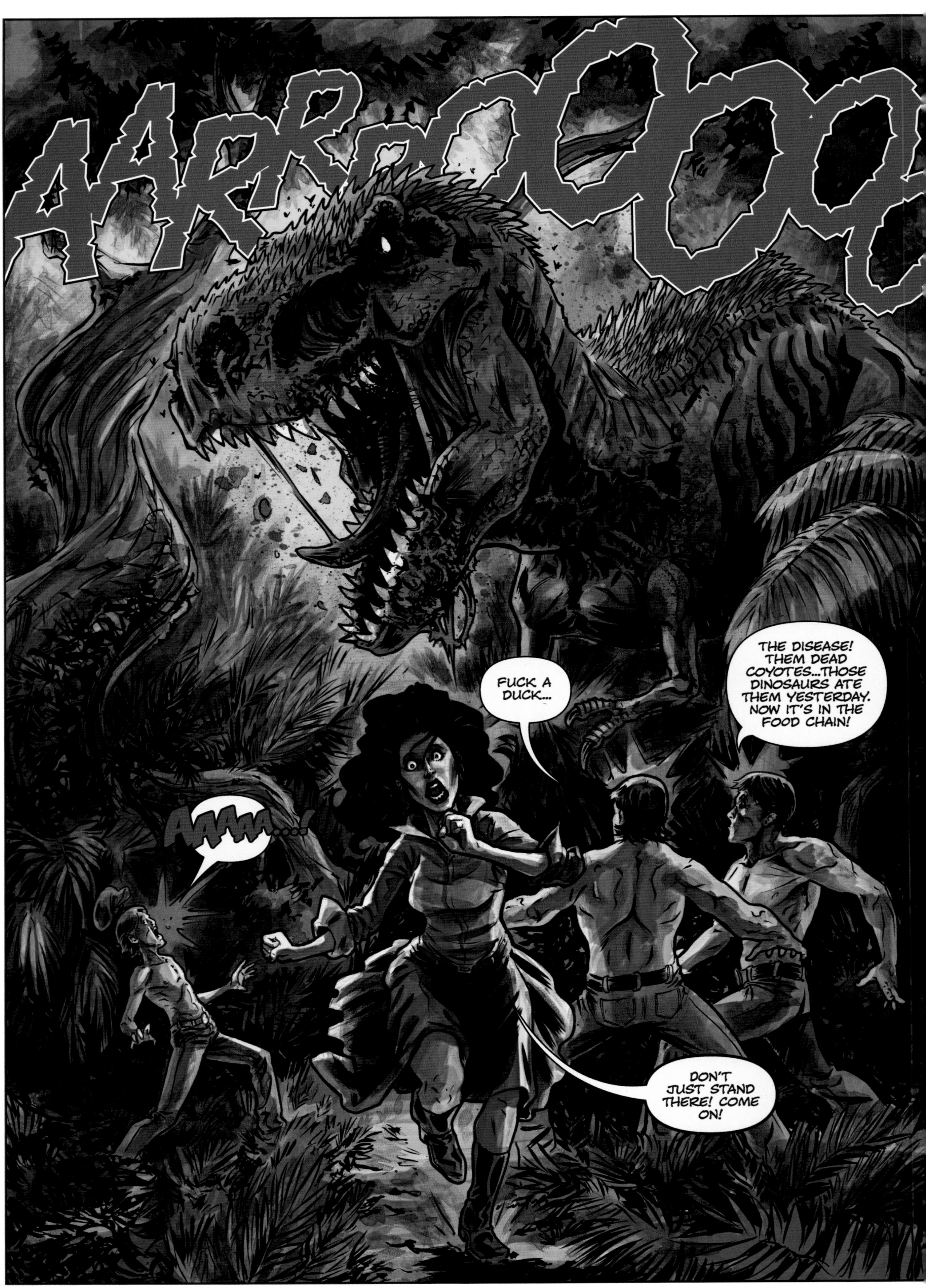
AARROOOOO
THE DISEASE! THEM DEAD COYOTES...THOSE DINOSAURS ATE THEM YESTERDAY. NOW IT'S IN THE FOOD CHAIN!
FUCK A DUCK...
AAAAA...!
DON'T JUST STAND THERE! COME ON!

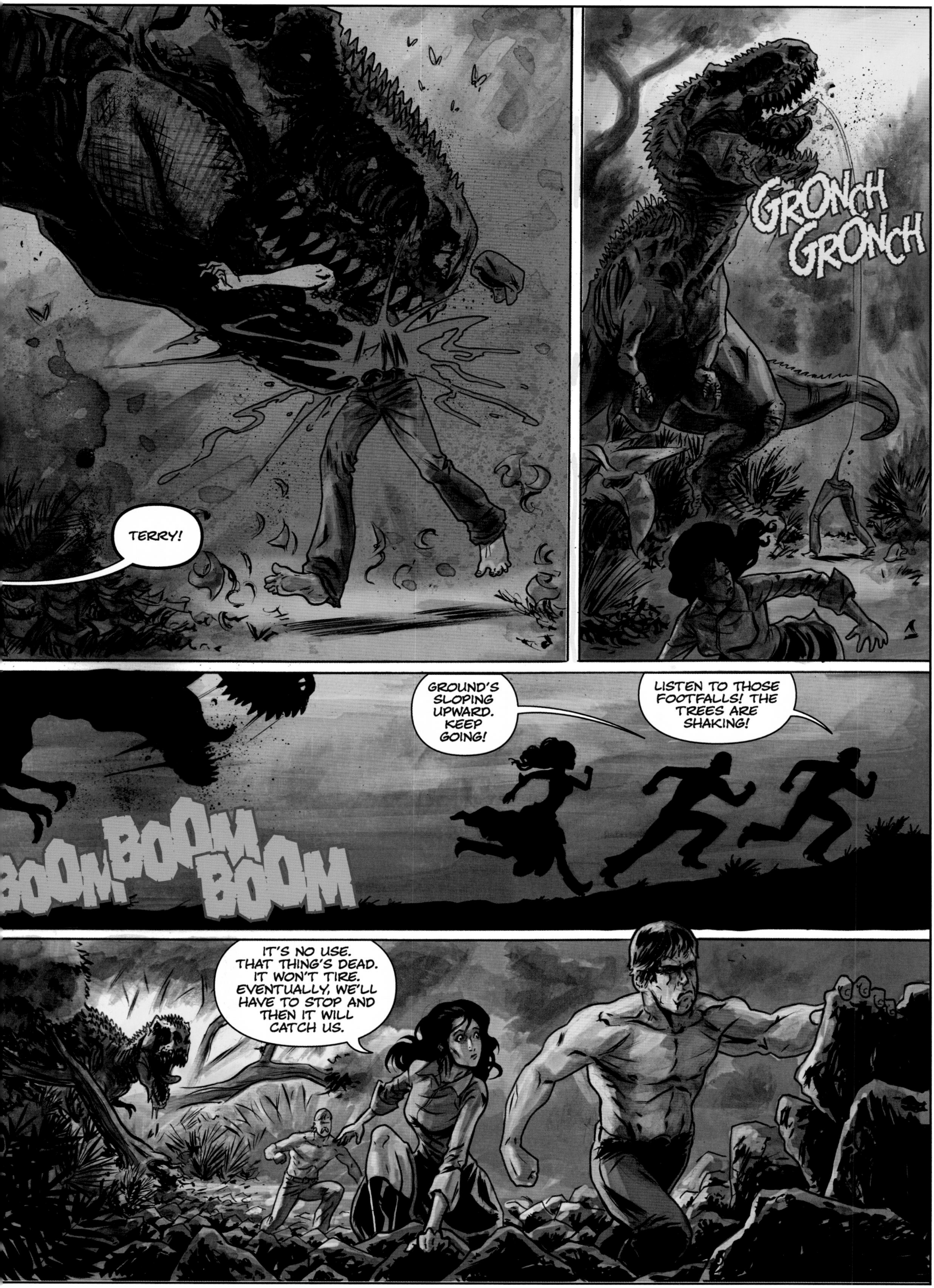
TERRY!
GRONCH GRONCH
GROUND'S SLOPING UPWARD. KEEP GOING!
LISTEN TO THOSE FOOTFALLS! THE TREES ARE SHAKING!
BOOM! BOOM BOOM
IT'S NO USE. THAT THING'S DEAD. IT WON'T TIRE. EVENTUALLY, WE'LL HAVE TO STOP AND THEN IT WILL CATCH US.

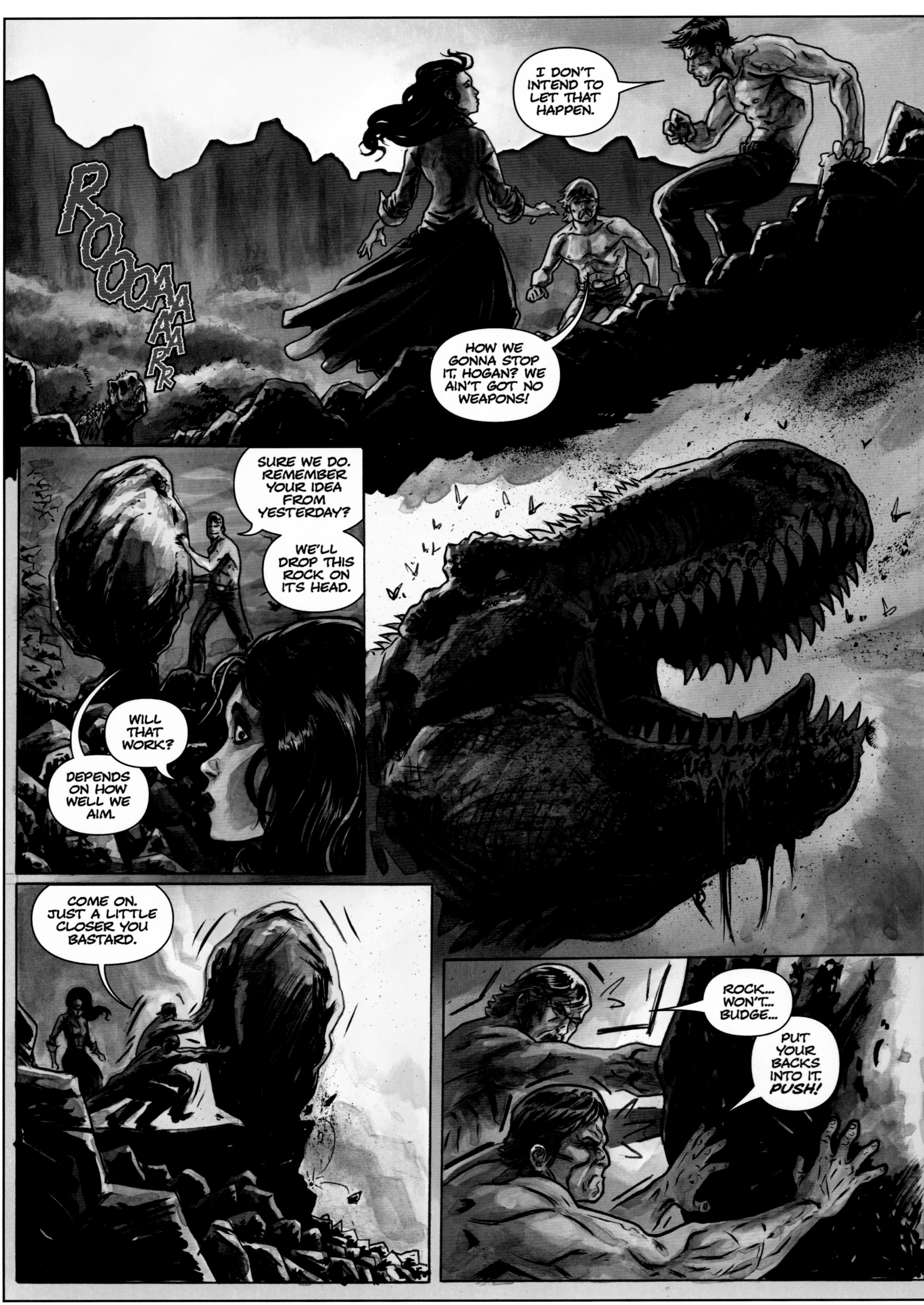
ROOOAAAARR
I DON'T INTEND TO LET THAT HAPPEN.
HOW WE GONNA STOP IT, HOGAN? WE AIN'T GOT NO WEAPONS!
SURE WE DO. REMEMBER YOUR IDEA FROM YESTERDAY?
WE'LL DROP THIS ROCK ON ITS HEAD.
WILL THAT WORK?
DEPENDS ON HOW WELL WE AIM.
COME ON. JUST A LITTLE CLOSER YOU BASTARD.
ROCK... WON'T... BUDGE...
PUT YOUR BACKS INTO IT. PUSH!

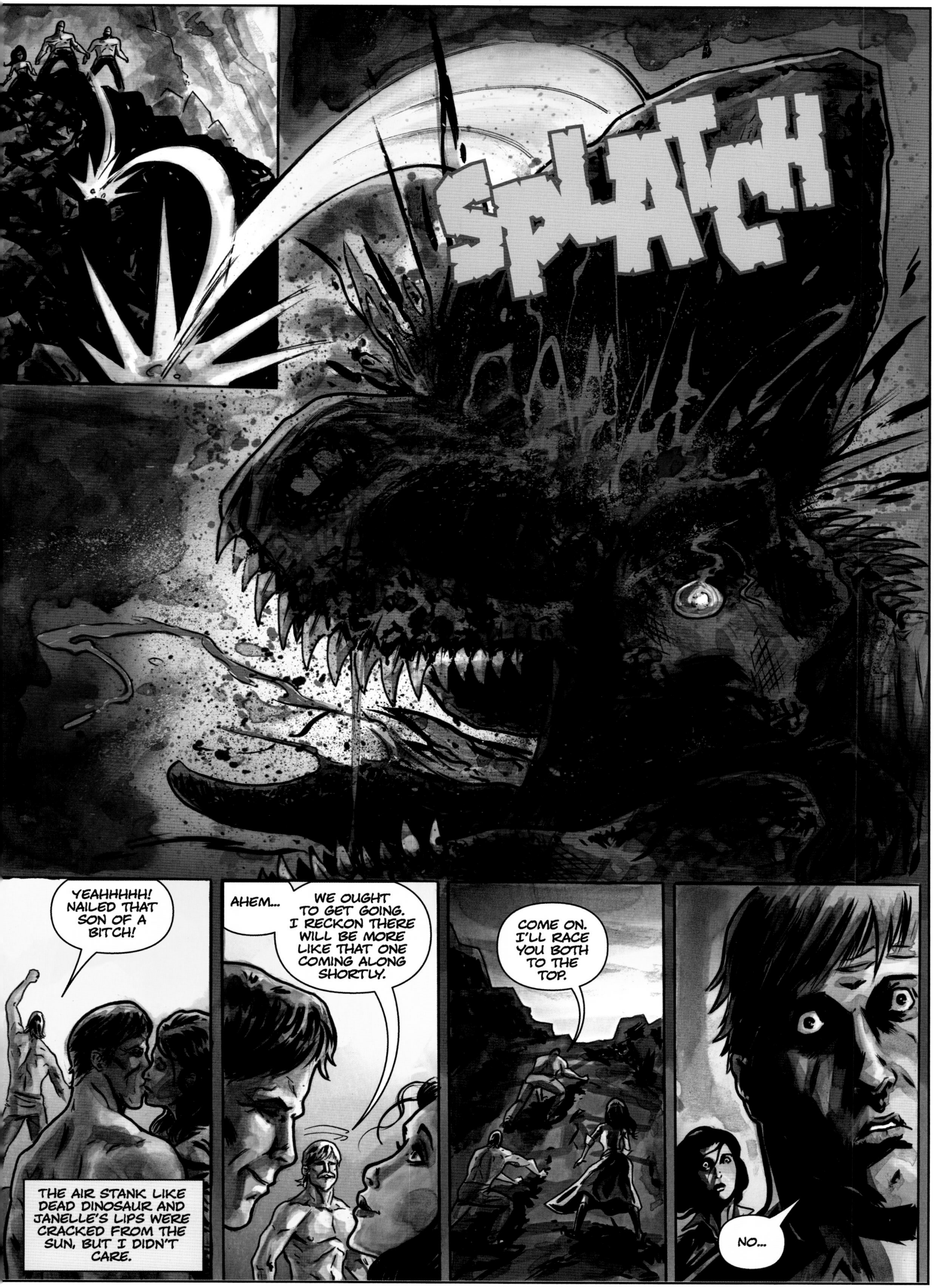
SPLATCH
YEAHHHHH! NAILED THAT SON OF A BITCH!
THE AIR STANK LIKE DEAD DINOSAUR AND JANELLE'S LIPS WERE CRACKED FROM THE SUN, BUT I DIDN'T CARE.
AHEM...
WE OUGHT TO GET GOING. I RECKON THERE WILL BE MORE LIKE THAT ONE COMING ALONG SHORTLY.
COME ON. I'LL RACE YOU BOTH TO THE TOP.
NO...

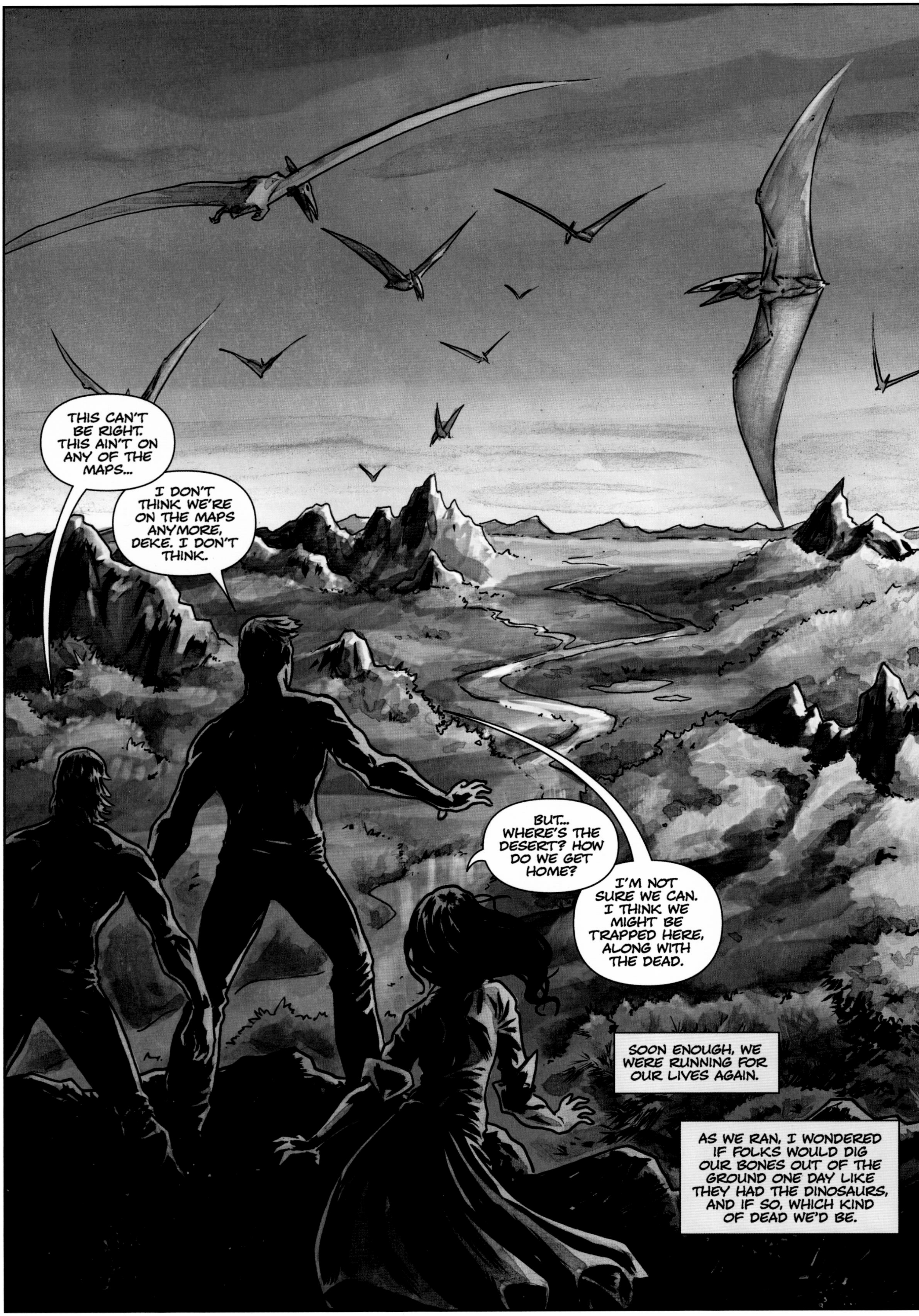
THIS CAN'T BE RIGHT. THIS AIN'T ON ANY OF THE MAPS...
I DON'T THINK WE'RE ON THE MAPS ANYMORE, DEKE. I DON'T THINK.
BUT... WHERE'S THE DESERT? HOW DO WE GET HOME?
I'M NOT SURE WE CAN. I THINK WE MIGHT BE TRAPPED HERE, ALONG WITH THE DEAD.
SOON ENOUGH, WE WERE RUNNING FOR OUR LIVES AGAIN.
AS WE RAN, I WONDERED IF FOLKS WOULD DIG OUR BONES OUT OF THE GROUND ONE DAY LIKE THEY HAD THE DINOSAURS, AND IF SO, WHICH KIND OF DEAD WE'D BE.

SET ME FREE

WRITER
JODY LEHEUP

ARTIST
DALIBOR TALAJIC

COLORIST
JIM CAMPBELL

LETTERER
ADAM WOLLET

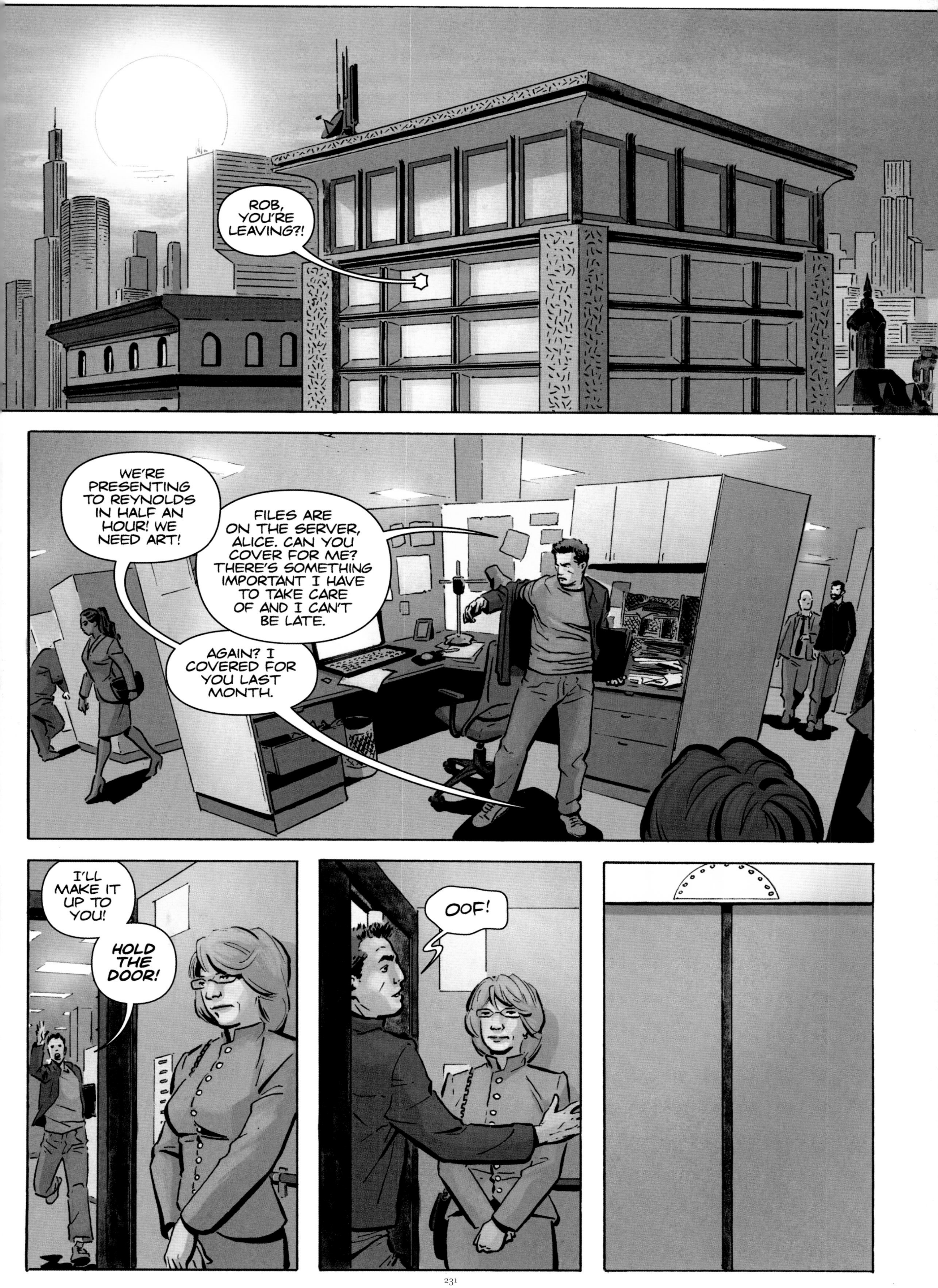
ROB, YOU'RE LEAVING?!
WE'RE PRESENTING TO REYNOLDS IN HALF AN HOUR! WE NEED ART!
FILES ARE ON THE SERVER, ALICE. CAN YOU COVER FOR ME? THERE'S SOMETHING IMPORTANT I HAVE TO TAKE CARE OF AND I CAN'T BE LATE.
AGAIN? I COVERED FOR YOU LAST MONTH.
I'LL MAKE IT UP TO YOU!
HOLD THE DOOR!
OOF!

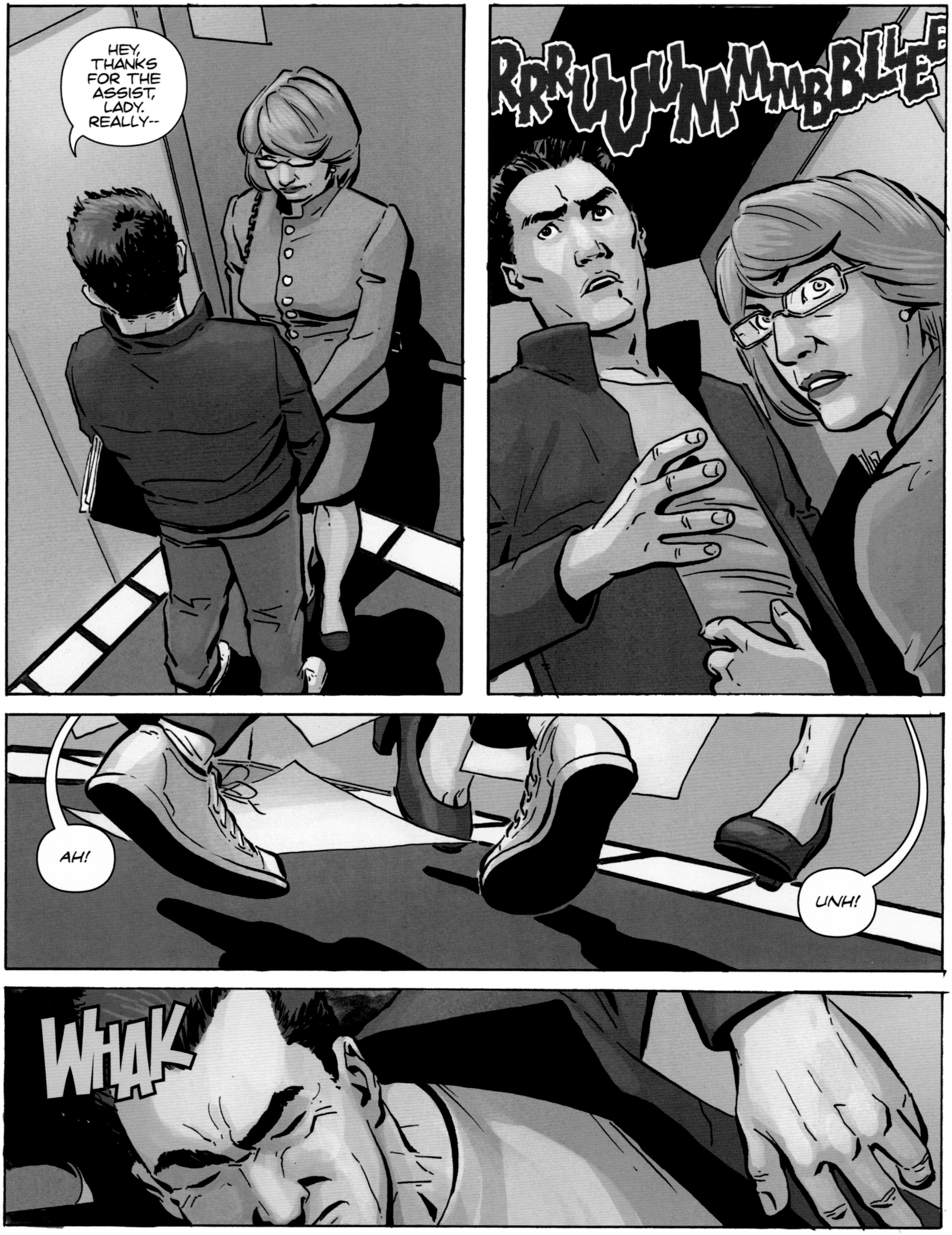
HEY, THANKS FOR THE ASSIST, LADY. REALLY--
RRRUUUMMMBBLLEE
AH!
UNH!
WHAK

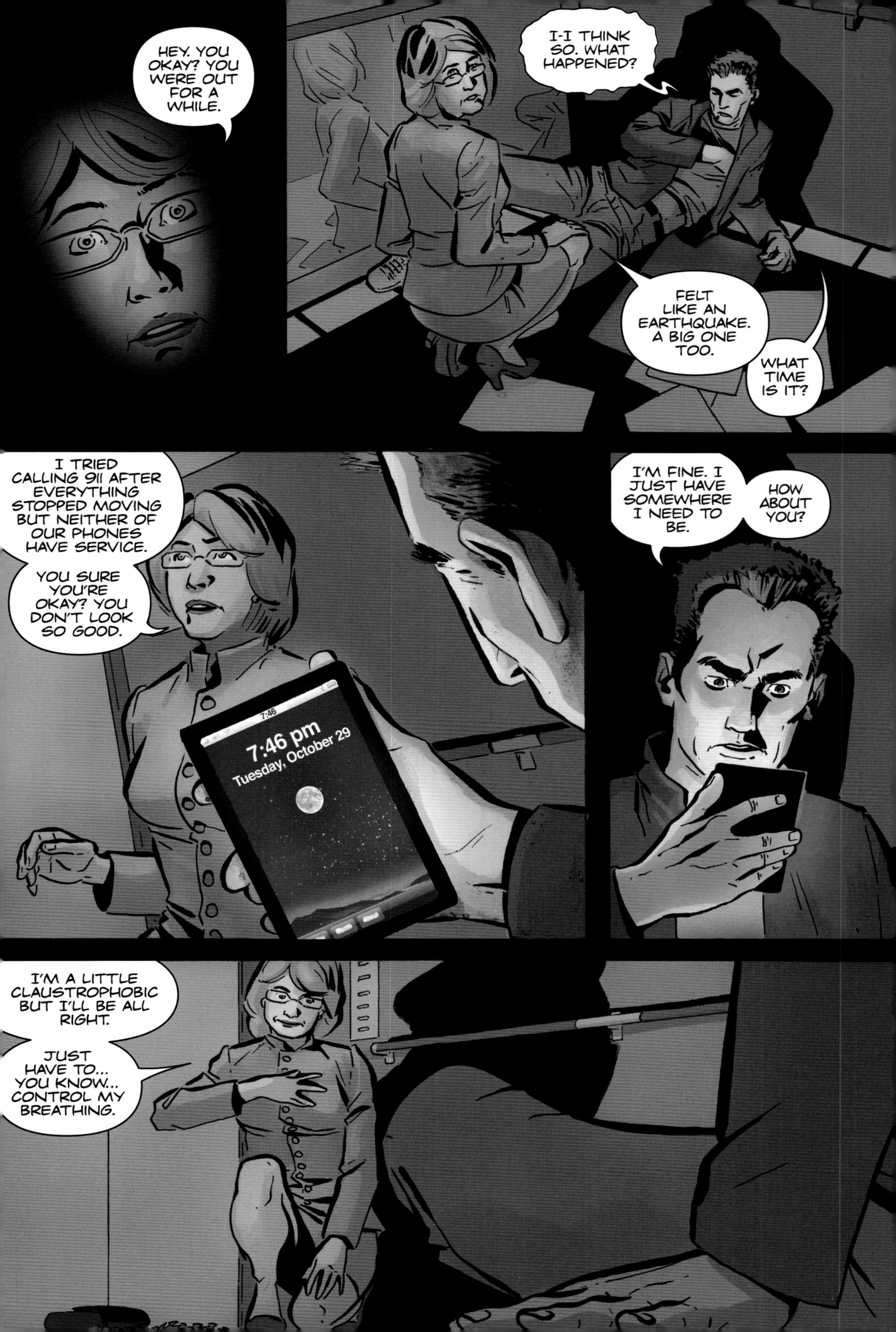
HEY. YOU OKAY? YOU WERE OUT FOR A WHILE.
I-I THINK SO. WHAT HAPPENED?
FELT LIKE AN EARTHQUAKE. A BIG ONE TOO.
WHAT TIME IS IT?
I TRIED CALLING 911 AFTER EVERYTHING STOPPED MOVING BUT NEITHER OF OUR PHONES HAVE SERVICE.
YOU SURE YOU'RE OKAY? YOU DON'T LOOK SO GOOD.
7:46
7:46 pm
Tuesday, October 29
I'M FINE. I JUST HAVE SOMEWHERE I NEED TO BE.
HOW ABOUT YOU?
I'M A LITTLE CLAUSTROPHOBIC BUT I'LL BE ALL RIGHT.
JUST HAVE TO... YOU KNOW... CONTROL MY BREATHING.

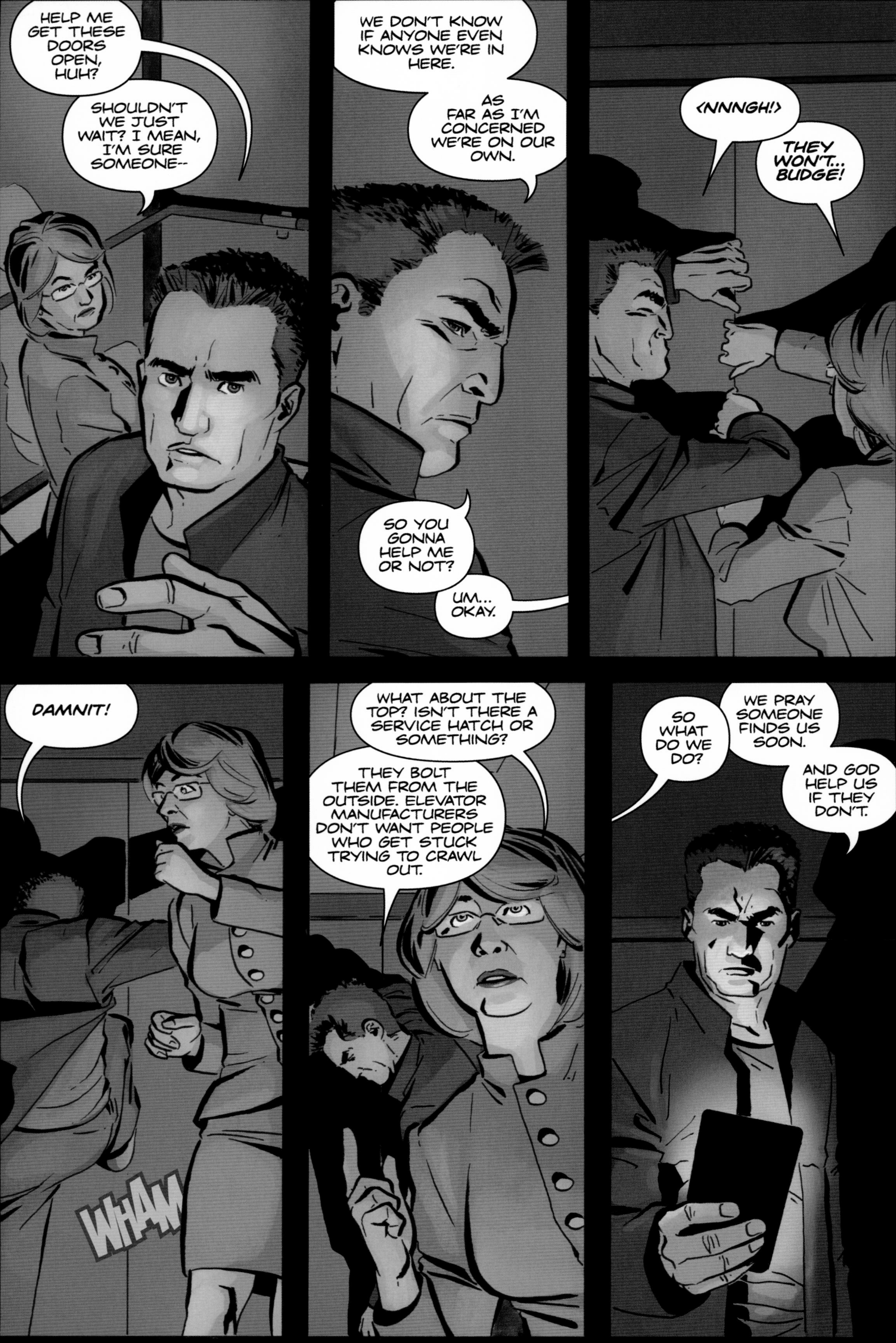

HELP ME GET THESE DOORS OPEN, HUH?
SHOULDN'T WE JUST WAIT? I MEAN, I'M SURE SOMEONE--
WE DON'T KNOW IF ANYONE EVEN KNOWS WE'RE IN HERE.
AS FAR AS I'M CONCERNED WE'RE ON OUR OWN.
SO YOU GONNA HELP ME OR NOT?
UM... OKAY.
<NNNGH!>
THEY WON'T... BUDGE!
DAMNIT!
WHAM
WHAT ABOUT THE TOP? ISN'T THERE A SERVICE HATCH OR SOMETHING?
THEY BOLT THEM FROM THE OUTSIDE. ELEVATOR MANUFACTURERS DON'T WANT PEOPLE WHO GET STUCK TRYING TO CRAWL OUT.
SO WHAT DO WE DO?
WE PRAY SOMEONE FINDS US SOON.
AND GOD HELP US IF THEY DON'T.

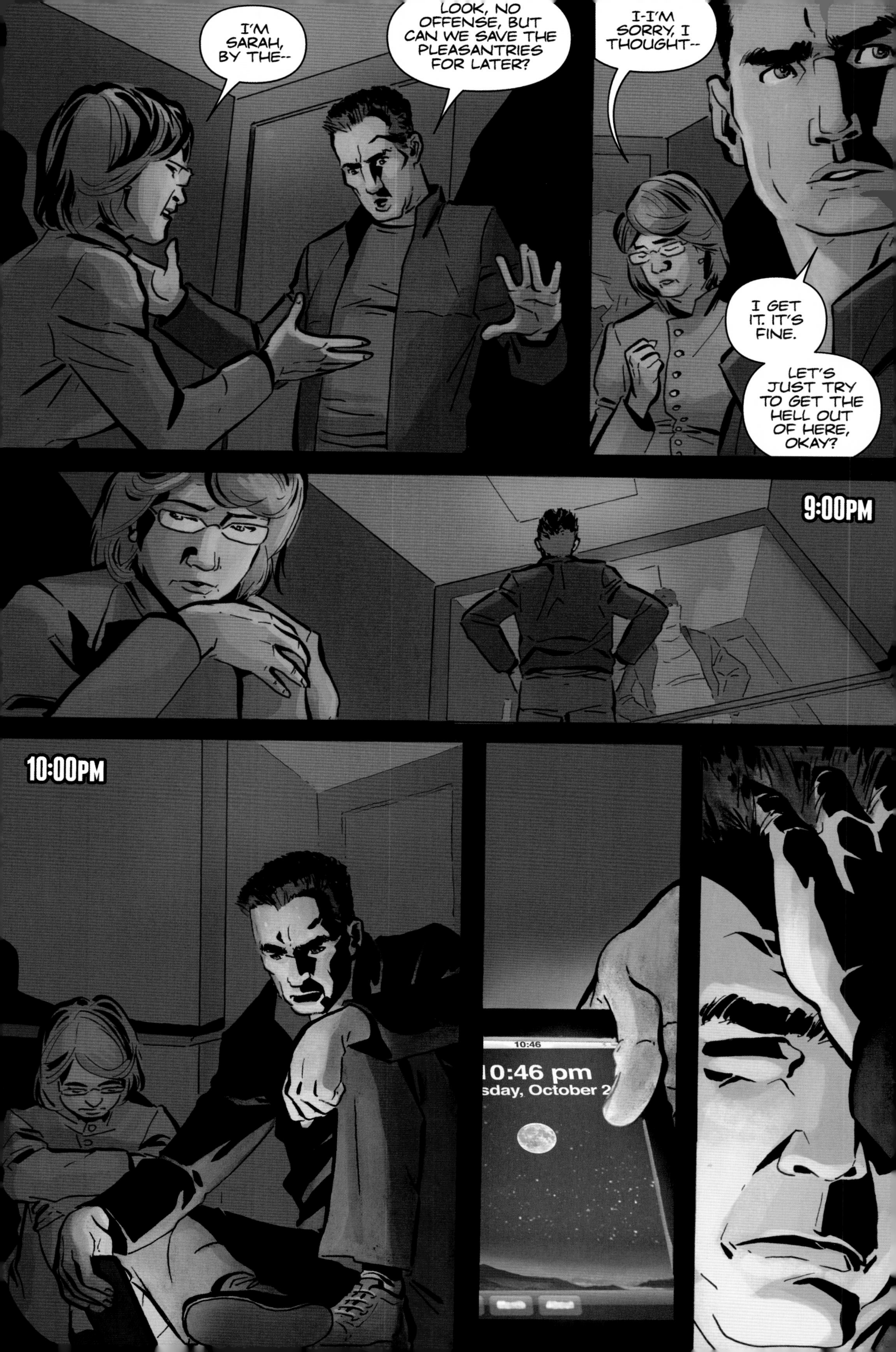
I'M SARAH, BY THE--
LOOK, NO OFFENSE, BUT CAN WE SAVE THE PLEASANTRIES FOR LATER?
I-I'M SORRY, I THOUGHT--
I GET IT. IT'S FINE.
LET'S JUST TRY TO GET THE HELL OUT OF HERE, OKAY?
9:00PM
10:00PM
10:46
10:46 pm
sday, October 2

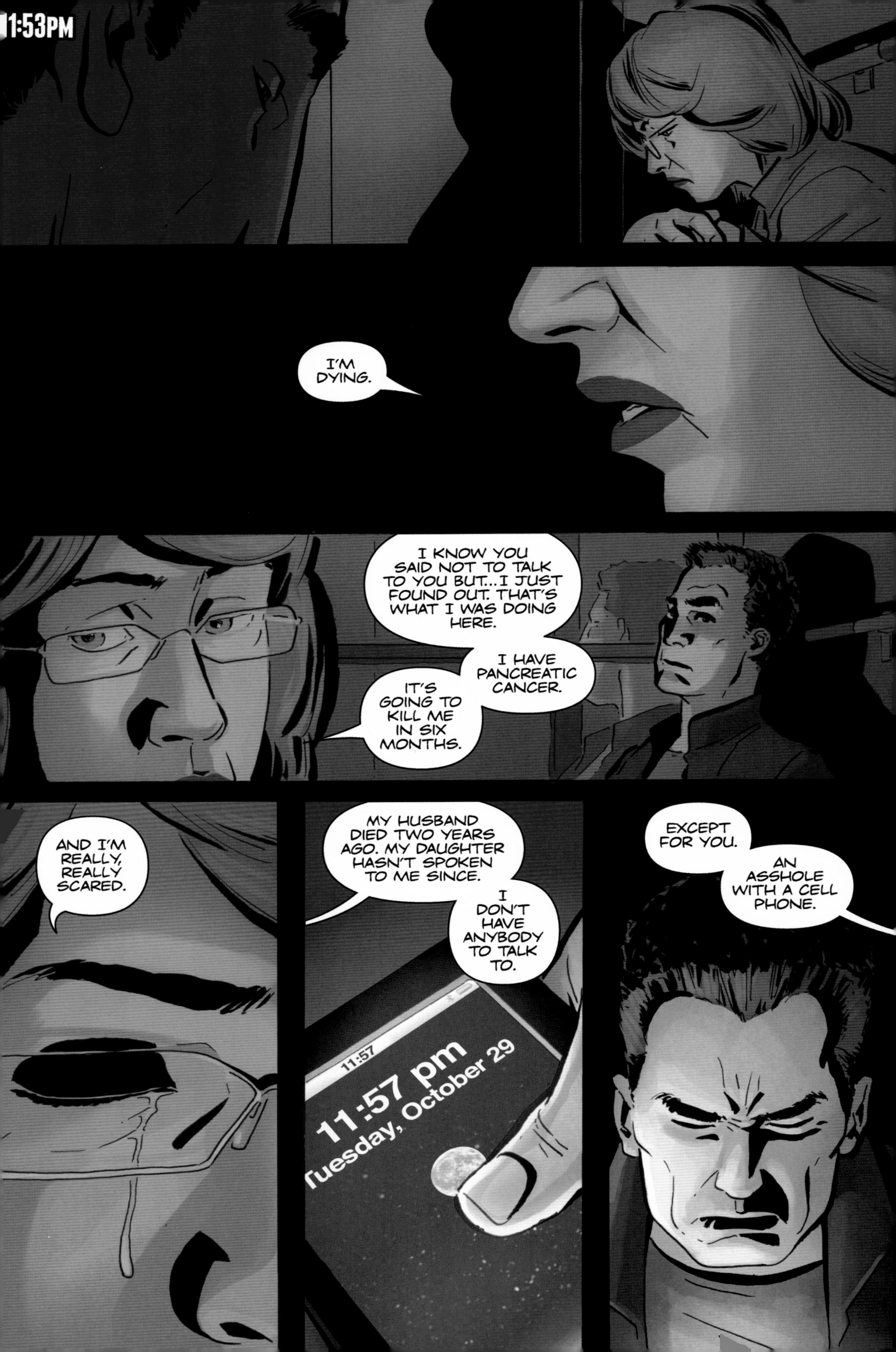
1:53PM
I'M DYING.
I KNOW YOU SAID NOT TO TALK TO YOU BUT...I JUST FOUND OUT. THAT'S WHAT I WAS DOING HERE.
I HAVE PANCREATIC CANCER.
IT'S GOING TO KILL ME IN SIX MONTHS.
AND I'M REALLY, REALLY SCARED.
MY HUSBAND DIED TWO YEARS AGO. MY DAUGHTER HASN'T SPOKEN TO ME SINCE.
I DON'T HAVE ANYBODY TO TALK TO.
11:57
11:57 pm
Tuesday, October 29
EXCEPT FOR YOU.
AN ASSHOLE WITH A CELL PHONE.

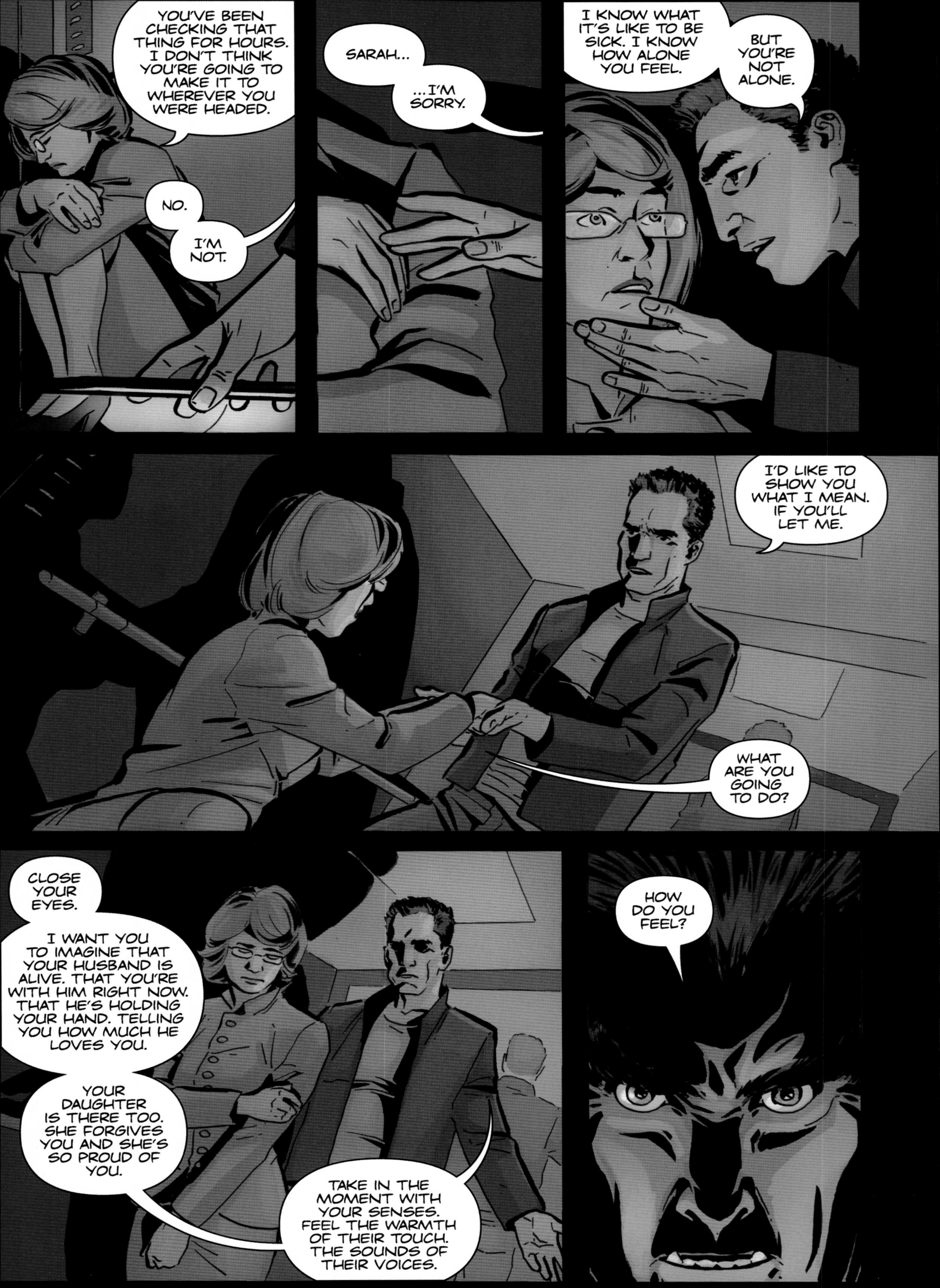
YOU'VE BEEN CHECKING THAT THING FOR HOURS. I DON'T THINK YOU'RE GOING TO MAKE IT TO WHEREVER YOU WERE HEADED.
NO.
I'M NOT.
SARAH...
...I'M SORRY.
I KNOW WHAT IT'S LIKE TO BE SICK. I KNOW HOW ALONE YOU FEEL.
BUT YOU'RE NOT ALONE.
I'D LIKE TO SHOW YOU WHAT I MEAN. IF YOU'LL LET ME.
WHAT ARE YOU GOING TO DO?
CLOSE YOUR EYES.
I WANT YOU TO IMAGINE THAT YOUR HUSBAND IS ALIVE. THAT YOU'RE WITH HIM RIGHT NOW. THAT HE'S HOLDING YOUR HAND. TELLING YOU HOW MUCH HE LOVES YOU.
YOUR DAUGHTER IS THERE TOO. SHE FORGIVES YOU AND SHE'S SO PROUD OF YOU.
TAKE IN THE MOMENT WITH YOUR SENSES. FEEL THE WARMTH OF THEIR TOUCH. THE SOUNDS OF THEIR VOICES.
HOW DO YOU FEEL?

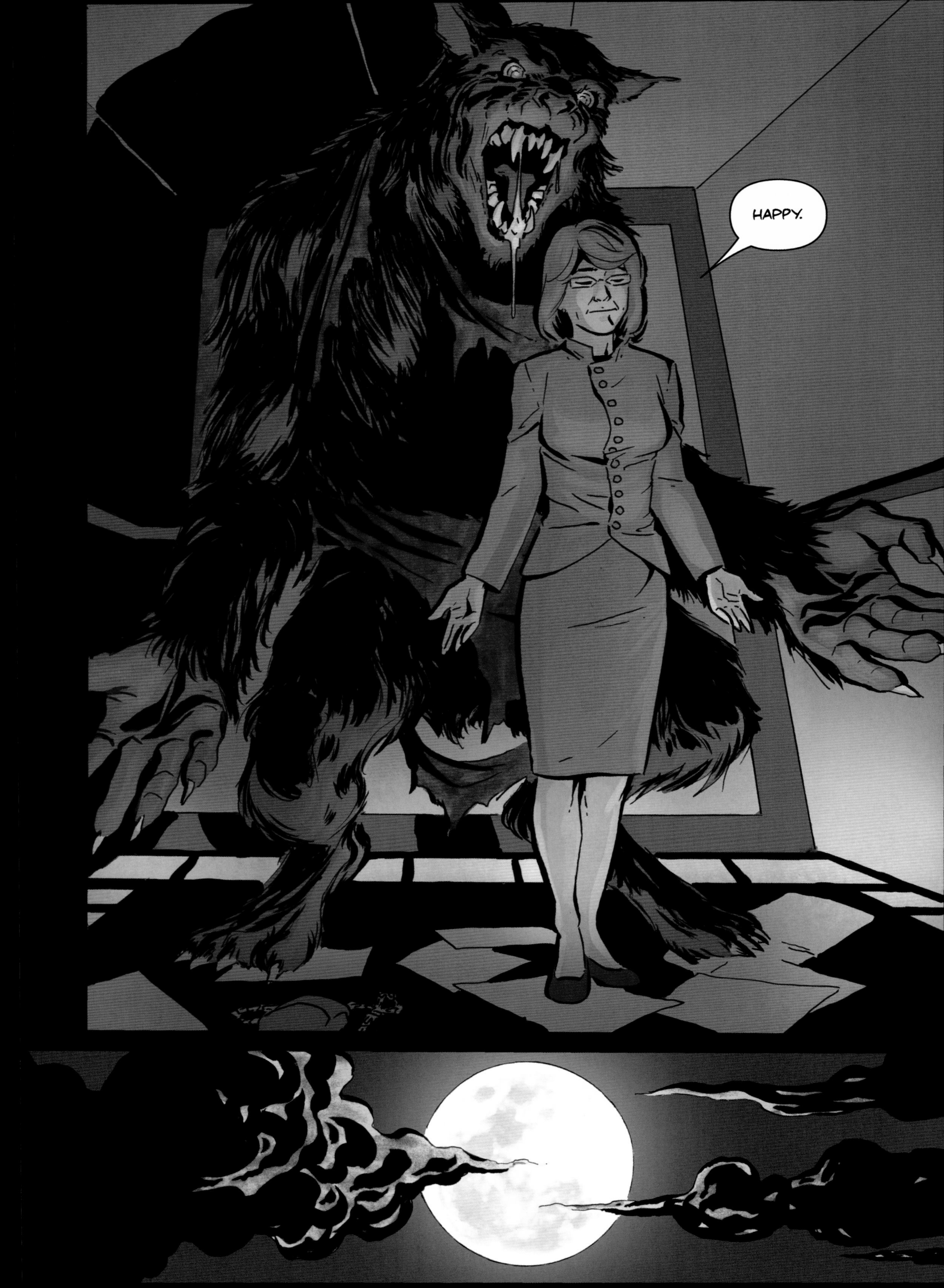
HAPPY.

STOP SMOKING

TOBACCO COUGH—TOBACCO HEART—TOBACCO BREATH—TOBACCO NERVES...
NEW, SAFE FORMULA HELPS YOU BREAK HABIT IN JUST 7 DAYS

No matter how long you have been a victim of the expensive, unhealthful nicotine and smoke habit, this amazing scientific (easy to use) 7-day formula will help you to stop smoking—IN JUST SEVEN Days! Countless thousands who have broken the vicious Tobacco Habit now feel better, look better—actually feel healthier because they breath clean, cool fresh air into their lungs instead of the stultifying Tobacco tar, Nicotine, and Benzo Pyrene—all these irritants that come from cigarettes and cigars. You can't lose anything but the Tobacco Habit by trying this amazing, easy method—You Can Stop Smoking!

• YOU CAN STOP

- **Tobacco Nerves**
  STOP
- **Tobacco Breath**
  STOP
- **Tobacco Cough**
  STOP
- **Burning Mouth**
  Due To Smoking
  STOP
- **Hot Burning Tongue**
  Due To Smoking
  STOP
- **Poisonous Nicotine**
  Due To Smoking
  STOP
- **Tobacco expense**

SEND NO MONEY

Aver. 1½-Pack per Day Smoker
Spends $125.90 per Year

Let us prove to you that smoking is nothing more than a repulsive habit that sends unhealthful impurities into your mouth, throat and lungs . . . a habit that does you no good and may result in harmful physical reactions. Spend those tobacco $$$ on useful, healthgiving benefits for yourself and your loved ones. Send NO Money! Just mail the Coupon on our absolute Money-Back Guarantee that this 7-Day test will help banish your desire for tobacco—not for days or weeks, but FOREVER! Mail the coupon today.

HOW HARMFUL ARE CIGARETTES AND CIGARS?

Numerous Medical Papers have been written about the evil, harmful effects of Tobacco Breath, Tobacco Heart, Tobacco Lungs, Tobacco Mouth, Tobacco Nervousness . . . Now, here at last is the amazing easy-to-take scientific discovery that helps destroy your desire to smoke in just 7 Days—or it won't cost you one cent. Mail the coupon today—the only thing you can loose is the offensive, expensive, unhealthful smoking habit!

ATTENTION DOCTORS:

Doctor, we can help you, too! Many Doctors are unwilling victims to the repulsive Tobacco Habit. We make the guarantee to you, too, Doctor. (A Guarantee that most Doctors dare not make to their own patients) . . . If this sensational discovery does not banish your craving for tobacco forever . . . your money cheerfully refunded.

YOU WILL LOSE THE DESIRE TO SMOKE IN 7 DAYS...OR NO COST TO YOU

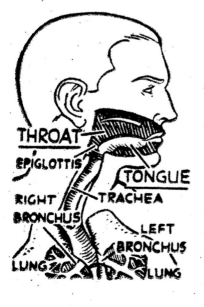

Here's What Happens When You Smoke . . .

The nicotine laden smoke you inhale becomes deposited on your throat and lungs . . . (The average Smoker does this 300 times a day!) Nicotine irritates the Mucous Membranes of the respiratory tract and Tobacco Tar injures those membranes. Stop Tobacco Cough, Tobacco Heart, Tobacco Breath . . . Banish smoking forever, or no cost to you. Mail the coupon now.

Don't be a slave to tobacco. . . . Enjoy your right to clean, healthful, natural living. Try this amazing discovery for just 7-Days. . . . Easy to take, pleasant, no after-taste. If you haven't broken the smoking habit forever . . . return empty carton in 10 Days for prompt refund. Mail the coupon now.

STOP SMOKING—MAIL COUPON NOW!

NO SMOK COMPANY, Dept HNS
400 Madison Ave., N.Y. 17, N.Y.

SENT TO YOU IN
PLAIN WRAPPER

On your 10 day Money-back Guarantee, send me No Smok Tobacco Curb. If not entirely satisfied I can return for prompt refund.

☐ Send 7-Day Supply. I will pay Postman $1.00 plus Postage and C.O.D.

☐ Enclosed is $1.00 for 7-Day Supply. You pay postage costs.

☐ Enclosed is $2.00 for 25-Day Supply for myself and a loved one. You pay postage costs.

NAME _____
(Please Print)
ADDRESS _____
TOWN _____ ZONE ___ STATE _____

ROAD TO CARSON

WRITER
NATE SOUTHARD

ARTIST
CHRISTIAN DIBARI

COLORIST
MIKE SPICER

LETTERER
NIC J. SHAW

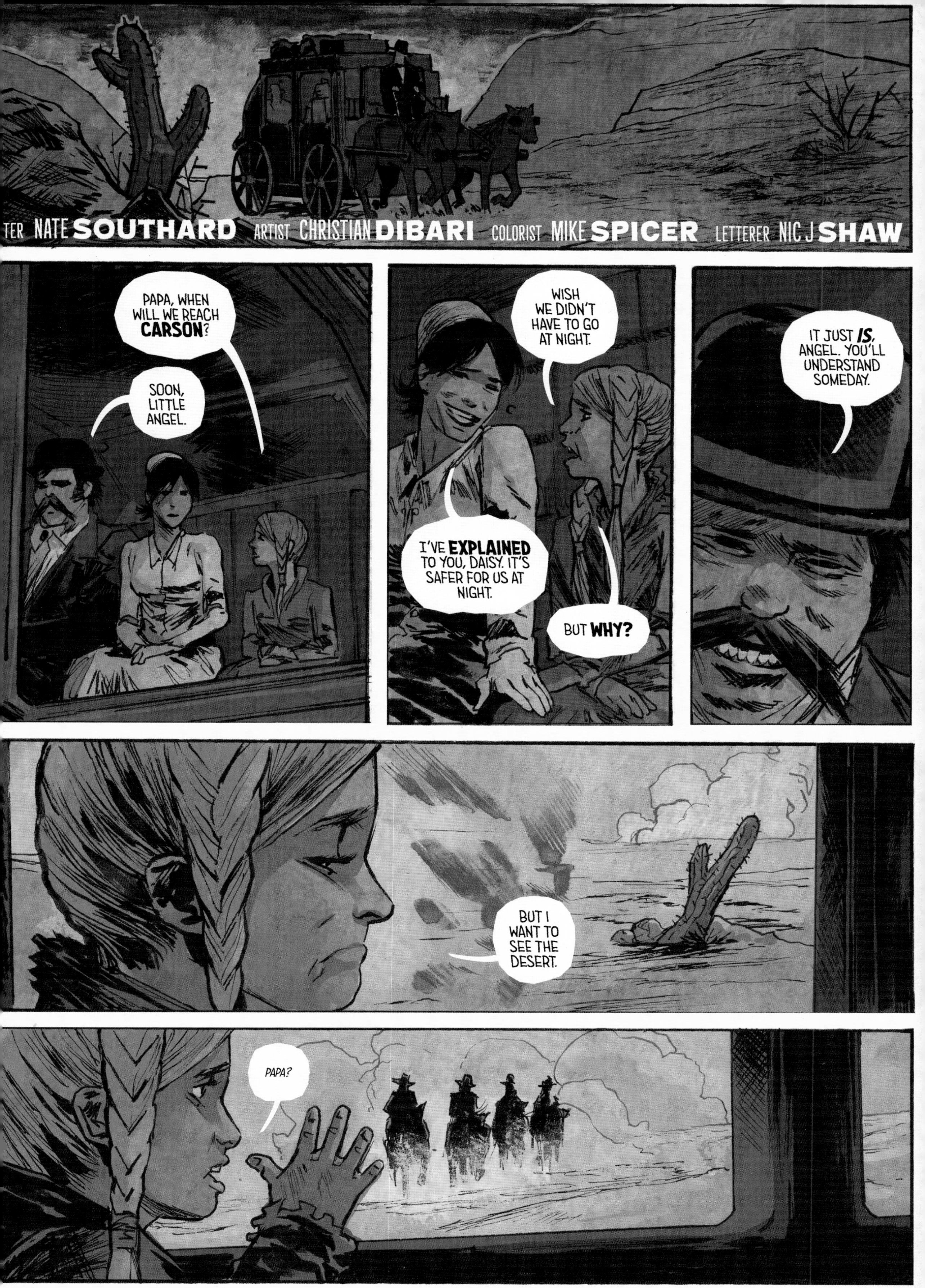
TER NATE SOUTHARD ARTIST CHRISTIAN DIBARI COLORIST MIKE SPICER LETTERER NIC J SHAW
PAPA, WHEN WILL WE REACH CARSON?
SOON, LITTLE ANGEL.
WISH WE DIDN'T HAVE TO GO AT NIGHT.
I'VE EXPLAINED TO YOU, DAISY. IT'S SAFER FOR US AT NIGHT.
BUT WHY?
IT JUST IS, ANGEL. YOU'LL UNDERSTAND SOMEDAY.
BUT I WANT TO SEE THE DESERT.
PAPA?

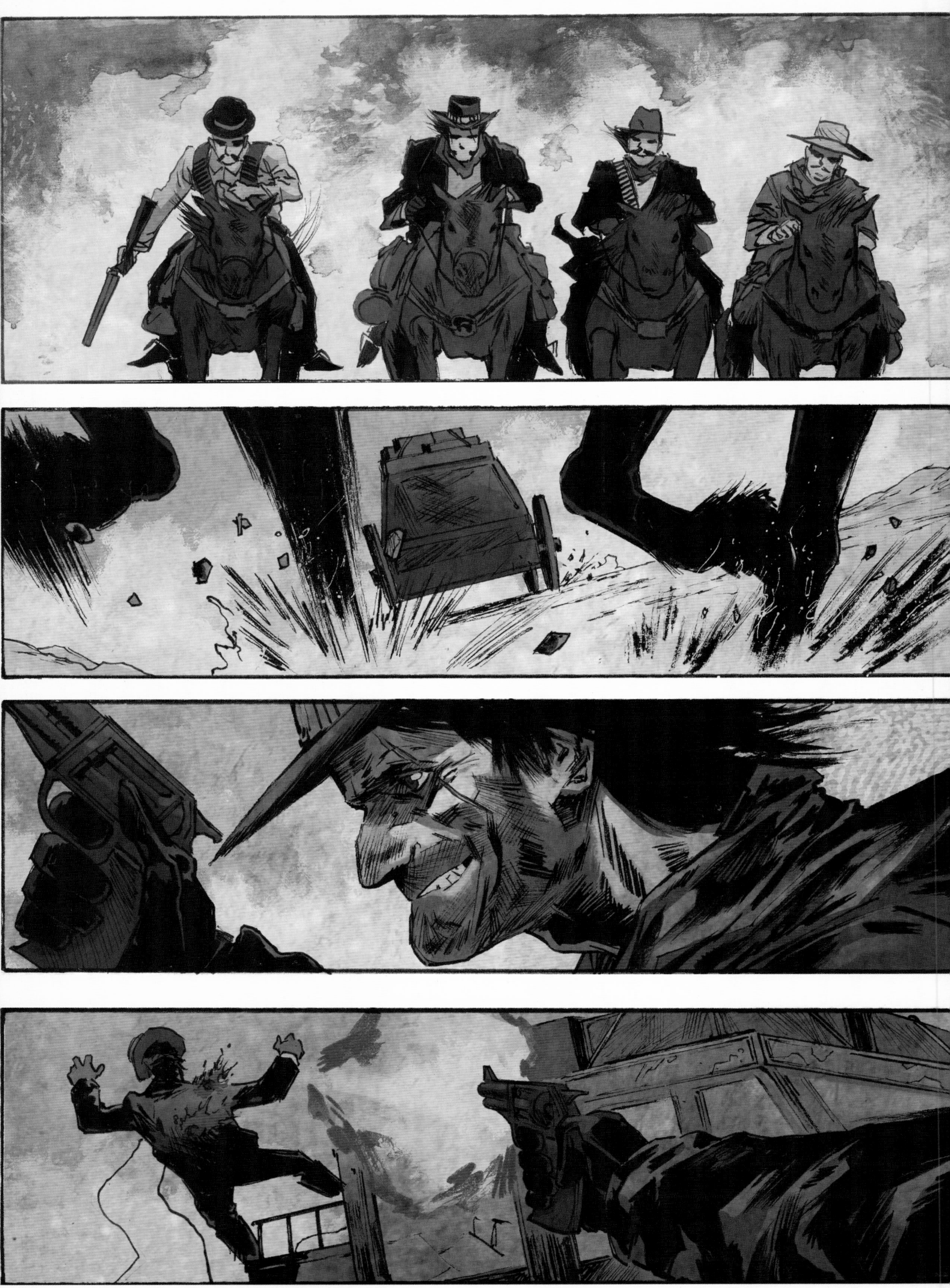

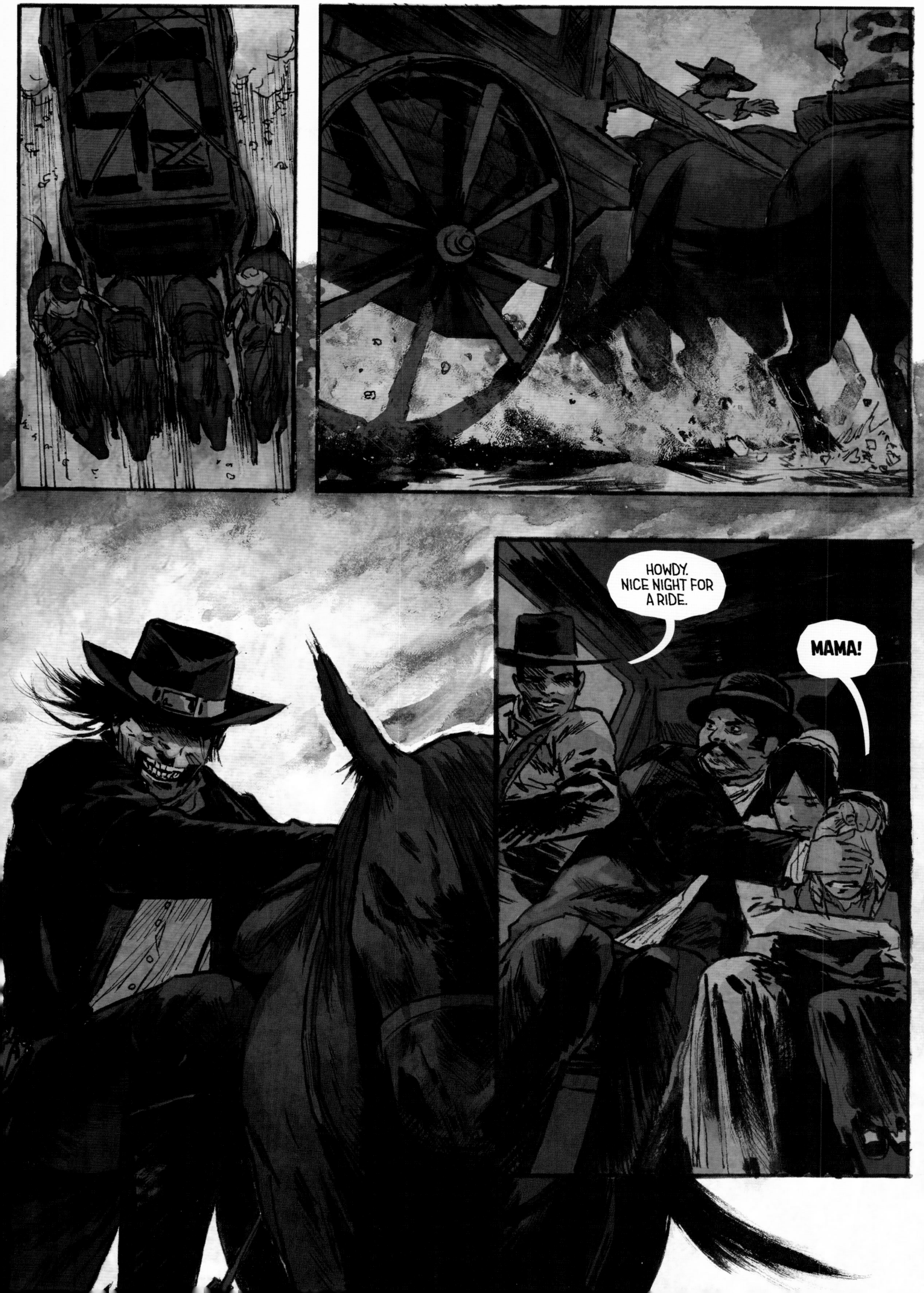
HOWDY. NICE NIGHT FOR A RIDE.
MAMA!

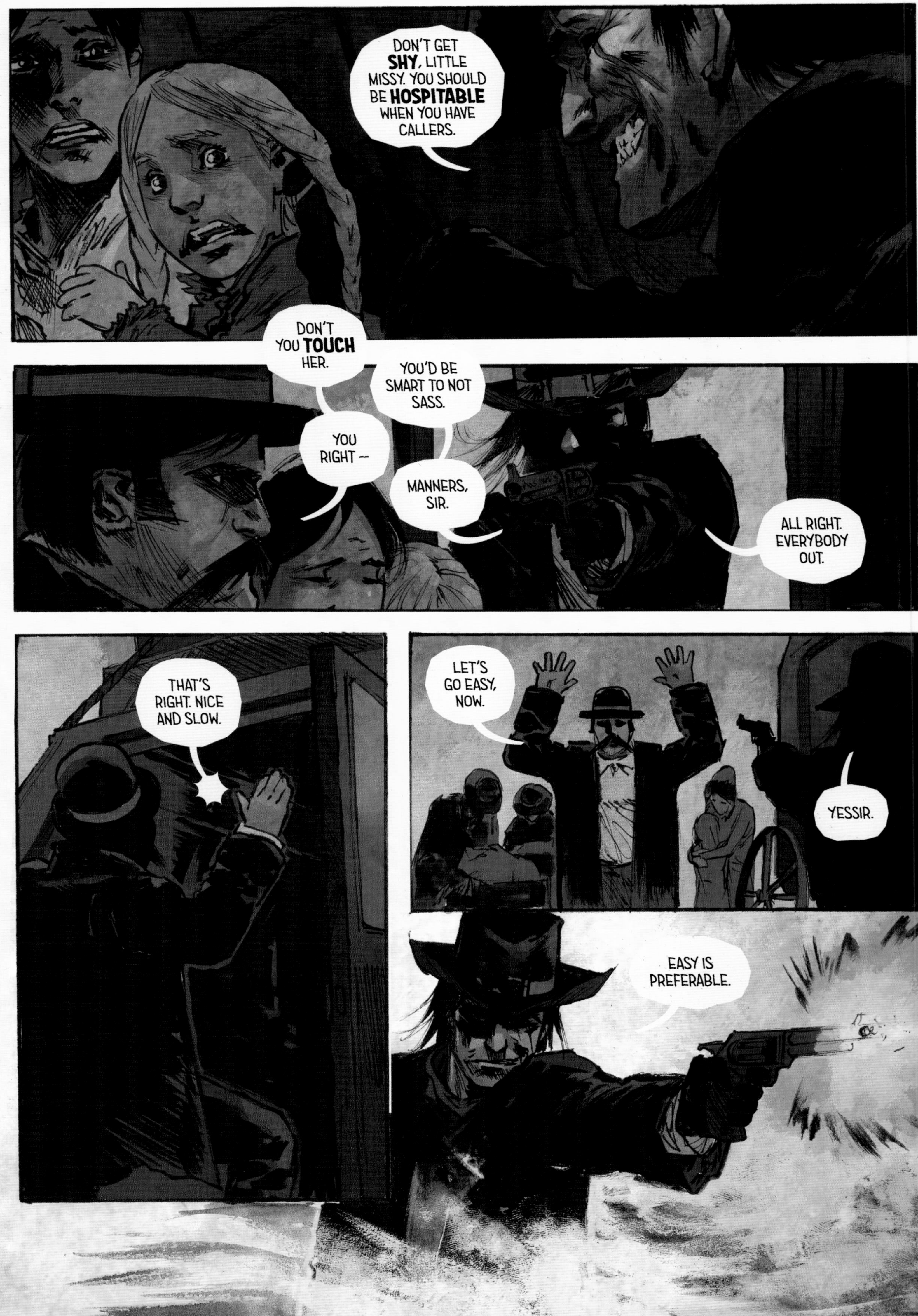
DON'T GET SHY, LITTLE MISSY. YOU SHOULD BE HOSPITABLE WHEN YOU HAVE CALLERS.
DON'T YOU TOUCH HER.
YOU'D BE SMART TO NOT SASS.
YOU RIGHT --
MANNERS, SIR.
ALL RIGHT. EVERYBODY OUT.
THAT'S RIGHT. NICE AND SLOW.
LET'S GO EASY, NOW.
YESSIR.
EASY IS PREFERABLE.

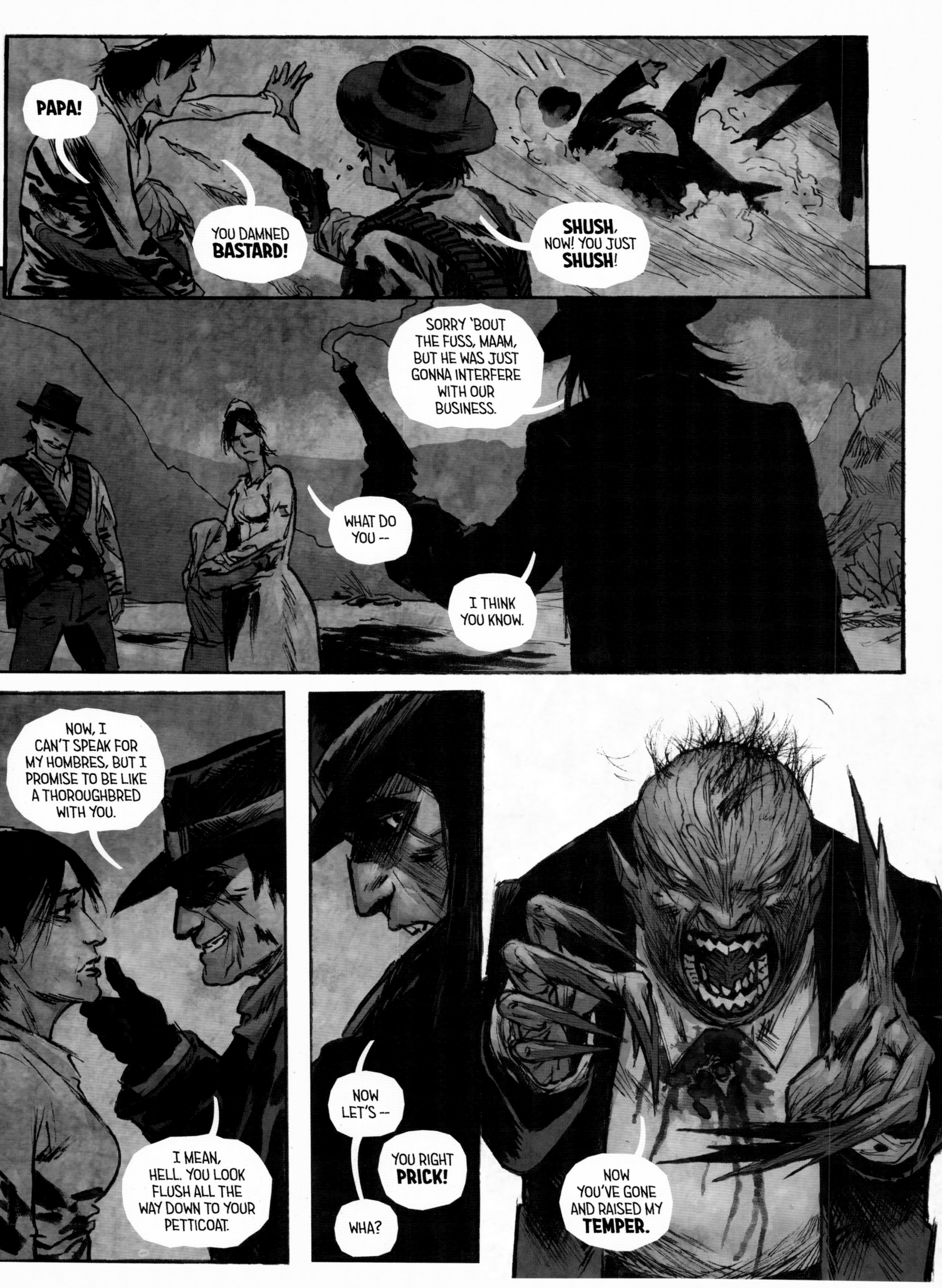
PAPA!
YOU DAMNED BASTARD!
SHUSH, NOW! YOU JUST SHUSH!
SORRY 'BOUT THE FUSS, MAAM, BUT HE WAS JUST GONNA INTERFERE WITH OUR BUSINESS.
WHAT DO YOU --
I THINK YOU KNOW.
NOW, I CAN'T SPEAK FOR MY HOMBRES, BUT I PROMISE TO BE LIKE A THOROUGHBRED WITH YOU.
I MEAN, HELL. YOU LOOK FLUSH ALL THE WAY DOWN TO YOUR PETTICOAT.
NOW LET'S --
YOU RIGHT PRICK!
WHA?
NOW YOU'VE GONE AND RAISED MY TEMPER.

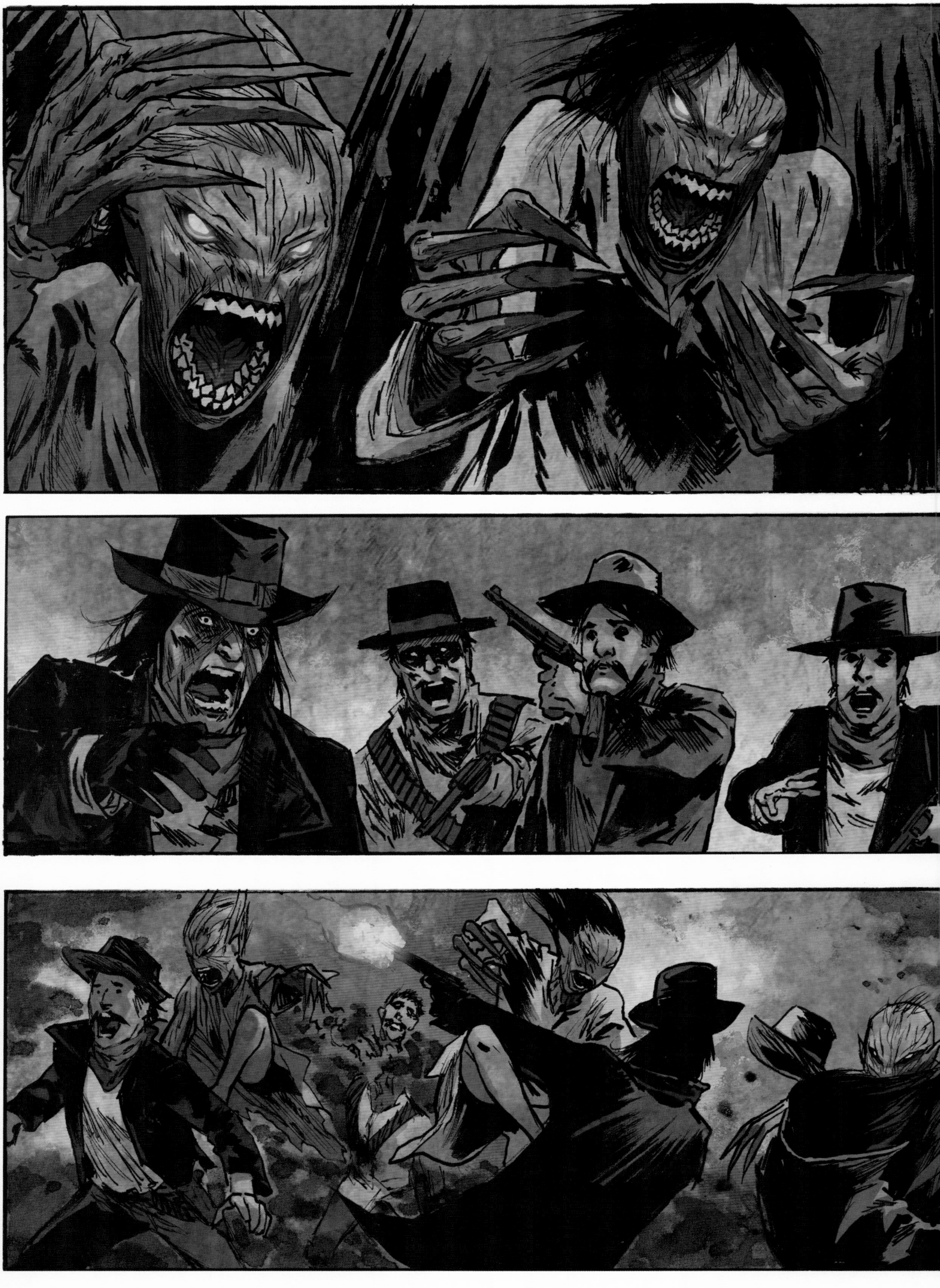

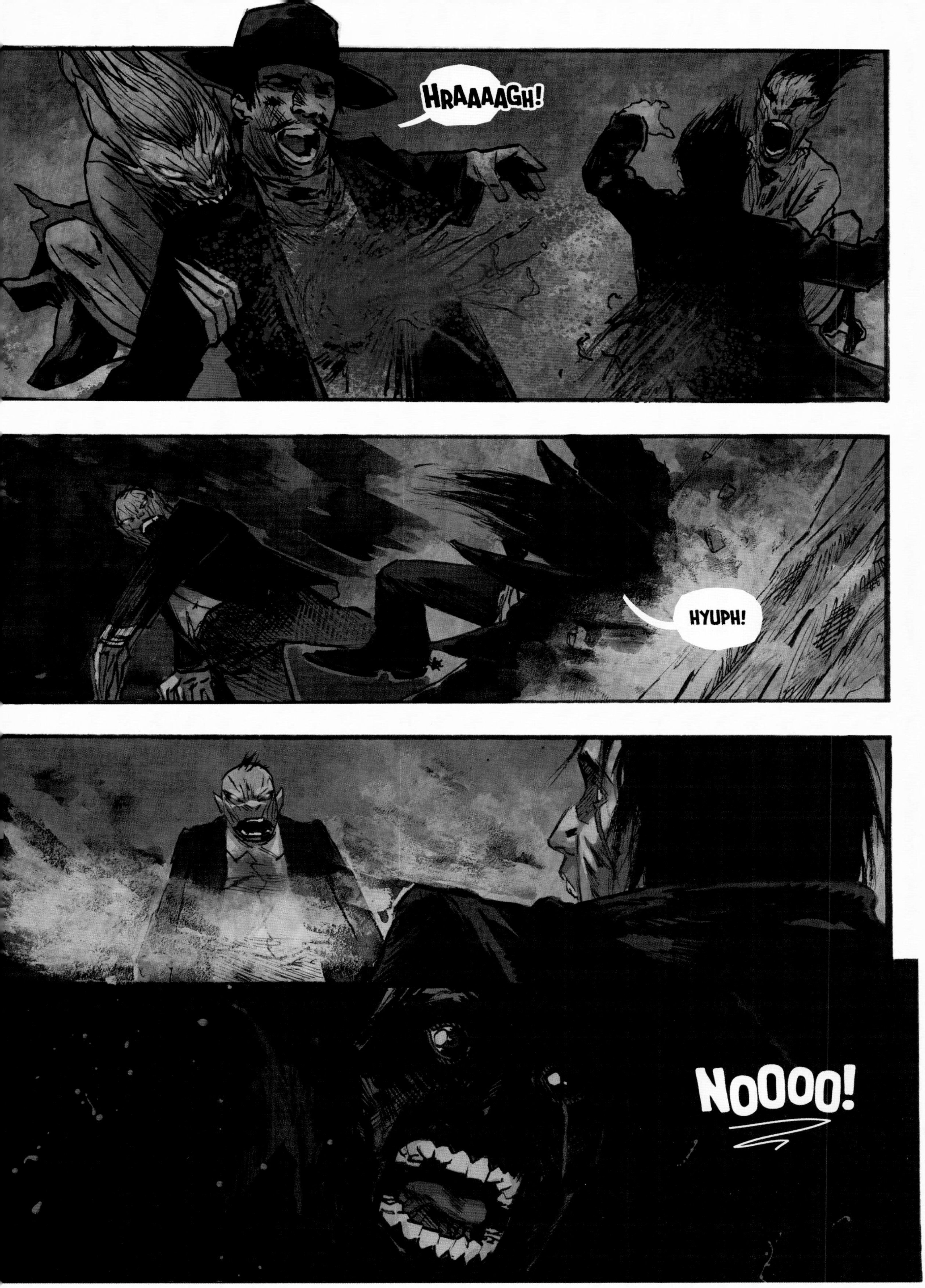
HRAAAAGH!
HYUPH!
NOOOO!

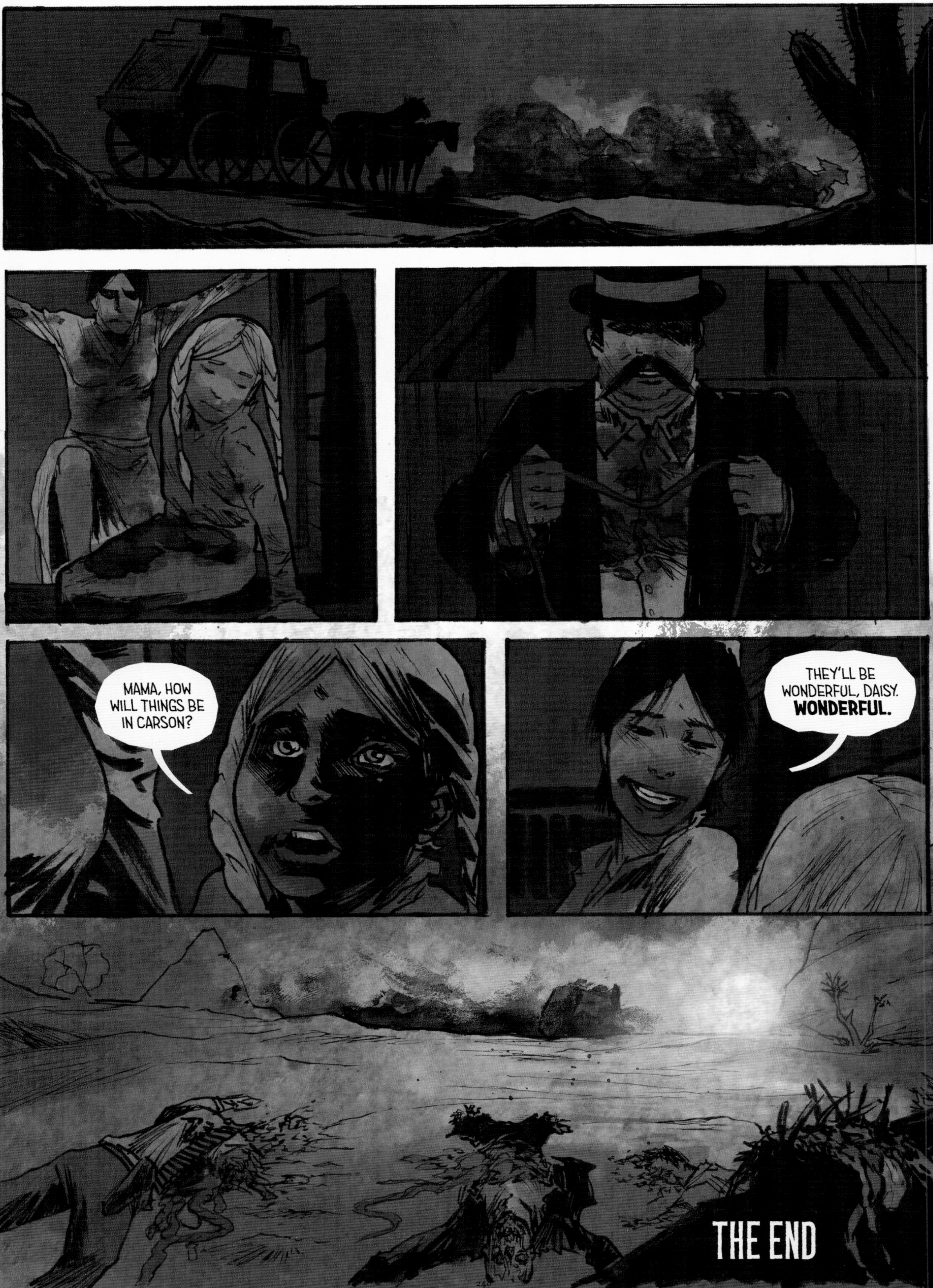
MAMA, HOW WILL THINGS BE IN CARSON?
THEY'LL BE WONDERFUL, DAISY. **WONDERFUL.**
THE END

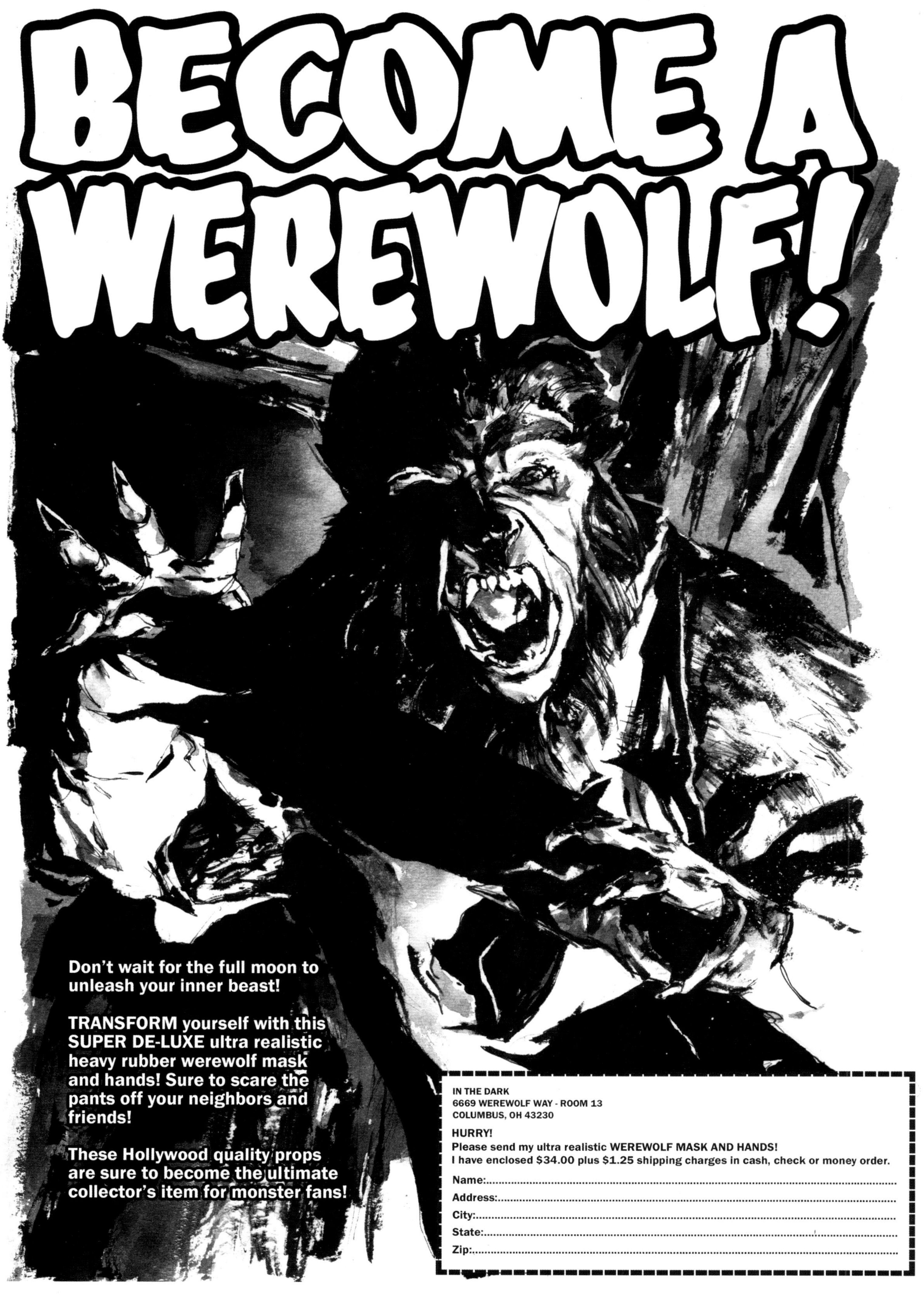
BECOME A WEREWOLF!
Don't wait for the full moon to unleash your inner beast!
TRANSFORM yourself with this SUPER DE-LUXE ultra realistic heavy rubber werewolf mask and hands! Sure to scare the pants off your neighbors and friends!
These Hollywood quality props are sure to become the ultimate collector's item for monster fans!
IN THE DARK
6669 WEREWOLF WAY - ROOM 13
COLUMBUS, OH 43230
HURRY!
Please send my ultra realistic WEREWOLF MASK AND HANDS!
I have enclosed $34.00 plus $1.25 shipping charges in cash, check or money order.
Name:
Address:
City:
State:
Zip:

BODY IN REVOLT

WRITER
THOMAS BOATWRIGHT

ARTIST
THOMAS BOATWRIGHT

COLORIST
THOMAS BOATWRIGHT

LETTERER
RACHEL DEERING

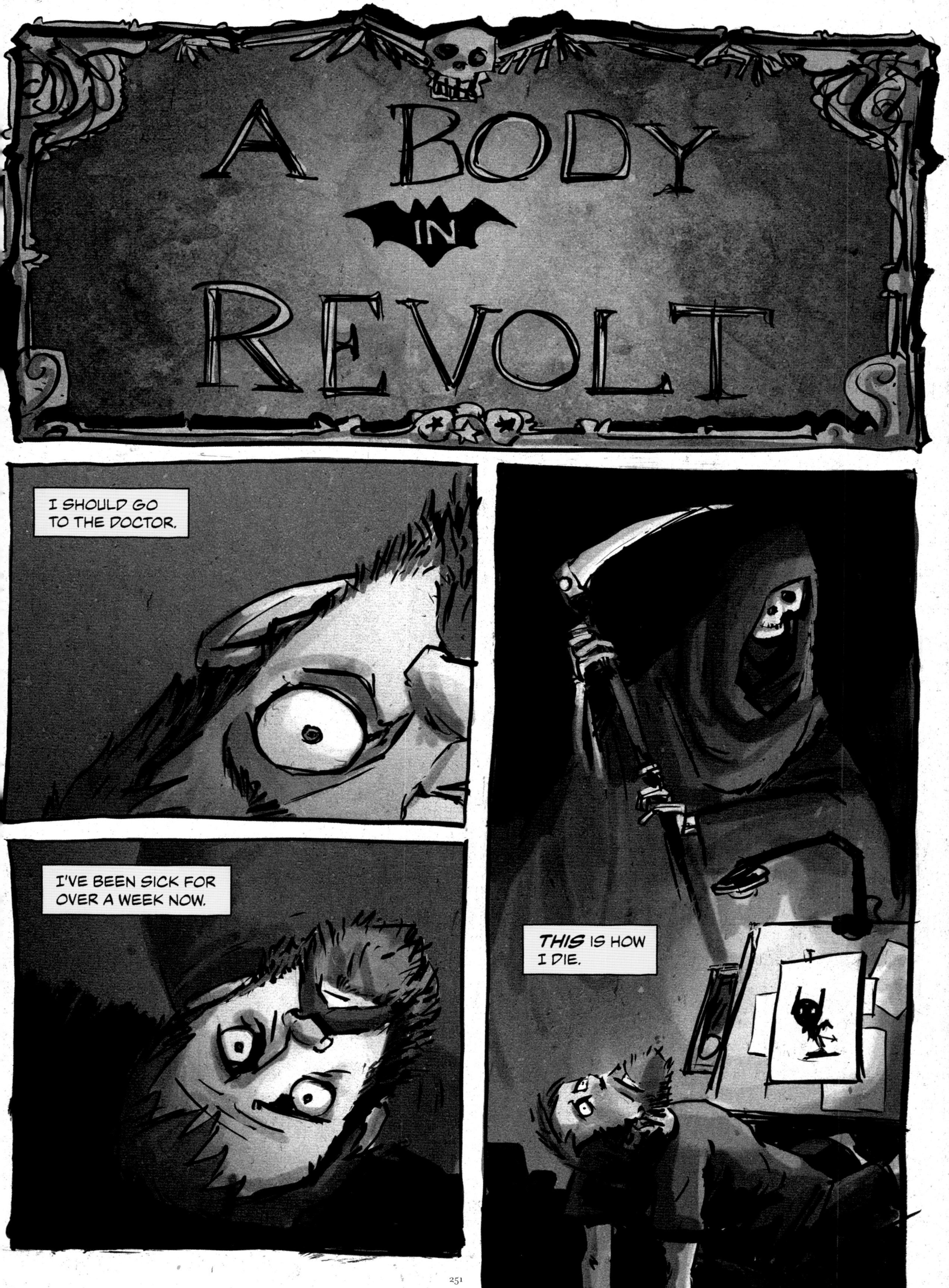
A BODY IN REVOLT
I SHOULD GO TO THE DOCTOR.
I'VE BEEN SICK FOR OVER A WEEK NOW.
THIS IS HOW I DIE.

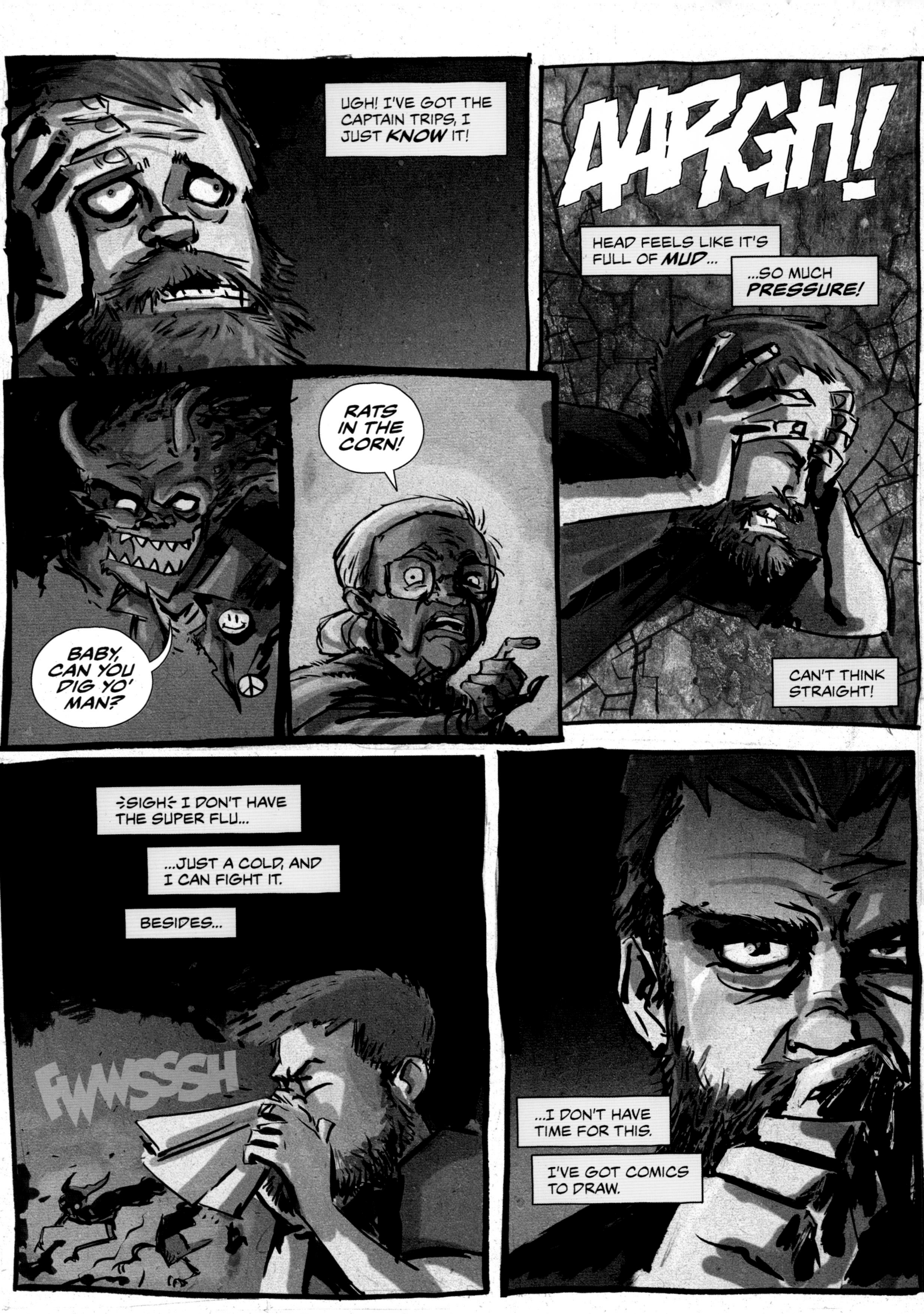
UGH! I'VE GOT THE CAPTAIN TRIPS, I JUST KNOW IT!
AARGH!
HEAD FEELS LIKE IT'S FULL OF MUD...
...SO MUCH PRESSURE!
BABY, CAN YOU DIG YO' MAN?
RATS IN THE CORN!
CAN'T THINK STRAIGHT!
-SIGH- I DON'T HAVE THE SUPER FLU...
...JUST A COLD, AND I CAN FIGHT IT.
BESIDES...
FWWSSSH
...I DON'T HAVE TIME FOR THIS.
I'VE GOT COMICS TO DRAW.

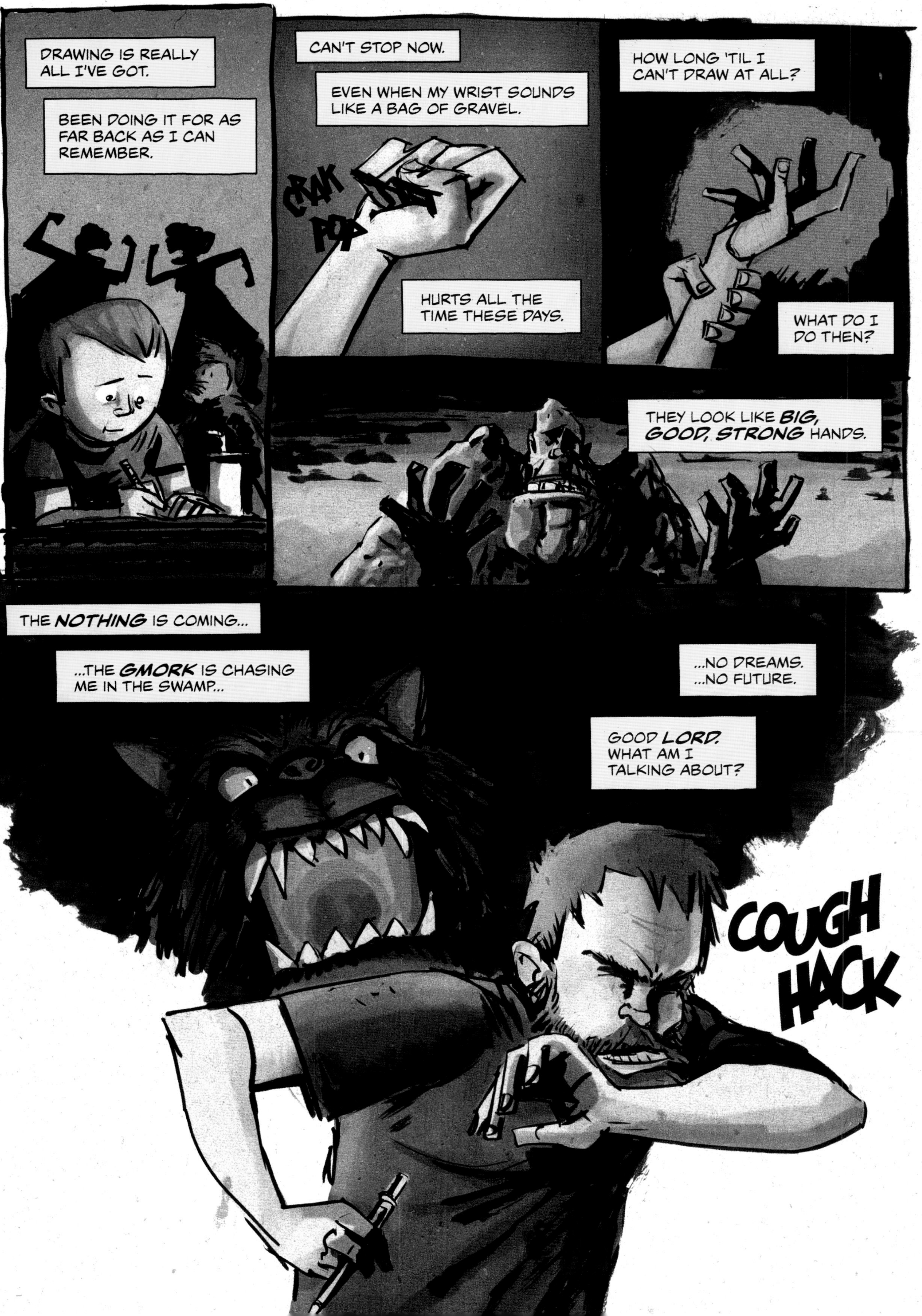
DRAWING IS REALLY ALL I'VE GOT.
BEEN DOING IT FOR AS FAR BACK AS I CAN REMEMBER.
CAN'T STOP NOW.
EVEN WHEN MY WRIST SOUNDS LIKE A BAG OF GRAVEL.
CRAK
POP
HURTS ALL THE TIME THESE DAYS.
HOW LONG 'TIL I CAN'T DRAW AT ALL?
WHAT DO I DO THEN?
THEY LOOK LIKE BIG, GOOD, STRONG HANDS.
THE NOTHING IS COMING...
...THE GMORK IS CHASING ME IN THE SWAMP...
...NO DREAMS. ...NO FUTURE.
GOOD LORD. WHAT AM I TALKING ABOUT?
COUGH
HACK

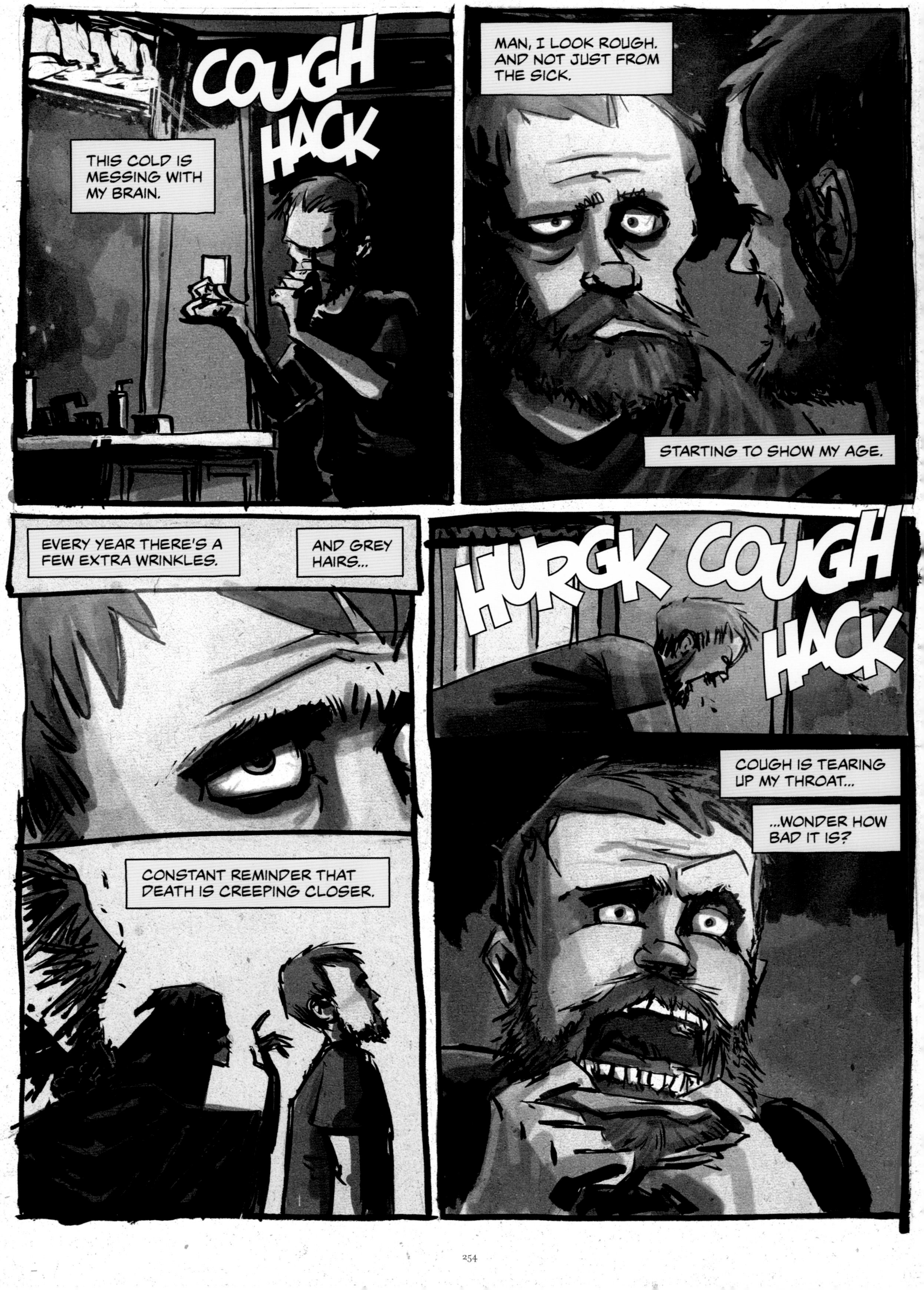
COUGH
HACK
THIS COLD IS MESSING WITH MY BRAIN.
MAN, I LOOK ROUGH. AND NOT JUST FROM THE SICK.
STARTING TO SHOW MY AGE.
EVERY YEAR THERE'S A FEW EXTRA WRINKLES.
AND GREY HAIRS...
CONSTANT REMINDER THAT DEATH IS CREEPING CLOSER.
HURGK COUGH
HACK
COUGH IS TEARING UP MY THROAT...
...WONDER HOW BAD IT IS?

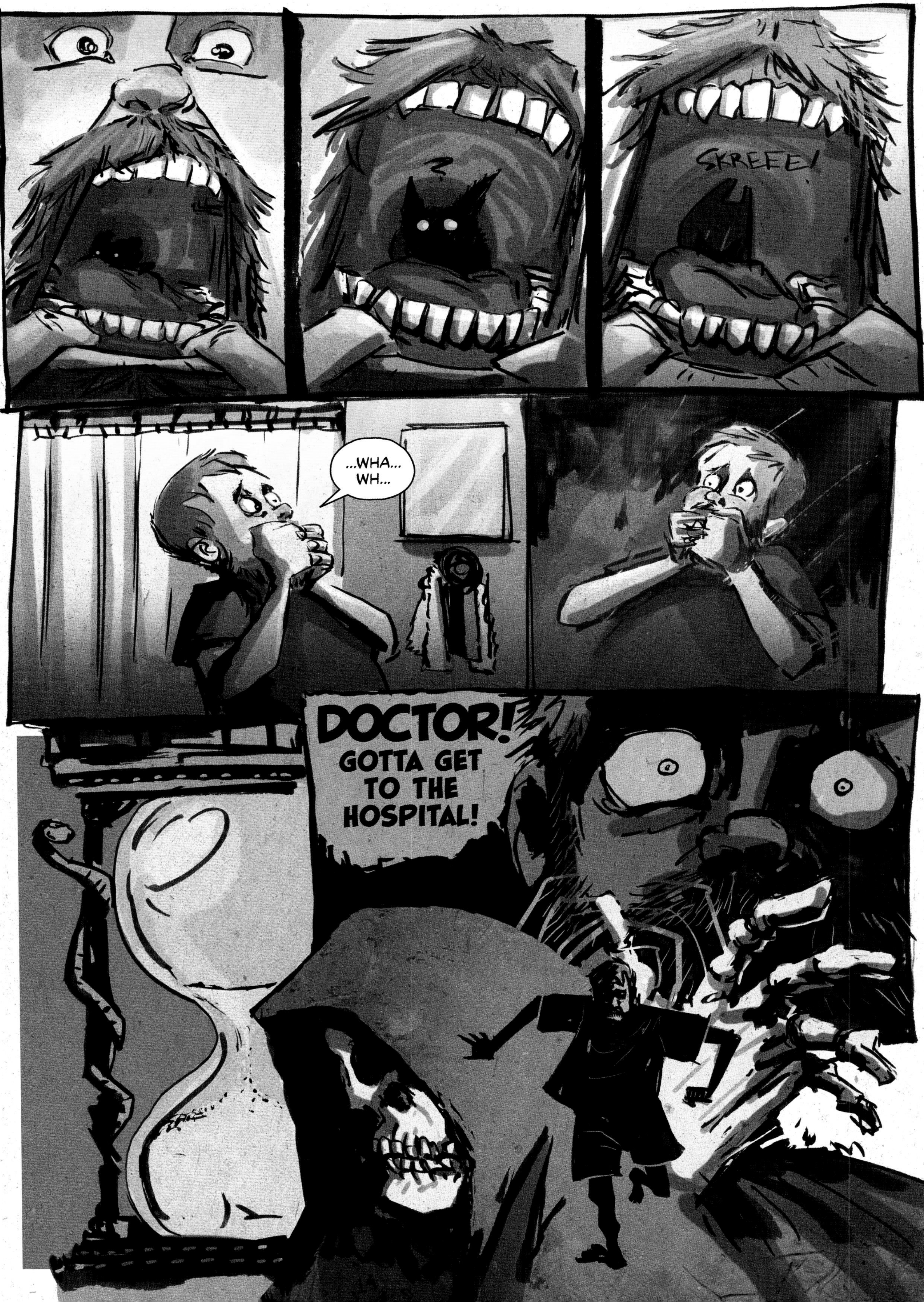
?
SKREEE!
...WHA...
WH...
DOCTOR!
GOTTA GET
TO THE
HOSPITAL!

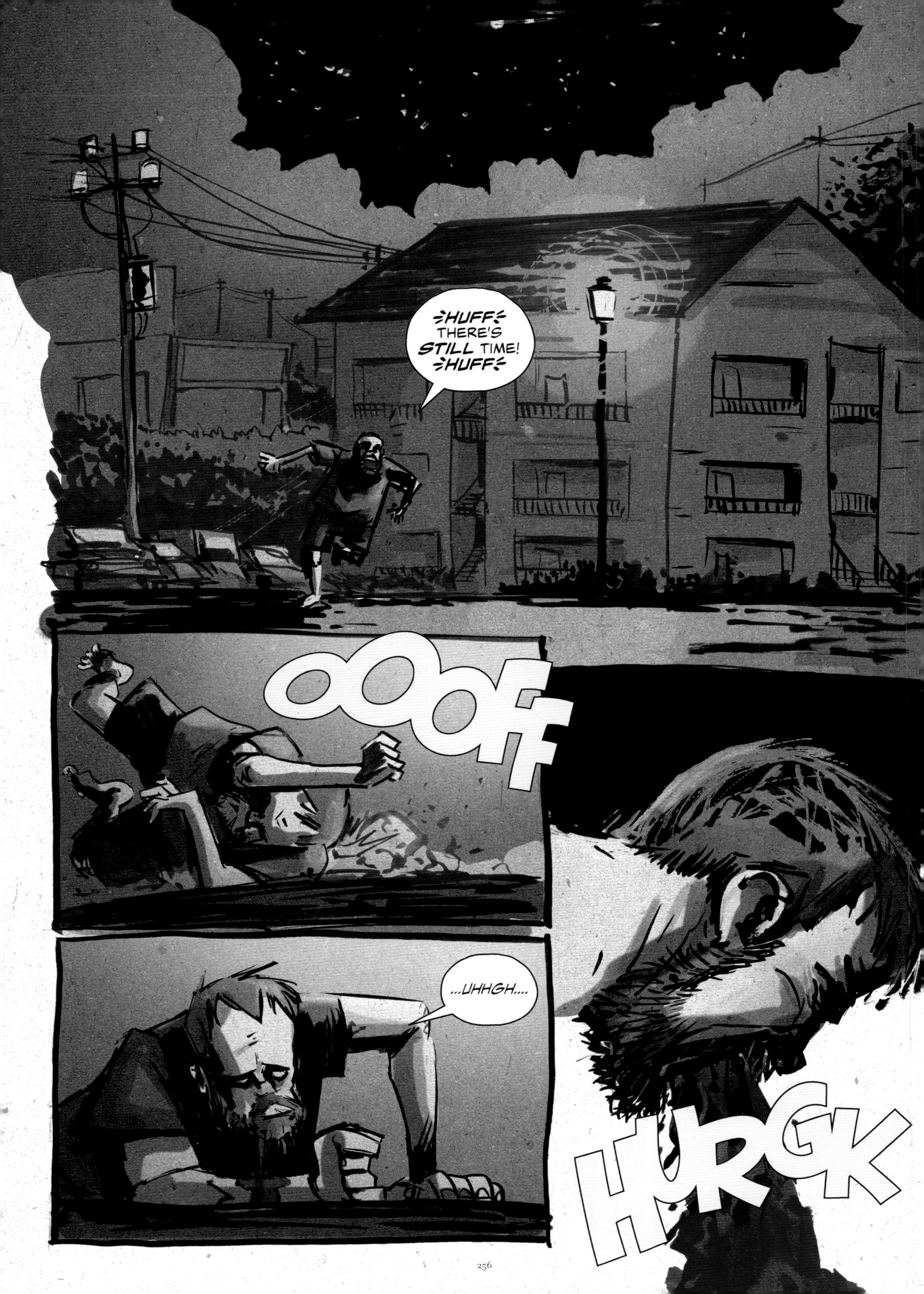
HUFF THERE'S STILL TIME! HUFF
OOOFF
...UHHGH....
HURGK

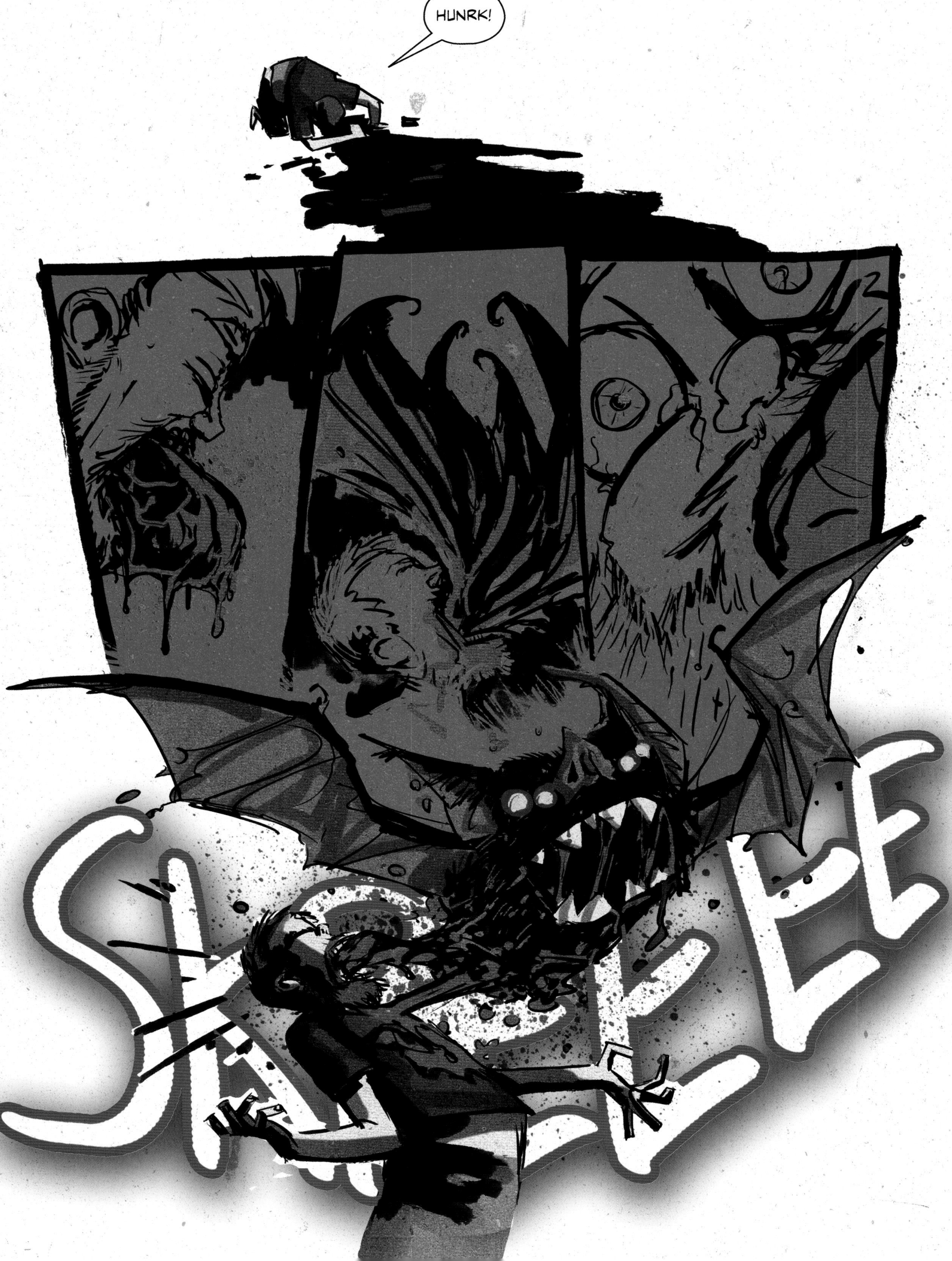
HUNRK!

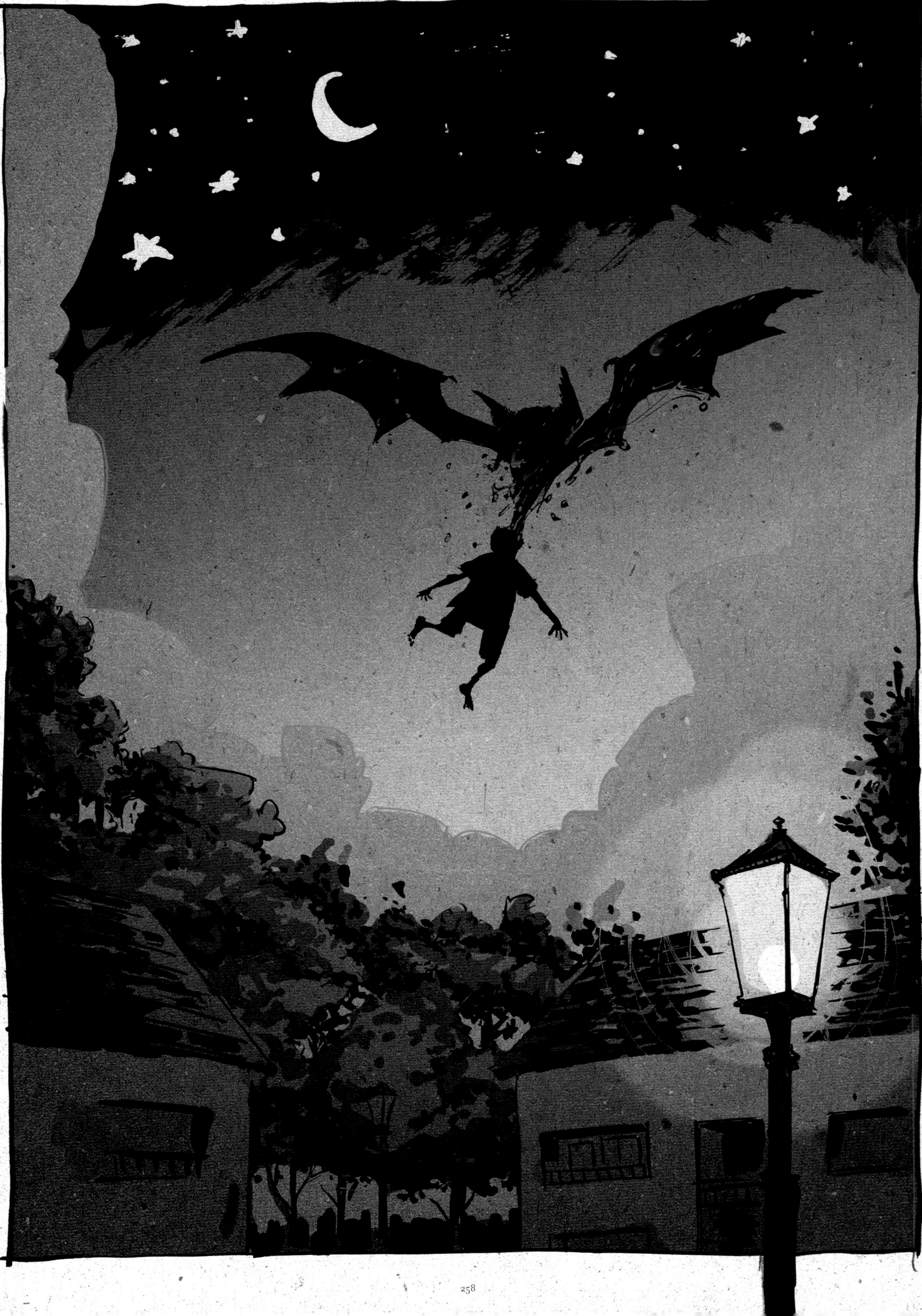

YOUR OWN AUTHENTIC VIAL OF VAMPIRE BLOOD!

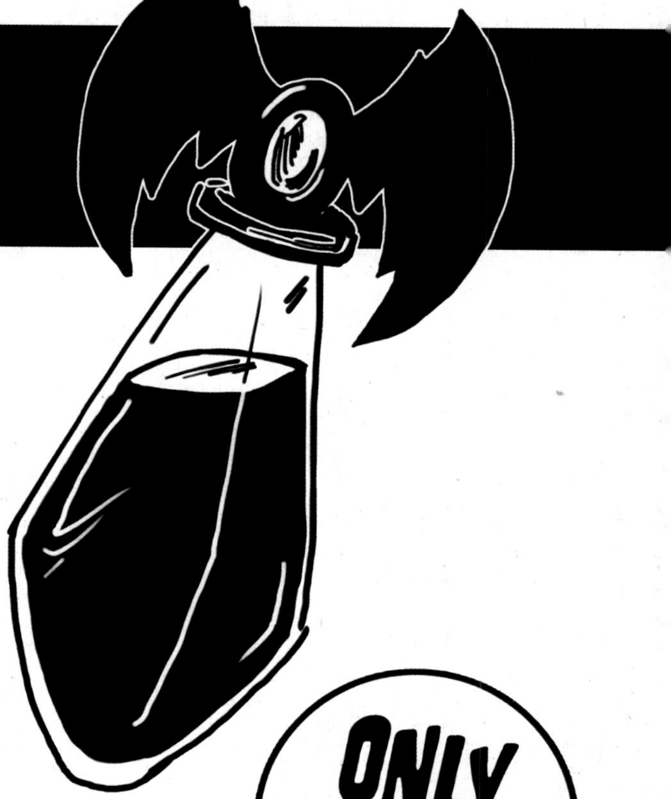

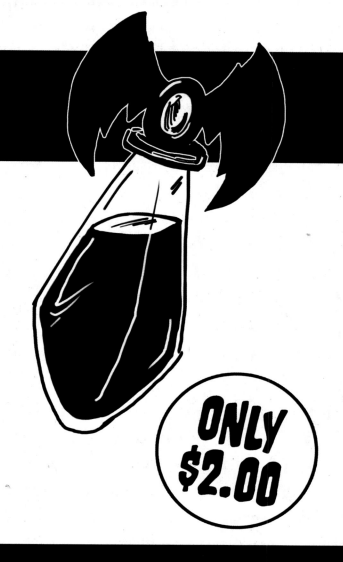

- **BECOME A VAMPIRE YOURSELF!**
- **TRANSFORM INTO A WOLF OR BAT!**
- **HYPNOTIZE ANYONE!**
- **STAY UP ALL NIGHT! SLEEP ALL DAY!**

IN THE DARK
6669 WEREWOLF WAY - ROOM 13
COLUMBUS, OH 43230

I COMPEL YOU!
Please rush my authentic vial of VAMPIRE BLOOD!
I have enclosed $2.00 plus $.25 shipping charges in cash, check or money order.

Name:..
Address:..
City:..
State:..
Zip:...

ONLY $2.00

ACK!

DO YOU DARE ORDER THE MAN-EATING PLANT?!

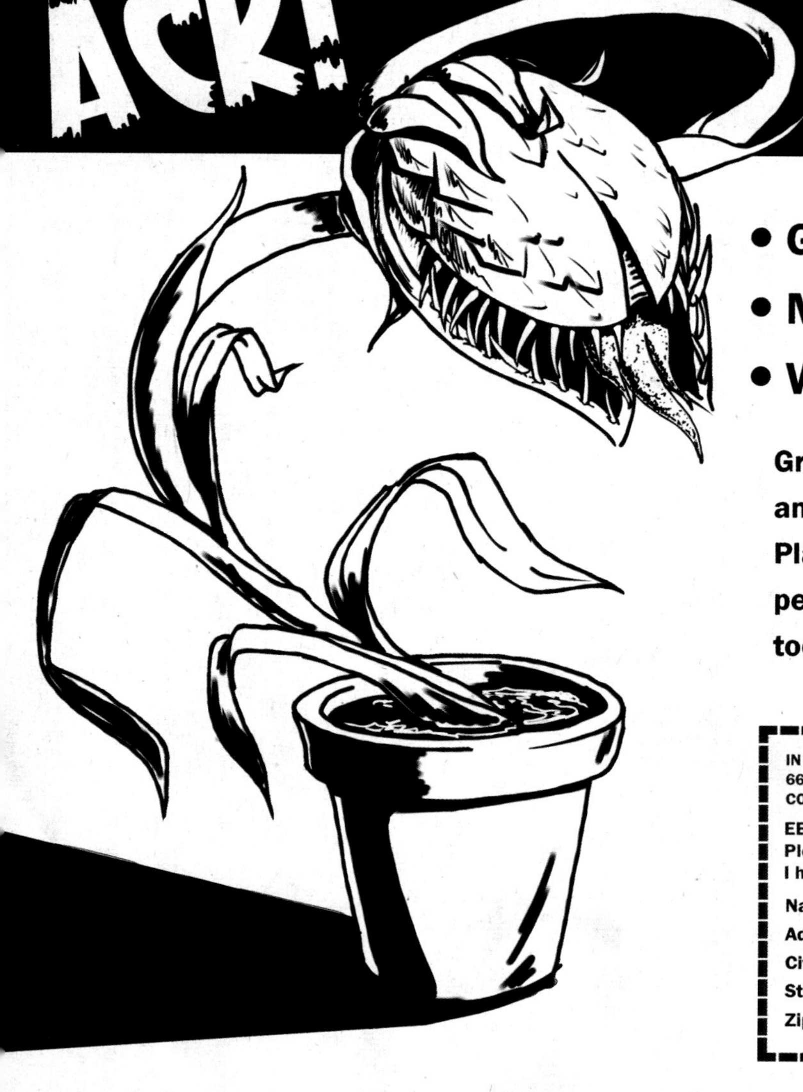

- **GET RID OF THAT NOISY NEIGHBOR!**
- **MAKE YOUR SISTER DISAPPEAR!**
- **WATCH IT GROW BEFORE YOUR EYES!**

Grown from special seeds of an unknown origin, this amazing flesh-eating plant is truly something to behold! Plant him in your flower bed and rid your house of those pesky pests forever! Be careful and don't let Fido get too close!

IN THE DARK
6669 WEREWOLF WAY - ROOM 13
COLUMBUS, OH 43230

EEK! I CAN'T WAIT!
Please send my very voracious MAN-EATING PLANT!
I have enclosed $3.00 plus $1.25 shipping charges in cash, check or money order.

Name:..
Address:..
City:..
State:..
Zip:...

THE CAGE

WRITER
ED BRISSON

ARTIST
BRIAN LEVEL

COLORIST
SHARI CHANKHAMMA

LETTERER
ED BRISSON

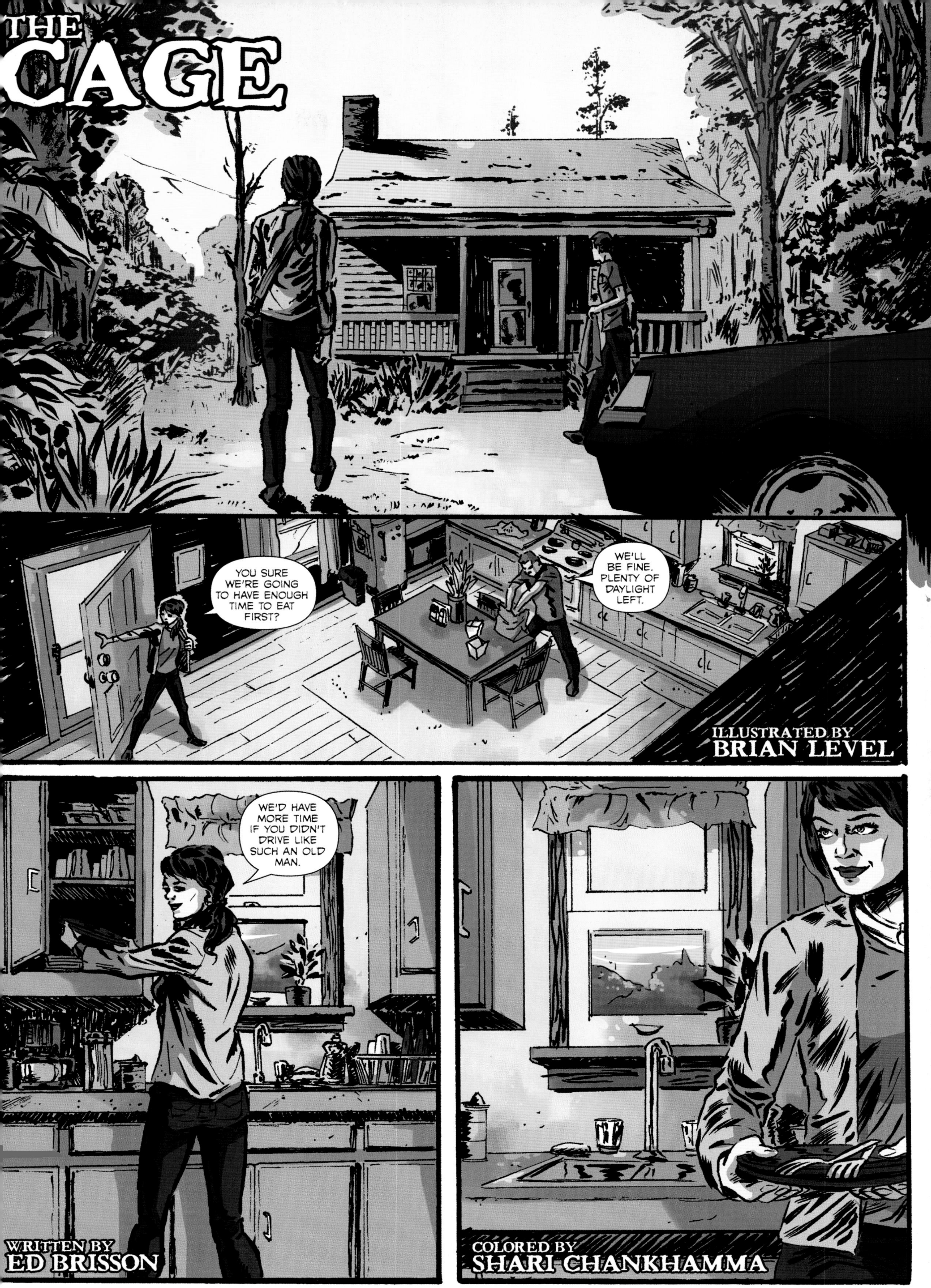
THE CAGE
YOU SURE WE'RE GOING TO HAVE ENOUGH TIME TO EAT FIRST?
WE'LL BE FINE. PLENTY OF DAYLIGHT LEFT.
ILLUSTRATED BY BRIAN LEVEL
WE'D HAVE MORE TIME IF YOU DIDN'T DRIVE LIKE SUCH AN OLD MAN.
WRITTEN BY ED BRISSON
COLORED BY SHARI CHANKHAMMA

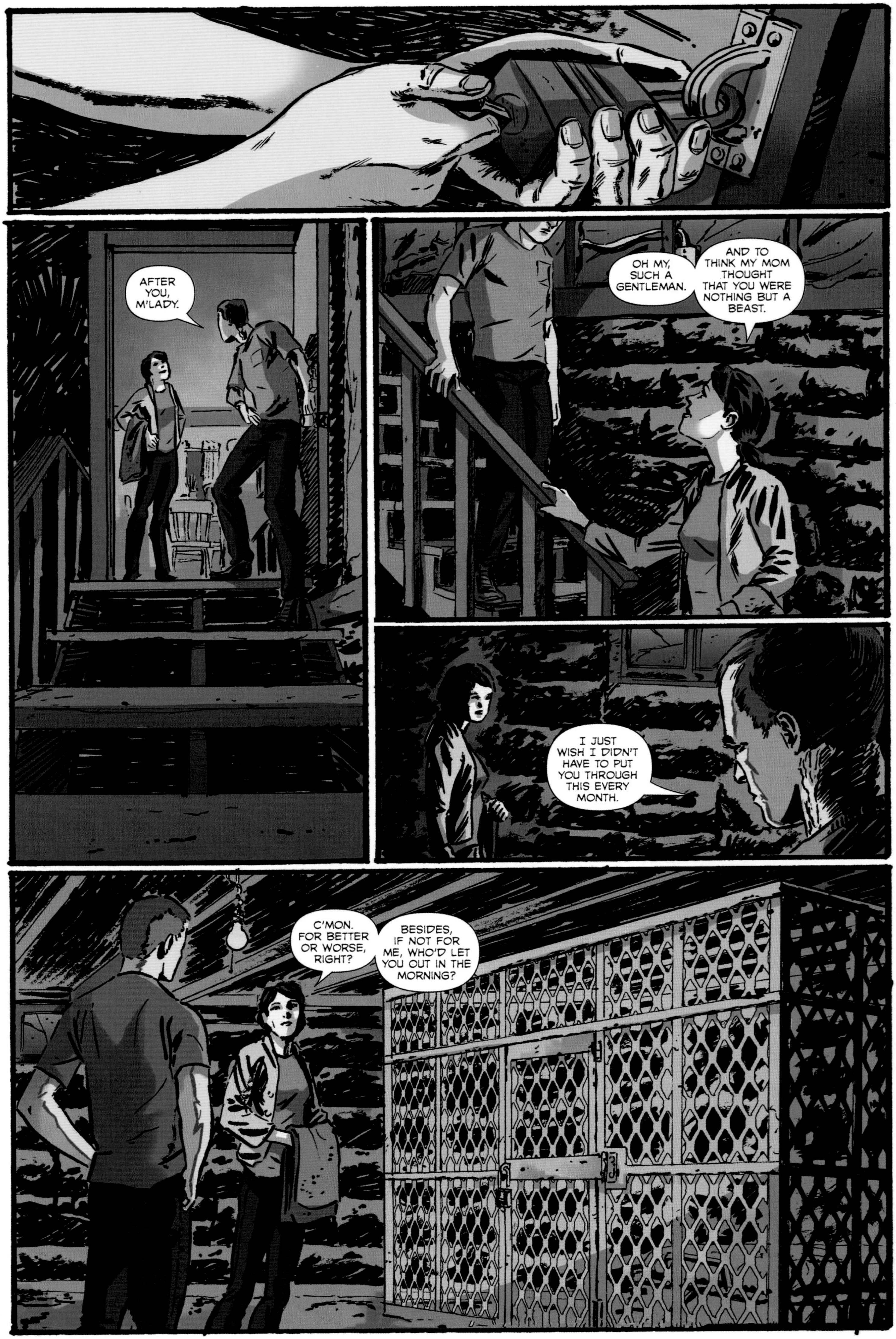
AFTER YOU, M'LADY.
OH MY, SUCH A GENTLEMAN.
AND TO THINK MY MOM THOUGHT THAT YOU WERE NOTHING BUT A BEAST.
I JUST WISH I DIDN'T HAVE TO PUT YOU THROUGH THIS EVERY MONTH.
C'MON. FOR BETTER OR WORSE, RIGHT?
BESIDES, IF NOT FOR ME, WHO'D LET YOU OUT IN THE MORNING?

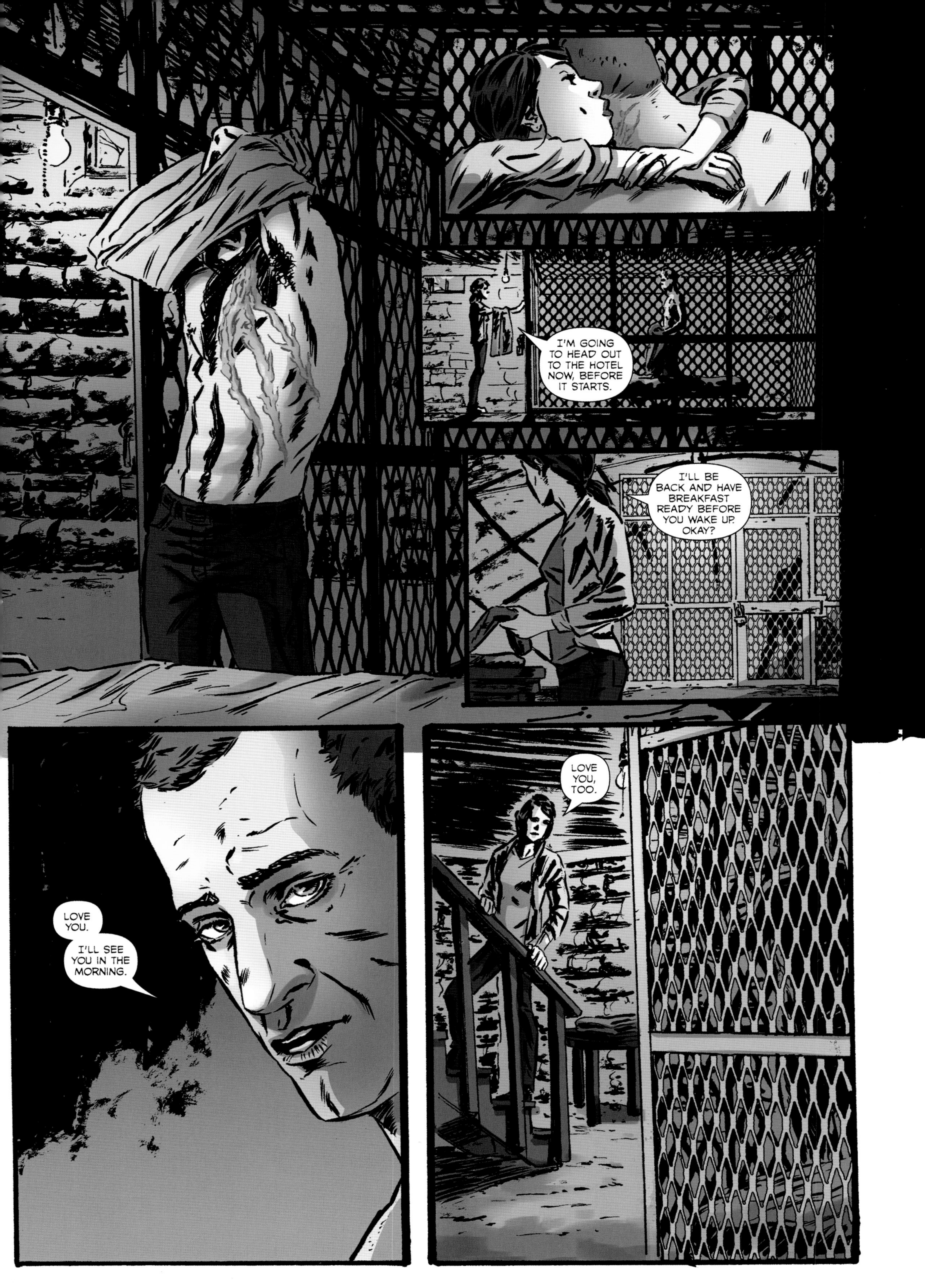
I'M GOING TO HEAD OUT TO THE HOTEL NOW, BEFORE IT STARTS.
I'LL BE BACK AND HAVE BREAKFAST READY BEFORE YOU WAKE UP. OKAY?
LOVE YOU.
I'LL SEE YOU IN THE MORNING.
LOVE YOU, TOO.

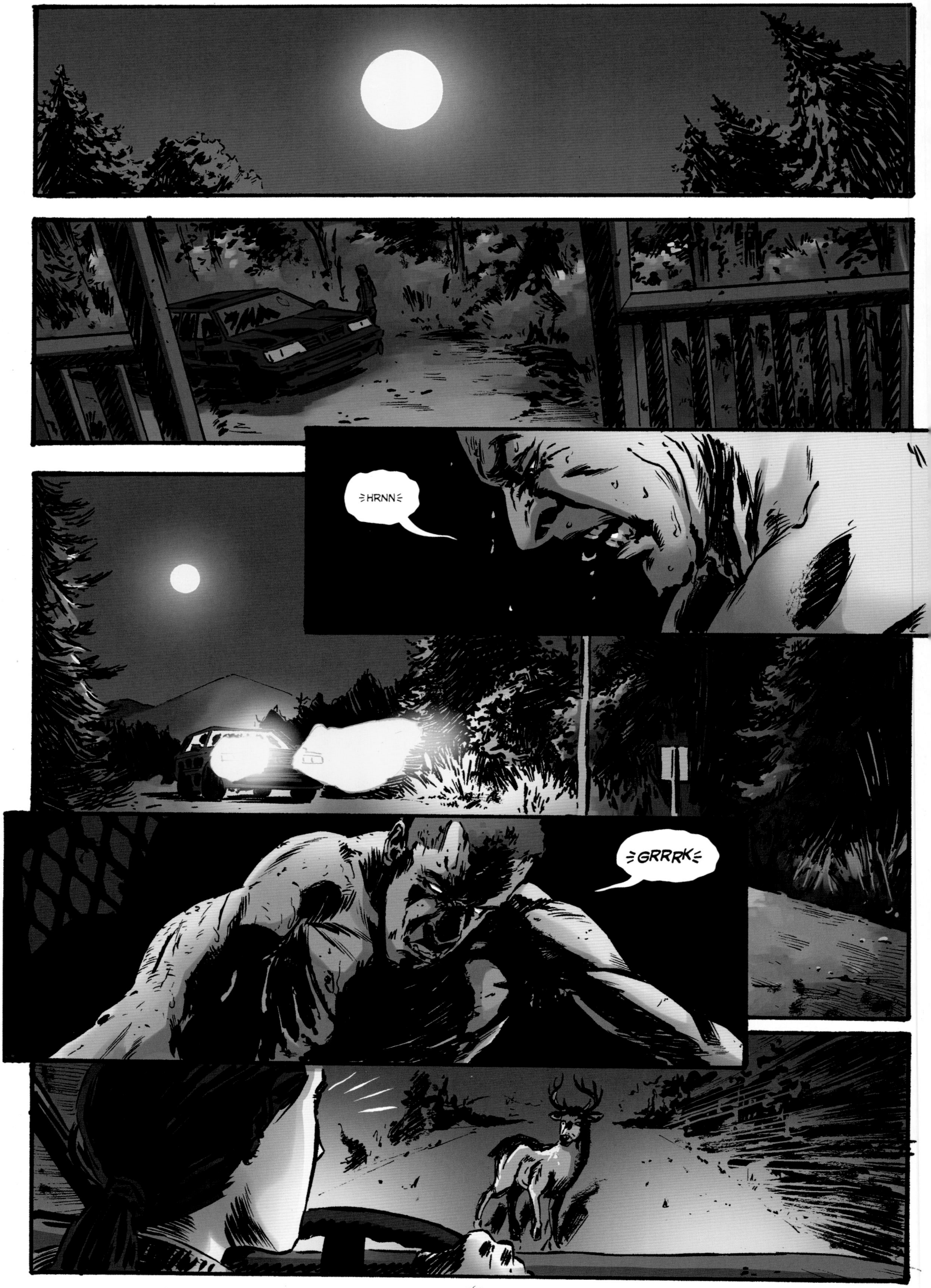
HRNN
GRRRK

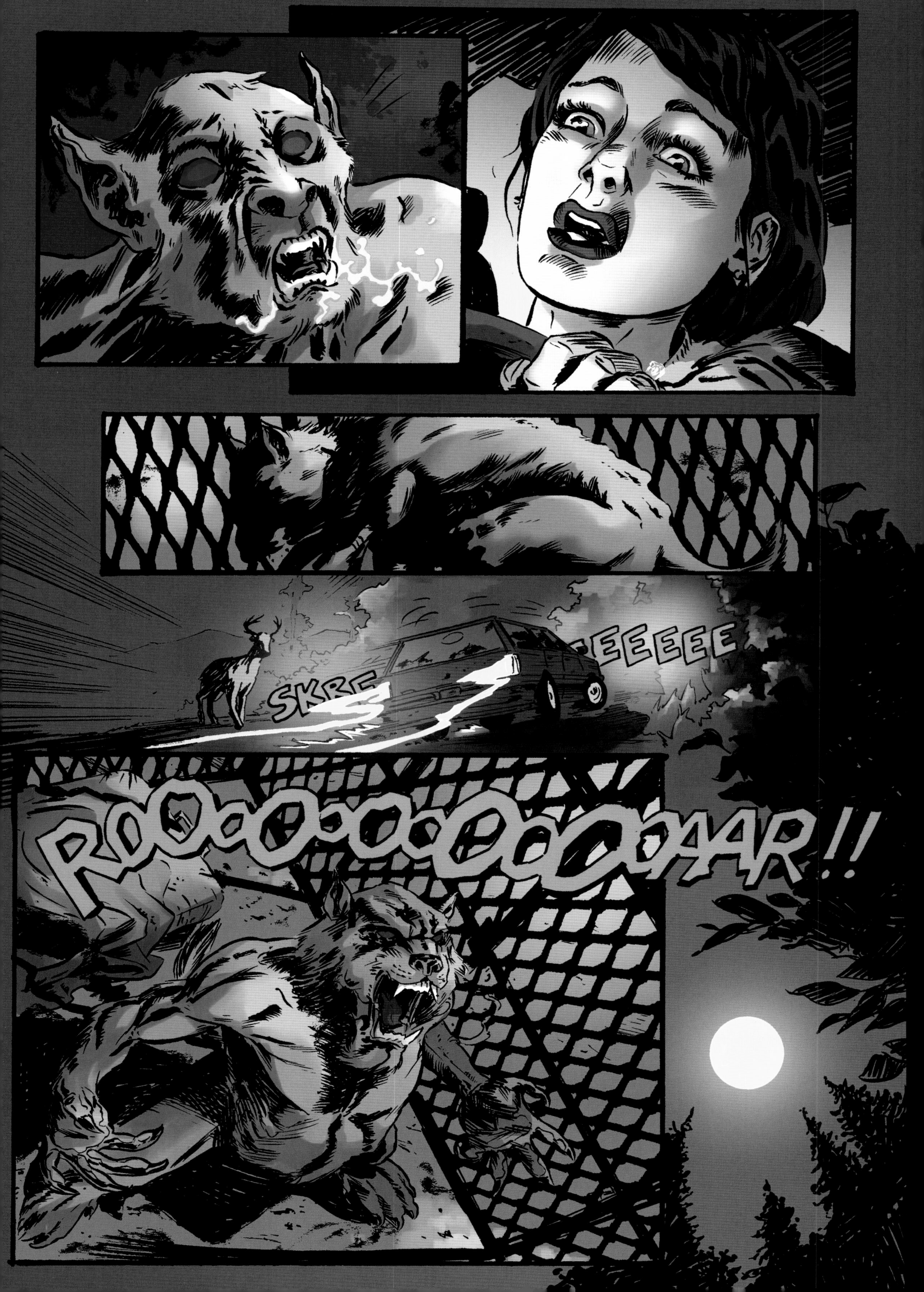

SKRE
EEEEEE
ROOOOOOOOOOOAAR!!

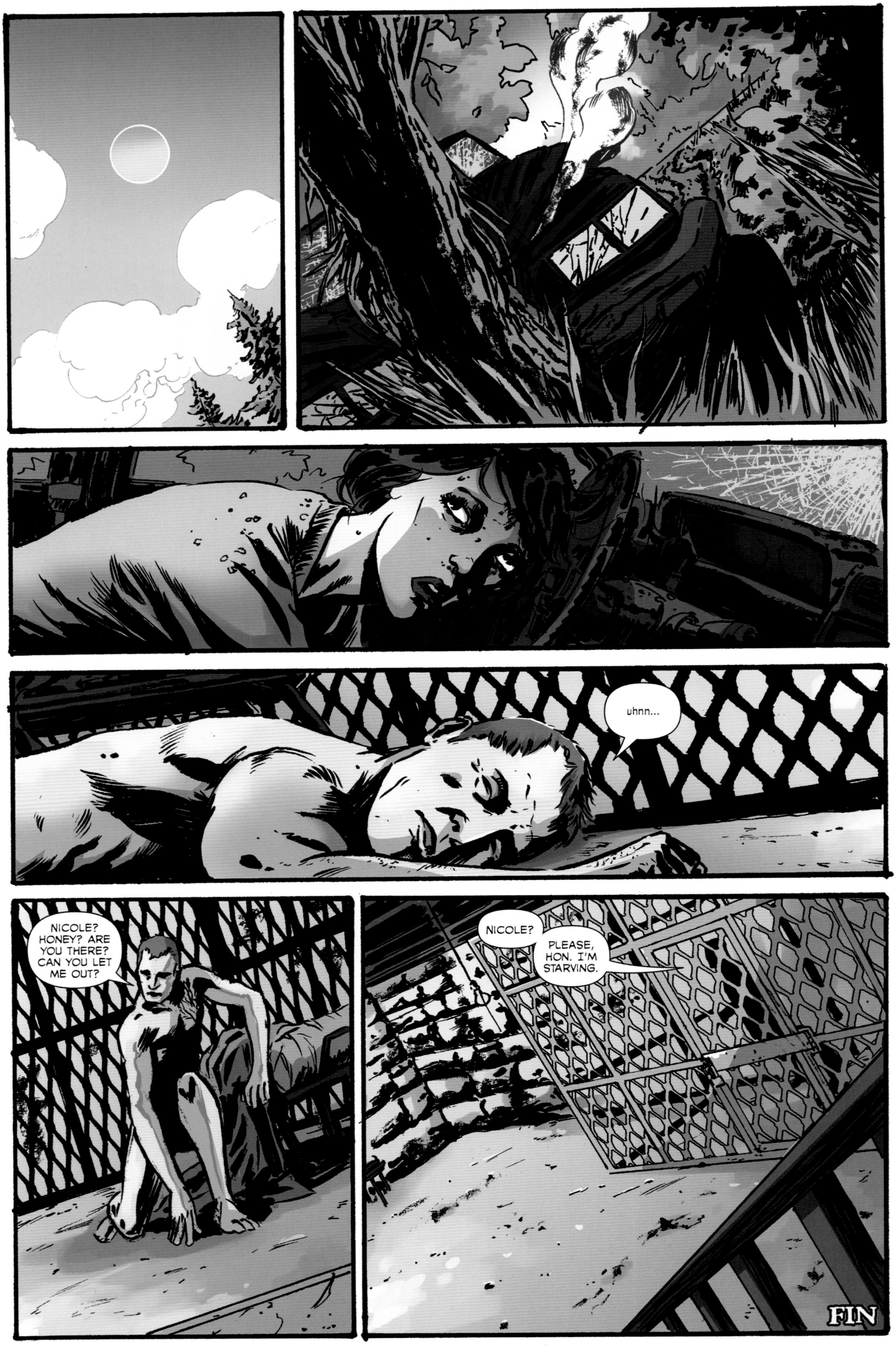
uhnn...
NICOLE? HONEY? ARE YOU THERE? CAN YOU LET ME OUT?
NICOLE?
PLEASE, HON. I'M STARVING.
FIN

AUTHENTIC HUMAN SKELETON!

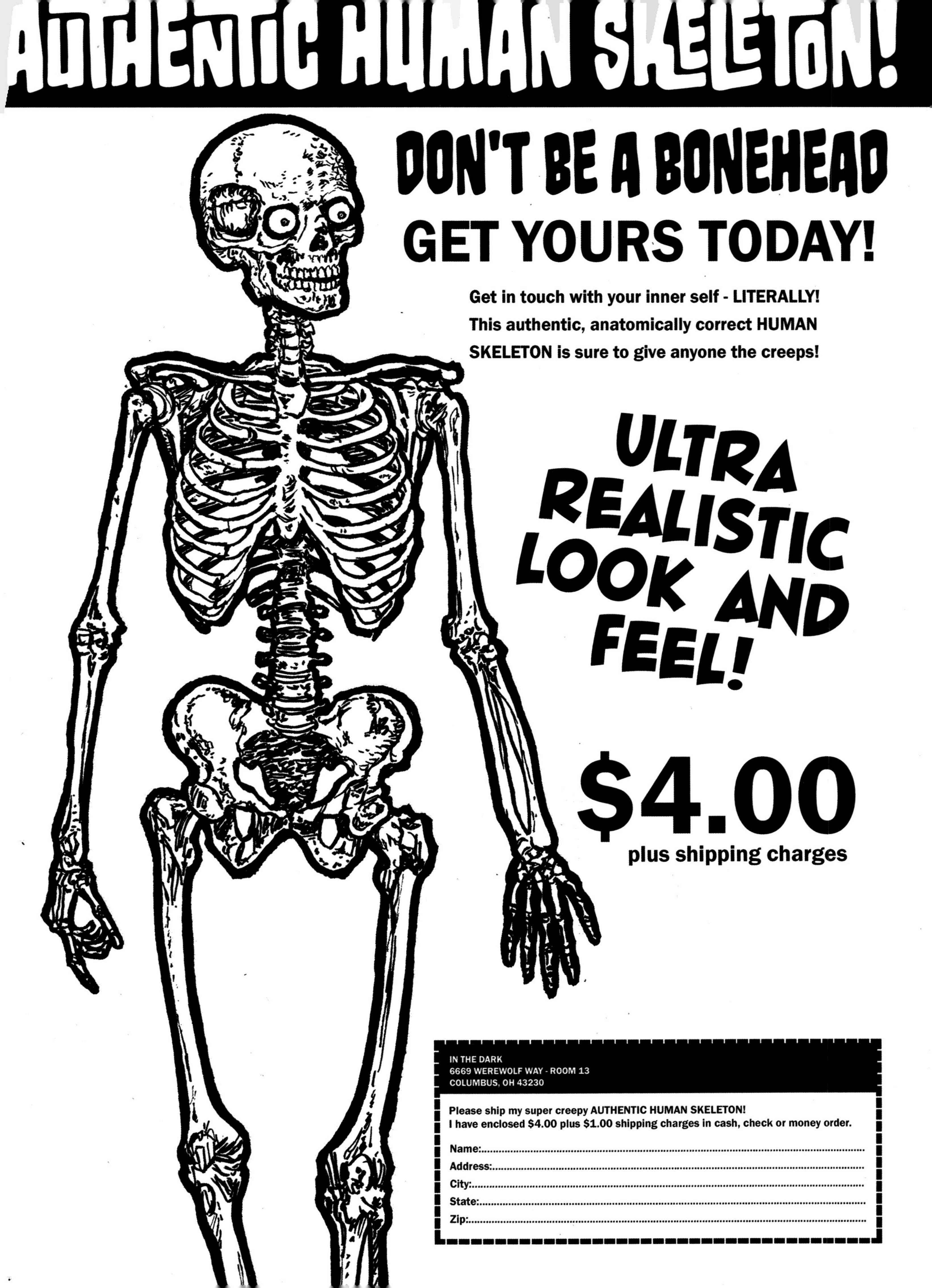

DON'T BE A BONEHEAD

GET YOURS TODAY!

Get in touch with your inner self - LITERALLY! This authentic, anatomically correct HUMAN SKELETON is sure to give anyone the creeps!

ULTRA REALISTIC LOOK AND FEEL!

$4.00

plus shipping charges

IN THE DARK
6669 WEREWOLF WAY - ROOM 13
COLUMBUS, OH 43230

Please ship my super creepy AUTHENTIC HUMAN SKELETON!
I have enclosed $4.00 plus $1.00 shipping charges in cash, check or money order.

Name:..

Address:..

City:..

State:..

Zip:..

THE GIRL ON THE CORNER

WRITER
PAUL TOBIN

ARTIST
ROBERT WILSON IV

COLORIST
MATT WILSON

LETTERER
NIC J. SHAW

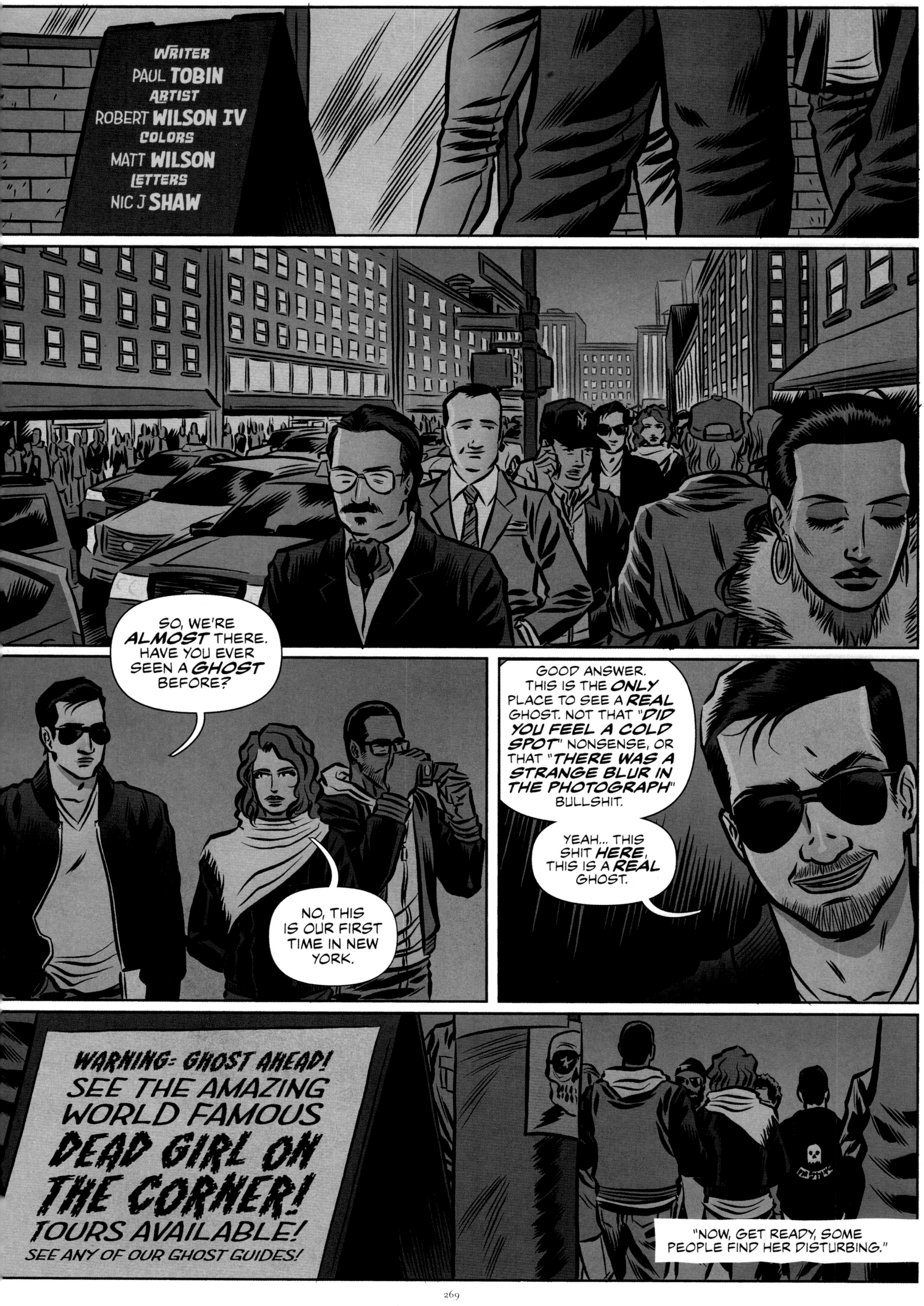
WRITER
PAUL TOBIN
ARTIST
ROBERT WILSON IV
COLORS
MATT WILSON
LETTERS
NIC J SHAW
SO, WE'RE ALMOST THERE. HAVE YOU EVER SEEN A GHOST BEFORE?
NO, THIS IS OUR FIRST TIME IN NEW YORK.
GOOD ANSWER. THIS IS THE ONLY PLACE TO SEE A REAL GHOST. NOT THAT "DID YOU FEEL A COLD SPOT" NONSENSE, OR THAT "THERE WAS A STRANGE BLUR IN THE PHOTOGRAPH" BULLSHIT.
YEAH... THIS SHIT HERE, THIS IS A REAL GHOST.
WARNING: GHOST AHEAD!
SEE THE AMAZING WORLD FAMOUS
DEAD GIRL ON THE CORNER!
TOURS AVAILABLE!
SEE ANY OF OUR GHOST GUIDES!
"NOW, GET READY, SOME PEOPLE FIND HER DISTURBING."

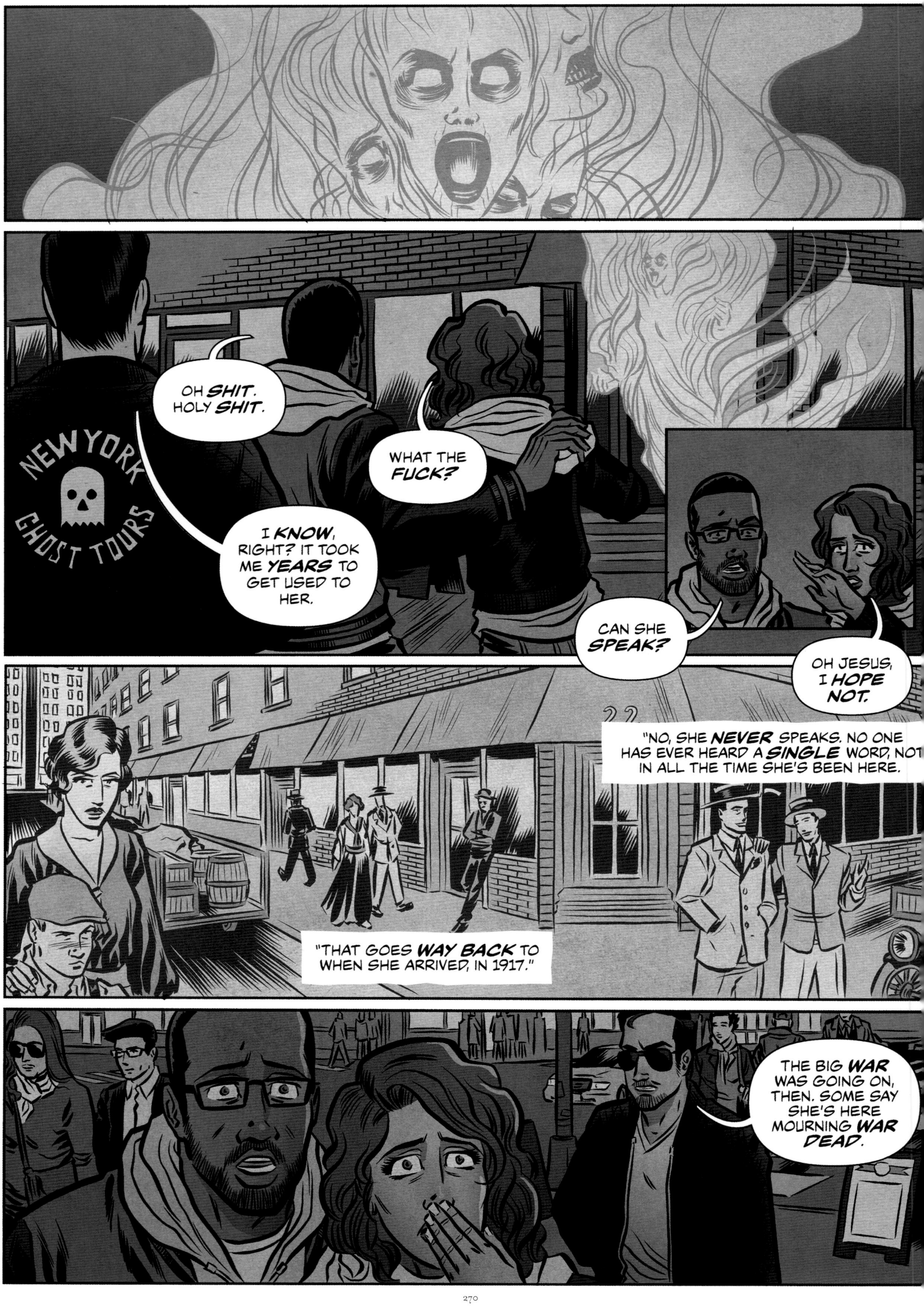
OH SHIT. HOLY SHIT.
WHAT THE FUCK?
I KNOW, RIGHT? IT TOOK ME YEARS TO GET USED TO HER.
NEW YORK GHOST TOURS
CAN SHE SPEAK?
OH JESUS, I HOPE NOT.
"NO, SHE NEVER SPEAKS. NO ONE HAS EVER HEARD A SINGLE WORD, NOT IN ALL THE TIME SHE'S BEEN HERE.
"THAT GOES WAY BACK TO WHEN SHE ARRIVED, IN 1917."
THE BIG WAR WAS GOING ON, THEN. SOME SAY SHE'S HERE MOURNING WAR DEAD.

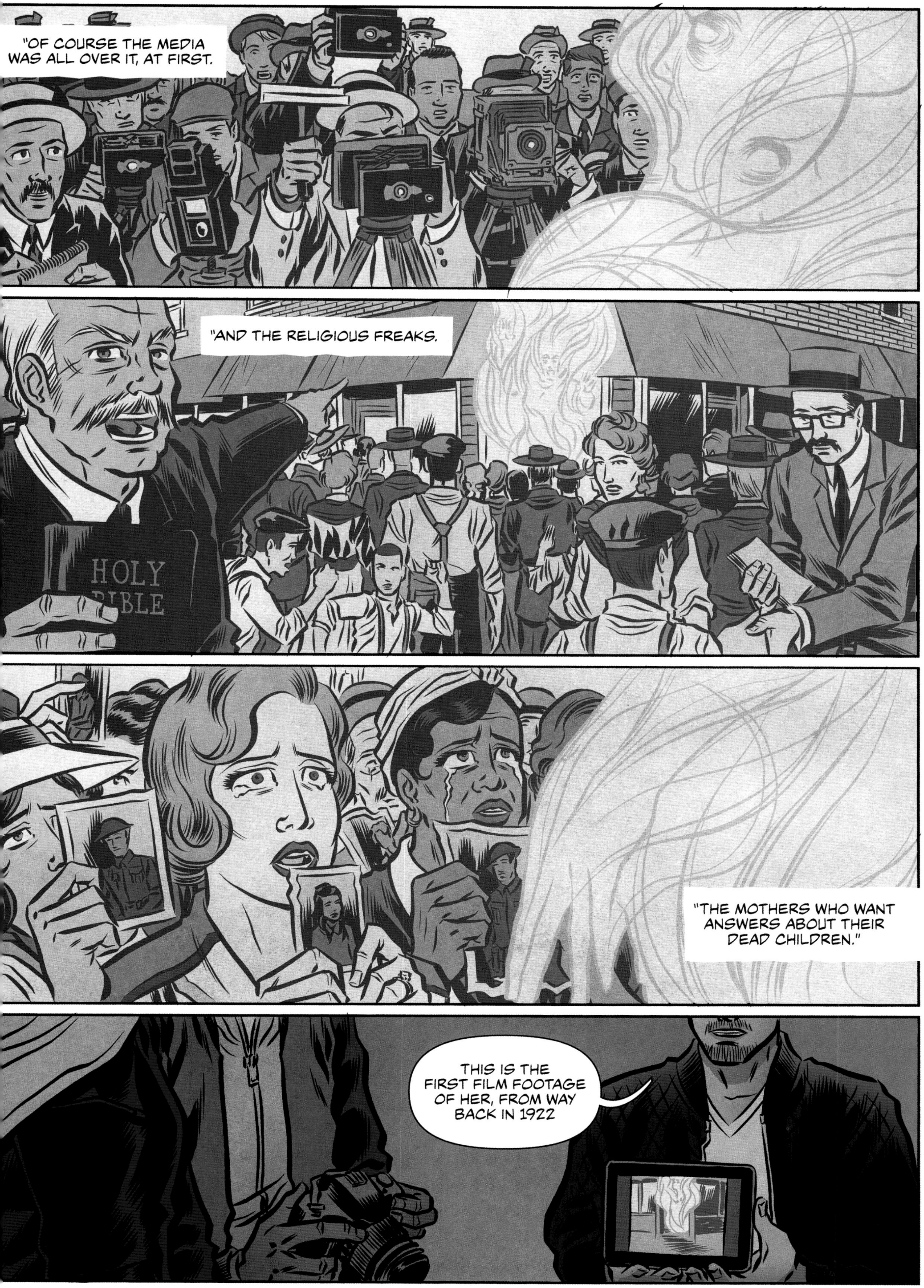
"OF COURSE THE MEDIA WAS ALL OVER IT, AT FIRST.
"AND THE RELIGIOUS FREAKS.
HOLY BIBLE
"THE MOTHERS WHO WANT ANSWERS ABOUT THEIR DEAD CHILDREN."
THIS IS THE FIRST FILM FOOTAGE OF HER, FROM WAY BACK IN 1922

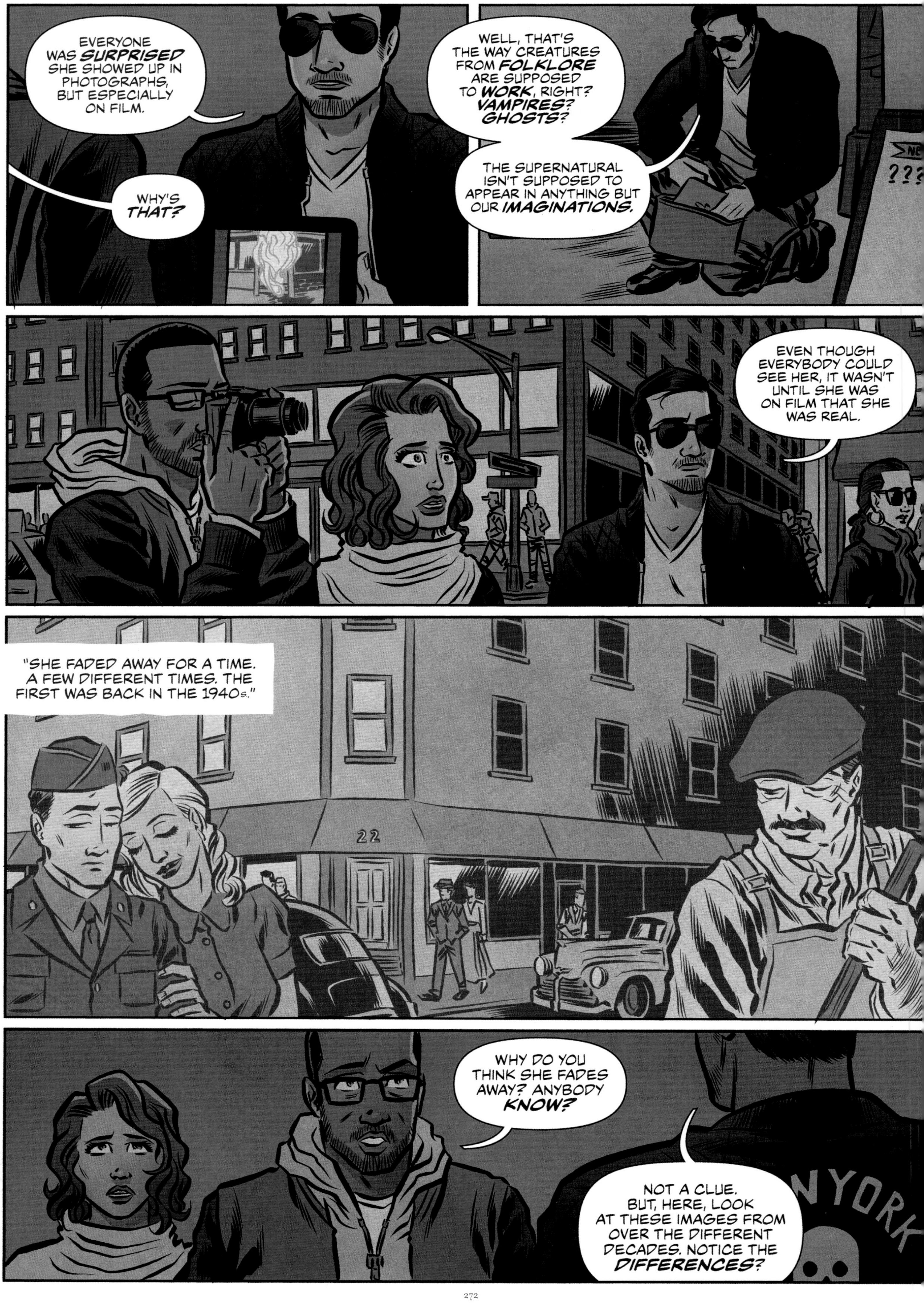
EVERYONE WAS SURPRISED SHE SHOWED UP IN PHOTOGRAPHS, BUT ESPECIALLY ON FILM.
WHY'S THAT?
WELL, THAT'S THE WAY CREATURES FROM FOLKLORE ARE SUPPOSED TO WORK, RIGHT? VAMPIRES? GHOSTS?
THE SUPERNATURAL ISN'T SUPPOSED TO APPEAR IN ANYTHING BUT OUR IMAGINATIONS.
???
EVEN THOUGH EVERYBODY COULD SEE HER, IT WASN'T UNTIL SHE WAS ON FILM THAT SHE WAS REAL.
"SHE FADED AWAY FOR A TIME. A FEW DIFFERENT TIMES. THE FIRST WAS BACK IN THE 1940s."
22
WHY DO YOU THINK SHE FADES AWAY? ANYBODY KNOW?
NOT A CLUE. BUT, HERE, LOOK AT THESE IMAGES FROM OVER THE DIFFERENT DECADES. NOTICE THE DIFFERENCES?
NYORK

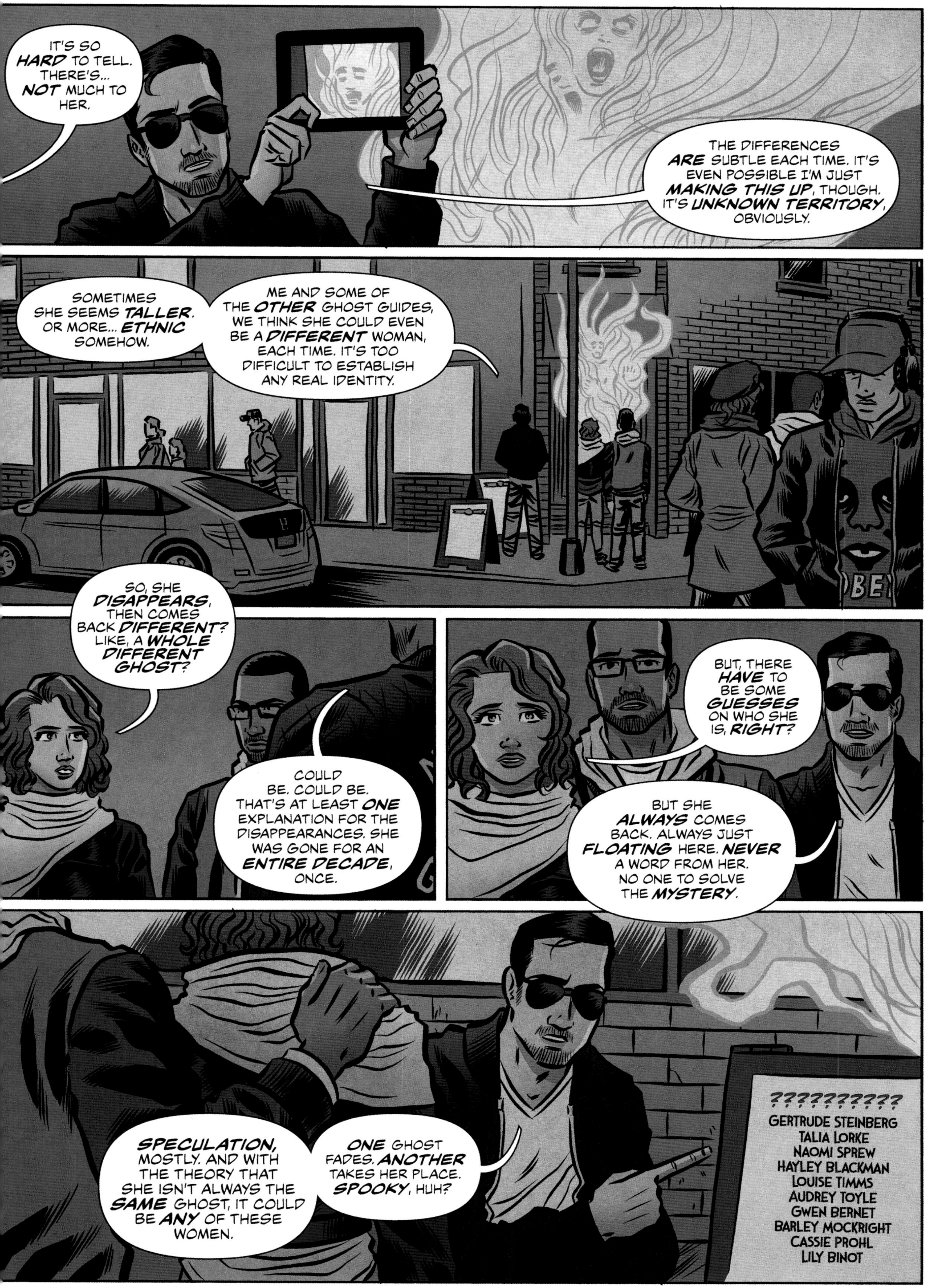
IT'S SO HARD TO TELL. THERE'S... NOT MUCH TO HER.
THE DIFFERENCES ARE SUBTLE EACH TIME. IT'S EVEN POSSIBLE I'M JUST MAKING THIS UP, THOUGH. IT'S UNKNOWN TERRITORY, OBVIOUSLY.
SOMETIMES SHE SEEMS TALLER. OR MORE... ETHNIC SOMEHOW.
ME AND SOME OF THE OTHER GHOST GUIDES, WE THINK SHE COULD EVEN BE A DIFFERENT WOMAN, EACH TIME. IT'S TOO DIFFICULT TO ESTABLISH ANY REAL IDENTITY.
SO, SHE DISAPPEARS, THEN COMES BACK DIFFERENT? LIKE, A WHOLE DIFFERENT GHOST?
COULD BE. COULD BE. THAT'S AT LEAST ONE EXPLANATION FOR THE DISAPPEARANCES. SHE WAS GONE FOR AN ENTIRE DECADE, ONCE.
BUT, THERE HAVE TO BE SOME GUESSES ON WHO SHE IS, RIGHT?
BUT SHE ALWAYS COMES BACK. ALWAYS JUST FLOATING HERE. NEVER A WORD FROM HER. NO ONE TO SOLVE THE MYSTERY.
SPECULATION, MOSTLY. AND WITH THE THEORY THAT SHE ISN'T ALWAYS THE SAME GHOST, IT COULD BE ANY OF THESE WOMEN.
ONE GHOST FADES. ANOTHER TAKES HER PLACE. SPOOKY, HUH?
??????????
GERTRUDE STEINBERG
TALIA LORKE
NAOMI SPREW
HAYLEY BLACKMAN
LOUISE TIMMS
AUDREY TOYLE
GWEN BERNET
BARLEY MOCKRIGHT
CASSIE PROHL
LILY BINOT

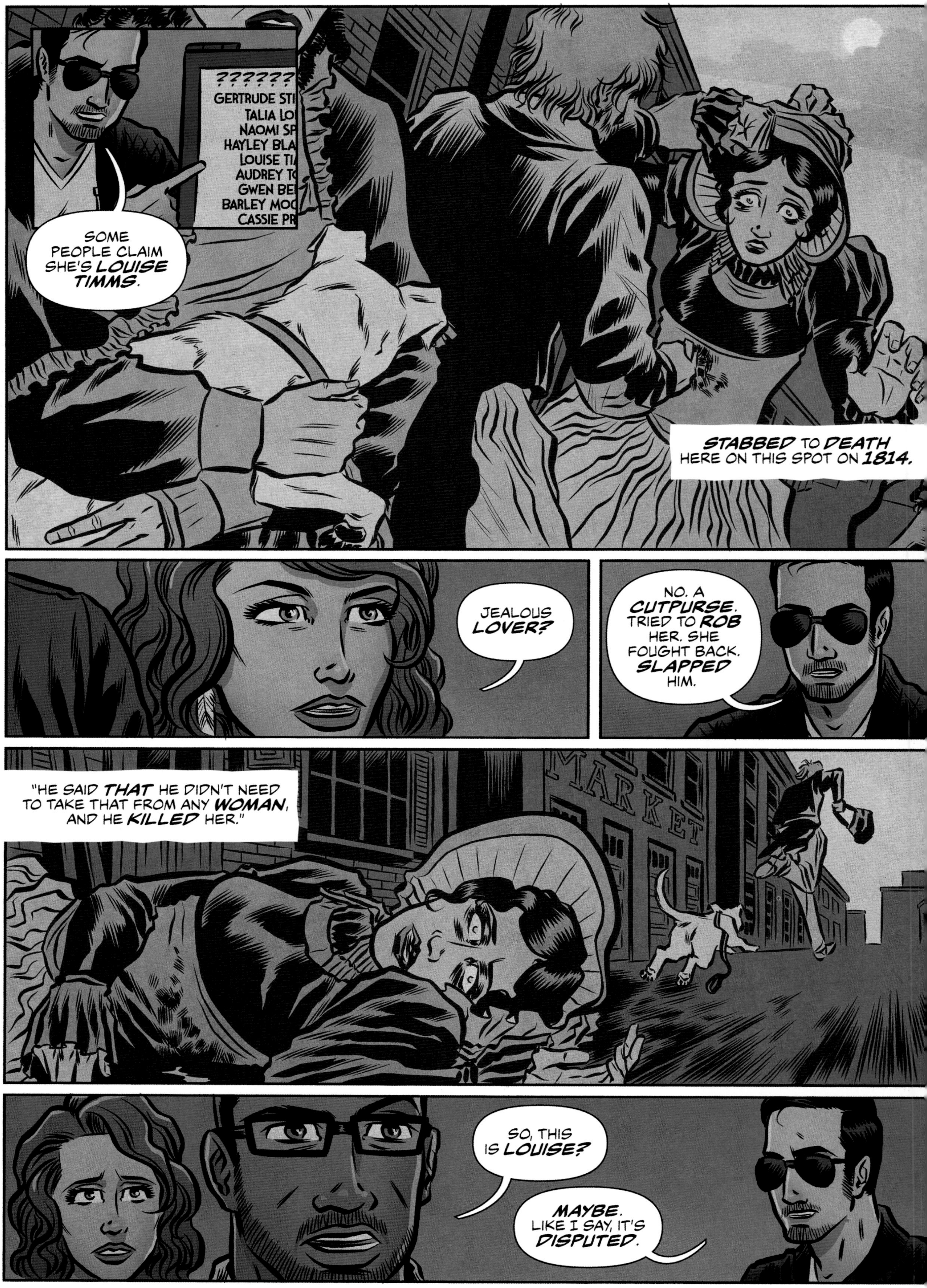

??????
GERTRUDE STI
TALIA LO
NAOMI SP
HAYLEY BLA
LOUISE TI
AUDREY T
GWEN BE
BARLEY MOO
CASSIE PR
SOME PEOPLE CLAIM SHE'S LOUISE TIMMS.
STABBED TO DEATH HERE ON THIS SPOT ON 1814.
JEALOUS LOVER?
NO. A CUTPURSE. TRIED TO ROB HER. SHE FOUGHT BACK. SLAPPED HIM.
"HE SAID THAT HE DIDN'T NEED TO TAKE THAT FROM ANY WOMAN, AND HE KILLED HER."
MARKET
SO, THIS IS LOUISE?
MAYBE. LIKE I SAY, IT'S DISPUTED.

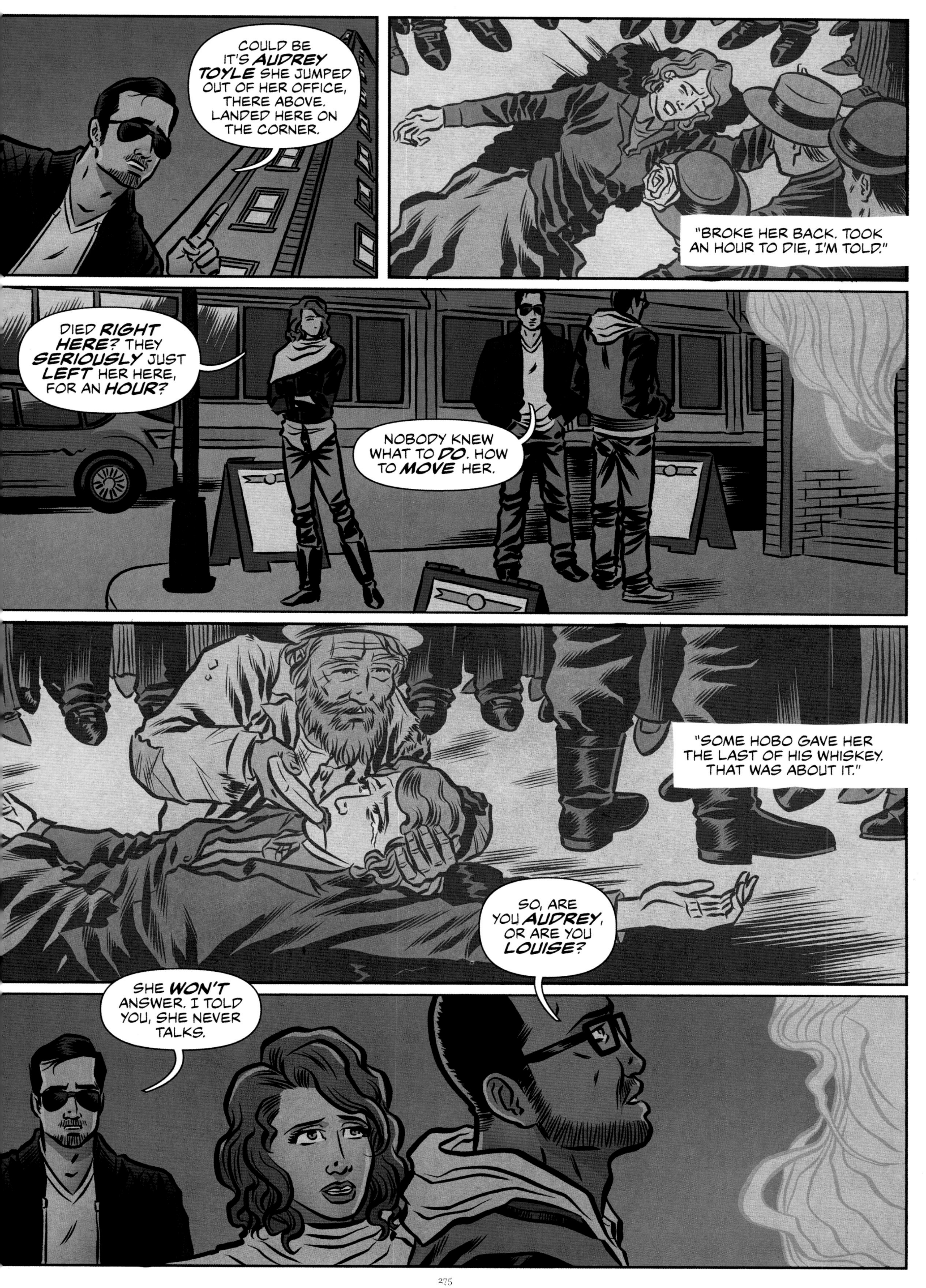
COULD BE IT'S AUDREY TOYLE SHE JUMPED OUT OF HER OFFICE, THERE ABOVE. LANDED HERE ON THE CORNER.
"BROKE HER BACK. TOOK AN HOUR TO DIE, I'M TOLD."
DIED RIGHT HERE? THEY SERIOUSLY JUST LEFT HER HERE, FOR AN HOUR?
NOBODY KNEW WHAT TO DO. HOW TO MOVE HER.
"SOME HOBO GAVE HER THE LAST OF HIS WHISKEY. THAT WAS ABOUT IT."
SO, ARE YOU AUDREY, OR ARE YOU LOUISE?
SHE WON'T ANSWER. I TOLD YOU, SHE NEVER TALKS.

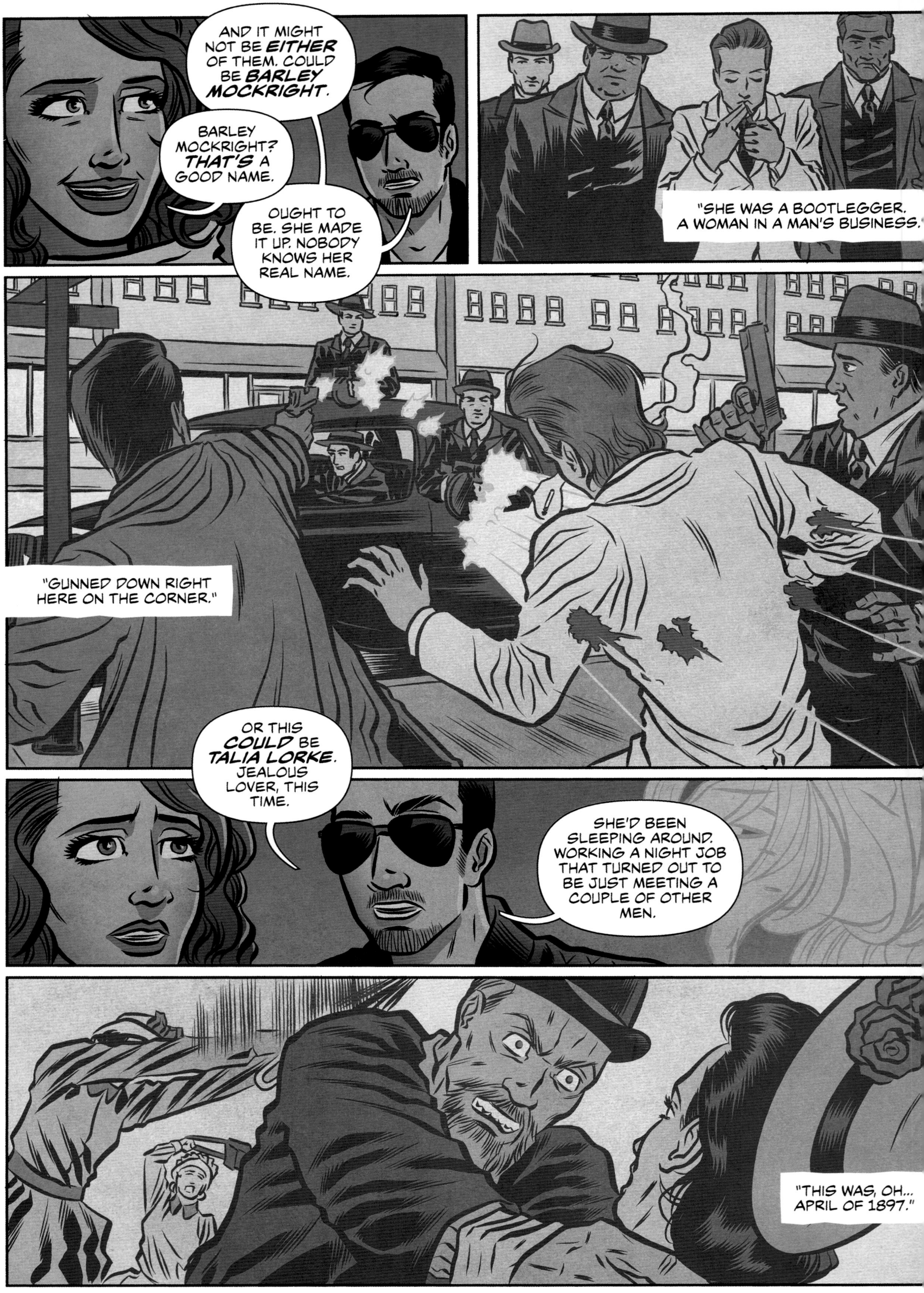
AND IT MIGHT NOT BE EITHER OF THEM. COULD BE BARLEY MOCKRIGHT.
BARLEY MOCKRIGHT? THAT'S A GOOD NAME.
OUGHT TO BE. SHE MADE IT UP. NOBODY KNOWS HER REAL NAME.
"SHE WAS A BOOTLEGGER. A WOMAN IN A MAN'S BUSINESS."
"GUNNED DOWN RIGHT HERE ON THE CORNER."
OR THIS COULD BE TALIA LORKE. JEALOUS LOVER, THIS TIME.
SHE'D BEEN SLEEPING AROUND. WORKING A NIGHT JOB THAT TURNED OUT TO BE JUST MEETING A COUPLE OF OTHER MEN.
"THIS WAS, OH... APRIL OF 1897."

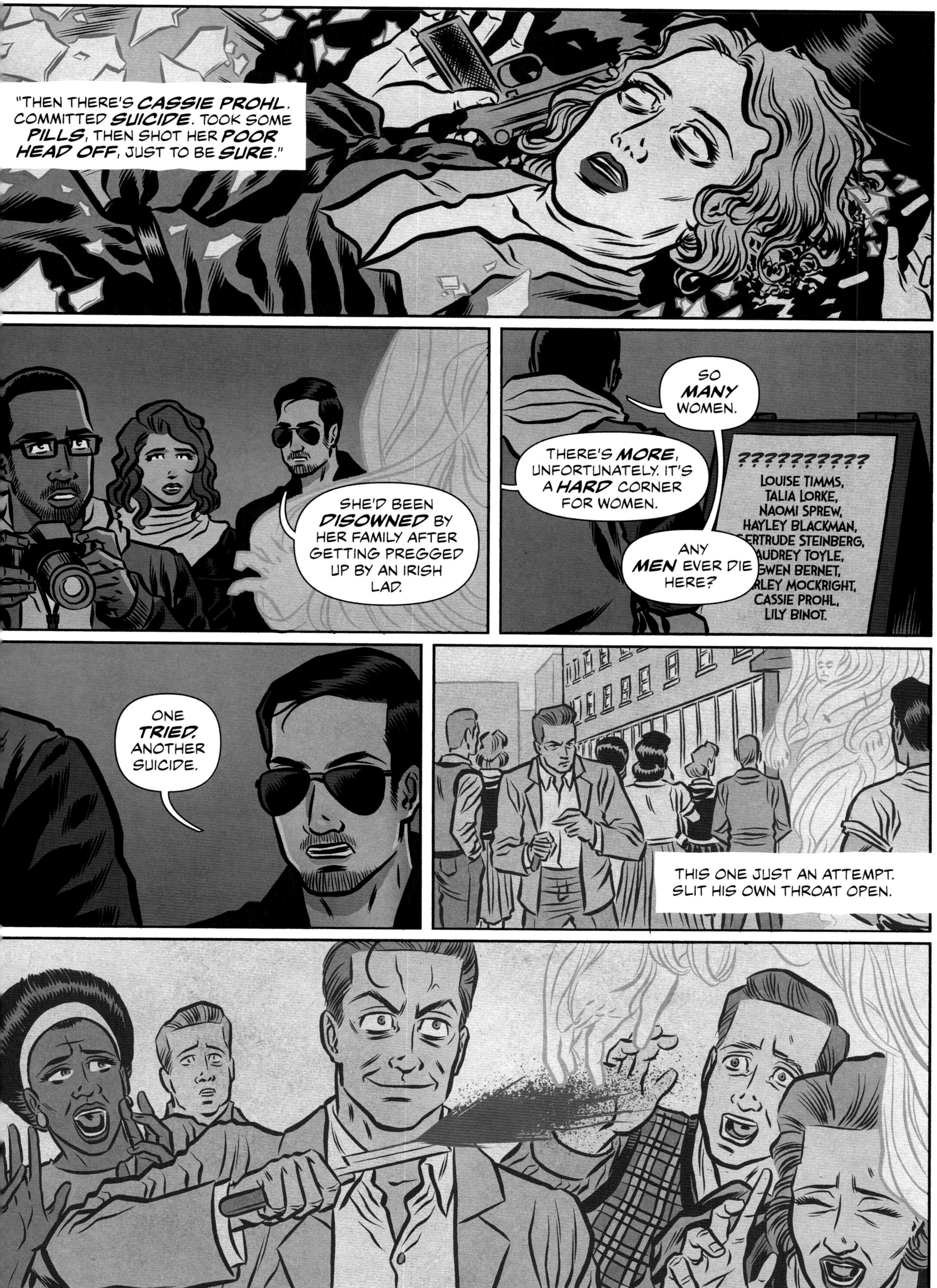
"THEN THERE'S CASSIE PROHL. COMMITTED SUICIDE. TOOK SOME PILLS, THEN SHOT HER POOR HEAD OFF, JUST TO BE SURE."
SHE'D BEEN DISOWNED BY HER FAMILY AFTER GETTING PREGGED UP BY AN IRISH LAD.
SO MANY WOMEN.
THERE'S MORE, UNFORTUNATELY. IT'S A HARD CORNER FOR WOMEN.
??????????
LOUISE TIMMS,
TALIA LORKE,
NAOMI SPREW,
HAYLEY BLACKMAN,
ERTRUDE STEINBERG,
AUDREY TOYLE,
GWEN BERNET,
RLEY MOCKRIGHT,
CASSIE PROHL,
LILY BINOT.
ANY MEN EVER DIE HERE?
ONE TRIED. ANOTHER SUICIDE.
THIS ONE JUST AN ATTEMPT. SLIT HIS OWN THROAT OPEN.

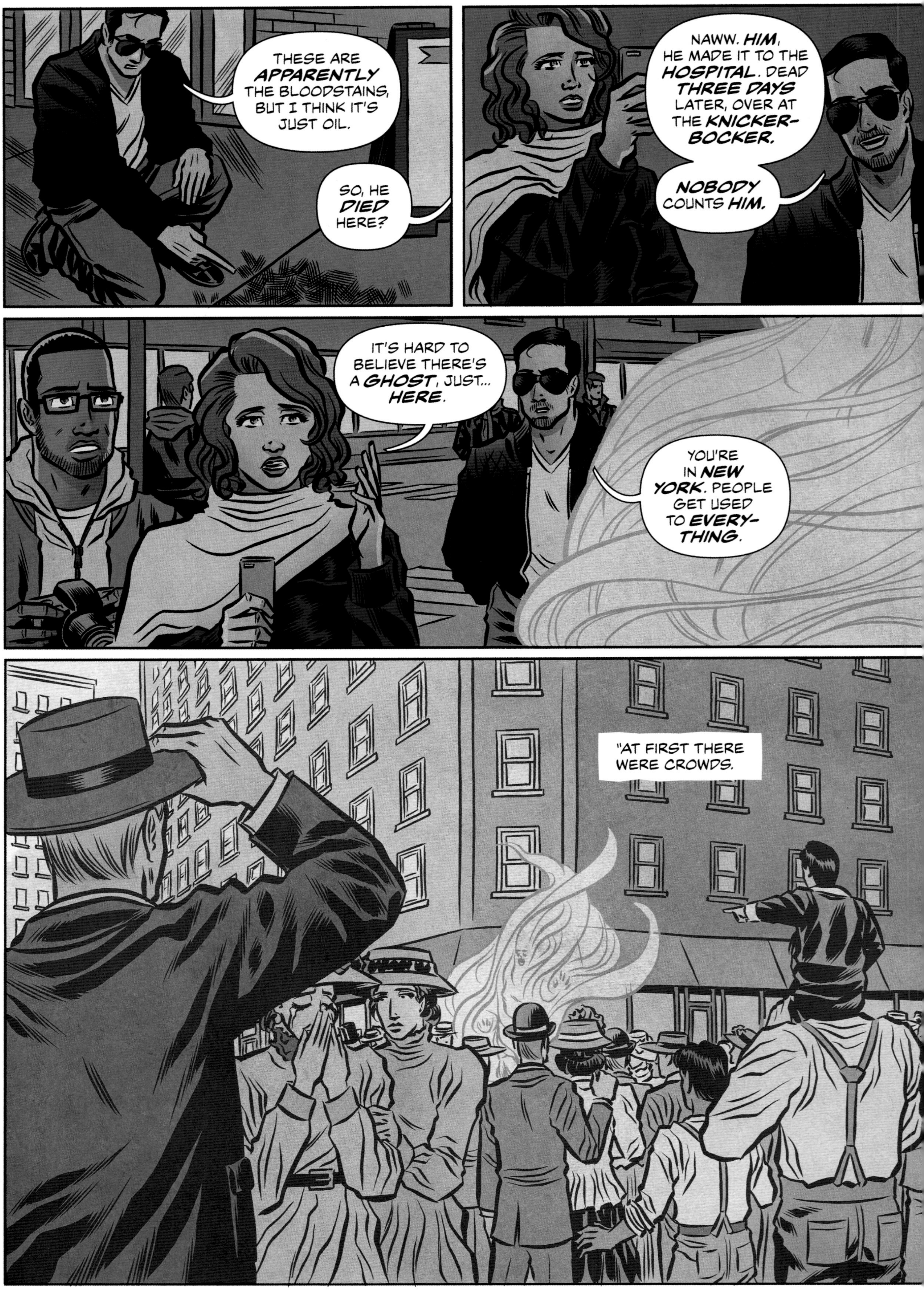
THESE ARE APPARENTLY THE BLOODSTAINS, BUT I THINK IT'S JUST OIL.
SO, HE DIED HERE?
NAWW. HIM, HE MADE IT TO THE HOSPITAL. DEAD THREE DAYS LATER, OVER AT THE KNICKER-BOCKER.
NOBODY COUNTS HIM.
IT'S HARD TO BELIEVE THERE'S A GHOST, JUST... HERE.
YOU'RE IN NEW YORK. PEOPLE GET USED TO EVERY-THING.
"AT FIRST THERE WERE CROWDS.

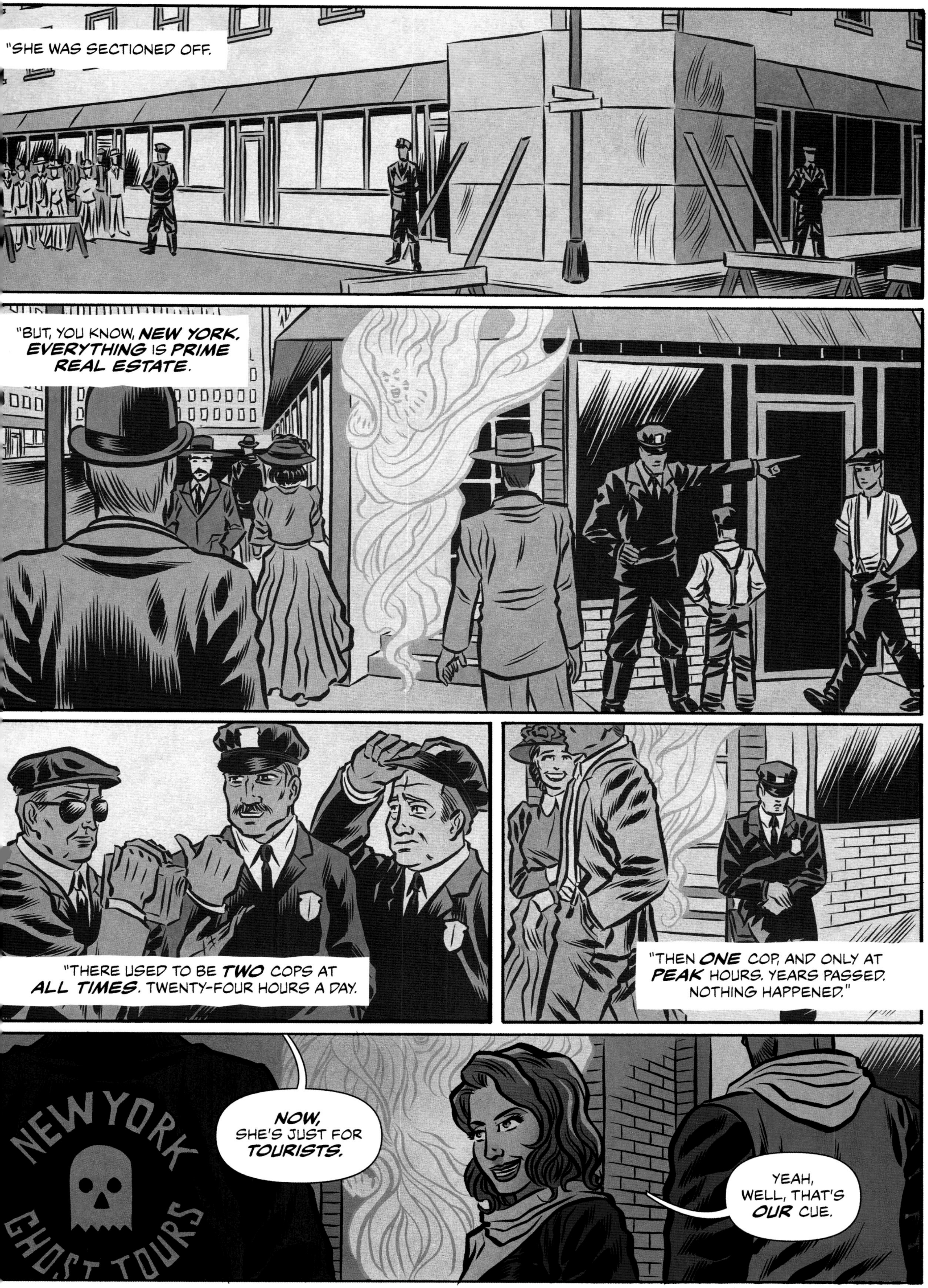
"SHE WAS SECTIONED OFF.
"BUT, YOU KNOW, NEW YORK. EVERYTHING IS PRIME REAL ESTATE.
"THERE USED TO BE TWO COPS AT ALL TIMES. TWENTY-FOUR HOURS A DAY.
"THEN ONE COP, AND ONLY AT PEAK HOURS. YEARS PASSED. NOTHING HAPPENED."
NEW YORK GHOST TOURS
NOW, SHE'S JUST FOR TOURISTS.
YEAH, WELL, THAT'S OUR CUE.

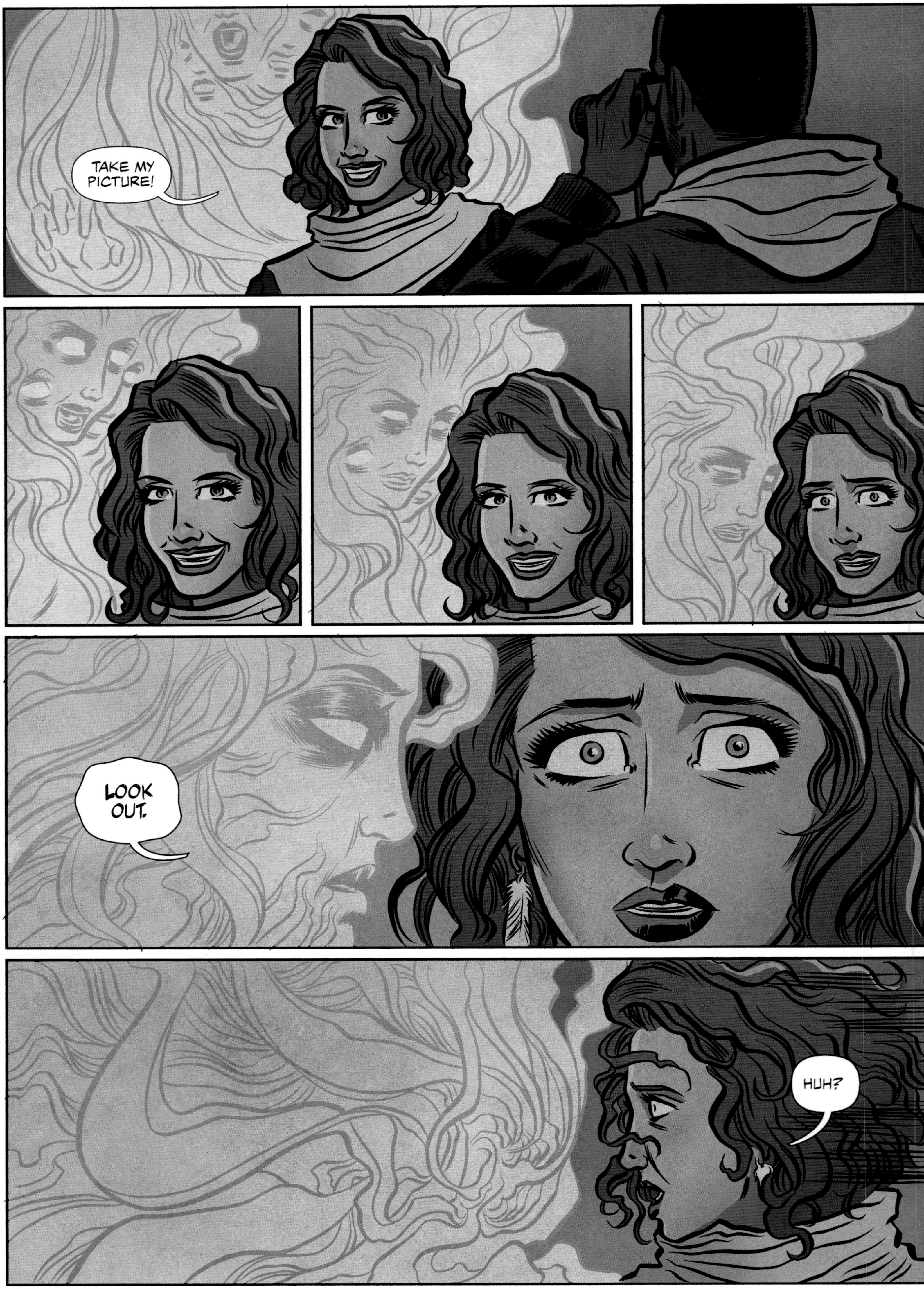
TAKE MY PICTURE!
LOOK OUT.
HUH?

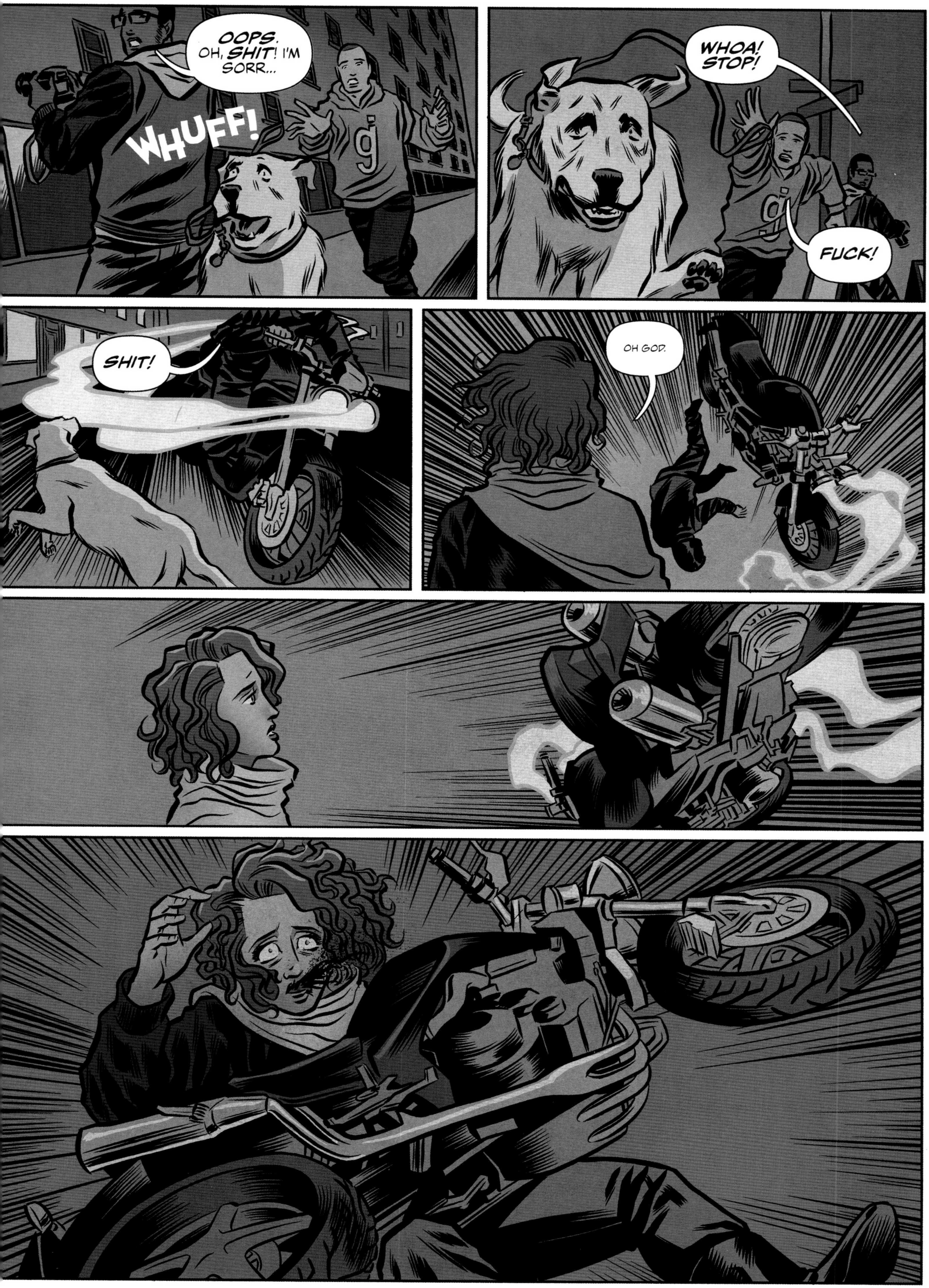
OOPS. OH, SHIT! I'M SORR...
WHUFF!
WHOA! STOP!
FUCK!
SHIT!
OH GOD.

JULIE!

OH *GOD*. OH *SHIT*. YOU HAVE TO BE OKAY. YOU *HAVE* TO BE...

SHE'S GONE, MAN. GONE. I'M SORRY. I'M SO SORRY.

YOU MIND TELLING ME HER NAME?

????????????
GERTRUDE STEINBERG
TALIA LORKE
NAOMI SPREW
HAYLEY BLACKMAN
LOUISE TIMMS
AUDREY TOYLE,
GWEN BERN
BARLEY MOCKRIGHT

POSSESS YOUR VERY OWN

SPOOKY SPIRIT!

- ADVICE FROM BEYOND THE GRAVE!
- SCARE YOUR FRIENDS TO DEATH!
- SEND IT TO SPY ON ANYONE!

The coffin-shaped vessel contains one real human ghost! You are guaranteed to have fun coming up with new and exciting tasks for your ghost to perform! The unlimited power and knowledge of the otherworld will be yours to command!

IN THE DARK
6669 WEREWOLF WAY - ROOM 13
COLUMBUS, OH 43230

QUICK!
Please ship my ultra creepy SPOOKY SPIRIT!
I have enclosed $3.00 plus $1.25 shipping charges in cash, check or money order.

Name:..
Address:..
City:..
State:..
Zip:...

WHO DO VOODOO? NOW YOU DO!

- GET ULTIMATE REVENGE ON YOUR ENEMIES!
- YOU CHOOSE THE AMOUNT OF TORTURE!
- SHOW THOSE BULLIES WHO'S BOSS!

Harness the power of the mysterious spiritual path of VOODOO! Use this authentic VOODOO DOLL, to cast curses and hone your hexes in no time! With this amazing artifact in your possession, you will earn instant respect and strike fear into the hearts of men!

IN THE DARK
6669 WEREWOLF WAY - ROOM 13
COLUMBUS, OH 43230

CURSES! DON'T MAKE ME WAIT!
Please send my frighteningly powerful VOODOO DOLL!
I have enclosed $2.00 plus $1.00 shipping charges in cash, check or money order.

Name:..
Address:..
City:..
State:..
Zip:...

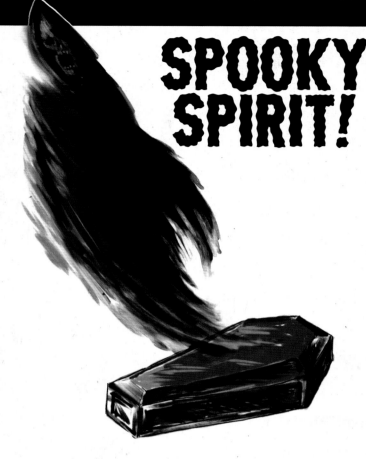

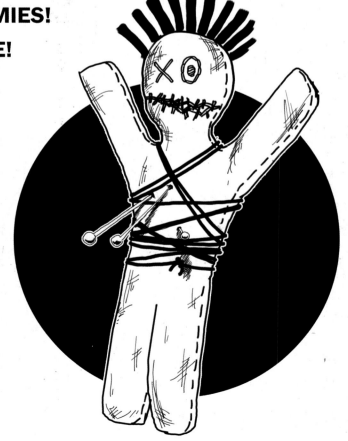

SWAN SONG

WRITER
RACHEL DEERING

ARTIST
MARC LAMING

COLORIST
JORDAN BOYD

LETTERER
RACHEL DEERING

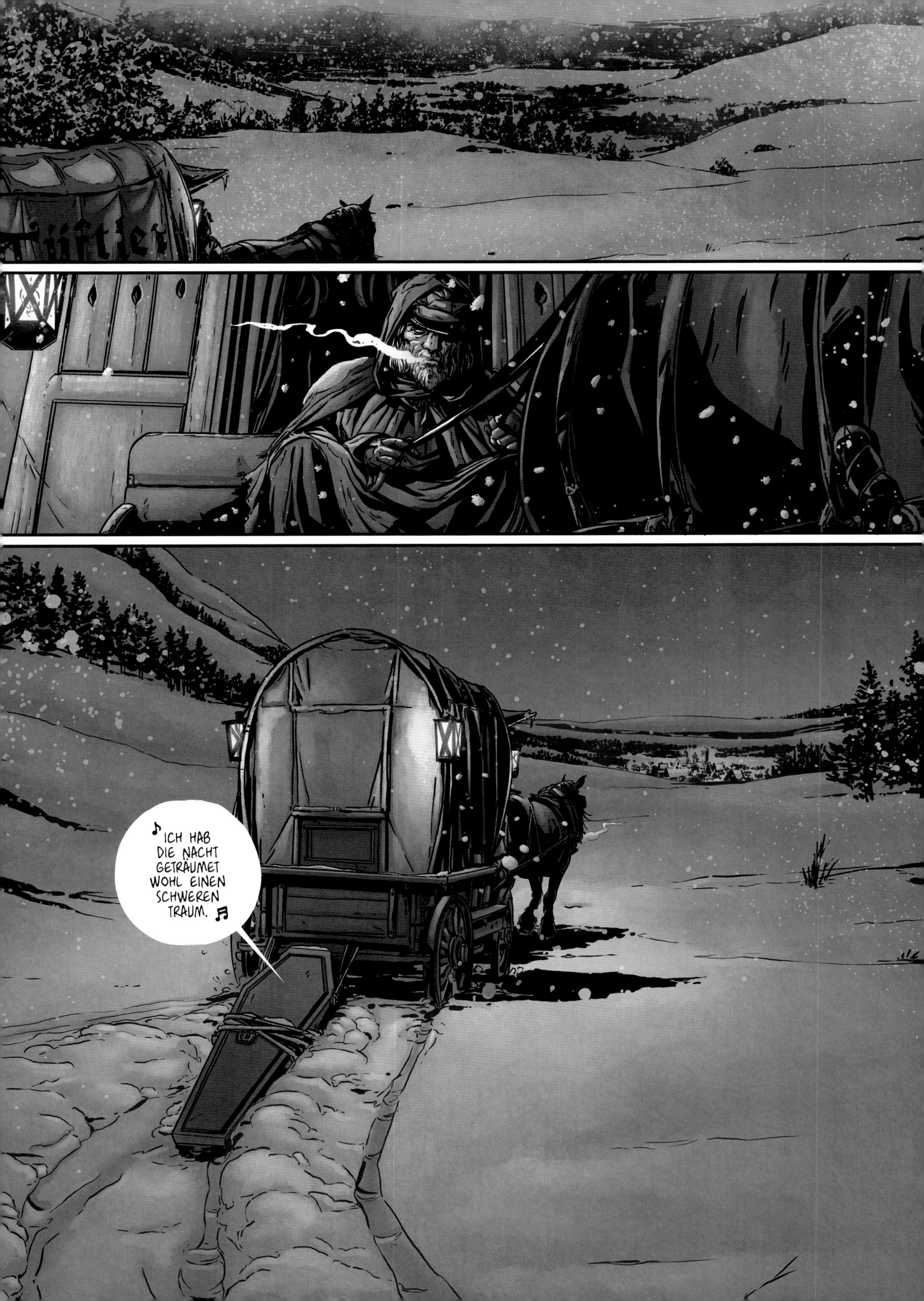
ICH HAB DIE NACHT GETRÄUMET WOHL EINEN SCHWEREN TRAUM.

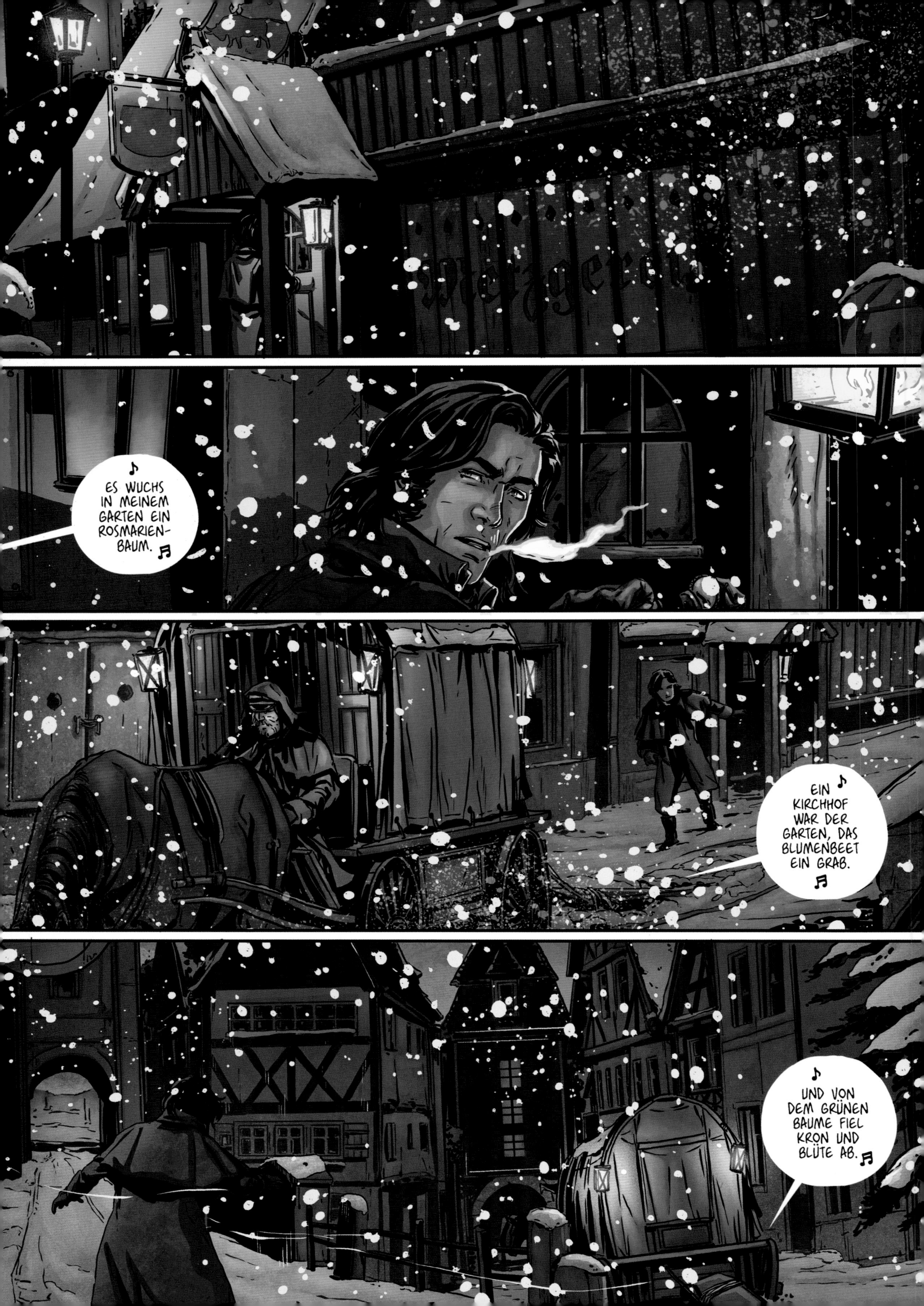
♪ ES WUCHS IN MEINEM GARTEN EIN ROSMARIENBAUM. ♫
♪ EIN KIRCHHOF WAR DER GARTEN, DAS BLUMENBEET EIN GRAB. ♫
♪ UND VON DEM GRÜNEN BAUME FIEL KRON UND BLÜTE AB. ♫

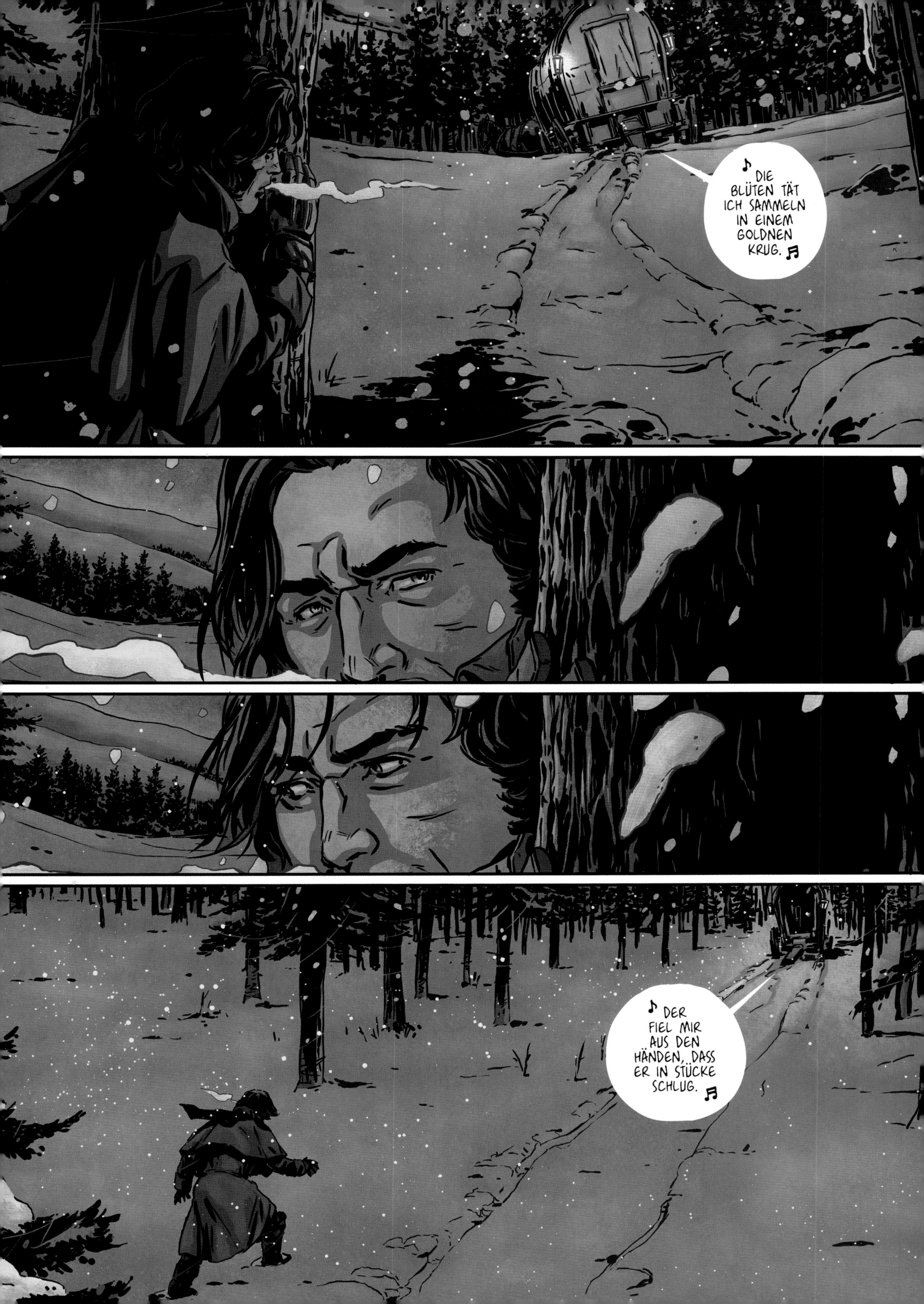
♪ DIE BLÜTEN TÄT ICH SAMMELN IN EINEM GOLDNEN KRUG. ♬
♪ DER FIEL MIR AUS DEN HÄNDEN, DASS ER IN STÜCKE SCHLUG. ♬

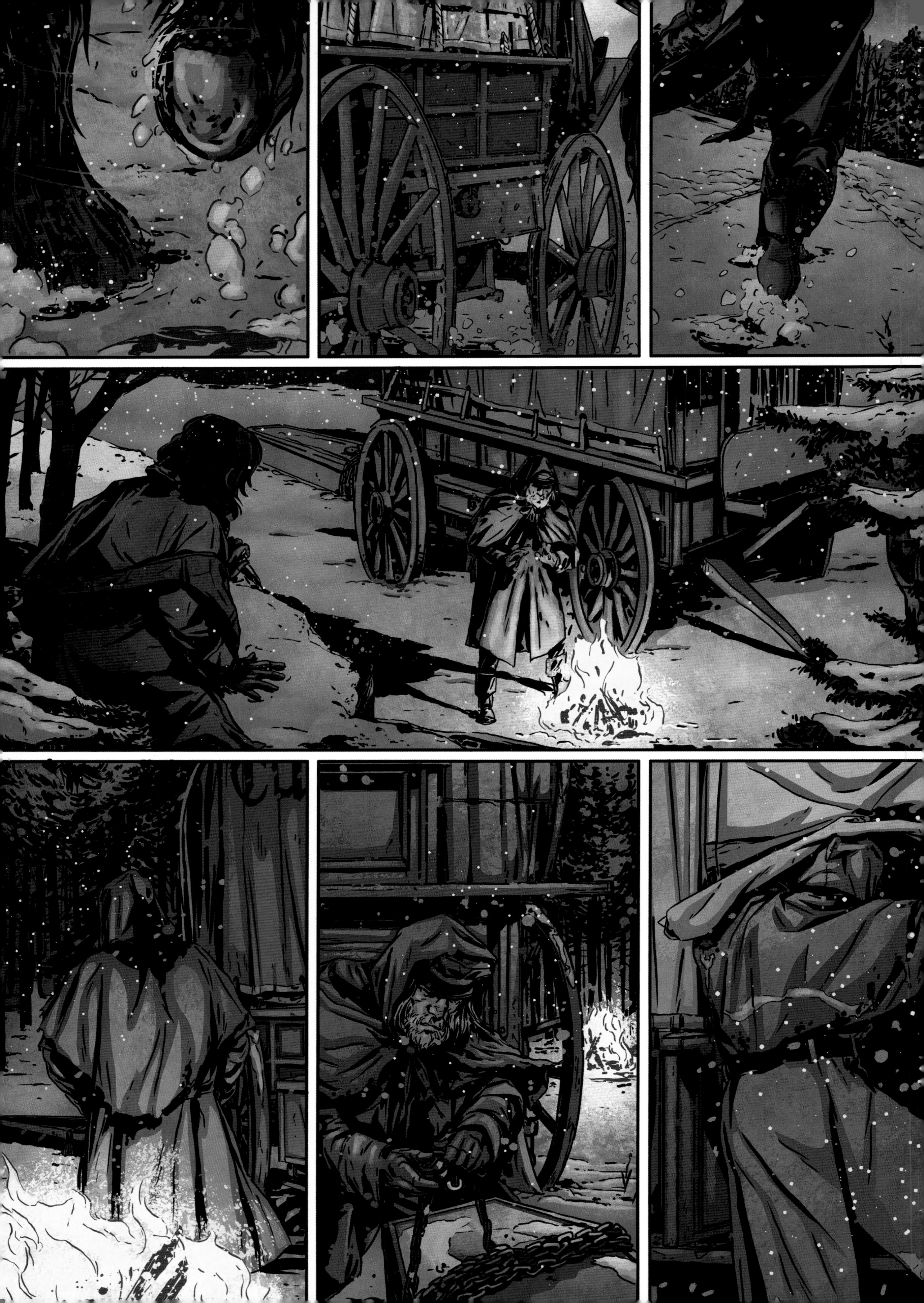

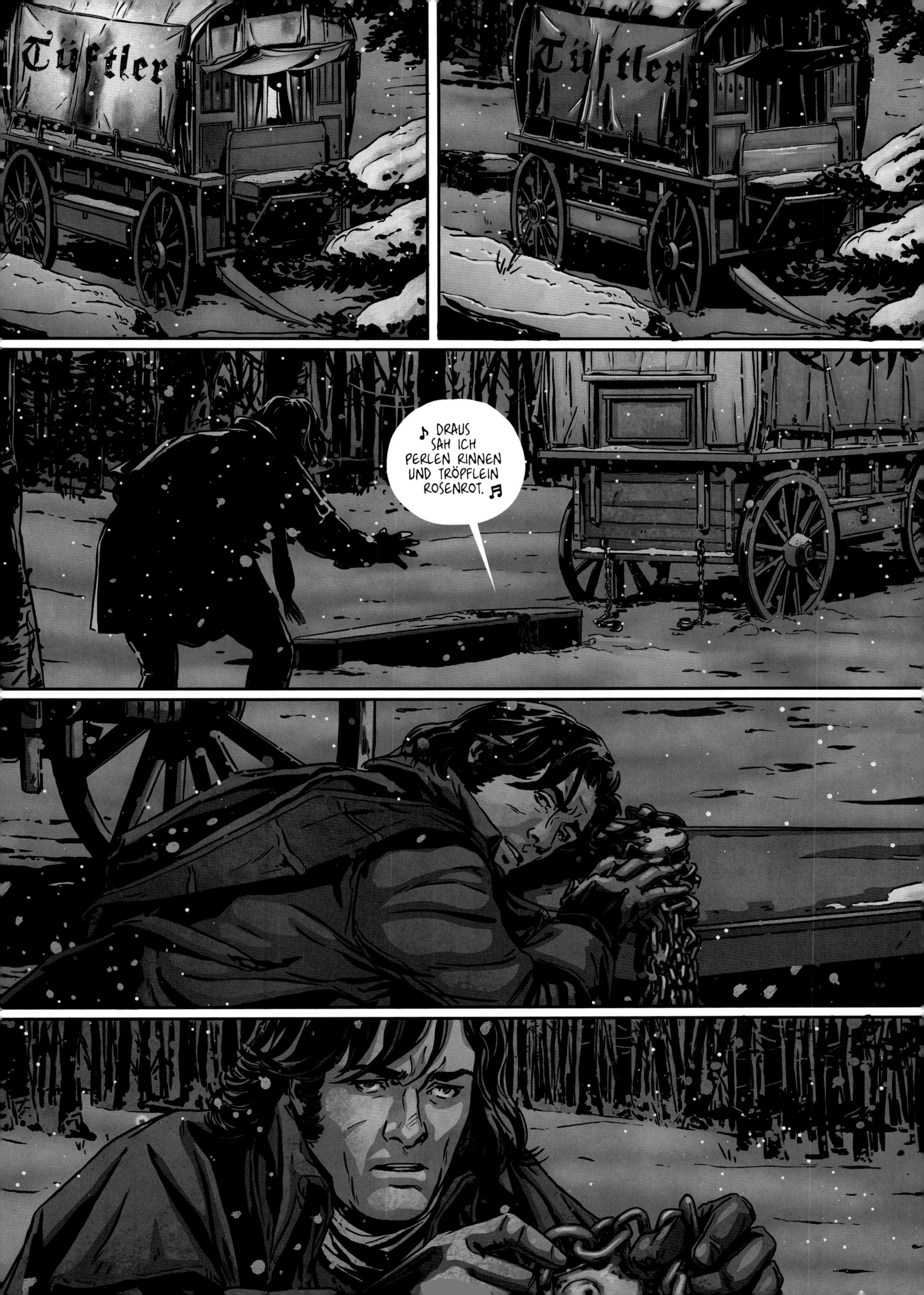

Tüftler
Tüftler
♪ DRAUS SAH ICH PERLEN RINNEN UND TRÖPFLEIN ROSENROT. ♬

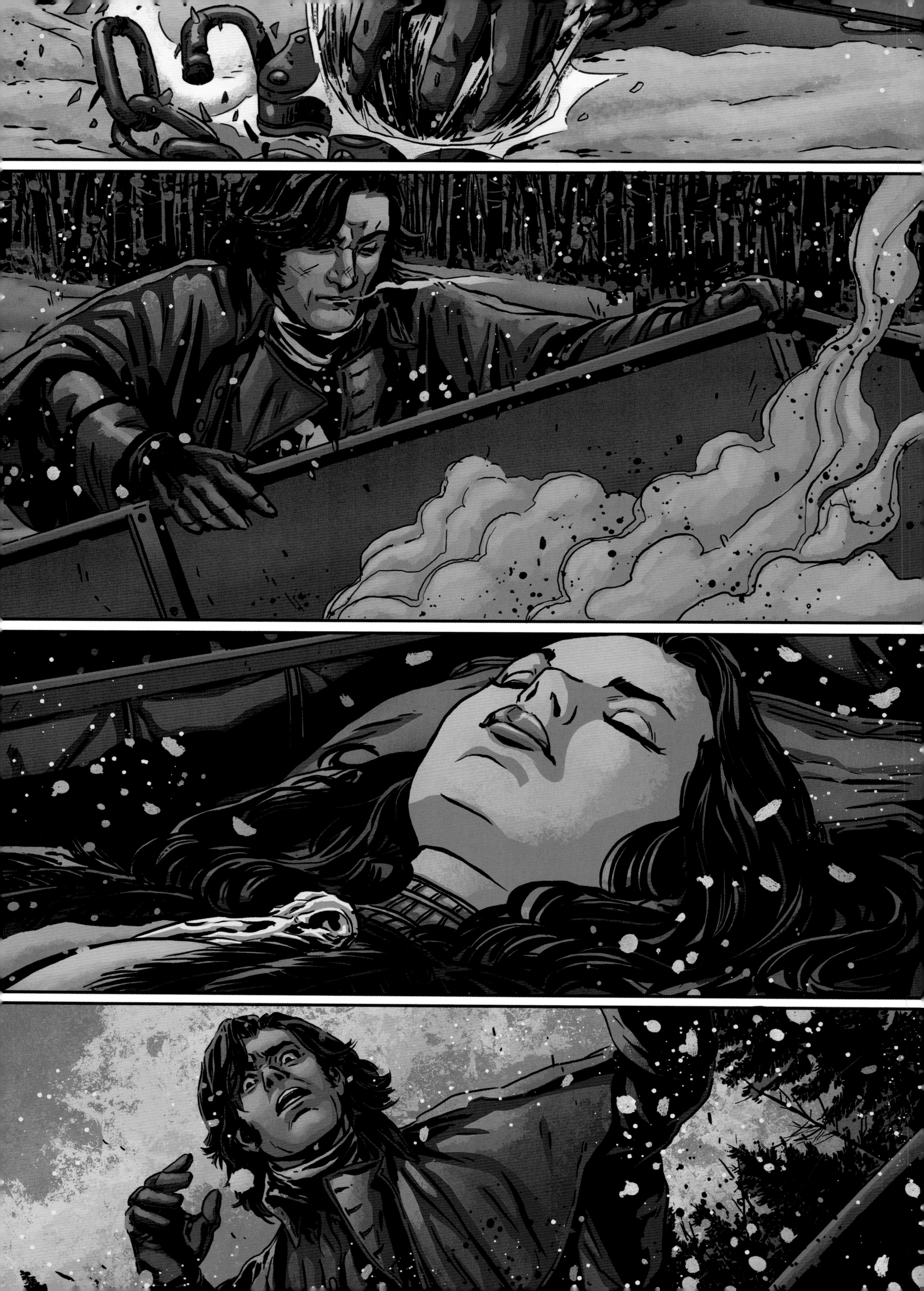

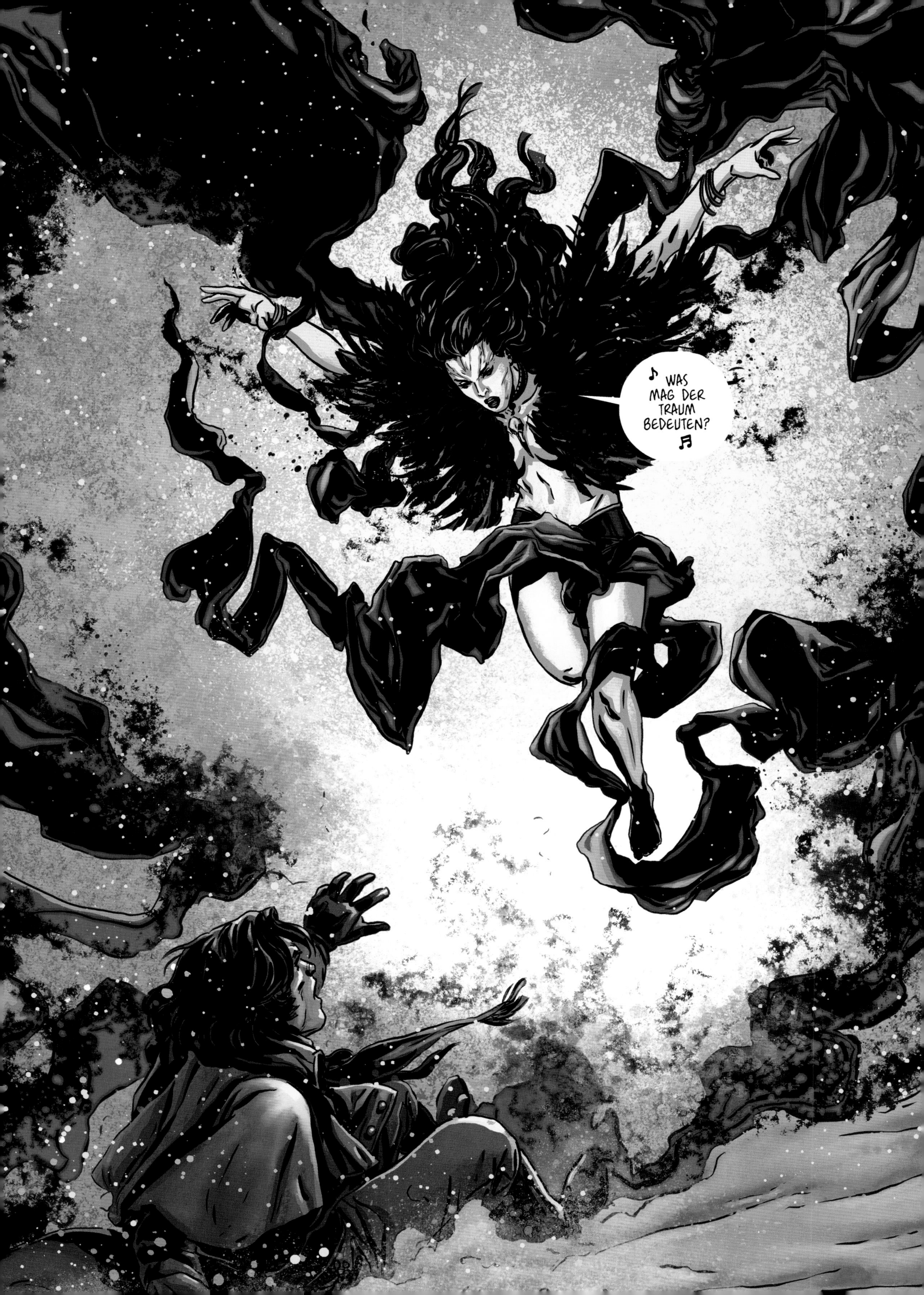
♪ WAS MAG DER TRAUM BEDEUTEN? ♬

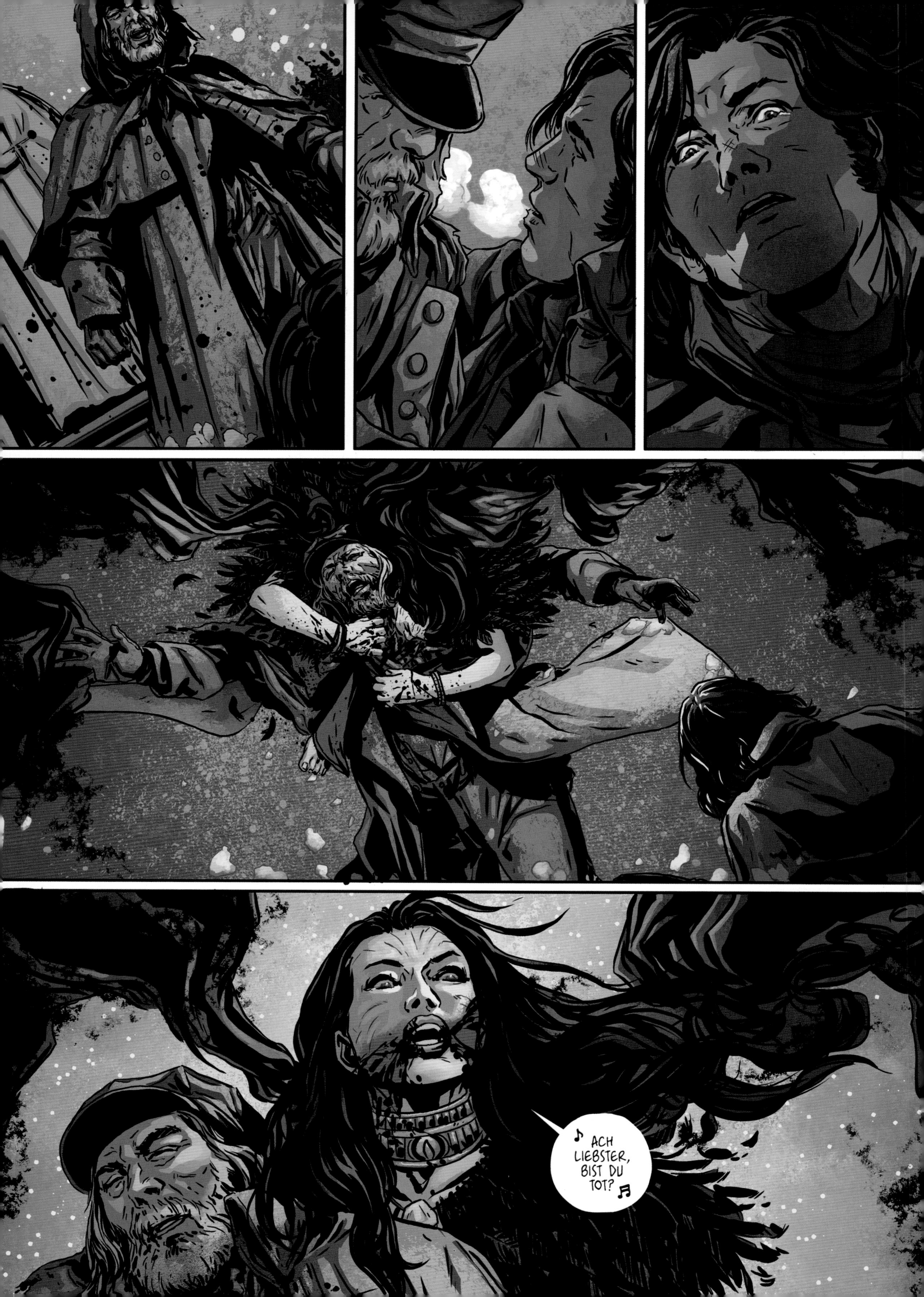
♪ ACH LIEBSTER, BIST DU TOT? ♬

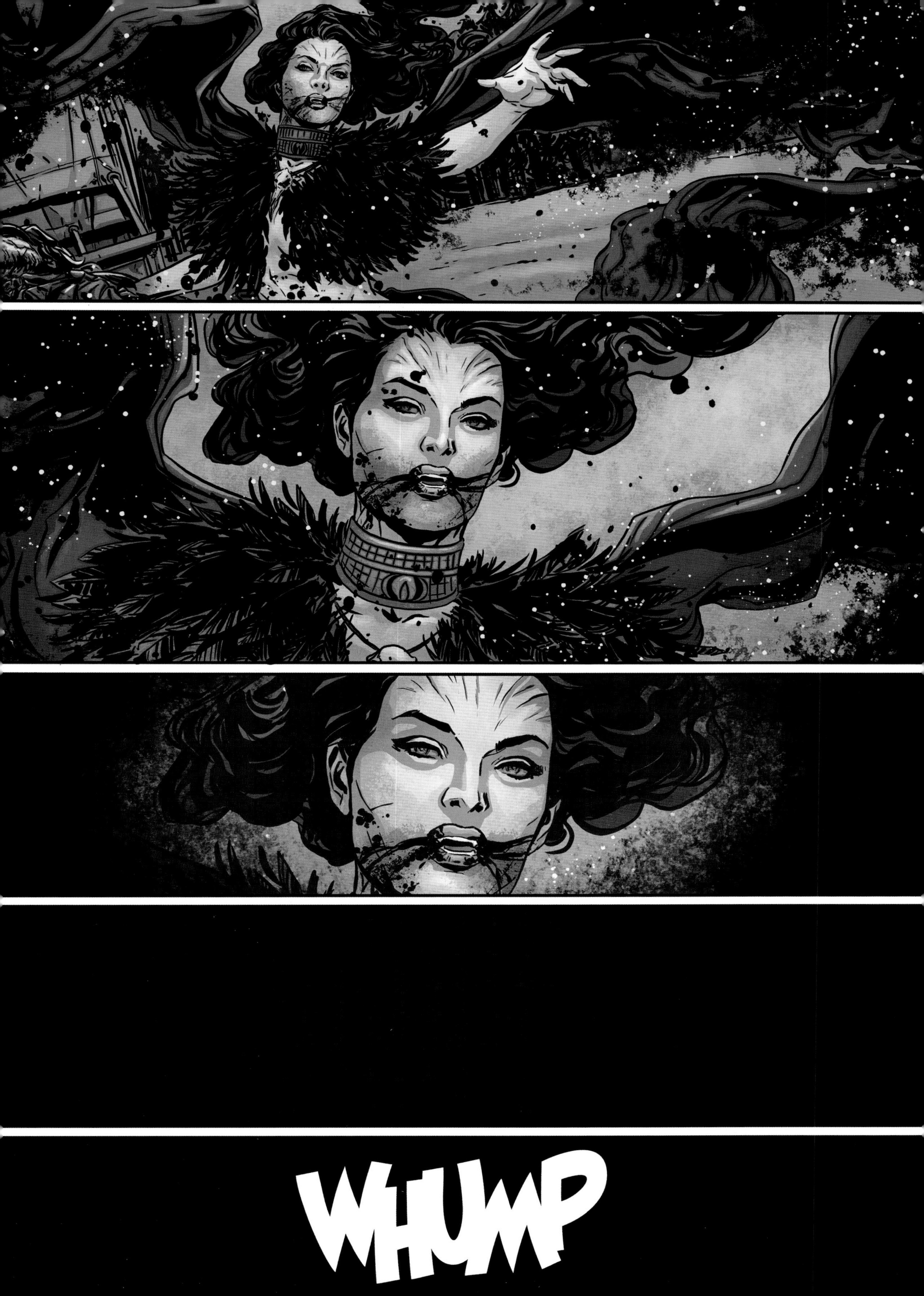
WHUMP

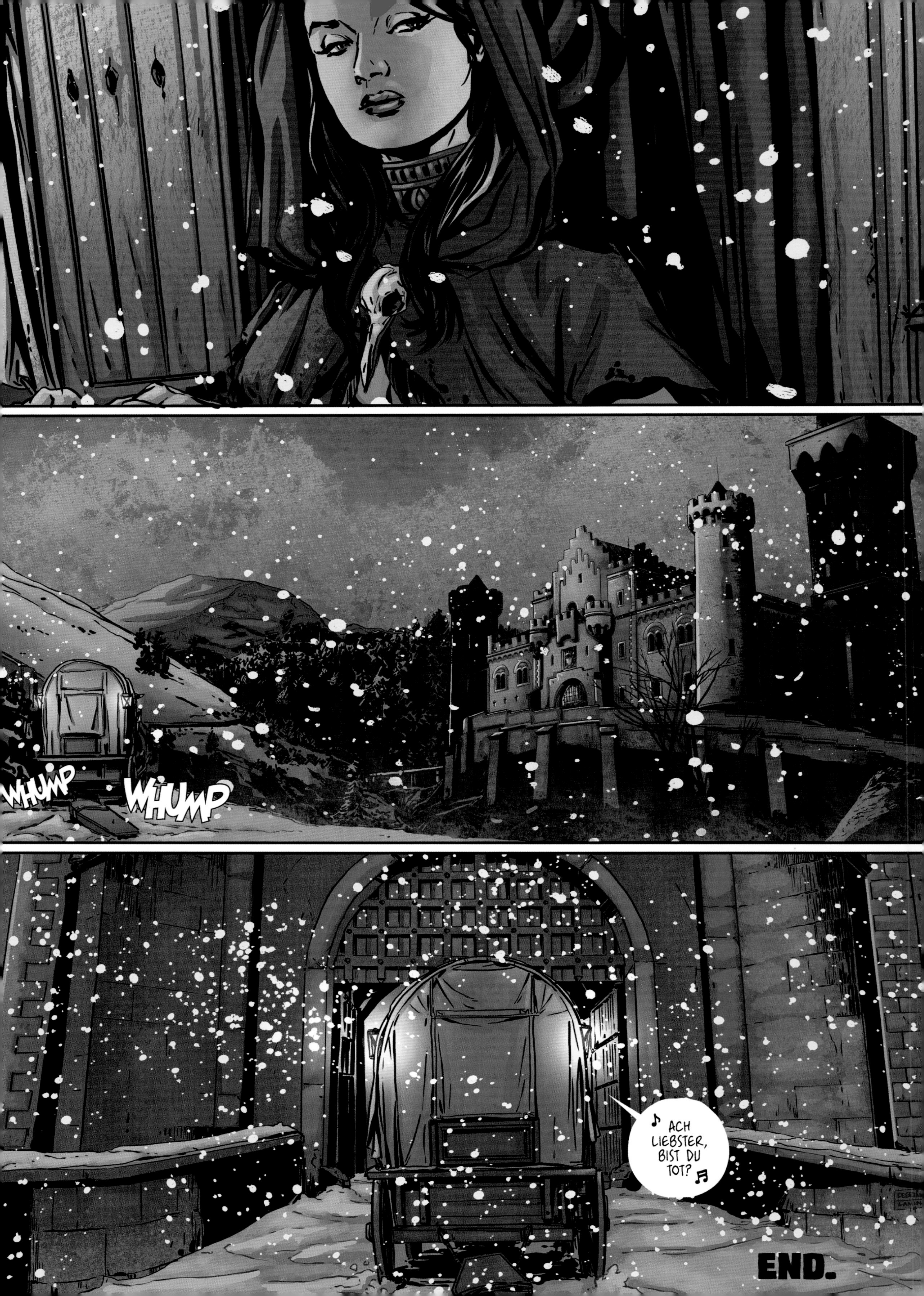
WHUMP
WHUMP
ACH LIEBSTER, BIST DU TOT?
END.

VICIOUS GIANT SNAKE!

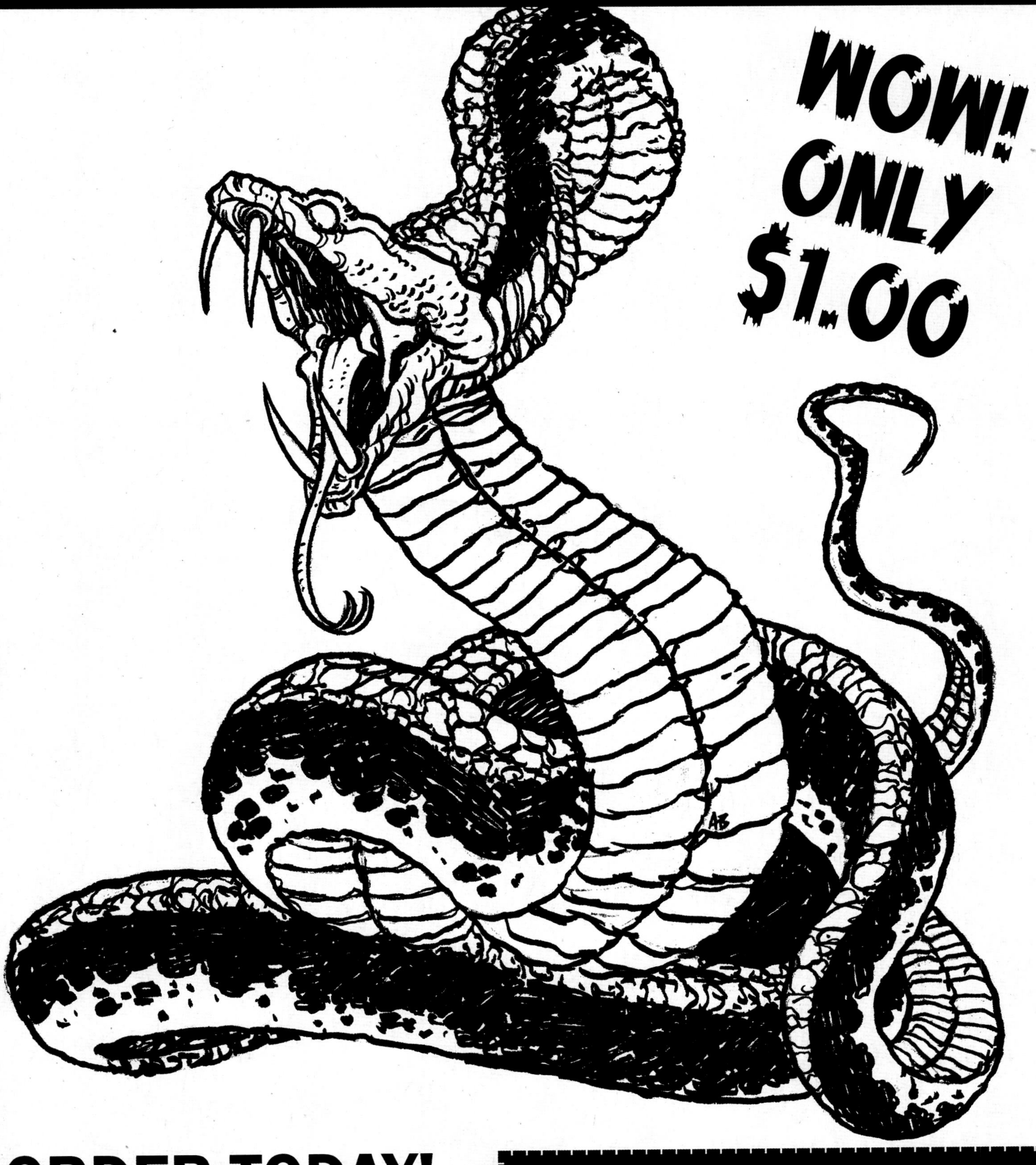
WOW!
ONLY
$1.00

ORDER TODAY!

From exotic, tropical lands on the other side of the earth comes your very own VICIOUS GIANT SNAKE! This is sure to be the coolest pet you will ever own. Wow your entire class at your next show-and-tell day!

IN THE DARK
6669 WEREWOLF WAY - ROOM 13
COLUMBUS, OH 43230

Pleasssse rush my very own exotic VICIOUS GIANT SNAKE!
I have enclosed $1.00 plus $.25 shipping charges in cash, check or money order.

Name:..

Address:..

City:...

State:...

Zip:..

INSIDE YOU

WRITER
VALERIE D'ORAZIO

ARTIST
DAVID JAMES COLE

COLORIST
TAMRA BONVILLAIN

LETTERER
ADAM WOLLET

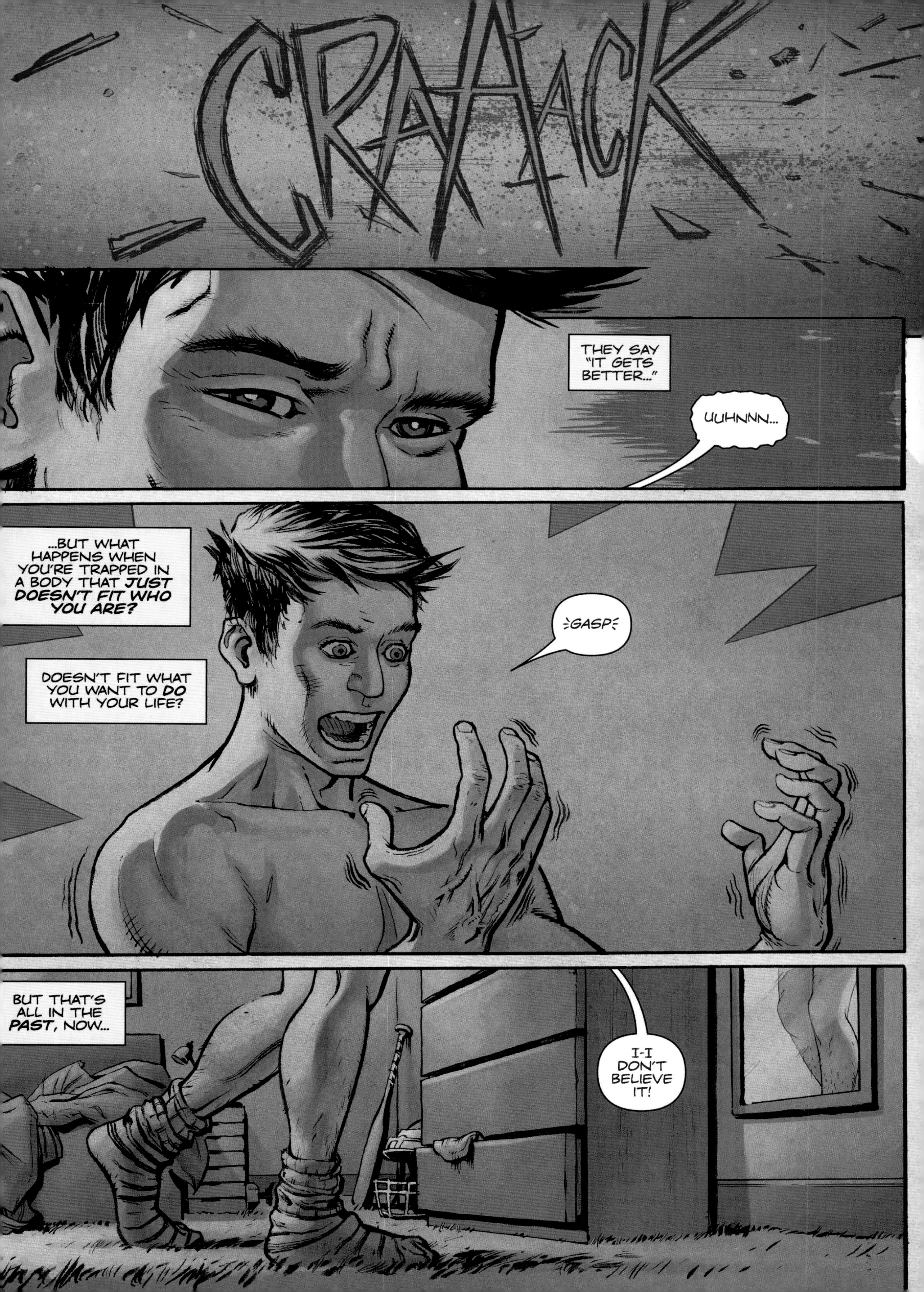
CRAAACK
THEY SAY "IT GETS BETTER..."
UUHNNN...
...BUT WHAT HAPPENS WHEN YOU'RE TRAPPED IN A BODY THAT ***JUST DOESN'T FIT WHO YOU ARE?***
DOESN'T FIT WHAT YOU WANT TO ***DO*** WITH YOUR LIFE?
GASP
BUT THAT'S ALL IN THE ***PAST***, NOW...
I-I DON'T BELIEVE IT!

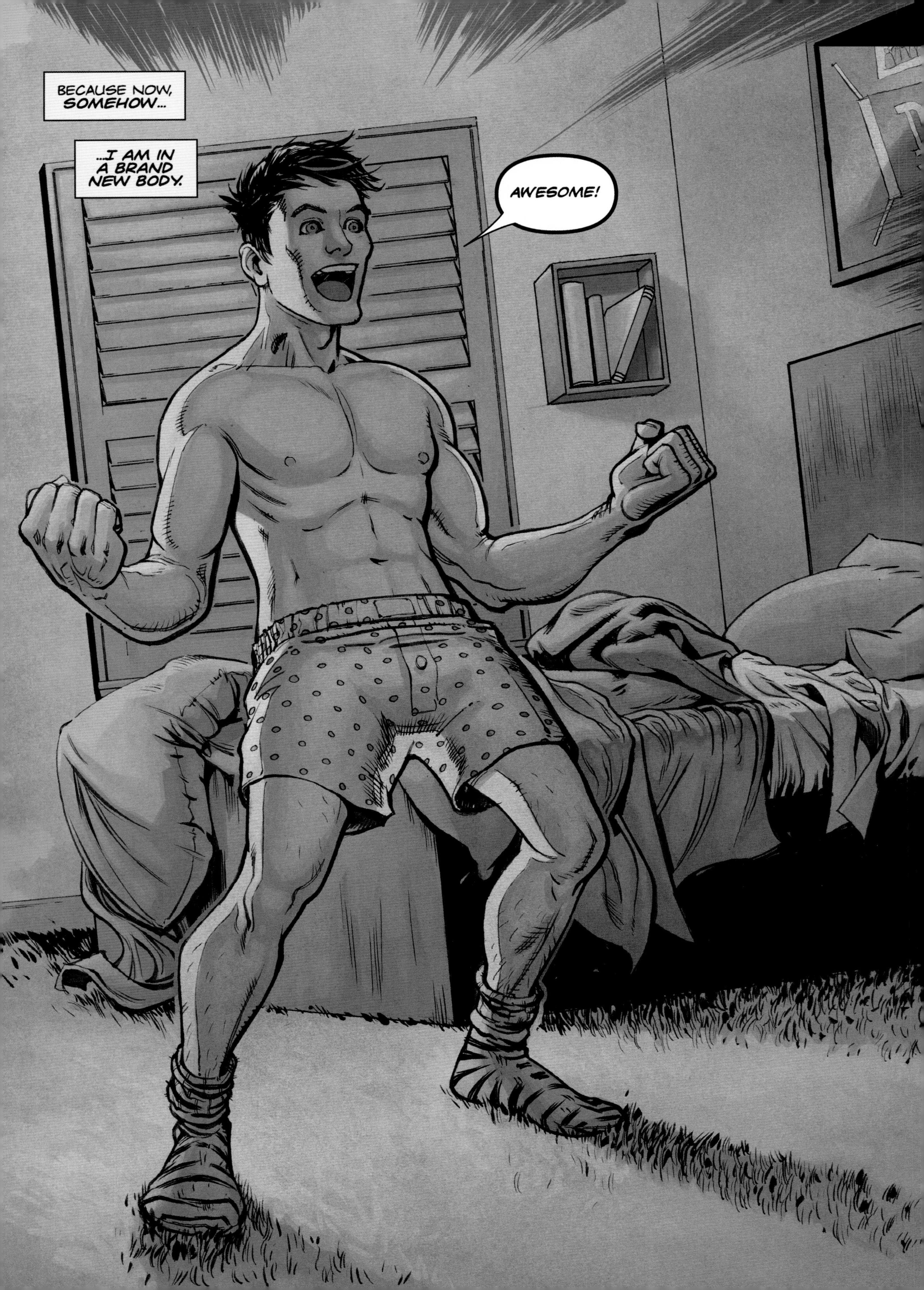
BECAUSE NOW, SOMEHOW...
...I AM IN A BRAND NEW BODY.
AWESOME!

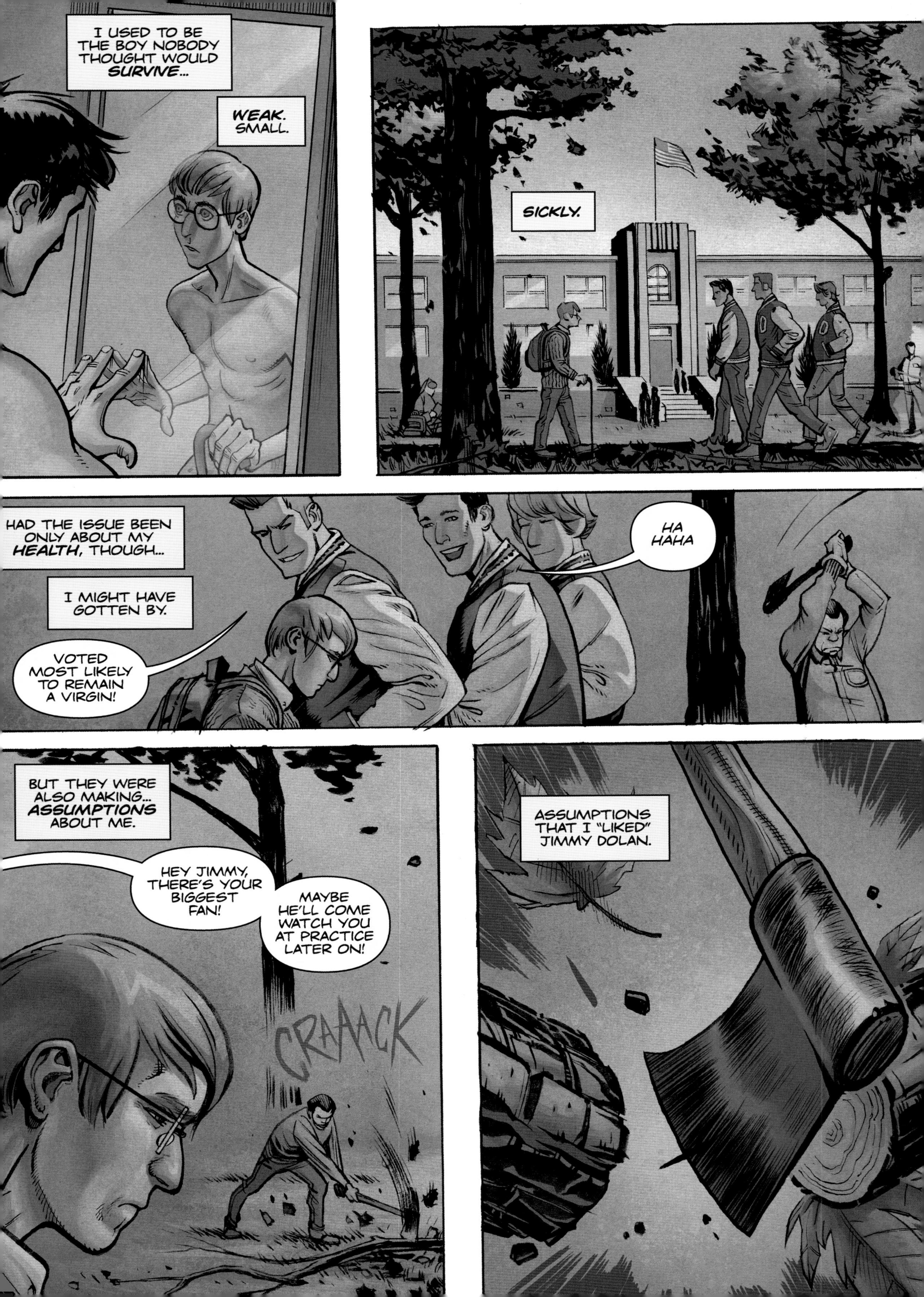

I USED TO BE THE BOY NOBODY THOUGHT WOULD **SURVIVE**...
WEAK. SMALL.
SICKLY.
HAD THE ISSUE BEEN ONLY ABOUT MY **HEALTH**, THOUGH...
I MIGHT HAVE GOTTEN BY.
VOTED MOST LIKELY TO REMAIN A VIRGIN!
HA HAHA
BUT THEY WERE ALSO MAKING... **ASSUMPTIONS** ABOUT ME.
HEY JIMMY, THERE'S YOUR BIGGEST FAN!
MAYBE HE'LL COME WATCH YOU AT PRACTICE LATER ON!
CRAAACK
ASSUMPTIONS THAT I "LIKED" JIMMY DOLAN.

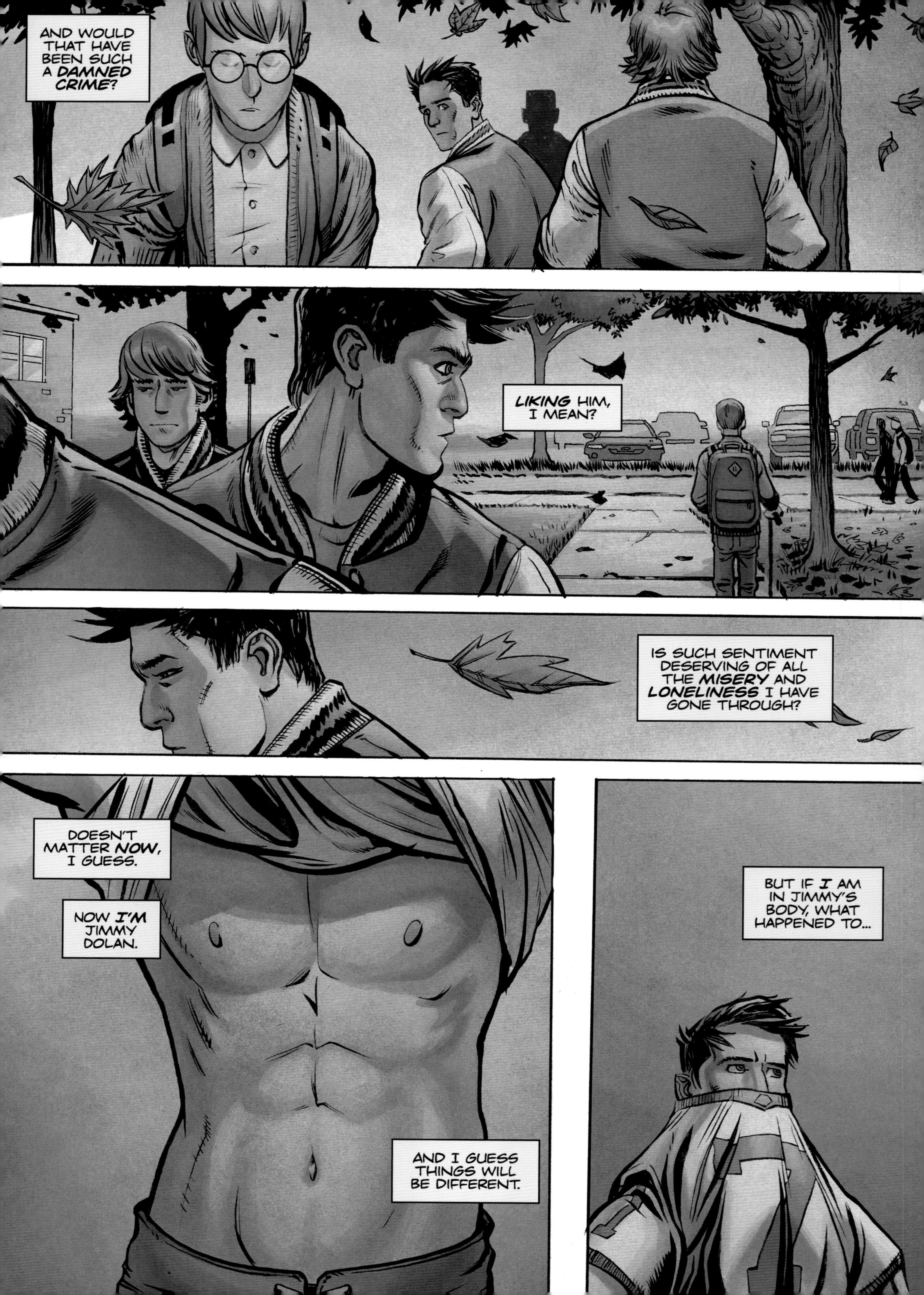
AND WOULD THAT HAVE BEEN SUCH A *DAMNED CRIME*?
LIKING HIM, I MEAN?
IS SUCH SENTIMENT DESERVING OF ALL THE *MISERY* AND *LONELINESS* I HAVE GONE THROUGH?
DOESN'T MATTER *NOW*, I GUESS.
NOW *I'M* JIMMY DOLAN.
AND I GUESS THINGS WILL BE DIFFERENT.
BUT IF *I* AM IN JIMMY'S BODY, WHAT HAPPENED TO...

OH.

...HIS LITTLE HEART JUST COULDN'T *TAKE* IT ANYMORE!

OHMIGOD, THAT'S *SO* SAD!

THE *STRESS* FROM THE BODY TRANSFER MUST HAVE *KILLED* HIM...

KILLED *ME*, RATHER.

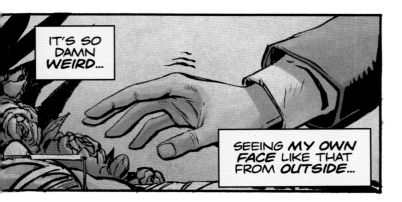

IT'S SO DAMN *WEIRD*...

SEEING *MY OWN FACE* LIKE THAT FROM *OUTSIDE*...

CRAAACK

AGH!

I SHOULDN'T BE HERE.

HORRIBLE YOUNG MAN!

HOW COULD YOU TOUCH HIM?!

I'M THE *LAST* PERSON WHO SHOULD BE HERE.

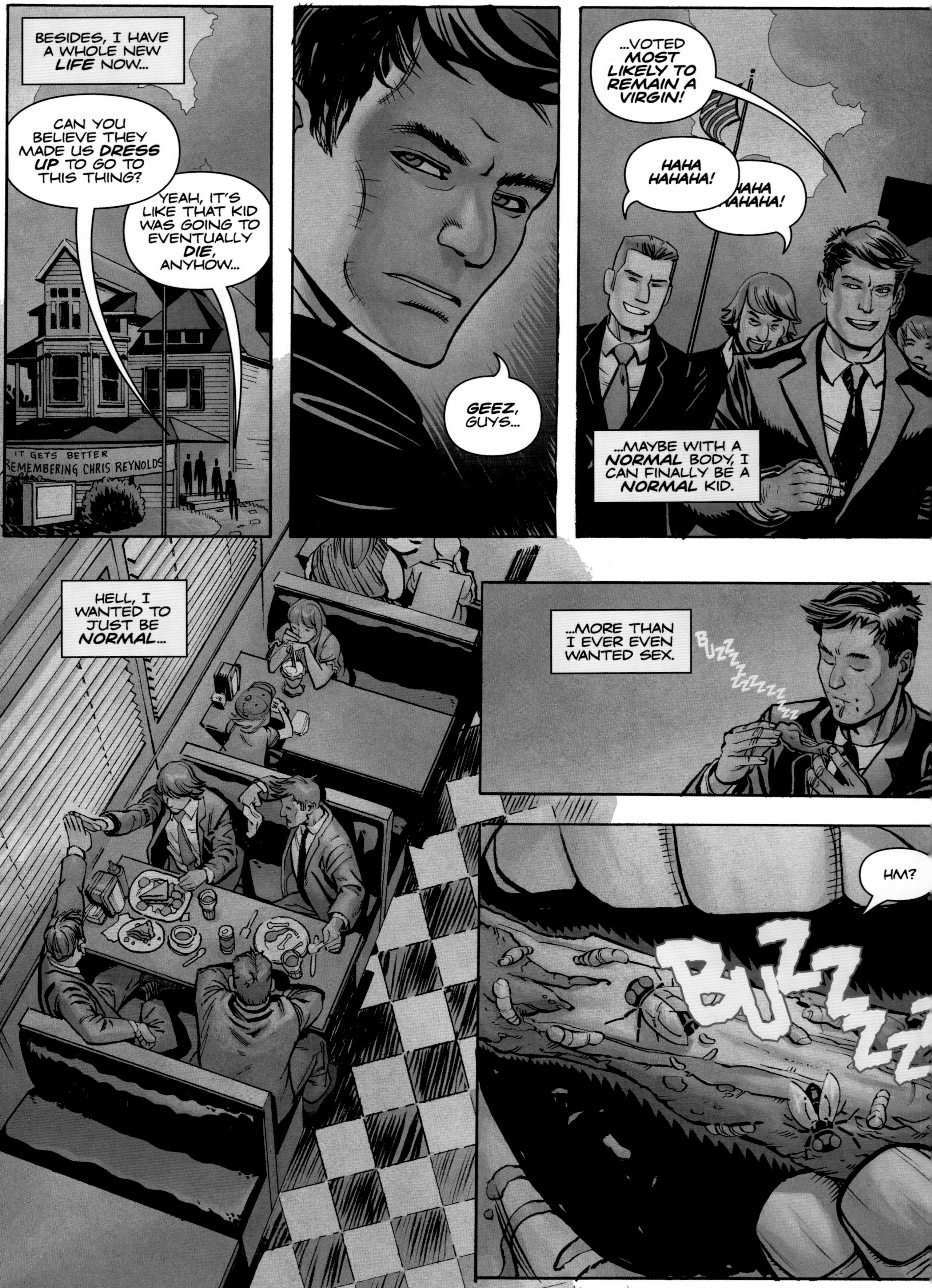
BESIDES, I HAVE A WHOLE NEW LIFE NOW...
CAN YOU BELIEVE THEY MADE US DRESS UP TO GO TO THIS THING?
YEAH, IT'S LIKE THAT KID WAS GOING TO EVENTUALLY DIE, ANYHOW...
IT GETS BETTER
REMEMBERING CHRIS REYNOLDS
GEEZ, GUYS...
...VOTED MOST LIKELY TO REMAIN A VIRGIN!
HAHA HAHAHA!
HAHA HAHAHA!
...MAYBE WITH A NORMAL BODY, I CAN FINALLY BE A NORMAL KID.
HELL, I WANTED TO JUST BE NORMAL...
...MORE THAN I EVER EVEN WANTED SEX.
BUZZZZZZZZZZ
HM?
BUZZZZ

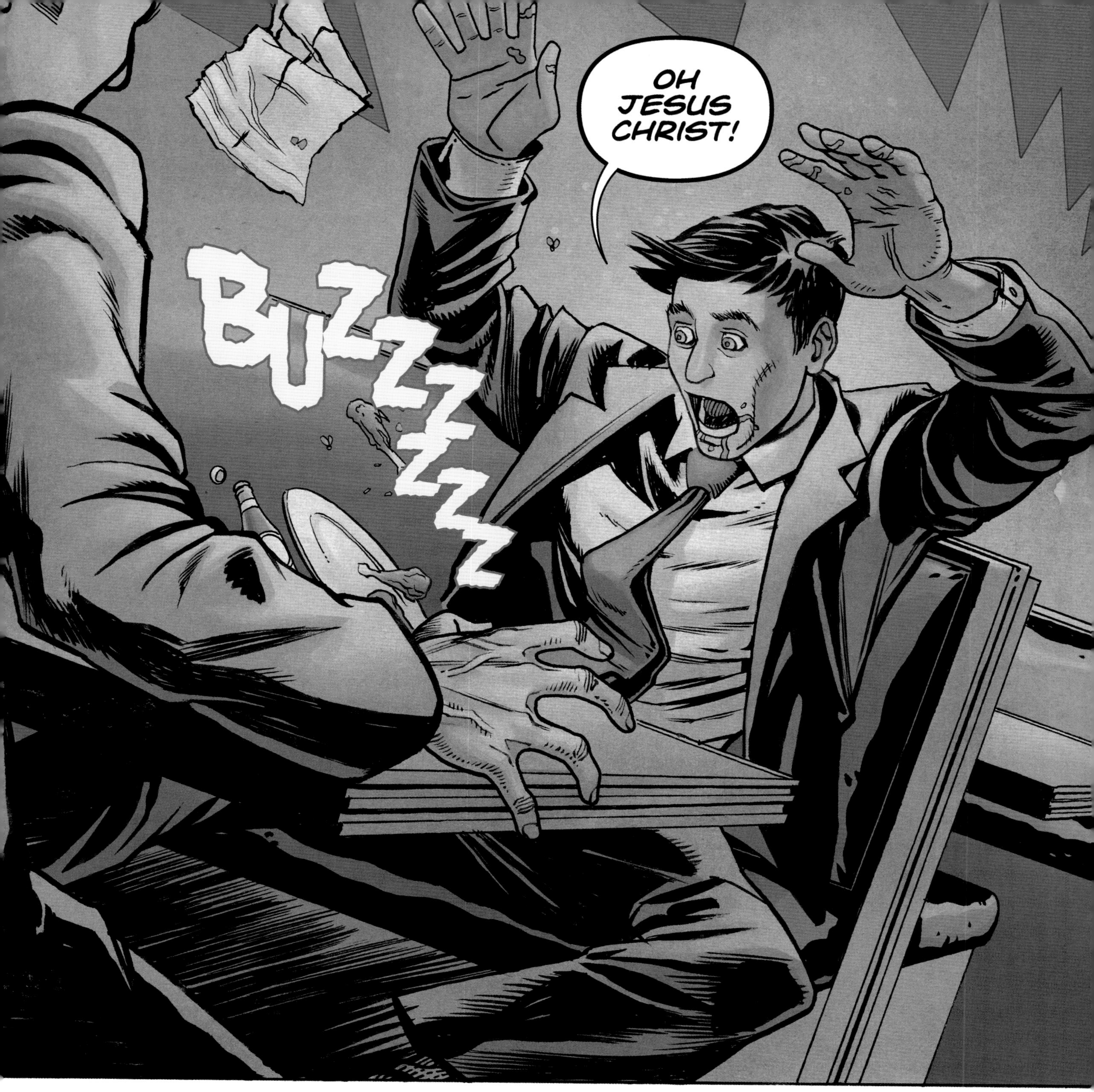
OH JESUS CHRIST!
BUZZZZZZZ

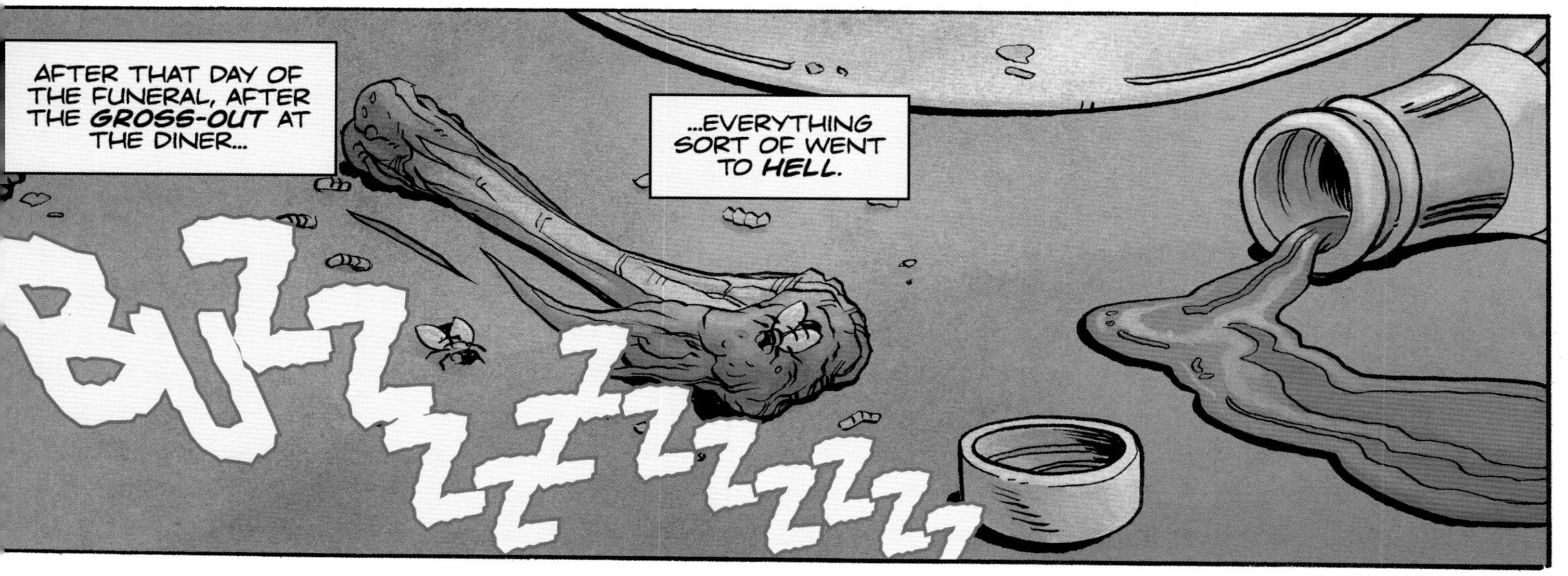
AFTER THAT DAY OF THE FUNERAL, AFTER THE **GROSS-OUT** AT THE DINER...
...EVERYTHING SORT OF WENT TO **HELL**.
BUZZZZZZZZZZZZZ

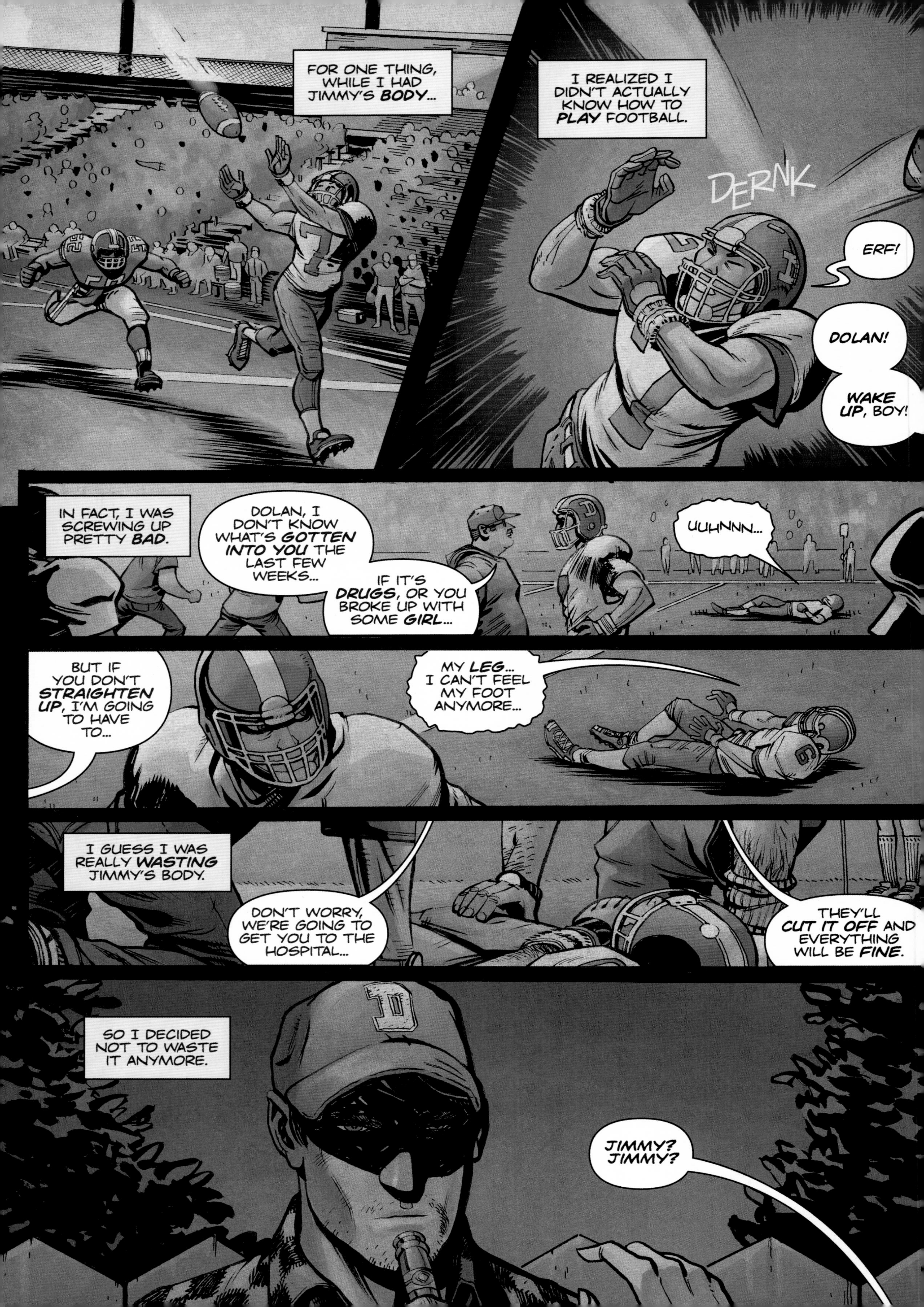
FOR ONE THING, WHILE I HAD JIMMY'S BODY...
I REALIZED I DIDN'T ACTUALLY KNOW HOW TO PLAY FOOTBALL.
DERNK
ERF!
DOLAN!
WAKE UP, BOY!
IN FACT, I WAS SCREWING UP PRETTY BAD.
DOLAN, I DON'T KNOW WHAT'S GOTTEN INTO YOU THE LAST FEW WEEKS...
IF IT'S DRUGS, OR YOU BROKE UP WITH SOME GIRL...
UUHNNN...
BUT IF YOU DON'T STRAIGHTEN UP, I'M GOING TO HAVE TO...
MY LEG... I CAN'T FEEL MY FOOT ANYMORE...
I GUESS I WAS REALLY WASTING JIMMY'S BODY.
DON'T WORRY, WE'RE GOING TO GET YOU TO THE HOSPITAL...
THEY'LL CUT IT OFF AND EVERYTHING WILL BE FINE.
SO I DECIDED NOT TO WASTE IT ANYMORE.
JIMMY? JIMMY?

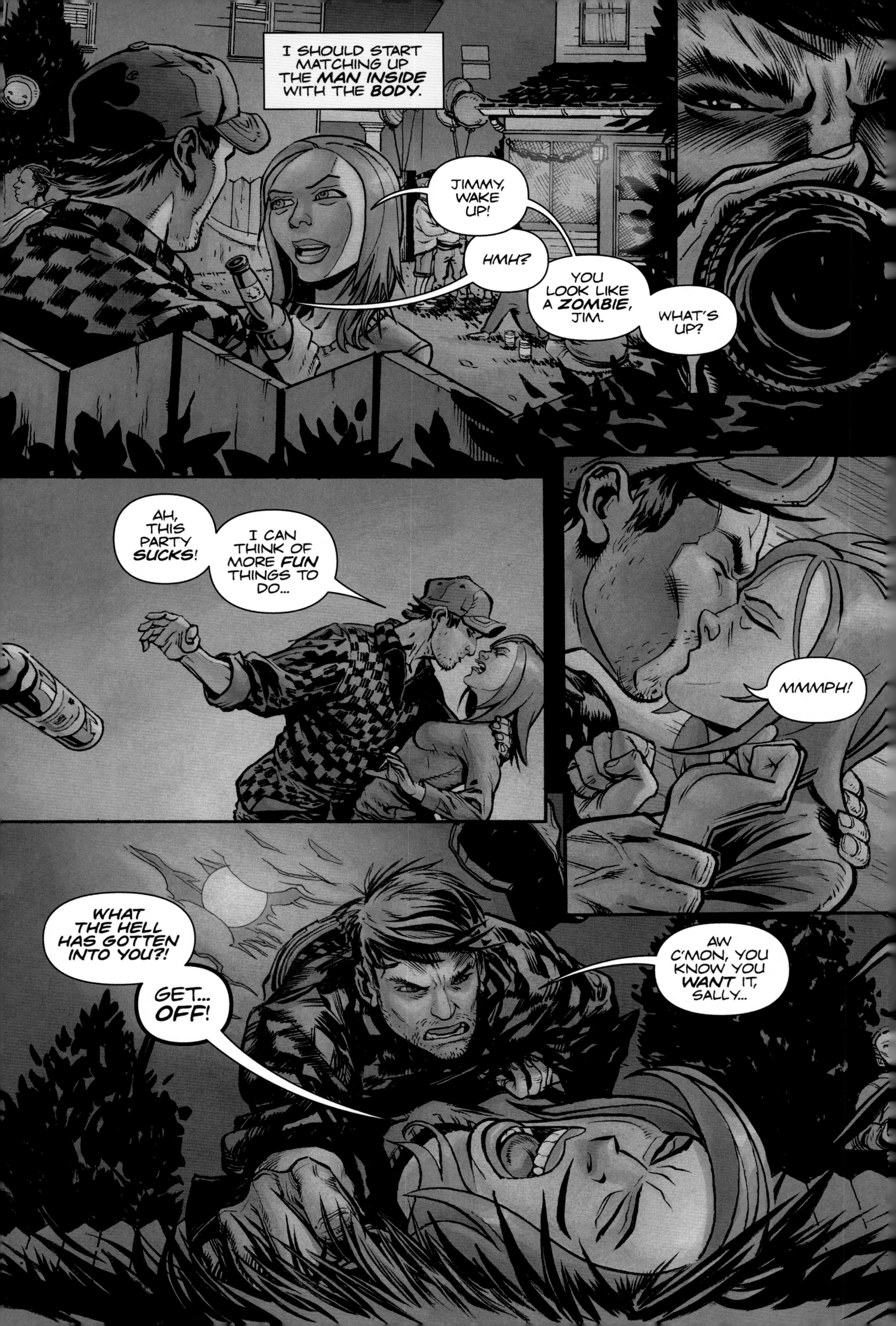
I SHOULD START MATCHING UP THE MAN INSIDE WITH THE BODY.
JIMMY, WAKE UP!
HMH?
YOU LOOK LIKE A ZOMBIE, JIM.
WHAT'S UP?
AH, THIS PARTY SUCKS!
I CAN THINK OF MORE FUN THINGS TO DO...
MMMPH!
WHAT THE HELL HAS GOTTEN INTO YOU?!
GET... OFF!
AW C'MON, YOU KNOW YOU WANT IT, SALLY...

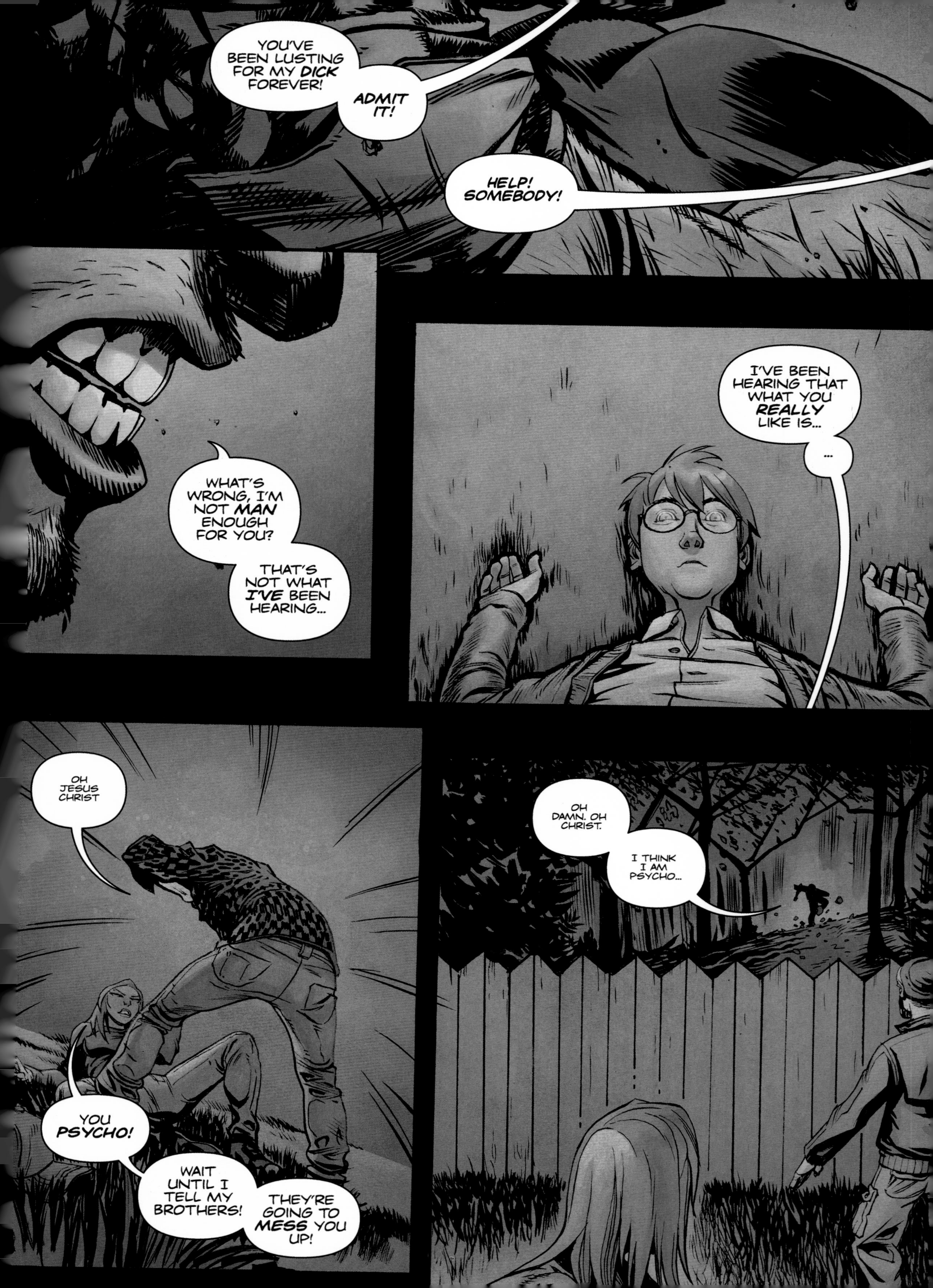
YOU'VE BEEN LUSTING FOR MY DICK FOREVER!
ADMIT IT!
HELP! SOMEBODY!
WHAT'S WRONG, I'M NOT MAN ENOUGH FOR YOU?
THAT'S NOT WHAT I'VE BEEN HEARING...
I'VE BEEN HEARING THAT WHAT YOU REALLY LIKE IS...
...
OH JESUS CHRIST
YOU PSYCHO!
WAIT UNTIL I TELL MY BROTHERS!
THEY'RE GOING TO MESS YOU UP!
OH DAMN. OH CHRIST.
I THINK I AM PSYCHO...

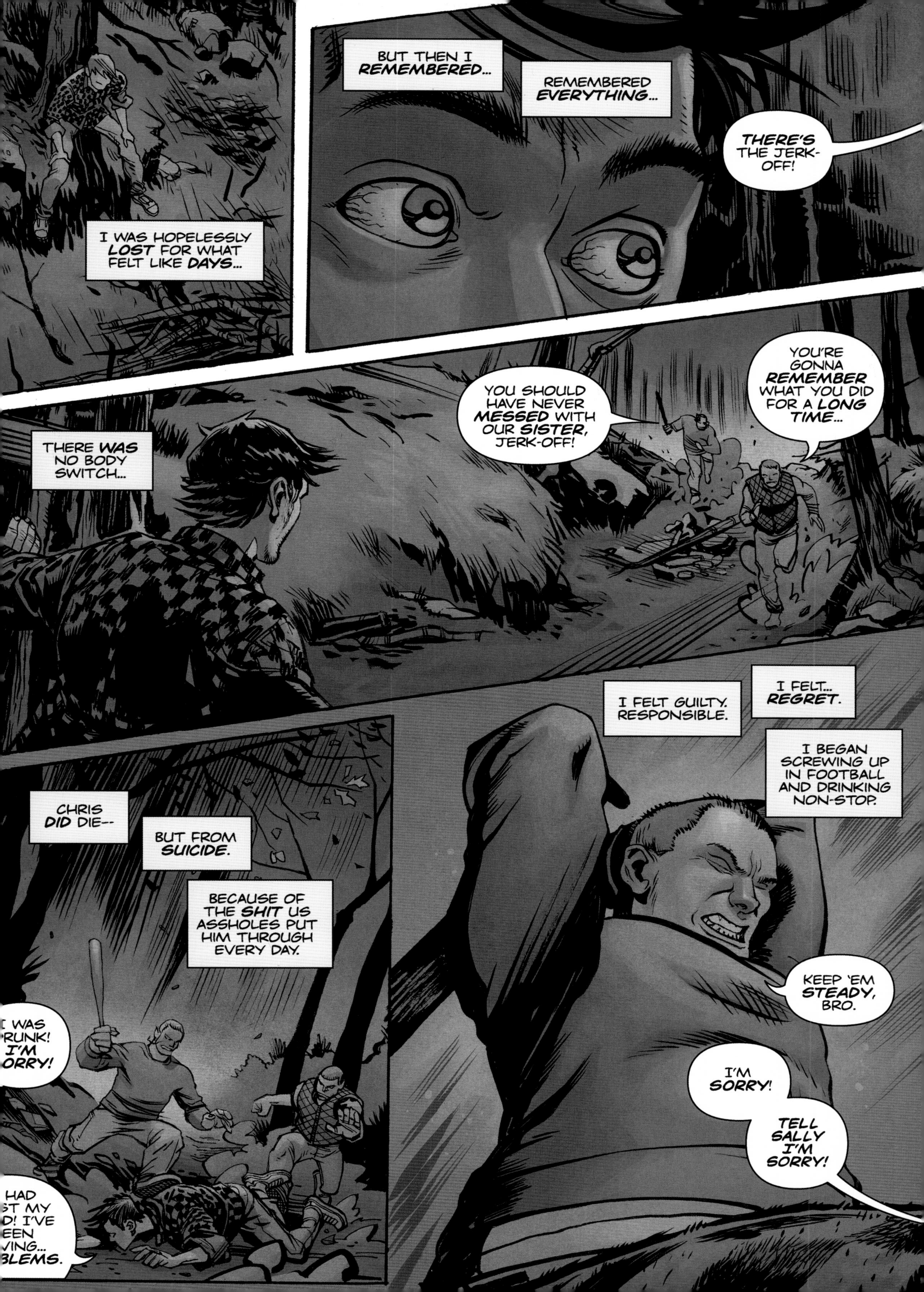
I WAS HOPELESSLY LOST FOR WHAT FELT LIKE DAYS...
BUT THEN I REMEMBERED...
REMEMBERED EVERYTHING...
THERE'S THE JERK-OFF!
THERE WAS NO BODY SWITCH...
YOU SHOULD HAVE NEVER MESSED WITH OUR SISTER, JERK-OFF!
YOU'RE GONNA REMEMBER WHAT YOU DID FOR A LONG TIME...
CHRIS DID DIE--
BUT FROM SUICIDE.
BECAUSE OF THE SHIT US ASSHOLES PUT HIM THROUGH EVERY DAY.
I FELT GUILTY. RESPONSIBLE.
I FELT... REGRET.
I BEGAN SCREWING UP IN FOOTBALL AND DRINKING NON-STOP.
KEEP 'EM STEADY, BRO.
I'M SORRY!
TELL SALLY I'M SORRY!

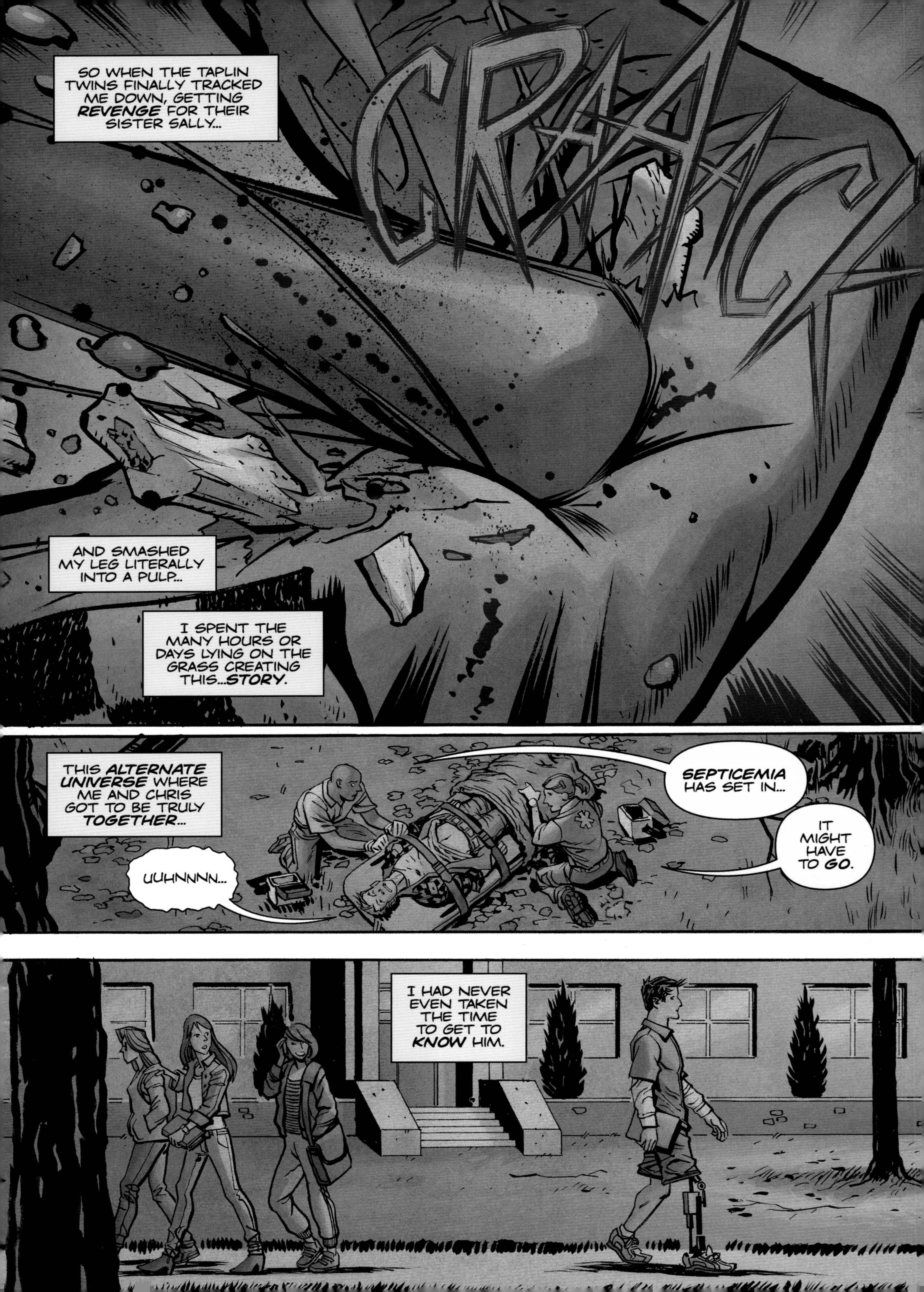
SO WHEN THE TAPLIN TWINS FINALLY TRACKED ME DOWN, GETTING REVENGE FOR THEIR SISTER SALLY...
CRAAACK
AND SMASHED MY LEG LITERALLY INTO A PULP...
I SPENT THE MANY HOURS OR DAYS LYING ON THE GRASS CREATING THIS...STORY.
THIS ALTERNATE UNIVERSE WHERE ME AND CHRIS GOT TO BE TRULY TOGETHER...
SEPTICEMIA HAS SET IN...
IT MIGHT HAVE TO GO.
UUHNNNN...
I HAD NEVER EVEN TAKEN THE TIME TO GET TO KNOW HIM.

TO ALL OUR GORE-DRIPPING, GHOULISH MONSTER-LOVERS: START A "YE-ECH-CHY"

HORROR PICTO-FICTION COLLECTION

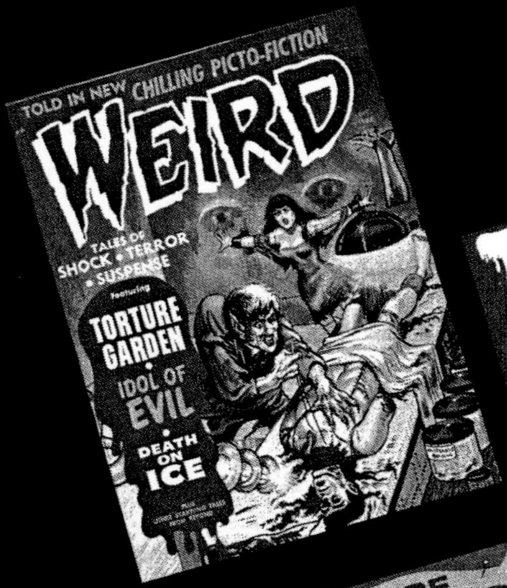
TOLD IN NEW CHILLING PICTO-FICTION
WEIRD
TALES OF SHOCK • TERROR • SUSPENSE
TORTURE GARDEN
IDOL OF EVIL
DEATH ON ICE

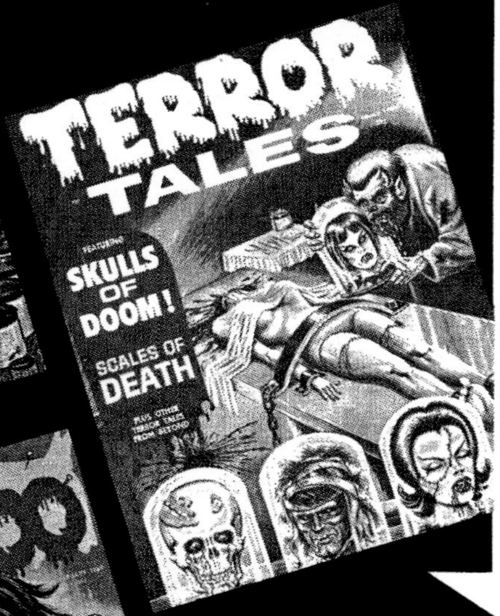
TERROR TALES
SKULLS OF DOOM!
SCALES OF DEATH

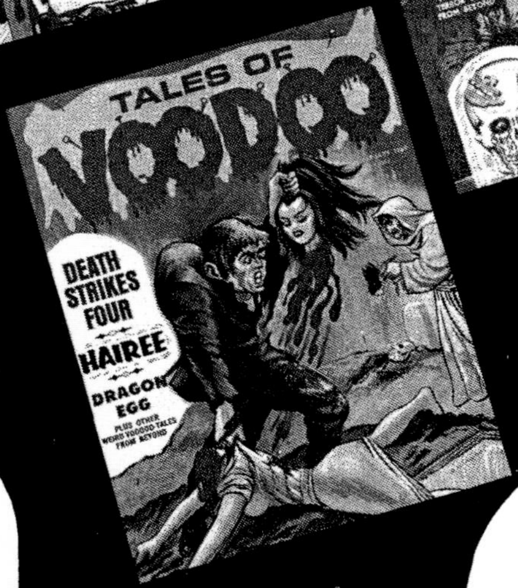
TALES OF
VOODOO
DEATH STRIKES FOUR
HAIREE
DRAGON EGG

Here's your golden opportunity to start a spine-chilling, terror-gripping, picto-fiction weirdo collection of the finest horror tales ever published in the world.

Get in on this "grave-bottom" offer, and—Who knows?—your startling, ghoulish, picto-fiction collection may be worth a small fortune as the bloody years roll by!

RUSH COUPON BELOW!

OR
EEPY
HOULS
ONLY

$1.00

POT-LUCK SPECIAL:

ANY 4 BACK ISSUES IN OUR FILES: $1.00! (We will send you what we have on hand, you lucky ghouls! Ye-ech-chy!)

EERIE PUBLICATIONS, INC.
150 Fifth Avenue
New York, N. Y. 10011

ENTER MY SUBSCRIPTION FOR (Check box below.):

☐ WEIRD (1 yr—5 issues): $1.50
☐ TERROR TALES (1 yr—5 issues): $1.50
☐ TALES OF VOODOO (1 yr—5 issues): $1.50
☐ $1.00 POT LUCK SPECIAL (Any 4 back issues.)

ENCLOSED, FIND (check or money order) for: $ ....

Name ....

Address ....

City .... State .... Zip ....

GESTATION

**WRITER
MARGUERITE BENNETT**

**ARTIST
JONATHAN BRANDON SAWYER**

**COLORIST
DOUG GARBARK**

**LETTERER
NIC J. SHAW**

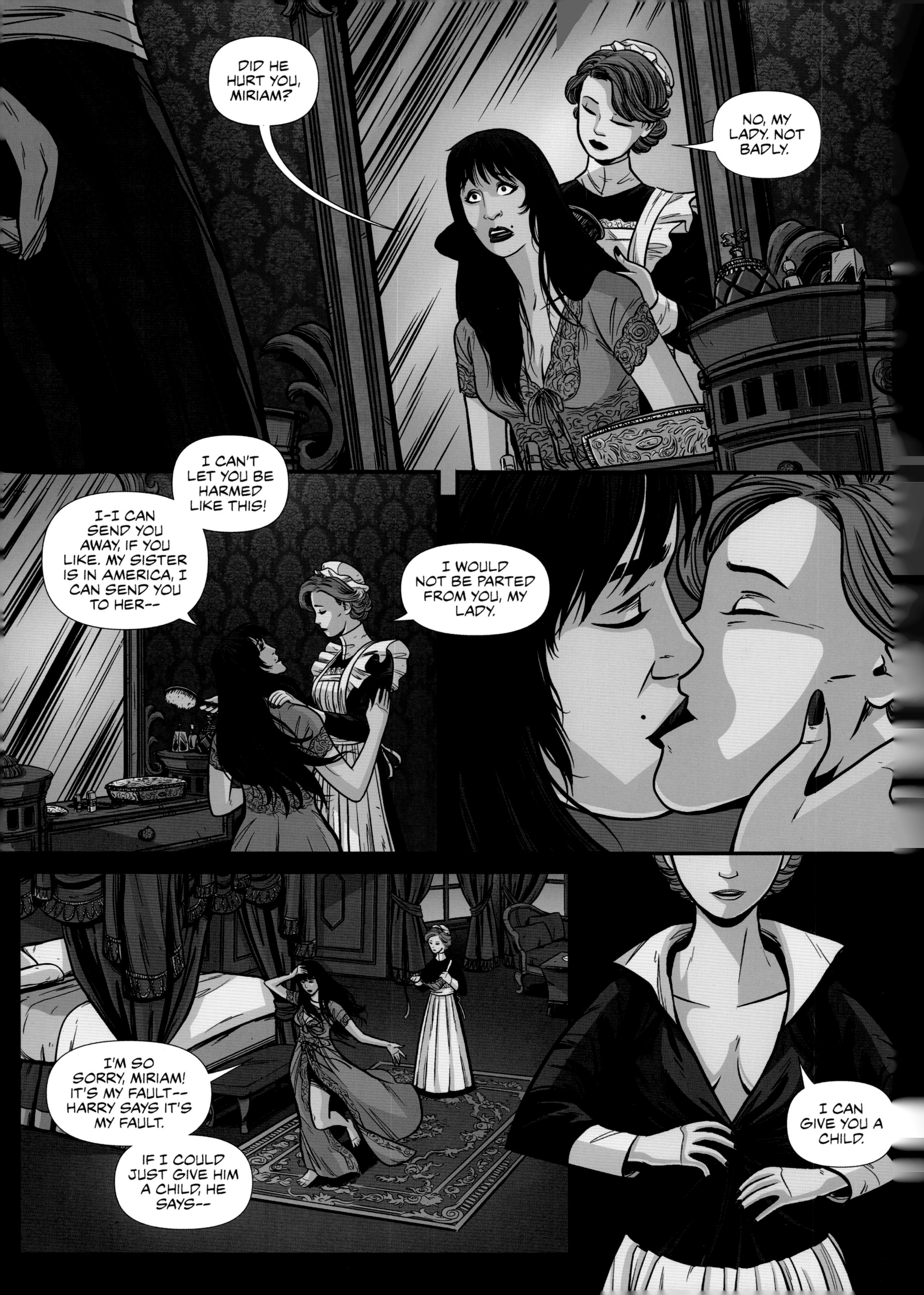
DID HE HURT YOU, MIRIAM?
NO, MY LADY. NOT BADLY.
I CAN'T LET YOU BE HARMED LIKE THIS!
I-I CAN SEND YOU AWAY, IF YOU LIKE. MY SISTER IS IN AMERICA, I CAN SEND YOU TO HER--
I WOULD NOT BE PARTED FROM YOU, MY LADY.
I'M SO SORRY, MIRIAM! IT'S MY FAULT-- HARRY SAYS IT'S MY FAULT.
IF I COULD JUST GIVE HIM A CHILD, HE SAYS--
I CAN GIVE YOU A CHILD.

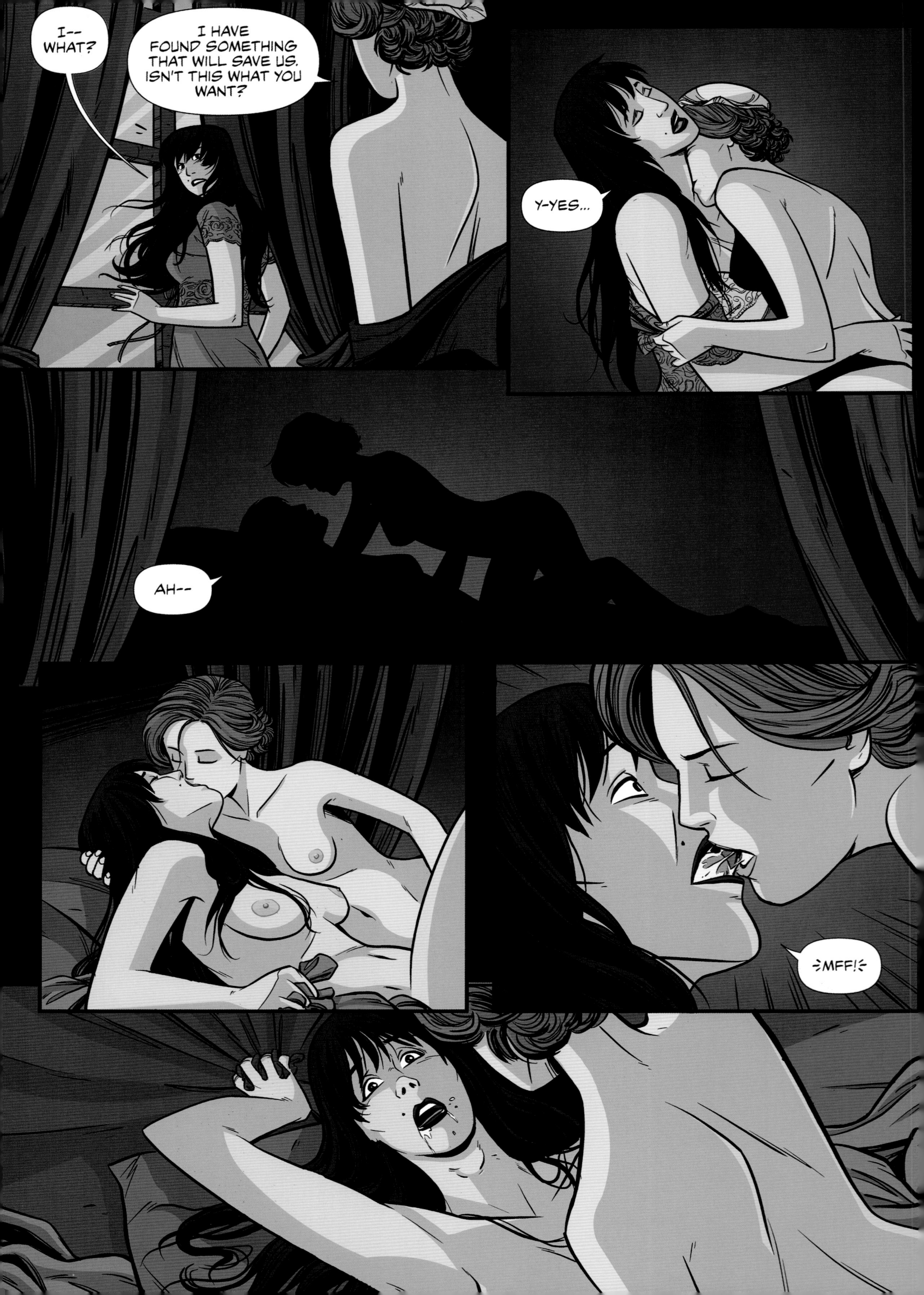
I-- WHAT?
I HAVE FOUND SOMETHING THAT WILL SAVE US. ISN'T THIS WHAT YOU WANT?
Y-YES...
AH--
MFF!

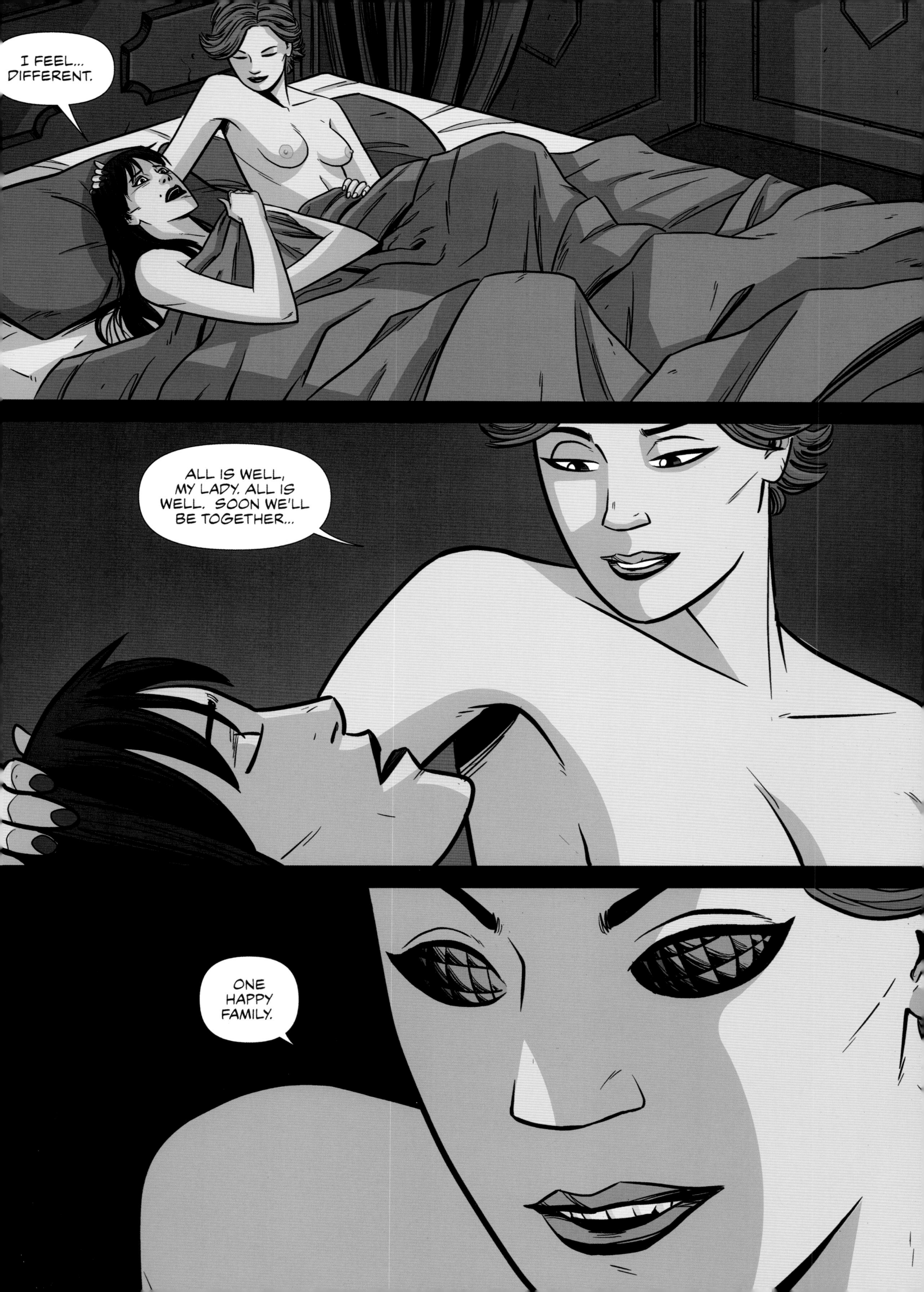
I FEEL... DIFFERENT.
ALL IS WELL, MY LADY. ALL IS WELL. SOON WE'LL BE TOGETHER...
ONE HAPPY FAMILY.

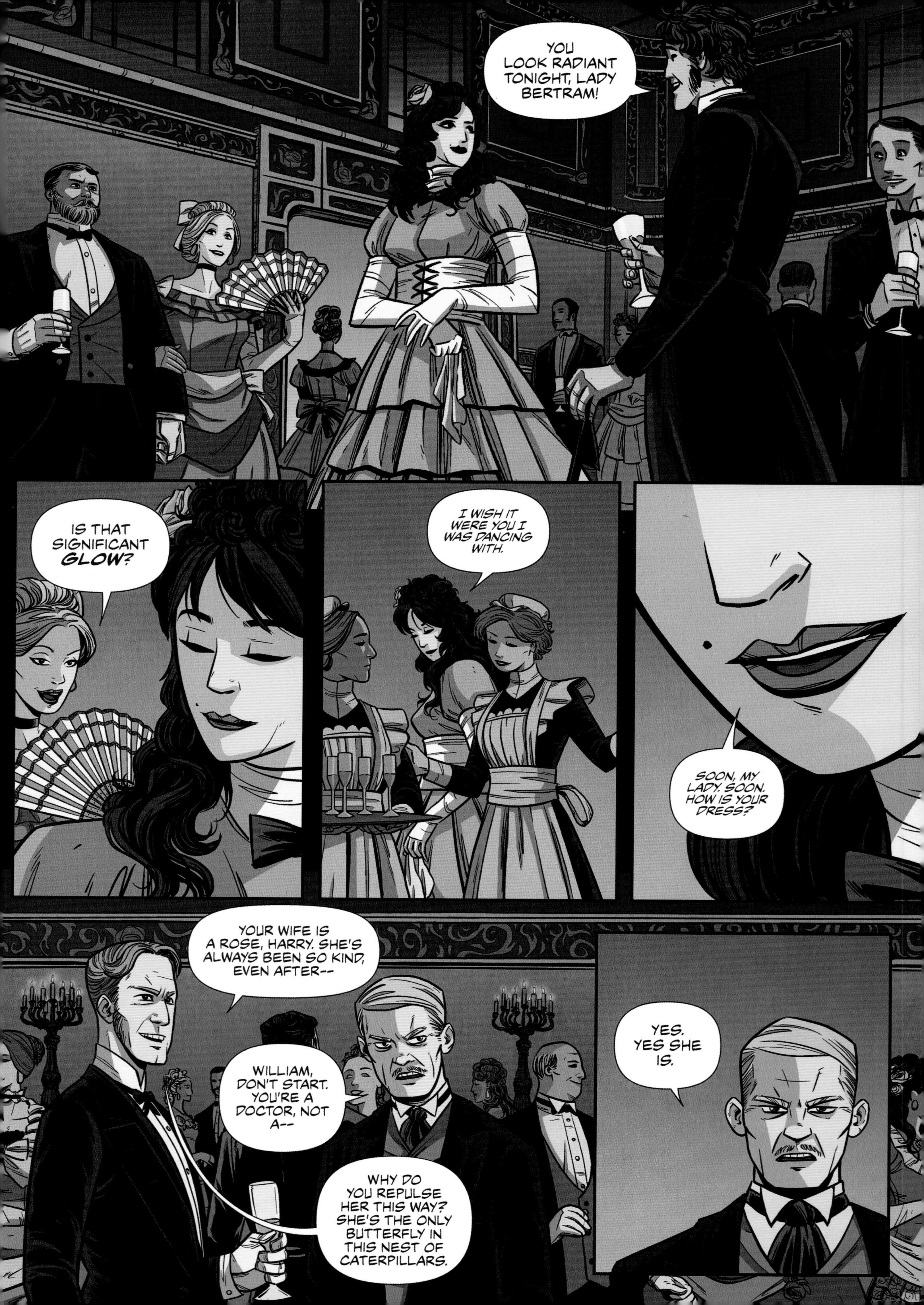
YOU LOOK RADIANT TONIGHT, LADY BERTRAM!
IS THAT SIGNIFICANT *GLOW*?
I WISH IT WERE YOU I WAS DANCING WITH.
SOON, MY LADY. SOON. HOW IS YOUR DRESS?
YOUR WIFE IS A ROSE, HARRY. SHE'S ALWAYS BEEN SO KIND, EVEN AFTER--
WILLIAM, DON'T START. YOU'RE A DOCTOR, NOT A--
WHY DO YOU REPULSE HER THIS WAY? SHE'S THE ONLY BUTTERFLY IN THIS NEST OF CATERPILLARS.
YES. YES SHE IS.

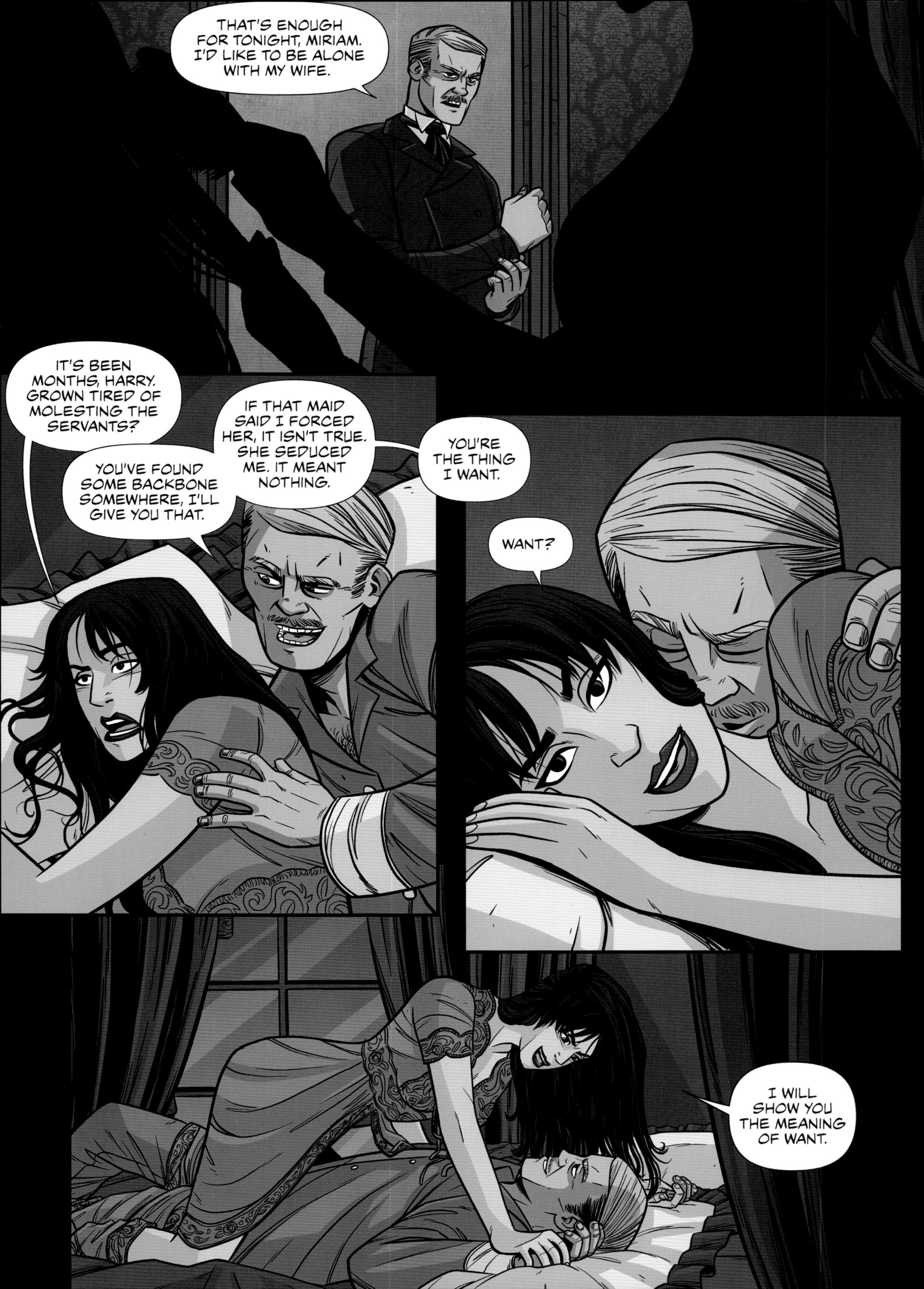
THAT'S ENOUGH FOR TONIGHT, MIRIAM. I'D LIKE TO BE ALONE WITH MY WIFE.
IT'S BEEN MONTHS, HARRY. GROWN TIRED OF MOLESTING THE SERVANTS?
YOU'VE FOUND SOME BACKBONE SOMEWHERE, I'LL GIVE YOU THAT.
IF THAT MAID SAID I FORCED HER, IT ISN'T TRUE. SHE SEDUCED ME. IT MEANT NOTHING.
YOU'RE THE THING I WANT.
WANT?
I WILL SHOW YOU THE MEANING OF WANT.

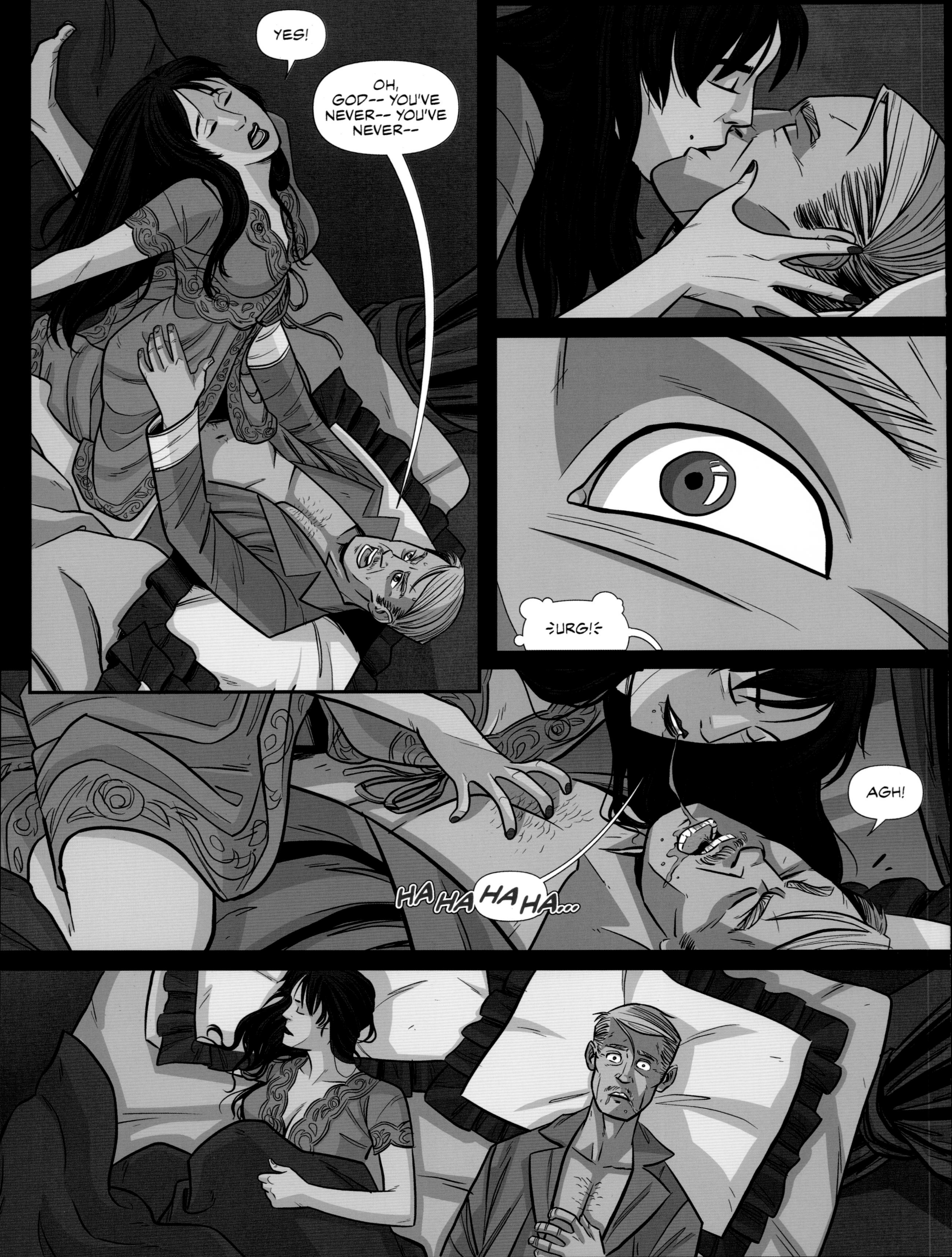
YES!
OH, GOD-- YOU'VE NEVER-- YOU'VE NEVER--
URG!
AGH!
HA HA HA HA...

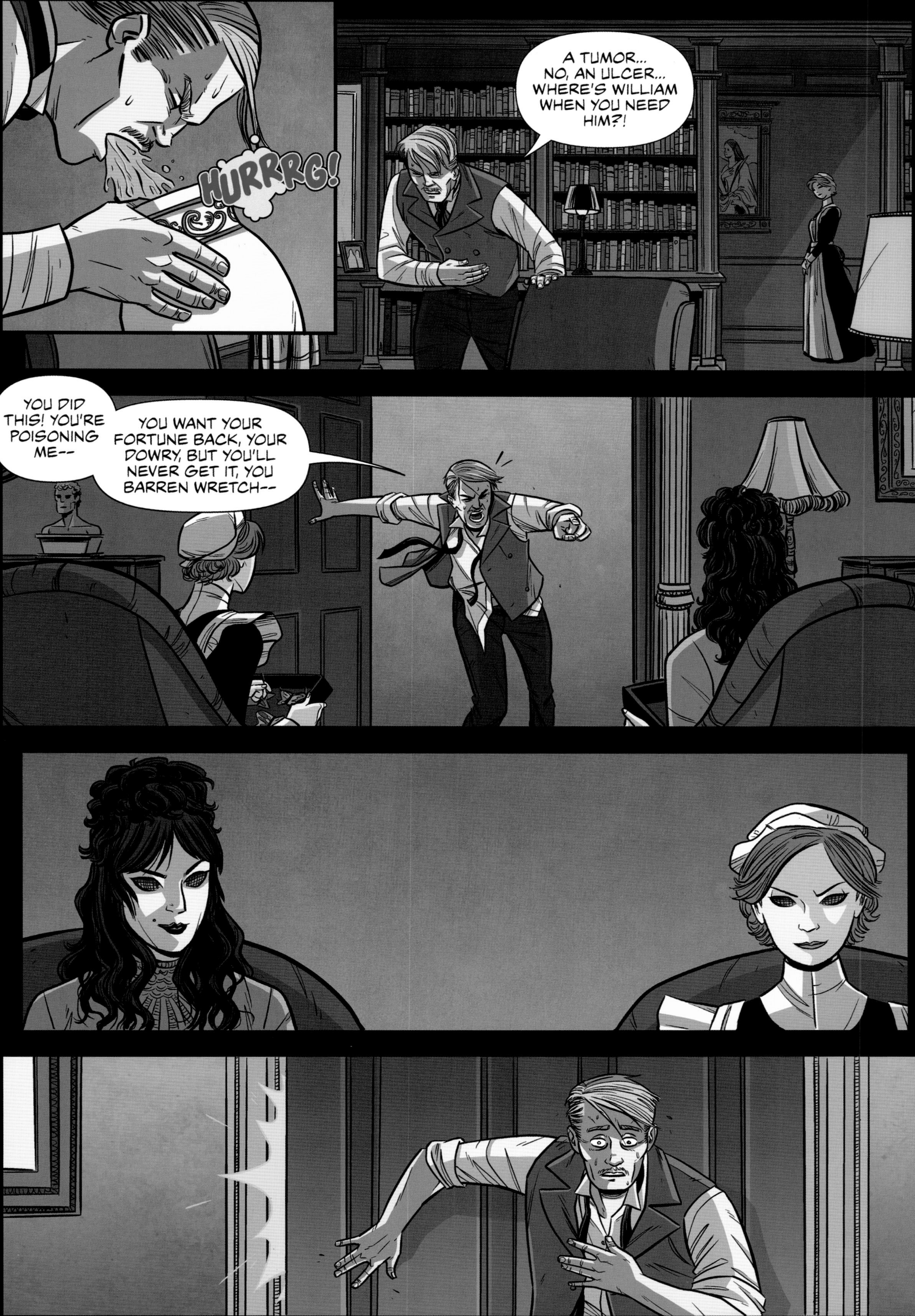
HURRRG!
A TUMOR... NO, AN ULCER... WHERE'S WILLIAM WHEN YOU NEED HIM?!
YOU DID THIS! YOU'RE POISONING ME--
YOU WANT YOUR FORTUNE BACK, YOUR DOWRY, BUT YOU'LL NEVER GET IT, YOU BARREN WRETCH--

WHERE DID IT COME FROM?

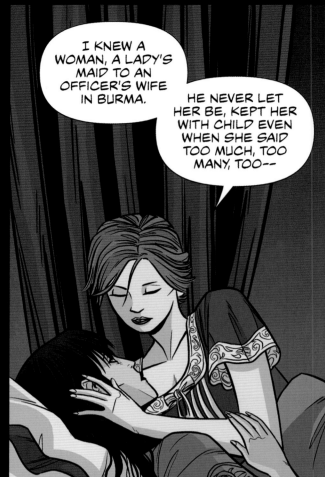

I KNEW A WOMAN, A LADY'S MAID TO AN OFFICER'S WIFE IN BURMA.

HE NEVER LET HER BE, KEPT HER WITH CHILD EVEN WHEN SHE SAID TOO MUCH, TOO MANY, TOO--

AAAAAAAAAAHHHH!

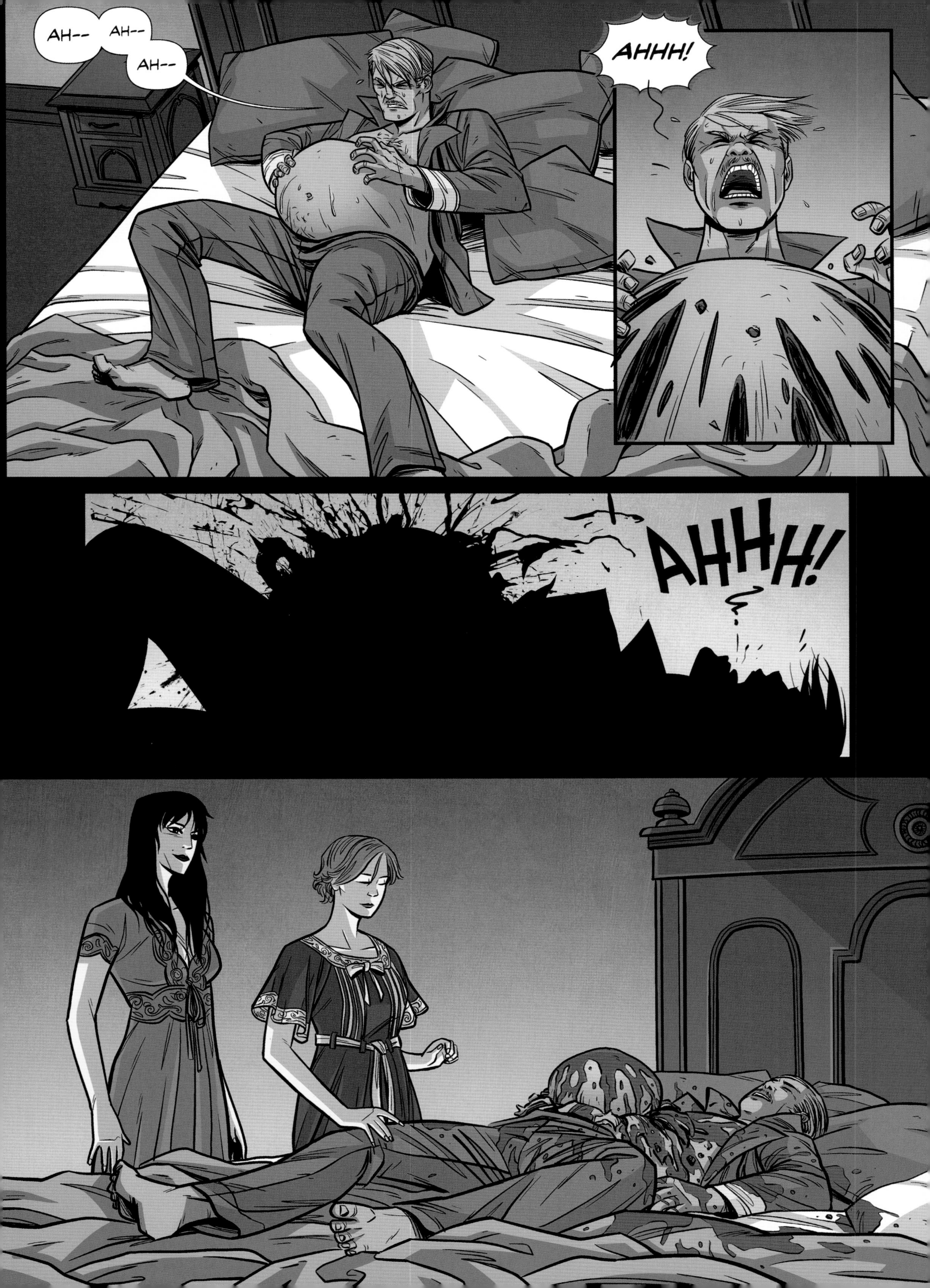
AH--
AH--
AH--
AHHH!
AHHH!

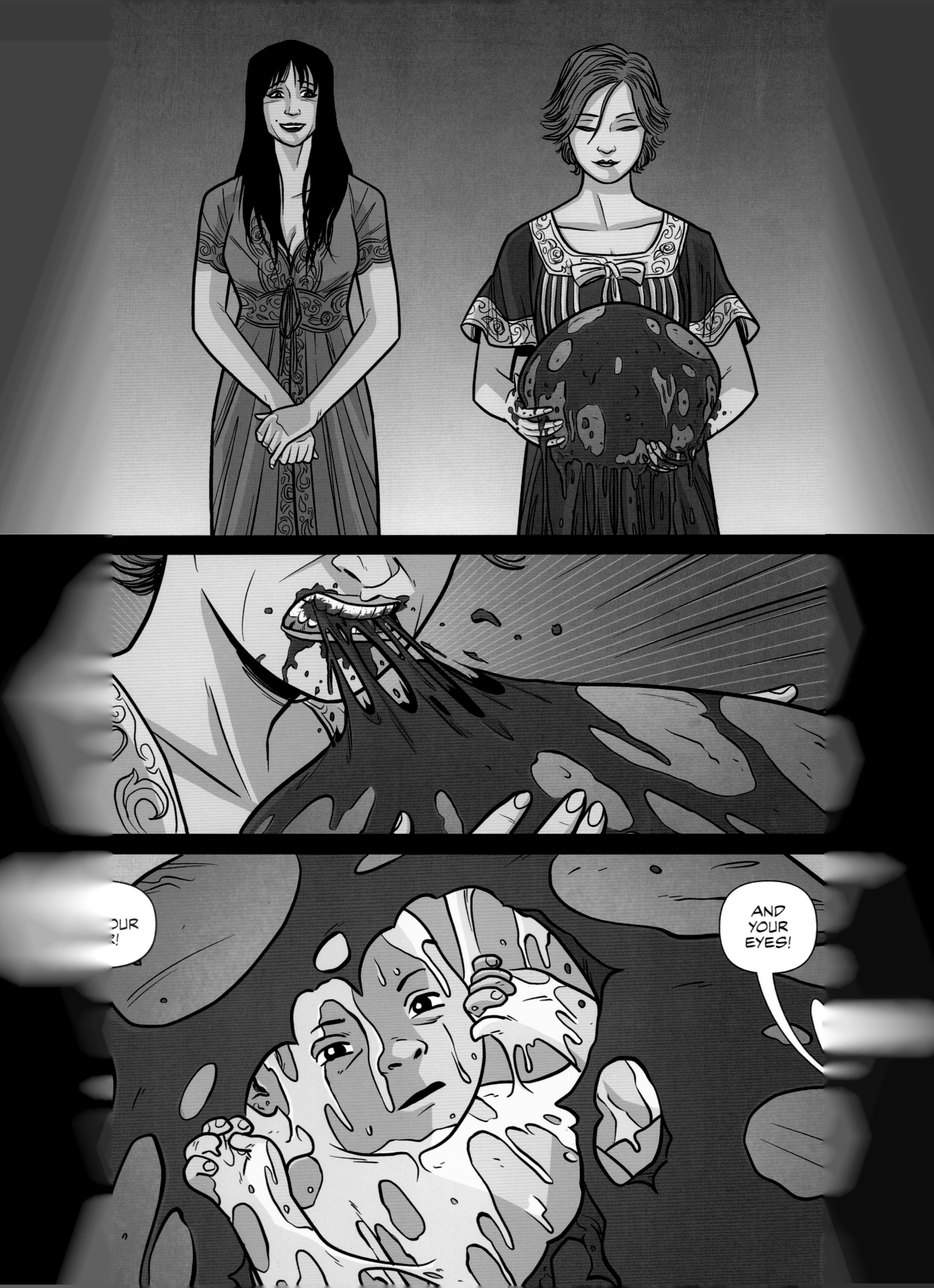
AND YOUR EYES!

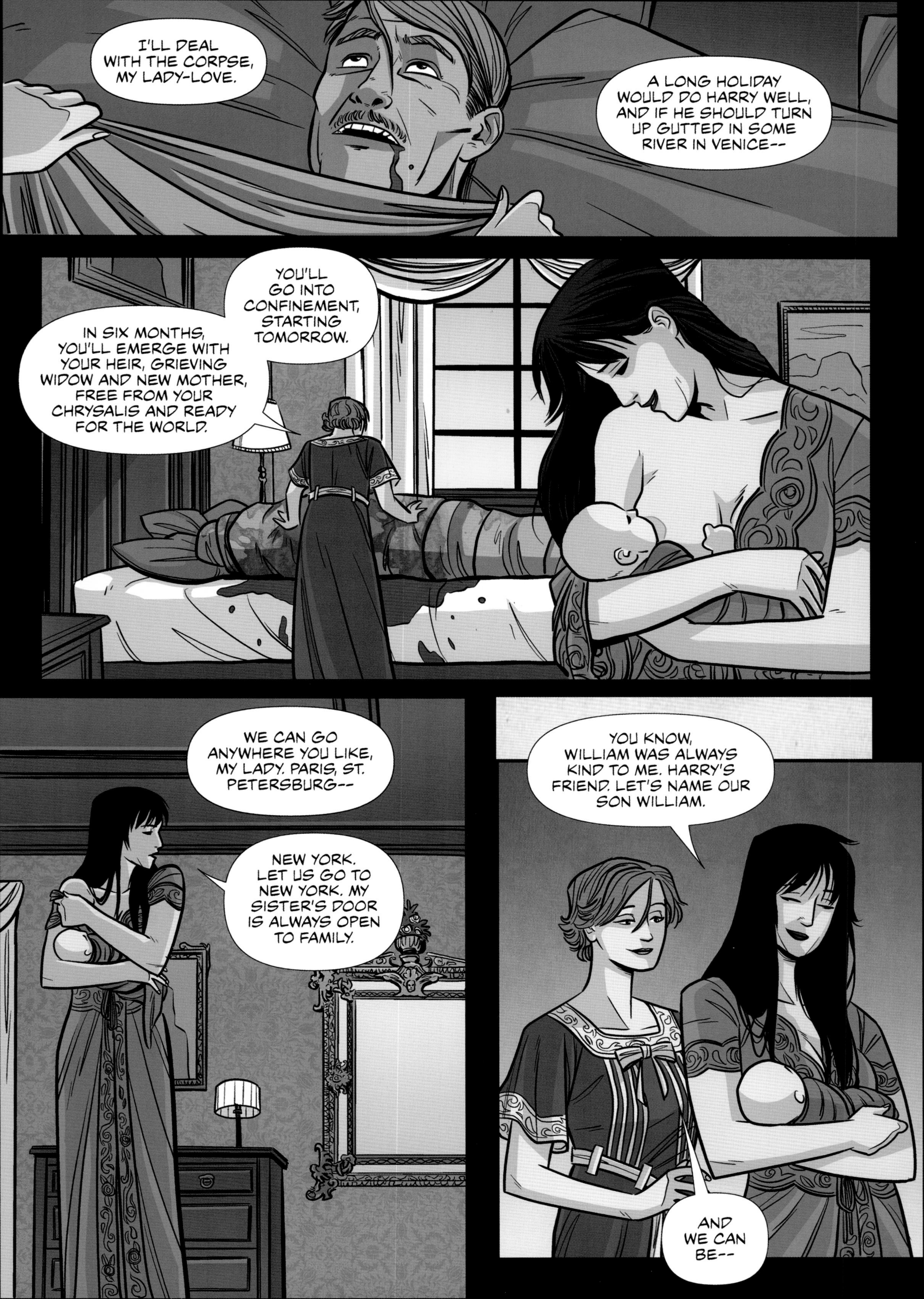
I'LL DEAL WITH THE CORPSE, MY LADY-LOVE.
A LONG HOLIDAY WOULD DO HARRY WELL, AND IF HE SHOULD TURN UP GUTTED IN SOME RIVER IN VENICE--
YOU'LL GO INTO CONFINEMENT, STARTING TOMORROW.
IN SIX MONTHS, YOU'LL EMERGE WITH YOUR HEIR, GRIEVING WIDOW AND NEW MOTHER, FREE FROM YOUR CHRYSALIS AND READY FOR THE WORLD.
WE CAN GO ANYWHERE YOU LIKE, MY LADY. PARIS, ST. PETERSBURG--
NEW YORK. LET US GO TO NEW YORK. MY SISTER'S DOOR IS ALWAYS OPEN TO FAMILY.
YOU KNOW, WILLIAM WAS ALWAYS KIND TO ME. HARRY'S FRIEND. LET'S NAME OUR SON WILLIAM.
AND WE CAN BE--

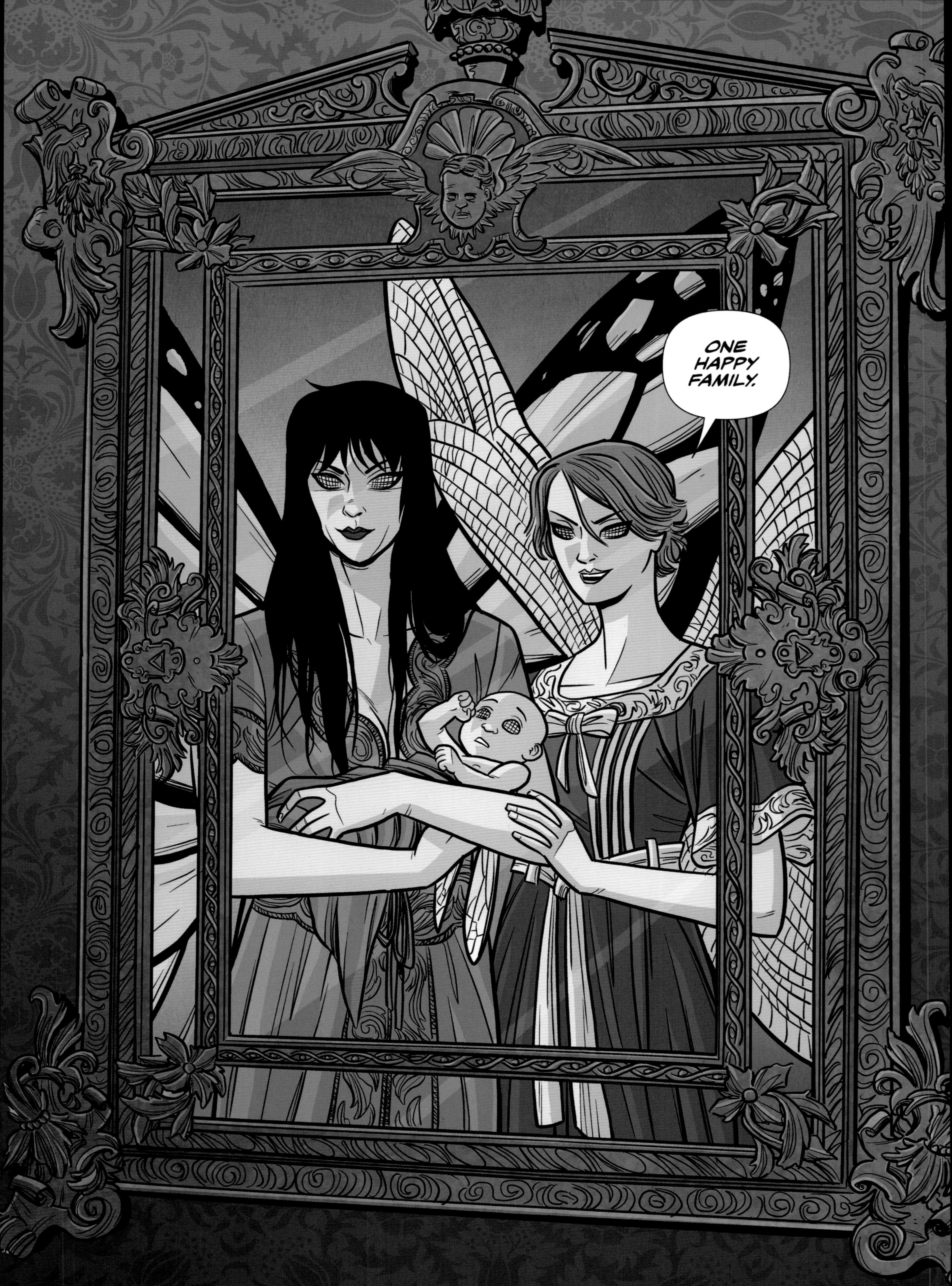
ONE HAPPY FAMILY.

PINUP GALLERY

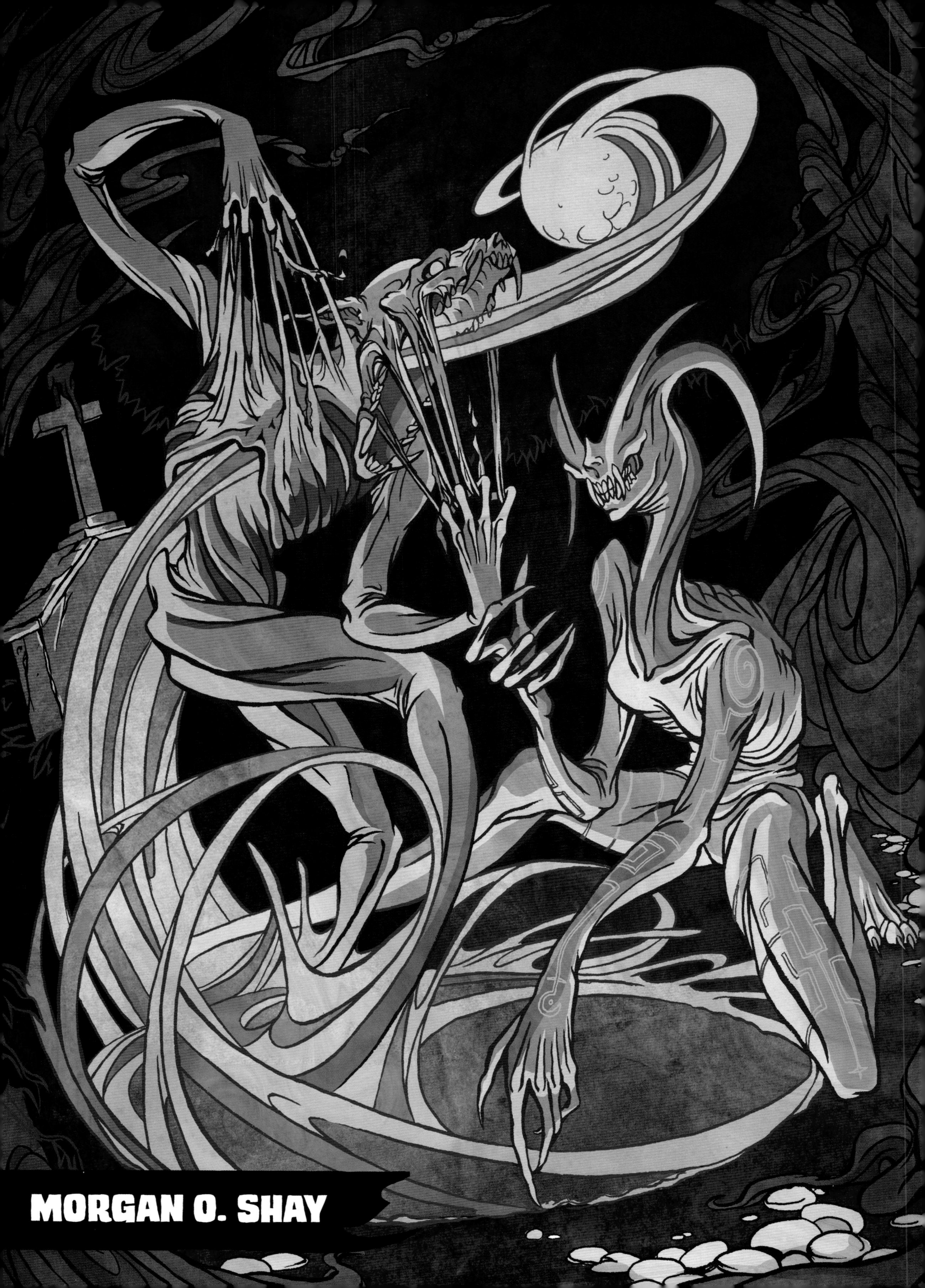

MORGAN O. SHAY

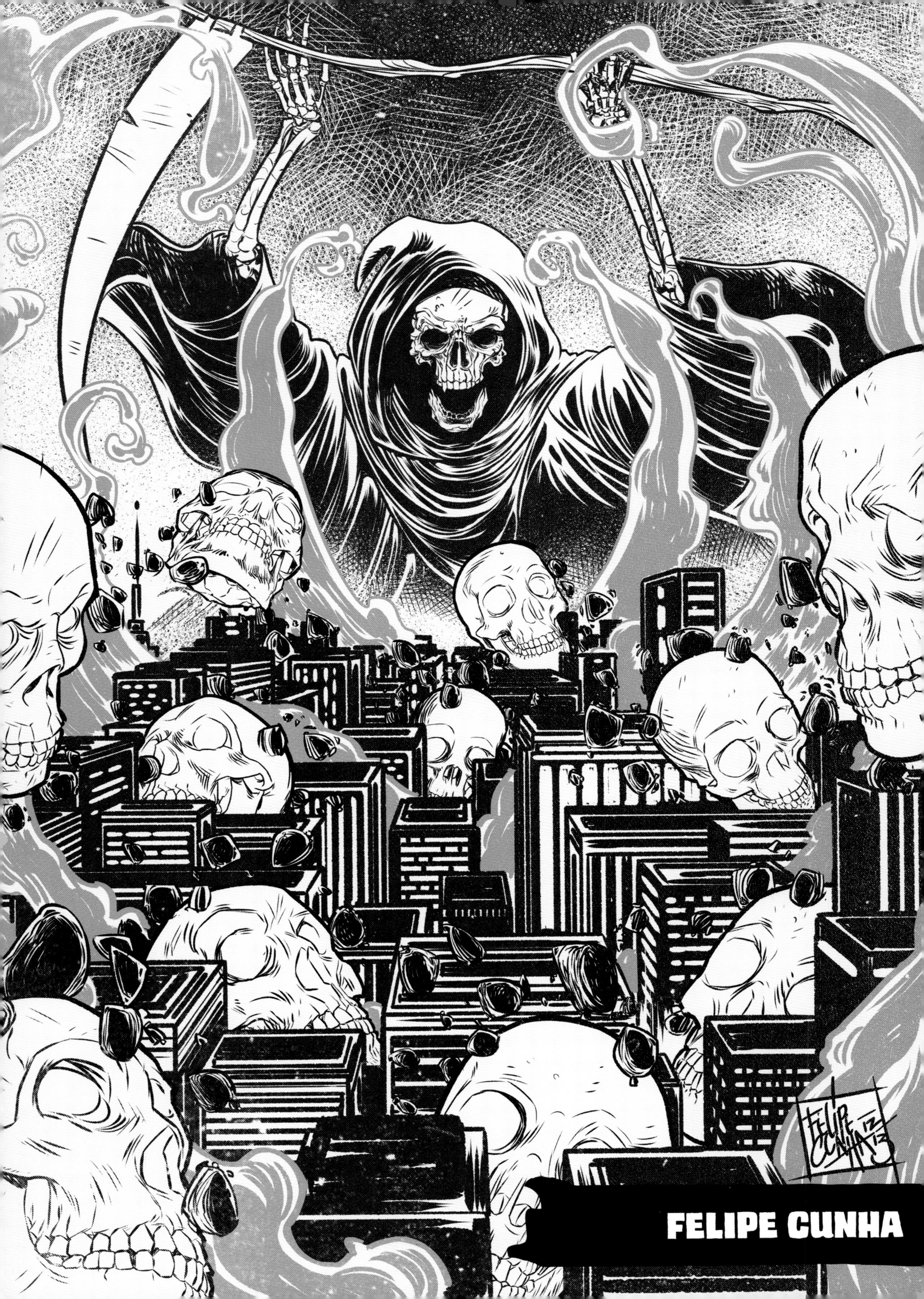

FELIPE CUNHA

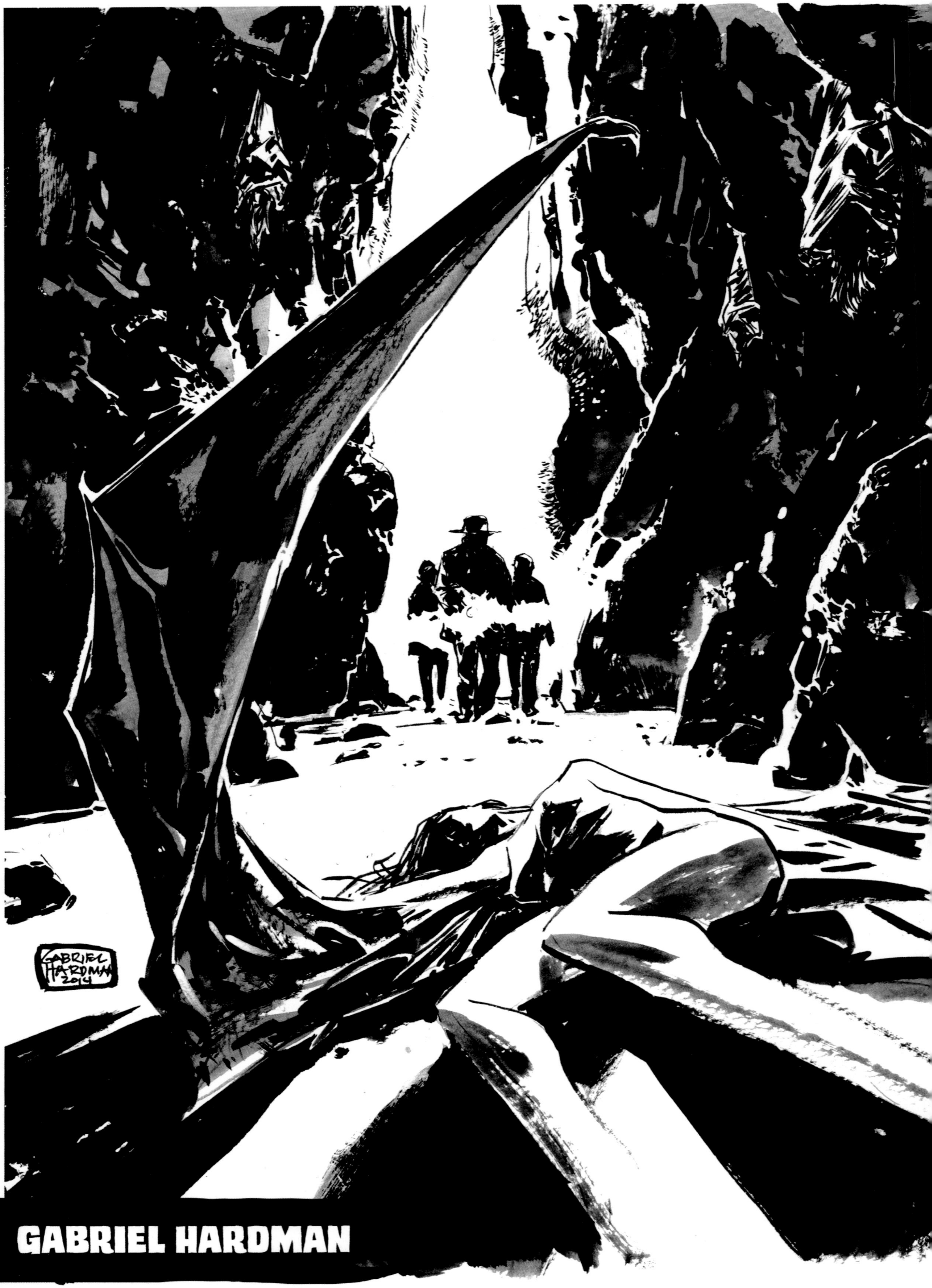
GABRIEL HARDMAN 2014

GABRIEL HARDMAN

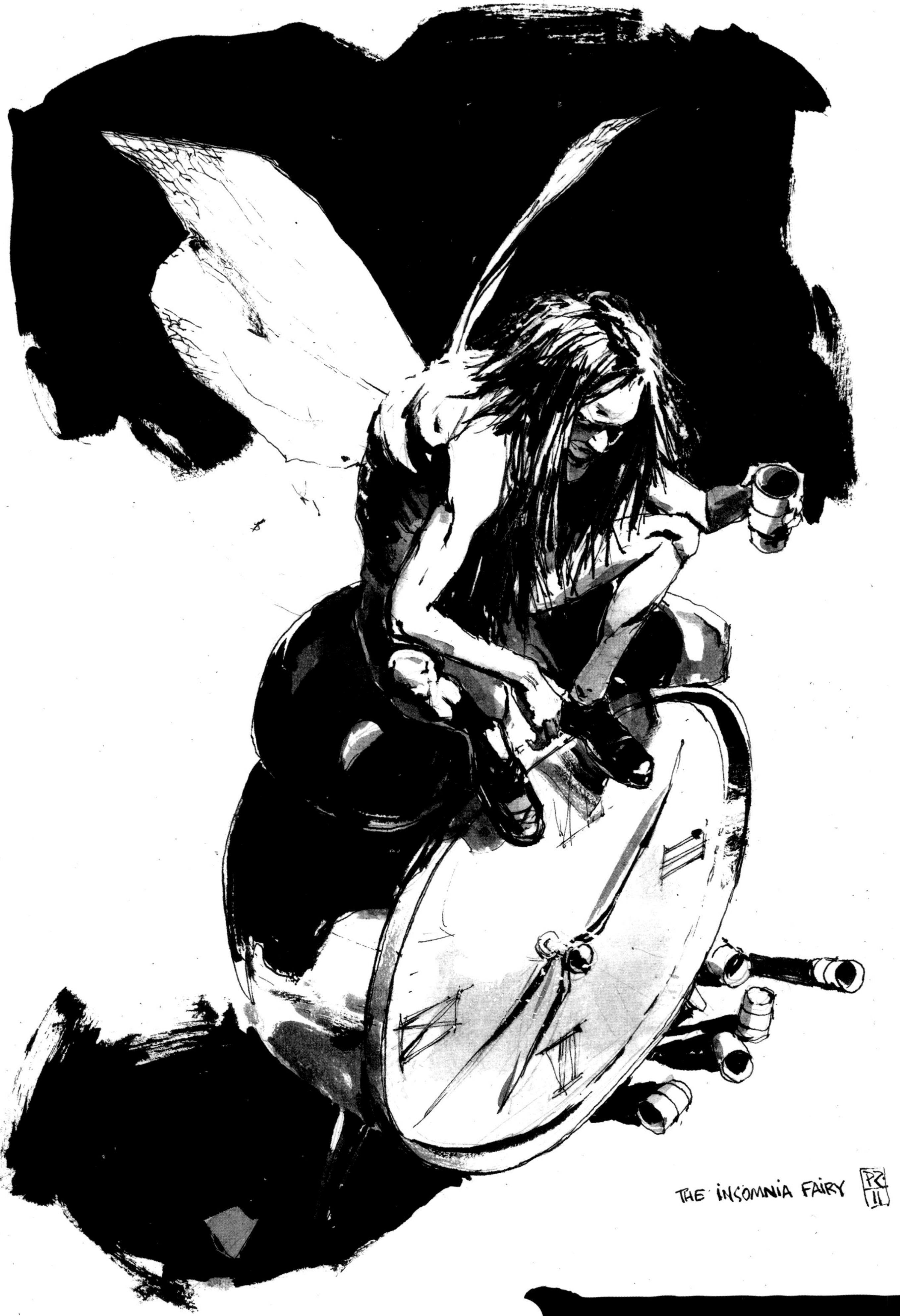
THE INSOMNIA FAIRY

PATRIC REYNOLDS

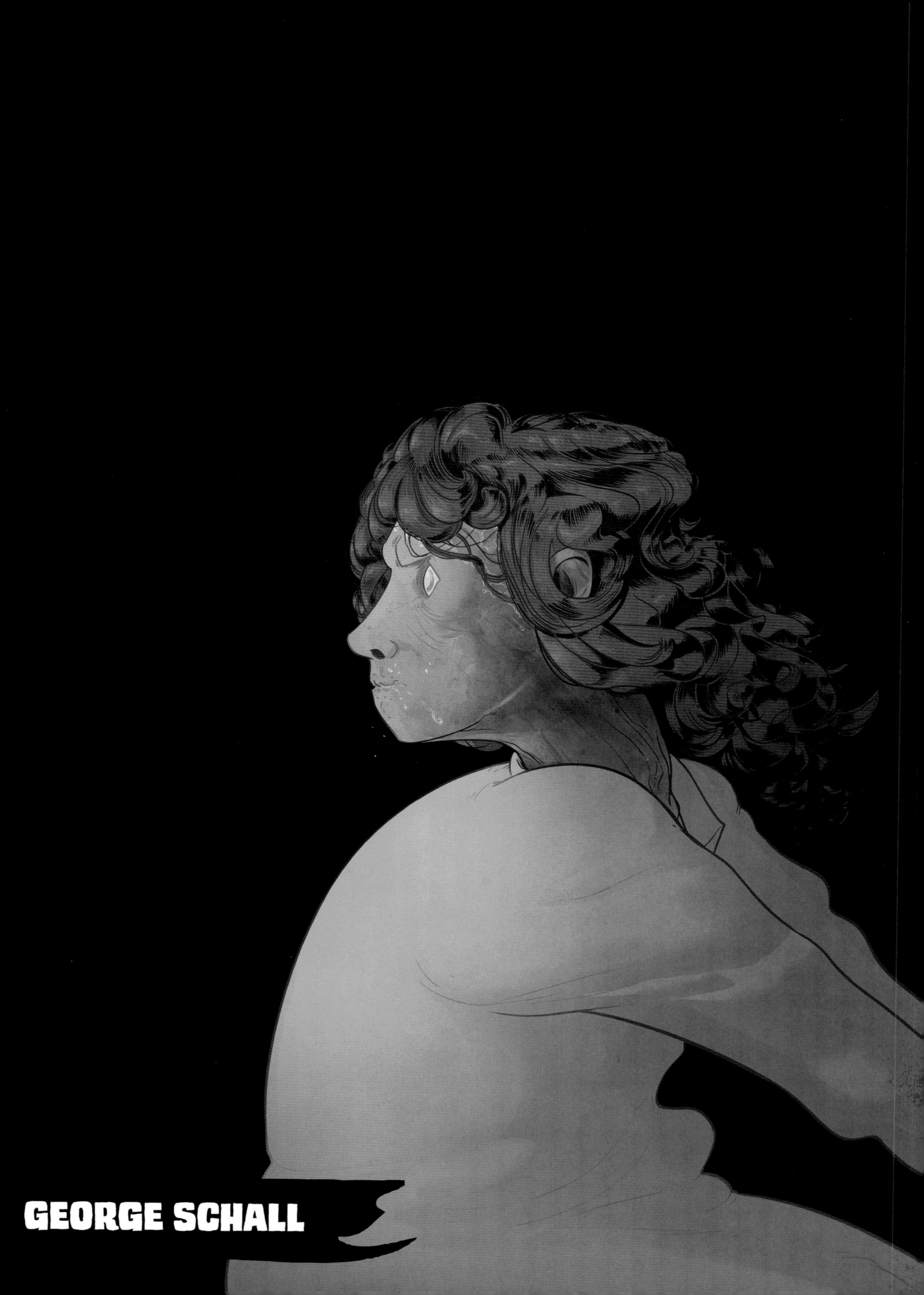
GEORGE SCHALL

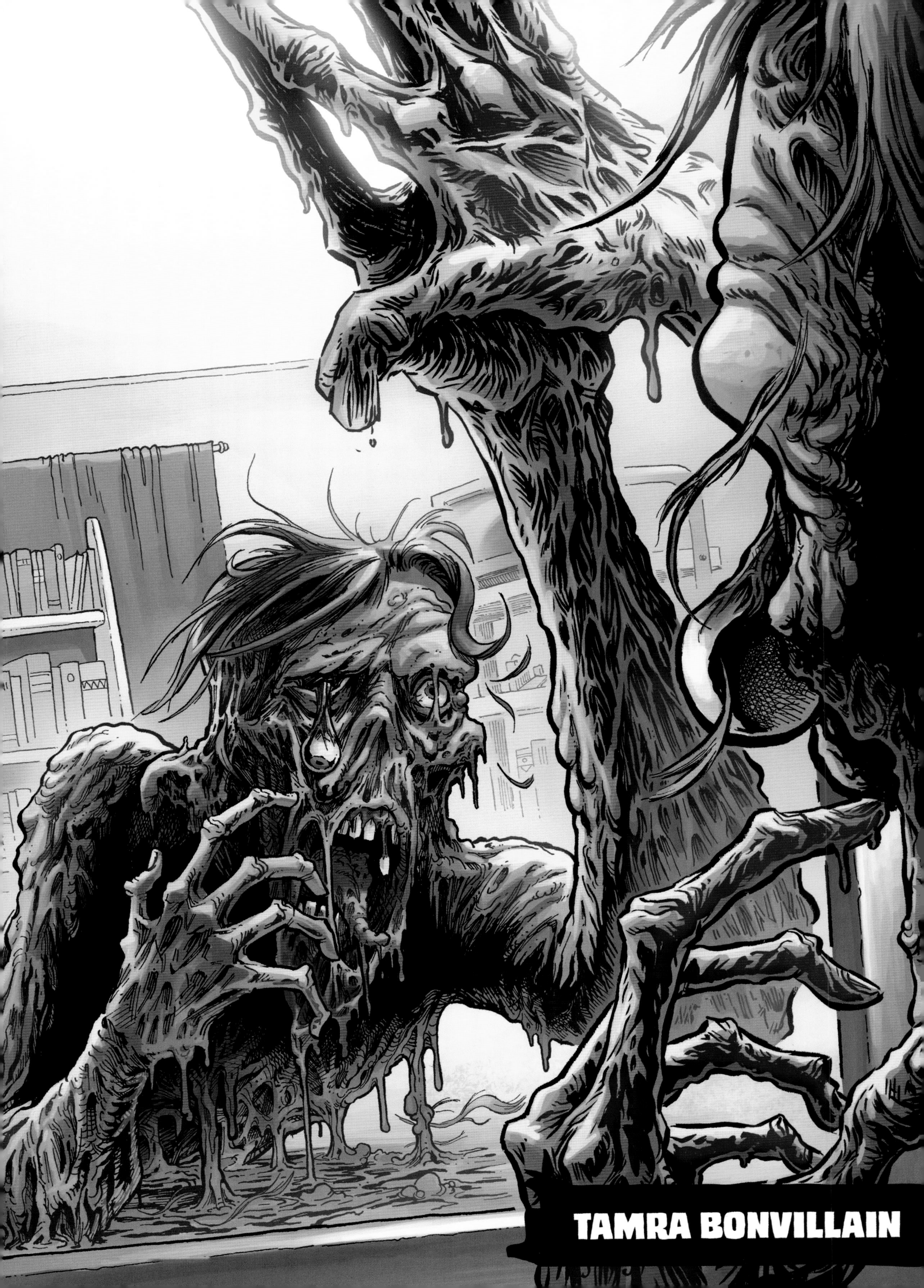
TAMRA BONVILLAIN

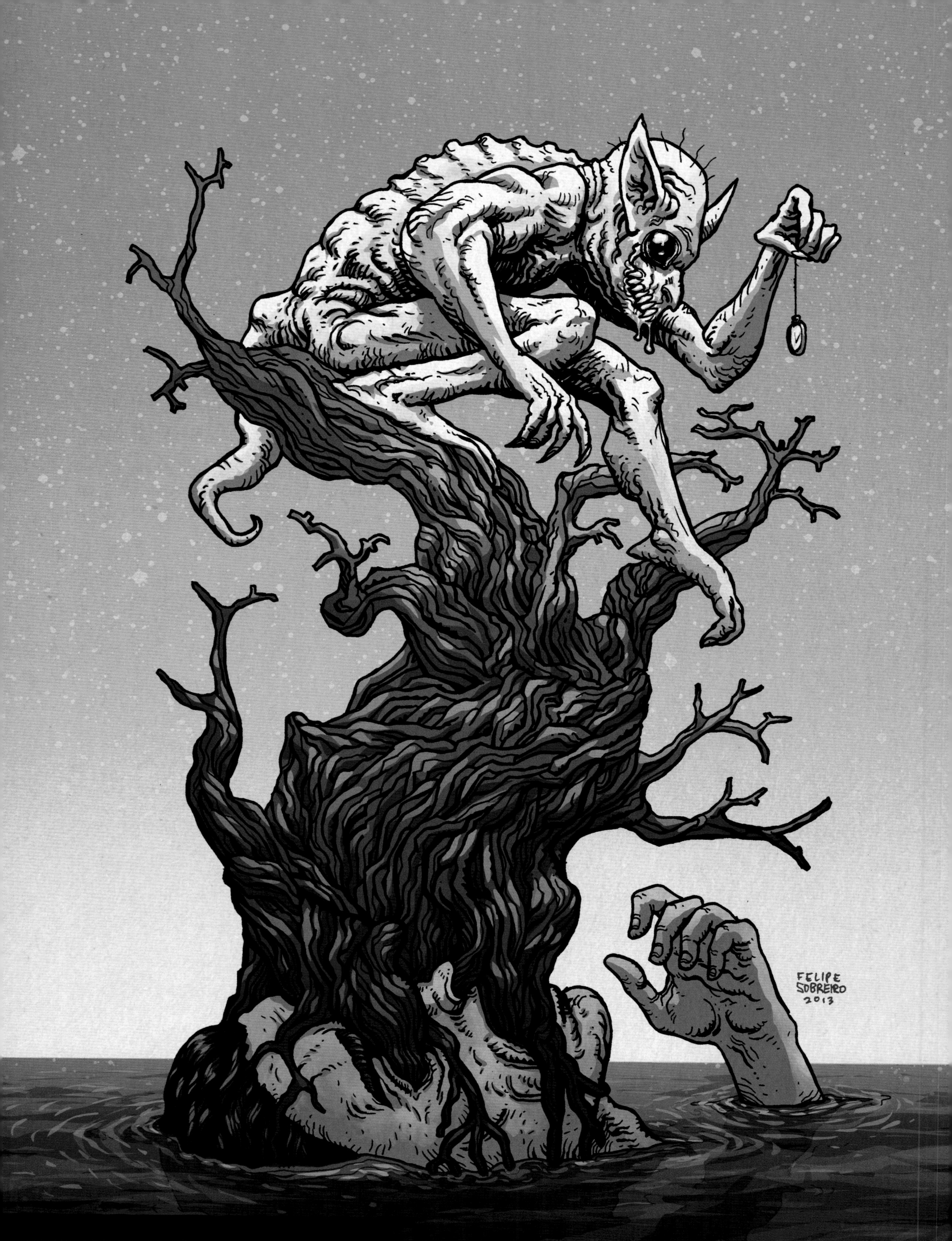
FELIPE
SOBREIRO
2013

FELIPE SOBREIRO

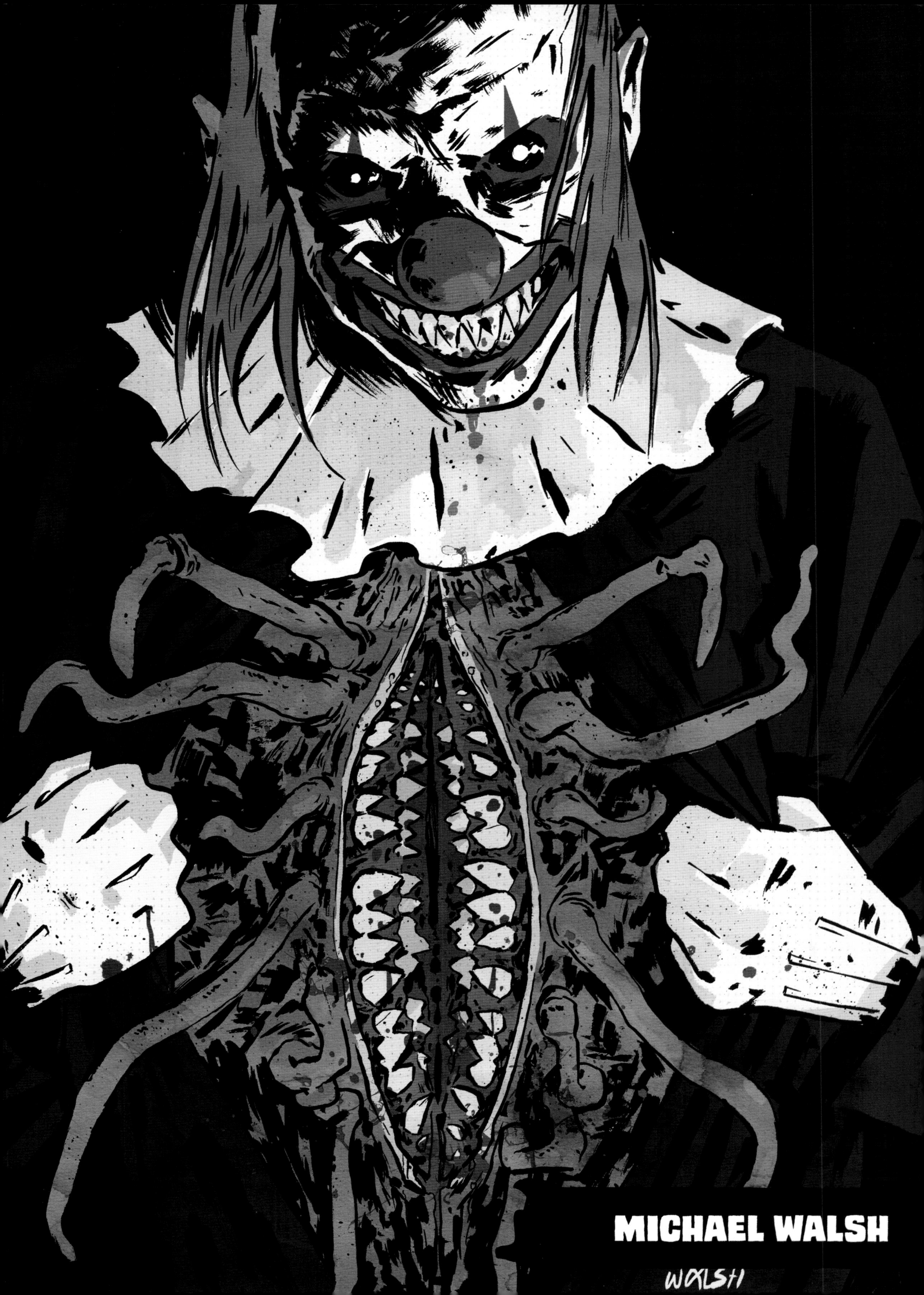
WALSH

MICHAEL WALSH

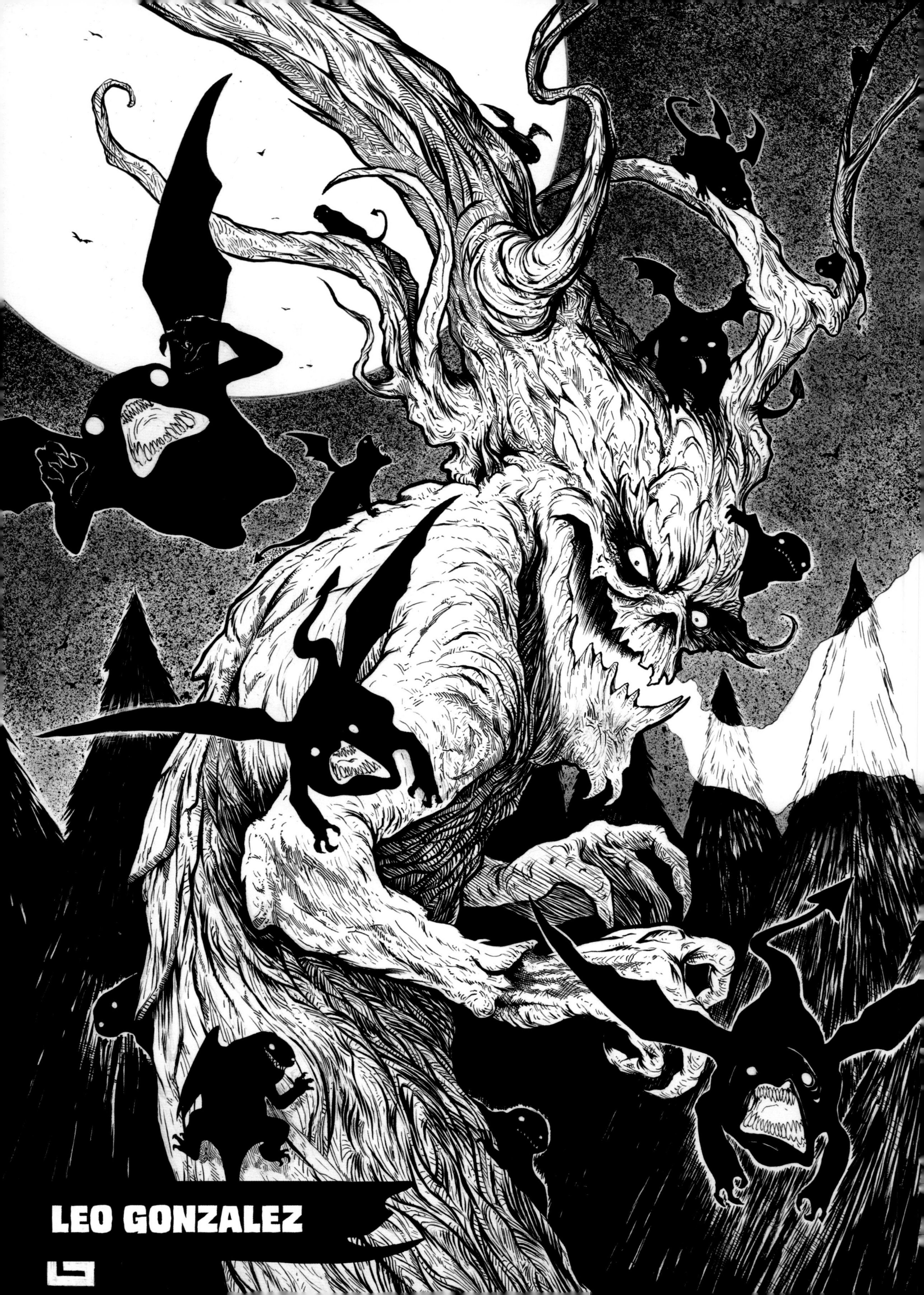
LEO GONZALEZ

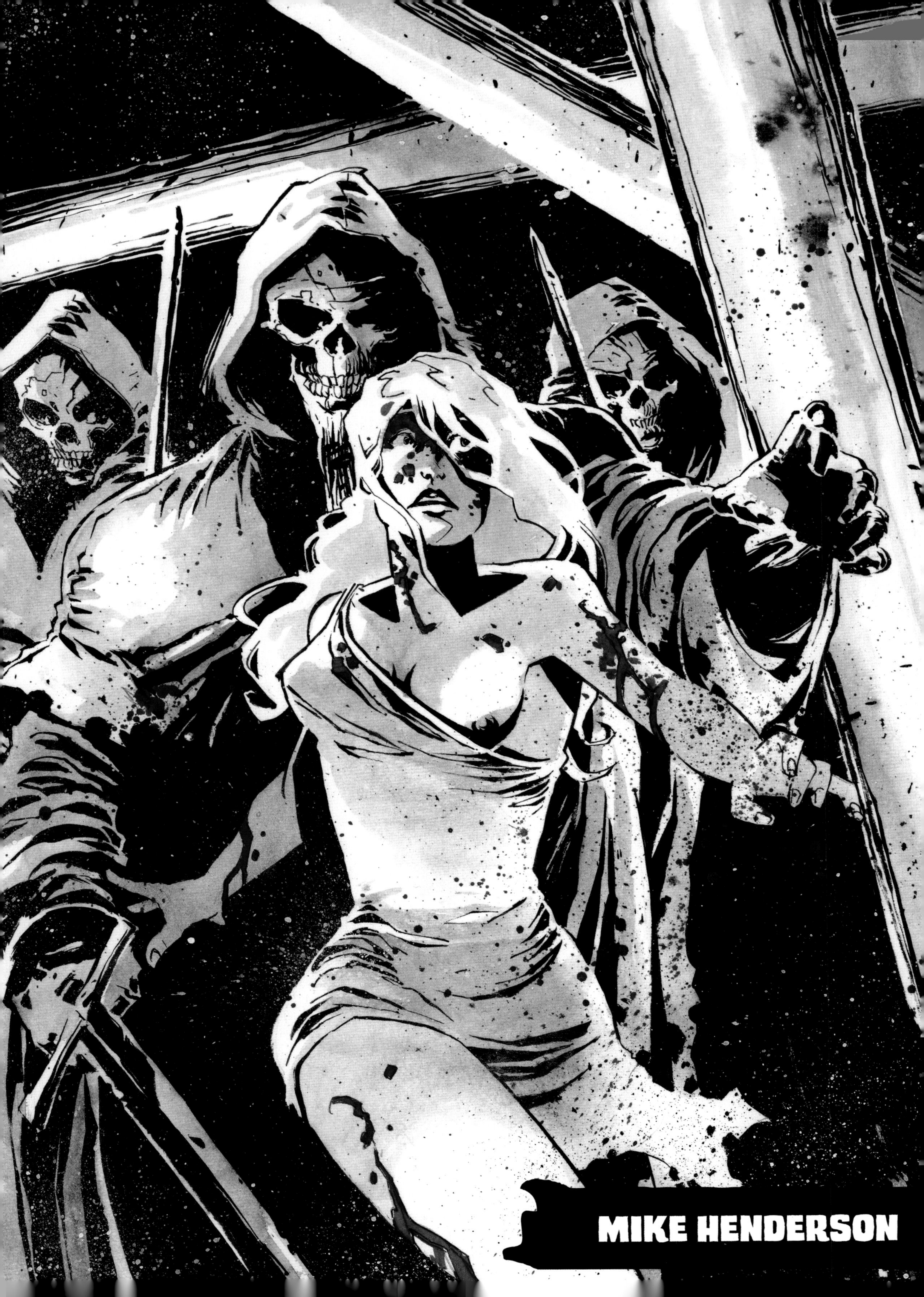
MIKE HENDERSON

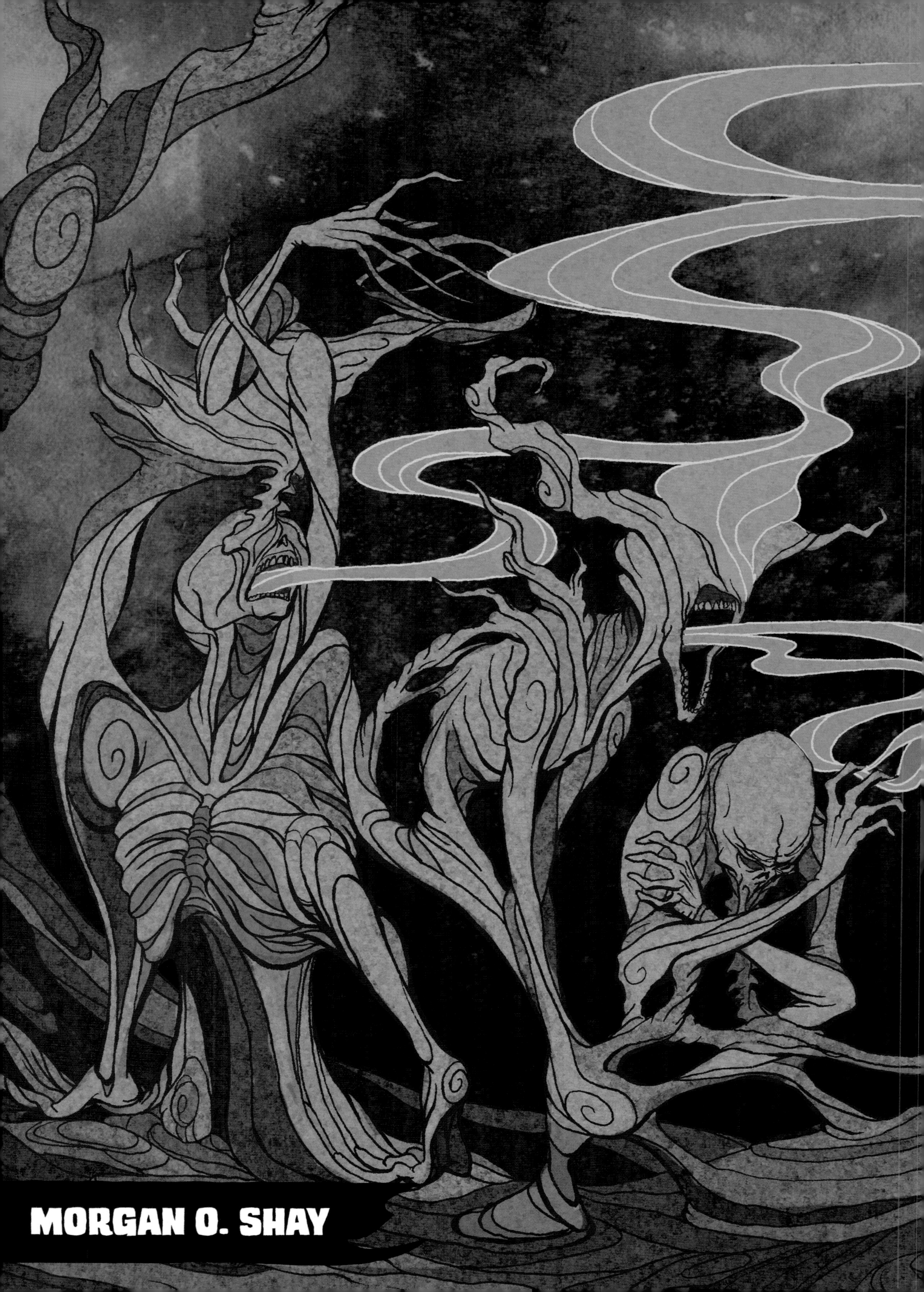

MORGAN O. SHAY

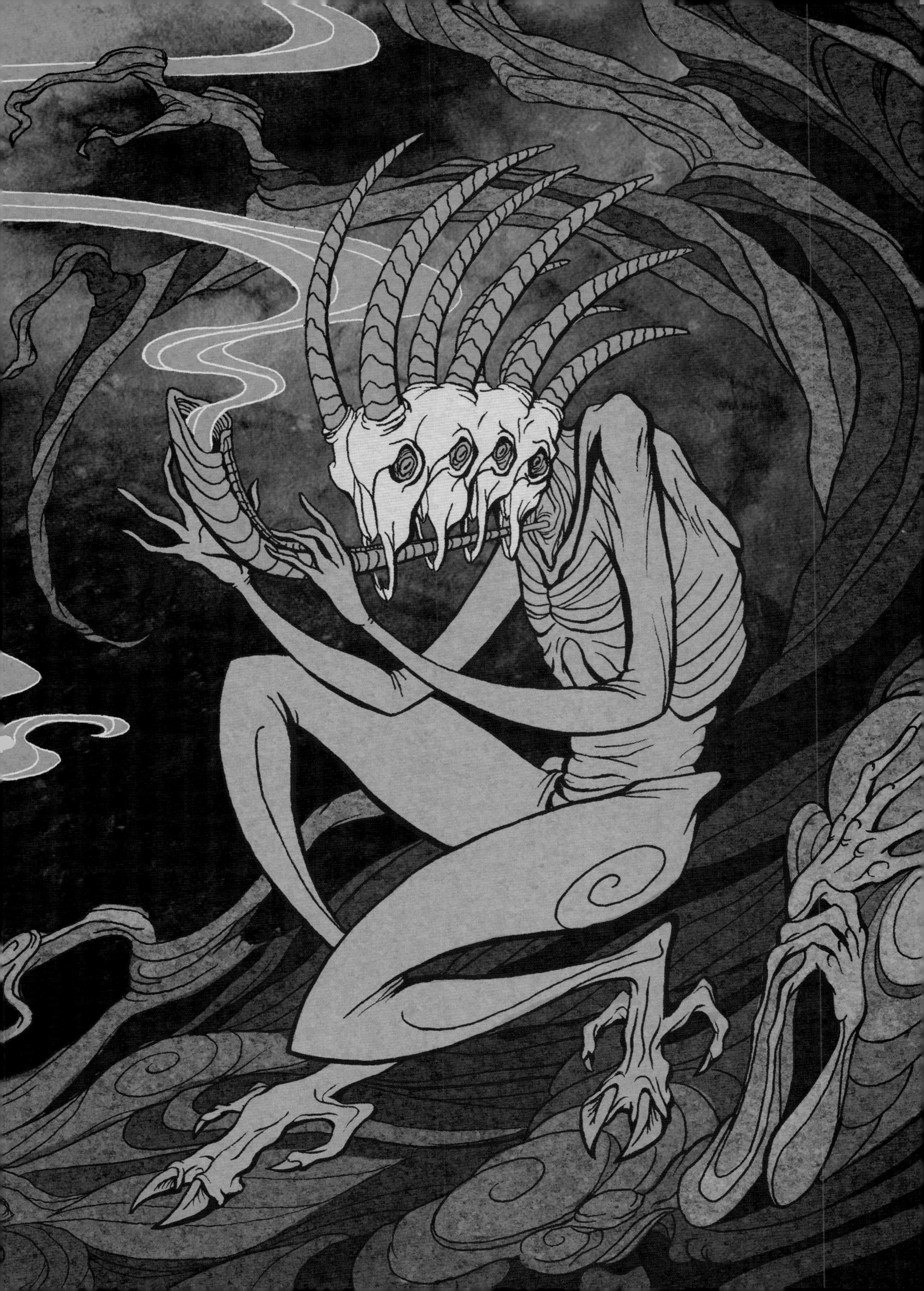

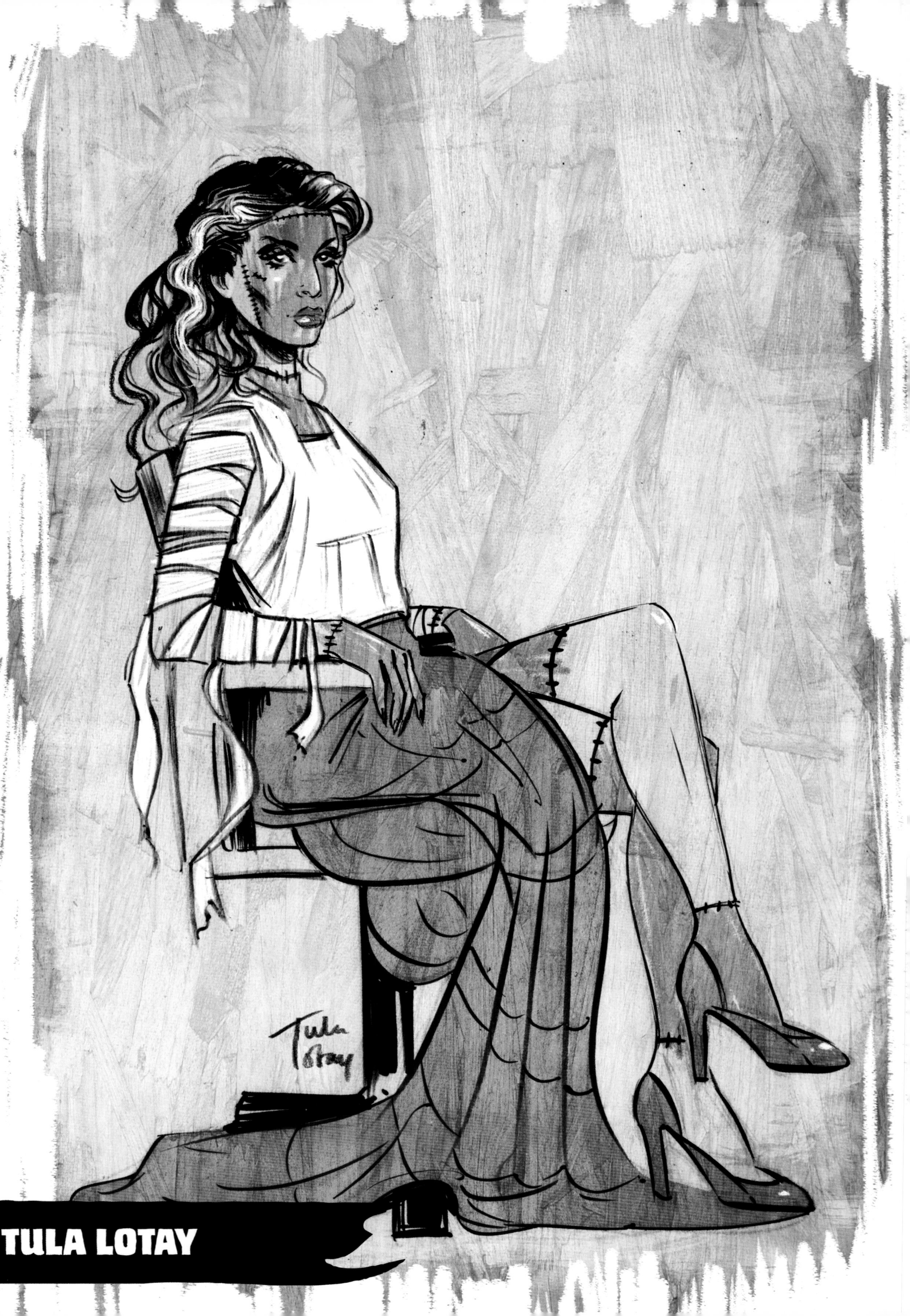
Tula Lotay

TULA LOTAY

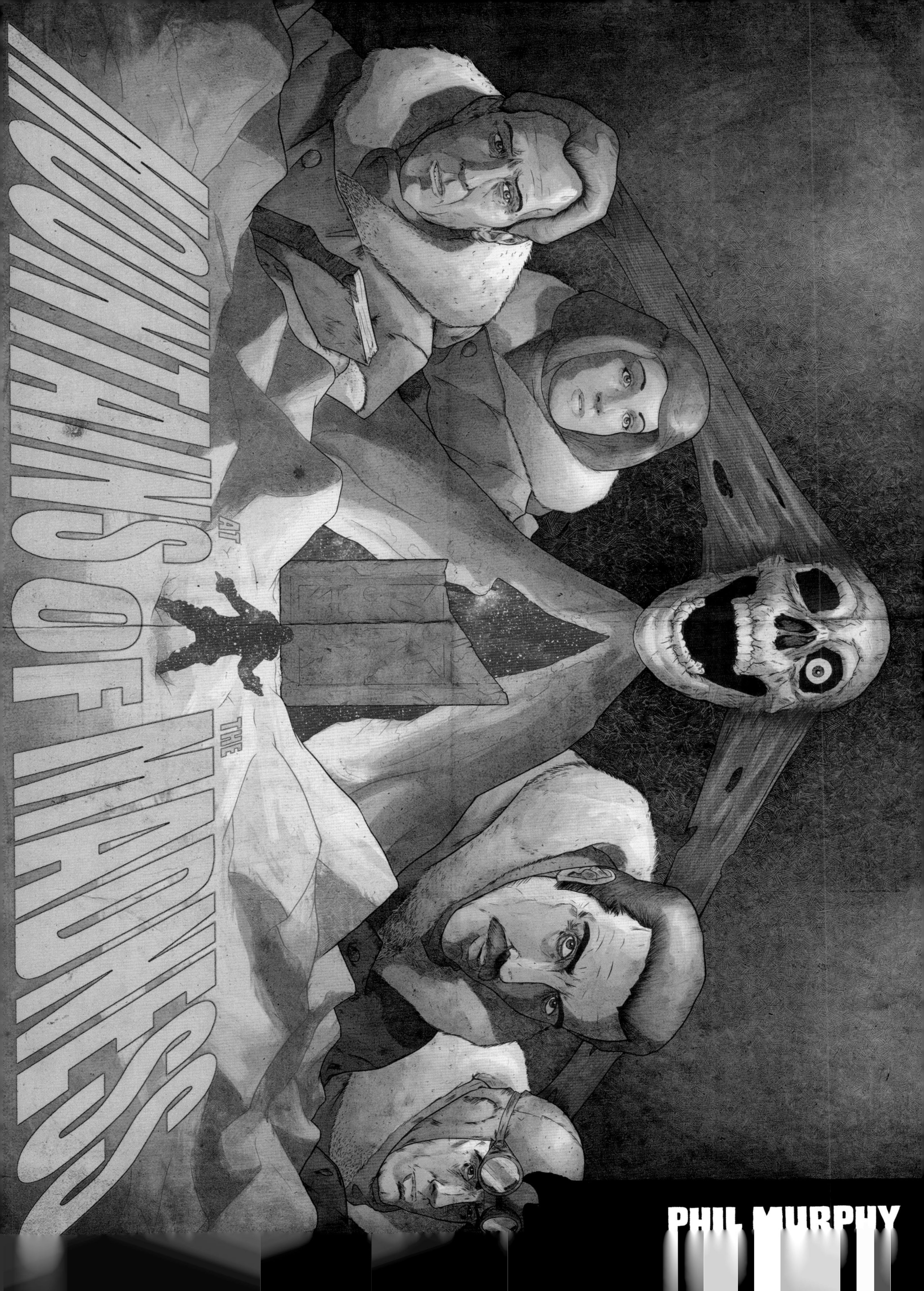
AT THE MOUNTAINS OF MADNESS
PHIL MURPHY

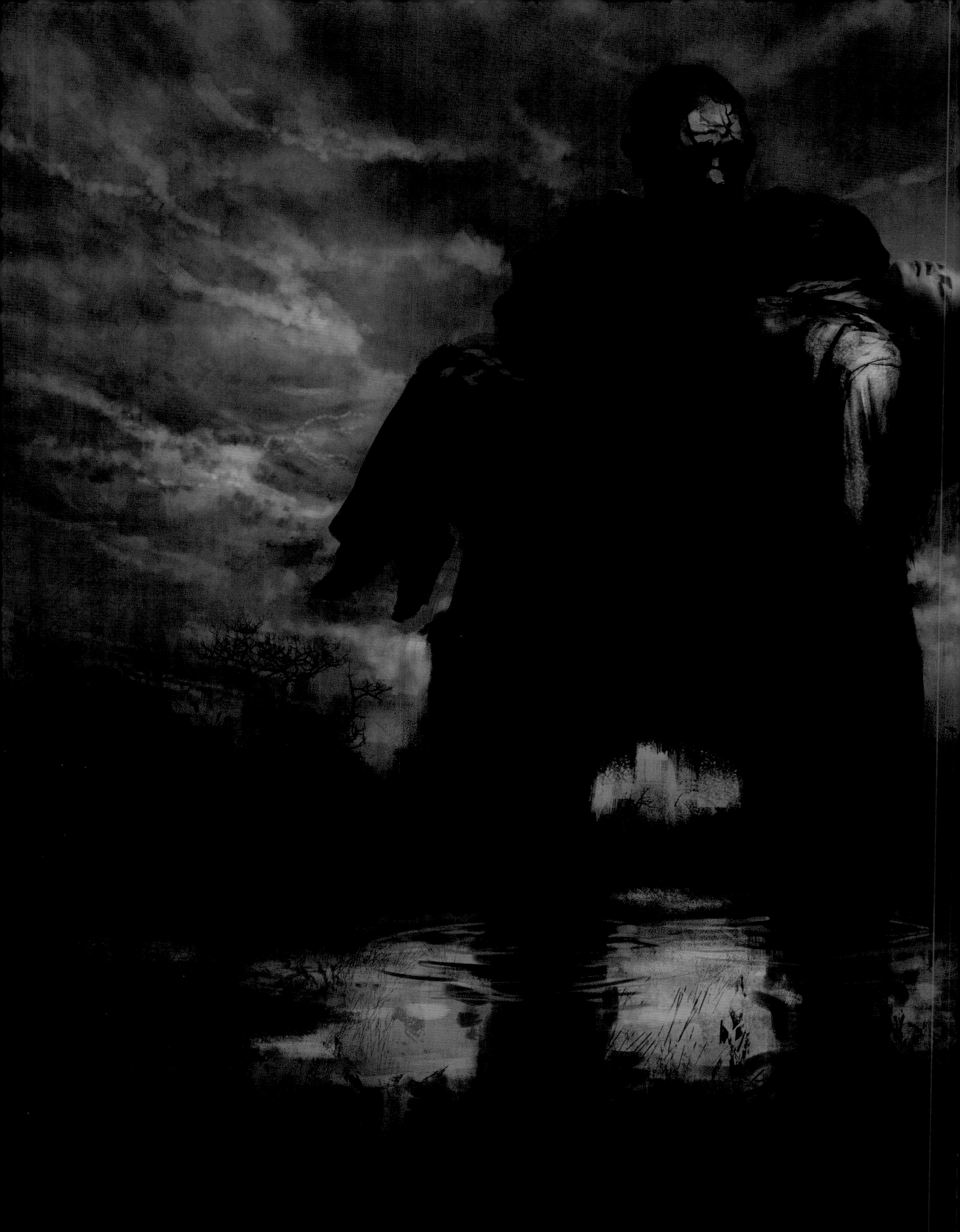

BILL THOMPSON

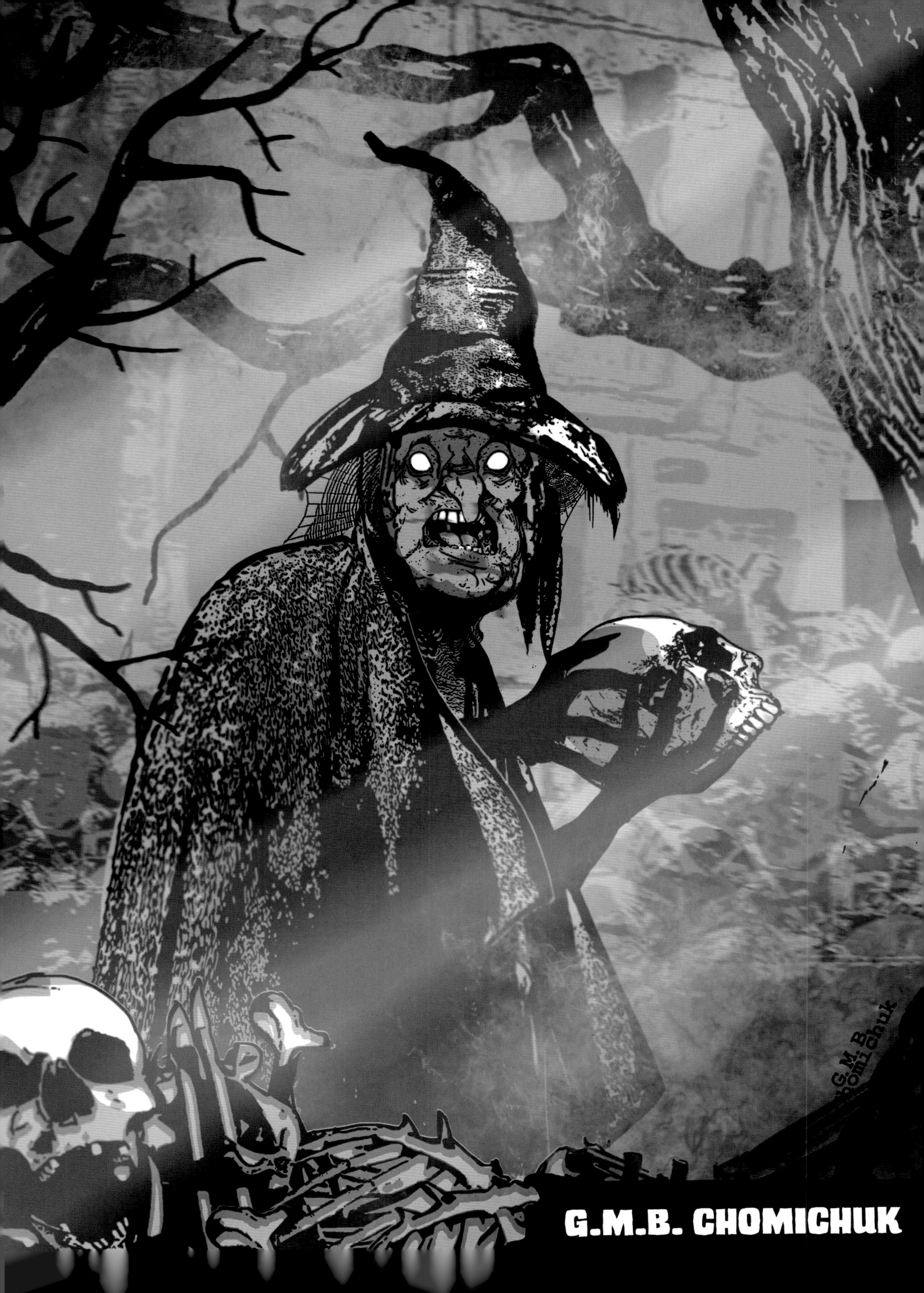
G.M.B. Chomichuk
G.M.B. CHOMICHUK

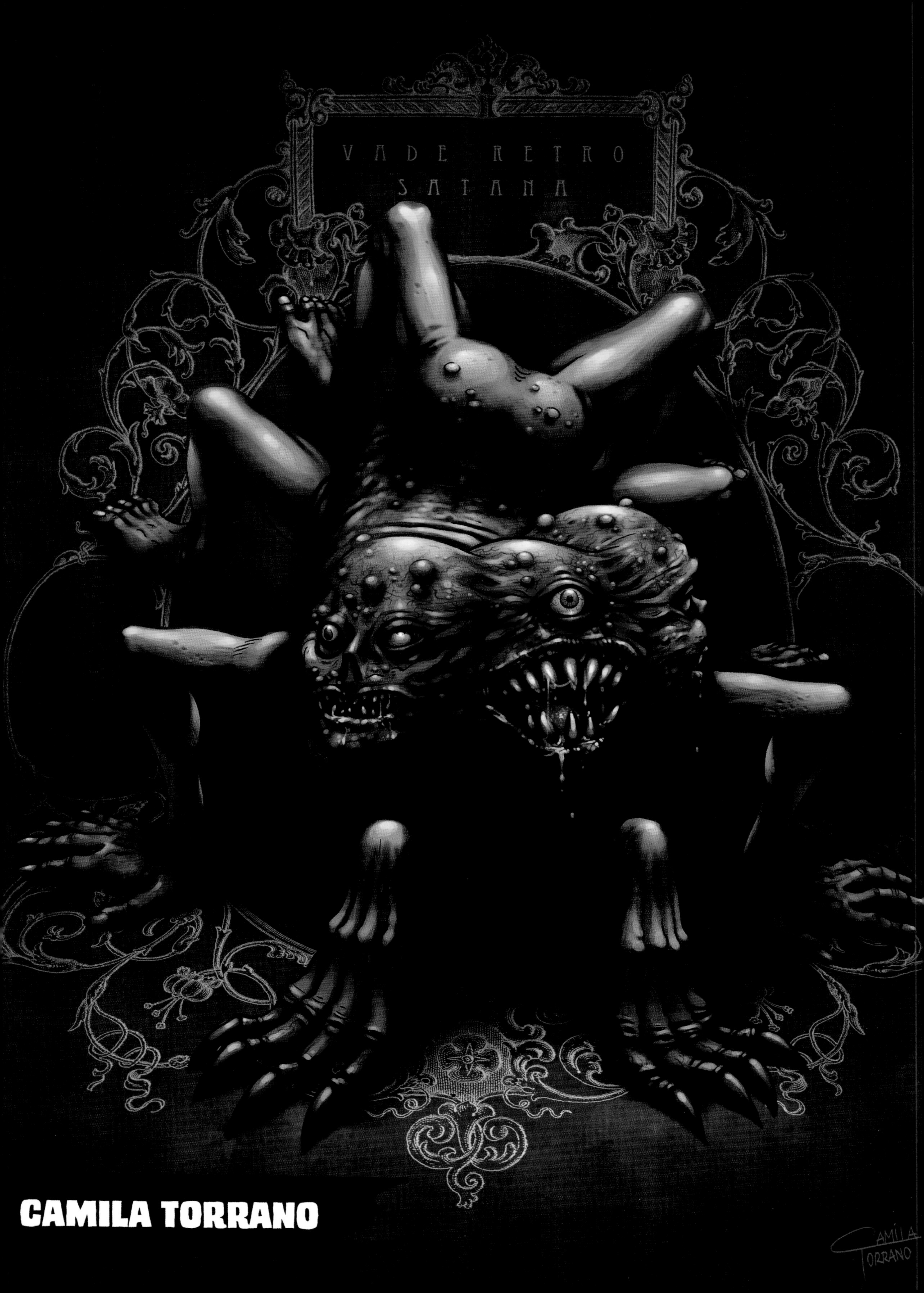
VADE RETRO
SATANA
CAMILA TORRANO

CAMILA TORRANO

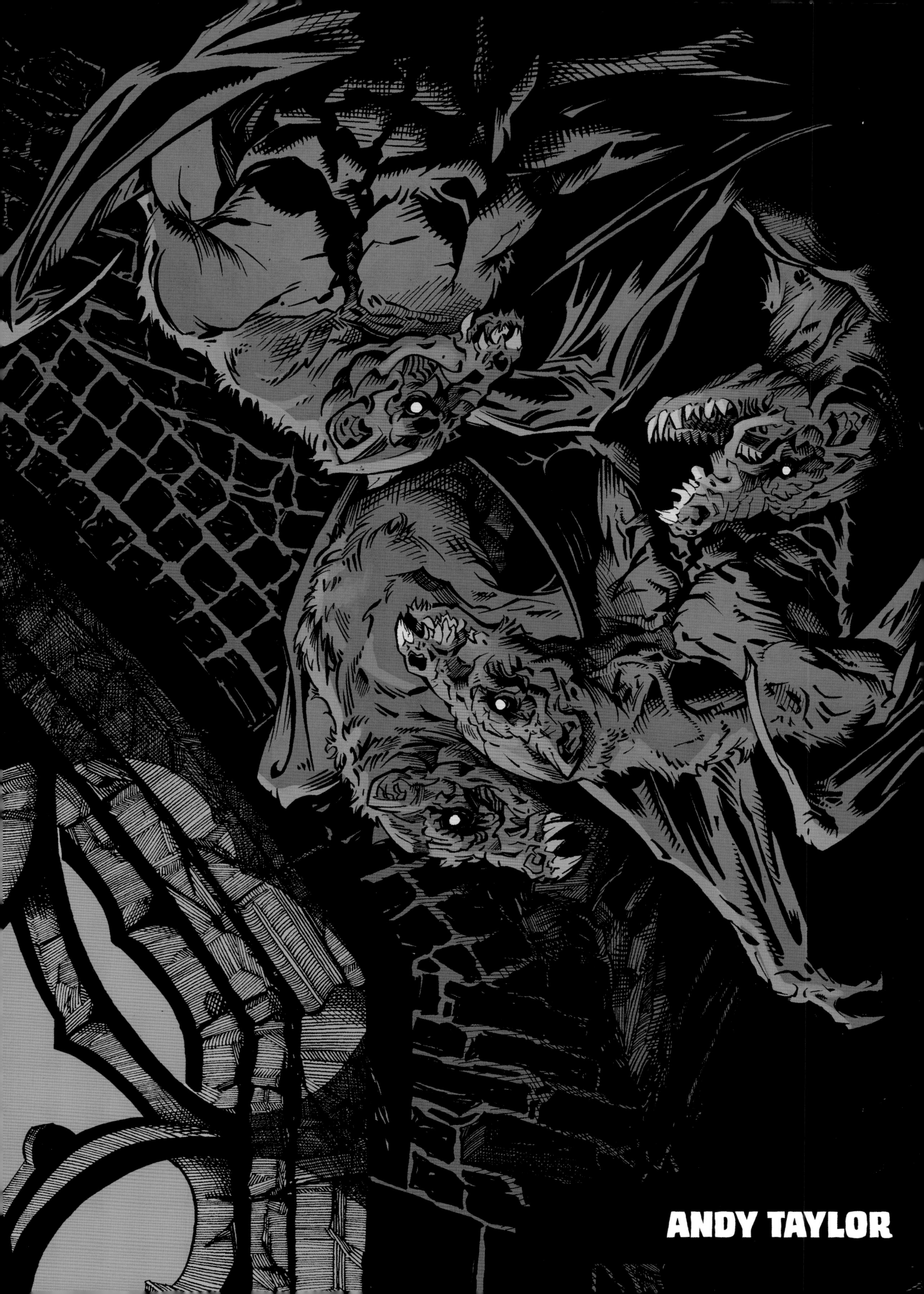
ANDY TAYLOR

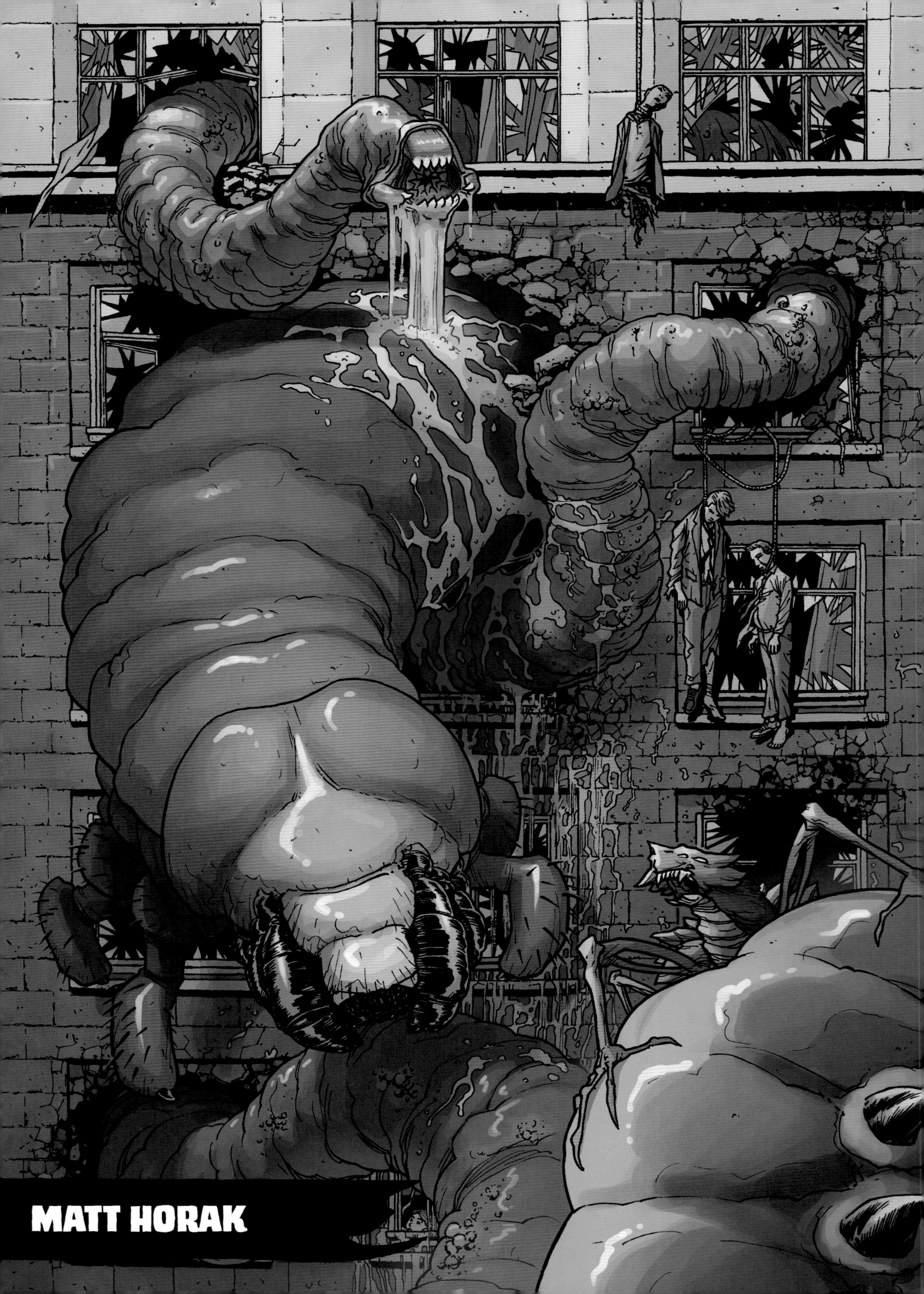
MATT HORAK

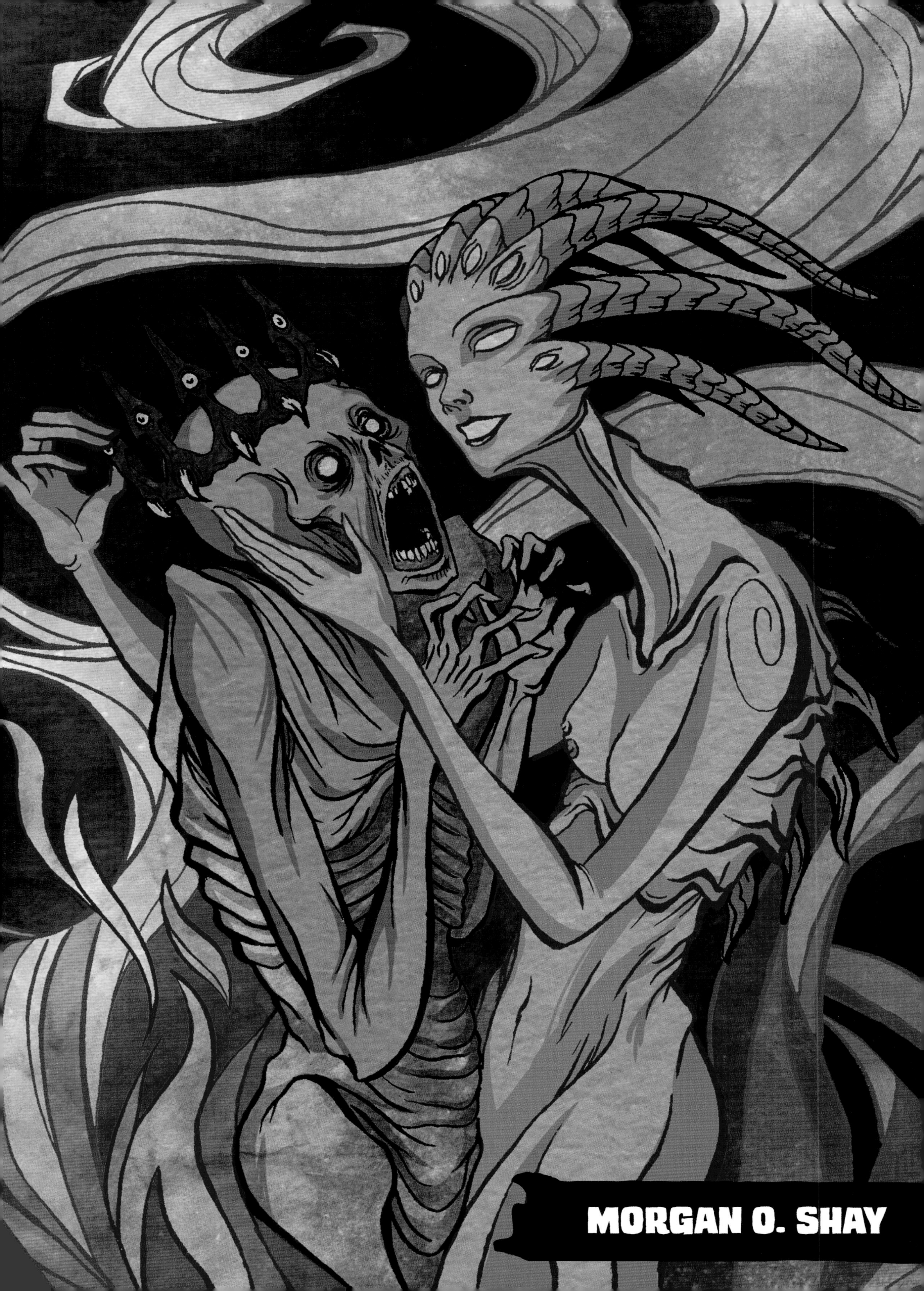
MORGAN O. SHAY

HOWLETT'S HYSTERICAL HORROR COMIC HISTORY

An Opinionated Essay by Mike Howlett

IN THE BEGINNING

Comic books, both as a form of entertainment and an industry, have had a checkered history. For every positive attribute, there has always been a downside; with every triumph, a failure. That notion has never been more clearly illustrated than with horror comics, the ugly kid sister of the medium. The genre has had a lot of critics over the years, but its true fans are rabid and loyal, if a bit unhinged. Parents, churches and even the government have tried to keep our horror comics from us. But like the zombies in their pages, they always seem to come back. Let's take a look at where it all started.

In the so-called "Golden Age" of comics, there were no horror titles. It's not that it wasn't a viable genre. Horror films had been popular for years, especially those from Universal Studios, like *Frankenstein, Dracula* (both 1931) and *The Mummy* (1932). Pulp magazines were also very popular, with titles like *Horror Stories, Terror Tales,* and *Weird Tales*, which featured stories by H.P. Lovecraft and a very young Robert Bloch, who remain titans of terror to this day. It took a while for horror to catch on with the Four-Color Crowd, however.

Of course, every superhero (which many of the popular comic characters were) needs a villain, every cop needs a criminal. Thus, several of the Golden Age ne'er-do-wells had horrific overtones, be they mad scientists or psycho murderers or some other unsavory character. In the beginning, most comics were anthology titles containing serials with continuing features and characters: a superhero, a reporter, a detective, etc. The December, 1940 issue of *Prize Comics* (#7) began serializing "The New Adventures of Frankenstein," written and drawn by the great Dick Briefer. While it was often more humorous or adventurous than horrific, some of the installments were pretty morbid.

Classic Comics (which later became *Classics Illustrated*, a series we all knew and pretended to love) adapted "Dr. Jekyll and Mr. Hyde" for its 13th issue in 1943, and later adapted other classic tales of terror (like "Frankenstein" in #27, 1945). Things were definitely headed in the right direction, however slowly.

In 1944, Charlton Comics, the pride of Derby, Connecticut, released the first issue of *Yellowjacket Comics*, another collection of adventure and superhero serials. Among the exploits of the do-gooders, however, was a feature called "Famous Tales of Terror." It figured into seven of the ten issues in the title's run. The first four installments were adaptations of Edgar Allan Poe stories, while the final three were hosted by an ancient witch storyteller. These were actual horror stories! Meanwhile, Briefer's Frankenstein earned his own book in 1945, although it was strictly a cartoon humor comic.

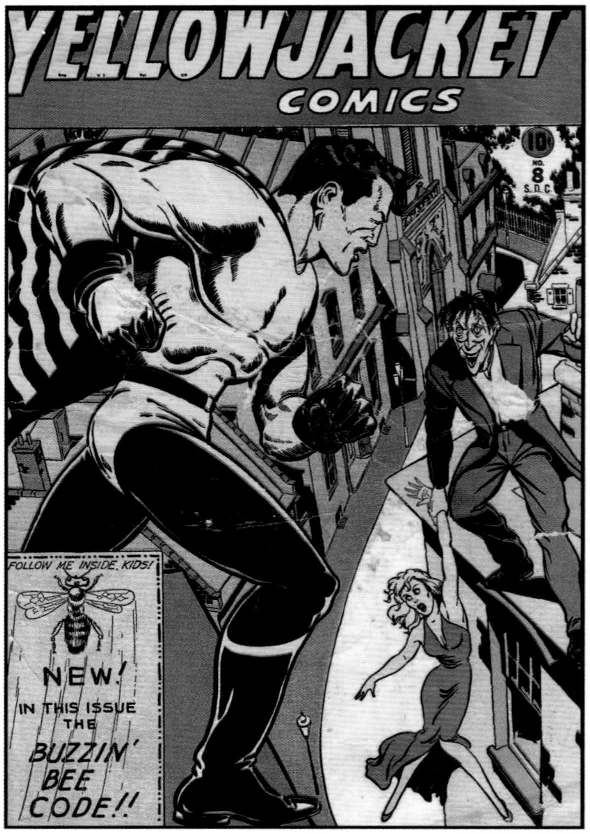
YELLOWJACKET
COMICS
10¢
NO. 8
FOLLOW ME INSIDE, KIDS!
NEW!
IN THIS ISSUE THE
BUZZIN' BEE CODE!!

Yellowjacket Comics #8 (Charlton- Feb. 1946)

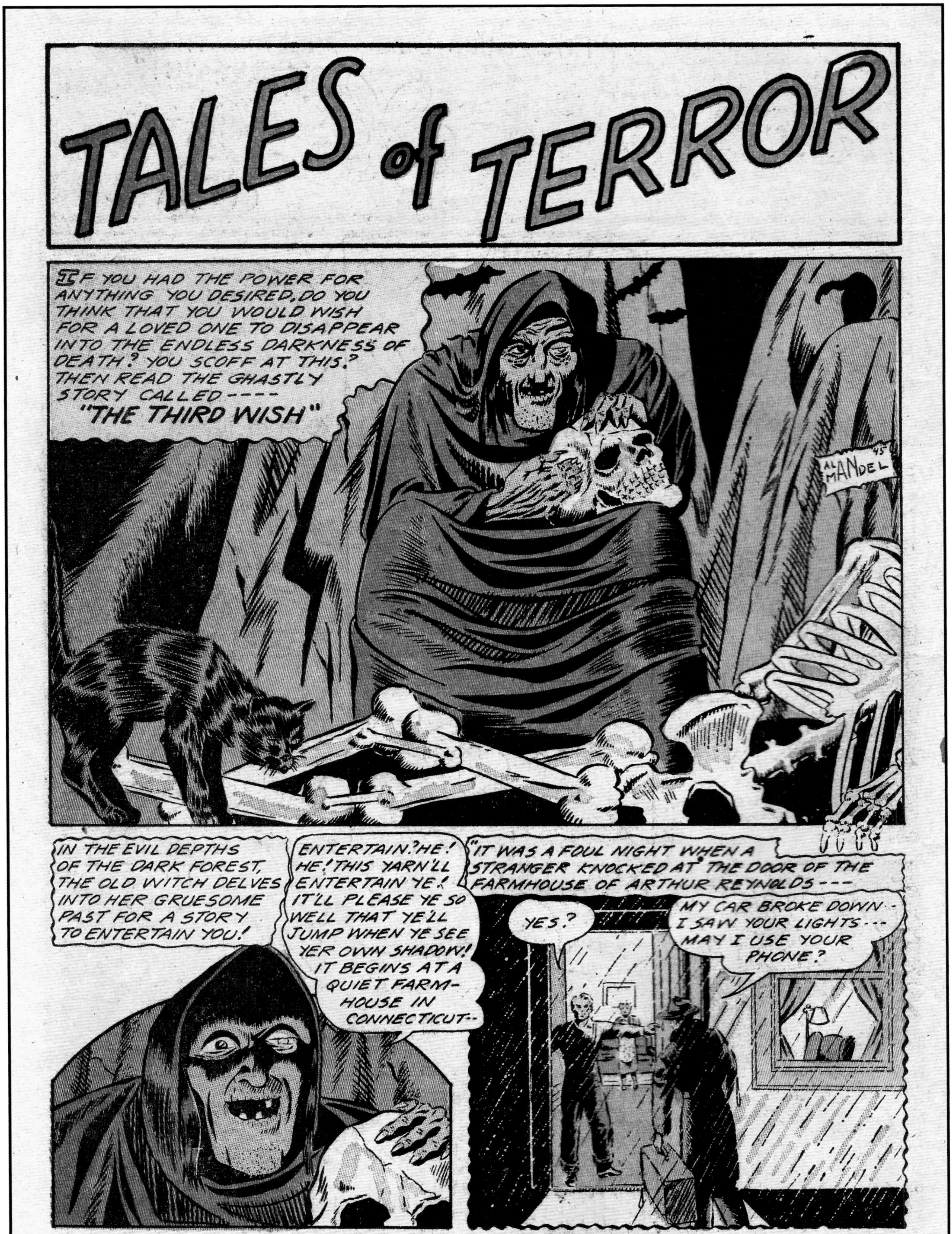
TALES of TERROR
IF YOU HAD THE POWER FOR ANYTHING YOU DESIRED, DO YOU THINK THAT YOU WOULD WISH FOR A LOVED ONE TO DISAPPEAR INTO THE ENDLESS DARKNESS OF DEATH? YOU SCOFF AT THIS? THEN READ THE GHASTLY STORY CALLED---- "THE THIRD WISH"
AL MANDEL '45
IN THE EVIL DEPTHS OF THE DARK FOREST, THE OLD WITCH DELVES INTO HER GRUESOME PAST FOR A STORY TO ENTERTAIN YOU!
ENTERTAIN? HE! HE! THIS YARN'LL ENTERTAIN YE! IT'LL PLEASE YE SO WELL THAT YE'LL JUMP WHEN YE SEE YER OWN SHADOW! IT BEGINS AT A QUIET FARM-HOUSE IN CONNECTICUT--
"IT WAS A FOUL NIGHT WHEN A STRANGER KNOCKED AT THE DOOR OF THE FARMHOUSE OF ARTHUR REYNOLDS---
YES?
MY CAR BROKE DOWN-I SAW YOUR LIGHTS---MAY I USE YOUR PHONE?

Tales of Terror splash from Yellowjacket Comics #8 (Charlton- Feb. 1946) art by Alan Mandell

DAWN OF AN ERA

With a cover date of January, 1947, Avon finally released the real deal... *Eerie Comics* #1. This was the first full-on horror comic book ever. Five complete horror tales (including "The Man-Eating Lizards," with artwork by Joe Kubert!), an eye-catching cover featuring a ghoul menacing a bound female victim (a fetish held over from the pulps) and even a scary text story. Avon was primarily a paperback publisher (they still are), but were also dabbling in comics at the time. Though the indicia says "published quarterly," only a single issue was released; Avon specialized in one-shots.

EERIE
COMICS
AN AVON COMIC
10¢
NO. 1

Eerie Comics #1 (Avon- Jan. 1947)

The next significant step in the history of horror comics came from American Comics Group (ACG), in the form of *Adventures into the Unknown*. The first issue, dated Fall 1948, had werewolves, ghosts and curses—just what horror fans had been craving. Best of all, the title wasn't going away soon. This was the first ongoing horror title of them all. Somewhat timid compared to what would soon come, the ACG horror stories were always very well drawn and intelligently written, if not particularly horrific. Let's call them "**spooky**."

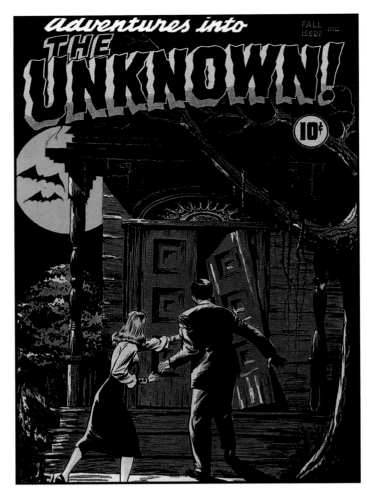

Adventures into
THE UNKNOWN!
FALL ISSUE
10¢

Adventures into the Unknown #1 (ACG- Fall 1948)
cover art by Edvard Moritz

That same year, creator Sheldon Moldoff pitched an idea for a "**supernatural**" comic to a very green William M. Gaines at EC Comics. Gaines had recently inherited the company upon his father's death and was looking for new ideas. He liked Moldoff's idea for *Tales of the Supernatural* and, so, agreed to publish it. Unfortunately, the deal for the new title fell through, but Gaines sprinkled the finished stories into issues of *Moon Girl* and *Crime Patrol* over the next two years.

At roughly the same time, Gaines had brought Al Feldstein on board at EC, originally for a teen comic. As that genre was losing popularity, the two looked into setting the trend, rather than following it. They were both horror fans, specifically of the old radio shows like *Lights Out* and *The Witch's Tale*, the latter hosted by a cackling, old—you guessed it—witch. They thought that a flat out horror comic could be the next big trend. The duo concocted some chilling tales and introduced them into the last two issues of EC's crime comics, *Crime Patrol* and *War Against Crime*. Like their beloved radio shows, each horror story had a scary host, the Crypt-Keeper in *Crime Patrol* and the Vault Keeper in *War Against Crime*. Of course, the stories were a huge hit and the face of comics was to change forever.

EC TERROR TALES

The crime titles were dropped in favor of *The Crypt of Terror* (changed to *Tales from the Crypt* after three issues) and *The Vault of Horror*, whose debut issues bore a cover date of April/ May 1950. The next month, a third title, *The Haunt of Fear* was introduced and the ball was really rolling. Early issues were still finding their way but the terror-trio soon hit their stride and begat an era of comics that will never be forgotten. Gaines and Feldstein wrote imaginative, adult stories with intelligent twist endings. They created not only the best horror comics, but perhaps the best comics of all time. Now, there will always be some contrarian who contends that EC was OK but so-and-so was better, but that's just someone trying to be confrontational. I mean, it's like saying the Gary Cherone era was Van Halen's high point. Gaines and Feldstein gathered the finest art staff and encouraged them (and paid them well) to go above and beyond. And they did.

The EC horror comics are the true blueprints of everything that would follow. They had their hosts (*The Haunt of Fear* introduced The Old Witch), their ever-present dark humor and four tight, well-written tales every issue. And that artwork… EC's stable of artists reads like a who's-who of comic art legends. Jack Davis, Johnny Craig, Jack Kamen, Reed Crandall, George Evans, Wally Wood, Joe Orlando, Al Williamson and editor Al Feldstein, among others, all created timeless artwork that still holds up over a half century later. Let us not forget "Ghastly" Graham Ingels, whose inimitable style is the very image of horror itself. Twisted, gnarled characters, with strings of drool stretching between their wormy lips, inhabited dank, murky landscapes, and putrescent graveyards. Ingels' spidery, fine inks spill into thick black shadows; his atmospheric artwork was a real study in lighting… or the lack of it. So deep and evil were Ghastly's shadows that Gaines and Feldstein played to his strengths and concocted a tale about a killer shadow for him to illustrate (*"Shadow of Death"* in *Tales from the Crypt* #39).

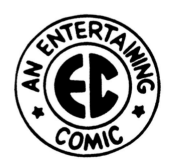

The EC Comics logo

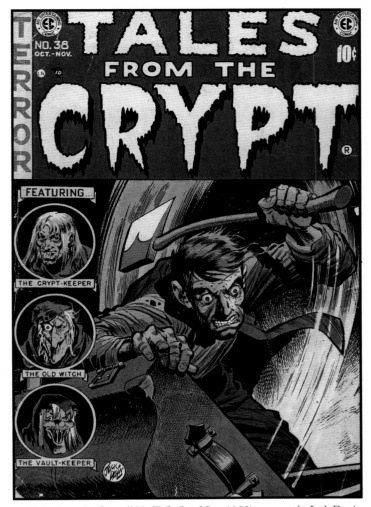

TALES FROM THE CRYPT
TERROR
NO. 38
OCT.-NOV.
10¢
FEATURING...
THE CRYPT-KEEPER
THE OLD WITCH
THE VAULT-KEEPER

Tales from the Crypt #38 (EC- Oct. Nov. 1953) cover art by Jack Davis

THE VAULT OF HORROR
NO. 34
DEC.-JAN.
10¢
FEATURING...
THE VAULT-KEEPER
THE CRYPT-KEEPER
THE OLD WITCH

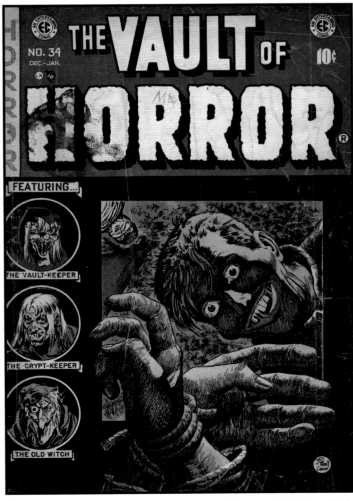

Vault of Horror #34 (EC- Dec. Jan. 1952-53) cover art by Johnny Craig

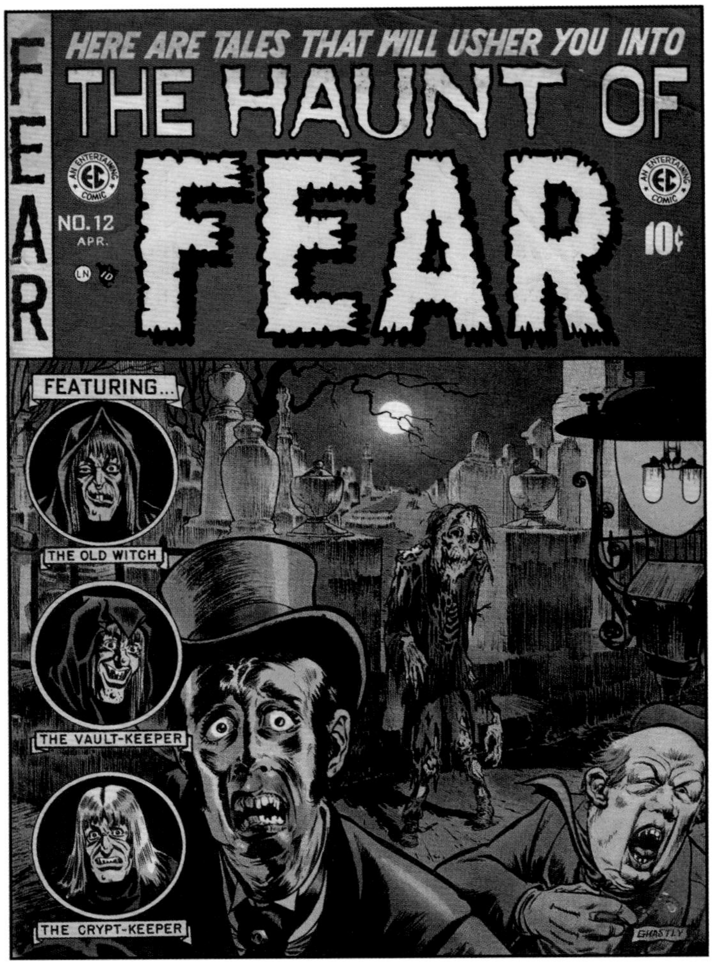
HERE ARE TALES THAT WILL USHER YOU INTO
THE HAUNT OF
FEAR
FEAR
NO. 12
APR.
10¢
FEATURING...
THE OLD WITCH
THE VAULT-KEEPER
THE CRYPT-KEEPER

Haunt of Fear #12 (EC- Mar. Apr. 1952) cover art by Graham Ingels

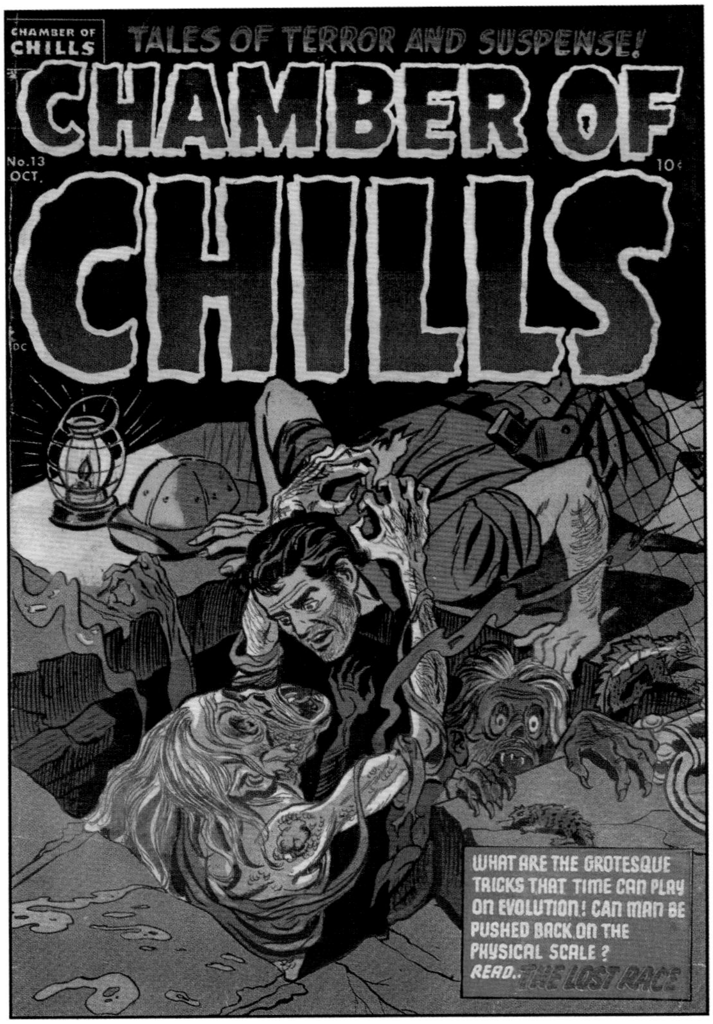
CHAMBER OF CHILLS
TALES OF TERROR AND SUSPENSE!
CHAMBER OF
CHILLS
No.13
OCT.
10¢
WHAT ARE THE GROTESQUE TRICKS THAT TIME CAN PLAY ON EVOLUTION! CAN MAN BE PUSHED BACK ON THE PHYSICAL SCALE? READ.. THE LOST RACE

Chamber of Chills #13 (Harvey- Oct. 1952) cover art by Al Avison

GROWING TERROR

The horror comics were huge sellers, and the bandwagon jumping was fast and furious. By 1952, there were over twenty different publishers with their own horror titles. Soon, there were 50 titles fighting for space every month on comic racks across the country. Some were great, some were dull, but in retrospect, all were of interest. Atlas Comics (now Marvel) had tested the horror waters in 1949 for two issues of *Amazing Mysteries*. They sure struck while the iron was hot; they had well over a dozen different horror titles on the market during the boom. Atlas horror comics featured excellent artwork from the likes of Bill Everett, Russ Heath and the great Joe Maneely. Harvey Comics, now known primarily for kiddie fare like *Richie Rich* and *Casper*, had a quartet of very good horror titles and a fine bullpen of creators, including Bob Powell, still a fan favorite.

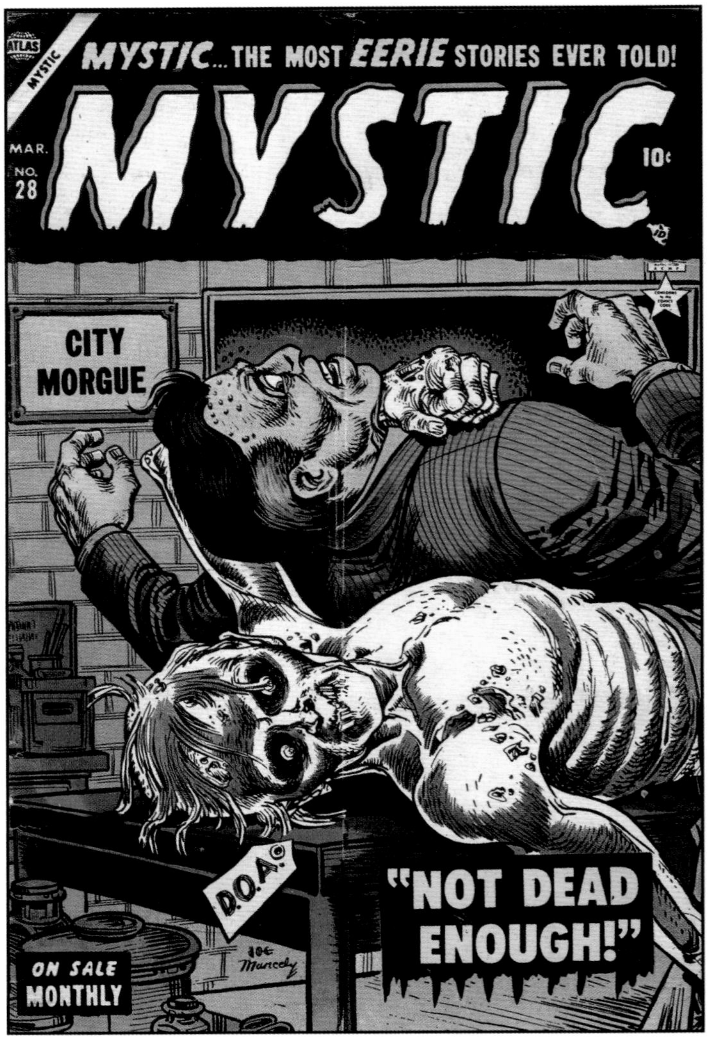
MYSTIC... THE MOST EERIE STORIES EVER TOLD!
MYSTIC
MAR.
NO.
28
10¢
CITY MORGUE
D.O.A.
"NOT DEAD ENOUGH!"
ON SALE MONTHLY

Mystic #28 (Atlas- Mar. 1954) cover art by Joe Maneely ▶

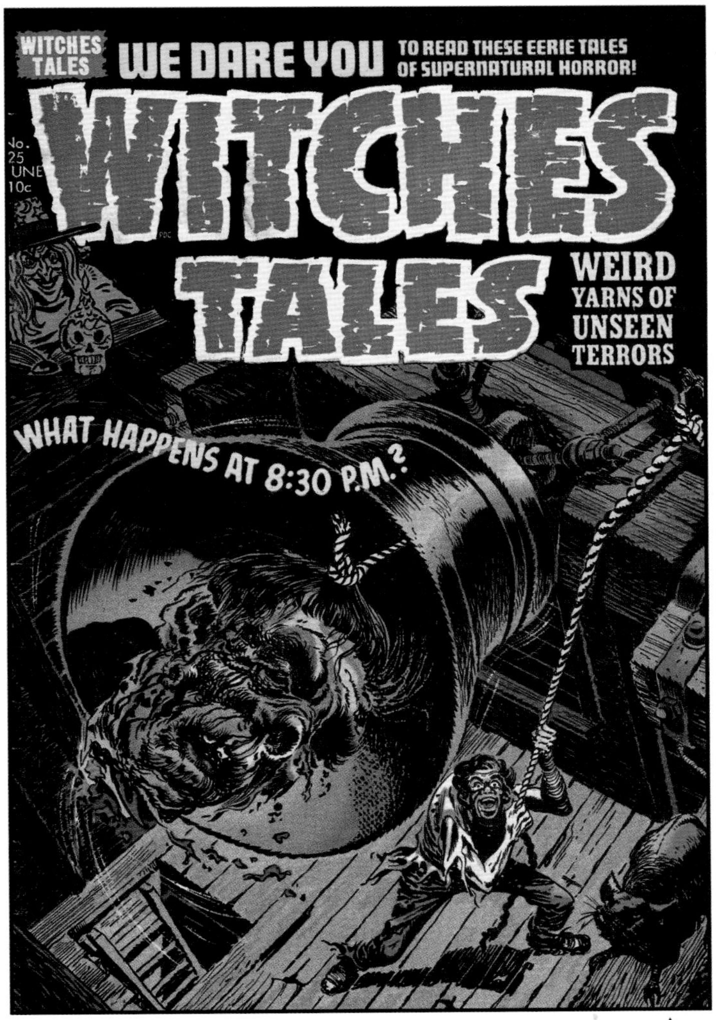
WITCHES TALES
WE DARE YOU
TO READ THESE EERIE TALES OF SUPERNATURAL HORROR!
No. 25
JUNE
10c
WITCHES TALES
WEIRD YARNS OF UNSEEN TERRORS
WHAT HAPPENS AT 8:30 P.M.?

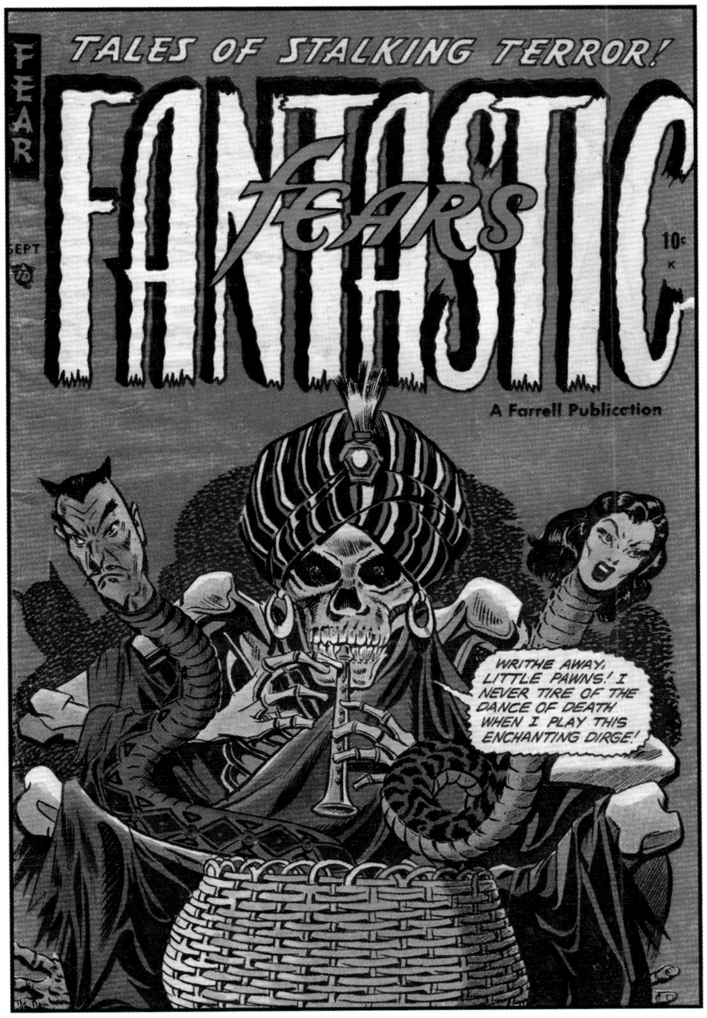
TALES OF STALKING TERROR!
FEAR
SEPT
FANTASTIC FEARS
10¢
A Farrell Publiccation
WRITHE AWAY, LITTLE PAWNS! I NEVER TIRE OF THE DANCE OF DEATH WHEN I PLAY THIS ENCHANTING DIRGE!

Witches Tales #25 (Harvey- June 1954) cover art by Warren Kremer ▲

▲ *Fantastic Fears #3 (Ajax- Sept. 1953) cover art by The Iger Shop*

Beware! Terror Tales #6 (Fawcett- Mar. 1953) ▼

▼ *Haunted Thrills #1 (Ajax- June 1951) cover art by The Iger Shop*

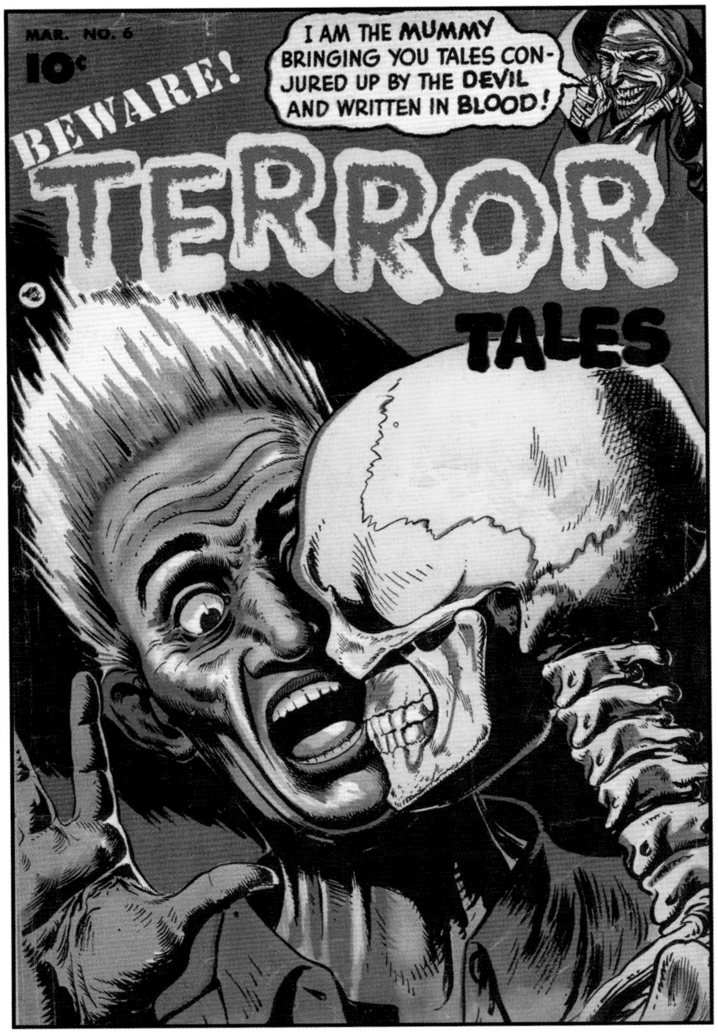
MAR. NO. 6
10¢
I AM THE MUMMY BRINGING YOU TALES CONJURED UP BY THE DEVIL AND WRITTEN IN BLOOD!
BEWARE!
TERROR
TALES

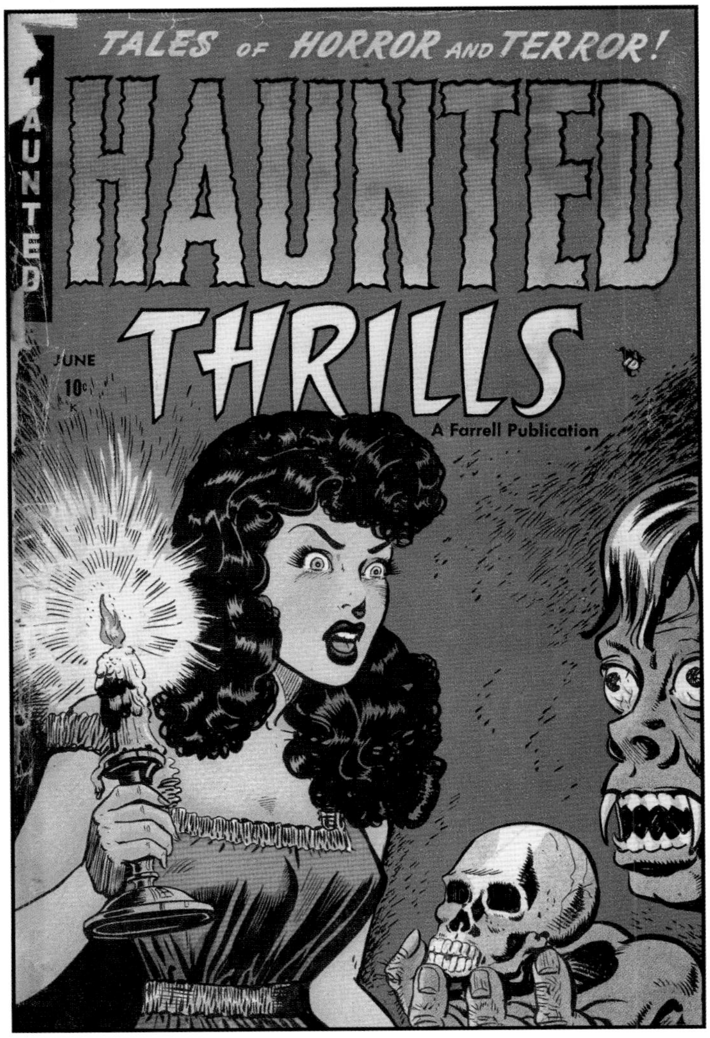
TALES OF HORROR AND TERROR!
HAUNTED
HAUNTED THRILLS
JUNE
10¢
A Farrell Publication

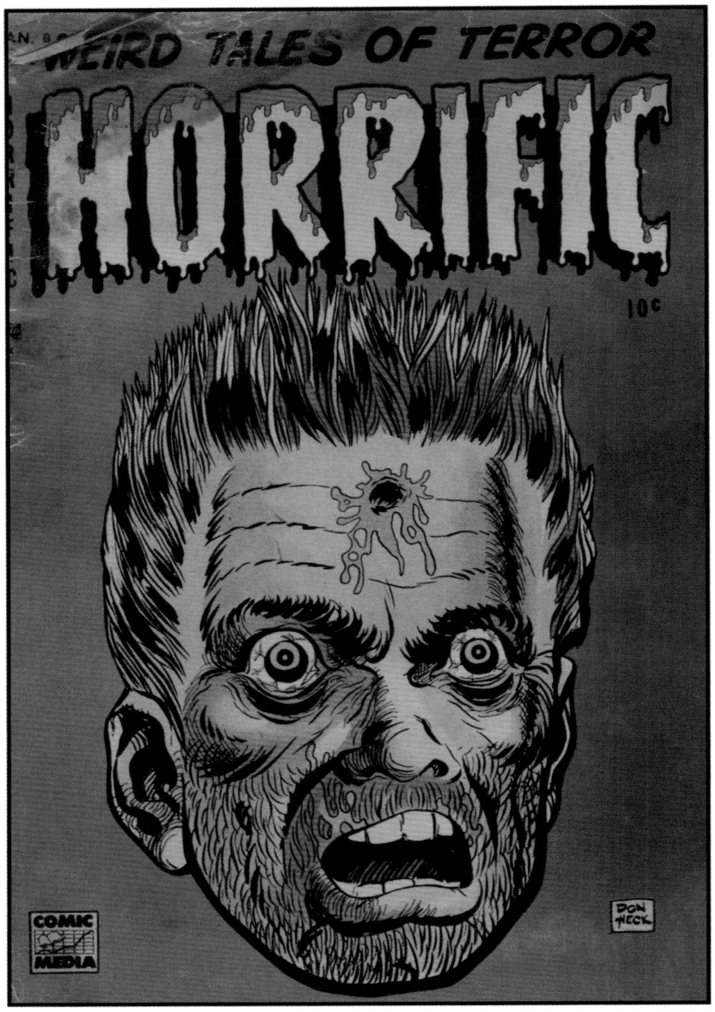
WEIRD TALES OF TERROR
HORRIFIC
10¢
COMIC MEDIA
DON HECK

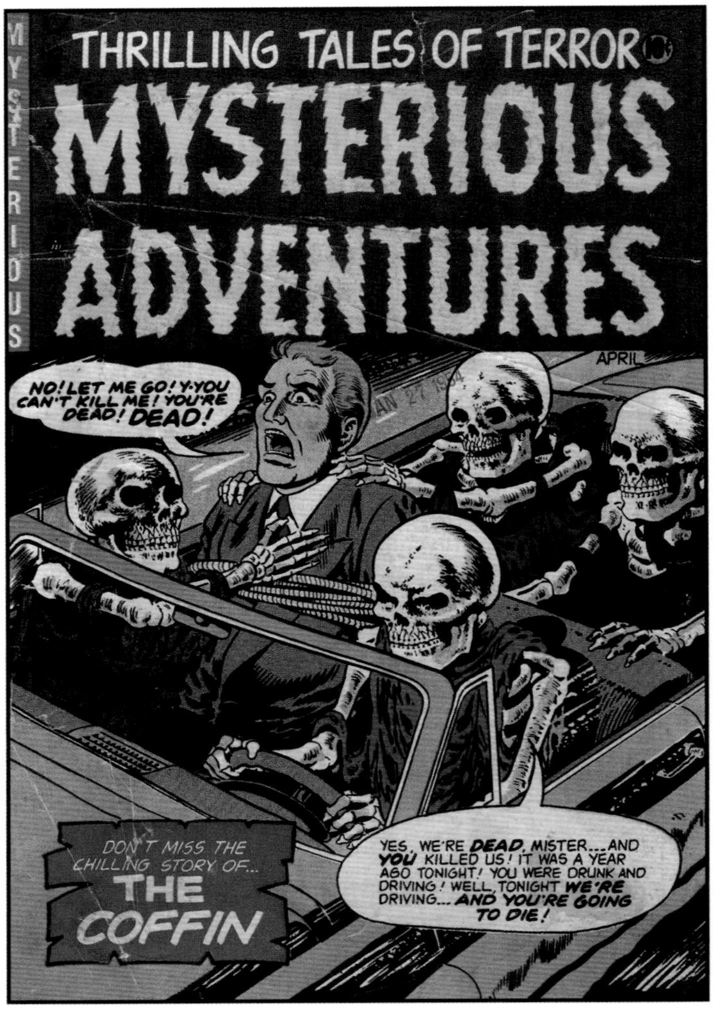
THRILLING TALES OF TERROR
MYSTERIOUS ADVENTURES
APRIL
NO! LET ME GO! Y-YOU CAN'T KILL ME! YOU'RE DEAD! DEAD!
DON'T MISS THE CHILLING STORY OF... THE COFFIN
YES, WE'RE DEAD, MISTER... AND YOU KILLED US! IT WAS A YEAR AGO TONIGHT! YOU WERE DRUNK AND DRIVING! WELL, TONIGHT WE'RE DRIVING... AND YOU'RE GOING TO DIE!

Horrific #3 (Comic Media- Jan. 1953) cover art by Don Heck ▲

▲ *Mysterious Adventures #19 (Story- Apr. 1954)*

Mister Mystery #13 (Gillmore- Sept. Oct. 1953) cover art by Bernard Bailey ▼

▼ *Out of the Shadows #7 (Standard- Jan. 1953) cover art by Jack Katz*

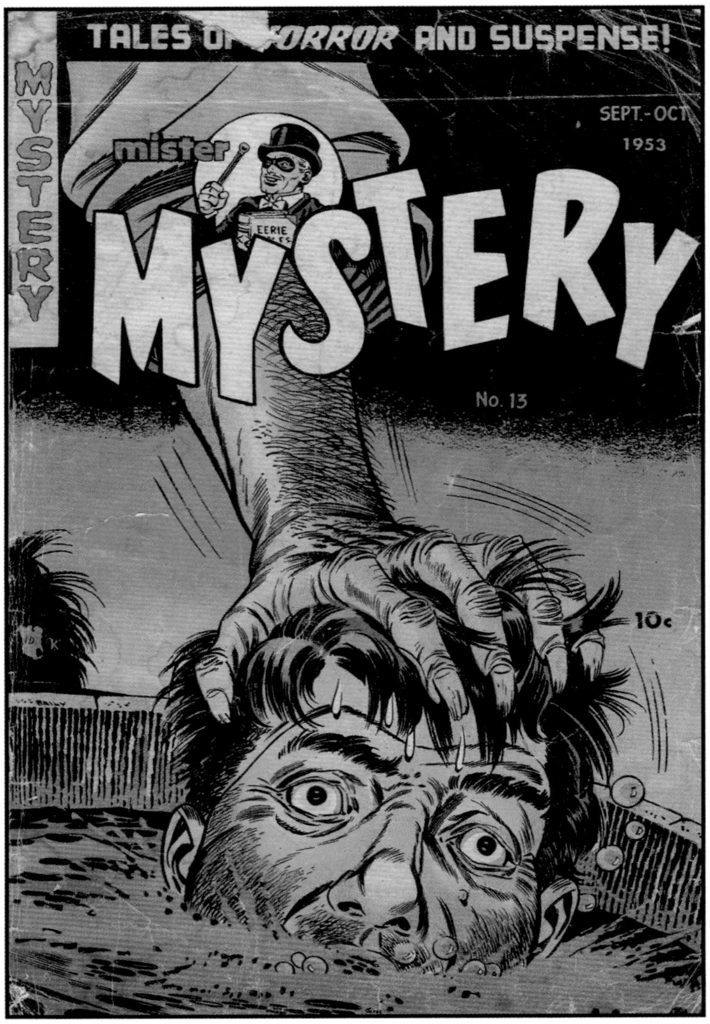
TALES OF HORROR AND SUSPENSE!
SEPT.-OCT 1953
mister MYSTERY
MYSTERY
No. 13
10¢

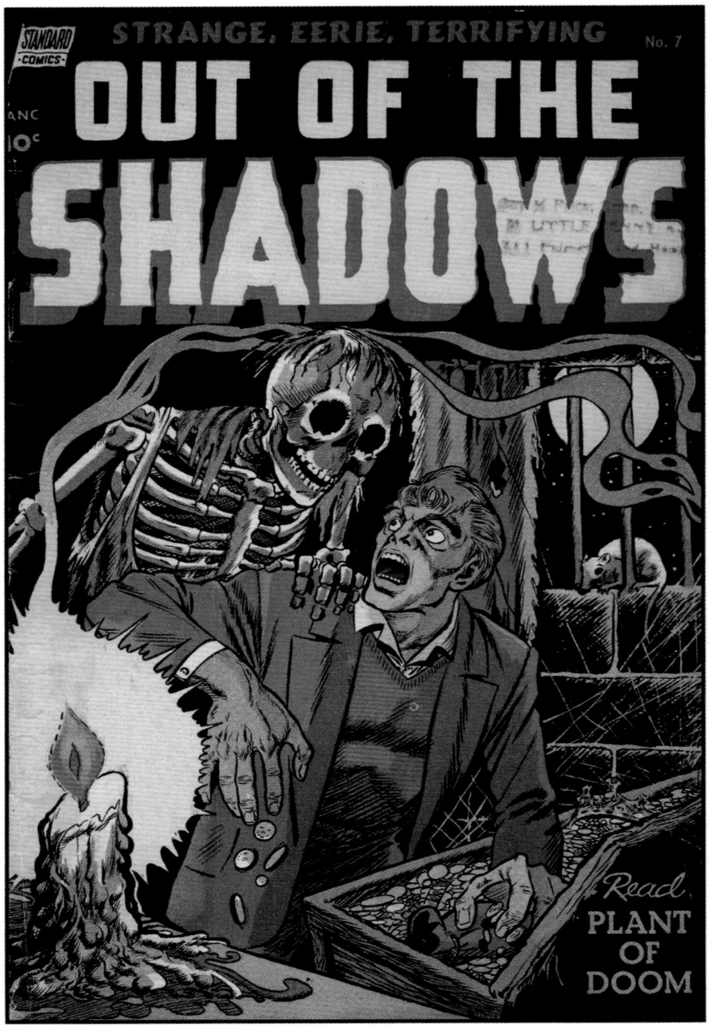
STANDARD COMICS
STRANGE, EERIE, TERRIFYING
No. 7
OUT OF THE SHADOWS
10¢
Read PLANT OF DOOM

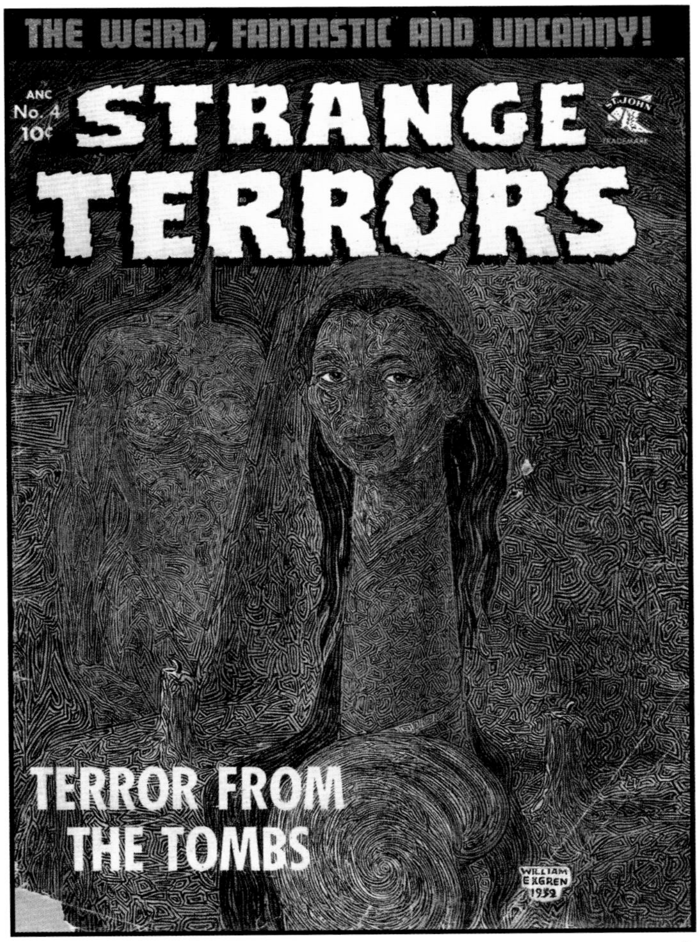
THE WEIRD, FANTASTIC AND UNCANNY!
ANC No. 4 10¢
STRANGE TERRORS
TERROR FROM THE TOMBS
WILLIAM EKGREN 1952

Strange Terrors #4 (St. John- Nov. 1952) cover art by William Ekgren ▲

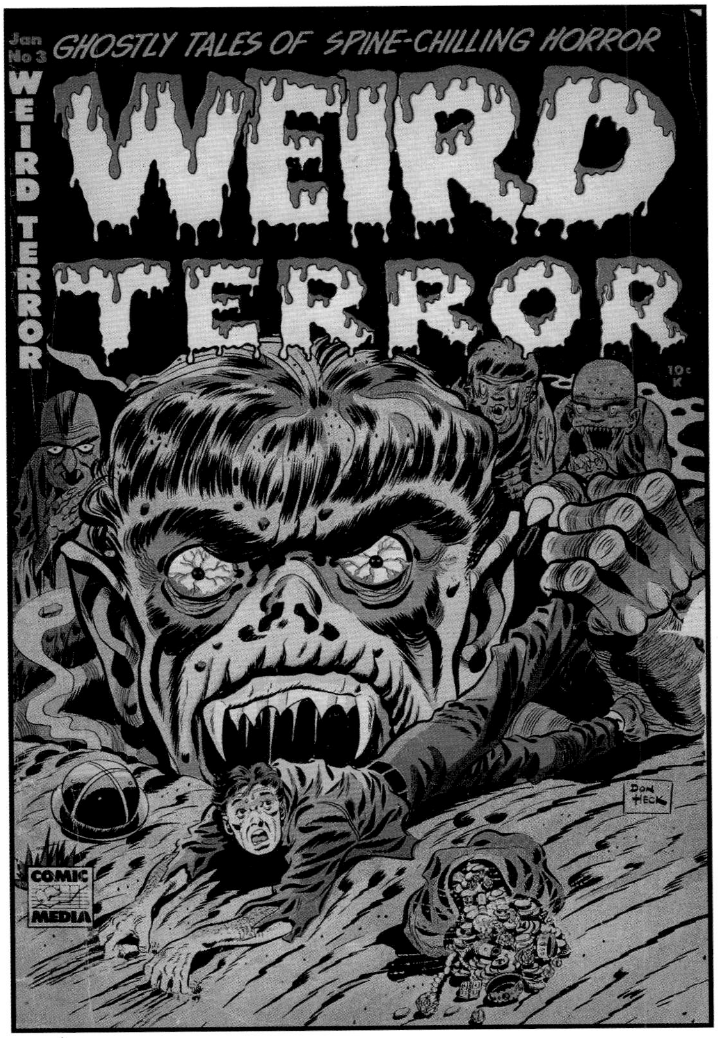
Jan No 3
GHOSTLY TALES OF SPINE-CHILLING HORROR
WEIRD TERROR
WEIRD TERROR
10¢ K
DON HECK
COMIC MEDIA

▲ *Weird Terror #3 (Comic Media- Jan. 1953) cover art by Don Heck*

Weird Mysteries #12 (Gillmore- Sept. 1954) cover art by Bernard Bailey ▼

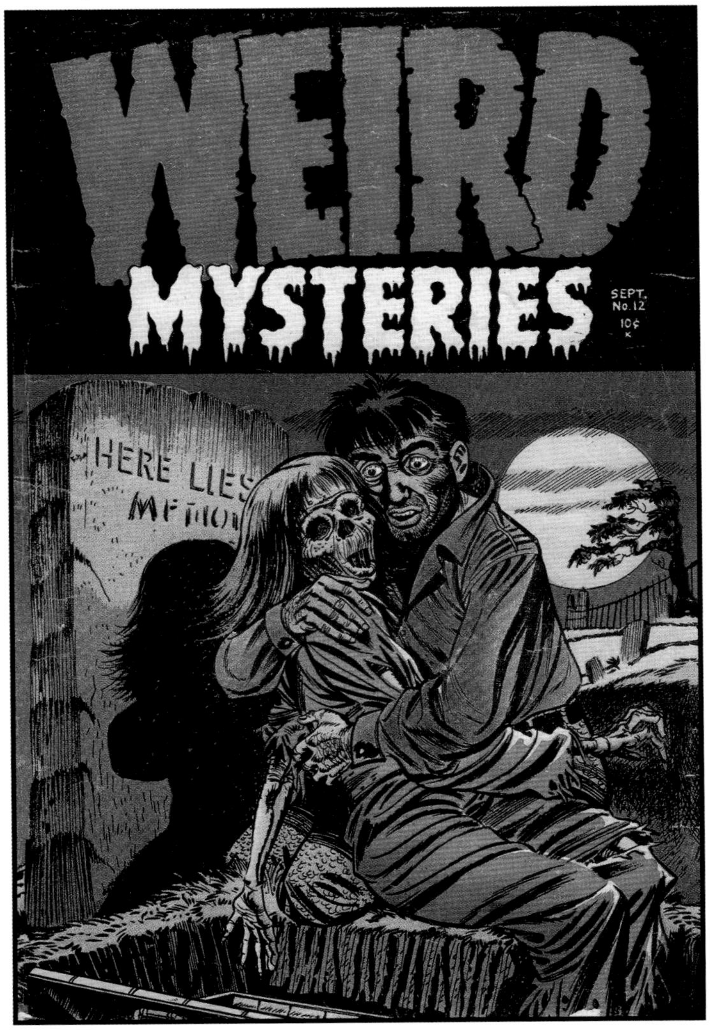
WEIRD MYSTERIES
SEPT. No. 12 10¢ K
HERE LIES

▼ *Worlds of Fear #9 (Fawcett- April 1953)*

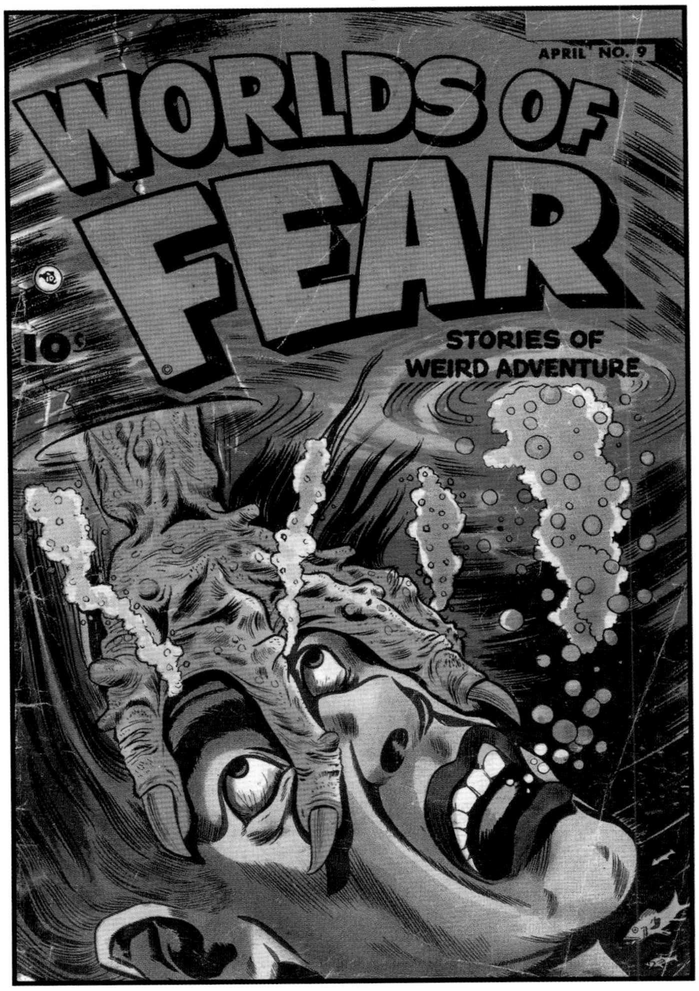
APRIL NO. 9
WORLDS OF FEAR
10¢
STORIES OF WEIRD ADVENTURE

SAVE OUR SOULS

With dozens of new horror comics jamming the stands every week, it was all important to be noticed. Comic Media did just that on their horror title *Horrific,* which featured close-up, terrifying faces on their covers, drawn by Don Heck. Both Gillmore and Fawcett utilized the talents of Bernard Bailey as a cover artist to catch the customer's eye. The stories inside all of these comics got more over the top in an effort to compete. Even Prize's *Frankenstein,* which had gone from cartoon humor to straight horror (while still being expertly written and drawn by Briefer) in early 1952, got in on the gory action. The titular character kills a victim by pouring molten metal down his esophagus in issue #30! Holy fuck! That would hurt! Vampires sucking blood, werewolves shredding flesh, ghouls eating the dead, decapitations, dismemberment, walking corpses seeking revenge, acid baths—it was the gory glory days of horror comics, all in blood-stained color, for a dime. It was a nightmare come true, but could this beautiful carnage last forever? Surely someone would step in and rain on the parade, surely our souls needed saving.

The world always has been and always will be populated with people who think they know what is best for us and need to tell us how to live. Our self-appointed "savior" at that time was psychiatrist Frederic Wertham. His book, *Seduction of the Innocent,* was released in early 1954 and whipped its readers into an anti-comic book frenzy. He purported that comic books led to juvenile delinquency. So many eyebrows were raised by his (sometimes falsified) data and case studies, that a Senate Subcommittee on Juvenile Delinquency was formed, to investigate these charges. Parents got involved, blaming comics for society's ills, because it was easier to have a scapegoat than to actually be a responsible parent. The hearings were a witch hunt. All comics were on trial, but horror and crime books took the brunt of the abuse. William Gaines was brought to the stand on behalf of the comic industry and he was raked across the coals.

Inevitably, the hearings proved nothing. Even if little Johnny wasn't going to pour molten metal down anyone's esophagus, like in the funny books, the damage had been done; the bad press was just too much. Pressure from pitiful, sheep-like parents who couldn't think for themselves (and were outraged by comics because they were told they were supposed to be) made it tough for news agents to display the verboten comics. The industry adopted a self-censorship program; a comic now had to display its seal of approval. Anything resembling a horror or crime comic would not get the seal. Ridiculous standards were set in order to rid the world of horror comics; no vampires, werewolves, ghouls, zombies, bloodshed, cannibalism, gruesome drawings or any other horror comic standards would pass muster. They couldn't use the word "terror," "horror," or even "weird" in a title.

GENERAL STANDARDS PART B

1. No comics magazine shall use the word horror or terror in its title.

2. All scenes of horror, excessive bloodshed, gory or gruesome crimes, depravity, lust, sadism, masochism shall not be permitted.

3. All lurid, unsavory, gruesome illustrations shall be eliminated.

4. Inclusion of stories dealing with evil shall be used or shall be published only where the intent is to illustrate a moral issue and in no case shall evil be presented alluringly nor as to injure the sensibilities of the reader.

5. Scenes dealing with, or instruments associated with walking dead, torture, vampires and vampirism, ghouls, cannibalism and werewolfism are prohibited.

We never stood a chance! This, from the actual comic code, forbids any of the good stuff!

Horror was outlawed. Some publishers tried releasing their books without the code but the product was returned, still tied in bundles. They would not be displayed. To this day, comic fans get angered by this part of our collective history. Hell, this all went down nearly ten years before I was born and I still take it personally!

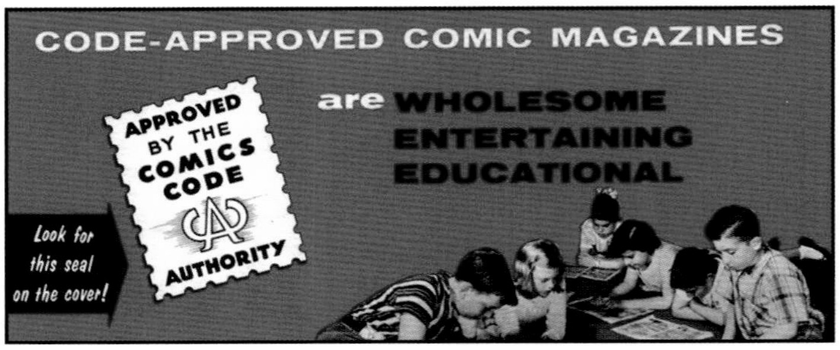
CODE-APPROVED COMIC MAGAZINES
are WHOLESOME
ENTERTAINING
EDUCATIONAL
APPROVED BY THE COMICS CODE AUTHORITY
Look for this seal on the cover!

Just what we wanted...

Of course, with the code in place, many comic companies went belly up; they closed shop or moved on to other ventures. Many creators were out of work. Some companies, like ACG and National (DC), who never pushed the envelope much to begin with, existed nicely within the code. Atlas changed over to a family-friendly fantasy format. Bill Gaines attempted to play by the rules with a few code-approved comics, but it just wasn't in his heart. Shed no tears for him, though; he put his energy into EC's only remaining title, *Mad,* which he had changed to a magazine format (thus bypassing the code) and stayed with it for the rest of his life. He died in 1992, a very wealthy man.

MONSTER MAGS

In 1956, when the Silver Age of comics was ushered in, there were no actual horror comics. The superhero genre became king and pretty much saved the industry. Fear fans were shit out of luck, and it stayed that way. Publishers were unwilling to test the code. Not everything was total crap. Charlton, Atlas, and a few others put out **suspense** and **mystery** titles with decent artwork and dark situations, but it was impossible to write a compelling (much less a scary) horror tale while handcuffed by the restrictions of the code.

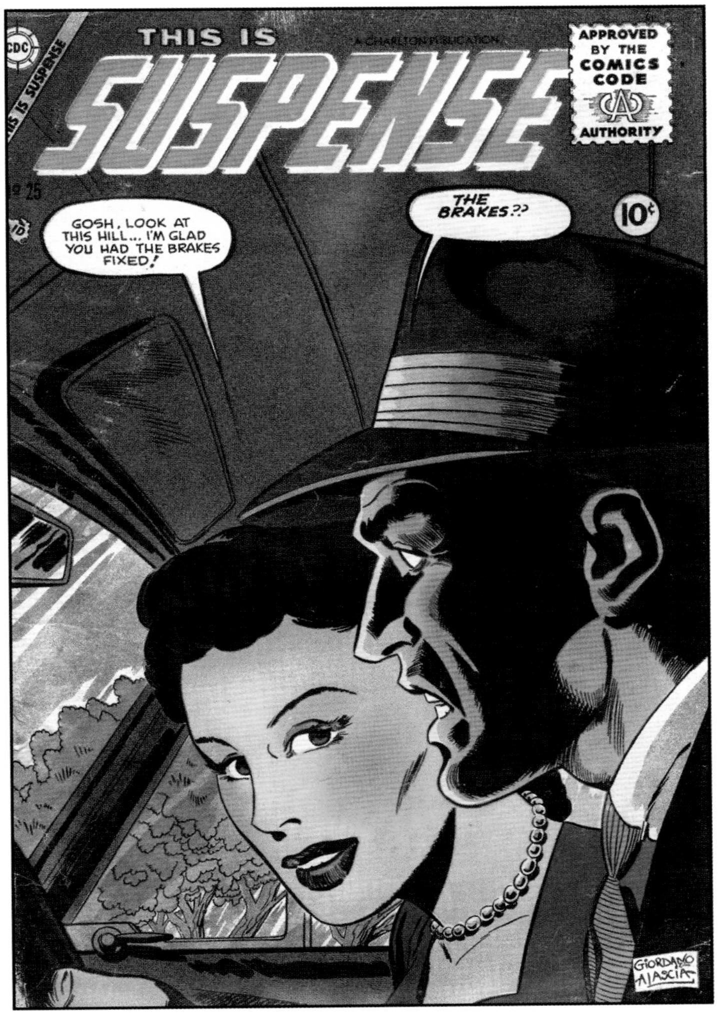
THIS IS
SUSPENSE
APPROVED BY THE COMICS CODE AUTHORITY
10¢
GOSH, LOOK AT THIS HILL... I'M GLAD YOU HAD THE BRAKES FIXED!
THE BRAKES??
GIORDANO ALASCIA

Sketchy brakes... not exactly a bloodthirsty werewolf, is it?
This Is Suspense #25 (Charlton- June 1955)

Horror fans went looking for thrills elsewhere. By 1957, American International Pictures was raking in the cash with movies about teenage werewolves, saucermen and she-monsters. Later that year, terror came to the television screen when the *Shock Theater* movie package was released, and the country was able to see Frankenstein, Dracula, and other Universal Studios monsters in their living rooms. Monster mania was sweeping the USA! Publisher James Warren and his editor Forrest Ackerman struck gold with the beautifully-timed release of their new monster mag, *Famous Monsters of Filmland.* Planned as a one-shot, they quickly decided to keep it going. It became the bible to the fans of the new monster craze.

Loads of monster magazine knock-offs followed, and monsters were invading comics again, as well. 1959 saw Joe Simon experiment with two black-and-white horror comic mags, *Weird Mysteries* and *Eerie Tales.* Funky distribution and ill timing thwarted any future issues, but these mysterious one-shots are rare and in demand today. Though clearly not horror comics, Atlas unleashed a slew of big monster, sci-fi/fantasy comics in the late '50s and early '60s. Drawn by Jack Kirby and usually inked by Dick Ayers, there were monsters with names like Rommbu, Kraa, and Bruttu, many of whom inexplicably wore a diaper or sarong (c'mon Jack, if you're not going to draw their junk, you don't need to be so modest!). Big monsters from space thwarted by milquetoast scientists; it was a formula that worked.

In 1962, Dell Comics (who never subscribed to the code, because their bread and butter comics were titles like *Bugs Bunny* and *Donald Duck*) put out two of the best actual horror comics of the era; *Ghost Stories* #1 (Sept. Nov.), and the one-shot *Tales from the Tomb* (October). The stories in both were written by John Stanley, best known for *Little Lulu*, who stepped outside of his comfort zone and penned some superior horror yarns that still hold up today.

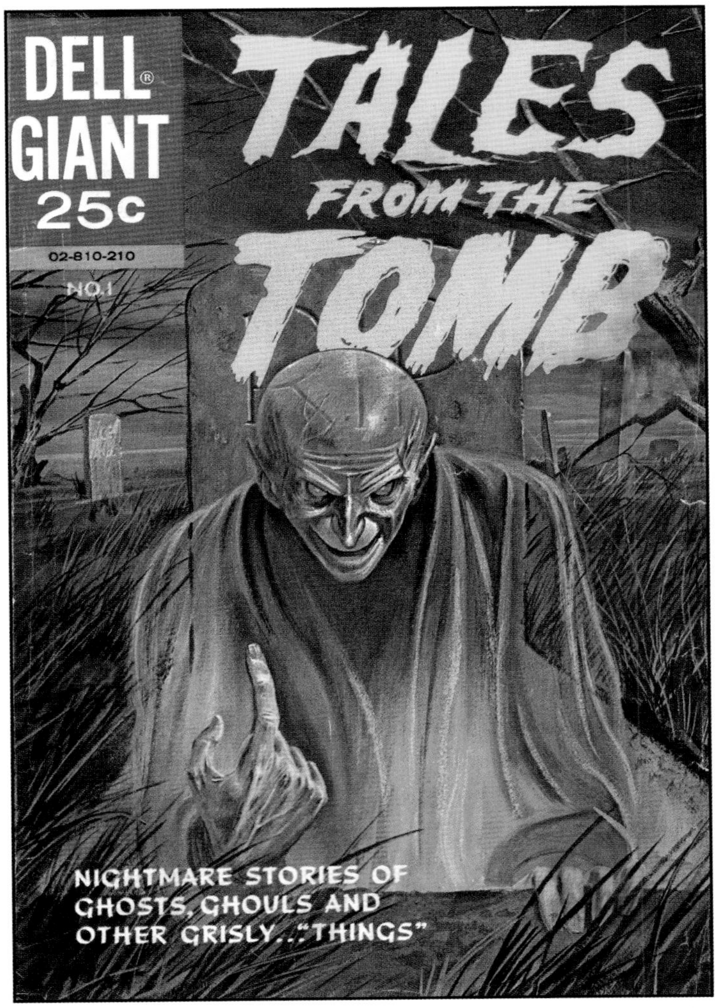
DELL GIANT
25c
02-810-210
NO.1
TALES FROM THE TOMB
NIGHTMARE STORIES OF GHOSTS, GHOULS AND OTHER GRISLY..."THINGS"

Tales from the Tomb #1 (Dell- 1962) cover art by L. B. Cole

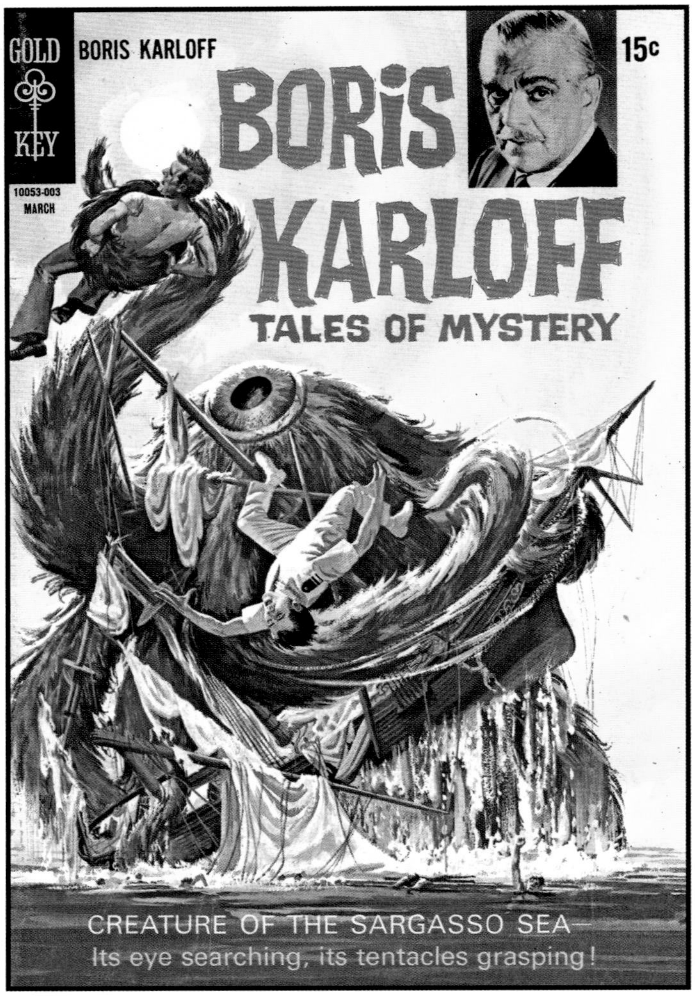
GOLD KEY
BORIS KARLOFF
15c
10053-003
MARCH
BORIS KARLOFF
TALES OF MYSTERY
CREATURE OF THE SARGASSO SEA—
Its eye searching, its tentacles grasping!

Boris Karloff Tales of Mystery #29 (Gold Key- Mar. 1970)

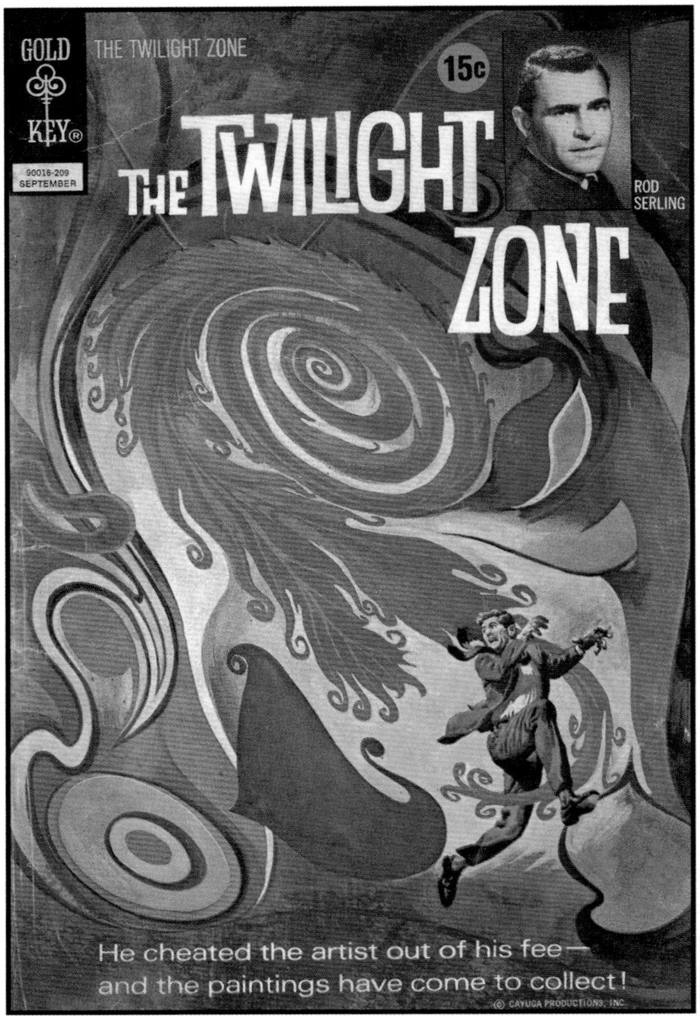
GOLD KEY
THE TWILIGHT ZONE
15c
90018-209
SEPTEMBER
THE TWILIGHT ZONE
ROD SERLING
He cheated the artist out of his fee—
and the paintings have come to collect!

Twilight Zone #45 (Gold Key- Sept. 1972)

That same year, Dell/ Gold Key licensed the rights to *The Twilight Zone* and *Boris Karloff Thriller*. Both titles had hosts (Rod Serling, for the former, of course) drawn into the splash panels and featured multiple stories in an anthology format. With Issue #3, *Thriller* became *Boris Karloff's Tales of Mystery* and enjoyed a long run. The stories dealt with the occult and supernatural, with a good dose of monsters, and they satisfied the horror itch to some extent. Dell also (very, very loosely) adapted popular monster films into comic form, like *The Creature* and *The Mummy*. They were also Code-free, but played it very safe.

The real draw of the Gold Key and Dell comics are the lush painted covers. Many of these colorful paintings remain uncredited but they are consistently good and eye-catching. Dell's film adaptations often used photo covers and movie-poster art, as well.

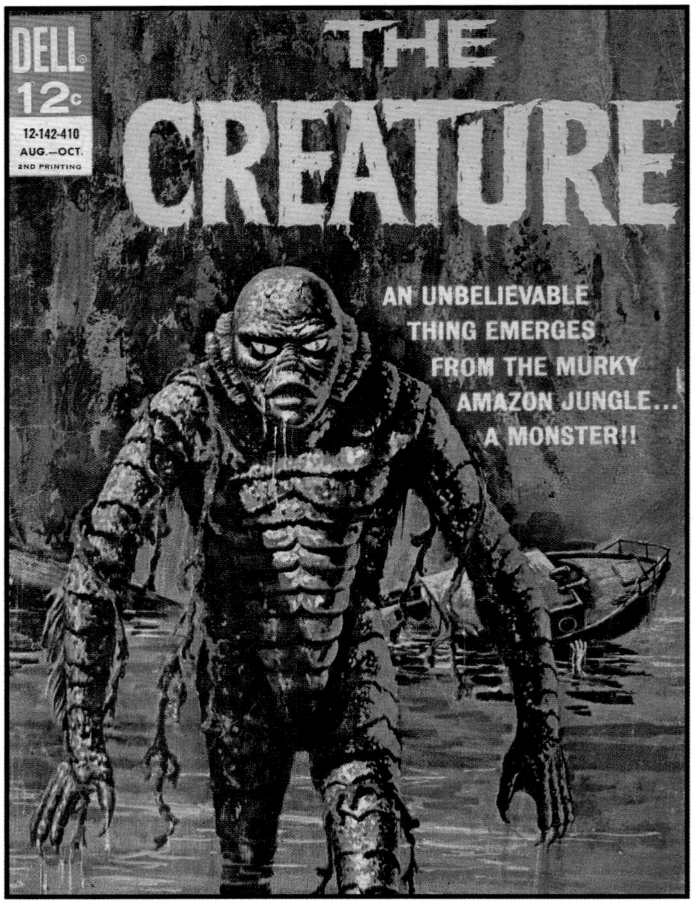
DELL
12c
12-142-410
AUG.—OCT.
2ND PRINTING
THE CREATURE
AN UNBELIEVABLE
THING EMERGES
FROM THE MURKY
AMAZON JUNGLE...
A MONSTER!!

The Creature #1 (Dell- Aug. Oct. 1964) cover art by Vic Prezio ▶

WARREN IS KING

One of *Famous Monsters of Filmland's* many knock-offs was Warren's own *Monster World*. Early issues found Warren presenting black-and-white comic versions of monster movies, with art by EC alums Wally Wood and Joe Orlando! The response must have been good because Warren's next move was a big one; a full-on horror comic magazine!

Warren's *Creepy* was introduced in 1964 and created a horror boom that reverberated for a decade. This code-free black-and-white horror comic magazine had it all… werewolves, vampires, blood and even a wise-cracking horror host in Uncle Creepy, who introduced brilliant stories with stunning artwork. Peppered with EC greats like Reed Crandall, Orlando, and Frank Frazetta, and with a cover by Jack Davis, this was what horror freaks were waiting for. Full tilt **HORROR!** It was an instant hit. Writer and (as of issue #3) editor, Archie Goodwin, was paying homage to his favorite comics, the EC horror line, and his readers were reaping the rewards. Warren introduced *Eerie* the next year and the game was afoot!

Like EC a decade earlier, Warren's magazines set the standard for everything that would follow. *Creepy* and *Eerie* sported gorgeous painted covers (many by the amazing Frazetta), top shelf horror writing (in addition to Goodwin, there were talents like Otto Binder and Larry Ivie) and the best collection of artists since the glory days. Johnny Craig, Angelo Torres, Gray Morrow, Alex Toth; the artist bullpen reads like a Best Horror Artists EVER list! Even when Warren resorted to reprints from earlier issues to flesh out a new one, the quality was always very high. As the guard changed and the elder EC statesmen stepped out, fresh new blood moved in to keep readers interested and to keep Warren's horror mags successful.

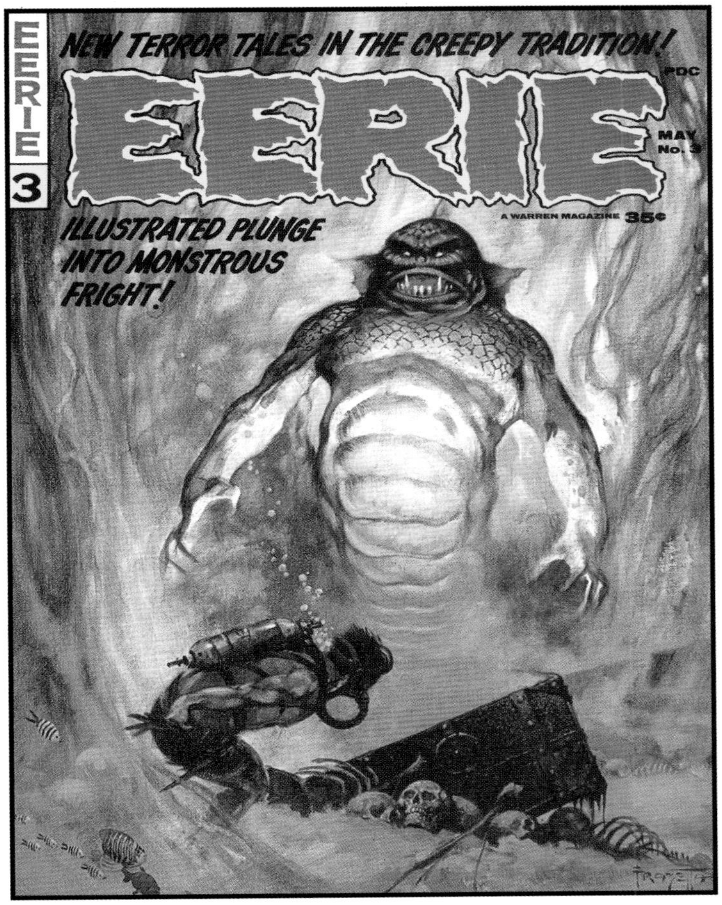
EERIE 3
NEW TERROR TALES IN THE CREEPY TRADITION!
PDC
EERIE
MAY No. 3
A WARREN MAGAZINE 35¢
ILLUSTRATED PLUNGE INTO MONSTROUS FRIGHT!

Eerie #3 (Warren- May 1966) cover art by Frank Frazetta

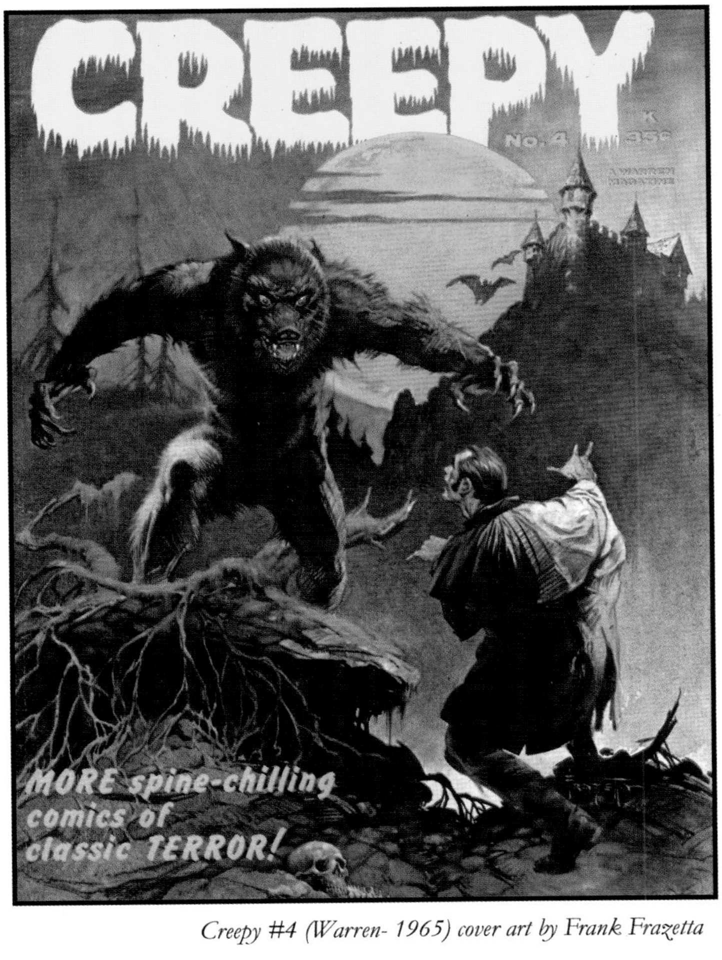
CREEPY
No. 4
35¢
MORE spine-chilling comics of classic TERROR!

Creepy #4 (Warren- 1965) cover art by Frank Frazetta

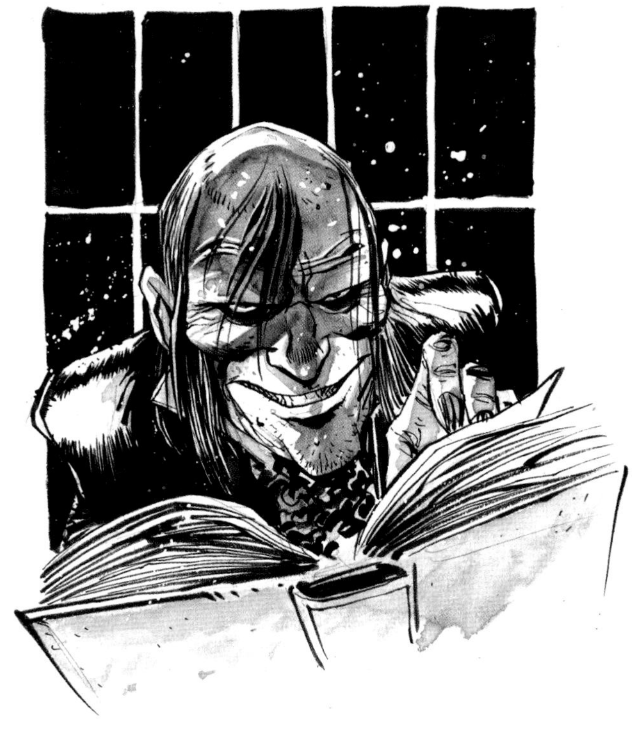

Uncle Creepy by Mike Henderson

GORE AND GHOSTS

Naturally, nothing inspires imitation like success, and it didn't take long for the knock-offs to step forward. Myron Fass and Carl Burgos entered into the fray with *Weird*, under the imprint of Eerie Publications. Fass had tried to secure the title *Eerie*, but Warren beat him to the punch; I suspect the imprint name was an "up yours" to Warren. The Eerie Pubs were very cheaply produced, and featured mostly reprints of pre-code horror comics from partner Robert Farrell's stash of Ajax-Farrell stories. They soon became infamous for excessive gore, and drawing extra blood into their reprints.

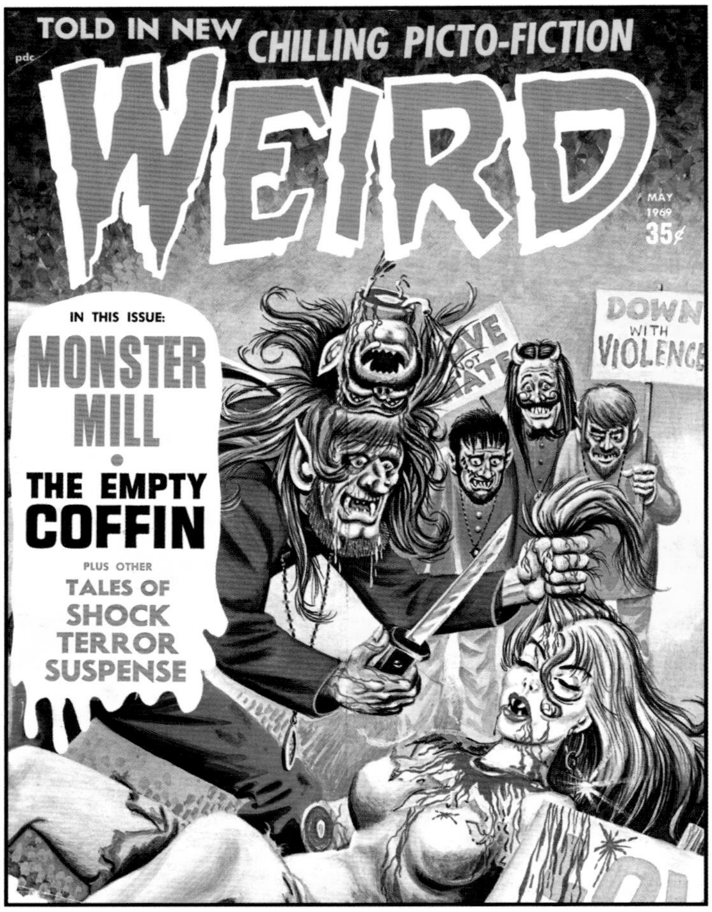
TOLD IN NEW CHILLING PICTO-FICTION
WEIRD
MAY 1969
35¢
IN THIS ISSUE:
MONSTER MILL
THE EMPTY COFFIN
PLUS OTHER
TALES OF SHOCK TERROR SUSPENSE
DOWN WITH VIOLENCE

Weird V3 #2 (Eerie Pubs- May 1969) cover art by Chic Stone

The good folks at Charlton, who had kept their feet wet with the suspense books throughout the horror drought, took a spirited step forward in 1966 with the first issue of *Ghostly Tales* (#55 April/May 1966), and added *The Many Ghosts of Dr. Graves* the next year. The Charlton ghost comics have a certain charm that is hard to describe. With the cheap paper, the subdued colors, and the creative team of Steve Ditko, Pat Boyette, Pete Morisi, Rocke Mastroserio, and Sanho Kim (among many others), these admittedly cut-rate comics are sometimes ugly and beautiful at the same time, and often as confusing as hell. Consider that a recommendation. Many more ghost titles soon popped up, to keep those presses running.

The Many Ghosts of Dr. Graves #6 (Charlton- May 1967) ▶

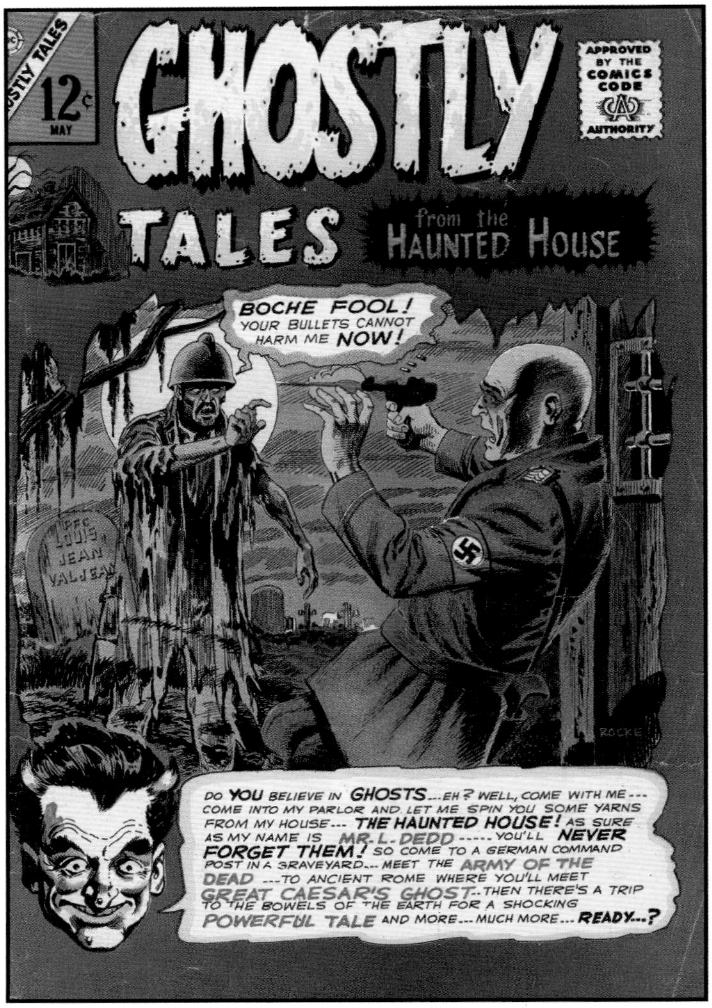
12¢
MAY
GHOSTLY
APPROVED BY THE COMICS CODE AUTHORITY
TALES from the HAUNTED HOUSE
BOCHE FOOL! YOUR BULLETS CANNOT HARM ME NOW!
PFC. LOUIS JEAN VALJEAN
ROCKE
DO YOU BELIEVE IN GHOSTS...EH? WELL, COME WITH ME--- COME INTO MY PARLOR AND LET ME SPIN YOU SOME YARNS FROM MY HOUSE--- THE HAUNTED HOUSE! AS SURE AS MY NAME IS MR. L. DEDD----- YOU'LL NEVER FORGET THEM! SO COME TO A GERMAN COMMAND POST IN A GRAVEYARD--- MEET THE ARMY OF THE DEAD ---TO ANCIENT ROME WHERE YOU'LL MEET GREAT CAESAR'S GHOST...THEN THERE'S A TRIP TO THE BOWELS OF THE EARTH FOR A SHOCKING POWERFUL TALE AND MORE... MUCH MORE... READY...?

Ghostly Tales #55 (Charlton- May 1969) cover art by Rocke Mastroserio

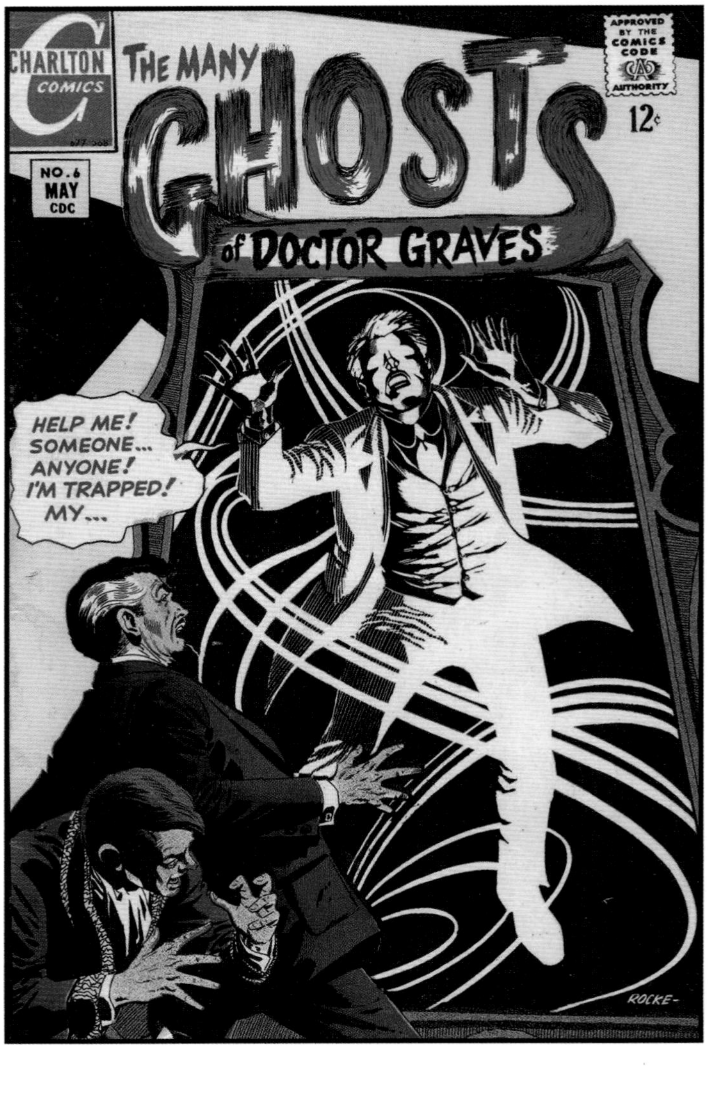
CHARLTON COMICS
THE MANY GHOSTS of DOCTOR GRAVES
APPROVED BY THE COMICS CODE AUTHORITY
12¢
NO. 6 MAY CDC
HELP ME! SOMEONE... ANYONE! I'M TRAPPED! MY...
ROCKE-

HORROR HOUSES

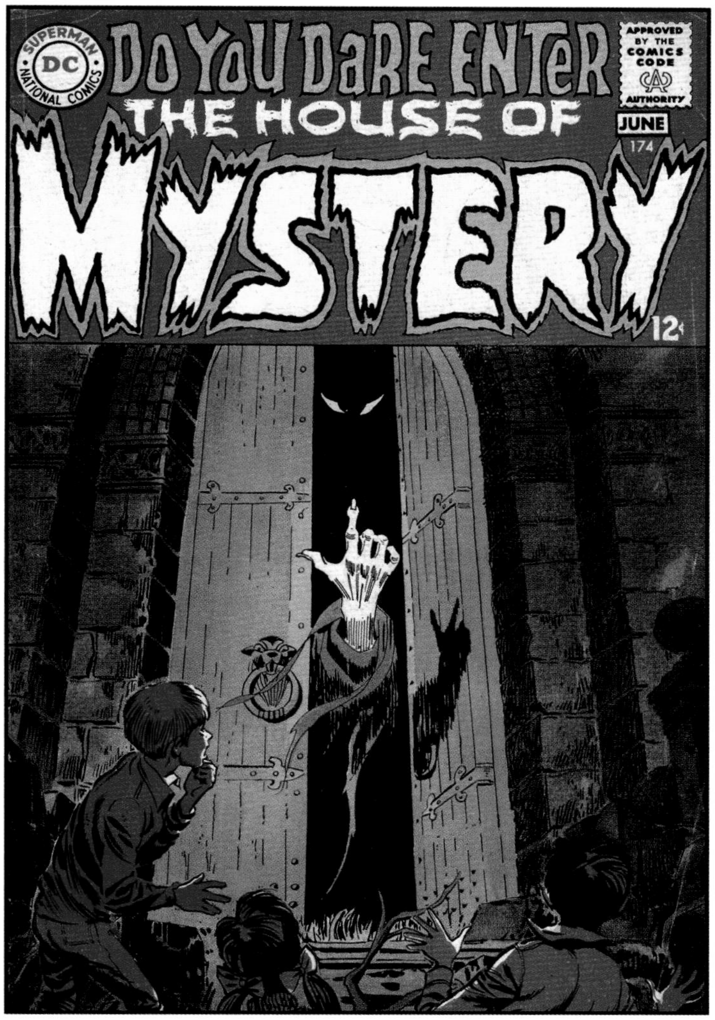
Do You Dare Enter
THE HOUSE OF
MYSTERY
JUNE
12¢

House of Mystery #174 (DC- June 1968) cover art by Nick Cardy

The next huge horror happening came from DC in 1968. *House of Mystery*, which had been around since the pre-code days, got a Gothic make-over thanks to new editor Joe Orlando, who was planning to model it after his old employer's comics, EC. Murray Boltinoff's *Tales of the Unexpected* dropped the "Tales of…" and likewise, started moving towards a "mystery" format. The H-word was still a no-no. It took a while but by the end of 1969, there were four DC titles waving the new "mystery" banner. *House of Secrets* made a similar style change and *The Witching Hour* was all new. These books were introducing readers to new talents who would soon become superstars, like Berni Wrightson, Len Wein, Mike Kaluta, and Marv Wolfman.

The DC "mystery" group became the best collection of four-color horror comics since the code came into effect. They adopted horror hosts, a la EC; Cain in *House of Mystery*, Abel in *House of Secrets*, and yes, even Eve arrived later to complete Orlando's biblical trio. They bickered, and teased, and cracked bad jokes, just like any self-respecting horror host should. Letter columns kept the fans involved, and horror was back in the good graces of readers.

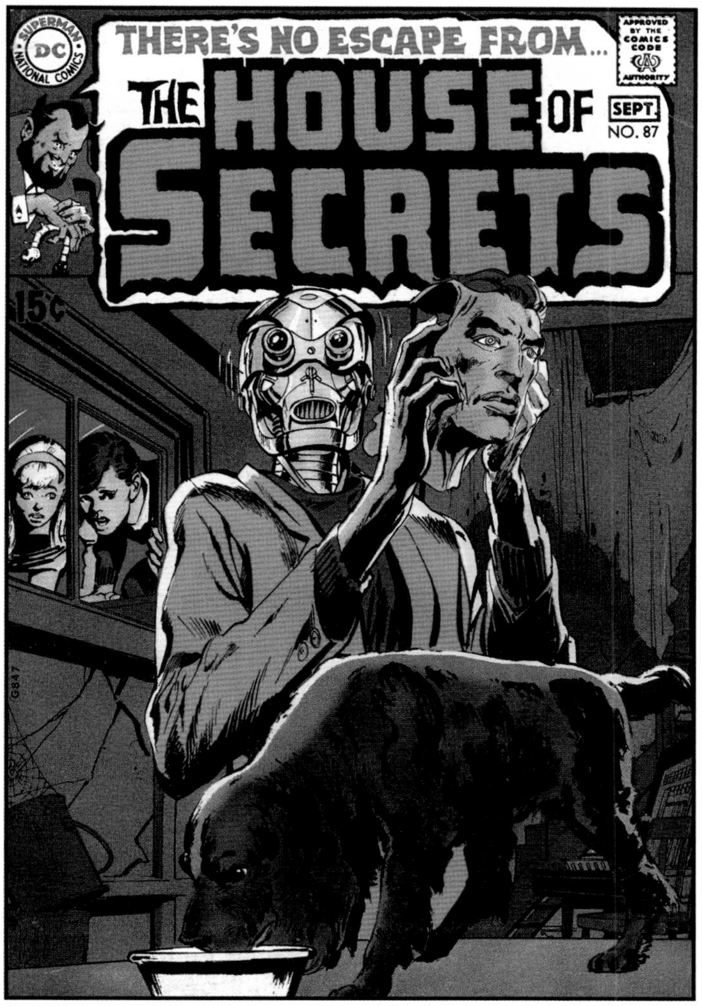
THERE'S NO ESCAPE FROM...
THE HOUSE OF SECRETS
SEPT. NO. 87
15¢

House of Secrets #87 (Aug. - Sept. 1970) cover art by Neal Adams

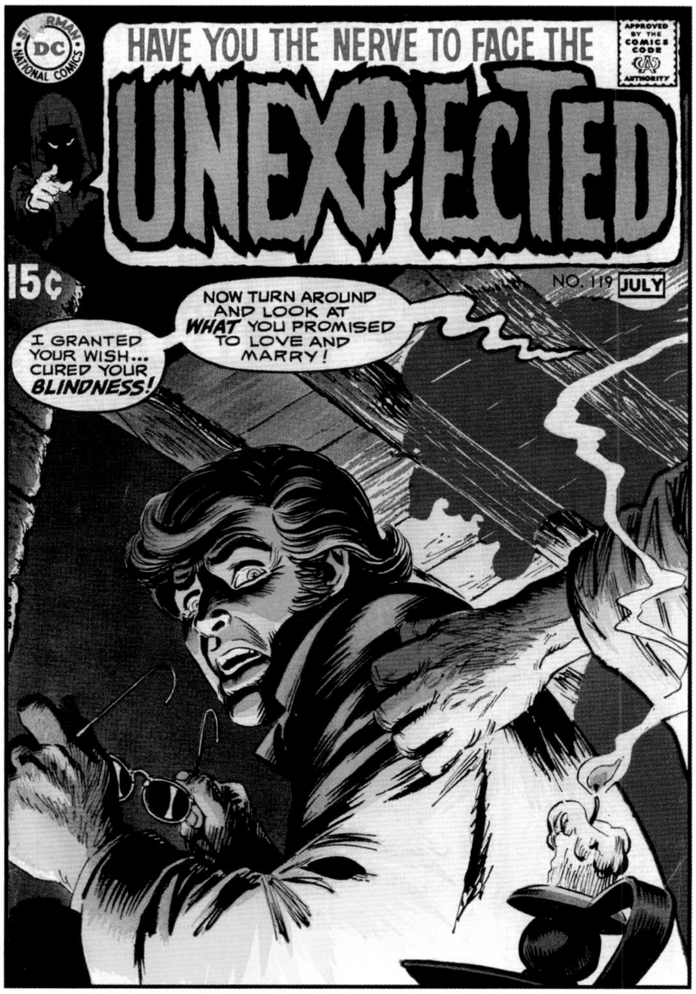
HAVE YOU THE NERVE TO FACE THE
UNEXPECTED
15¢
NO. 119 JULY
NOW TURN AROUND AND LOOK AT WHAT YOU PROMISED TO LOVE AND MARRY!
I GRANTED YOUR WISH... CURED YOUR BLINDNESS!

Unexpected # 119 (June - July 1970) cover art by Nick Cardy

HORRORSPLOSION

Not just limited to the DC offices, horror comics were exploding everywhere in 1969! Warren introduced another title, *Vampirella*, which owed as much to good-girl art as it did to horror. The hostess was a slinky, barely-clothed space vampire, and it was an immediate hit.

ILLUSTRATED TALES TO BEWITCH & BEDEVIL YOU
VAMPIRELLA
VAMPI #12 JULY/71
A WARREN MAGAZINE PDC 60¢
THE END OF VAMPIRELLA?
WITH ONE FATAL
THIS SHADOWY WINGED CREATURE
CAN KILL! READ...
DEATH'S DARK ANGEL!
PAGE 6

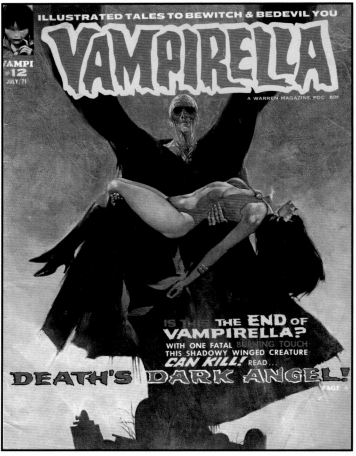

Vampirella #12 (Warren- July 1971) cover art by Sanjulian

Eerie Publications countered by upping their title count to six. All of the titles were interchangeable, but the covers were super gory. By the end of the year, they were introducing new art, not just reprints, though they were stealing scripts from pre-code comics. Stanley Morse dug into his treasure trove of pre-code horror stories for Stanley Publications' mags *Shock* and *Chilling Tales of Horror*. His books were so poorly put together that they made the Eerie Pubs look slick, but I still like 'em. He would soon introduce two more.

Robert Sproul, publisher of the successful *Mad* knock-off, *Cracked*, entered the black-and-white horror mag race with a very good horse; *Web of Horror*. With top-shelf artwork by Wrightson, Kaluta, and Jeff Jones, superior writing by editor Terry Bisson and Binder, and even a horror host (a spider named Webster), this title was a real treat. Sadly, it only lasted three issues, but those three issues are coveted by horror comic aficionados.

WITCHES' TALES
pdc
DEC. 1969
35¢
HEAD TRANSPLANTS
IN THIS ISSUE:
DEVIL'S MONSTER
DOOM CREATURES
NIGHTMARE
PLUS OTHER BEWITCHING TERROR TALES

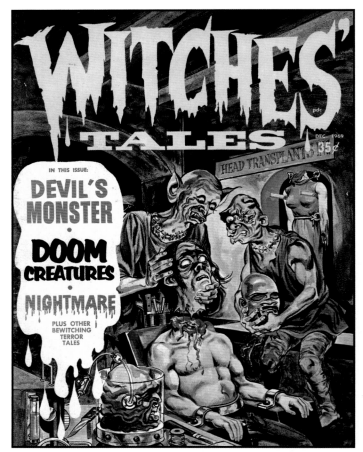

Witches' Tales V1 #9 (Eerie Pubs- Dec. 1969) cover art by Bill Alexander

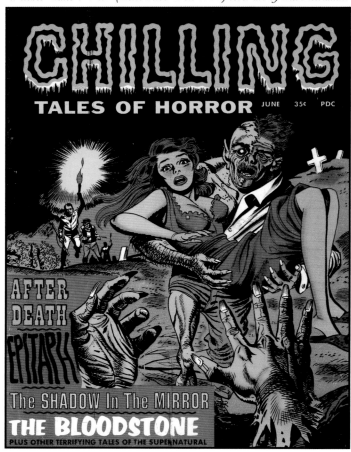

CHILLING
TALES OF HORROR
JUNE 35¢ PDC
AFTER DEATH
EPITAPH
The SHADOW In The MIRROR
THE BLOODSTONE
PLUS OTHER TERRIFYING TALES OF THE SUPERNATURAL

Chilling Tales of Horror (Stanley- June 1969) cover art by Bernard Bailey (reprinted from Weird Mysteries #11, July 1954)

BRONZE AGE ICK

It is said that 1970 is the beginning of the "Bronze Age" of comics. Unlike the beginning of the Silver Age, comic racks were filthy with horror product this time around. From 1970 to 1974, a bonafide horror **BOOM** was taking place. Joe Orlando's *House of Secrets* hit the big time with issue #92 (June/July 1971). The lead story, an 8-pager written by Len Wein and illustrated by Berni Wrightson, was a runaway hit and eventually led to its own title. The story was called "Swamp Thing."

Sex and drugs and horror mixed in the underground comics that started to surface in the new decade. Notable horror titles like *Insect Fear* by Print Mint and *Skull* and *Fantagor*, both by Rip-Off Press, pushed the limits of good taste, but did so with clever storytelling and some wildly imaginative art. Richard Corben, who often signed his name as "Gore" (a la "Ghastly" Ingels), cut his teeth in these counterculture comics years before becoming a star at Warren.

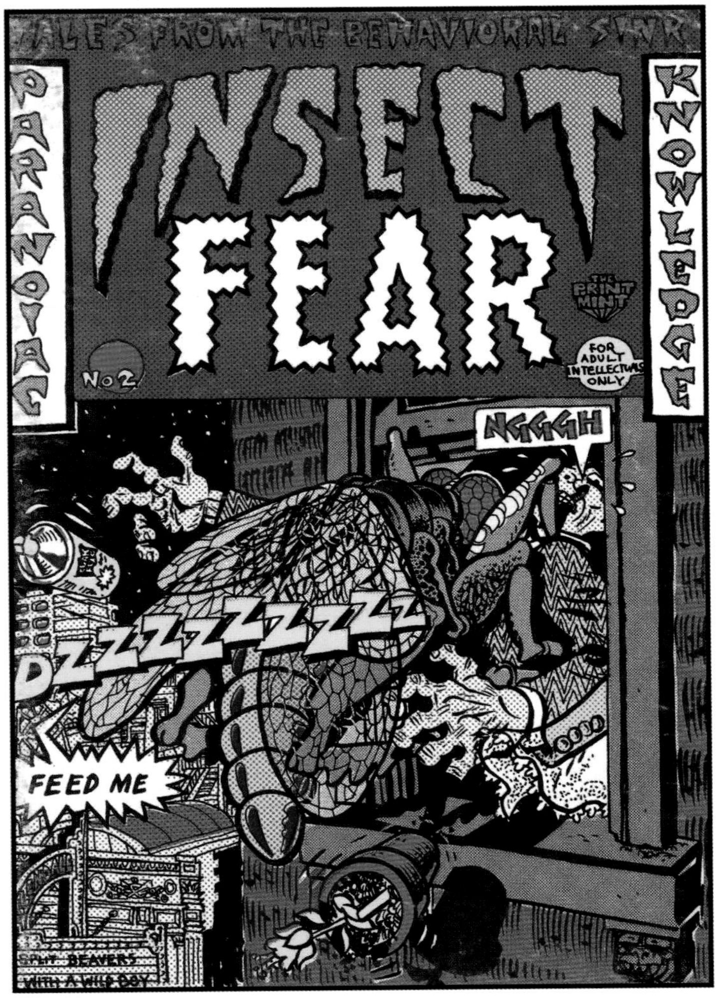
TALES FROM THE BEHAVIORAL SINK
INSECT FEAR
PARANOIAC
KNOWLEDGE
No 2
FOR ADULT INTELLECTUALS ONLY
NGGGH
DZZZZZZZZZ
FEED ME

Insect Fear #2 (1970) cover art by Spain Rodriguez

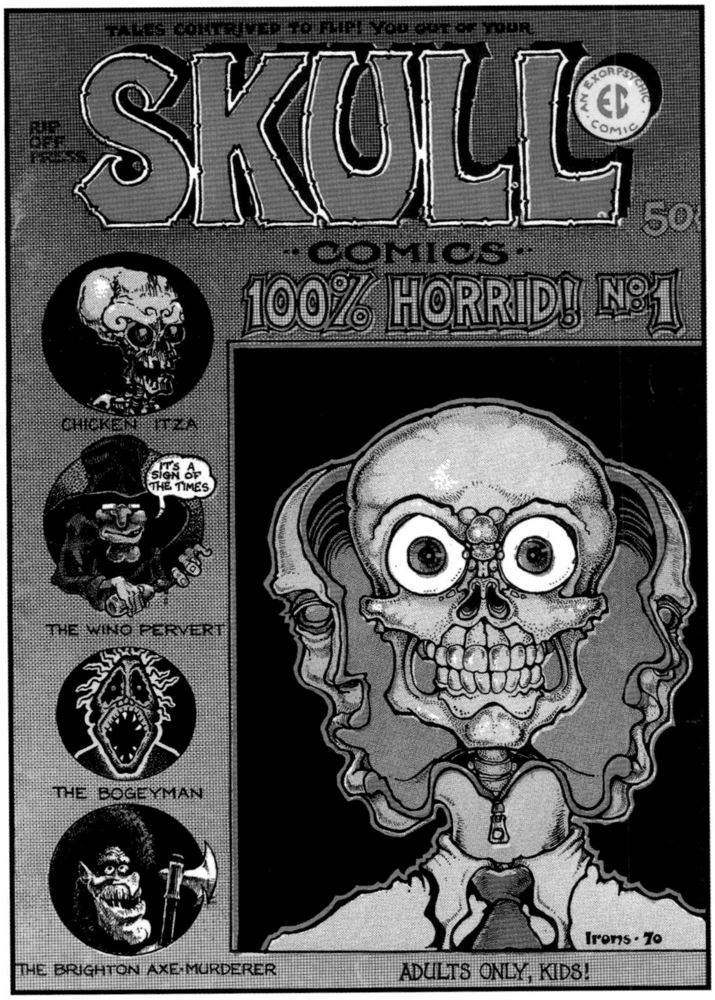
TALES CONTRIVED TO FLIP! YOU OUT OF YOUR
RIP OFF PRESS
SKULL
AN EXORPSYCHIC EC COMIC
50¢
COMICS
100% HORRID! No 1
CHICKEN ITZA
IT'S A SIGN OF THE TIMES
THE WINO PERVERT
THE BOGEYMAN
THE BRIGHTON AXE-MURDERER
Irons · 70
ADULTS ONLY, KIDS!

Skull #1 (1970) cover art by Greg Irons

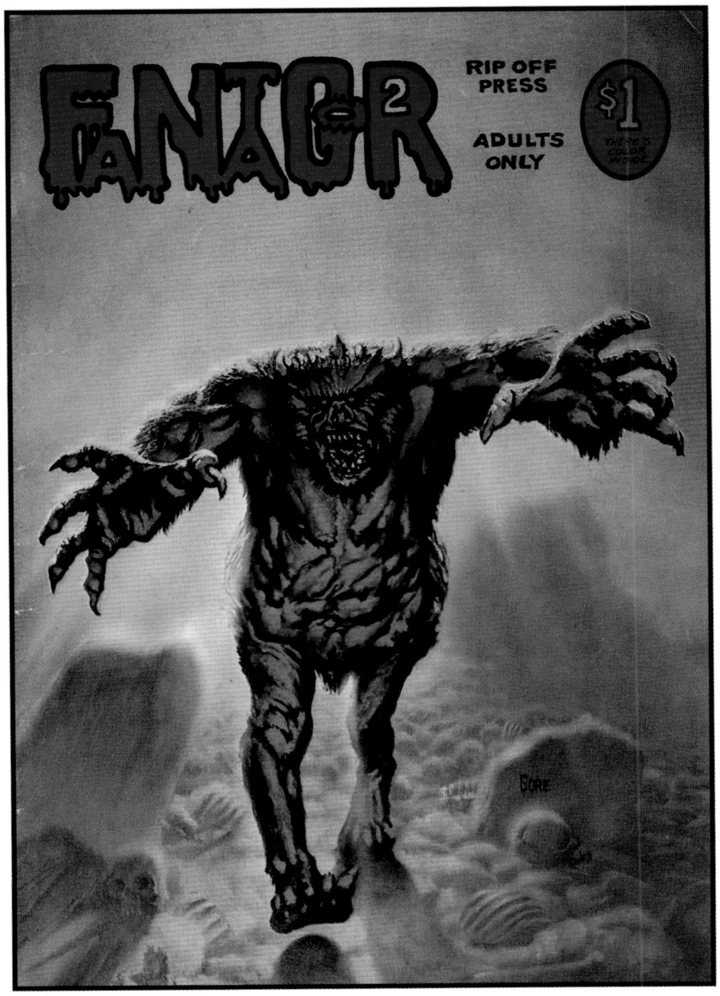
FANTAGOR 2
RIP OFF PRESS
$1
ADULTS ONLY
GORE

Fantagor #2 (1972) cover art by Richard Corben

DC's Mystery titles were multiplying like bunnies, all with very good stories by writers like EC veterans Jack Oleck and Carl Wessler, and illustrated mostly by a phenomenal group of artists from the Philippines. These DC twenty-cent titles were some of the finest color horror comics since the demise of EC. With covers by Neal Adams (whose specialty was moody "kids in peril" covers), Wrightson, Nick Cardy, and Luis Dominguez, and with inside art by Alfredo Alcala, Nestor Redondo, and Alex Niño, new titles like *Ghosts*, *Weird Mystery Tales*, and *Secrets of Sinister House* all delivered the goods in spades. The code had loosened up a little, so vampires and werewolves again stalked the printed comic page. Joe Orlando gave us horror hounds what we wanted.

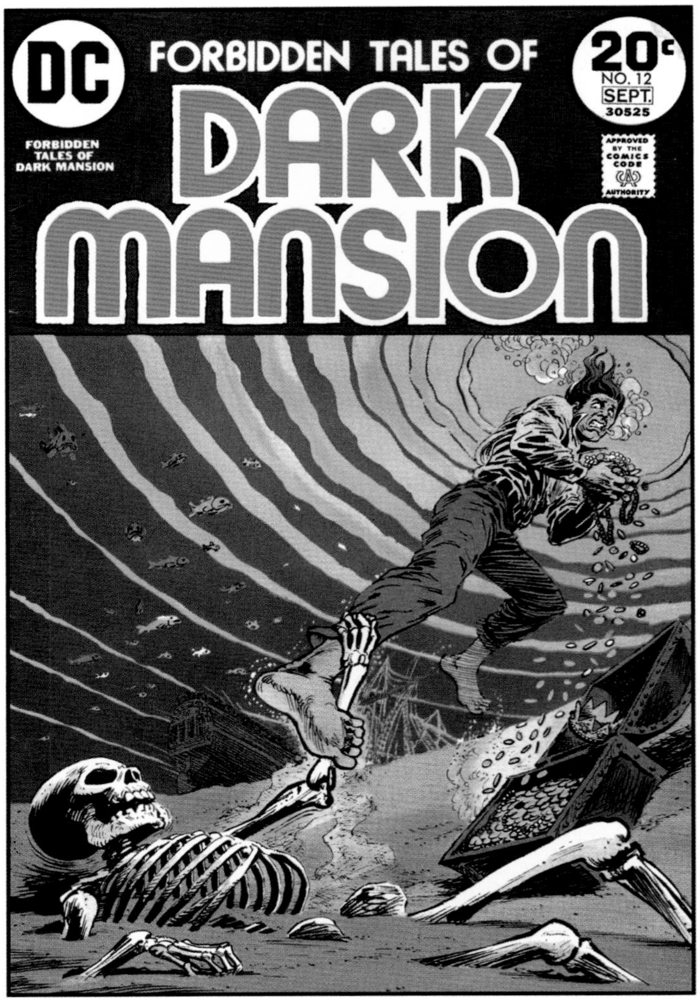
DC
FORBIDDEN TALES OF
20¢
NO. 12
SEPT.
30525
FORBIDDEN TALES OF DARK MANSION
DARK MANSION
APPROVED BY THE COMICS CODE AUTHORITY

Forbidden Tales of Dark Mansion #12 (Aug. - Sept. 1973) cover art by Nick Cardy

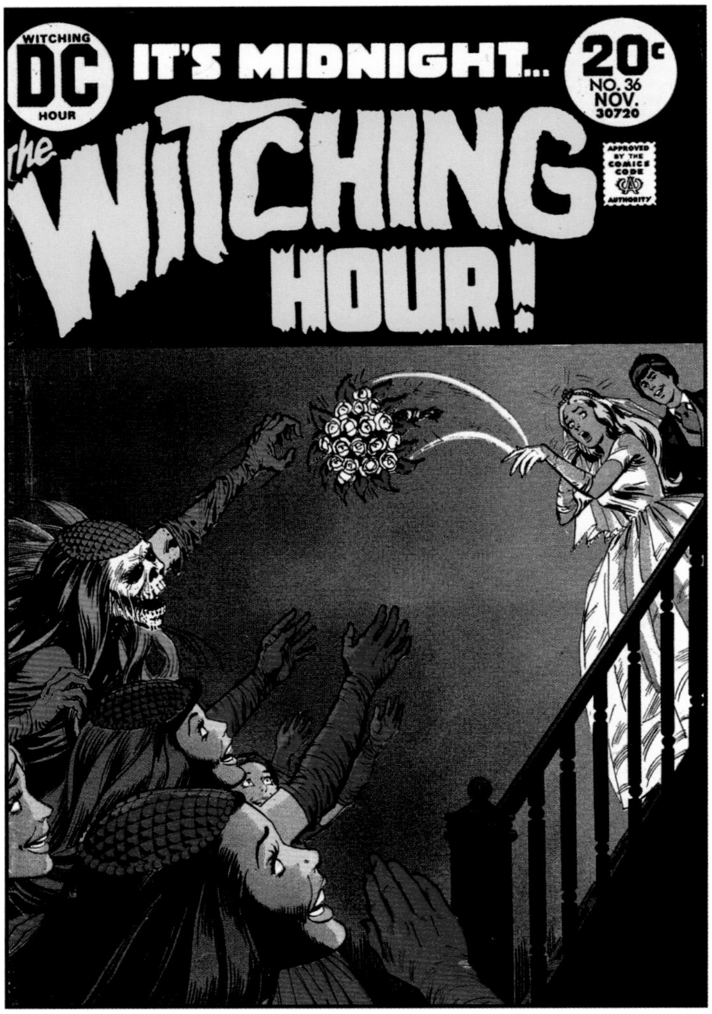
WITCHING DC HOUR
IT'S MIDNIGHT...
20¢
NO. 36
NOV.
30720
the WITCHING HOUR!
APPROVED BY THE COMICS CODE AUTHORITY

The Witching Hour #36 (Nov. 1973) cover art by Nick Cardy

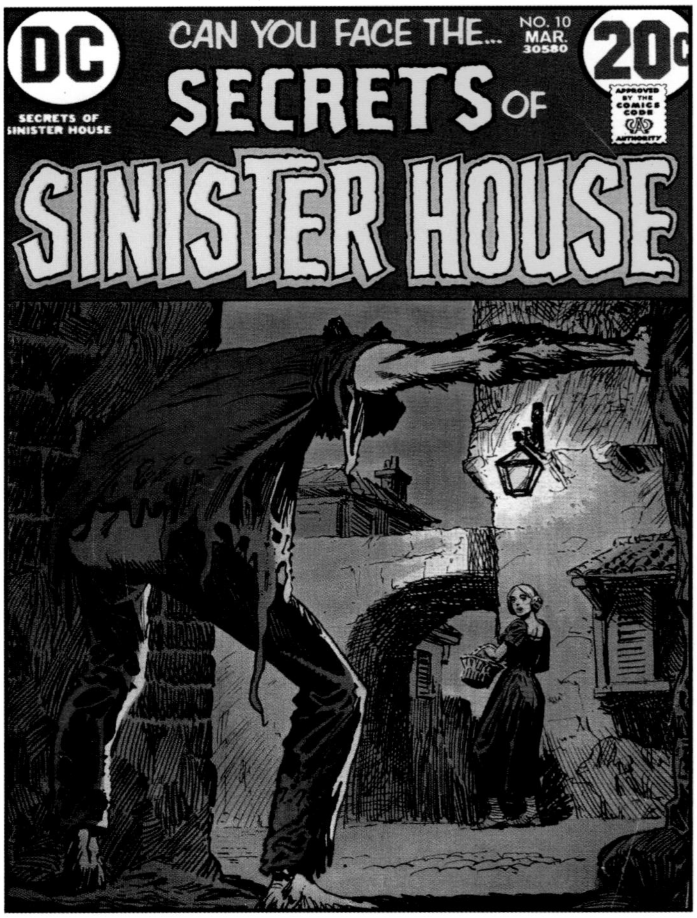
DC
CAN YOU FACE THE...
NO. 10
MAR.
30580
20¢
SECRETS OF SINISTER HOUSE
SECRETS OF
SINISTER HOUSE
APPROVED BY THE COMICS CODE AUTHORITY

Secrets of Sinister House #10 (Mar. 1973) cover art by Alfredo Alcala

Orlando really took advantage of the word "weird" when it was deemed OK to use under the code. Everything became weird: *Weird War Tales, Weird Western Tales, Weird Worlds,* and the "mystery" artists were working overtime. *Weird Western Tales* was the home of Jonah Hex, a scarred bounty hunter and anti-hero whose exploits bordered on horror. *Weird War Tales*, which featured the same writers and artists as the straight-up horror titles, was hosted by none other than Death himself.

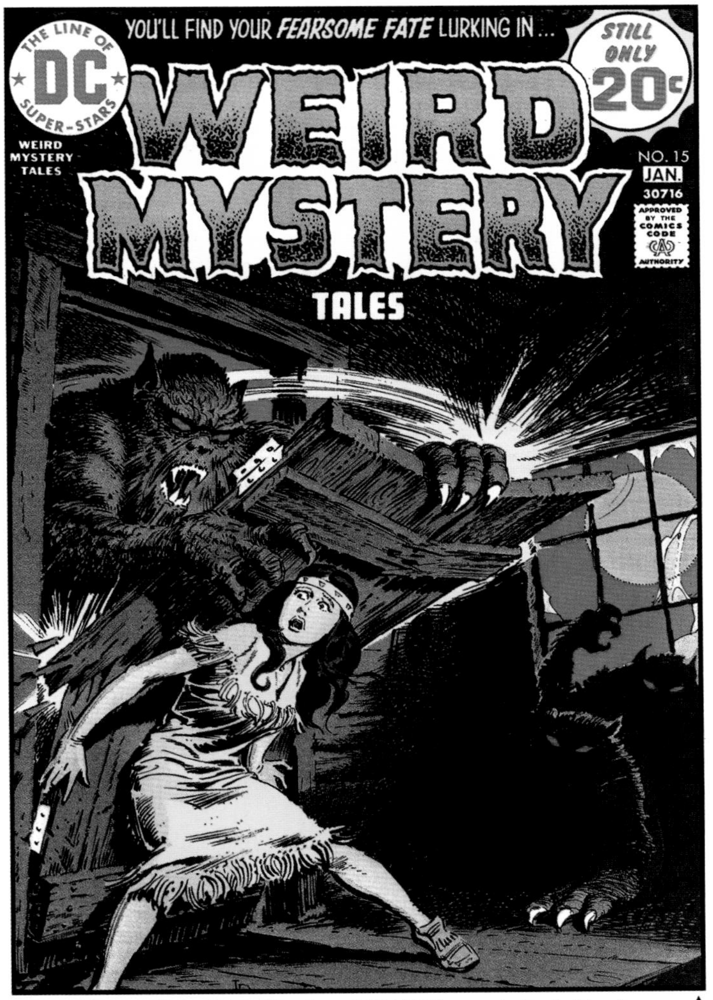
YOU'LL FIND YOUR FEARSOME FATE LURKING IN...
STILL ONLY 20¢
DC
WEIRD MYSTERY TALES
NO. 15
JAN.
30716
APPROVED BY THE COMICS CODE AUTHORITY

Weird Mystery Tales #15 (Dec. Jan. 1974/75) cover by Luis Dominguez ▲

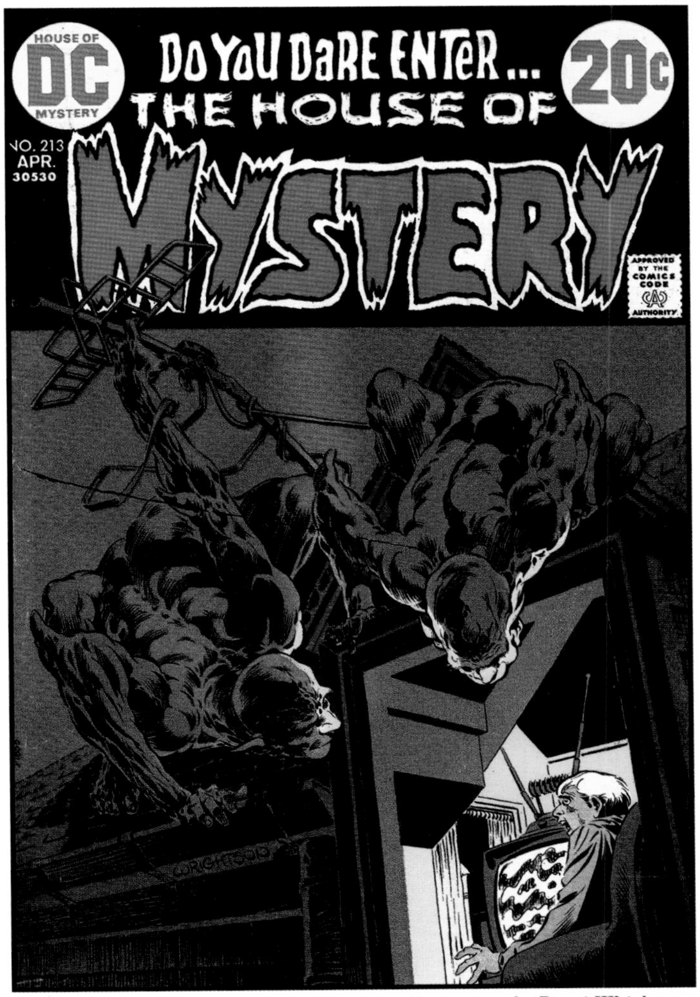
HOUSE OF MYSTERY
DC
DO YOU DARE ENTER...
THE HOUSE OF
MYSTERY
20¢
NO. 213
APR.
30530
APPROVED BY THE COMICS CODE AUTHORITY

▲ *House of Mystery #213 (Apr. 1973) cover art by Berni Wrightson*

Ghosts #28 (July 1974) cover art by Nick Cardy ▼

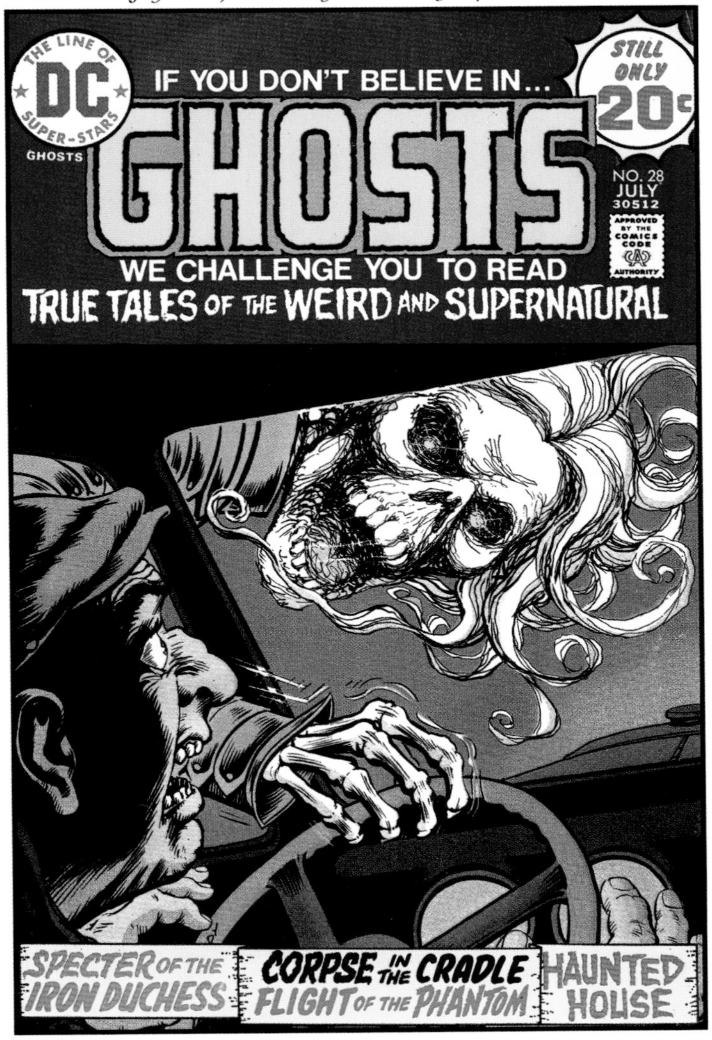
THE LINE OF DC SUPER-STARS
GHOSTS
IF YOU DON'T BELIEVE IN...
STILL ONLY 20¢
GHOSTS
NO. 28
JULY
30512
APPROVED BY THE COMICS CODE AUTHORITY
WE CHALLENGE YOU TO READ
TRUE TALES OF THE WEIRD AND SUPERNATURAL
SPECTER OF THE IRON DUCHESS
CORPSE IN THE CRADLE
FLIGHT OF THE PHANTOM
HAUNTED HOUSE

▼ *Unexpected #149 (Aug. 1973) cover art by Nick Cardy*

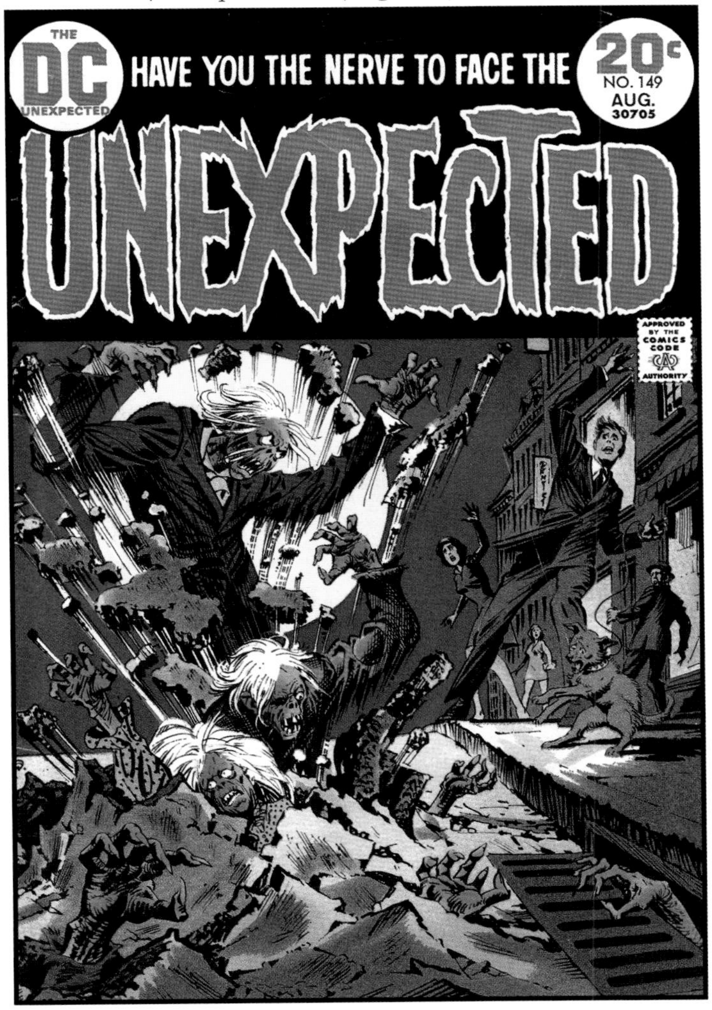
THE DC UNEXPECTED
HAVE YOU THE NERVE TO FACE THE
20¢
NO. 149
AUG.
30705
UNEXPECTED
APPROVED BY THE COMICS CODE AUTHORITY

HORROR MOOD

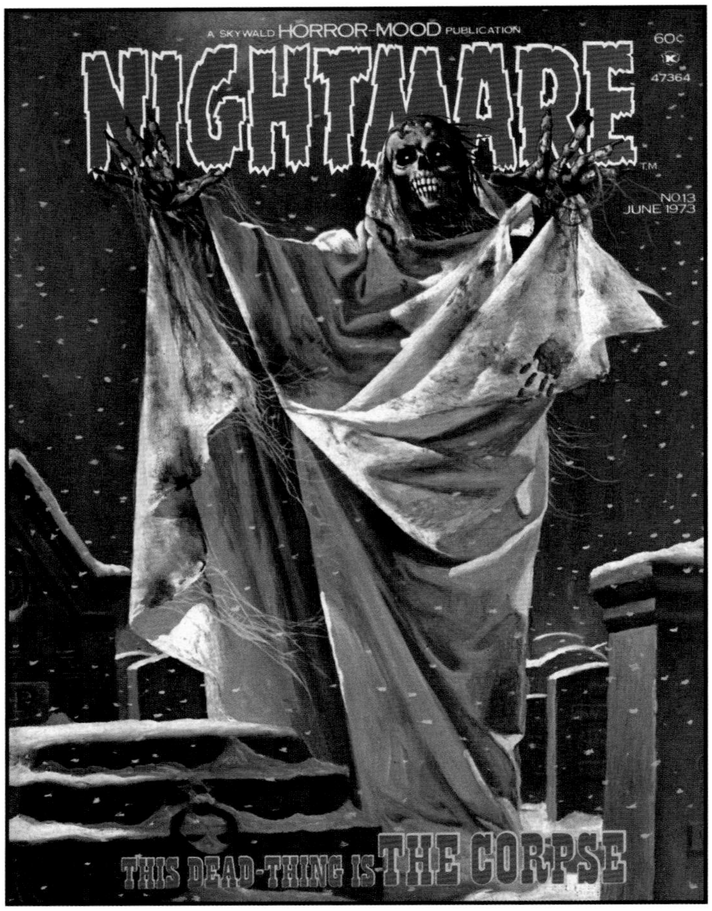
A SKYWALD HORROR-MOOD PUBLICATION
60¢
47364
NIGHTMARE
TM.
NO.13
JUNE 1973
THIS DEAD-THING IS THE CORPSE

Nightmare #13 (Skywald- June 1973) cover art by Segrelles

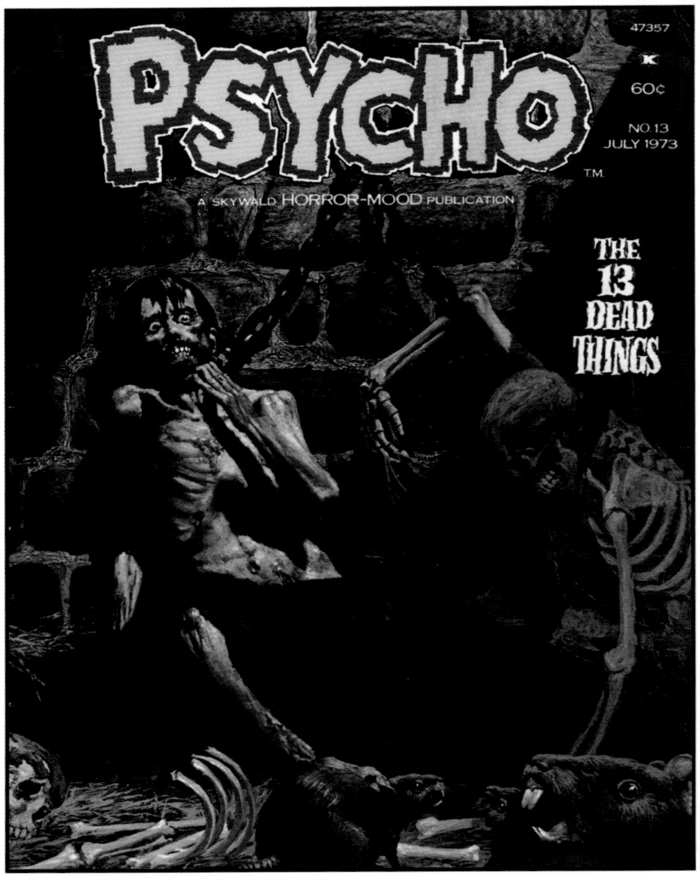
47357
60¢
PSYCHO
NO.13
JULY 1973
T.M.
A SKYWALD HORROR-MOOD PUBLICATION
THE 13 DEAD THINGS

Psycho #13 (Skywald- July 1973) cover art by Segrelles

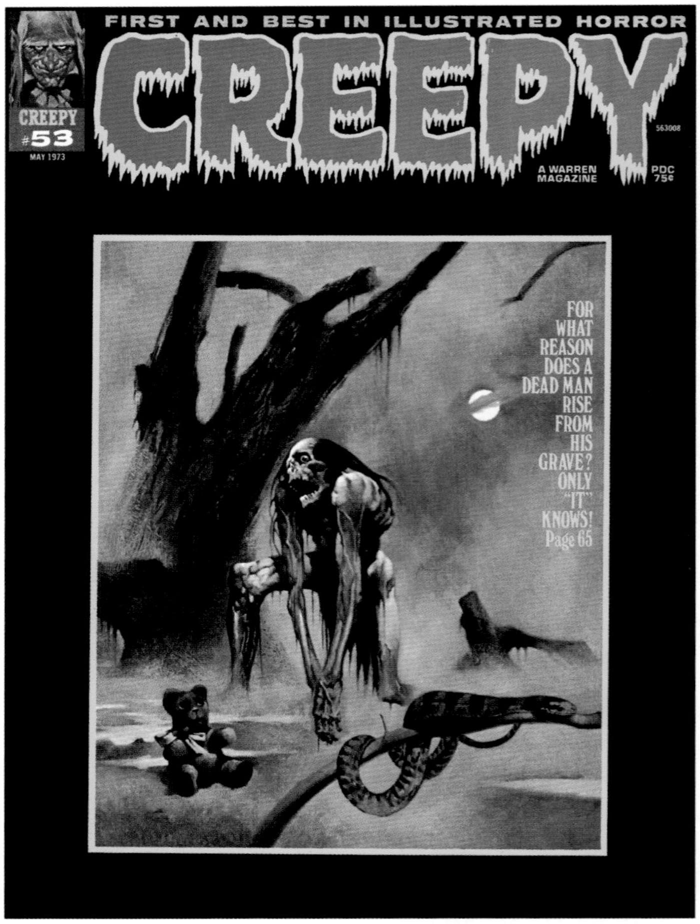
FIRST AND BEST IN ILLUSTRATED HORROR
CREEPY
CREEPY #53
MAY 1973
A WARREN MAGAZINE
PDC 75¢
FOR WHAT REASON DOES A DEAD MAN RISE FROM HIS GRAVE? ONLY "IT" KNOWS! Page 65

Creepy #53 (Warren- May 1973) cover art by Sanjulian

In addition to the Warren mags (who had started importing art talent from Spain and again raised the bar with some absolutely stunning pen-and-ink artwork), and the DC and Charlton comics, Skywald had entered the black-and-white horror mag market in 1970. They put out what was, in my opinion, the best horror of the day. Their titles *Nightmare, Psycho*, and *Scream* were part of the self-proclaimed "**Horror-Mood,**" and Editor Al Hewetson wrote some of the most fun, Lovecraftian tales this side of hell. Early issues had yet to find their way, but once Hewetson was in charge, these were as good as anything published at the time.

I'll admit that I was really lucky. 1972 through 1974 was a fantastic time to be a burgeoning horror nut; it was my personal golden age. The shelves were bursting with horror comics, both color and black-and-white. I used to make Creepy Crawlers (little rubber bugs) and sell them to kids after school. As soon as I had 20¢, I'd run over to Bill's Variety and plunk it down for the new *Unexpected* or *Forbidden Tales of Dark Mansion.* If that makes me an old codger now then so be it, but I had it made back then. I also saw the original Alice Cooper band in 1973, and Thin Lizzy open for Queen in 1977, so **fuck you! Get off my lawn!**

HERO OR HORROR

So where was Marvel during all of this, you might ask. The House of Ideas had, of course, changed the face of comics in the early '60s with their own brand of superhero comics; *The Fantastic Four*, *The Amazing Spiderman*, and *The X-Men* all made Marvel very wealthy and gave all comics a boost of adrenaline. They were the big cheese in the genre, even with DC's iconic heroes still being extremely popular. As for horror, they didn't really jump onto the bandwagon until 1969, with *Chamber of Darkness* and *Tower of Shadows*. Early issues featured all new stories with some excellent artwork, but they both soon started being sprinkled with old Atlas reprints. Both titles were dropped by 1971. But they were far from over.

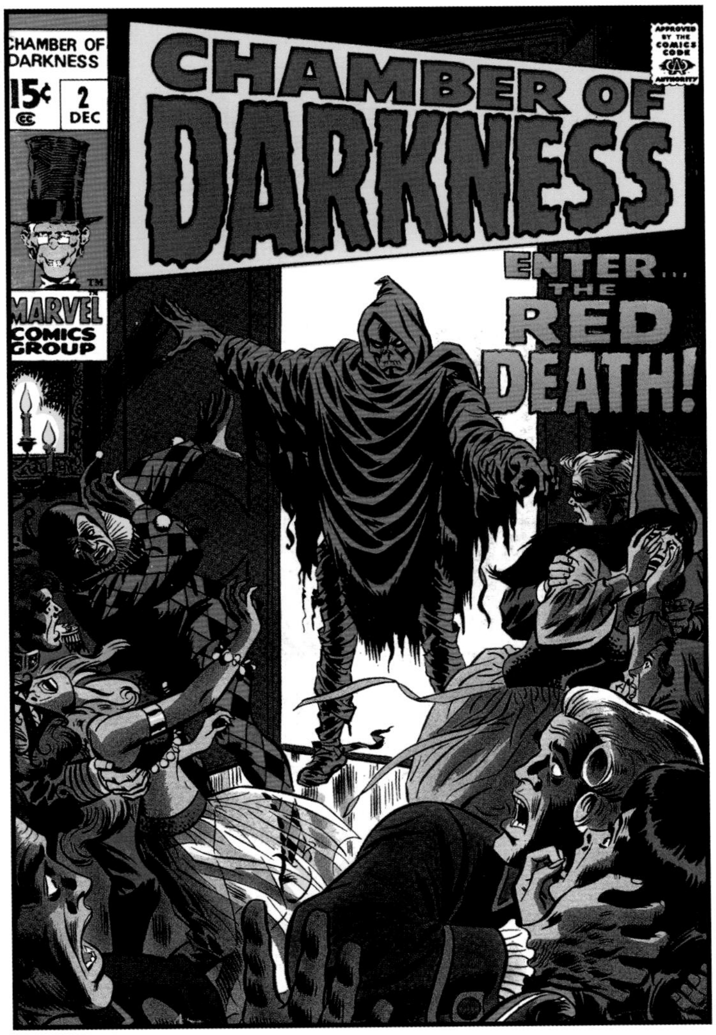

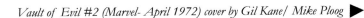

CHAMBER OF DARKNESS
15¢
2
DEC
APPROVED BY THE COMICS CODE AUTHORITY
CHAMBER OF DARKNESS
MARVEL COMICS GROUP
ENTER... THE RED DEATH!

Chamber of Darkness #2 (Marvel- Dec. 1969) cover art by John Romita

With the vast supply of Atlas material, Marvel opened the floodgates. Between 1970 and 1973, they put out multiple comics utilizing that stash of giant monster and pre-code horror reprints. *Chamber of Chills*, *Crypt of Shadows*, *Where Monsters Dwell*, *Vault of Evil*, and *Uncanny Tales from the Grave*… the hits just kept on coming. Some of these titles had a few new stories mixed in but most of the content was old Atlas reprints. Still, the material was new to most of the readers of the time.

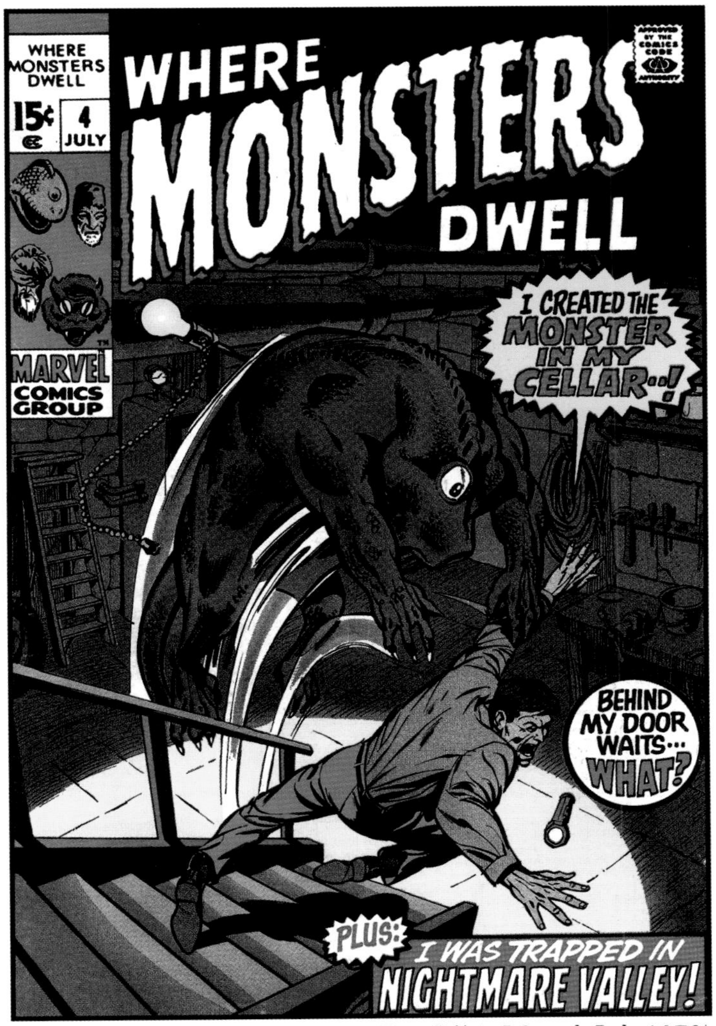

WHERE MONSTERS DWELL
15¢
4
JULY
APPROVED BY THE COMICS CODE AUTHORITY
WHERE MONSTERS DWELL
MARVEL COMICS GROUP
I CREATED THE MONSTER IN MY CELLAR..!
BEHIND MY DOOR WAITS... WHAT?
PLUS: I WAS TRAPPED IN NIGHTMARE VALLEY!

Where Monsters Dwell #4 (Marvel- July 1970)

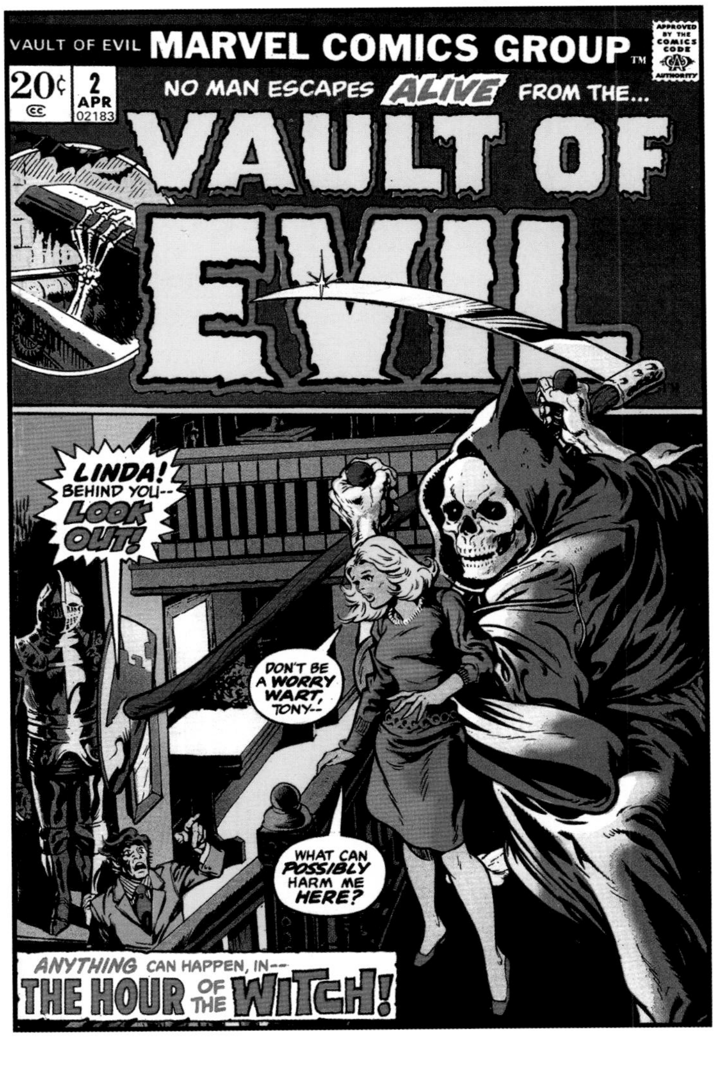

VAULT OF EVIL
MARVEL COMICS GROUP
APPROVED BY THE COMICS CODE AUTHORITY
20¢
2
APR
02183
NO MAN ESCAPES ALIVE FROM THE...
VAULT OF EVIL
LINDA! BEHIND YOU-- LOOK OUT!
DON'T BE A WORRY WART, TONY--
WHAT CAN POSSIBLY HARM ME HERE?
ANYTHING CAN HAPPEN, IN-- THE HOUR OF THE WITCH!

Vault of Evil #2 (Marvel- April 1972) cover by Gil Kane/ Mike Ploog ▶

CHAMBER OF CHILLS
MARVEL COMICS GROUP
20¢
8 JAN
02160
CHAMBER OF
CHILLS
I WAIT IN THE DUNGEON!

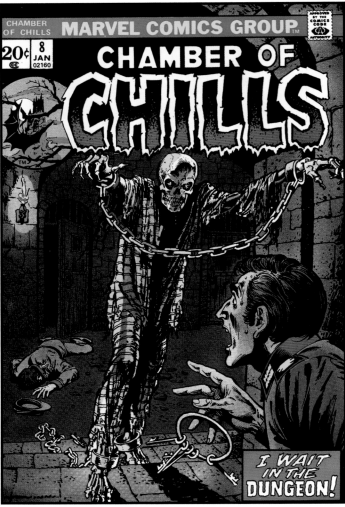

Chamber of Chills #8 (Marvel- Jan. 1973) cover art by Ernie Chua

Marvel also scored big with their continuing character monster series *Tomb of Dracula* and *Werewolf by Night.* Top notch writing and artwork gave both of these titles a long life. Here is where I have to be all bull-headed and controversial and stir the pot. I have a very tough time considering *Tomb of Dracula* and Marvel's other continuing character titles actual horror comics. Really, horror is a situation, not a character, no matter how evil one may be. You just can't successfully express horror over a long run… a short run or mini-series, sure. Marvel, in particular, also made their monsters feel a bit like superheroes to me. After all, that was what the company did best. For me, the anthology format is the purest form of horror comic. I back that up by saying that, in my opinion, the short story is the purest form of horror fiction as well. Can you think of Lovecraft, Bloch, or Barker without thinking first of their short-form masterpieces? Of course, I have to include Warren's *Eerie,* which featured many continuing characters. I'm sorry… Dax the Warrior was not horror, no matter how beautifully written and drawn it was. These comics have frightening moments and scary characters, but are they really horror? And I'll be honest, when I was a kid, it really frosted my balls when I got to the end of a comic only to be confronted by a "to be continued…"

My anal-retentive nitpicking aside, there were scores of worthwhile comics to choose from at the time, with more constantly popping up. In 1973, Marvel added a line of black and white "horror" mags to the mix as well. This boom couldn't last forever and, indeed, the market couldn't support so much product.

ALL NEW
CHARLTON COMICS
25¢
CREEPY THINGS
NO. 1 JUL
00122 75/CDC

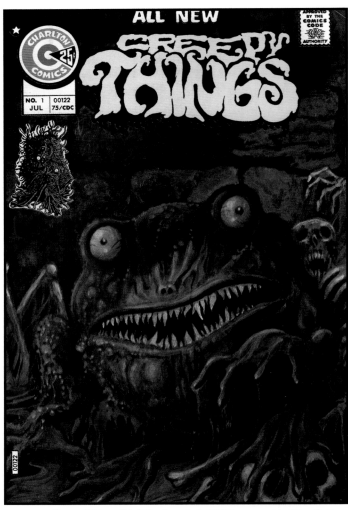

Creepy Things #1 (Charlton- July 1975) cover art by Tom Sutton

Many of DC's Mystery titles started to disappear in 1974. The black-and-white market imploded within a year, with Eerie Publications and Skywald both folding, and Marvel discontinuing their "horror" magazines. Warren soldiered on, as they were still the best of the bunch, with the Spanish masters still going strong, and with unique artistic contributions from Wrightson and Corben keeping buyers interested. DC's main mystery titles like *House of Mystery* and *Unexpected* continued serving up good artwork and passable stories. The shelves had been pruned, but they were still bearing fruit. Charlton and Gold Key kept releasing their interesting, if spotty, comics throughout the decade, though many issues were burdened with more reprints than original material. The Eerie Pubs resurfaced in 1976 in an even more compromised form and sputtered along into the early '80s.

RISE OF THE INDIE

Another big change to the comic industry was happening throughout the '70s; the advent of the comic shop. No longer were drug stores, newsstands and candy shops the only place to find your books. This also led to the Direct Sales market, where the publisher could get their product right to the outlet, bypassing distributors. This encouraged many independent comic companies to be born, and get their product right where it belonged with no bullshit, and no code. Plus, with the indies, most titles were creator-owned, meaning the creators held on to their own rights. While the early '80s brought the eventual demise of Warren's and DC's books, there were independents standing in the wings to usher in the next phase of sequential horror.

Bruce Jones had been one of the more successful horror writers for the Warren books in the '70s. In 1982, he and his partner, April Campbell, put together the seminal indie horror comic *Twisted Tales*, for Pacific Comics. Code-free, full color, and on quality paper, the comic was a revelation. Artwork was provided by Corben, Wrightson, and British horror great, John Bolton, among others, including some of the underground artists of yore, all illustrating Jones' sinister stories. These were violent, mature and often controversial stories, definitely not for the children. Their sci-fi sister publication for Pacific, *Alien Worlds*, was likewise very horrific at times.

PC
"For the NEW Era in Comics"
$1.50 US
$2.00 Canada
TWISTED TALES
NO.2
WRIGHTSON

◀ *Twisted Tales #2 (Pacific- April 1983) cover art by Berni Wrightson*

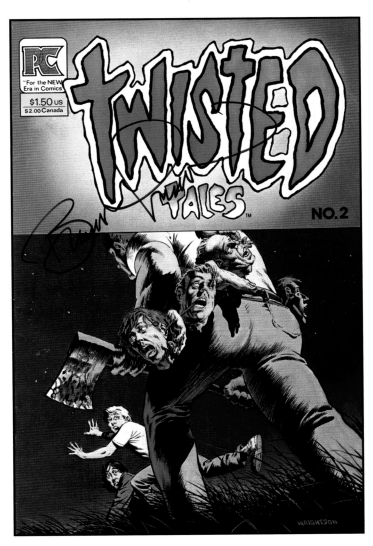

Pacific closed up shop in 1984 and Eclipse Comics stepped up to release the last two issues of both of Jones' titles, but Jones and Campbell weren't interested in continuing with them. Eclipse then launched *Tales of Terror* with many of the same artists as *Twisted Tales*, and it had a successful 13-issue run.

ECLIPSE COMICS
FIRST ISSUE!
The Illustrated Horror Magazine for Mature Readers
$1.75
$2.25 in Canada
Tales of
TERROR
VINCENT

Tales of Terror #1 (July 1985) cover art by Eric Vincent

Denis Kitchen revived his old underground title *Death Rattle* around this same time, showcasing the artistic talents of some of his old underground crew. One of the most fondly remembered titles from the mid-'80s was Fantaco's *Gore Shriek*, whose crazy, subversive stories and art, and a no-holds-barred editorial style spiced up a short but potent run. One name common to many of these titles is Stephen Bissette, arguably the top name in '80s horror. Not only did he have stories in most of the aforementioned titles, but he took over as managing editor of *Gore Shriek* on the fifth issue. He was also knee-deep in the retelling of the *Saga of the Swamp Thing* for DC. Bisette was busy and prolific, but he never skimped; he always delivered high quality.

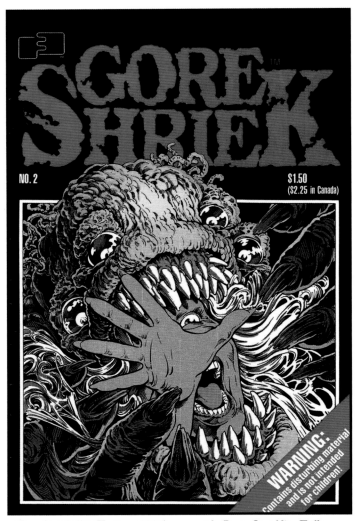

GORE SHRIEK
NO. 2
$1.50
($2.25 in Canada)
WARNING:
Contains disturbing material
and is not intended
for children!
Gore Shriek #2 (Fantaco- 1986) cover art by Bruce Spaulding Fuller

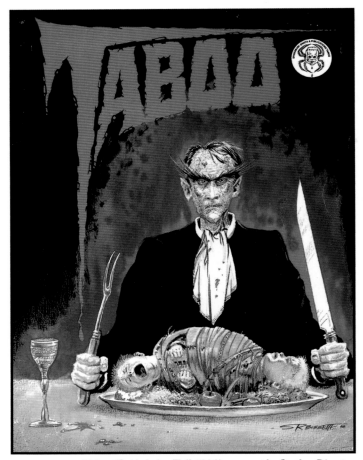

Another horrific bright spot of the time was the many reprint titles available. Russ Cochran had been reprinting the EC classics for some time, in various formats. Some of the other, less visible companies started getting noticed again. Eclipse led the way with *Seduction of the Innocent* and a handful of titles put together by Michael Gilbert. These comics brought Basil Wolverton's surreal horror and sci-fi to many new, disbelieving eyes. New England Comics published *Tales Too Terrible to Tell.* It not only served up pre-code reprints, but scholarly information about the lesser known comics and publishers, serving as a real springboard for young comic historians (read: geeks) like myself.

Besides the *Swamp Thing* redux, DC introduced other "horror" characters that enjoyed long runs; *Hellblazer* (created by Alan Moore with the ubiquitous Bissette) and *Sandman* by Neil Gaiman. The big news for real horror fans at the end of the decade was the introduction of Bissete and (his *Swamp Thing* partner) John Totleben's *Taboo*, a decidedly strong, adult horror anthology. Creators like S. Clay Wilson, Moore, Gaiman, Bissette, Tim Lucas, and Charles Burns let their imaginations and dark sides run rampant; these are some of the most jolting horror comics ever. The first seven issues were published by Bissette's own Spiderbaby Graphix.

TABOO
Taboo (Spiderbaby- Fall 1988) cover art by Stephen Bissette

In the mid-'80s, Stanley Harris, Myron Fass' former partner and the man who took the Eerie Pubs reprints into the new decade, purchased the rights to Warren's defunct comic titles in a fire sale. He made a weak attempt to reinstate *Creepy* and *Vampirella* with one-shot continuations of the original run, but found sales to be lacking. By 1991, however, the timing was better and Harris reintroduced *Vampi* in a handful of titles, some reprint and some new, and had a huge hit on his hands.

For better or worse, the new era of "horror" bad girls was upon us. Besides Vampirella, there was Lady Death, first seen in *Evil Ernie* #1 (Eternity Comics, 1991) and, in my opinion, the saving grace of the genre, Dawn. The raven haired goddess only appeared on the covers of Joseph Monks and Joseph Michael Linsner's very adult comic *Cry for Dawn.* It was an extremely confrontational but beautiful horror comic, started in 1989. Linsner's art and obvious love of the female form attracted many fans, and Dawn eventually starred in her own comic series. The original nine issues of *Cry for Dawn* are definitely strong and not to everyone's tastes, but come recommended to fans of disturbing entertainment.

Harris's Vampirella was a far different character than Warren's; she was tough and mean and whereas the vintage Vampi found her vampirism to be an impediment, the new model embraced her violence and used it against her enemies. Writers Kurt Busiek and Tom Sniegoski made the Vampi redux into an ass-kicking tigress. It should also be noted that the various new artists were drawing her with bigger tits than the Warren version. She must have had a Drakulonian boob-job.

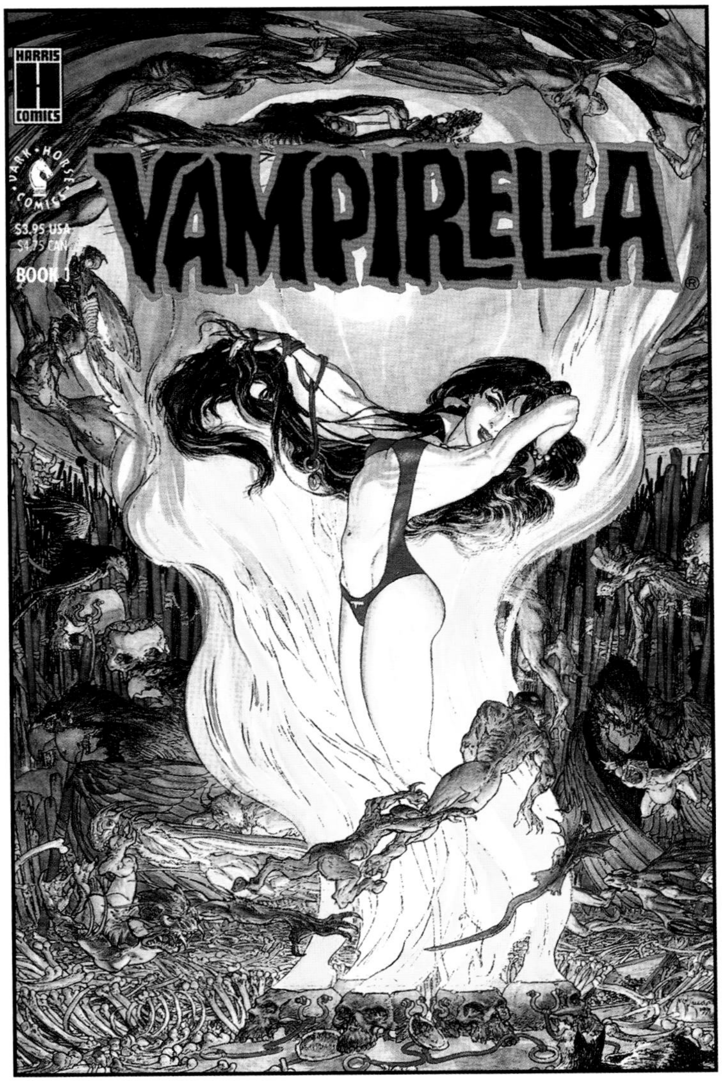
HARRIS COMICS
VAMPIRELLA
$3.95 USA
$4.75 CAN
Vampirella: Morning in America #1 (Harris- Sept. 1991)

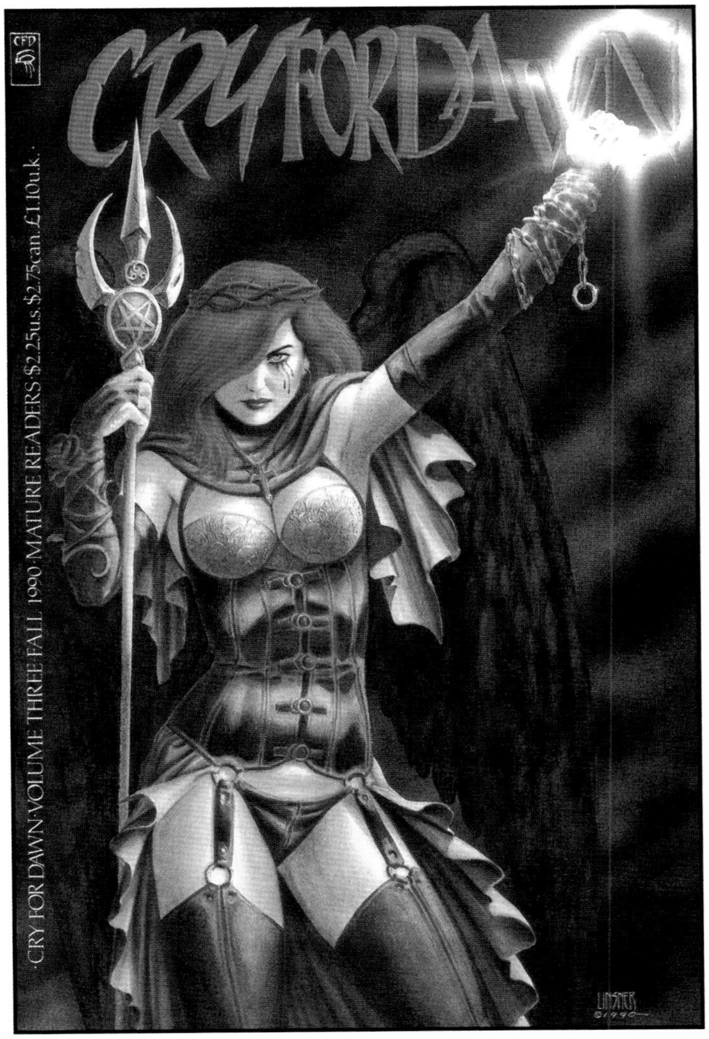
CRY FOR DAWN
CRY FOR DAWN·VOLUME THREE·FALL 1990·MATURE READERS $2.25us.$2.75can.£1.10u.k.
Cry for Dawn Vol. III (Fall 1990) cover art by Joseph Michael Linsner

NAUSEOUS '90S

A small black-and-white wave rippled through the pond in late 1991. Bruce Hamilton (who had formed Gladstone Publishing with Russ Cochran to reprint the EC comics) published a trio of terror mags; *Grave Tales, Dread of Night,* and *Maggots*. Though each title only lasted a few issues, they are all very good and worth seeking out. They feature fun, twist endings, and good artwork by veterans Gray Morrow and Joe Staton.

Meanwhile, Steve Geppi's Gemstone Publishing took over the EC comics, reprinting every title in order; the horror and suspense stories, as well as the war, science-fiction and "New Direction" titles. Readers newly discovering the greatness of EC could relive the excitement of getting a "new" issue of the best comics ever. Long-time collectors, who could never afford the premium prices that some of the originals fetch, finally had a way to fill in their collections. Even the text stories were reprinted, so readers didn't lose any of their grue.

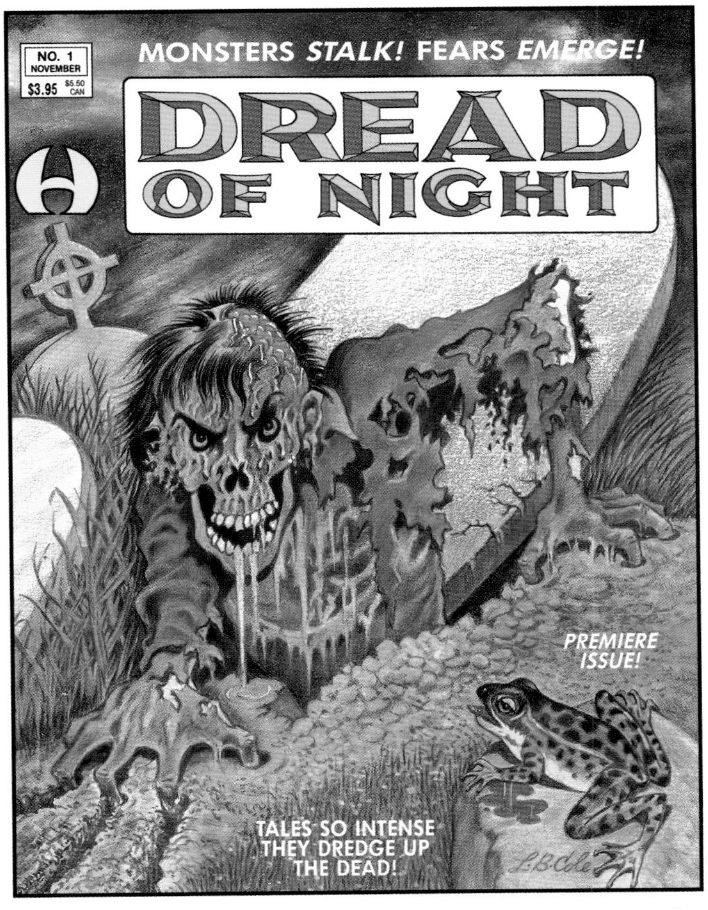
NO. 1
NOVEMBER
$3.95
$5.50 CAN
MONSTERS STALK! FEARS EMERGE!
DREAD OF NIGHT
PREMIERE ISSUE!
TALES SO INTENSE THEY DREDGE UP THE DEAD!
Dread of Night #1 (Nov. 1991) cover art by L. B. Cole

In all honesty, horror comics throughout the '90s were a pretty mixed bag. Horror films became fodder with properties like *Texas Chainsaw Massacre* (1974), *A Nightmare on Elm Street* (1984) and *Hellraiser* (1987) all getting the comic treatment. One-shots and independent horror titles came and went without much of a trace. Some were excellent, but with skimpy distribution and a disinterested market (superheroes ruled the day, and still do), it was hard to get the comics into the right hands. This is still an area where the advanced (read: super-geeky) collector like myself can unearth some forgotten relic and discover something "new."

One of the more entertaining comics from the '90s came from the mysterious Phantomb Publishing. Seven issues of *Tomb Tales* came out between 1997 and 1999, and had a very heavy EC vibe. So heavy, in fact, that each cover was illustrated by an EC great! George Evans, Jack Kamen (who surprisingly contributes the most grisly cover), Johnny Craig, and even Jack Davis all drew covers. The insides are all very good, with an EC-like layout (including the familiar typeface), hosts, and art that understood what was required of a horror comic. "Horrid" Hal Robins drew many nice, detailed stories that were collected in 1999 for Phantomb's only other comic, *Grave Yarns* #1. Back covers advertised mouth-watering lithographs by Feldstein and Kamen. My only quibble with this wonderful series is the black border around each cover, filled with loud, distracting text.

LURID THRILLS!
CRYPTIC
TOMB TALES
$3
JUNE-JULY
NO. 2
WITH YOUR HORRID HOSTS...
THE TOMB KEEPER
THE CHILLER
CRUMBLIN' CHARLIE
GRISLY CHILLS!

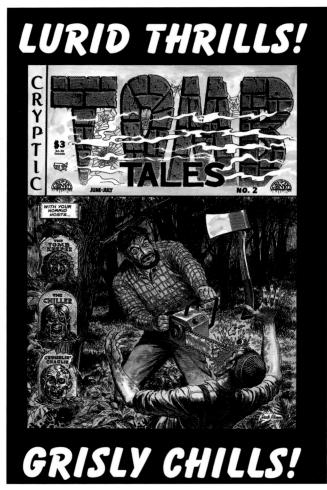

Tomb Tales #2 (June- July 1997) cover art by Jack Kamen

TODAY'S TOMBS

DC's line of "mature" comics, under the Vertigo imprint, had taken over the series *The Sandman*, *Swamp Thing*, and *Hellblazer* and added a good horror anthology in 1999 to keep it real. *Flinch* killed off the '90s and rang in the new millennium with well-written horror stories and some good, if sometimes over-stylized, artwork. 16 issues were published over two years, and they stand as one of the last good color horror comics.

VERTIGO
DC COMICS
the vertigo HORROR anthology
flinch
NO. 2
JULY 99
$2.50 US
$3.95 CAN
DOWN TO THE BONE
three trips into the darkness by
DEAN MOTTER & BILL SIENKIEWICZ
BRIAN AZZARELLO & EDUARDO RISSO
BOB FINGERMAN & PAT McEOWN
DIRECT SALES

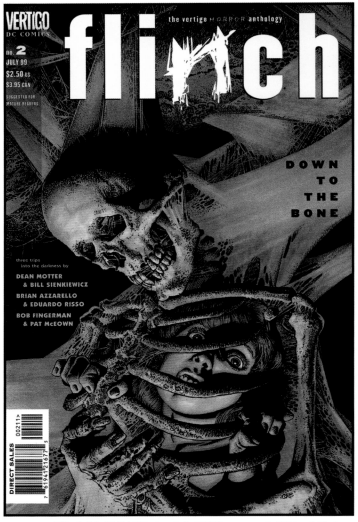

Flinch #2 (DC/ Vertigo- July 1999) cover art by Richard Corben

IDW Comics entered the ring in the early part of this century with *30 Days of Night*, initially a 3-part vampire mini-series written by Steve Niles, and drawn by Ben Templesmith. It was a massive hit and launched Niles into the comic spotlight. Many more *30 Days* mini-series followed, as did a film, and a number of novels.

Two other series that are worth mentioning due to their paranormal ideas are Mike Mignola's *Hellboy* and Eric Powell's *The Goon*; both are very successful, long running characters. *Hellboy* has even become a movie franchise and an industry unto itself, complete with toys, shirts, and coffee mugs. *The Goon* might not be far behind, with movie rumors always circulating.

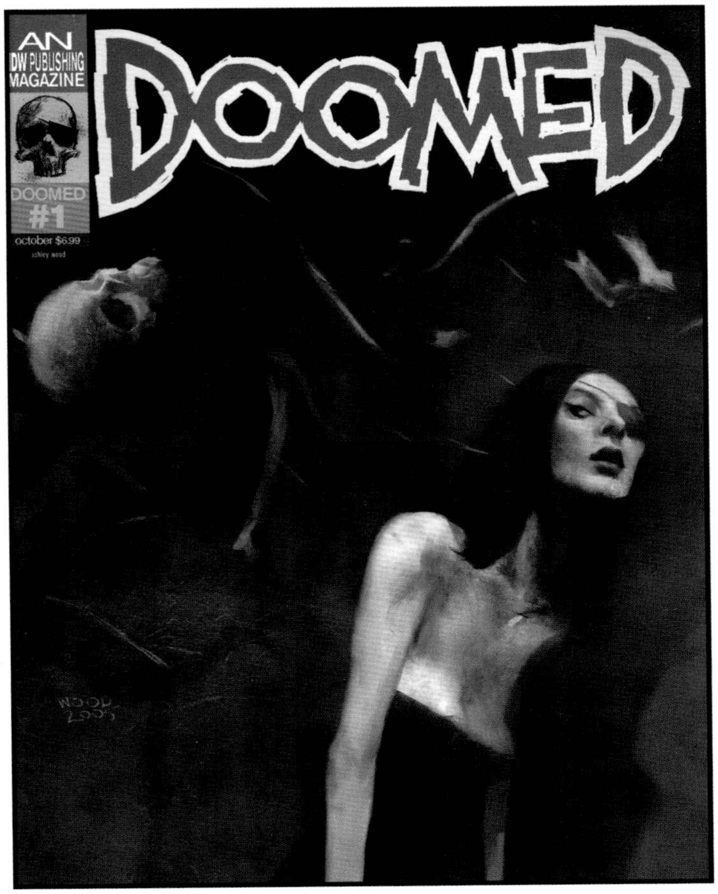
AN
IDW PUBLISHING
MAGAZINE
DOOMED
DOOMED
#1
october $6.99

Doomed #1 (Oct. 2005) cover art by Ashley Wood

In the classic anthology tradition, IDW produced a short-lived, black-and-white horror magazine titled *Doomed*. Starting in 2005, four handsome issues were released, sporting lovely painted covers and a very Warren aesthetic. While I thought it was great to see such a magazine at that time, I must have been among the few, as the title lasted only four issues.

FETID FUTURE?

So where do we stand now? Image Comics has *The Walking Dead*, a soap-opera with horror trappings, which is immensely popular and has spawned a top-rated TV series. Zombies have become almost **too** popular in the last decade. Even Marvel zombied up their superheroes for… wait for it… *Marvel Zombies*. James Warren pried the rights to his *Creepy* and *Eerie* from Stanley Harris and sold them to New Comics Company, who licensed them to Dark Horse. They have not only been reprinting every issue in beautiful archive collections, but have also resurrected both titles as ongoing series with mostly new material. Pre-code reprints are everywhere! Horror comics, in whatever form, are still loved. In 2011, the Ghastly Award was developed to give recognition to those who still dare to dabble in the horror comic craft. New blood is constantly flowing into the genre, inspired by the great books of the past. Perhaps, with a little luck, we can look forward to another horror comic boom that will piss off parents, scare the neighbors, and satisfy our bloodthirsty need for terror.

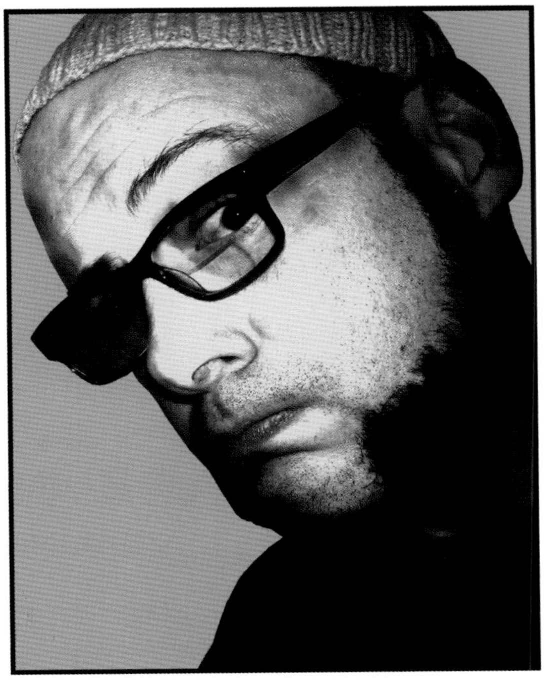

Mike Howlett *is a lifelong horror geek. He is the author of* The Weird World of Eerie Publications *(Feral House) and its companion tome,* The Weird Indexes of Eerie Publications *(made to order from Lulu and Amazon). Because the world always needs more Eerie, he is also preparing* The Worst of Eerie Publications *for IDW/Yoe Books, due in 2014. His work has apeared in* Famous Monsters, Comic Book Marketplace, Vintage Guitar, *and more fanzines than you can shake a petrified pelican dick at.*

Suggested Reading (*other than my own great books*)

The Illustrated History: Horror Comics by Mike Benton (Taylor Publishing 1991)

Tales Too Terrible to Tell #1 through 10, *Terrorology* #11 (New England Comics 1989- 1993)

The Warren Companion by David A. Roach and Jon B. Cooke (Twomorrows 2001)

The Complete Illustrated History of the Skywald Horror-Mood by Alan Hewetson (Headpress 2004)

Tales of Terror by Fred von Bernewitz and Grant Geissman (Gemstone/ Fantagraphics 2000)

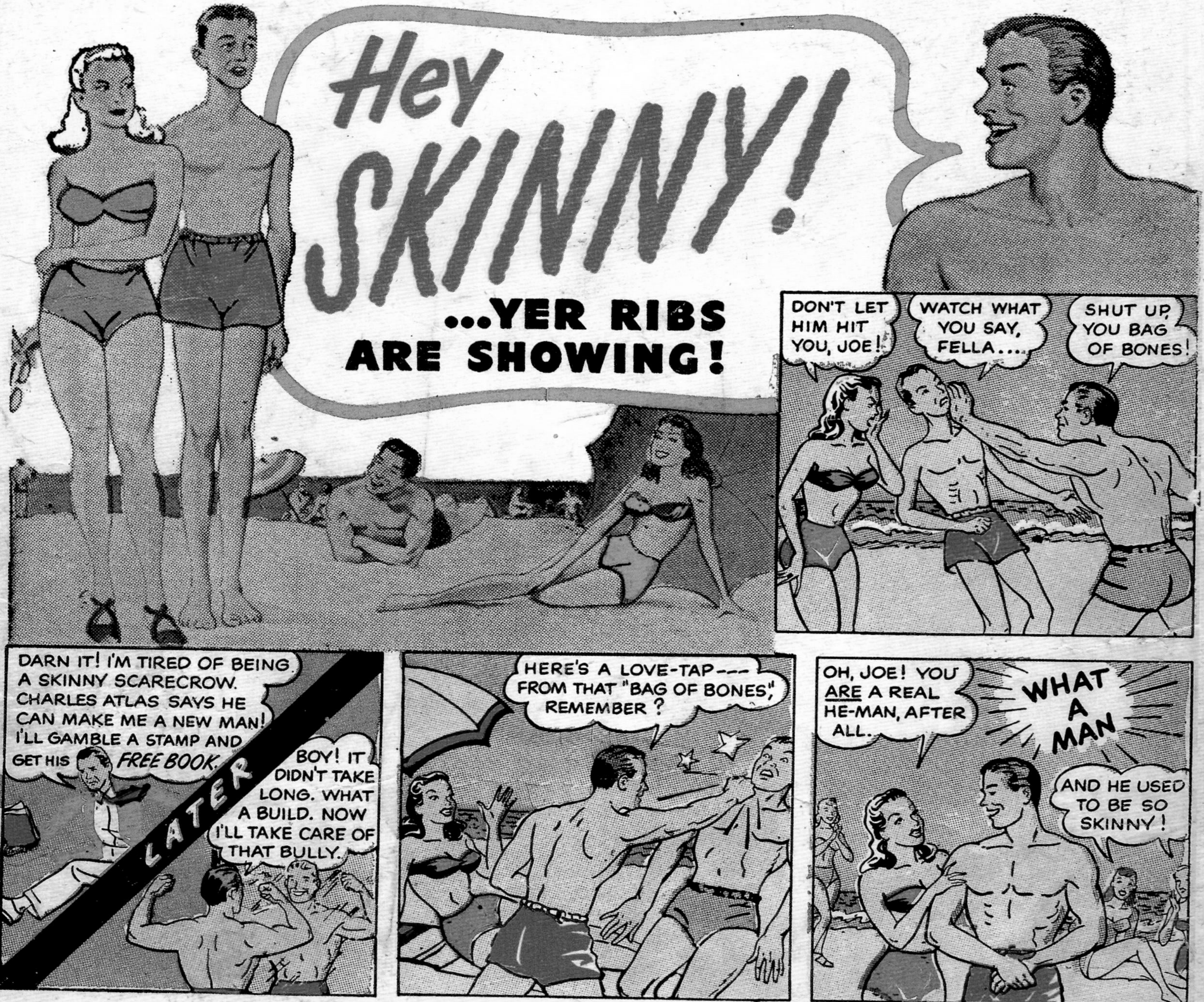
Hey SKINNY!
...YER RIBS ARE SHOWING!
DON'T LET HIM HIT YOU, JOE!
WATCH WHAT YOU SAY, FELLA....
SHUT UP, YOU BAG OF BONES!
DARN IT! I'M TIRED OF BEING A SKINNY SCARECROW. CHARLES ATLAS SAYS HE CAN MAKE ME A NEW MAN! I'LL GAMBLE A STAMP AND GET HIS FREE BOOK.
LATER
BOY! IT DIDN'T TAKE LONG. WHAT A BUILD. NOW I'LL TAKE CARE OF THAT BULLY.
HERE'S A LOVE-TAP--- FROM THAT "BAG OF BONES," REMEMBER ?
OH, JOE! YOU ARE A REAL HE-MAN, AFTER ALL.
WHAT A MAN
AND HE USED TO BE SO SKINNY!

I Can Make YOU a New Man, Too, In Only 15 Minutes a Day!

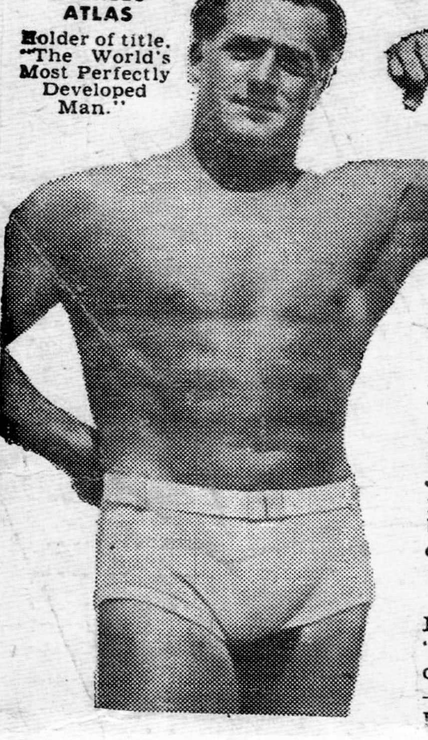

CHARLES ATLAS
Holder of title, "The World's Most Perfectly Developed Man."

PEOPLE used to laugh at my skinny 97-pound body. I was ashamed to strip for sports or for a swim. Girls made fun of me behind my back. THEN I discovered my body - building system. "*Dynamic Tension*." It made me such a *complete* specimen of manhood that I hold the title, "The World's Most Perfectly Developed Man."

What's My Secret?

When you look in the mirror and see a healthy, husky, fellow smiling back at you — then you'll be astonished at how fast "*Dynamic Tension*" GETS RESULTS! It is the easy, NATURAL method and you can practice in the privacy of your own room — JUST 15 MINUTES EACH DAY. Just watch your scrawny chest and shoulder muscles begin to swell . . . those spindly arms and legs of yours bulge . . . and your whole body starts to feel "alive," full of zip and go!

Thousands are becoming husky — my way. I give you no gadgets to fool with. With "*Dynamic Tension*" you simply utilize the dormant muscle-power in your own body — watch it grow and multiply into real, solid LIVE MUSCLE.

FREE My 32 Page Illustrated Book is Yours — Not for $1.00 or 10c — But FREE

Send for my book, *Everlasting Health and Strength*. 32 pages of photos, valuable advice. Shows what *Dynamic Tension* can do, answers vital questions. A *real prize* for any fellow who wants a better build. I'll send you a copy FREE. It may change your whole life. Rush coupon to me personally: *Charles Atlas, Dept. 324-W 115 E. 23rd Street, New York 10, N. Y.*

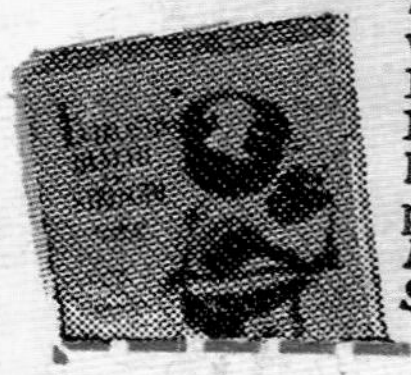

CHARLES ATLAS, Dept. 324-W
115 East 23 St., New York 10, N.Y.

Send me — absolutely FREE — a copy of your famous book, *Everlasting Health and Strength* — 32 pages, crammed with photographs, answers to vital questions, and valuable advice. This book is mine to keep, and sending for it does not obligate me in any way.

Name __________ Age ____
(Please print or write plainly)

Address __________

City __________ State ____

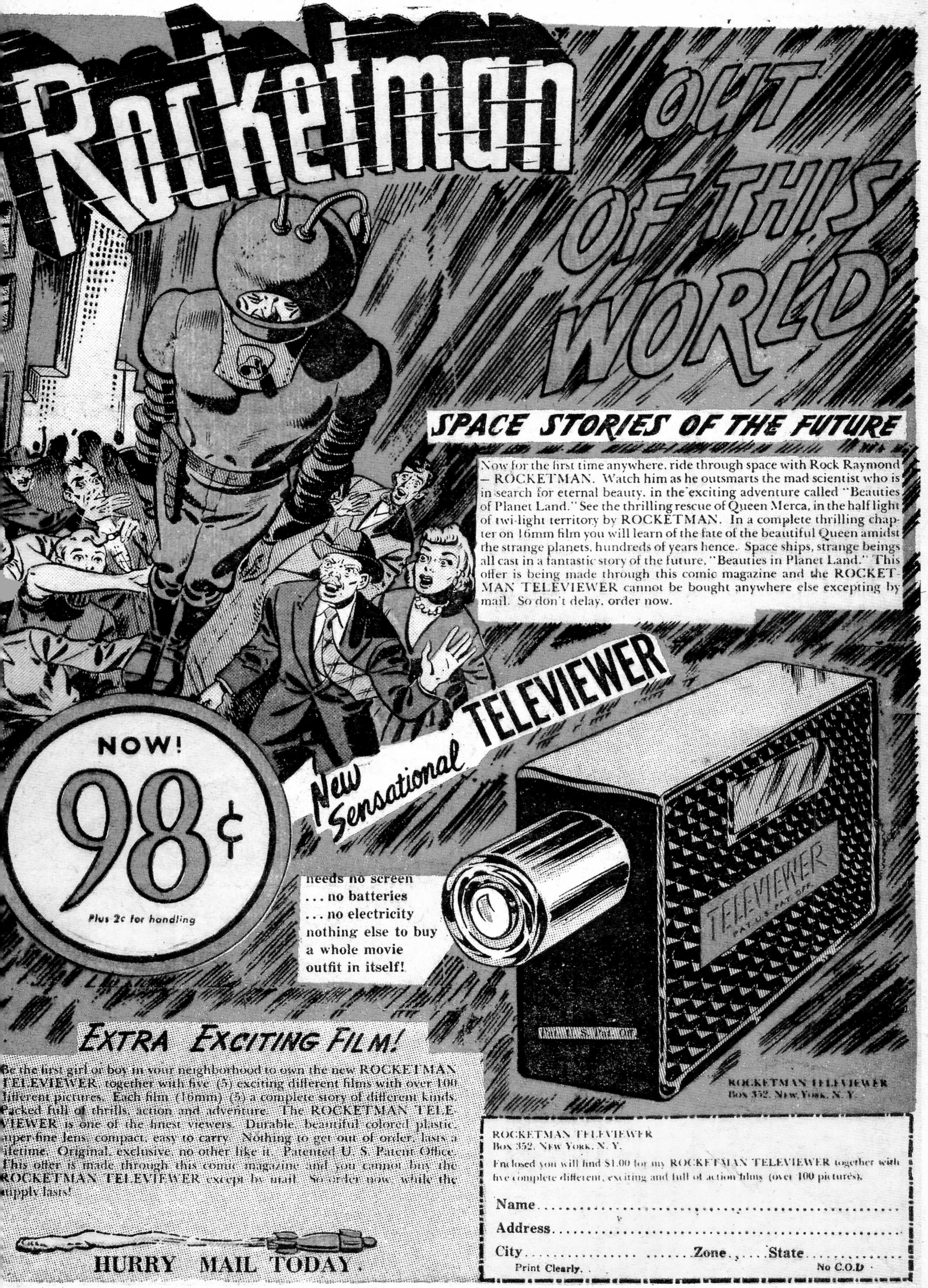
Rocketman
OUT OF THIS WORLD
SPACE STORIES OF THE FUTURE
Now for the first time anywhere, ride through space with Rock Raymond – ROCKETMAN. Watch him as he outsmarts the mad scientist who is in search for eternal beauty, in the exciting adventure called "Beauties of Planet Land." See the thrilling rescue of Queen Merca, in the half light of twi-light territory by ROCKETMAN. In a complete thrilling chapter on 16mm film you will learn of the fate of the beautiful Queen amidst the strange planets, hundreds of years hence. Space ships, strange beings all cast in a fantastic story of the future, "Beauties in Planet Land." This offer is being made through this comic magazine and the ROCKETMAN TELEVIEWER cannot be bought anywhere else excepting by mail. So don't delay, order now.
NOW!
98¢
Plus 2¢ for handling
New Sensational TELEVIEWER
needs no screen
... no batteries
... no electricity
nothing else to buy
a whole movie outfit in itself!
TELEVIEWER
EXTRA EXCITING FILM!
Be the first girl or boy in your neighborhood to own the new ROCKETMAN TELEVIEWER, together with five (5) exciting different films with over 100 different pictures. Each film (16mm) (5) a complete story of different kinds. Packed full of thrills, action and adventure. The ROCKETMAN TELEVIEWER is one of the finest viewers. Durable, beautiful colored plastic, super-fine lens, compact, easy to carry. Nothing to get out of order, lasts a lifetime. Original, exclusive, no other like it. Patented U. S. Patent Office. This offer is made through this comic magazine and you cannot buy the ROCKETMAN TELEVIEWER except by mail. So order now, while the supply lasts!
HURRY MAIL TODAY.
ROCKETMAN TELEVIEWER
Box 352, New York, N. Y.
ROCKETMAN TELEVIEWER
Box 352, New York, N. Y.
Enclosed you will find $1.00 for my ROCKETMAN TELEVIEWER together with five complete different, exciting and full of action films (over 100 pictures).
Name
Address
City
Zone
State
Print Clearly.
No C.O.D

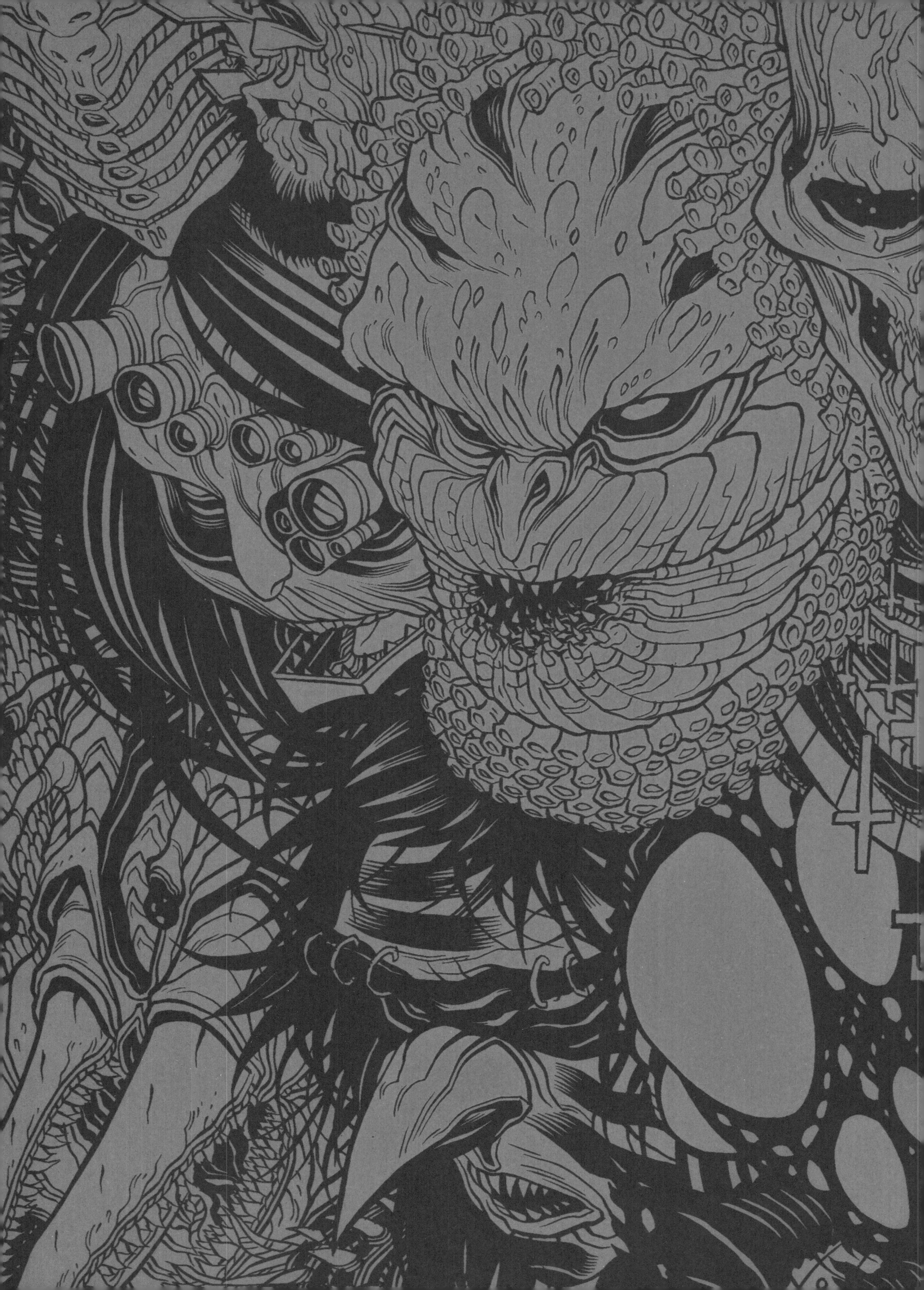